KIERKEGAARD AS HUMANIST
Discovering My Self

The self is the central and unifying theme of Søren Kierkegaard's writings. In *Kierkegaard as Humanist,* Arnold Come provides a comprehensive exposition of Kierkegaard's understanding of what it means to be a self and the problems and possibilities that every human being faces in the task of becoming a self.

Come limits his discussion to the humanist dimensions of Kierkegaard's writings—to what is open to the experience of every human being without reference to or assistance from any particular religious insight or revelation. He concludes that Kierkegaard's ontology is independent of his Christian theology but includes an openness to and a relation with the eternal as inherent natural possibility in the experience of every human being.

Come lets Kierkegaard speak for himself rather than exploring how his thought is derived, or differs, from his predecessors and contemporaries or related to major philosophical and psychological positions and schools. The basic outline of the self, drawn from the opening pages of *The Sickness unto Death,* is explored in all of Kierkegaard's works, both pseudonymous and acknowledged, and the importance of the self thus revealed for understanding determinism/indeterminism and the philosophy of action is discussed.

Kierkegaard as Humanist is an exciting exploration of the humanist dimensions of the self.

Arnold B. Come is Professor Emeritus of systematic theology, San Francisco Theological Seminary and the Graduate Theological Union.

McGILL-QUEEN'S STUDIES IN THE HISTORY OF IDEAS

1 Problems of Cartesianism
Edited by Thomas M. Lennon, John M. Nicholas, and
John W. Davis

2 The Development of the Idea of History in Antiquity
Gerald A. Press

3 Claude Buffier and Thomas Reid:
Two Common-Sense Philosophers
Louise Marcil-Lacoste

4 Schiller, Hegel, and Marx:
State, society, and the Aesthetic Ideal of Ancient Greece
Philip J. Kain

5 John Case and Aristotelianism in Renaissance England
Charles B. Schmitt

6 Beyond Liberty and Property:
The Process of Self-Recognition in Eighteenth-Century
Political Thought
J.A.W. Gunn

7 John Toland: His Methods, Manners, and Mind
Stephen H. Daniel

8 Coleridge and the Inspired Word
Anthony John Harding

9 The Jena System, 1804–5: Logic and Metaphysics
G.W.F. Hegel
Translation edited by John W. Burbidge and George di Giovanni
Introduction and notes by H.S. Harris

10 Consent, Coercion, and Limit:
The Medieval Origins of Parliamentary Democracy
Arthur P. Monahan

11 Scottish Common Sense in Germany, 1768–1800:
A Contribution to the History of Critical Philosophy
Manfred Kuehn

12 Paine and Cobbett:
The Transatlantic Connection
David A. Wilson

13 Descartes and the Enlightenment
Peter A. Schouls

14 Greek Scepticism
Anti-Realist Trends in Ancient Thought
Leo Groarke

15 The Irony of Theology and the Nature of Religious Thought
Donald Wiebe

16 Form and Transformation
A Study in the Philosophy of Plotinus
Frederic M. Schroeder

17 From Personal Duties towards Personal Rights
Late Medieval and Early Modern Political Thought, 1300–1600
Arthur P. Monahan

18 The Main Philosophical Writings and the Novel *Allwill*
Friedrich Heinrich Jacobi
Translated and Edited by George di Giovanni

19 Kierkegaard as Humanist
Discovering My Self
Arnold B. Come

KIERKEGAARD AS HUMANIST
Discovering My Self

Arnold B. Come

McGill-Queen's University Press
Montreal & Kingston • London • Buffalo

© Arnold B. Come 1995
ISBN 0-7735-1019-2
Legal deposit 3rd quarter 1995
Bibliothèque nationale du Québec

Printed in the United States on acid-free paper

The author wishes to express his personal gratitude, and the indebtedness of the world of Kierkegaard scholarship, to Princeton University Press for its long tradition in Kierkegaard publication and especially for its new edition of *Kierkegaard's Writings*. The present book would be much the poorer without the remarkable research that informs the new series and without its fresh and faithful translations.

Canadian Cataloguing in Publication Data

Come, Arnold B. (Arnold Bruce), 1918–
Kierkegaard as humanist: discovering my self
(McGill-Queen's studies in the history of ideas: 19)
Includes bibliographical references and index.
ISBN 0-7735-1019-2
1. Kierkegaard, Søren, 1813–1855. 2. Self (Philosophy).
I. Title. II. Series.
B4378.S4C65 1995   198'.9   C95-900250-2

This book was typeset by Typo Litho Composition Inc.
in 10/12 Baskerville

Dedicated to
Alastair McKinnon
A Friend in Deed!

Contents

Preface xvii

1 MY SELF: AN OVERVIEW 3

   General Definition 3

   The Five Qualifications
   1. A Relation 5
   2. A Relation Which Relates to Itself 8
   3. Established by an Other 11
   4. A Failure 13
   5. Transparent Rest in the Power 14

2 MY SELF: A SYNTHESIS OF TWO 18

   The Essential Duality: Inward, Outward 19

   The Procedure of Abstraction for Procuring an Anthropological Ontology 23

   Body/Soul 25

   Finitude/Infinitude 31

   Necessity/Possibility 40

   Summary 44

3 MY SELF: A TASK 46
   Part 1: Coming to Consciousness 46

   Angst: The Birth-Pangs of Self-Consciousness 47
   1. The General Character of Angst 49
   2. The Object of Angst 50

3. The First Evocation of Angst: Nothingness   52
4. The Second Evocation of Angst: A Conversation   54
   a. First Question: "Am I Able?"   56
   b. Second Question: "Will I Fail?"   57

Reflection: The First Step toward Self-Consciousness   60
1. The Self before and after Angst   61
2. The First Step beyond Angst: Reflection   62

Consciousness of My Self   64
1. The Object of Consciousness: The Self   65
2. The Attitude of Consciousness: Earnest Interestedness   67
3. The Methodology of Consciousness   71
   a. The Awakening of Consciousness through the Dichotomy of Reflection   71
     (1) About Finitude: Sexuality   74
     (2) About Infinitude: The Negative Self   76
   b. The Unity of Consciousness in Subjectivity   77
     (1) Reason and Understanding   79
     (2) Thinking and Being   84
     (3) Objective Reflection   85
        (a) Assumes Continuity   85
        (b) Seeks Generalities   87
        (c) Is Disinterested   88
        (d) A Current Example   89
     (4) Subjective Reflection   90
        (a) Rejects Abstraction   90
        (b) Occurs in Inwardness   93
        (c) Accepts Isolation   102
        (d) Compels Indirect Communication   105
4. The Limits of Consciousness   107

4 MY SELF: A TASK   109

Part 2: Freedom: The Dialectical in Temporality/Eternity   109

The Relevance of the Dyad Temporal/Eternal for the Self   109

Kierkegaard's Concept of Time   111
1. Ordinary Time   111
2. The Dialectic of Past/Future   112
3. The Dialectic of Temporality/Eternity   114

The Resultant Nature of Freedom   114

1. Freedom as *Act* to Unite Possibility and Necessity   115
2. Requires Relation to the Eternal   115
3. The Limited Nature of Freedom   117

Freedom in Relation to the Past   118
1. Means: Choosing Oneself Which ...   119
   a. Must Be Done Absolutely   120
   b. Must Be Done Concretely   121
   c. Must Be Done Repentantly   121
2. Choosing Transforms the Self   122
3. To Choose Is Not to Create Oneself   123

Freedom in Relation to the Future   125
1. Choosing Future Possibility   125
2. Possibility as Indeterminate Future   126
3. Freedom as Integration of Future with Past   127

Freedom and the Eternal   128
1. The Move from Ethical to Religious   129
2. Relation to Self vis-à-vis Relation to the Eternal   130
3. The Eternal as "God"   132
4. God Is: "All Things Are Possible"   133
5. Implications for Human Freedom   134

5 MY SELF: A TASK   137
Part 3: Freedom: The Dialectical in Possibility/Necessity   137

Introduction   137
1. Dialectic of Finite/Infinite   137
2. Dialectic of Necessary/Possible   138
3. Major Issue in Kierkegaardian Interpretation   139
4. Issue Set in Context of Logic   140
5. Emergence of the Dialectic in Kierkegaard's Study   140
   a. Lectures of Martensen and Schelling   140
   b. In *Either/Or*   142
   c. Tennemann, Trendelenburg, and Aristotle   142

Major Formulations on Possibility by Kierkegaard   145
1. Possibility as "Future" in *Fragments* and *The Concept of Anxiety*   146
2. New Perspective in *Postscript*   148
3. Possibility in *The Sickness unto Death*   152
   a. Continuity with *Fragments* and *Postscript*   152
   b. The Role of Imagination   153

      c. The Possible Self as Impetus   156
      d. A Serious Dilemma: Potentiality versus Contingency   159
      e. Resolution Formulated in *Sickness*   161
          (1) The Self as Duality-in-Unity   162
          (2) Possibility vis-à-vis Becoming   164
              (a) Possibility as *between* the Universal Human and the Concrete Individual   164
              (b) Possibility as Essential Gestalt   166
              (c) Its Role in Becoming   169
              (d) An Illustration   170
          (3) Possibility vis-à-vis Actuality   172
              (a) *Fragments* versus *Sickness*   173
              (b) Actuality as Fulfilled Possibility   172
              (c) Continuity of Self as Possibility   177

Major Formulations on Necessity by Kierkegaard   178
1. Necessity in *Either/Or*, *Fragments*, and *Postscript*   178
    a. Necessity in *Either/Or*   179
    b. Necessity in *Fragments*   181
        (1) Summary   181
        (2) Concepts of "Ground" and "Cause"   182
        (3) Concepts of Nature and History   186
    c. Necessity in *Postscript*   189
2. The Change in Concept of Necessity after *Postscript*   191
    a. The *Corsair* Affair   191
    b. As Expressed in *Upbuilding Discourses in Various Spirits*, *Journals*, *Works of Love*, and *Christian Discourses*   192
3. The New Formulation on Necessity in *Sickness*   200
    a. Three Forms Not Labelled "Necessity"   201
    b. Necessity Internal to Becoming Self   203
        (1) The Self as κατα δυναμιν   203
        (2) The Inner Self as "Necessary"   210
        (3) Growth in the Self's Necessity   216
4. Resolution of the Conflict between *Fragments* and *Sickness*   221

Summary of Analysis of the Dialectical in the Determinants Possibility and Necessity   224

6 MY SELF: A TASK   232
    Part 4: The Leap as Freedom's Form   232
    The Issue of Determinism/Indeterminism   234

Origin and Development of the Concept of the Leap   242

The Variety of Leaps   249

The Leap as μεταβασις εις αλλο γενος   250

The Leap as Concerned with the Infinite/Eternal   258

The Leap as a Passionate Transition   267
1. Definition of "Pathos" and Its Object   267
2. Interpretation in the Language of Philosophy of Action   271
3. Kierkegaard's Concept of the Unconditional   273
4. Obedience Enabled by Confession and Repentance   276

The Leap as Transition from Ethical to Religious   281
1. Religiousness A Distinguished from Religiousness B   283
2. How the Religious Goes beyond the Ethical   285
3. Teleological Suspension of the Ethical   287
4. Exposition of Religiousness A in *Postscript*   290
5. Exposition of Religiousness A in *Sickness*   294
6. The Breach in Religiousness A   297
   a. The Experience of Isolation and "Death"   300
   b. The Experience of Silence   303
   c. The Leap and Faith's Healing   306
7. The Transformation of Human Existence in Religiousness A   309
   a. Question of Content of "Good" or "Blessedness"   312
   b. Definition by Negation   318
   c. "Personhood" versus "Virtue"   319
   d. Positive Definition: "Higher Nature" and "Love"   323

7 MY SELF: A TASK   324

Part 5: Love as Freedom's Content   324

Distinction between Higher and Lower Natures   325

"Willing" Located between the Two   330

Love as Content of Freedom   330
1. Introduction   330
2. Use of *Works of Love* for Religiousness A   333
3. Five Specifications of "Spiritual" Love   340

The Object of Love   341

Unconditional Love versus Preferential Love   342
1. Self-Denial versus Self-Love   342

2. Are They Mutually Exclusive?   345

Love's Triad   350
1. The Use of Religious Language in *Works*: A or B?   351
2. Love Is "God"   351
3. The Triad: Lover, Beloved, Love-Itself   354
4. Love and Conscience   358

Love Presupposes Love   359
1. Principle of Like-for-Like   359
2. Requires Faith in Love-Itself   363
3. Principle of Reduplication   364
   a. Background in *Postscript*   364
   b. Occurrence in the Eternal   366
4. Reduplication and the Triad   368
5. The Issue of Communal Love   374

Works of Love Transform Human Existence   377
1. The Requirement of a "Work" or "Deed"   377
2. Examples in *Works of Love*   379
3. Resulting Definition of an Act of Love   384
4. The "Revolution" of Love: No "Mine" and "Yours"   388
   a. Does It Actually Occur?   391
   b. How Concrete Is Its Specification?   394

Final Question: Is the Act of Love Indeterminate?   397

8   MY SELF: A TASK   398
Part 6: The Leap of Love Is Indeterminate   398

The Leap in Terms of the Three Breaches   398
1. The First Breach: Immediacy versus Absolute Telos   399
2. The Second Breach: The Self versus the Eternal   400
3. The Third Breach: Intention versus Act   403

"Willing" as Decisive in Transition from Intention to Act   411
1. Definition of Willing   412
2. The Point of Indeterminacy   414
3. A Messy Problem: Weakness of Will and Self-Deception   414

Willing and the "Darkening" of the Understanding   416

Kierkegaard's Concept of Self-Deception   419
1. Occurs in Conflict of Higher and Lower Natures   420
2. Self-Deception according to Philosophy of Action   421

3. Kierkegaard's View in Those Terms   423
   a. His Concept of Stages and Spheres   423
   b. His Concept of Higher and Lower Truth   426
4. The Development of Kierkegaard's View   431
   a. In *Postscript*   431
   b. In "On the Occasion of a Confession"   432
   c. In *Works of Love*   434
5. Summary   440

Willing as "Uncaused," Free   441
1. Kierkegaard's Use of "the Unconditional"   442
   a. Illustrations   443
   b. Formulation in Kierkegaard's Own Terms   449
   c. In Terms of Philosophy of Action   451
2. His Contribution to Analysis of Decision-Making   453
3. Kierkegaard Not a Determinist in Rigid Sense   455
   a. Critique of Nordentoft's Interpretation   456
   b. Kierkegaard's Indeterminism   459
   c. Illustrations of Kierkegaard's Position   460

Interlude: Ontology and Theology   465

Bibliography   475

Index   481

Preface

Sooner or later, the greatest mystery to appear in every human being's life is the mystery of human existence itself, more particularly, the mystery of one's own self, one's own existence, the mystery of "My Self." Many persons pass through their lives placidly, with no sense of awe or wonder, with their consciousness totally absorbed by the routines of life—working, playing, raising a family, fighting with relatives, fishing, golfing, making a few friends, seeking financial security, watching television, reading the newspaper. But sooner or later that surface calm is punctured, and the continuity of life is broken, either by a sudden touch of beauty (the smile of a baby, sunset over the Grand Canyon), or by an unaccountable tragic suffering (automobile accident, swift death by cancer). I am disturbed: is beauty more valuable than money in the bank? And why *me* that has to suffer?

Many persons respond to this wonderment with not much more than a shrug, an unreflective Oh! before beauty, and with a dull sense of fate or bad luck before tragedy. But other possible responses are opened up to us, often unconsciously, by the music we listen to, the novels we read, the movies and plays we see, our religious feelings and thoughts however vague and uncertain, our being moved by social and political conditions and events, and through discussions and arguments with family and friends.

It is the thesis and burden of this present study that, beyond the mysteries of the origin of the universe, the beginning of life on this planet, the atomic structure of all things that exist here, the functioning of our bodies, the dynamic forces and movements of history and society, the greatest and most significant mystery is that of the emergence of the unique individual human self and its unlimited potentialities in community with other humans and the rest of the natural order.

There are those who contend that the self, as an entity with continuity, is an illusion, an ephemeral pattern that appears temporarily from the accidental concatenation of diverse forces. And little wonder! The self, as it has come to consciousness in the great religious and philosophical traditions and especially in contemporary humanistic culture, is as elusive as water being caught in the hand, as fragile as a blade of grass under foot, as sensitive as the retina of the eye poked by a needle. Yet this self is also as indestructible and inescapable as the force of gravity, because the human self, unlike any other species of life we know, is capable of understanding and participating in the creative movement of energy and life in this universe—even to the point of transforming its own genetic structure and almost to the point of creating life itself, and certainly to the point of being able to destroy itself with nuclear weapons. The human community has created "history" in the sense of racial memory and record in which is accumulated the insights and wisdom, as well as the follies, of human experience.

The human self, therefore, transcends the confines of time and space and shares in that hidden "eternity" of continuity of structure and purpose that binds all things together. This character of the human self is the conviction of all of the great religions of the world and of many of its philosophies. It is expressed in the wonderful symbolism of the Jewish (and Christian) scriptures when it is said that humankind is created in the image of God. The mode by which the individual self participates in eternity varies among the religions and philosophies, but they share the central conviction that this capacity is definitive of what it means to be a human being.

The present study of "my self" takes Søren Kierkegaard as its guide into the mysteries. Why Kierkegaard? The present writer was immersed as a child in the ethos of American individualism; I lived through the Esalen phenomenon in California (and it still goes on); I have dealt, agonizingly, with the "me" orientation of several generations of students; I have talked at length with humanistic psychologists and watched transactional analysts at work in the "OK corral" of Marin County; I have listened to Freudians and Jungians and to Erik Erikson himself with great benefit, and have tried to fathom some of the complex depths of Heidegger and Sartre. But during and after all this, the greatest help I have received for understanding "my self" has come from Kierkegaard.

Preface xix

This present study attempts, therefore, to present a summary of what he has to offer, in the form of a fairly thorough and rather technical interpretation of Kierkegaard on this theme. Its background consists of twenty-five years of reading and contemplating his writings as I led, once a year, a seminar on the subject for graduate theological students, and guided several doctoral candidates who chose Kierkegaard as one of their major resources for their dissertations. But then in the freedom of retirement, I spent practically all my time and energies for an eight year period in reading, reflecting, and writing for this present volume. A few words about how it evolved are essential for an intelligent reading of it and, especially, for understanding why the study has been divided into two parts on Kierkegaard as Humanist, and Kierkegaard as Theologian—which was not part of my original intention.

After struggling for a long time to determine which topics should be covered and in which order, I finally settled on Kierkegaard's own topics and order as presented in the first two pages of *The Sickness unto Death*. So the "Overview" summarized in chapter 1 provided the outline for the entire study of Kierkegaard's own exploration of the mysteries of "my self." I anticipated five chapters on "My Self" as: A Synthesis of Two, A Task, A Gift, A Failure, In Need of the Eternal, with a concluding chapter on my own topic of the implications of Kierkegaard's view of the self for human community and history. I worked my way slowly but fairly easily, without any major surprises, through the outline (as presented in the table of contents) of chapters 2, 3, and 4. But then I came to the topic of "Freedom as the Dialectical in the Determinants: Possibility and Necessity," and I became vividly aware of what I had given only tangential attention before, namely, that Kierkegaard's use of the categories possibility and necessity had at first been derived from and had been significantly influenced by their use in the field of logic.

Before proceeding with my outline, I found it necessary to make several background studies. First, I wrote up a survey of how these categories had been dealt with in the history of logic, from Aristotle on (about twenty-five pages). But at the end of this review I discovered that the philosophical study of logic in the last couple of generations has branched out into a number of fields and, for my purposes, most significantly into a philosophy of human action which draws on both logical and psychological materials. A summary of these developments, especially as exemplified in the writings of Donald Davidson, required some seventy pages. Then, I wrote up an account of how Kierkegaard himself became educated in the field of logic (about fifteen pages). But this led me to a specialized question, namely: what specific influence did the German philosopher Friedrich Adolf Trendelenburg have on Kierkegaard's formulation of his own use of the concepts of possibility and necessity? I canvassed the secondary literature expecting to find a lot of help on this topic, since Kierkegaard had lavished such high praise on Trendelenburg as the "modern philosopher from whom I have profited" the most, and had declared that "[m]y relation to him is very special." I found nothing but bits and pieces. Becoming intrigued with this topic, I proceeded to read parts of Trendelenburg's major work, *Logische Untersuchungen*, especially the chapter on "*Die modalen Kategorien*," that is, the categories of possibility and necessity. This produced a careful summary of Trendelenburg's views and a comparison, point for point, with Kierkegaard (some eighty pages, which have been published under the title *Trendelenburg's Influence on Kierkegaard's Modal Categories*, Montreal: Inter Editions 1991).

The result of these studies was an explosion in my exploration of Kierkegaard's own unique interpretation of the self (freedom) in the terms of the modal categories of logic: possibility and necessity. And it was the analysis of the dialectic of possibility/necessity (and especially of the shift in his view of necessity from *Fragments* to *Sickness*) that forced an even more extensive exploration of the concept of the "eternal" in the "religious sphere." And this involvement compelled me to ask: just how far does Kierkegaard see human fulfilment as occurring within the limits of the ethical-religious sphere of religiousness A? To my amazement I was thus led to draw a line within all of the major works of Kierkegaard, a line between the views of Kierkegaard the humanist and Kierkegaard the theologian, or as he puts it in *Sickness*, between the depiction of "the merely human self" and "the theological self." And being as honest and objective as I could be in my reading of the materials in both the pseudonymous works and the upbuilding discourses, I again was amazed at what Kierkegaard the humanist ascribed as possible for human accomplishment through ethical striving within the confines of religiousness A, including an authentic measure of both the form of freedom (the leap) and the content of freedom (love).

Following out these leads has led to this rather lengthy and complicated treatment of "My Self: A Task," and forced the treatment of Kierkegaard the theologian to be dealt with later by itself. I can only plead that it was Kierkegaard himself that forced this procedure to be followed.

In general, four basic principles guided me in this study. (1) I was committed to let Kierkegaard speak for himself, and not let his thinking get blurred or lost in comparison with that of others, or through my engaging in lengthy debate with other interpreters. I have read widely in the secondary literature, but no one can keep up with the international flood of writings about Kierkegaard during the last twenty-five years. So I refer to only a few other writers and mainly in the footnotes (Mark C. Taylor being the only exception). But my major concern is not to drown Kierkegaard's own thought in the complexities of debate about it. (2) I am convinced that the concept of "my self" is the unifying focus of all of Kierkegaard's writings, and that he was aware of this fact (see Malantschuk in *Kierkegaard's Thought* [Princeton: Princeton University Press, 1971], pp. 12f.). (3) I have taken *The Sickness unto Death* as Kierkegaard's most mature work, his masterpiece, and have used it as normative in judging all that went before it and all that came after it in the Kierkegaardian corpus. Kierkegaard himself so regarded it (see Howard and Edna Hong's *Kierkegaard's Journals and Papers*, entries #6337, 6238, 6361). (4) I contend that Kierkegaard's methodology is essentially phenomenological, and those interested in this thesis can find my defence of it in *Kierkegaardiana* 14 (1988), 14–28.

I need to make two other introductory comments. First, I hope that the full outline in the table of contents will be of help in following the line of argument here presented. Secondly, I hope that the repetitive use of certain passages from both Kierkegaard's works and the journals will not bother the reader. Each time I hope a new insight into their meaning will appear.

It should also be noted that every quotation from Kierkegaard has been read in Danish and that I have often modified the standard English translations, and so the reader at times may have to search the English page for the materials being quoted. We all are deeply indebted to Howard and Edna Hong for the new translations and background materials that are being provided in the publication of *Kierkegaard's Writings* by Princeton University Press. I have used them with great profit as far as they were available at the time of the writing of this study. I do not pretend to be an expert in the Danish language, but I do claim to have developed over the years, ever since I first read *Philosophical Fragments* in the autumn of 1939, an intense and sharpened feeling for and intuition of what Kierkegaard is trying to say in much of his language—which is often difficult to fathom even for Danish scholars. Every translation is an interpretation, and its "accuracy" depends as much on understanding *what* is being said in the original as on understanding *how* it is said linguistically (vocabulary, grammar, syntax, etc.). We always *mean* more than we can *say*. There is no final and perfect translation of Kierkegaard because there can be no final and perfect interpretation of him. He invites us into a process of appropriation of the truth for ourselves.

Finally a personal note. I wish to express my deep appreciation to Jim and Nancy Johnson, James and Jane Bryson, and Leslie and Dorothy Dobbins for their generous help in making the publication of this book possible.

Arnold B. Come
San Francisco Theological Seminary, San Anselmo, California
Graduate Theological Union, Berkeley, California

EXPLANATIONS

References to Kierkegaard's collected works include (in this order): (a) page number(s) in the older English translations (see "Other English Translations" in Bibliography); (b) in parentheses, the volume and page number(s) for the same reference in *Kierkegaard's Writings* (KW) if published (Howard V. Hong and Edna H. Hong, editors, Princeton University Press, publishers); in volumes of KW that appear after the publication of this book, references may be found by using the page references of the first edition of SV [item (d) below] which are marked in the margins of the volumes of KW; (c) the volume and page number(s) for the same reference in the third edition of *Søren Kierkegaard: Samlede Værker* (abbreviated as SV), edited by Peter P. Rhode and published by Glydendal, Copenhagen, 1962; (d) in parentheses, the volume and page number(s) for the same reference in the first edition of *Samlede Værker*, edited by A.B. Drachman, J.L. Heiberg, and H.O. Lange and published in Copenhagen 1901–6.

References to *Søren Kierkegaards Papirer* include (in this order): (a) the entry number (1–6969) for the English translation as (and if) contained in *Søren Kierkegaard's Journals and Papers* (abbreviated as *Journals*), vols. 1–7, edited and translated by Howard V. Hong and Edna H. Hong (Bloomington: Indiana University Press 1967–78); (b) the standard reference to the same item in the Second Enlarged Edition of *Papirer*, edited by Niels Thulstrup and published in Copenhagen by Glydendal, 1968, consisting of twenty-two volumes or part-volumes of papers, plus three volumes of index compiled by Niels Jørgen Cappelørn.

KIERKEGAARD AS HUMANIST
Discovering My Self

1

My Self: An Overview

Kierkegaard says that a physician has a view of sickness different from that of the patient. Why? "Because the physician has a definite and developed conception of what it is to be healthy and ascertains a person's condition accordingly."[1] When he came to the climax of his creative vision in 1848, Kierkegaard believed that he had captured a comprehensive understanding, "a definite and developed conception," of spiritual health. Typically, he explores and depicts this vision of ideal human "health" as the reverse implication of a detailed analysis of the universal human "sickness unto death," namely despair.

In the first six paragraphs of his masterpiece, however, he gives us a summary definition of spiritual health, of ideal human selfhood, in a series of formulas that are so exact and coherent that they may rightly be called "algebraic" in their precision and intensiveness. Many people, on first reading these words, are inclined to denounce them as gibberish and deliberate mystification, without any exact meanings. In this study the attempt will be made to demonstrate that Kierkegaard has "definite and developed" content in mind for each word and phrase. This content is not there on the page as such but only by infinitely complex allusion and connotation. Everything that he had previously written, in both books and journals, and everything that follows in *The Sickness unto Death*, must be poured into the stark structure of these paragraphs in order to enflesh their bare bones and to bring them to life. The present study is one limited attempt to do so.

However, before we get lost in the endless and criss-crossing paths of the labyrinth of Kierkegaard's thought, before we try to trace the inter-

---

1 *The Sickness unto Death*, p. 156; (KW 19:23); SV 15:82; (11:137).

weavings of the infinitely rich variety of figures and designs in the single fabric of his authorship, let us try to see the bare bones, their joints, and their overall gestalt.

Two preliminary points must be made. First, in these opening paragraphs, as throughout *The Sickness unto Death*, Kierkegaard is describing what all human beings have in common, what he elsewhere (in *Works of Love*) calls "the universally human" (*det Almene-Menneskelige*), "the eternal likeness, the equality." Hence the first word, *Mennesket*, must be understood in this sense: the universal human being that "constantly shines in every individual [*Enkelte*]" through all the unique particular differences of each one of us. So he formulates his equation: "The human being is spirit. But what is spirit? Spirit is the self." Secondly, in equating spirit with self, he departs from the tendency of previous Western thought to identify the spiritual life with a realm that is antimaterial and otherworldly, and makes the startling assertion that the "spiritual" includes all aspects of the unitary self. At least, it was startling in the context of early nineteenth-century thinking, and much of twentieth-century psychology, anthropology, and theology had to work hard to accept this concept and to draw its implications. George Schrader is probably right that this is one of the many points at which Kierkegaard learned something positive from Hegel, namely, "the conception of spirit as encompassing the totality of man's being."[2] The dramatic significance of this equation of spirit with self will become clear in the next two chapters.

Kierkegaard next asks, "But what is the self?" Ah, at last! After hovering and circling around this question ever since his commitment to "anthropological contemplation" (1840) and his posing the question in *Either-Or*, now at the height of his confidence in his own genius, he can at last face the question directly and propose an answer that gathers together most (but not all) of the diverse threads of his contemplation. This answer, as proposed in these first six paragraphs, states five qualifications for the mature or fulfilled self. Each qualification assumes and brings forward the preceding ones, and each is structured proleptically in anticipation of those that follow. As indicated in the Preface, our study of these five qualifications will be divided into two parts, the humanistic (the first two) and the theological (the last three). But it will be helpful for following those prolix treatments to hear and see the five in their simplest possible statement and in their interrelationships. This

---

2 George A. Schrader, *Existential Philosophers*, p. 21.

task will require rather detailed exposition of some of the words and definitions contained in what Kierkegaard himself calls his "formula."³ Our study will treat a sixth and final topic, namely an aspect of the life of the self that is, without doubt deliberately, omitted from Kierkegaard's formula as stated in *Sickness unto Death*, but is treated on and off throughout the entire authorship including his last great work, *Practice in Christianity*. I refer to what Reinhold Niebuhr called *The Self and the Dramas of History*.

So: "What is the self?" The five qualifications in the formula are these:

(1) The self is a relation.
(2) The self is a relation which relates to itself.
(3) The self, as a relation which relates to itself, is established by an other (*et Andet*), and in relating to itself relates to this other.
(4) The self, as a relation, fails to relate to itself and fails to relate to the other, and so finds itself in a dual disrelation of despair.
(5) The self finds its despair completely rooted out (healed) when the self rests transparently in the power that established it.

Since each of these qualifications will be exposited at length in our total study that follows, only a few basic statements of clarification will be made now on each of them.

(1) By saying that the self is a "relation," Kierkegaard is asserting that the human being is composed of a basic indissoluble and irreducible duality or polarity. He makes the same point by saying that "the human being is a synthesis," and "a synthesis is a relation between two." The basic polarity Kierkegaard always starts with is "infinitude and finitude," but here he adds two other controlling pairs, "the temporal and the eternal" and "freedom and necessity." The meaning and interrelationship of these polarities will be exposited in detail in the next three chapters. But Kierkegaard makes clear, in a later section of *Sickness*, that in what he means by a "synthesis" neither pole is ever eliminated, and the polarity of the two is never overcome in a higher unity. He says that when the relation becomes a concrete self as "the conscious synthesis of finitude and infinitude," this means "neither to become finite nor to become infinite, for that which is to become concrete is indeed a synthesis." And he says, "The dialectic inherent in the self as a synthesis" means

---

3 *Sickness*, p. 147; (KW 19:14); SV 15:73f.; (11:143).

that "the one [constituent] constantly is its opposite."[4] In other words, the interplay of the infinite and the finite is an inherent, inescapable, and permanent condition of human existence.

However, to return to the first paragraphs of *Sickness*, Kierkegaard states flatly that "the self is not the relation," that is, the relation in its character as a simple polarity. "A synthesis is a relation between two. Considered in this way, the human being is still not self. In the relation between two, the relation is the third as a negative unity, and the two relate to the relation, and in the relation to the relation." What he means by a "negative unity," and by the puzzling language that follows, requires detailed analysis if we are to be clear about what he means when he says that the self is a "positive third" or unity. Much of this analysis will be done in the next chapter but at least the basic terms must be clarified here in order to have an accurate translation.

What then does Kierkegaard mean by a "negative unity" in a "relation between two?" In the subordinate sentence, following this statement in paragraph two, he gives us a very significant illustration. "Under the qualification soul, the relation between soul [the psychical] and body [the sensuous] is such a relation."[5] The key to the meaning of this illustration is to be found in a passage in *Either/Or*. There it is said, "As a determinant [qualification] of spirit, sensuousness was first posited by Christianity. ... Sensuousness already existed in the world, but not spiritually determined. How then did it exist? It was determined psychically. ... But sensuousness psychically determined is not opposition, exclusion, but harmony and consonance."[6] This is the stage or sphere of life which Kierkegaard calls the aesthetic or immediacy. In immediacy, he says,

> there is no infinite consciousness of the self. ... The *immediate one* (in so far as immediacy occurs in reality without any reflection) is merely psychically determined; his self, he himself, is a something within the dimensions of temporality and secularity, ... and has but an illusory appearance of having anything eternal in it. The self is bound up in immediacy with ... desiring, craving, enjoyment, etc., yet passively.[7]

---

4 Ibid., pp. 162ff.; (KW 19:30); SV 15:87f.; (11:143).

5 Contrary to the new Hong translation, I occasionally retain Kierkegaard's own words "soul" and "body" to illustrate that he is here once again deliberately instilling radically new understandings and meanings into traditional terminology. I also use "sensuous" instead of "physical" in order to tie this passage in with the one that follows from *Either/Or*.

6 *Either/Or*, 1:60; (KW 3:61f.); SV 2:60; (1:44f.).

7 *Sickness*, p. 184; (KW 19:50f.); SV 15:106f.; (11:162f.).

In other words, a human being living at the level of a simple relation between two, where the psyche passively accepts what there is to enjoy in the way of sensuous desires, is not yet spirit or self, indeed is unaware that there is an other self, a "third" that transcends the relation which is immediate interplay of psyche and sense. The key statement in the above quotes is this: "Sensuousness psychically determined is not opposition [*Modsætning*] ... but harmony." Because there is no *opposition* in it, the relation between psyche and sense is a *negative* unity. Why "negative"? Because this immediacy blocks the emergence of consciousness of that self which is not yet, blocks the awareness of the task of becoming one's self. Here Kierkegaard typically reverses Hegelian language: any harmony or unity that involves the "mediation" and "annulment" of opposites and contradictions is "negative" because it prevents or destroys authentic human selfhood. That harmony or unity is "positive" which calls into play and preserves those opposites which give rise to self-consciousness and ethical determination to become self.

Now we are in a position to give an interpretation to those puzzling words that follow Kierkegaard's statement: "In the relation between two, the relation is the third as a negative unity," namely, "and the two relate to the relation, and in the relation to the relation." The latter sentence can now be translated as follows: "the two [the sensuous and the psychical] relate [find fulfilment] to the relation [in immediacy], and in the relation [and in this immediacy] to the relation [there is no awareness of contradiction or of a transcendent other self]." Kierkegaard says, "*Immediacy is fortune*, because in immediacy there is no contradiction [*Modsigelse*]; the immediate individual is essentially seen as a fortunate individual. ... The immediate individual never comes to any understanding with misfortune, for he never becomes dialectical in himself."[8] In *Either/Or* he gives the ancient Greek as a prime example of this kind of immediacy.

In the Greek consciousness, the sensuous was under control in the beautiful individuality, or, more rightly stated, it was not controlled; for it was not an enemy to be subjugated, nor a dangerous rebel who should be held in check; it was liberated into life and joy in the beautiful individuality. ... The psychical which constituted the beautiful individuality was unthinkable without the sensuous. So

---

[8] *Postscript*, p. 388; (KW 12.1:433–4); SV 10:121; (7:376). For a restatement of Kierkegaard's "puzzling words," see below at note 4 in chapter 3.

sensuousness indeed existed in the world before Christianity "but not spiritually determined."⁹

What, then, does it mean to be "spiritually determined"? If "the human being is not yet self" when regarded simply as a "relation," as a synthesis of two in immediacy where there is no opposition or contradiction *within* the relation, then what more is needed? This question brings us to the second qualification of the self in Kierkegaard's formula.

(2) In answer to the question, "What is the self?", Kierkegaard gives us a key formula that he uses repeatedly throughout *The Sickness unto Death*. The full formula does not occur in any other writing, although there are pieces of it in several other works.¹⁰ The formula is: "*Selvet er et Forhold, der forholder sig til sig selv.*" The Danish is given because a translation that is different from that of Lowrie and of the Hongs is proposed here, and space is given to this issue because it is significant for understanding the formula. The Hong translation (a definite improvement on Lowrie) is: "The self is a relation that relates itself to itself." We propose: "The self is a relation, which relates to itself." The comma and the relative pronoun are used (as in the Danish) to show that the first point of the formula is to stress the fundamental polarity in the structure of the self.¹¹

But the main point is that, by not translating the reflexive pronoun (*sig*), emphasis is put on the *act* of the "relation," i.e., the relation itself (*sig*) is taking the initiative to "relate" to itself. This is certainly the intention of the Hong translation also, as indicated by the fact that in the next paragraph the Hongs translate the same construction without the reflexive pronoun in English: "... and the two relate [*forholde sig*] to the relation" (not "relate *themselves*"—as in the Lowrie translation). In other words, the movement of "relates" (*forholder sig*) as reflexive is not transitively forward

---

9 *Either/Or*, 1:60f.; (KW 3:61f.); SV 2:61; (1:45).

10 See especially *The Concept of Anxiety*, p. 40; (KW 8:44); SV 6:138; (4:315): "How does the spirit relate to itself (*forholder ... sig til sig selv*)?"; and *Stages on Life's Way*, p. 387; (KW 11:427); SV 8:224; (6:398): "he, in a presentiment of a possibility, is unwilling to relate to himself (*forholde sig til sig*) in his religious idea. ..." There is another startling anticipation in *Fragments*, which will be discussed in the next note.

11 Howard Hong argues that the comma and relative pronoun "which" detract from the main point of the definition, namely, that the relation *relates to itself*. Granted, that is the main point. But its real significance and meaning is lost if one blurs Kierkegaard's first point, namely, that the relation is a synthesis of two *in and for itself* in order to be able to relate to itself. Kierkegaard makes this point in two notes written for *Sickness* (*Journals*, 6, 749; VIII² B 168:5, 6). In the first he says, "To be a human being is to be a relationship." And in the second, "The composite of the finite and the infinite, freedom and necessity, the divine and the human, is a relationship for itself."

toward an object but reflexively backward in reference to some hidden action of the relation within itself. To say that "the relation relates itself to itself" could too easily be understood (in English) as positing two objective entities or selves that are being interrelated. So, in this text, I will use the simpler translation, "... a relation, which relates to itself."[12] The question is: what is the hidden action or behaviour that transforms the relation, in its immediacy, into a "positive third" which is "the self"?

---

12 Without wishing to exaggerate the point, yet I will add the following comments because they will help to clarify the meaning of Kierkegaard's formula-definition of the self.

(1) In a generously lengthy response to my inquiry, Howard Hong made clear that he is concerned that my translation might be read as meaning that "relates to" is not an action but a passive state of affairs, such as when we say for example, "This war relates to (that is, has to do with) economic conditions." That is certainly not my intent. But the possible reading of his translation (which I mention in my text) is equally misleading. The key to the meaning of this formula lies in Kierkegaard's later statement [*Sickness*, p. 162; (KW 19:29); SV 15:87; (11:142)], "this synthesis [of infinitude and finitude] is a relation, and a relation that, even though it is derived, relates to itself [*forholder sig til sig selv*], which is freedom. The self is freedom." So he is saying that the act of *forholder sig til sig selv* is "freedom." Since "freedom" (as we shall come to see) means the voluntary leap of decision to act in a certain way, the occurrence of this event as "the dialectic in the determinants possibility and necessity" is best indicated (I think) by the non-commital phrase "relates to itself," thus leaving the occurrence of "freedom" to be the indeterminate event it is. Incidentally, I came to this conclusion, and wrote this first chapter, sometime in 1984. I was recently encouraged to hold to my conclusion when I came across Alastair Hannay's translation of *The Sickness unto Death* in which he also uses "relates to itself" (see pp. 43 and 59).

(2) It should be noted that on many occasions throughout the rest of the works and the journals the Hongs translate "*forholder sig til*" as "relates to."

(3) Finally, we should take note of one very problematic use of the formula *forholder sig til sig selv* and note that the Hongs have vacillated on its translation. The passage occurs in *Fragments*, and curiously the formula is applied not to freedom but to the nature of "necessity" (i.e., the necessity of "nature" as formulated rationally in natural "law"). Climacus has just made the point that "the change of coming into existence is the transition from possibility to actuality," and then asks, "Can the necessary come into existence?" His answer, as it stands in the original Danish (SV³ 6:68; SV¹ 4:237), literally reads, "Coming into existence is a change, but the necessary cannot be changed at all, since it always relates to itself [*forholder sig til sig selv*], and relates to itself in the same way." In the first English translation of *Fragments* in 1936 (p. 60 of the second printing of 1942), David Swenson translated the key words as "the necessary cannot undergo any change, since it is always related to itself, and related to itself in the same manner." In Howard Hong's 1962 revision of Swenson's translation (p. 91), he gave this version: "the necessary cannot be changed, since it always relates itself to itself and relates itself to itself in the same way." But in Howard and Edna Hong's own new translation of 1985 (vol. 7 of *Kierkegaard's Writings*), they reverted to Swenson's original language, so we read, "since the necessary is always related to itself and is related to itself in the same way, it cannot be changed at all." I believe that the Hongs were correct to adopt the latter translation, for reasons I will give presently.

That this question is Kierkegaard's concern here comes out in the second part of the sentence, where he gives a supplementary definition of the self. Here translation is again difficult and critical. Continuing from the previous Danish quotation, it reads: "*eller er det i Forholdet, at Forholdet forholder sig til sig selv.*" This time I believe that Lowrie is closer to Kierkegaard's meaning than is the Hong translation. The latter reads: "or is the relation's relating itself to itself in the relation." This is certainly a possible translation, but what does "in the relation" mean in this case? It would seem to mean what, in the second paragraph, is called "a negative unity" wherein "the two relate to the relation and in the relation to the relation," whereas Kierkegaard certainly means this formula to be a description of the self as a "positive third."

A straightforward translation precisely poses the question asked at the end of the previous paragraph: "or [the self] is that [quality? structure? condition? act?] in the relation that [explains the fact that] the relation relates to itself." In other words, this second description of the self adds to the first an element of complexity or a depth-dimension to the term "relation," pointing to something interior to and hidden in the relation, and revealing the true character of the act of "relating to itself." What is this something interior and hidden? Kierkegaard gives a very direct answer. Later in *Sickness* he says, "The self is composed of infinitude and finitude. But this synthesis is a relation, and a relation which, even though it is derived, relates to itself, which is freedom. The self is freedom. But freedom is the dialectical [element] in the determinants possibility and necessity."[13] So "relating to itself" is the freedom, the choosing which the relation gets involved in and which disturbs its immediacy when, out of the *opposition* of finitude and infinitude, there emerges awareness of possibilities which have not yet been actualized in the relation. How these possibilities are both inward and outward, both present and absent, how they "come into existence" not of necessity but in freedom, how this involves the emergence of consciousness and *self-consciousness*, as well as a relationship with the eternal—all this Kierkegaard had previously explored in *Either/Or, Philosophical Fragments,* and *Postscript,* and in a number of "edifying discourses." And we will explore it with him in some following chapters. But here it must be clear that all this, and more, is implied by that simple phrase, "a relation, which relates to itself." The self is all "*that* in the relation" that, put together, adds up to *freedom*, because "the self is freedom." Or to put it in

13 *Sickness*, p. 162; (KW 19:29); SV 15:87; (11:142).

other words, the phrase, "a relation which relates to itself," is a *description* of an event, of an act or behaviour (taking "relate" or *forholde sig* in its initial sense), an event in which the relation chooses to become a self that is "there" but only as a possibility which must be actualized. This event does not happen "in the relation" when the relation is "between two," but this event breaks the relation open to a new stage or sphere of existence in which the relation becomes a "positive third."

It should be clear, therefore, that this language is highly figurative. These words cannot be taken as an abstract technical definition with a literal meaning. They are meant to connote a whole series of rich images which invite the reader to explore their significance in her/his own existence and self-understanding. As already noted, Kierkegaard himself felt that the dialectical and rigorous language and thought structure of *Sickness* requires a parallel rhetorical treatment in which "every single individual form should at the same time be depicted poetically."[14] In later sections of *Sickness* he supplies some such poetical images, and we shall draw others from previous works to fill in the figurative meanings of the "geometrical" language of this formulaic definition of the self.

(3) In the next place, in the third of his opening six paragraphs, Kierkegaard makes the flat statement: such a complicated being as the human self "must either have established [*sat* from *sætte*] itself or have been established by an other." And in the next paragraph he draws the inescapable inference: "If the relation which relates to itself has been established by an other, then the relation is indeed the third, but this relation, the third, is yet again a relation [that] relates to that which established the entire relation." And immediately he flatly states his own position: "The human self is such a derived, established relation, a relation which relates to itself and in relating to itself relates to an other."

Humanist existentialists must wish that Kierkegaard had never written these words. Some of them make much of the fact that human existence is "given," or that we have been "thrown" (another meaning of *sætte*) into existence (Heidegger). But they see no grounds for talking about "an other" which/who has done the giving or throwing. Moreover, this basic assumption of Kierkegaard about the human self must be embarrassing to those who claim to be able to derive from Kierkegaard's writings an anthropological ontology which omits this element of a transcendent "other." It is Kierkegaard's clear meaning that the two acts of relating, "to itself" and "to an other," are inseparable. One cannot do

14 *Journals*, 6137; VIII[1] A 652.

the one without doing the other simultaneously. In other words, his anthropological ontology integrally includes a "religious" dimension. He had worked out this point very carefully at the beginning of his authorship in *Either/Or*, and summarizes it in this way: "In case what I chose did not exist but absolutely came into existence with the choice, I would not be choosing, I would be creating [*skabte*]; but I do not create myself, I choose myself."[15] And he makes the same point in *The Sickness unto Death* when he is describing defiance as the ultimate form of despair.[16] At the end of these opening six paragraphs he names this "other" as "the power that established it [the self]". And later he unabashedly calls this power "God." And in a later chapter we will show that when Kierkegaard, in the first paragraph, says that the human self is also a synthesis of the temporal and the eternal, it is this power, this God, that he means by the "eternal."

The question remains: in spite of his own convictions and his intentions in his writings, are Kierkegaard's anthropology and theology really inseparable? It was one of the keenest interests in the writing of this book to search for an honest answer to this question. One of the main justifications for writing this book is the fact that one constantly finds bits and pieces, or whole strains, of Kierkegaard's anthropology in novels, plays, poetry, and even (especially?) detective fiction, also in psychologies, philosophies, and even sociologies, also in the columns of commentators on politics, society, and sports—all without a single trace of his theology. Are they justified in borrowing one without the other? Can anyone see and embrace the truth of many of his depictions of human existence, as living, frightening, revealing images of our everyday life—and yet not even cast a glance at his plumbing of (what he believed to be) the transcendent infinite heights and depths that surround and permeate and give substance to these images? There are even theologians who claim to learn much from Kierkegaard and who follow him all the way through his religiousness A (which requires no special revelation), but who totally reject his religiousness B derived (he says) from encounter with and faith in the intrusion of the eternal into time in the figure of Jesus.

Are these enterprises legitimate? Should they be encouraged, even if oneself goes all the way with Kierkegaard? These are questions without easy answers, perhaps no final answers. This present study struggles with

15 *Either/Or*, 2:219f.; (KW 4:215f.); SV 3:200; (2:193).
16 *Sickness*, pp. 201ff.; (KW 19:68); SV 15:122; (11:179).

them as openly and honestly as possible throughout its entirety. The rest of this present volume is written as if the basic anthropology were experienceable and describable without any reference to religiousness B (Christianity) and without dependence on its theology. Then there is a pause to ask about the realism of such a project. What forces this pause and this question is the fact of the human failure to move in a straight line to the realization of all the good human possibilities. How does one understand the origin, the meaning, and the scope of this failure and its attendant evils? Kierkegaard believed that the Christian religious experience, Christian faith, (with its sense of being "created," its sense of "sin," its sense of "salvation"), gives the only adequate answer to this question, and, more important, possesses a unique power to free us from sin and its despair.

His perspectives on these issues will be explored in another volume, and readers of a humanist or religiousness-A point of view are invited to listen carefully to Kierkegaard the theologian, to see if they can detect points where his appeal to religiousness B is unnecessary for the validation of his depiction of human origin, failure, and renewal. The resolution of this issue can help decide the legitimacy of the widespread borrowing from Kierkegaard, and will be of great assistance to Christians (other than fundamentalists) as they struggle again with the pressing question of the uniqueness of Christian faith in relation to other living faiths of our world.

(4) The fourth qualification of the self in Kierkegaard's summary formula is the assertion of universal human failure. This failure takes two distinguishable but interdependent forms. The self as a relation fails to relate to itself, and it fails to relate to the power that established it. They are interdependent because "the self cannot by itself arrive at and be in equilibrium and rest, but only by, in relating to itself, [also] relating to that which has established the entire relation." Hence the failure of the relation to relate to itself "reflects itself infinitely in the relation to the power that established it."

Already in this paragraph (the fifth) Kierkegaard uses two key terms. He calls the failure to relate (in either form) a "disrelation" (*Misforhold*).[17] He calls the attendant human condition "despair" (*Fortvivlelse*). What is

---

17 The Hongs translate *Misforhold* as "misrelation." It is not an important point but I prefer "disrelation" because the prefix mis- in English connotes "badly, wrongly, unfavourably," while dis- connotes "to do the opposite of, deprive of, exclude, expel." So dis- has a stronger sense of action, and of negative action, while mis- is more passive. *Misforhold* is not simply a misfortune that has befallen a human being, or simply a mistaken relation. It is a broken relation traceable to human failure.

meant by each of these and how they are related will require considerable analysis later on. But he does raise the question (in the next section), "Where does despair come from?" It must at least be noted here that Kierkegaard does not treat this question, in any systematic way, in *Sickness*. But here he gives the very concise answer that disrelation occurs in and despair comes out of the self, the spirit, as a relation which relates to itself. That is to say, their source lies in human freedom and its responsibility. This failure of human freedom Kierkegaard has already analysed and depicted in great detail in *The Concept of Anxiety*. So we will have to bring all of that material to bear in the exploration of despair's disrelation as a universal (but not inherent) qualification of the human self.

However, whether or not there is agreement about the origin of despair and about who or what is responsible for it, Kierkegaard submits detailed analysis and overwhelming evidence that despair is not just an occasional human feeling but is the universal "human condition." There are those, of course, who contend that Augustine projected his own "original sin" on the human race, and that likewise this "despair" is Kierkegaard's projection of his own introspective melancholy and depression. Judgment about the force and validity of Kierkegaard's entire vision of human existence hangs in the balance on this issue. Even more critical for this judgment is his insistence, again, on the interdependence of anthropology and theology. The purely human levels of despair, attendant on the broken relations of self to itself and of self to neighbour, are seen as reflective of the broken relation of self to the Eternal, God. Thus the ultimate and normative form of despair is called "sin," that is, despair "before God." For Kierkegaard the ultimate mystery is not the greatness and goodness of human existence. That is what life is given and structured for. The deepest mystery is that the self, when confronted by and offered love, may take offence and withdraw into itself and its "sickness unto death."

(5) The final qualification of the human self, as depicted in these first six paragraphs of *Sickness*, is for many a strange note, perhaps an unbelievable note, for Kierkegaard to make. It is a note of hope. He is popularly known, if at all, as the prophet of hopelessness, despair, death, and nothingness, of human brokenness and defeat. This is the picture given in that distorted account of his life by Josiah Thompson.[18] It is also the

---

18 Josiah Thompson, *Kierkegaard*. After having talked personally with Mr Thompson about my accusation of "distortion," I understand better his reasons, but I still do not accept his conclusions. More on this later.

conclusion of that much more sophisticated and sympathetic analysis of Kierkegaard's concept of the self by Mark C. Taylor in his *Journeys to Selfhood*. One of the conclusions of this present study is that such interpretations are based on a total misunderstanding, if not a deliberate misreading, of the authorship, and derive too much from a judgment of the writings in the light of Kierkegaard's own personal life and character, whereas Kierkegaard himself constantly protests that he in no way claimed to be himself the perfect example of the God-inflected humanity which he was describing as the fulfilment of human potentiality, even though he always adds, "I am striving."

The note of hope at the beginning of *Sickness* is given as a "formula" for the complete conquest and elimination of despair. It is: "in relating to itself and in willing to be itself, the self rests transparently in the power that established it." Kierkegaard did not mean this formula as a facetious afterthought. He did not mean to dangle it as an impossible possibility at the end of his crushing depiction of universal human despair in all its various forms. Thus, in the last paragraph of *Sickness*, he repeats this formula and insists that it was the major theme running throughout the entire book. Then he concludes, "This formula in turn, as has been frequently pointed out, is the definition of faith." This recalls how he finishes his other reputedly "pessimistic" book, *The Concept of Anxiety*. Its last chapter is entitled "Anxiety as Saving through Faith."

In other words, the central focus, the main theme, the purpose and goal of Kierkegaard's entire authorship, and hence of his entire life, is the depiction of what it means to live "by faith" or "in love," of how one comes to self-actualization in the synthesis of the temporal and the eternal, or in terms relevant to his own situation, of how one may become a Christian while living in Christendom. Thus in *Either/Or* he says, "When all has become still around one, ... when the soul is alone in the whole world, then there appears before one, not a distinguished man, but the eternal power itself. The heavens part, as it were, and the I chooses itself—or rather, receives itself."[19] And again, "I choose the absolute, which chooses me. I establish [*sætter*] the absolute, which establishes me."[20] Thus, in *Philosophical Fragments* and *The Concept of Anxiety*, the one who has fallen from innocence and lost the truth is encountered by the truth in the absolute paradox and is enabled to return to the truth through faith/love. One comes to know "the fullness of time" when the

---

19 *Either/Or*, 2:181; (KW 4:177); SV 3:166; (2:160f.).
20 Ibid., 2:217; SV 3:198; (2:191).

eternal invades one's time and brings the past and future together. Thus in *Stages, Postscript,* and *Upbuilding Discourses in Various Spirits* the fulfilment of self requires that one goes on beyond the aesthetic and the ethical into the religious stage or sphere, and even at the level of religiousness A, as described in these works, a significant measure of self-fulfilment is held out as a possibility. Finally, Kierkegaard makes a very self-conscious turn in his authorship in order to explore and to depict more deeply and fully that ultimate stage of the self's pilgrimage in religiousness B, i.e. the stage of *faith,* which, he says, "is a totally distinct sphere ... paradoxically distinguished from the aesthetic and metaphysical ... and the ethical."[21] This he does mainly in <u>Works of Love, The Sickness unto Death,</u> and <u>Practice in Christianity.</u> Six months before he died, he said, in the exaggerated language of that period, that in all the previous works he had given a version of Christianity that he had "finished and left behind," and that in the latter works he sought to "get further forward in the direction of discovering the Christianity of the New Testament."[22] He certainly did not "leave behind" everything from his earlier works, and it will be shown at length that there is much exposition of the possibilities of religiousness A in *Works of Love* and *The Sickness unto Death.* Nevertheless, he did "get further forward" in the later works.

The main point here, however, is that his climactic depiction of faith and love is deliberately described as ideal and impossible not in order to discourage pilgrims from striving forward "on the way." He believed that he was actually helping and encouraging them. But he did want to make it impossible for anyone to identify that "way" with any aesthetic, ethical, philosophical, cultural, institutional, political approximation and compromise—which was what he saw happening in the church and state of his contemporary world.

Thus concludes our summary of the five qualifications of the mature or fulfilled self as briefly defined by Kierkegaard in the first six paragraphs of *The Sickness unto Death.* The formula for the self (a relation, which relates to itself and simultaneously to the power that established it) can now be translated as follows: the self is an essential polarity of finitude and infinitude out of whose interplay as opposites emerge consciousness of freedom to choose the enactment of certain potentialities (possibilities) in harmony with one's given (necessitated) conditions (both inward and outward), a unity enabled by freedom's (simulta-

---

21 *Postscript,* p. 514; (KW 12.1:580); SV 10:246; (7:506).
22 *Kierkegaard's Attack upon "Christendom,"* p. 52; SV 19:69; (14:76f.).

neous) joyful acceptance of loving affirmation and support by the eternal giver of existence, and acceptance of eternity's inescapable demand that one become this concrete self.

As already noted, this definition blatantly and deliberately omits two of the prime qualifications of selfhood as understood by the social sciences as well as by most theology of our own day. It omits any reference to the *communal* and the *historical* character of the self, in its origins, development, and maturation. Kierkegaard does not deny but quite clearly acknowledges these dimensions of human existence as being operative at each of the "stages" on life's way. We will see how he does this as we take up each of his five qualifications one by one. We will especially take pains to explore how he interrelates the love of God and the love of neighbour. But we will leave to the end of our total study a consideration of the overall significance of these omissions in the formula and their critical implications.

2
My Self: A Synthesis of Two

"The view which sees life's doubleness [*Duplicitæt*] or duality [*Dualisme*] is higher and deeper than that which seeks unity."[1]

These words, a journal entry of 1844, could be inscribed as the motto above everything Kierkegaard wrote. Not that he did not yearn and seek after unity, and find it in the experience of Christian faith/love. But his fundamental conviction was that any unity, however arrived at, which erased, "annulled," or even blurred "life's doubleness" would lead to the loss of freedom and to the absorption and destruction of the human individual, of human "existence." This duality is at the base of "having a self, being a self," and therefore is integral to "the greatest, the infinite concession made to every human being, but also eternity's demand upon her/him."[2]

Kierkegaard has therefore been accused of a reversion to "Kantian dualism," and has been derided for not embracing Hegel's vision of human fulfilment in the unity of divine *Geist* (Spirit/Mind). But Kierkegaard is not to be understood either as Kantian or as an anti-Hegelian. He was greatly helped in his conceptualization by both of these philosophers, but the wellsprings of his own vision are to be traced elsewhere.

Malantschuk agrees that "Kierkegaard's point of departure for an understanding of the human is the perception that the human is a synthesis of two opposite qualities."[3] Malantschuk traces the origin of this perspective to Kierkegaard's own reading of the New Testament and to his hearing A.N. Clausen's lectures on dogmatics in 1834–35 and H.L.

---

1 *Journals*, 704; IV A 192.
2 *Sickness*, p. 154; (KW 19:21); SV 15:80; (11:135).
3 G. Malantschuk, *Fra Individ til den Enkelte*, p. 14.

My Self: A Synthesis of Two

Martensen's lectures on "Speculative Dogmatics" in 1838-39, and especially to the latter's treatment of "Augustine's System." He claims that the decisive concept that Kierkegaard thus derived was "the formula 'the unity of freedom and necessity'."[4] Be that as it may, Kierkegaard responded to these elements in his education because they confirmed and described the actualities of his own experience. The real roots of this basic perspective were "phenomenological," analysis of the conditions and events of his own existence. "Existence begins with contradiction," he said. "As long as I live, I live in contradiction, because life itself is contradiction."[5]

[margin note: Life is Contradiction]

So he came to know himself as "a synthesis of two." Two *what?* He finds and gives no single, easy, definitive answer. In his summary definition of the self in the first paragraph of *Sickness*, he tells us "The human being is a synthesis of the infinite and the finite, of the temporal and the eternal, of freedom and necessity." But along the way he explores many others: body and soul, the sensuous and the psychical, the ideal and the actual, the comic and the tragic, the metaphysical and the accidental, the male and the female, sin and faith, etc..

Probably the primal duality experienced by Kierkegaard, and used by him as the key to depicting and understanding the adventure of becoming a self, was the antithesis between the outward (*Udvortes*) and the inward (*Indvortes*). These terms, and the integral dimensions and overwhelming magnitudes of human existence indicated by them, appear repeatedly throughout *Either/Or* (written in 1841-42), *Eighteen Upbuilding Discourses* (1842-45), and *Stages on Life's Way* (1844-45). They serve as the basis for his later, more subtle and complex distinctions between subjective-objective and infinite-finite. But the "outward" and "inward" of these earlier works point to the fundamental structure of human nature as experienced by every human being, whether or not they ever move on to the more mature stage of "subjectivity" and "inwardness" (an inadequate translation of *Inderlighed*) as explored so extensively in *Postscript*.

Kierkegaard's consciousness, from early childhood onward, was overwhelmed with awareness of these two opposing spheres or worlds of his existence. He later chose two terms which capture the essential tone and mood and meaning of these two magnitudes within which he lived and moved and had his being. The "outward" is the realm of the fortu-

---

4 Ibid., p. 15.
5 *Journals*, 703, 705; IV A 57, V A 68.

itous and accidental (*det Tilfældige*). The "inward" is the realm of fantasy and imagination (the Danish *Fantasi* means both). In the next chapter we will see that the outward as "objectivity" can also be the realm of scientific and philosophic abstraction and speculation, while the inward as "subjectivity" can also be the realm of freedom, ethical choosing, and religious faith. But prior and more fundamental are fantasy and the fortuitous.

For Kierkegaard as a child, the inward world was more real than the outward. He learned to live in and by his imagination. In his usual hyperbole, he says that he was born an old man and "leapt completely over childhood and youth." In his retrospective account of how he became an author, he says that when he was a child, "and the other children play or jest or whatever else they do," and when he was a youth, "and the other young people make love and dance or whatever else they do," he was living a life of "spirit" and "melancholy." But "with the help of imagination" he says he performed "the trick of appearing to be the youngest of all," and hid his melancholy "under an apparent gaiety and *joie de vivre*."[6] If he absorbed his melancholy from his father, so was his power of fantasy heightened by his father. In a story generally taken as autobiographical, Kierkegaard tells about a child who would ask to go out to play but was usually refused by his father. Instead, the father would take the child by the hand and ask him where he wanted to go. Then, walking him up and down the room, the father would describe in glowing detail every step of the way there and back, including everyone they would meet. For the child "it was as if the world was being created as they conversed. ... The life in his paternal home thus contributed to the development of his imagination [*Phantasie*]." And when this child went to school and in Greek grammar was taught that the accusative implies extension in time and place, "then everything expanded for him. The preposition disappeared, and the extension in time and space became like a huge empty picture for his intuition. His imagination was once more set in motion."[7]

It was on this experiential base that Kierkegaard was able to use his "phenomenological method" to generalize about the human soul, that is, about the inwardness of human existence. We will see how he does this later in this chapter. But here we must note that the human capacity

---

6 *The Point of View for My Work as an Author*, pp. 81, 76; SV 18:130, 127; (13:567, 564).
7 *Johannes Climacus, or, De Omnibus Dubitandum Est*, pp. 105f.; (KW 7:120f.); *Papirer* IV B 1, pp. 106f.

to fantasize, to live in a world of the imagination, becomes a key for him in his definitive exposition of infinitude in *The Sickness unto Death.* There he says, "As a rule, imagination is the medium for the process of infinitizing. ... Imagination is infinitizing reflection. ... The self is reflection, and the imagination is reflection, is the re-presentation of the self as the self's possibility."[8] So what he liked to call the hidden, secret inwardness of the human being is seen as an essential operative factor or force in the coming into existence of the self.

However, in Kierkegaard's own basic consciousness or awareness, outwardness with its character as the fortuitous and accidental increasingly loomed as just as real as inwardness, and it becomes for him an integral and positive constituent element of human existence. And ultimately, we shall see, outwardness plays an equally important role in the coming into existence and the maintenance of the self. The fortuitous/accidental becomes a major and permanent concept in Kierkegaard's exploration and exposition of his understanding of authentic selfhood over against that of the Hegelian system.

The emergence of this concept is also rooted in Kierkegaard's own personal experience. He entered university at the age of seventeen and for the first time in his life experienced some freedom from the influence of his family and particularly from his father. Gradually his mind expanded and went wild in the exploration of all of the alternative ways of understanding life. He threw himself into the social whirl of the university and adopted the fashionable life-style of his fellow students. Five years later (he stayed at the university for eleven years) he was in open rebellion against his father, Christianity, and even God. He was living a life of dissipation and, on his own confession, was on "the path of perdition." He wanted to reject and to obliterate all the fortuitous and accidental elements of his past life: his father's melancholy, his father's adultery, his own melancholy, his lost childhood, his fragile body, the narrow moralism and morbid form of Christian piety he had imbibed at home. His sense of being bound and confined within these fixed limits lasted his whole life, so that, near the end, he wrote that "my poet, when he comes, ... will say [of me], 'He suffered from being a genius in a provincial town.' "[9]

However, he came quickly to a radical revision of his evaluation of these elements of his "outward" existence. Within the next three years

8 *Sickness*, pp. 163f.; (KW 19:30f.); SV 15:88f.; (11:144).
9 *Point of View*, p. 100; SV 18:142; (13:580).

(1835-38), he left his dissolute ways, sought serious goals, made a lifelong friend in Emil Boesen, came to a new sense of Christian faith, and reconciled with his father. After his father's death soon thereafter, he committed himself to finishing his theological studies and passed his exam for the degree *magna cum laude* on 3 July 1840.

The very next day he made that critical entry in his journal already quoted above. In it his revised evaluation is clearly stated. He contrasts the fortuitous/accidental (*Tilfældige*) with the metaphysical, by which he means the eternal, transcendent, universal (inward) dimension of existence. He says that the two occur in unity in the historical and in the individual. For the individual, this unity occurs in "self-consciousness, which is the point of departure for personal-individuality [*Personlighed*]. I become conscious simultaneously in my eternal validity, ... and in my accidental finitude [*tilfældige Endelighed*]" (emphasis added). In other words, self-consciousness requires that both factors be operative "at once" (*paa eengang*). This point will be important for our argument later, but here we ask: Just what does Kierkegaard mean by "fortuitous/accidental finitude"? He gives a specific answer: "that I am this particular being, born in this land, at this time, under all the multifarious influences of these changing circumstances." And does he decry and bemoan all his particular fortuitousness? Does he seek to escape it into his "eternal validity, [or] so to speak, divine necessity?" No! "On the contrary, the true life of the individual is its apotheosis, which does not mean that this empty contentless *I* steals, as it were, out of this finitude, in order to become volitalized and diffused in its heavenward emigration, but rather that the divine inhabits and finds itself in the finite."[10]

Malantschuk is certainly correct, that the character of the fortuitous/accidental as worked out by Kierkegaard at this early date "is constantly maintained in his later use of the concept."[11] We find almost the same language in *The Sickness unto Death*. In the section delineating the interrelationship of finitude and infinitude, he says that the self, in refusing to fear others, ought "to dare to be itself in its more essential fortuitousness [*Tilfældighed*] ... in which one is yet himself for himself." And what is this characteristic which is definitive of one's self? In the later section on despair as defiance, he tells us: "One's concrete self or concretion has indeed necessity and limitations, is this very particular being with these capabilities, aptitudes, etc., in this concretion of relationships,

---

10 *Journals*, 1587; III A 1
11 Malantschuk, *Fra Individ til den Enkelte*, p. 16.

etc."[12] Kierkegaard had an intuitive conviction that, with this characteristic of human existence, he was in touch with one of the irreducible ineluctable dimensions of cosmic reality. He once remarked, "It is strange [that] it is the fortuitous/accidental and the insignificant in life which acquire significance." This insight came to him as he heard an organ-grinder playing and singing in the street below, and as an image of some Laplanders on the deck of a ship flashed across the screen of his memory.[13]

It is not too much to say, then, that understanding Kierkegaard's depiction of the self and its coming into being depends as much on a clarification of the role of the fortuitous/accidental as of subjectivity/inwardness. How they interrelate and interact in the process of the self's coming into existence will be described in the next chapter. But first we must give added substance and clarity to this basic duality or polarity of which the self is comprised in its fundamental nature prior to and as presupposition of its becoming conscious of the task of becoming a self. To do this we will depict, at a simple and initial level, the various dyads used in the opening paragraphs of *Sickness* to describe the "synthesis" which comprises the self considered simply as a "relation." They are: (1) soul/body, (2) infinitude/finitude, (3) possibility/necessity. But first some explanatory remarks must be made.

The procedure followed in this chapter yields an abstract view of human nature that might seem to be untypical of, if not unfaithful to, Kierkegaard. The human being is described as a synthesis of two, without any reference to universal human failure, despair, and relation to the eternal. This basic neutral anthropology is developed by Kierkegaard as a set of reverse implications from his analysis of sin, despair, and the aid of the eternal. Thus his method remains phenomenological rather than speculative. But in this chapter we will try to deduce these implications and let them stand by themselves. They will thus be gathered together in a summary form and possess a seeming clarity, which occur nowhere in Kierkegaard's authorship. This procedure is justified in two ways.

Kierkegaard himself does experiment with the development of certain aspects of this abstract anthropology through the voices and thoughts of some of his pseudonymous authors. So we will draw on some of this material from *Either/Or* and *Stages on Life's Way*, as well as from the works more closely "edited" by Kierkegaard himself, *Philosophical*

---

12 *Sickness*, pp. 166, 201f.; (KW 19:33, 68); SV 15:91, 122; (11:147, 179).
13 *Journals*, 5522; III A 167.

Fragments and *Postscript.* Then it must be noted that, in the work most closely related to *The Sickness unto Death* in subject matter, Kierkegaard has Virgilius Haufniensis compose *The Concept of Anxiety* as a purely psychological study of the preconditions of original sin. Even more to the point, however, is that in *Sickness* itself he himself commits a notable act of abstraction which serves as a basis for our present chapter. In his first attempt to clarify the nature of despair (as the disrelation in the relation which relates to itself), he analyses "despair considered in such a way that one does not reflect upon whether it is conscious or not, so that one reflects only upon the constituentelements [*Momenter*] of the synthesis."[14] As a matter of fact, there is considerable phenomenological reporting of autobiographical and religio-experiential material in this "abstract" analysis. But this attempt to "reflect only upon the constituent elements of the synthesis" has two results with significant implications.

It must be noted, first, that Kierkegaard omits from this entire section any mention of one of the dyads which he lists in his definition of the human being as a synthesis in the opening paragraph of *Sickness*, namely, "the temporal and the eternal." Obviously, he does not consider the "eternal" to be a constituent element of the basic structure of the human being as a synthesis or relation of two. This omission is often overlooked by interpreters of Kierkegaard, especially by the more philosophically inclined. But it is clear that when Kierkegaard says that the human can be understood and fulfilled only in relation with the eternal, and that there is "something of the eternal" in the human, he in no way is modifying his basic assumption that the human as such, by itself, on its own, is not eternal, that there remains to all eternity "an infinite distinction of quality" between the human and the eternal.

Secondly, when Kierkegaard reflects only on the constituent elements of which the synthesis is composed, he makes a significant change in the name he uses for one of the elements as listed in the opening paragraph. In that paragraph he says that the human being is a synthesis of "freedom and necessity." In this section on the "constituent elements" of the synthesis he speaks instead of "possibility/necessity." It is important for the analysis made in this chapter to see that "possibility" in the basic structure of human nature is not identical with what Kierkegaard means by "freedom." How the two are related will be explored in the next chapter.

14 *Sickness*, p. 162; (KW 19:29); SV 15:87; (11:143).

Thus our first justification for the abstract deduction of what Kierkegaard means by the self as synthesis is that Kierkegaard himself lays the groundwork for it. The second justification can be stated more simply. The extensive statement, analysis, and summary of these materials from the authorship in this form (throughout the rest of this volume) will set the stage for a clearer delineation of the issues involved in the question as to whether Kierkegaard's anthropology contains an ontology which is independent of and separable from his theology. In other words, is the "clarity" thus achieved real or deceptive? The answer to this question in this present study is not an unequivocal yes or no. Some materials even from Kierkegaard himself will be adduced in support of a kind of "both-and" reply. This issue will be explored throughout the rest of this book. We now turn to the three dyads noted above.

BODY/SOUL

In his definition of the human being as a synthesis in the opening paragraph of *Sickness*, Kierkegaard does not list this dyad along with the basic three, but mentions it only as an illustration in the second paragraph. Yet he continues to use the duality of body/soul at several key spots throughout the book. It is considered separately here because it is not strictly identical with finitude/infinitude but says something even more fundamental about human nature. And the traditional terms are sometimes used instead of the Hongs' more contemporary "physical/psychical" because Kierkegaard was deliberately trying to inject new and fresh meanings into the old language (although "psychical" is used as an adjective because "soulish" is awkward).

What then is this something fundamental, this given condition of existence in which every human being shares, which is suggested by the designation or determinants "body and soul"? In *Sickness* Kierkegaard says, "Every human being is a psychical-bodily synthesis naturally fitted for being spirit; that is the construction, but he/she prefers to live in the basement, that is, in the determinants of the sensuous [*Sandselige*]."[15] He is clearly recalling and alluding to the entire conceptuality which he had worked out four years earlier in *The Concept of Anxiety*, where he says, "The human being is a synthesis of the psychical [*det Sjelelige*] and the bodily [*det Legemlige*]. But a synthesis is unthinkable if the two are not united in a third. This third is the spirit." Then he adds some words

15 Ibid., p. 176; (KW 19:43); SV 15:100; (11:156).

which shed startling light on what he means by "living in the basement." He continues, "In innocence the human being is not merely animal, for if one were at any moment of life merely animal, one would never become human. So spirit is present, but as immediate, as dreaming."[16]

In this pregnant sentence, Kierkegaard makes some very significant connections. In the original and basic state of human existence, three characteristics obtain: (1) the essential human duality is a synthesis; that is, the two are held together in a unity (called "spirit"); (2) but this unity is still only "dreaming," or even can be said to be "asleep;" that is, the "two" are related to each other in "immediacy"; (3) in this original or "first" immediacy, the human being is in a state of "innocence." Each of these points will be treated more fully later, but each requires a brief explication under our present topic.

(1) Kierkegaard is making a very explicit and positive assertion when he says that the self, as a relation between two, is a *synthesis*. To repeat: "To become oneself is to become concrete. But to become concrete is neither to become finite nor to become infinite, for that which is to become concrete is indeed a synthesis." And from the next paragraph, "the dialectic inherent in the self as a synthesis" means that "the one [constituent] constantly is its opposite."[17] I repeat these statements here to stress the point that to see Kierkegaard's dyads as mutually exclusive opposites and as forming an absolute and irresolvable dualism is to misunderstand him totally. We have indeed heard him say that seeing "life's doubleness is higher and deeper" than just seeing unity. And we will see the reasons for this insistence when we understand that "the self is freedom" and that the "third term" which unites the temporal and the eternal is faith. But Kierkegaard insists that the doubleness of human life is not a dualism of irreconcilable opposites. Rather this basic doubleness is given in an unbreakable, inescapable unity. That is what he means by a "synthesis." And this synthesis of two is "dialectical"; that is to say, the two of this synthesis are so structured in their relation that together they are fitted, inclined, even intended by nature to become and to be a unity called "self." So Kierkegaard makes the radical assertion that each one of the dyad "constantly is its opposite" (*det Ene bestandigt er sit Modsatte*). The force of the "is" means: you never have the one without the other. That is the ontological reality of the unity pointed to by the term "synthesis." And the orientation of this synthesis toward selfhood is so ontologically inherent

---

16 *The Concept of Anxiety*, p. 39; (KW 8:43); SV 6:137; (4:315).
17 *Sickness*, pp. 162f.; (KW 19:30); SV 15:87; (11:143).

My Self: A Synthesis of Two

that it is irresistible and indestructible. So the unity, the self as the third, is already present but asleep or dreaming, as a potentiality.

The importance of this point cannot be exaggerated. Kierkegaard has been accused of the exact opposite position. For example, Mark Taylor has written,

> For Hegel, the structure of spirit is essentially self-referential negativity that binds together coimplicated opposites. Kierkegaard denies that contraries are identical in their difference, or that opposites are related in such a way that each in itself is at the same time its other. His adherence to the rules of traditional logic persuades him that opposites are mutually exclusive and actually antithetical. Consequently, spirit, as the structure of self-relation within which opposites meet, cannot be the "negative unity" of internal relationality, but must be a "positive third" constitutive of a genuine coincidentia oppositorum. In other words, since opposites are not implicitly identical or necessarily related, they must be contingently conjoined.[18]

This is a clear misreading of Kierkegaard. As throughout his book, Taylor here poses only two alternatives, rightly asserts that Kierkegaard does not subscribe to Hegel's, and so nails him to the other alternative—which is not Kierkegaard's either.

Kierkegaard *does* assert a "'negative unity' of internal relationality" which irrevocably ties together in the human being the opposites body/soul, finitude/infinitude, possibility/necessity, and even temporal/eternal whether or not "spirit" ever emerges as an actuality. He explicitly says that each one "is constantly its opposite." But at the same time, contra Hegel, he also asserts that human freedom (with the help of the eternal) plays an integral role, not in the impossible task of bringing and holding together mutually exclusive opposites, but in actualizing another kind of relation which is already *given* as a potentiality within the negative unity of internal relationality. Kierkegaard loved to say that "actuality is the unity of possibility and necessity," as opposed to Hegel's "necessity is the unity of possibility and actuality."[19] Or as Mark Taylor puts it, Hegel shows that "actuality and possibility are coimplicates whose extricable unity constitutes necessity."[20]

---

18 Mark C. Taylor, *Journeys to Selfhood*, pp. 169f.
19 *Sickness*, p. 169; (KW 19:36); SV 15:93; (11:149). See the Hongs' note on this quote for other instances in Kierkegaard and for references in Hegel.
20 Taylor, *Journeys*, p. 156.

We will return to this important and difficult question at several places below, but it must be made clear here that Kierkegaard's position is an alternative that Taylor does not describe or seem to understand. For Kierkegaard the opposites are "implicitly identical" in the sense that they are "necessarily related." The human being is a "relation," a "synthesis" of opposites, so that one can never be just one or the other. My body is constantly modified by my psyche, and the reverse. My finitude is constantly modified by my infinitude, and the reverse. My necessity is constantly modified by my possibility, and the reverse. My temporality can never escape its relation to the eternal, and the eternal will never desert me in the prison of my temporality. Even the demand that this negative unity become a positive unity is implicit and necessary within this given unity. BUT: contra Hegel, this possibility does not become actuality of necessity but in freedom.

That Kierkegaard's concept of freedom is radically different from Hegel's, and the reasons for it, will be spelled out later. The point insisted on here is simply that, for Kierkegaard, the "two" of life's doubleness are bound together in an indissoluble unity, in a given unbreakable synthesis. The *existential* importance of this conceptual issue becomes clear in Taylor's allegation that Kierkegaard's prescription for the cure of the sickness of despair is in the end a tragic failure. He concludes:

Kierkegaard's coincidentia oppositorum inevitably breaks down, leaving spirit fragmented. Torn between exclusive opposites and conflicting contraries, the existing individual yearns for a reconciliation that is ever transcendent, never present. Historical existence becomes a period of exile—the self an estranged wanderer. Rather than representing the realization of authentic selfhood, this form of life is the desperate expression of self-alienated spirit.[21]

Such a conclusion is possible only on the basis of several critical failures in interpretation: one, a misunderstanding of Kierkegaard's concepts of synthesis, freedom, and faith; two, an ignoring of the essential hopefulness that characterizes Kierkegaard's major works; three, total neglect of the concept of "grace" as the help of the eternal that enables and energizes faith and love; four, the distorting (sometimes malicious) misuse of materials from the journals and the "attack upon Christendom" written the last few years of his life. The use of the latter materials by Taylor, in such a crude ad hominem way, in the conclusion of his book is disap-

21 Ibid., p. 275.

pointing. He does not invalidate Hegel's prescription for a cure on the basis of Hegel's own self-admitted disillusionment with German society of his day and his retreat, as a member of "an isolated order of priests," into the "separate sanctuary" of philosophy.[22] Alternative positions on these issues supported by alternative interpretations will be developed throughout the present study. But now we turn to the second of the three characteristics of basic human nature as indicated by Kierkegaard's dyad body/soul.

(2) Kierkegaard says that the human being, as a "psychical-bodily synthesis," first lives in a state of "immediacy" where the "spirit" is only "dreaming," and thus lives in the "basement" of one's structure under "the determinants of the sensuous." In the concept of "immediacy" we have another one of those very important themes that run throughout Kierkegaard's works and which cannot be adequately treated in our space.[23] We have already noted that at this level or state of human existence, there is no opposition or contradiction in its polarity, and therefore there is no reflection about becoming a self. In an interesting note about the difference between "dizziness" and "despair" (written while composing *Sickness*), Kierkegaard says that there is "an ambiguous common-boundary" between the psychical and the bodily; so the psychical/bodily form a "relation" or "composite" in which it is often difficult to tell which one takes the initiative. Thus Kierkegaard is able to say that life at this level may be described either as under "the determinants of the sensuous," or as "sensuousness psychically determined" because there is "not opposition but harmony." Dizziness can occur at this level, but not despair, because "despair is related to spirit, to freedom, to responsibility."[24] Life in immediacy therefore is a matter of fortune and the accidental. "In immediacy the individual is rooted in the finite." So, "as the immediate he is the fortunate unity of finitude and infinitude, to which there corresponds fortune and misfortune as coming from outside."[25] The "self in its immediacy is accidentally determined." And Kierkegaard can say the same things about the "aesthetical" life: "it is that in a man whereby he is immediately the man he is; ... he develops by necessity not by freedom, no metamorphosis takes place in him, no infinite movement."[26]

---

22 Ibid., p. 268.
23 See the Hongs' *Søren Kierkegaard's Journals and Papers*, 2:594, for a comprehensive list of passages in the works and journals where Kierkegaard treats this theme.
24 *Journals*, 749; VIII^2 B 168:6.
25 *Postscript*, pp. 367, 406; (KW 12.1:410, 453); SV 10:102, 138; (7:356, 394).
26 *Either/Or*, 2:261, 229; (KW 4:256, 225); SV 3:237, 209; (2:230, 201).

Later we will see that such a state of being can continue throughout one's life as "unconscious despair," or the "despair of ignorance." But at the present level of human existence, immediacy is seen as a fundamental neutral state that is original and natural. This leads to the third characteristic indicated by the dyad body/soul.

(3) In the quotation from *The Concept of Anxiety*, immediacy is also characterized as "innocence." This is another complex concept in the Kierkegaardian corpus, and there will be further explications of it in relation to the nature of *angst* (dread, anxiety) and in relation to human failure (original sin). At this point the concept is helpful in shedding further light on the nature of the human being as synthesis at the basic level of the psychical/sensuous unity. (Everything from *The Concept of Anxiety* is quoted here as being Kierkegaard's own because it is clearly assumed as presupposed and carried forward in *The Sickness unto Death*.)

First, it must be stressed that innocence is not identical with immediacy.[27] Something more is being pointed to by this term. He does say, "In innocence the human being is not qualified as spirit [self] but is psychically qualified in immediate unity with one's natural condition. The spirit is dreaming. ... In this state there is peace and repose."[28] What then does "innocence" add to "immediacy"? Kierkegaard is indicating something about the nature of the transition out of immediacy, when the self that was "dreaming" comes "awake." With this point, Kierkegaard makes one of his most critical differentiations of his understanding of the human self from that of Hegel.[29]

Kierkegaard asserts that "The concept immediacy belongs in logic, but the concept innocence belongs in ethics." So the "movement" (κινησις) out of immediacy is one of immanence, but the movement out of innocence is one of transcendence. "Immanence" means that "mediacy presupposes immediacy." So immediacy is "a nothing" in itself but simply points to the coinherence (entailment) of two factors, as in logic. To say, therefore, that the psychical and the sensuous are in a state of immediacy means that each presupposes the other, that any "opposition" between them in a movement toward mediacy is only secondary and temporary, and the movement toward reunion is assured and necessary. On the contrary, "innocence is *something*. Innocence is a quality, it is a

---

27 *The Concept of Anxiety*, p. 32; (KW 8:35); SV 6:130; (4:307).
28 Ibid., pp. 37f.; (KW 8:41); SV 6:135; (4:313).
29 Quotations in the next two paragraphs are from ibid., pp. 32–4; (KW 8:35–8); SV 6:130–2; (4:307–9).

state that may very well endure." Therefore, "when innocence is cancelled by transcendence, something entirely different comes out of it."

In the context of his discussion of innocence, Kierkegaard simply calls this movement of transcendence a "leap" (his favourite figure for one of his major concepts). In a later chapter, this figure will be elaborated into a full description of what he means by the "ethical" as "choosing" and "freedom." And he calls the "something different" simply "guilt." In the next volume this will be given a full elaboration as sin and despair. But here we must note that "innocence" points to a quality of human existence *before* any choice is made. It is, he says, not a perfection (what the human is designed to become), but neither is it an imperfection (something evil that causes one to sin). Innocence is "ignorance," that is, ignorance of any distinction between right and wrong or good and evil, ignorance that something more than innocence is intended, that the self of which one is aware in the immediacy of innocence is only a "dream" and not the real thing.

So, in summary, human existence at the level of body/soul (the psychical/sensuous) is (1) a real synthesis of two, (2) which are related in the immanence of immediacy, and (3) it exists in the state of innocence. But if this is all there is to human existence, how can there be any movement out of innocence? Kierkegaard posits other "constituent elements" in human nature in its basic given state before there is any question of choice and failure. So now we proceed to see how finitude/infinitude and possibility/necessity qualify and transform the simple immediacy of the psychical/sensuous.

FINITUDE/INFINITUDE

When Kierkegaard first turns, in *The Sickness unto Death*, to "reflecting upon the constituents of which the self as a synthesis is composed," his first statement is: "The self is composed of infinitude and finitude."[30] He gives a general indication of what he means by these two determinants of human existence by saying that the whole process of becoming a self "consists in infinitely moving away from itself in the infinitizing of the self, and in infinitely coming back to itself in the [process of] finitizing." Both clearly "belong to the self." The human being exists in the constant interplay of the two. My finitude, however, is something more than my bodily sensuousness, and my infinitude is more than a particular

30 *Sickness*, p. 162; (KW 19:29); SV 15:87; (11:142).

function of my psychicality. Furthermore, these two constituents of my being cannot be described without inferring at least some disturbance to the peace and harmony of my psychical/sensuous immediacy. There is movement in two directions, even if the movement is circular. What are these two directions or dimensions of my being and existence?

(1) *Finitude.* My bodily physicality or sensuousness is part of my finitude but not all of it. My body, my whole individual physical/sensuous being, is the product of and is in continuing continuity with the entire natural and human world. In *Works of Love*, Kierkegaard says, "As little as a Christian can live without the body, so as little without the distinctions of earthly life which belong to everyone by birth, by position, by circumstance, by education etc.—no one of us is pure [ideal] humanity."[31] In his definition of our "essential fortuitousness" in *Sickness*, we have heard him speak of the "limitations" imposed by particular "capabilities and aptitudes, in this concretion of relationships." In *Either/Or* he spells this out in greater detail. He says, "Whoever chooses oneself ethically chooses oneself concretely as this specific individual, ... with these capacities, these dispositions, these drives, these passions, influenced by this specific social milieu, as this specific product of a specific environment." A little later he repeats that the "concrete self stands in living interaction with these specific surroundings, these conditions of life, this order of things." Then he adds, "This self ... is not simply a personal self, but a social, a civic self."[32] And throughout *Either/Or* and *Postscript* he readily acknowledges that this social, civic self is involved in what he calls "world-history" (*Verdenshistorie*).

It must be immediately and readily acknowledged that Kierkegaard spent much of his writing career attacking the allegedly negative character and impact of this whole world of finitude, especially in its social and historical manifestations. True selfhood is described as lost and in despair when human existence is lived at the level of aesthetic immediacy, when the self as psyche submits passively to live within the dimensions of temporal worldliness and knows nothing but desiring, craving, enjoying, when one's whole finite existence is allowed to be shaped by the dictates of external social standards, and when ultimately the individual is merged as just another indistinguishable number in the mass movements of world history. So the phrase "a civic self" would certainly stick

---

31 *Works of Love*, p. 81; SV 12:73; (9:71).
32 *Either/Or*, 2:255, 267; (KW 4:250f., 262); SV 3:232, 242; (2:225, 235).

in Kierkegaard's throat. But this perspective should not blind us to his very positive evaluation of human finitude in its every aspect.

I simply do not exist or become my self except in and with the concreteness of my very specific and unique finitude. On the one hand, it is what gives my existence its actuality, in being bound into the whole physical, sensuous, natural, animal, racial, human, social, historical world. On the other hand, it is (at least in part) my finitude in its concreteness and uniqueness that sets me off and separates me as over against every other creature and human being. "Remember what you have so frequently rejoiced in seeing, remember the beauty of the fields! There is no discrimination in love—yet what a difference among the flowers! Even the slightest, most insignificant, the most plain-looking, ... it is as if this too had said to love: let me be something for myself, something distinctive." Likewise with every "insignificant person—if he has had courage before God to be himself, so he has his own-distinctive-individuality [*Eiendommelighed*]" (although later we shall see that *Eiendommelighed* also refers to the individual's most inward spiritual identity and character). In fact, this concrete individuality is what gives the human being actuality and life over against God also, because it is God's will that "creation over against God shall not be nothing."[33]

This finitude, therefore, in all its multifarious forms, is an integral positive constituent of basic human nature in every individual person. This is Kierkegaard's pervasive perspective throughout his authorship, in spite of his unrelieved attack upon the ecclesiastical and social institutions of his day, and in spite of his own failures in interpersonal relations. Obviously, much has to be done, as Bruce H. Kirmmse has said, "to dispel the unfortunate notion that Kierkegaard was an asocial, ahistorical individualist who had no real interest in the ramifications of the social and political realities in which every individual is implicated."[34] The present study hopes to be a contribution to that end.

What really frightens and concerns Kierkegaard is not the continuing presence and operation of our finitude in the shaping of our lives and therefore our selfhood. This is inescapable, indeed must be welcomed, if we are to become unique concrete selves. But he considers it to be "the sickness unto death," utter despair and hopelessness, when this finitude

---

33 *Works of Love*, pp. 252f.; SV 12:259ff.; (9:257ff.).

34 Bruce H. Kirmmse, "Psychology and Society: The Social Falsification of the Self in *The Sickness unto Death*," in Joseph H. Smith, ed., *Kierkegaard's Truth*, pp. 167ff. Kirmmse has himself made a significant contribution to this task in his recent major work, *Kierkegaard in Golden Age Denmark*.

shapes us without our awareness, *unconsciously*, without our choice also playing a role in the continuous process of our coming into existence. Despite his central concern with self-consciousness and deliberate choice, he has a profound sense of the power of racial memory, of family environment and heredity, of social and historical conditions, of one's own bodily condition, of the accumulated experience and personality traits in one's own individual life—the power of all this to influence and to shape, moment by moment, the emerging self with only a dim or even no awareness on the part of the subject.

A clear and forceful statement of this perspective is to be found in *Either/Or.* Judge William is beginning his own disquisition on the nature of choice, which we will draw upon at length when dealing with this topic in a later chapter. Here it is his anthropology or psychology which is relevant. And Kresten Nordentoft is certainly correct that whatever Kierkegaard's own critique of Judge William's ethical idea may be, he assumes and uses the Judge's psychology.[35] The first major point is the inseparability of the chooser and the things chosen. The two "stand in the deepest relationship" to each other. "The choice is crucial for the content of personal-individuality [*Personlighed*]; through the choice personal-individuality submerges itself in that which is being chosen." Thus the person is not an "ethereal thought" or sprite that remains untouched and unchanged within, while participating in the movement outside. There is indeed an instant of deliberation between alternatives to be chosen, but the already-formed person does not remain aloof and indifferent to the alternatives as if they were strictly outside or objective. The instant of deliberation cannot be extended so as to hold the alternatives apart indefinitely. Something else happens. It is an illusion to think that, in delaying the choice or in not choosing, nothing happens.

The second major point is that when conscious choice fails, the unconscious takes over. And what works through the unconscious is the entirety of an individual's finitude. When one neglects to choose, the alternatives are no longer open, because "others have chosen for him." And how do these "others" have their influence? Through what is called "the inner bent [*Drift*] of the personal-individuality" already formed, which "has no time for imaginary constructions of thought, so that it continually speeds ahead and in one way or another posits either the one or the other, making the choice more difficult the next instant

---

35 Kresten Nordentoft, *Kierkegaard's Psychology*, p. 195. The following quotations are from *Either/Or*, 2:167f.; (KW 4:163f.); SV 3:154f.; (2:148f.).

because what thus has been posited must be withdrawn." So "the moment of choosing is very earnest ... because there is danger involved, that in the next instant a choice may not be at my disposal, that something already has been lived which must be lived over again. For to think that for an instant one can keep one's personal-individuality blank and bare, or that strictly speaking one can stop and break off one's personal life, is a delusion. Already prior to one's choosing the personal-individuality is interested in the choice, and if one puts off the choice, the personal-individuality, or obscure forces within it, chooses unconsciously."

This passage makes clear that for Kierkegaard my finitude, both in its original, given, totally unchosen form, and in its cumulative character through moment by moment experience, is an integral and powerful factor in the unity of my selfhood. It is more than my sensuousness or physicality. It is the totality of what *I am*, including everything I have been, now present and operative in ways of which I am unaware and which I do not understand. And this totality which I am "stands in living interaction" with my entire natural, physical, and social/historical environment. My potentialities and freedom are strictly limited and defined within the confines of my particular place in this "order of things" (*Tingenes Orden*).

Kierkegaard understood himself—and so all other humans—in this way to his dying day. In a journal entry of 1852, he is musing about his motivation for continuing his writing at the expense of his financial security and comfort. He notes that "one could say that it was pride, arrogance." Probably someone had so accused him (his own brother?). Then he makes the very telling comment: "Is it that? Well, who knows oneself in this way?"[36] And in a long paragraph, he agonizes over the pros and cons of this accusation, admitting that at the height of one's self-consciousness and self-acceptance, one cannot be sure how the "obscure powers" in one's personality are working to influence one's decisions. But he knows what he believes to be God's will, and he dares to risk his decision on that belief. The unconscious or subconscious impact of finitude, in all its multifarious dimensions, was very clear to Kierkegaard. But that was not the focus of his concern and exploration. It was the individual self, in concrete existence, centred in freedom, which he chose as his "category," as the human terrain which called out for exploration, explication, and defence against the ravagement of the self by the intellectual and social systems of his day. This should not blind us,

36 *Journals*, 6805; x⁴ A 559.

however, to the fact that Kierkegaard saw vividly the all too powerful social, communal character of human individual selfhood.

(2) *Infinitude.* How, then, did he understand the emergence of any real freedom of the individual under the massive impact of one's finitude? He saw the fundamental ground for this freedom in another basic constituent of human nature. He called it "infinitude." Again, we will take our point of departure from his definitive treatment in *The Sickness unto Death.*

✓ As already noted, something must disturb the harmony and repose of the immediacy of the self living simply at the sensuous/psychical level—if the self is to come into existence, is to realize its full potentialities in freedom and responsibility. This something must be prior and fundamental to the angst (dread, anxiety) which disturbs the "dreaming" self. What, then, is this "dreaming"? It must be admitted that it is very difficult to get down inside and behind Kierkegaard's despairing self and his reflecting subject in such a way as to discern, in its pristine form, this basic constituent of human nature called "infinitude." All of his discussions of it are entwined with his analyses of the reflective self coming to self-consciousness.

A first clue comes from the point made at the beginning of this chapter: the basic distinction between the outward and the inward in human existence and awareness. In *Either/Or* we read, "Even the humblest individual has a doubleexistence."[37] Everyone has "a history," but also "the inward work." At first, one seeks harmony and repose and finds it in the immediacy of sensuous/physical unity which originally is a state of innocence. But whether in innocence or unknowing despair, immediacy is never complete or perfect. The human psyche withdraws its attention and subservience to the sensuous and the finite, in all their enthralling forms and extensions. What does it do? Figuratively, it turns inward. The line of demarcation between outward and inward awareness is often very hazy and indistinct. Yet the inward awareness is clearly hidden and secret, not open to the direct observation of others.

Kierkegaard says that our finitude is "the limiting constituent" of our being, but it is matched by another which he calls "the expanding constituent, ... the fantastic, the limitless." This is the basic characteristic of our infinitude: to be able to "dream," to "fantasize," without regard to the limiting rules and forces of our finitude. So "The fantastic [*Det Phantastiske*], of course, is most closely related to the imagination [*Phanta-*

---

37 *Either/Or*, 2:179; (KW 4:175); SV 3:165; (2:159).

sien]." And, "As a rule, imagination is the medium for the process of infinitizing. ... The fantastic is generally that which leads a person out into the infinite." But this happens in such a way that "it only leads him away from himself and thereby prevents him from coming back to himself. ... The self, then, leads a fantasized existence in abstract infinitizing or in abstract isolation, continually lacking itself, from which it only moves further and further away."[38]

The psyche, then, sometimes turns outward and seeks to achieve a state of relative peace and harmony in immediacy with its world of sensuousness and finitude. But the psyche also turns sometimes inward to another world, the world of fantasy and imagination. In an early (1842–43) unpublished work (*Johannes Climacus, or, De Omnibus Dubitandum Est*), Kierkegaard makes a similar distinction but with different terminology. He speaks of the duality (*Dupplicitet*) of our "reality" (*Realitet*) and "ideality" (*Idealitet*). He uses this distinction to define the nature of and the difference between reflection and consciousness (which will be described at length in the next chapter). But he also says some interesting things which shed light on the basic duality of human nature. By "reality" he means immediacy, and "*Immediacy* is simply *indeterminateness*. In immediacy is no relationship, because as soon as the relationship is there, immediacy is cancelled."[39] So this is the psyche living in harmony with its finitude. It makes no distinctions. Everything is equally true and untrue; in fact, "in immediacy the very issue of truth is abrogated." But the psyche is engaged in another way. In this case, "ideality" is not the activity of fantasy but of language. Reality is in a sense "cancelled" by "talking about it." So "language is ideality." The interesting point is that there can be an interchange or alternation between the two "without reciprocal contact" between the two. Here Kierkegaard calls this state "reflection," the awareness of *two* without bringing the two into relation or contradiction. And "as long as the alternation occurs without collision, consciousness does not really exist." Thus the formula emerges: "Reflection is the *possibility* of the *relationship*; consciousness *is* the relationship, whose first form is contradiction."

38 *Sickness*, pp. 163–6; (KW 19:30–3); SV 15:88–90; (11:143–6).

39 *Johannes Climacus, or, De Omnibus Dubitandum Est*, p. 147; (KW 7:167); *Papirer* IV B 1, p. 145. All the following quotations are from pp. 147–50 (KW 7:167–70) of the English, pp. 145–7 of the Danish. The translation by T. H. Croxall often is a paraphrase and includes insertions from the variant readings; so Hongs' newer translation and edition should be used if available.

The major point is that my infinitude disturbs the harmony and repose of immediacy in my finitude. As Kierkegaard says, "The moment I express reality [i.e. in words], the contradiction is there." The collision of the "two" has not been joined by my conscious interrelating of the two, but the duality is "there" implicitly at some dim level of awareness as I alternate between the two. In *Johannes Climacus*, Kierkegaard says that doubt now makes its appearance when reflection inevitably raises the question: where does truth lie, in reality or in ideality? And he makes a significant correlation between reflection and imagination in *Sickness*: "whatever feeling, knowing and willing one has depends upon what imagination one has, upon how that person reflects, that is, [depends] on imagination. Imagination is infinitizing reflection. ... The self is reflection, and imagination is reflection, is the re-presentation of the self, which is the self's possibility. Imagination is the possibility of all reflection, and this medium's intensity is the possibility of the self's intensity."[40]

Whatever else this means (and we will return to this passage in the next chapter), we can gather that as consciousness presumes the prior work of reflection, so reflection presumes the prior operation of imagination. In other words, the "language" of "ideality" (infinitude) may be either the language of imagery and fantasy, or the language of abstract ideas and concepts. Surely for Kierkegaard, as for all other human beings, fantasy precedes concepts. For many, fantasy remains the only, or at least the dominant, mode of the inward life of infinitude. In any case, the immediacy of my sensuous/psychical existence is not left to have its harmony and repose shattered and shocked only if by chance I am the object of outrageous misfortune in the realm of my finitude. Rather, there is a given structure in my very being that guarantees this disturbance. My finitude is always accompanied by, and could not escape if it would, an inward world of fantasy which is infinite, is without limits, and which can carry me off into a realm of images and ideas in contrast with the "realities" of my finitude. Of course it is also true that this "expanding constituent" of my being, this infinitude with its imagination, is always accompanied by, and could not escape if it would, the "limiting constituent" of my existence, the finitude of my body and its incorporation into nature, society, and history.

In the following chapters we will see how crucial this basic duality of the human being is to Kierkegaard in his depiction of the emergence of consciousness, self-consciousness, freedom, and the coming into exist-

40 *Sickness*, pp. 163f.; (KW 19:31); SV 15:88f.; (11:144).

ence of the self. But at this point we simply note that Kierkegaard sees fantasy and imagination as the basic, fundamental, initial human capacity that arouses a human being out of the false and unstable harmony of sensuous/psychical immediacy, and that leads this human to an inward vision of another world, another kind of existence, which at first seems to have its own reality or truth, and which only gradually—through reflection and consciousness—may take on the character of "possibility" for that human's world of actual finitude. We have already heard him say that "whatever feeling, knowing, and willing a person has depends upon what imagination he has." So he also says that imagination "is not just any capacity like other capacities—it is the capacity *instar omnium*."[41] It is first and primary among all the others. The images of the world of imagination are all derived from and seem identical with the images of the world of sense impressions from finitude. But they operate according to different rules. They employ the same words but have different meanings. And when the two are brought together at the level of human "spirit" (self-consciousness), the language of sense takes on a figurative power which gives it a secret and hidden meaning except for those who have spiritual ears to hear.[42]

For Kierkegaard the language of rational abstraction and conceptualization is a further remove, one more step away from the concrete actuality of human existence than the language of imagery in imagination. Certainly, the world of fantasy is no more the world of actuality than is the world of abstract concepts. But it is closer. The images of fantasy carry with them and therefore can project more of the richness and substance of the sensuous/psychical reality. So while his pseudonyms were developing the essential categories and concepts in his major "works," Kierkegaard was writing, under his own name, his edifying (upbuilding) discourses in more "poetic" form. Actually, he intermingles the two "languages" in all his writings. But the language of fantasy possesses a certain primacy for Kierkegaard.

So Nordentoft is misleading when he says, "Kierkegaard does not make any attempt to go behind language into a preverbal or preconscious, presymbolic cognition of the surrounding world, which he regards as illusory, but he clings fast to language as the condition for the boundary of cognition."[43] Nordentoft is speaking in the context of the

---

41 Idem.
42 See *Works of Love*, pp. 199f.; SV 12:203f.; (9:201f.).
43 Nordentoft, *Kierkegaard's Psychology*, p. 334.

language of abstract conceptualization, whereas Kierkegaard regards the imagery of the imagination as a kind of "language." In the role Kierkegaard assigns to imagination and the poetic, he is hinting at an aesthetic (a critique of judgment) which does get behind the conscious, symbolic verbiage of conceptual cognition to a prior more primitive level of human cognition at the point of transition from sense-immediacy to the mediacy of primary imagery that is more directly related to the concrete complexity of actual human existence.

So the human self, in its basic given structure, is composed of finitude and infinitude—never one without the other. What then is added by saying that every human being is also composed of necessity and possibility? We come to our last dyad.

NECESSITY/POSSIBILITY

By qualifying my finitude as "necessity," and by qualifying my infinitude as "possibility," Kierkegaard indicates another form, an intensification, of my awareness and reflection. And this occurs prior to the "collision" of the two opposites, which gives rise to self-consciousness, consciousness of another self, namely, the self I must become.

As long as I consider only my finitude, it remains *mine*: *my* body, *my* family, *my* schooling, *my* friends, etc. It is mine in the sense that I have the vague feeling that I can do with it what I please: accept it or reject it, inhabit it or escape it. But then my finitude asserts itself as "necessity," and it all seems more restrictive and binding. It lays a hand on my fantasy so that it seems not so free and "infinite."

As long as I consider only my infinitude, the illusion continues that it is a realm unto itself, totally inward and hidden, beyond the reach of any restrictions imposed from without. But when the fantasies of my imagination present themselves as "possibilities," these fantasies carry an extra charge. They vaguely hint at the question: possible when, how, for whom? This is not yet the self-conscious question, "Who am I?" But "possibility" takes on the more definite character of "potentiality" as something related to my finitude and with the tone of demand and expectation.

My finitude and infinitude are thus brought closer together as I reflect on them (alternately) as necessity and possibility. Kierkegaard says, "Just as infinitude and finitude belong to the self, so also do possibility and necessity." Thus the first shadow of self-consciousness is cast across my awareness because "possibility and necessity are equally essential for becoming (and the self has the task of freely becoming itself). ... A self that has no possibility is in despair, and likewise a self that has no necessity."[44] The self, in its basic given composition, becomes aware of its finitude as necessity, and of its infinitude as possibility. These two categories (necessity and possibility) play such key roles in Kierkegaard's thinking that they require some further analysis here (with a full treatment in a later chapter).

As already noted, his description of these basic constituents of the human being is always in the context of his description of the human self coming to selfconsciousness and choosing in freedom to become itself. So again we will have to make an abstraction from such statements. His summary definition is this: "The self is *kata dynamin* [potentially] just as much possible as necessary: because it is indeed itself, and yet it is obliged to become itself. Insofar as it is itself, it is the necessary, and insofar as it must become itself, it is a possibility."[45] This statement obviously alludes to Climacus's more abstract and quite different treatment of possibility and necessity in the "Interlude" of *Philosophical Fragments*. There he says, "the necessary can never be changed, since it always relates to itself ... in the same way. ... The necessary *is*. ... Necessity ... is not a determinant of being but a determinant of essence, since the essence of the necessary is to be."[46]

In complete contrast to necessity is something called "possibility." If one had to pick one concept which is the key to all others in Kierkegaard, this might be it. The Danish word (*Mulighed*) may be translated as "potentiality," that is, something which already lodges in what is, with the ability to come into existence. Or it may be translated as "possibility," that is, something lying in an indeterminate future with a vague chance of coming into existence, contingent on several unpredictable circumstances. Kierkegaard, in his works from *Fragments* to *Sickness*, only gradually clarifies the tension between these two uses, coming finally to include them both in his concept. But here in *Fragments* the word designates something which has a kind of being, which yet is non-being. He uses the example of a plan, which has being (*Væren*) in that it is lodged in my mind and is a potentiality of the conditions of existence as I judge them. But it is non-being in that it has not yet come-into-existence (*blive*

---

44 *Sickness*, p. 168; (KW 19:35); SV 15:92; (11:148).
45 Idem.
46 For this and the following quotations, see *Philosophical Fragments*, pp. 90–3; (KW 7:73–5); SV 6:68–70; (4:236–9).

til or *Tilblivelse*) and thus has the character of a future, contingent possibility. "Such a being, which yet is non-being, is precisely possibility." When the plan comes-into-existence, then it is "actual being, or actuality [*Virkelighed*]." The plan as possibility and the plan as actuality are one (identical) in *what* they are, in essence (*Væsen*). They differ in their mode of being (*væren*).

In *Fragments*, furthermore, Kierkegaard is centrally concerned with possibility as over against necessity rather than with the two of them as equally important determinants of human nature. So he uses his distinctions between the two to stress (over against Hegel) that the kind of change involved in coming-into-existence, the movement (κινησις) in the transition from possibility to actuality, is not one of necessity but one of freedom. So the realm of human existence or actuality is not ruled by a principle of necessity, either in the sense of natural causation or of logical entailment. Likewise, in *The Concept of Anxiety*, the focus is on freedom and its relation to the possible and the future. There he says, "Possibility is to *be able.*" And, "The possible corresponds exactly to the future." Thus "the opposite of freedom is guilt," not necessity.[47] But this emphasis on freedom makes our point that necessity and possibility are fundamental characteristics of human nature which lie at a more basic level than their dialectical interrelationship where self-consciousness and freedom come into play. And this also explains why Kierkegaard, on the first page of *Sickness*, says that the human being is a synthesis of *freedom* and necessity, but later changes it to *possibility* and necessity when he is considering the constituents of human nature without regard to *consciousness*. (The complex relation of freedom to possibility and necessity will be analysed in a later chapter on "Freedom as the Dialectical in the Determinants Possibility and Necessity.")

The material concerning this dyad in *Sickness*, therefore, is more helpful for understanding their basic meanings. In contrast to his thinking in *Philosophical Fragments* and *The Concept of Anxiety*, Kierkegaard presents a qualitatively different concept of "necessity" and its role in the self's coming-into-existence. Necessity is not seen as at war with possibility. Rather, for its own good, "the self's possibility" must come to terms with "the self's necessity." When one's infinitude (which finds expression in

---

47 *The Concept of Anxiety*, pp. 44, 82, 91; (KW 8:49, 91, 108); SV 6:142, 179, 194; (4:320, 361, 377). Kierkegaard also uses "abstract possibility" in a related sense in *Postscript* to designate the realm of abstract ideas in speculative philosophy, and also to indicate the formation of ideas about what other persons mean and are like. This use will be described in the next chapter.

the "medium of imagination") takes on the quality of "possibility," then imagination acquires a more specific orientation than fantasy's aimless daydreaming in immediacy, as an end or pleasure for itself. "Inasmuch as the self as synthesis of finitude and infinitude is established *kata dynamin* [in potentiality], now for the task of becoming, it [the self] reflects in the medium of imagination, and thereby the infinite possibility appears." And this reflection in imagination "is the self's re-presentation [depiction], which is the self's possibility." But Kierkegaard warns that this depiction "must be used with extreme caution," because "the mirror of possibility ... is, in the highest sense, untrue. That a self appears to be such and such in the possibility of itself is only a half-truth, for in the possibility of itself, the self is still far from or is only half itself. Therefore, the question is how this self's necessity defines it more specifically."[48]

First it should be noted that "possibility" is the product of reflection, not in the medium of rational ideas and concepts, but in the medium of the images and pictures of the imagination. Secondly, although this possibility has an aura of telos and task about it, possibility is not yet actuality. Although it may be a potentiality that is inherent in what already is, it may or may not actually come-into-existence. In the gap between the "possibility" of imagination and the actuality of existence, "freedom" must occur. So freedom is something in addition to possibility and thus is not the opposite of necessity. (The nature of freedom and how it occurs will be explored in later chapters.) Possibility is a more fundamental constituent of human nature that makes itself felt prior to freedom and its task. Indeed, imagination may resist the tug of telos and task inherent in possibility and keep wandering on into the extended realms of possibility. "The self becomes an abstract possibility; it flounders in possibility until exhausted. ... Thus possibility seems greater and greater to the self; more and more becomes possible because nothing becomes actual. Eventually everything seems possible, but this is exactly the point at which the abyss swallows up the self, ... the moment when the individual him/herself becomes entirely a mirage."[49]

The nature of "necessity" now becomes clear (in a preliminary way). As my finitude sets a limit on the fantasies of my infinitude, so the quality of necessity "holds back" the extravagances of the possibilities I envision

---

48 These three quotes are from *Sickness*, consecutively: pp. 168, 164, 170; (KW 19:35, 31, 37); SV 15:93, 89, 94; (11:148, 144, 150).
49 Ibid., p. 169; (KW 19:36); SV 15:93; (11:149).

for my self to become. Thus we have heard Kierkegaard say that necessity "belongs to the self" and is "equally essential" to the self as is possibility. "To become oneself is precisely a movement in place," and "necessity is literally that place." Therefore, the self that wanders off into "abstract possibility" does not lack actuality; "it is really necessity it lacks," because "actuality is the unity of possibility and necessity." In other words, prior to my consciousness that I have the task freely to choose to enact and so become my possible self in actuality, there is something in my finitude that makes me question and doubt my vision that "all things are possible" for me. When

possibility outruns necessity so that the self runs away from itself in possibility, it has no necessity to which it must return. ... What is missing is essentially the power to obey, to submit to the necessity in one's self, to what may be called one's limitations. ... The tragedy is that ... such a self ... did not become aware of itself, aware that the self one is is a very definite something and thus the necessary. ... Therefore, the question is how this self's necessity defines it more specifically.[50]

In this way, my finitude with the added quality of necessity disturbs and unsettles not only the immediacy of my sensuous/psychical harmony but also the infinitude of my fantasies as real possibilities of *this* self. (And later we will see that the self's necessity is not limited to a quality of the self's finitude but is also a quality of the self's possibility, but some groundwork is required before this more complicated point can be made.)

We come to the end of a consideration of "my self: a synthesis of two," of an analysis of the self in such a way that "one reflects only upon the constituent-elements of the synthesis." A brief summary of this basic duality-in-unity is in order, before we proceed to a description of the emergence of consciousness and freedom. The following are the main points that have come to light in our foregoing analysis.

(1) The fundamental duality of the human being is a complex duality. There is the complexity manifest as we move from bodily sensuousness,

---

50 Ibid., pp. 168–70; (KW 19:35–7); SV 15:93–4; (11:148–50). As noted, the critical question as to the difference between Kierkegaard's concept of necessity in *Fragments* and his concept in *Sickness* will be treated at length in a later chapter under the topic: "Freedom as the Dialectical in the Determinants Possibility and Necessity."

to enlarged and extended finitude, to the quality of necessity. There is the complexity manifest as we move from simple psychical awareness, to the infinite reaches of imagination, to the quality of possibility. There is the complexity of the increasing tension between the two elements of each dyad as we move up this ladder. What we have seen in Kierkegaard's basic view of humanity is not a static dualism of two mutually exclusive, qualitatively irreconcilable entities or realms, but a dynamic dialectic operating between multileveled and multifaceted constituent-elements which are equally integral to the existence of the single individual.

(2) The duality, therefore, is also an indissoluble unity. My being, as it is tied inescapably into my sensuous, finite, necessitated existence, is *always* qualified by my psychic awareness, my fantasy-world, and my sense of telos and task of possibility. "The one constantly is its opposite." I never am or have one side without the other.

(3) Nevertheless, the synthesis as originally constituted is unstable. Not in the sense that either side of the duality could withdraw and be unqualified by the other, let alone exist on its own. Yet each side has the tendency to wander off to explore its own medium as an end in itself and to ignore the other's limitation of its activity. The achievement of a sense of innocent immediacy occurs by the psychical dimension being willing to live under sensuous categories of the beautiful and the enjoyable. But the imagination carries most individuals into an exploration of a realm of fantasy and possibility that far outruns their rather meagre finitude. Thus a sense of alternation between outward and inward increases.

(4) This instability, although seeming to be a negative and disturbing factor, serves a positive function. Fantasy acquires the character of possibility, which then induces an inchoate sense of purpose and task. This instability points to a something else, as yet undefined. The individual is ready for the emergence of *angst* and a critical movement out of and beyond one's duality to something new and different.

(5) This movement does not happen automatically. One is not catapulted or carried into this transition by an irresistible force. "Necessity" appears as a determinant of both my finitude and infinitude, but never as a force that creates the synthesis of my possibility and actuality. How, then, do I move out of my duality to the something new? This question compels us to move to an analysis of the emergence of consciousness of the self.

3

My Self: A Task
Part 1: Coming to Consciousness

Kierkegaard says, quite simply, that the task set for every human being is to become a self. In this deceptively plain word "task" (*Opgave*), he concentrates all the complexities of his understanding of the human self. By explicating the ramifications of this term, we will come to see how Kierkegaard understands the emergence of the self as a "third" (entity, or reality, or structure) beyond but including the polarities of body/soul, finitude/infinitude, necessity/possibility.

It is important to note that this term runs throughout the authorship. In *Either/Or*, Kierkegaard has Judge William use it as a key way of distinguishing the ethical from the aesthetical. "The one who lives ethically has oneself as one's task. One's self in its immediacy is determined as accidental; the task is to work the accidental and the universal together [as a whole]." "The ethical individual ... distinguishes between the essential and the accidental. Everything that is posited by one's freedom belongs to him/her essentially; ... everything that is not posited [in one's freedom] is for her/him accidental. ... Only that belongs to me essentially which I ethically take on as a task."[1] In *Concluding Unscientific Postscript*, on his way to the conclusion that "subjectivity is the truth," Kierkegaard says that "becoming subjective is the task, the highest task, set for every human being," and "becoming subjective gives to a human being fully enough to do as long as one lives."[2] In *The Sickness unto Death* Kierkegaard says that when a human being comes to the ultimate form of despair, viz. defiance, "one does not want to put on one's own self, does not want to see one's task in that self given to him/her." He puts it an-

---

1 *Either/Or*, 2:260f., 264; (KW 4:256, 260); SV 3:237, 240; (2:230, 233).
2 *Postscript*, pp. 141, 146; (KW 12.1:159, 163); SV 9:131, 136; (7:130, 135).

other way by saying, "to have a self, to be a self, is the greatest, the infinite concession made to the human being, but it is also eternity's claim [or requirement: *Fordring*] upon her/him." In other words, to be my self is to possess something, but this self is also something that I still have to do or accomplish. And this self as potentiality is something I "cannot get rid of."[3]

The first step in and the absolute prerequisite for the accomplishment of this task of becoming oneself is coming to consciousness that one *is* a self.

ANGST: THE BIRTH PANGS OF SELF-CONSCIOUSNESS

In the last chapter, we saw two parallel tracks in the experience of the human individual finally beginning to bend toward each other in the consciousness of that individual. On the one track the psyche moved out on its own into infinitude by the power of its imagination, and then its fantasies began to take on the quality of "possibilities." On the other track human sensuousness was seen as a link with one's more inclusive finitude of accumulated past experience, social relations, and cultural context, and this finitude began to take on the quality of "necessity." Kierkegaard says that in the existence of the individual, these two tracks are in a "synthesis," that is, they form a unity in which my fantasies are always limited by my finitude, and my possibilities are always held in check by my necessity. But this unity is said to be "negative" because, at this initial level, the interrelation of the two dimensions of my being is not something I choose but is simply a given. So each dimension "relates to the relation" (that is, exists only in immediacy with the other), "and in the relation to the relation" (that is, in this immediacy the two do not assert themselves as opposites, which would evoke a need for harmonization).[4]

When, however, my fantasies suggest themselves as being "possibilities," and my finitude asserts itself as "necessity," the immediacy of my "innocence" is disturbed. I begin to ask *where* these possible fantasies might become real or actual, and I am disturbed by the undeniable inescapable restrictions imposed by my finitude. I begin to ask *when* this actualization might take place, and I am disturbed by the first appearance of what is called "future," as if my past and present were not enough to

---

3 *Sickness*, pp. 202, 154; (KW 19:68, 21); SV 15:122, 80; (11:179, 135).
4 For another treatment of this language, see text at note 8 in chapter 1.

worry about. I begin to ask *how* this vaguely defined future might move into my actual present, and I am frozen in my tracks, immobilized.

Kierkegaard's analysis and description of the movement out of innocence is one of his more profound accomplishments, and it perhaps has had a deeper and broader impact on subsequent thinking than any other item in his writings. His leading concept in this analysis (angst) has been borrowed to label part (or all) of the twentieth century as "the age of anxiety." This impact may be seen in the fact that philosophers, psychologists and literary artists have felt free to employ this concept without having to accept and to use Kierkegaard's notion of "the eternal" and religiousness A, let alone his theology (God, sin, Christology, faith, etc.). He seems to encourage them in this direction by giving as a subtitle to his book on this subject (*The Concept of Angst*, i.e., of "anxiety" or "dread"): "A simple psychologically-demonstrative consideration." Later, in *Postscript*, he also says that this "simple demonstrative psychological examination" is "essentially different from the other pseudonymous writings in that its form is straightforward and even a little didactic."

We have already noted that when Kierkegaard characterizes the immediacy of human psychical-sensuous existence as "innocence," he is adding a new characteristic. This difference is indicated by the phenomenon that the movement out of immediacy is "an immanent movement within immediacy," whereas the movement out of innocence is a movement of "transcendence."[5] What kind of a movement is transcendence, and how does it take place? Kierkegaard's major analysis of this movement is performed under the pseudonym of Vigilius Haufniensis in the work entitled *The Concept of Anxiety* (we will use Reidar Thomte's rendering of *angst* [*angest* in Kierkegaard's day] for the new translation of this work). Kierkegaard assumes and uses this interpretation throughout the rest of the authorship.

The movement out of innocence and its immediacy is the movement of possibility into actuality. In the previous chapter we summarized the nature of possibility (potentiality) as exposited in *Philosophical Fragments*. The transition from possibility to actuality is a change in being, not in essence. Thus a possibility has both being and non-being: being, in that *what* it is (its essence) is already determined; non-being, in that it has not yet come into existence and thus lies as yet in the "future." The transition from possibility to actuality, the movement of coming-

---

5 *The Concept of Anxiety*, p. 34; (KW 8:37); SV 6:132; (4:308).

into-existence, is not one of necessity. The necessary *is*. The transition occurs only as an act of freedom, which may be characterized as a "leap." It would seem that we are ready for a full analysis of the nature of freedom. But Kierkegaard calls a halt.

Along with *Fragments*, he published *The Concept of Anxiety* as a companion volume. In the latter work he says that "in a logical system" (i.e. Hegel's) it is simply assumed that "possibility passes over into actuality," but "in actuality it is not so easy." An "intermediate term" is required to describe how the psychical-sensuous immediacy of innocence gets so disturbed, gets broken open, that the stage is set for the "qualitative leap" of freedom, by which that which already *is* as a potentiality becomes an actuality, comes-into-existence. But, be it noted, this description, this "middle term," "no more explains the qualitative leap than it justifies it ethically." Kierkegaard proposes *angst* as the middle term to indicate that strange phenomenon wherein the human individual is aroused so as to cease contemplating a fantasy as a possibility and to take the fateful step to enact it.[6]

The first and most important thing to note about Kierkegaard's peculiar and unique usage of this term is this: it designates the simultaneity of two opposite feelings toward a common object. So he defines it as a "sympathetic-antipathy and an antipathetic-sympathy." On the one hand, in angst one feels allured, enticed, tempted and so one desires and seeks the object; on the other hand and at the same time, one feels alarmed, frightened, repulsed and so one fears and flees the object. He had worked this definition out in a journal entry two years previously, where he says very simply, "Angst is a desire for what one fears, a sympathetic antipathy."[7]

Obviously, no single word carries this double meaning, neither the original German *angst*, nor the French *angoisse*, nor either of the English words "anxiety" and "dread." The difficulty with all of these words is that they connote almost exclusively the negative antipathy and not the positive sympathy. And this is true also of the Danish *angst* and its verbal root, *ængste*, which means to make anxious or uneasy, to alarm. Yet it is precisely the allurement and desire one feels that break the dominating contentment of the immediacy in the state of psychical-sensuousness. On the other hand, it is the ambiguity of the desire-fear relation that

---

6 Ibid., pp. 44f.; (KW 8:49); SV 6:142; (4:320).

7 Ibid., p. 38; (KW 8:42); SV 6:136; (4:313f.); also *Journals* 94; III A 233; quoted in full in KW 8:235.

both serves as the ground for Kierkegaard's understanding of freedom and explains why the move out of innocence is one of transcendence and discontinuity rather than one of immanence and continuity. For Kierkegaard, "angst" is a very complex phenomenon which is assumed as being operative at every level and in every sphere of human existence. Therefore, it calls for a detailed analysis here. And since "angst" is a perfectly good English word now, we will use it instead of the variants "dread" and "anxiety." The richness of his concept is good cause for its serving as the inspiration for a main theme in two such different and complex philosophies of human existence as those of Heidegger and Sartre.

Angst, we have said, is a kind of "feeling" (more on this term later) that seizes a person as one faces a certain possibility, that is, as one's psychical sensitivity projects a vague image or adumbration which acquires the quality of being "possible," of being capable of (or even demanding) enactment in one's finitude. Kierkegaard describes angst as "an alien power which grasps" a person. Thus the simple "peace and repose" of innocence is pervaded by angst, as when a dream appears and disturbs undifferentiated sleep. But what is it about the possibility that evokes the ambiguity of feeling both enticement and alarm? Obviously, this feeling is not evoked by such possibilities as wearing my brown suit instead of the blue one, as going to the movies tonight instead of watching TV, etc. A certain degree of angst may be felt by a child who is about to enter the "ghost house" at an amusement park, or by an adult who is deciding what kind of work to do or whether to marry a certain person. But none of these are the decisive, qualitative angst which, Kierkegaard asserts, seizes *every* human being, beginning at the moment of leaving innocence and throughout the rest of life.

The particular possibility which evokes this existential angst appears when, "[d]reaming, the spirit projects its own actuality," that is to say, when my finitude and infinitude so interact that my innocence is disturbed by a shape "outside itself," a *positive* unity of the two, a unity which appears as a "third," a third something which is different from either of the two, and different from the two in their synthesis of immediacy, and yet includes the two. This "third" Kierkegaard calls "spirit" or "self." He summarizes this view of things by saying,

The human being is a synthesis of the psychical and the sensuous. But a synthesis is unthinkable if the two are not united in a third. This third is the spirit. ... The spirit is present, but as immediate, as dreaming. Inasmuch as it is now present, it is in a sense a hostile power, because it constantly disturbs the relation between soul and body. ... On the other hand, it is a friendly power, which precisely wants to constitute the relation. What, then, is the human being's relation to this ambiguous power; how does the spirit relate to itself and to its condition? It relates as angst. Get rid of itself, the spirit cannot; neither can it grasp itself as long as it has itself outside of itself; nor can the human being sink down into the vegetative, because he is qualified as spirit; one cannot flee from angst, because one loves it; yet one cannot really love it, because one flees from it. Innocence has now reached its uttermost point.[8]

This spirit or self, as a "third," is like a dream, then, in that it has not been actualized. It is a possibility; it has being in that it is a potentiality suggested by one's concrete synthesis of finitude/infinitude, but it is also non-being in that it has not yet passed over the great divide between possibility and actuality.

Why, then, do I not simply reach out and grasp this wonderful possibility which is the positive unity of what I already am as a negative unity? What could be more "natural"? Are they not linked by an identity, a coinherence or coimplication, which is more fundamental than their opposition (Hegel!)? Why should the transition be made to look so difficult? Is it not really a necessary, an irresistible movement? Why is the human being's relation to this particular possibility to be characterized as one of "angst" with its duality of enticement and alarm, filled with desiring and fleeing?

In answer to this question, Kierkegaard says that there are two complex reasons. And here we have the first occasion for testing whether or not Kierkegaard's basic methodology is phenomenological. Does his analysis of the reasons for angst answer to universal human experience or merely reflect the peculiar, some would say tragic, conditions of his childhood, especially his relations with his parents? What, then, are the two reasons that the projected potential self evokes double-sided angst in the dim consciousness of the immediate self?

Before we look at these two reasons, it must be made clear that throughout all of his authorship, Kierkegaard assumes and repeatedly asserts that the major fact of human existence is that the human being is composed and structured in such a way that a self is one's destiny. He

---

8 The quotes in the last two paragraphs are from *The Concept of Anxiety*, pp. 38–40; (KW 8:42–4); SV 6:136–8; (4:313–15). The last phrase in the last quote, "its uttermost," should be understood as "its point of crisis."

agrees (with Hegel) that it is "natural" and inevitable that the human being becomes aware of, desires, seeks the possibility of transcending one's self as innocent immediacy in order to be a self which consciously and responsibly affirms and accepts that immediate self and the task of actualizing its potentialities. But Kierkegaard disagrees totally (with Hegel) that the transition, the movement, from immediate self to conscious self is one of immanence and inevitability. The possible self fills one not only with enticement but also alarm; one not only desires (*elske*) it but also simultaneously flees or avoids (*fly*) it. Why?

Kierkegaard's first answer is this: indeed, it is true that "the spirit projects its own actuality, but this actuality is nothing [*Intet*]." And "what effect does nothing have? It begets angst. ... The actuality of the spirit constantly appears as a form which entices its possibility but is gone as soon as it grasps after it, and is a nothing which can only alarm [*ængste*]. More it cannot do as long as it merely shows itself." That is to say, as long as my spirit (self) appears to me only as an unactualized possibility, "the difference between my self [*mig selv*] and my other [*mit Andet*] ... is an intimated [adumbrated] nothing."9

What does Kierkegaard mean by "nothing"? For him, the nothing that begets angst is the ignorance that obtains in innocence. The original self, which is merely a synthesis of finitude/infinitude in immediacy, is simply ignorant of *what* this projected possible self might be. Kierkegaard says that this "angst that is posited in innocence" has at first no quality of guilt or troublesome burden of suffering "that cannot be brought into harmony with the blessedness of innocence." Although it alarms, it also captivates "by its pleasing anxiousness." But then innocence "reaches its uttermost point [of crisis]." It is profoundly enticed and captivated by this "dream," this dimly adumbrated possibility of its true self which transcends the immediacy of innocence. But the innocent immediate self is also alarmed and put off by this vision, because the projected self is totally undefined, is as yet nothing. So innocence comes to the startling awareness that "it is ignorance; however, it is not an animal brutality but an ignorance qualified by spirit, and as such innocence is precisely angst, because its ignorance is about nothing. Here there is no knowledge of good and evil, etc., but the whole quality of knowledge projects itself in angst as the enormous nothing of ignorance."

---

9 Ibid., p. 38; (KW 8:41f.); SV 6:136; (4:313).

Finally, what really alarms innocence is not just its inability to define or put content into its vision of the possible self, but even more its inability to reach out and grasp this possibility. It is tantalized by the fact that while this vision of a new possibility of self will not disappear, "neither can it grasp itself as long as it has itself outside of itself." The actuality of the projected self is not only "nothing," but "innocence constantly sees this nothing outside of itself." It "appears as a form which entices its possibility, but is gone as soon as it grasps after it."[10]

For Kierkegaard, then, "nothing" is not a metaphysical being or a cosmic force that intrudes itself into human existence and consciousness. Rather, it is a characteristic of one's possible self, experienced in the process of becoming oneself. And angst is what we have called a "feeling" that seizes and overwhelms the simple consciousness of a self-in-innocence when faced by this characteristic of its "dreaming" self. But, as already noted (and to anticipate material in the next several chapters), this feeling is not a simple urge or impulsive desire but has "dialectical determinants" (sympathy/antipathy). Hence it comprises a basic attitude or disposition involving a rudimentary, unreflective, intuitive evaluation of the possible self as, on the one hand, a good which I desire and seek after, but, on the other hand, a threat which I fear and flee. At this point, one may retreat into innocence and its ignorance, or one may leap into the uncertainty of the self's undefined "nothingness." So, even though he has not considered the requirement of self-consciousness, Haufniensis anticipates *Postscript* and *Sickness* when he says, "angst is freedom's actuality as possibility for possibility," which roughly means that the leap of freedom is grounded in the fundamental nature of the human individual's "being able" to "choose" at the point of the dialectic feeling of sympathy/antipathy.[11]

The reason, therefore, why the immediate self cannot reach out and grasp the possible self in immediacy is explicated in Kierkegaard's understanding of freedom, which we will explore later. But in this context, he insists that this sense of one's self as a "nothing" that fills one with "fearful fascination"[12] is common among children, and it takes the form of what he calls "melancholy" in many adults. One has only to ask the average teenager what she/he wants to "do" or "be" when schooling is finished, to see the shrug of ignorance before "nothing"—"I don't know,

---

10 Ibid., pp. 40, 38; (KW 8:44, 41f.); SV 6:138, 136; (4:315, 313).
11 Ibid., p. 38; (KW 8:42); SV 6:136; (4:313).
12 See Robert B. Parker, *The Judas Goat*, p. 138.

yet"; and to see the shadow of angst pass over the face. And in the adult world it is even more embarrassing to view the consternation aroused if one asks the forbidden question of another person, "Who are you?" What does one even mean by such a question? As Kierkegaard says,

> A person can go on living fairly well, seem to be a human being, be occupied with temporal matters, marry, have children, be honoured and esteemed—and it may not be detected that in a deeper sense this person lacks a self. Such things do not create much of a stir in the world, for a self is the last thing the world cares about and the most dangerous thing of all for a person to show signs of having. The greatest hazard of all, losing the self, can occur very quietly in the world, as if it were nothing at all. No other loss occurs so quietly; any other loss—an arm, a leg, five dollars, a wife, etc.—is sure to be noticed.[13]

And of course if one is forced to recognize the loss or the absence of one's self, the usual feeling or "attitude" that seizes an adult is not angst—too late for that—but melancholy. Heidegger insists that the ultimate "Nothingness" of death compels everyone to "care" for one's "being" and to seek for its ground in "Being." But any pastor who has conducted dozens of funerals for unbelievers will tell you that the usual reaction to death is numbness, followed by melancholy, followed by indifference.

Kierkegaard, however, sees another quite different source of angst than the initial undefined nothing of the possible self. There is quite another reason why this shadowy apparition fills one's innocent immediacy with an even sharper sense of enticement and alarm. He calls it "a higher form of ignorance" which evokes "a higher expression of angst." And "in this way, innocence is brought to its uttermost." We arrive at the "last approximation" in our psychological analysis of the "state that precedes" the movement or transition from possibility to actuality, which analysis however does not pretend to explain that movement, which Kierkegaard describes as a "leap."[14] What, then, is this "higher form of ignorance," which evokes a "higher expression of angst"?

The undefined "nothing" of my possible self made its appearance and disturbed (caused to be anxious) the contented innocent immediacy of my psychical/sensuous synthesis. Now "angst's nothing" does not remain as a mere projection of an "outside" possibility to be looked at;

---

13 *Sickness*, p. 165; (KW 19:32f.); SV 15:90; (11:146).
14 *The Concept of Anxiety*, pp. 40f., 68f., (KW 8:45, 77); SV 6:138f., 166; (4:316, 345).

rather, it "comes within," it penetrates and pervades my innocence. With what result? Innocence begins to speak to itself. Kierkegaard makes (what is for some) the startling proposal that the words attributed to God ("of the tree of the knowledge of good and evil you shall not eat, for in the day that you eat of it, you will die" Gen.2:17), and the words attributed to the serpent ("You will not die" Gen.3:4), are actually words spoken by every human being to him/herself in innocence. He says, "Innocence can indeed speak, inasmuch as in language it possesses the manifestation for everything spiritual. Accordingly, one need merely assume that Adam talked to himself," even though he was not able "to understand what was said." So "the myth allows something that is inward to take place outwardly. ... The speaker is language."[15]

Haufniensis is assuming here the first beginnings of what Climacus (in *Postscript*) calls "reflection" and therefore of consciousness of self. The nature of this process will be dealt with in detail in the third section of this chapter. But its first dim form occurs within innocence, and we cannot understand Kierkegaard's view as to how angst occurs and sets the (psychological) stage for the radical movement (leap) out of innocent immediacy without a preliminary characterization of this stage of reflection.

In an alternative formulation of his position, developed in his unpublished work *Johannes Climacus*, Kierkegaard says that consciousness cannot stay in immediacy if we are to transcend our animal nature, that is, become self. And "it is language that annuls immediacy; if the human being could not talk he/she would remain in the immediate."[16] But what kind of "talking" and reflection goes on at this stage of human existence? It is the kind that is appropriate to that structure of the human being which is oriented, even in innocence, toward becoming "spirit" or self. And this language, Kierkegaard says, is figurative language rather than literal or abstract language.[17] So the first level of inward reflection or conversation (that is evoked within innocence by encounter with the nothing of the projected possibility of one's "other" self) may be almost wordless. Two inchoate questions take shape in the emerging consciousness of the self, and the answers that are "heard" reveal a "higher form of ignorance" which evokes a "higher expression of angst."

---

15 Idem. (pp. 40–3).
16 *Journals*, 2320, IV B 14:6.
17 *Works of Love*, pp. 199f.; SV 12:203f.; (9:201f.).

The first question that arises in innocence is: *why* is the projected, possible self an undefined "nothing"? Am I not able to select and reject, to judge what is right or wrong for the content of my possible self? And the answer that innocence must say to itself is "No!" But then an amazing thing happens: as a reflex to this negative, innocence becomes aware that it has raised a new question: not "Do I like or dislike?" or "Do I find pleasure or pain?" but "Am I able?" Even though I cannot decide *what* I should do, I become aware *that* I am able to do something. Kierkegaard says, "The prohibition awakens in him freedom's possibility. ... He has no conception of what he is able to do. ... Only the possibility of being able is present as a higher form of ignorance, ... because in a higher sense it both is and is not." That is to say, one has become aware of the *possibility* of choice (freedom), but one has not actually enacted it. So "here again it is a nothing" which again alarms, "the anxious possibility of *being able.*" So now there is also a "higher expression of angst, ... because in a higher sense one both loves it and flees from it."[18]

This is Kierkegaard's initial exposition of freedom in its first form, as it is first intimated in innocence. Although a full treatment of his concept of freedom will come later, we must make here a few preliminary remarks about freedom in order to clarify the origin and nature of angst as the condition and power that disturbs innocence and that thus prepares the immediate self to seek its "other" self through the "qualitative leap" out of innocence in order to actualize the projected possible self.

Kierkegaard uses the term "freedom" in two senses in order to indicate the two forms of this definitive element of human existence. First, there is what he calls "freedom's possibility," the sheer capacity of "being able" without any definition of what one is able to do. Secondly, freedom is the *act* of choosing, choosing to *be* what one *is*, and especially choosing to actualize (become) one's possible self. So he sometimes uses "freedom" and "possibility" interchangeably, as when he speaks of "freedom's actuality as possibility for [not "of"] possibility," by which he means: "being able" for the sake of "choosing." In the later exposition of freedom, we will explain the reason why innocence hears the word of prohibition when it asks whether it can determine what its self will be. And we will explore what Kierkegaard means when he says that freedom is *hildet*, a strange word meaning "snared" or "prejudiced."[19]

---

18 *The Concept of Anxiety*, pp. 40f.; (KW 8:45); SV 6:138f.; (4:316).
19 Ibid., pp. 38, 45; (KW 8:42, 49); SV 6:136, 143; (4:313, 320).

Lowrie translated it "trammelled," while Reidar Thomte uses "entangled." I will suggest "oriented" or "directed."

At this point, however, we are concerned only with "being able" and its relation to angst. Kierkegaard asserts clearly that angst is not a determinant either of necessity or of freedom (i.e., possibility).[20] Rather angst is that dual sense of enticement/alarm produced in the consciousness of innocence by the "nothing" (indeterminateness) both of the possible self and of "being able" (freedom's possibility). On the one hand, one yearns and desires to become that other self and to become it *freely*. On the other hand, one is alarmed and repelled because one does not know (ignorance) either *what* that self may be, or the limits of one's sensed but unused freedom. Kierkegaard insists that angst, with its simultaneous attraction/repulsion, "is altogether different from fear and similar concepts that refer to something definite." He says that "if the object of angst is a something, then we get no leap but a quantitative transition," that is, an unfree transition.[21]

The final intensity of angst, however, has not yet been described. Something more is added even to the "higher expression of angst" that has been evoked by the word of prohibition about the limits of "being able." We said that innocence speaks two questions to itself and hears two answers. The second question arises something like this: since there are limits on my freedom and I do not know what I am able to do, am I certain that I really am able? Or might I make a mistake and fail? Do I even know what it means to "fail" ("die")? To the frustrating, bewildering, repelling ignorance and angst of a limited freedom is now added a qualitatively new kind of ignorance, and it evokes an angst with an element not simply of alarm but of *terror*. "In this case, the terror is simply angst." Because one does not understand what it means to fail, "there is nothing but the ambiguity of angst. The infinite possibility of being able that was awakened by the prohibition now draws closer, because this possibility points to another possibility as its consequence." So the answer comes: yes, you may fail—with dire results. One now senses that the misuse of the "possibility of being able" will result in the possibility of "death," failure, the total loss of the possible self one longs, yet fears, to become.

The "nothing" innocence faces is now total: the projected possible self is "nothing"; the consequent terrifying possibility of failure is "nothing."

---

20 Idem. (p. 45).
21 Ibid., pp. 38, 69; (KW 8:42, 77); SV 6:136, 166; (4:313, 345).

And with each increase in the depth and complexity of its "nothing," innocence has experienced an ever-intensifying enticement/alarm (angst): from the mild interest in an "other" possible self and the disturbing fact that it is undefined; to the exciting sense of "being able" but with the disconcerting, confusing awareness that this freedom is strictly limited; to the bewildering challenge of the possibility of failure, accompanied by the terrifying certainty of reprisal.[22]

What does one do when one's innocence has been so profoundly aroused and terrified by these phantom possibilities which come like disturbing dreams in the darkness and night? Would it not be better to slip back into the undifferentiated immediacy of sleeping innocence? Some try. But one cannot get rid of the self. The harder one tries to fling it away, the more persistently does the self come back to haunt one's dreams. This possible self is both "a hostile power, because it constantly disturbs the relation between soul and body," and also "a friendly power, since it is precisely that which constitutes the relation. What then is one's relation to this ambiguous power? How does spirit [self] relate to itself and to its condition? It relates as angst. Do away with itself, the spirit cannot; neither can it grasp itself, as long as it has itself outside of itself."[23] So "angst is of all things the most self-centred [*Selviske*], and no concrete expression of freedom is as self-centred as the possibility of every concretion. This again is the overwhelming [factor] that determines the individual's ambiguous [relation], sympathetic and antipathetic. In angst there is the self-centred infinity of possibility, which does not tempt like a choice but ensnaringly disquiets [*ængster*] with its sweet anxiousness [*Beængstelse*]."[24]

What, then, does one do? At this extreme point of crisis, a fateful move occurs: "Freedom gazes down into its own possibility."[25] There is no more pregnant sentence in all of Kierkegaard's writings, and we will look at it more closely at several points throughout this study. Basically it means: I am able (free) to look at, to reflect about, the fact that I am able (free). In another place, Kierkegaard has more to say on the matter. "As freedom with all its passion wishfully stares at itself and would keep guilt at a distance so that not a single particle of it might be found in freedom, it cannot refrain from staring at guilt, and this staring is the

---

22 Ibid., p. 41; (KW 8:45); SV 6:139; (4:316).
23 Ibid., pp. 39ff.; (KW 8:43ff.); SV 6:137ff.; (4:314ff.).
24 Ibid., p. 55; (KW 8:61); SV 6:153; (4:331).
25 Idem.

ambiguous [staring] of angst."[26] Of course, innocence does not know what it means to be "guilty," but this dim intimation is the reflex of the awareness of the possibility of failure and its reprisal. So "freedom gazing down into its own possibility" is not yet guilt, but it does have a strange effect: "dizziness." The "ambiguous staring of angst" produces "the dizziness of freedom."[27] We will have to return to this concept several times in what follows, but with it we have reached the "last approximation" to the point of movement out of innocence. "In this way, innocence is brought to its uttermost. In angst it is related to the forbidden and the retribution. Innocence is not guilty, and yet there is an angst as though it were lost."[28]

But what if freedom does not "gaze down into its own possibility," but keeps its attention on its proper object, namely, the projected possible self? What if freedom overcomes its alarm and terror and dares to step out into the unknown in order to accomplish the positive unity of its possibility and necessity in its authentic selfhood? After all, according to Kierkegaard failure is not necessitated. So before we proceed to Kierkegaard's scenario of human failure and its consequences (in another volume), we will follow the positive possibility in order to see how he conceives the ideal, fulfilled self. In this way, the "task"—which is set for every human being by the very structure of human existence in the context of reality as a whole—will be clarified. And, Kierkegaard says, it is especially apposite to call the realization of this ideal self a "task" because it is something which is never completed; this self is not a "result," not an objective truth or state which is arrived at and finished. The self's being is in the doing. To become one's self, he says, is identical with "possessing the way [*Vei* or *Vej*, i.e. road, route, path]," with being "in the-process-of-becoming [*i Vorden*]." So "the truth is not the truth, but the way is truth, that is, the truth is only in the becoming, in the process [*Proces*] of appropriation; consequently, there is no result."[29]

It should be noted that, by following this "way" immediately subsequent to the foregoing topic of angst as the end of innocence, we are omitting (at this time) any reference either to human failure and its consequences (sin and despair), or to the human need for help from beyond the human (faith in the eternal in the sense of religiousness B,

26 Ibid., p. 97; (KW 8:109); SV 6:194; (4:377).
27 Ibid., p. 55; (KW 8:61); SV 6:152; (4:331).
28 Ibid., p. 41; (KW 8:45); SV 6:139; (4:316).
29 *Postscript*, pp. 68, 72; (KW 12.1:73, 77); SV 9:63, 67; (7:55, 59).

i.e., Christianity—although, be it noted, "the human" for Kierkegaard includes integrally the dimension or "sphere" of religiousness A as an immanent relation with the eternal and this relation involves a "teleological suspension of the ethical" and a "total guilt-consciousness"). In other words, we are exploring the possibility (using Kierkegaardian ideas) of understanding human existence as self-explanatory and self-realizing, that is (in Kierkegaard's language), exploring "the self whose criterion is the human," or "the merely human self," rather than "the theological self."[30] Can Kierkegaard's anthropology stand on its own, without his theology? As we shall see in this study of "Kierkegaard as Humanist," Kierkegaard provides profound grounds for exploration of this thesis, even though in the "second authorship" as theologian he increasingly loses interest in this project. Finally, he argues, human existence is most profoundly understood from within the paradoxical religiousness of the eternal-in-time with its peculiar experience of sin and grace. But in this present study we suspend those considerations in order to see what human existence is capable of on its own terms—terms that Kierkegaard himself supplies.[31]

REFLECTION: THE FIRST STEP TOWARD
SELF-CONSCIOUSNESS

We have made a basic distinction between two different forms or states of the self. The first is the potential or possible self, which projects itself in a person's consciousness like a dream. Yet it is the dreaming possibility of a particular, concrete, unique individual, with all of his/her unique bodily, psychical, social, temporal finitude. The second is the actualized self, which comes-into-existence through a person's free enactment of those possibilities which were already "present" as potentialities inherent within the given finitude/infinitude of the person. The infinite possible self and the finite concrete self are brought together in the actuality of a positive unity. The "self" (or "spirit") in this form, therefore, is a "third" factor or entity which brings together, and forms a new concrete whole of, one's given factual finitude and the infinitude of one's possibilities.

---

30 *Sickness*, p. 210; (KW 19:79); SV 15:133; (11:191).
31 For a defence of this possibility, see John W. Elrod, *Being and Existence in Kierkegaard's Pseudonymous Works*, part one. We will comment on Elrod's position in the Interlude at the end of this volume.

This *act* of transition from possible to actual self is definitive of what it means to be a human being. This is the task for which the human being is structured. In its accomplishment alone does the human person come to an ultimate sense of meaning and fulfilment. But, as we have seen in the previous section, this transition does not happen automatically and easily. It involves great agony. The passage is filled with "angst." Indeed, it is angst alone that prepares us, that sets the stage for the transition.

Let us now assume, then, that in spite of the alarm evoked by the vague undefined quality of my possible self, and in spite of the terror evoked by the vague sense of my possible failure and its reprisal, I respond to the enticement of and to my passionate desire for this possible self. I dare to risk the "leap" into an undefined and uncertain possibility. "I," that is "my self," comes-into-existence. What, then, is the nature, the character, the inner structure and dynamic of this event? Kierkegaard's first answer is that the event involves the retention—in fact, the accentuation—of the bipolar structure that was already present in innocence but sublimated in its sensuous/psychical immediacy. Before angst disturbs the ignorance of innocence, one's sensuous and psychical dimensions abide in an undifferentiated unity and harmony.

Kierkegaard contends that "most people virtually never advance beyond what they were in their childhood and youth: immediacy with the admixture of a little dash of reflection." These adults seek to avoid or to quiet any inroads of angst about becoming a self. "Immediacy actually has no self, it does not know itself; thus it cannot recognize itself and therefore generally ends in the fantastic." Kierkegaard uses an intriguing image to describe such a person: "The whole question of the self becomes, in a deeper sense, a kind of blind door in the background of one's soul, behind which there is nothing." Then he gives this very telling description of such a male in modern society:

He takes on what he in his language calls his self, that is, whatever capacities, talents, etc. he may have; all these he takes on but in an outward direction, towards what is called life, the real, the active life. He behaves very discreetly with the little bit of reflection he has within himself, fearing that what he has in the background might emerge again. Little by little, he manages to forget it; in the course of time, he finds it almost ludicrous, especially when he is together with other competent and dynamic men who have a sense and aptitude for real life. Charming! He has been happily married now for several years, as it says in novels, is a dynamic and enterprising man, a father and citizen, perhaps even an important man; at home in his own house the servants call him "He Himself";

downtown he is among those addressed with "His Honour"; his conduct is based on respect of persons or on the way others regard one, and others judge according to one's social position. In Christendom he is a Christian.[32]

Becoming oneself, consciously and responsibly, therefore, requires a willingness to shatter and desert this immediacy, to refuse submission of one's entire psychic awareness to one's outward sensitivities in the aesthetic and social realms of experience. One must welcome angst as a friendly power, and take the first step of opening one's awareness to the radical difference between one's finitude and one's infinitude. As Kierkegaard puts it in his precise terms, "In the moment the spirit [self] posits itself, it posits the synthesis, but in order to posit the synthesis, it [the self] must pervade it [the synthesis] differentially [separately]."[33] In other words, the consciousness of self, as a third reality that is on the "way," in the "process," of becoming itself, integrally and constantly involves and requires the distinction and opposition between my "self" as finite, as bodily, sensuous, social, worldly, and, on the other hand, my "self" as infinite, as fantastic, unlimited, abstract possibility. Kierkegaard is very clear: the "concrete" or "actual" self, the conscious self in contrast to the childish immediate self, is neither simply finite nor simply infinite but retains and *uses* the contrast of the two in achieving the new positive unity and harmony of the two. He says that deliberate reflection on this dichotomy is the prerequisite of *self*-consciousness, is "the advancing impetus in the whole process by which a self infinitely assumes responsibility for its actual self."[34]

The nature and role of this initial form of reflection will become clear in the next section on "Consciousness of My Self," but Kierkegaard stresses its importance by pointing out that "with this certain degree of reflection begins the act of discrimination wherein the self becomes aware of itself as essentially distinct from the environment and external-world [*Udvortesheden*] and [from] their influence upon it."[35] The major point is that even when this self comes-into-existence responsibly and consciously, with its new form of positive unity and harmony, it retains its

---

32 For the quotes in this paragraph, see *Sickness*, pp. 191, 186, 189f.; (KW 19: 57f., 53, 56); SV 15:113, 109, 111f.; (11:170, 165, 168).

33 *The Concept of Anxiety*, p. 44; (KW 8:49); SV 6:142; (4:319).

34 *Sickness*, pp. 162, 188; (KW 19:30, 55); SV 15:87f., 111; (11:142, 167). Kierkegaard worked this view out in more technical form in his unpublished work, *Johannes Climacus, or, De omnibus dubitandum est*, which will be used below.

35 Ibid., p. 188; (KW 19:54); SV 15:110; (11:166).

fundamental duality or dichotomy of finitude/infinitude, necessity/possibility. Without this duality, the new self is not a "third" but becomes homogeneous, a result; it loses its dialectical character and thus its freedom and thus its character as an ongoing living "task." It becomes homogeneous with its environment and loses its self-identity.

Kierkegaard illustrates this point with numerous descriptions of the "concrete self," but here the point must again be stressed that he regards the continuing, lifelong interplay of my finitude and infinitude as a positive good, without which I lose my power of self-determination and so my identity as a self qualitatively distinguished from every other human being, and even (especially) from God. The opposition (*Modsætning*) and contradiction (*Modsigelse*) between the two do not make them mutually exclusive factors which make unity and harmony impossible. Rather, it is the interplay of two different but inseparable dimensions of a single entity that determines the quality of the movement by which unification and harmonization is achieved: namely, a movement of freedom rather than by necessity. As Kierkegaard loves to say: my concrete, actual self emerges from bringing the fantasies of my possibility (infinitude) into the delimiting structures of my necessity (finitude or given specificity). Hence, "it is not so, as the philosophers explain," that the fantasies of my possibility "pass over" into my actuality by necessity.[36]

The importance of this point cannot be exaggerated. How one understands the interrelationship between a human being's inner and outer modes of being, between one's subjectivity and objectivity, determines or reflects one's whole view of the nature and meaning of human existence. There are strong intellectual and political forces in our present world culture which vociferously and persistently reject and oppose any view which sees this interrelationship as the focal point for the emergence of a free and responsible self whose unique personal identity has ultimate worth in the social-historical-natural scheme of things. But it is out of place here to attempt a comprehensive cataloguing of these forces.

In summary, then, the first step beyond angst, the first step toward the conscious responsible self, is a moment of reflection. The focus of this

---

36 Kierkegaard makes a telling statement of this point in a journal entry (*Journals and Papers*, 77, X³ A 186): "Two heterogeneous qualities can never become homogeneous through continuous self-relating to each other; on the contrary, the difference, the qualitative difference, the heterogeneity becomes more obvious." This statement is under the heading: "Is the essence [nature] of the human being, Christianly understood, a unity or a duality (*Dobbelthed*)?"

reflection is not the actual self I may become but the distinction and contrast between what I am and what I dream of becoming. And in this moment comes the realization that I am all alone in this gap, that nothing in all the world around me will close this gap for me. This moment of reflection is prerequisite, is "prior," to self-consciousness and self-actualization at the beginning of my journey but also is experienced in "repetition" at every moment throughout it. This is why my self is a "task." And this task is set for me, unavoidably, precisely because of that gap between the neural and the mental, because of that "intermediate area" between my inner and outer reality, because there is not only psychological continuity but also discontinuity which requires choices, choices that are not settled by one's desires no matter how refined, because natural process and social justice find their point and meaning in *me* as a unique personal subject. In Kierkegaard's terms, "the self is a synthesis [of finitude/infinitude, of necessity/possibility] wherefor each [constituent] always is its opposite [*Modsatte*]."[37]

The next step occurs if one does not stifle this reflection, if one does not push the first dim intimation of self behind that "blind door" in the back of one's soul and forget it. If one encourages this reflection and lets it flow, then a whole new state of consciousness takes shape and becomes a major absorbing focus of one's life. We have heard Kierkegaard say (at note 33 above) that "most people never advance beyond ... immediacy with the admixture of a little dash of reflection"—which is tragic because "immediacy actually has no self; it does not know itself." But this pessimistic view expressed in *Sickness* runs counter to his more generous representations of the possible achievement of selfhood within the limits of religiousness A, as described in such works as *Fear and Trembling, Eighteen Upbuilding Discourses, Postscript, Upbuilding Discourses in Various Spirits,* and *Works of Love*—as we shall see in chapters 6 and 7 below. The question as to the "why?" and as to the validity of the more pessimistic view of *Sickness* will have to wait for our treatment of Kierkegaard as Theologian and his interpretation of human sin and failure.

CONSCIOUSNESS OF MY SELF

The nature of consciousness in the human individual, and the role it plays in self-actualization, are an enormously complex and uncertain

37 *Sickness,* p. 163; (KW 19:30); SV 15:88; (11:143).

subject. After more than a century of explorations, psychology's insights on the matter are as far from composing a "science" as ever. The results of research by neurophysiology are no more clear or final. But for our present purposes, these limitations are not critical, because our concern is with a very limited scope and operation of consciousness. Kierkegaard was profoundly interested in the emerging field of psychology in the early nineteenth century, and he realized that much of his analysis and description of human experience lay within this field (as we have seen in his delineation of the complexities of angst). But his major focus was not psychological, and thus he was not interested in developing a general inclusive concept of consciousness.[38] He was clearly aware of the workings of the subconscious and of psychosomatic interchange, but he had no interest in trying to fathom their modes of operation.

The limited scope of consciousness with which he was concerned, and which is relevant to our subject of the self, will be described under four headings: (1) the object of consciousness, (2) the attitude of consciousness, (3) the methodology of consciousness, (4) the limits of consciousness.

1 The Object of Consciousness

The proper object and ultimate import of human consciousness is one's self, the achievement of which is one's lifelong task. As we have heard Kierkegaard say, "Every human being is a psychical-bodily synthesis naturally fitted for being spirit [self], that is the construction."[39] But, he adds, this human being usually "prefers to live in the basement, that is, in the determinants of the sensuous." Does this mean that he denies any consciousness in this form or level of human existence? Of course not. In an early unpublished essay (*Johannes Climacus or De omnibus dubitandum est*), Kierkegaard describes how his pseudonym set out to explore "consciousness as it is in itself, as that which explains every specific consciousness, yet without being itself a specific [consciousness]." He begins by asking what the consciousness of a child is like. It is "indeterminate" or "immediate." And what is immediacy? "In immediacy there is no relationship," that is, no sense of opposition between one's "reality" and

---

[38] This is why I believe that Adi Schmueli's *Kierkegaard and Consciousness*, while insightful and helpful on some aspects, is mistaken in its general approach. He describes all aspects of the self according to Kierkegaard as different forms of consciousness. One may make a case for this perspective, but it was not Kierkegaard's usage of the concept.

[39] *Sickness*, p. 176; (KW 19:43); SV 15:100; (11:156).

"ideality," or, in his later terminology, no opposition between one's finitude and infinitude, "because as soon as there is a relationship, immediacy is cancelled." Then he adds this disconcerting remark: "Cannot consciousness then remain in immediacy? This would be a foolish question, because if it could, there would be no consciousness at all." In other words, consciousness as it occurs in immediacy, whether in a child or an adult, is a specious consciousness; it "exists only according to its possibility [*Mulighed*]."[40]

In his later mature work, *The Sickness unto Death*, Kierkegaard speaks of "degrees of consciousness" ranging from minimum to maximum, and we will trace this process of intensification in the section on "the methodology of consciousness." But even in *Sickness*, he wants to reserve the term "consciousness" for the recognition of that ultimate definitive task of becoming one's self. As we have seen, he asserts that many adults never mature but retreat into and live on in an "immediacy" similar to that in which they lived as children. "The sensuous in them usually far outweighs their intellectuality." They "live in the sensuous categories, the agreeable and the disagreeable, wave goodby to spirit, truth, etc." So it can be said of "every human existence which is not conscious as spirit [self]" that it "vaguely rests in and merges into some abstract universal (state, nation, etc.) or, in the dark about itself, regards its capacities merely as powers to produce without becoming deeply aware of their source."[41] It can be said of such individuals that they have some kind of "awareness" of the complexities of the physical social world in which they live, and a very different kind of "awareness" in the fantasies and dreams of what they wish their world might be. And some times they even reflect a little about the discrepancies between the two. But Kierkegaard would prefer to reserve the term "consciousness" for that peculiar awareness that comes when a person begins to envision and be grasped by the task of bringing these two worlds together, through deliberate responsible choice.

Of course, in this state of immediacy one can speak of an "immediate self," that is, the self that is there potentially. But the reflection that occurs here is only "quantitative," and therefore "there is no infinite consciousness of the self." That is to say, one's powers of fantasy and imagination (in one's infinitude) are not used to project the wondrous

---

40 *Johannes Climacus, or De omnibus dubitandum est*, pp. 147–9 (Croxall); (KW 7:167–8); *Papirer*, IV B 1, pp. 145–7.
41 *Sickness*, pp. 176, 179; (KW 19:43, 46); SV 15:99, 102; (11:155, 158).

possibility of a unique responsible self, but are used only to depict *more* pleasure, more riches, more fame, more power, etc. So one can say that "immediacy actually has no self, it does not know itself; thus it cannot recognize itself. ... The one living in immediacy ... quite literally knows himself only by the clothes he wears, he knows what it means to have a self by externalities. There is hardly a more ludicrous mistake, because a self is indeed infinitely distinct from externalities." For Kierkegaard, then, a self existing in such "immediacy" cannot be said to possess consciousness. "Consciousness—that is, self-consciousness [*Selvbevidsthed*]— is decisive with regard to the self. The more consciousness, the more self; the more consciousness, the more will; the more will, the more self. A person who has no will at all is not a self; but the more will he has, the more self-consciousness he has also."[42]

Consciousness is defined by its proper object: the self.

2 The Attitude of Consciousness

How does one regard this self of which one has become conscious? As will become clear in a later chapter, the term "attitude" carries significant content in our contemporary psychology and philosophy of action, and it is not to be confused with "mood." Kierkegaard has specifically denied "mood" as the apposite term for describing the proper stance toward the object of consciousness.[43] For him, "mood" is too passive, because one must take an active deliberate stance toward the self. So what attitude should one assume? Actually, this is part of the larger question of *how* one becomes self-conscious (methodology), which will be taken up in the next section. But it is so critical that it deserves to be given a preliminary treatment.

As one's awareness is aroused out of its psychic-sensuous immediacy, and one begins to glimpse the possibility of becoming a conscious responsible self, one could take an attitude of curiosity, or of indifference. One could approach it analytically and thus coolly consider the

---

42 Ibid., pp. 184, 186f., 162; (KW 19:50, 53, 29); SV 15:106, 109, 87; (11:162, 165, 142).

43 See *Three Discourses on Imagined Occasions* translated by David F. Swenson as *Thoughts on Crucial Situations in Human Life* pp. 79–81; (KW 10:74–6); SV 6:298–300; (5:228–30). For an interesting and perceptive treatment of "mood" in Kierkegaard, see Vincent A. McCarthy, *The Phenomenology of Moods in Kierkegaard*. His thesis is that irony, angst, melancholy, and despair are all properly termed "moods" in Kierkegaard's treatment of them, but we have argued above that angst is a "feeling" for Kierkegaard and therefore an "attitude."

alternatives. One could be guided by the methods of psychology and psychoanalysis. All of these attitudes and approaches, Kierkegaard maintains, would be self-defeating. None of them would lead to authentic self-consciousness, to the understanding of one's self which will prepare one to take the first step toward self-actualization. Authentic consciousness of self as one's imperious possibility demands a very different attitude; it requires (what Kierkegaard calls) "interestedness" (*Interesse* or *Interesserethed*) and "earnestness" (*Alvor*).[44] These two are not the same but closely related.

Interestedness arises from the consciousness that my self is neither just an abstract idea in a larger scheme of concepts, nor a mere undifferentiated thing in a world of things. Rather, human existence is an inescapable duality of thinking *and* being, of infinitude with its imagination of possibilities *and* finitude with its conditions of necessity. And "I" (as the "third," the self coming to consciousness) cannot ignore either side of this duality but must hold them in dialectical tension and not allow either one to absorb the other. *Self*-consciousness is the coming to awareness that a continuing alternation between the two sides is an inadequate, an immature form of existing, that *human* existing requires that I seek to interrelate the two, that "I" (my self) am that act of interrelating the two, and that this task is never "done," never completed. Therefore, nothing is more important to me (my self). In Kierkegaard's language, "For the existing one, the fact of existing is to him his highest interest [*Interesse*], and interestedness [*Interesserethed*] in existing is [his] actuality. What actuality is, cannot be indicated in the language of abstraction. The actuality [of an existing human being] is an *inter-esse* between abstraction's hypothetical unity of thought [on the one hand] and being [on the other hand]."[45] Since, then, actuality as an authentic human self means "existing-in-between" (*inter-esse*) "a tremendous contradiction ... in which one has to remain," therefore one's "eternal blessedness" requires that one brings to this task "infinite passionate interest," rather than seeking to escape this task by being content with disinterested abstract ideas about existence, or by losing all consciousness of self by

---

44 Kierkegaard formulates his special meaning of "interest" in *Johannes Climacus* (1843) and uses it in *Postscript* (1845). His special use of "earnestness" appears in several "edifying discourses" and in *The Concept of Anxiety*, all in 1844, but he continues to use it, especially in his journals, to the end of his life.

45 *Postscript*, p. 279; (KW 12.1:314); SV 10:21; (7:270). Kierkegaard enjoyed this play on the double meaning of *inter-esse*, and uses it repeatedly throughout *Postscript*. He had worked out this usage in *Johannes Climacus* and in *Journals*, 197, IV C 100.

allowing one's awareness to be absorbed into the immediate sensibilities of things and social relationships.[46] In other words, my fulfilment as a self in the conditions of human existence requires that I focus my ultimate interest on this task, without any reservations and with total earnestness.

So we come to our second word, "earnestness." Obviously, the addition of a couple of adjectives to "interestedness" is very important. One can be more or less, even slightly, interested in something. This is not the attitude of self-consciousness. If, seized by the profound dialectical feeling of angst, one is to have the venturesomeness to step out toward the actualization of the self's possibilities, then one's interest must indeed be without limits (infinite) and totally serious (earnest) and ultimately all-absorbing (passionate). We will see in the next section that Kierkegaard means something more by "passion" (*Lidenskab*) than by "earnestness" (*Alvor*), but the latter is a basic quality of interestedness that makes it passionate. So without it, there is no self-consciousness, because "all existence-issues are passionate, because existence, if one becomes conscious of it, yields passion."[47]

Kierkegaard makes this equation in his direct treatment of earnestness. He says, "Earnestness denotes the personality itself, and only an earnest personality is an actual personality, ... because to do something with earnestness requires first and foremost to know what is the object of earnestness. ... This object every human being has, because it is *oneself.*"[48] So to have the self as the object of consciousness requires that one focuses total and profoundly earnest interest on the task of becoming that self. Otherwise, it is not true to say that one is *self*-conscious. What, then, are some of the characteristics of this earnestness?

Perhaps the greatest instiller of earnestness is death—not the death of others no matter how dear, which yields only a mood of sadness, but *my*

---

46 Ibid., pp. 313, 28, 30, 33, 51; (KW 12.1:350, 27, 29, 33, 52); SV 10:52; 9:27, 29, 32, 49; (7: 303, 16, 18, 21, 39). In the latter four pages, one finds several different versions of "infinite passionate interest" which are not translated very exactly by David Swenson (or Walter Lowrie). They are as follows: "personal, infinite interestedness with passion," "infinite, personal interestedness with passion," "infinite, personal, interested passion," "infinite, passionate interest." This is a good example of Kierkegaard's refusal to use fixed formulas, of his conviction that existence cannot be captured in conceptual and verbal abstractions capable of exact definition and formulation.

47 Ibid., p. 313; (KW 12.1:350–1); SV 10:52; (7:304).

48 *The Concept of Anxiety*, p. 133; (KW 8:149f.); SV 6:229f.; (4:415). Kierkegaard here goes on to equate earnestness with inwardness (*Inderlighed*), but that will be treated in the next section.

death, whose contemplation reveals that only two things exist: death and myself. Then I become profoundly earnest—not about death, which is a nothing, or about speculations of what comes after death, which I cannot know. In earnest, I know one thing about death: life is over. Death is night. So while there is day, I must earnestly pursue one thing: I must seek out myself. I become aware of a difference: not the difference from others but the distance between what I am and the goal that is set before me. "Death, in earnestness, produces vitality (lifepower) as nothing else does." So the earnestness taught and instilled by death is focused on my self, my life. "And so earnestness comes to consist in living each day as if it were the last, and at the same time the first in a long life."[49]

Interestedness is "earnest," therefore, when I regard its object as having "absolute significance for me," and when I approach it with "fear and trembling," with "all my strength and utmost exertion."[50] Earnestness moves me toward "decisiveness," toward the enactment of my self "recklessly, absolutely," toward that moment of "achieved originality," the leap of freedom. But (Kierkegaard cautions) one must always "have a sense of humour to control one's earnestness," must constantly "dare to submit one's earnestness to the test of jest."[51] Why? Because one must not equate *consciousness* of self, no matter how intense its interest and earnestness, with the actual enactment of self. "Earnestness ... stands in no relation (except a comic one) to the leap. ... To have been very near to doing something has even its comic side, but to have been very near making the leap is absolutely nothing, because the leap is the category of decision."[52] One must always see the humorous (ridiculous) aspect of the assumption that being deeply interested and in earnest about becoming one's self is the same as having done it. This amounts to being satisfied with the fantasy of the imagination in place of the actuality of

---

49 For this paragraph, see Kierkegaard's edifying discourse, "At a Graveside," in *Three Discourses on Imagined Occasions*, Swenson's *Thoughts on Crucial Situations in Life*, especially pp. 81, 90–1, 98, 107; (KW 10:75, 82–3, 89, 96); SV 6:300, 306–7, 311–12, 317; (5:229–30, 236, 241–2, 247).

50 *Stages on Life's Way*, p. 335; (KW 11:365–6); SV 8:170; (6:341); *Postscript*, p. 123; SV 9:114; (7:111f.).

51 For this series of terms, see *Journals*, 1853, X^1 A 455; 235, IX A 387; 3795, V B 69; 1743, VI A 3.

52 *Postscript*, p. 91; (KW 12.1:99); SV 9:85; (7:79). See the index of the English translation for passages throughout *Postscript* where Kierkegaard repeatedly returns to the role of "humour" and jest in the process of becoming self.

existence, or (as will be shown at length later) with having an intention to do something rather than doing it.

Nevertheless, our point here is that unless consciousness is moved by ultimate interestedness and intense earnestness about the self, it will never come to the point of decision and have the courage to risk stepping off toward an unknown and uncertain goal. The sympathetic aspect of angst, with its allurement and desire for one's self, must not be allowed to be numbed and paralysed by the terror of the unknown and the uncertain, and thus lead to the loss of self-consciousness by its being absorbed into the immediacy of sense enjoyment and into the priority of external relations to things and society.

The proper object of consciousness is the self.
The effective attitude of consciousnes is earnest interestedness.

3 The Methodology of Consciousness

How, then, does *self-*consciousness come into being? How does one break out of the merely sensuous awareness and quantitative reflection of the immediate self? How does one come to a vision of one's other self as a fantastic possibility still to be actualized? How does an infinite, passionate, personal interest in *this* self arise? Kierkegaard worked out a few experimental, preliminary answers to these questions in *Johannes Climacus or De omnibus dubitandum est* (1842-43), but two years later he gave detailed and thorough attention to these issues in his philosophical magnum opus, *Concluding Unscientific Postscript.*

In the *Postscript,* Kierkegaard does not use the language of "self" or "consciousness," but he discusses the same phenomenon with the terms "spirit" and "subjectivity." His major thesis is that we usually approach the question of truth "objectively," that is, historically or philosophically, seeking to demonstrate truth by the support of empirical fact or rational argument. But there is an entirely different kind of truth which he calls "subjective." Here one is concerned with "appropriation" (*Tilegnelse*) of the truth, with "one's relation to the truth"; that is to say, one has an "infinite, personal, passionate interest as regards one's own eternal blessedness."[53] So after some preliminary considerations, ostensibly about Lessing, Kierkegaard begins his own analysis of the nature of truth (in *Postscript*) with a chapter entitled, "Becoming Subjective" (*Det at blive sub-*

---

53 Ibid., p. 23; (KW 12.1:21); SV 9:23; (7:11).

jektiv).[54] We will follow the process of becoming subjective under two topics: (1) reflection as a prerequisite of subjectivity (self-consciousness), and (2) the differences between objective thinking and subjective thinking.

The first step out of immediacy toward subjectivity (self-consciousness) Kierkegaard calls "reflection." And as usual, he gives the term his own special twist in meaning.[55] As already indicated above, reflection is that first stirring beyond angst wherein one becomes aware of and admits the contradiction between one's finite, necessary self and one's infinite, possible self. "The determinants of reflection are always dichotomous; e.g. ideality and reality, soul and body, knowing and the true, willing and the good, desiring and the beautiful, God and the world, etc. are determinants of reflection. In reflection they touch each other in such a way that a relation becomes possible." This contradiction is "the first pain of becoming." Therefore, "reflection is the *possibility of relation*, consciousness is *the relation, whose first form is the contradiction*."[56] Thus, in authentic reflection there is already a looking toward and an anticipation of consciousness of self, of self as a "third" entity in which the duality of finitude/infinitude, and the tension between the two, is not annulled, but in which the two relate to each other in a positive way. *Either:* one pushes this disturbing reflection behind the "back door" of one's psyche, locks the door tightly and returns to immediacy; *or:* the duality of one's being as revealed in reflection is welcomed, and one begins to look in the direction of that possible self pointed to by the duality.

In a couple of paragraphs in *The Sickness unto Death*, Kierkegaard gives a vivid portrayal of the state of the human psyche in this tentative, tenuous moment of transition. He says that "when immediacy is assumed to have some reflection, ... a somewhat greater consciousness of self comes about." Then there occurs "a certain degree of pondering over one's

---

54 Ibid., p. 115; (KW 12.1:129); SV 9:107; (7:104).

55 In *Johannes Climacus, Postscript*, and *The Sickness unto Death*, Kierkegaard uses the German spelling, *Reflexion*, to signify this special meaning. But I do not find him making the distinction indicated by Mark Taylor: "reflexion" as a differentiation of opposites, "reflection" as abstraction from concrete existence (*Journeys*, p. 173, note 104). In *Postscript*, "reflexion" does have to do with the treatment of opposites, but there are two alternatives: "objective reflexion" which annuls the difference through abstraction from existence, and "subjective reflexion" which preserves the difference and the tension in existence (*Postscript*, pp. 171ff.; (KW 12.1:192ff.); SV 9:159ff.; (7:159ff.).

56 *Johannes Climacus*, p. 150 (Croxall); (KW 7:168f, 257); *Papirer* IV B 1, p. 147; and B 14:9, p. 180.

self," and from that comes an awareness of being "essentially distinct from the environment and external-world and from their influence." There emerges a willingness "to be responsible for oneself." "One's imagination discovers a possibility which, if it eventuated, would thus become the break with immediacy." One begins to consider that one can lose many things "without losing the self." So one gains "a dim idea that there may even be something eternal in the self." Nevertheless, one still "does not have the self-reflection or the ethical reflection" required for "a total break with immediacy."[57]

Reflection, therefore, although it does not arrive at a full consciousness of the self as the potential *unity* of human duality, does nevertheless awaken consciousness at its primary level as a startling sense of what human existence actually is in its fundamental individual form: "an immense contradiction," an "absolute, qualitative disjunction" at the core of one's being. If one is to become and to remain an authentically human individual, one must "hold fast to the qualitative disjunction," must accept this "immense contradiction" as a condition of existence "in which one has to remain." This is not an easy task. For an existing human being, the temptation is to abstract from existence, "to understand one thing one moment and another thing in another moment." But this "is not to understand one's self [*sig selv*]." Admittedly, "to understand the greatest oppositions together, and to understand one's self existing in them, is very difficult." But if one is not to "disregard the concrete, the temporal, the becoming of existence," then this condition must be acknowledged as the inescapable "affliction of existence arising from being composed of the eternal and the temporal located in existence." This "difficulty of existence constitutes the interest of the existing individual, who is infinitely interested in existence."[58]

How, then, does the concrete specific human being handle this distressing difficulty of finding that existence is irrevocably composed of this immense contradiction, this qualitative disjunction? How does one "pervade it differentially [separately]"? Kierkegaard says that each side of the duality [synthesis] must be explored intently and exclusively before any attempt can be made to actualize the self as the positive unity (although one must have come "awake" to the self as that still-undefined

---

57 *The Sickness unto Death*, pp. 187f.; (KW 19:54f.); SV 15:119f; (11:166f.).
58 *Postscript*, pp. 313, 316, 267; (KW 12.1:350, 353–4, 301); SV 10:51, 55, 9f.; (7:303f. 307, 258).

"nothing," and begun to reflect on one's condition).[59] What then is the specific content of this reflection which conducts the exploration? How does one reflect intently about one's finitude, about one's infinitude?

On human finitude, Kierkegaard makes the flat assertion: "The ultimate point of the sensuous is precisely the sexual."[60] Others might argue that for them the thing they most desire is food, or diamonds, or money, or power over others, etc. But Kierkegaard believes that none of these—or anything else a human desires—touches, modifies, influences the human being as person (spirit, self) as universally and as profoundly as does one's sexuality. Clearly, the vow of chastity, or the vow of fidelity, are simply two of the more extreme ways of recognizing sexuality's inescapable demands. And these demands are equally imperious whether they take the form of heterosexual or homosexual desire.

Kierkegaard was convinced that "the whole question of the significance of the sexual ... has undeniably been answered poorly until now." And he deplored the situation in his own day when the same people heard two contradictory views of sexuality from the stage and the pulpit, the former praising it as the ultimate beauty of our worldly existence while the latter condemned it as bestial and sinful, each embarrassed by the view of the other. And, even worse, both views were admitted to have meaning by most hearers, but no one sought to reconcile them, leaving this "heavy burden" to be borne by the ordinary human being.[61] Kierkegaard would probably wonder if we have made much progress in this area 140 years later, in spite of the advent of Freud and the extensive treatment of sex by religionists. He agreed that "psychology is what we need," but that we also need a "more human" approach based on "a thorough knowledge of human life as well as sympathy for its interests." And then added, "herein lies the task, and until this is resolved there can be no question of completing a Christian view of life." And he derided "the system" (Hegel) "which presumably has explained everything ... but has been unable to explain the simplest things, namely, that which almost every person is interested in, whether he has lived as a pagan or as a Christian in his marriage."[62]

---

59 *Concept of Anxiety*, p. 44; (KW 8:49); SV 6:142; (4:319).
60 Idem.
61 Ibid., pp. 6of.; (KW 8:67f.); SV 10:158f.; (4:337).
62 *Papirer*, V B 53:29. Translation in *The Concept of Anxiety*, KW 8:190–3.

Did Kierkegaard "resolve" these issues for himself in order to complete his Christian view of life? He said, "I obligate myself forthwith to draw up a number of sketches that will exhibit the prodigious conflicts that may arise in this area." But he never did. (Many an unsuspecting reader has been misled into reading his "Seducer's Diary" in *Either/Or*, expecting a juicy account of sexual exploits.) His most extensive treatment of sexuality remained what he had already written in chapter 11 of *The Concept of Anxiety*. *Works of Love* and later journal entries do not add anything substantial. In fact, many of the journal entries of his last five years reflect an increasingly negative perspective. And his entire view of the nature and role of the female in relation to the male makes most males today uneasy and makes most females livid. (For example, when he says, "Woman is more sensuous than man," or "Silence is not only woman's greatest wisdom but also her highest beauty," or "Viewed ethically, woman culminates in procreation.")[63] Possibly these views could be interpreted positively when fully understood and placed in context. But a full analysis of his understanding of sexuality would be out of place at this point. Our concern here is to see sexuality as the ultimate form of the problem faced by the self when it seeks to come to terms with its finitude.

The self, remember, is a third factor which is a positive unity of finitude and infinitude, of the sensuous and the psychical. So, as Kierkegaard repeatedly asserts, the sensuous and the sexual *as such* are not sinful. The self is empty without the concreteness of its finitude. The self *exists* only in its unique, singular (*enkelt*) actuality. So when Kierkegaard says that spirit "must first pervade the synthesis separately," he means that I must come to terms with the inescapable finitude/necessity of *my* being. The first step toward *self*-consciousness is reflection on, and an unblinking awareness of, the whole range of my sensate being, starting with my body but including its entire physical and social environment. This is what (at least in part) defines "me" and differentiates me from every other human being. In the task of becoming a self, every human being is universally the same and equal, but the self each is to become is absolutely, eternally unique.[64]

---

63 *Concept of Anxiety*, pp. 58f.; (KW 8:64, 66); SV 6:156f.; (4:334, 336).
64 The importance of this point will become clear in the next chapter on freedom, and in the treatment of "love" in chapter 7. For Kierkegaard's best development of this point, see *Works of Love*, pp. 80f., 96f., 252f.; SV 12:72–4, 89f., 259f.; (9:70–2, 86f., 257f.).

Thus, when Kierkegaard takes sexuality as the most intense and ultimate expression of our finitude, he still insists that as spirit or self "there is no difference between man and woman."[65] But in the spheres of sensuous being and behaviour, one cannot escape one's specific sexual makeup and determination, whether it be female, male, heterosexual, homosexual, or non-sexual (rare!). Without reflection on this fact, and awareness of it as an integral dimension of one's existence, one will not achieve self-consciousness.[66]

Now we must turn to see that there is another entirely different focus of reflection as the initial methodological step toward self-consciousness: our infinitude/possibility. As already noted, reflection is always dichotomous, because the basic duality of human nature asserts itself, even if we try to ignore it by living at the purely aesthetic level in psycho-sensuous immediacy. And reflection is precisely the turning of our awareness willingly to explore this dichotomy. If, then, sexuality is the ultimate specific content of my reflection about my finitude, what is the content of my reflection about my infinitude?

This content is what Kierkegaard calls "the infinite form" of my self, my "negative self" (explicated in chapter 5). We have already seen that by the capacity of imagination and fantasy, the human psyche explores images of one's self without any consideration of the limits set by one's finitude. And when one begins to consider these fantasies as "possibilities," then they are bent back toward the actualities of one's finite conditions. This is a kind of reflection which begins to be sensitive to the "immense contradiction" between one's actual self and one's possible self. But reflection that produces the infinite, negative form of the self is something else. This begins when one gains "a dim idea that there may be something eternal in the self." Then by reflection, one becomes "conscious of a self that is won by infinite abstraction from every externality, this naked abstract self, which, compared with immediacy's fully dressed self, is the first form of the infinite self and the advancing impetus in the whole process by which a self infinitely becomes responsible for its actual self with all its difficulties and advantages."[67]

In other words, in "reflection" the fanciful images of the imagination do not bend themselves under the judgment of one's finitude as to

---

65 *The Concept of Anxiety*, pp. 63, 57; (KW 8:70, 64); SV 6:161, 155; (4:340, 334).

66 How one, as a mature self, accommodates to sexuality will be treated later (though briefly) under the topic of love in chapter 7.

67 *Sickness*, p. 188; (KW 19:55); SV 15:111; (11:167).

what is really possible. Rather, reflection is the process by which one *abstracts from* these limitations. It is spirit (self) "pervading the synthesis differentially (separately)"—in this case, exploring the infinite possibilities of self on their own terms, without any reference to external limitations. Kierkegaard notes that this process is usually called "selfishness" (*Selviske*), but he thinks it more appropriate to call it "self-centredness," a form of authentic self-concern on the part of the unique individual (*Enkelte*).[68] In order to will to be one's self, "there must be consciousness of an infinite self." When reflection explores one's infinitude at its extreme,

> this infinite self is the most abstract form, the most abstract possibility of the self. ... With the help of this infinite form, the self wants ... to create itself, to make one's self into the self one wants to be, to determine what one will have or not have in one's concrete self. One's concrete self or concretion has necessity and limitations, is this very specific being with these natural capacities, predispositions, etc. in this specific concretion of conditions etc. But with the help of the infinite form, the negative self, one wants first of all to take upon oneself the transformation of all this in order to fashion out of it a self such as one wants, produced with the help of the infinite form of the negative self—and in this way one wills to be oneself.[69]

This infinite form of the self is "negative" in a double sense. On the one hand, it lacks the positive concreteness of actuality. On the other hand, the actual self is in "existence" and shares in its fluid uncertainty, whereas the infinite self in its purity negates this uncertainty. This dialectical negativity is inherent in the process of becoming self. So one who "is conscious of this negativity of the infinite in existence ... constantly keeps the wound of the negativity open."[70] This "duplicity" and uncertainty of existence is the beginning point and the constant point from which one becomes a self.

We have now seen how "reflection" is the process by which consciousness, at its initial level, explores the opposites of that "immense contradiction" and "qualitative disjunction" of which human existence is composed. It pursues our finitude to the extremity of sensuousness in

---

68 See his discussion in *The Concept of Anxiety*, pp. 69–71, (KW 8:77–9); SV 6:166–8; (4:346–348).
69 *Sickness*, pp. 201f.; (KW 19:68); SV 15:122f.; (11:179).
70 See *Postscript*, pp. 74–9; (KW 12.1:80–6); SV 9:69–74; (7:62–7), for Kierkegaard's discussion of the concept of "negativity," especially as opposed to Hegel.

our sexuality. It pursues our infinitude to the extremity of a pure possible self totally abstracted from all external restrictions. But reflection is dichotomous; it does not succeed in bringing the two opposites together in a way that both are seen as integral dimensions of the authentic self, each accepting the modification of the other. To accomplish this relationship something more is required. Kierkegaard calls it: "subjectivity." This brings us to the second and decisive step in the "methodology" or process of becoming authentically self-conscious.[71]

"Subjectivity," for Kierkegaard, is achieved when the existing individual comes to full consciousness that one's own self is the ultimate task of one's existence, and that this task consists of the achievement of a functioning unity of one's finite self and one's infinite self. As such, the "self" of which one becomes conscious is a true "third." It is "other," but not totally other because it is composed as a unity of the finite self and the infinite self. "Subjectivity" is consciousness of my self as this peculiar unity in which there is a continuing dialectical interplay of these two seemingly contradictory, opposite dimensions of my being, but which are *in actuality* interdependent, inseparable and strangely open to and in need of each other. In this sense, "subjectivity is truth" for me. Not that the extended, finite world (my body, my physical and social environment, history) is not a kind of truth also for me. Not that my fantasies, my thoughts, my contemplation of pure abstract possibility are not also a kind of truth for me. But *I*, my *self*, as the peculiar unity of these two kinds or spheres of truth, cannot find myself in either one of these in isolation from the other, but only in the truth of "subjectivity," the truth of being this unique, particular, individual subject.

How does consciousness-as-subjectivity come into being? How is it a development beyond the dichotomy of reflection? Kierkegaard explores this question in *The Concept of Anxiety* (1844) as the "positing of spirit" in the resolution of angst. In *Concluding Unscientific Postscript* (1846), he speaks often of "spirit" but chiefly elaborates the nature of "subjectivity." In *The Sickness unto Death* (1849), he talks almost exclusively about the different levels of "consciousness of self." This refusal to settle on a definitive language illustrates again Kierkegaard's conviction that the reality of the human being of the unique individual can never be captured in any language or conceptuality. As already indicated, his most detailed analysis as to how consciousness of self emerges, after reflection has

---

71 See above at note 59.

"pervaded differentially" the bipolarity of the human individual, is to be found in *Postscript*'s description of "subjectivity."

Two preliminary points are important to note. First, subjectivity is a kind of thinking or knowing, an awareness and consciousness of self, which is still short of *enactment* of the self. Subjectivity, Kierkegaard likes to say, is a preparation for the ethical. And the ethical is more than knowing, it is action. So the description of the ultimate "movement" or "transition" to selfhood requires a consideration of freedom (in the next several chapters). Secondly, therefore, the task of subjectivity or self-consciousness is not yet the enactment of self as the synthesis but the preliminary holding together of the two opposite dimensions of human existence as integral to the self one is to become. "To remain in existence so as to understand one thing one moment and another thing another moment is not to understand one self. But to understand the extreme opposites together, and to understand oneself existing therein, is very difficult." So the question must be raised "where the place is which is the unity of infinitude and finitude, where one is at once infinite and finite and may speak at once of one's infinitude and finitude, whether it is possible to find a place so dialectically difficult, which yet is so needful."[72] Kierkegaard answers that this place may be found in what he calls "subjective reflection," which is the way an individual who has "subjectivity" *thinks*.

In attempting to clarify what Kierkegaard means by "subjective reflection," we arrive at one of the most controversial issues in all Kierkegaardian interpretation—both of his thought and of his person. There is a large body of opinion that represents Kierkegaard, in both his thought and person, as totally committed to irrationalism, as apotheosizing the paradox, as ultimately believing in the irreducible absurdity of human existence. For example, we have the reductio ad absurdum version in Josiah Thompson's *Kierkegaard*. Kierkegaard is presented as a schizoid who cannot deal with normal social existence and withdraws into an interior world of fantasy. There, behind drawn drapes, he spends his life writing—not about philosophy, theology, or psychology, but a literature of self-reference exploring the imaginative act, ending in failure. In *The Sickness unto Death*, we are told, despair is seen as man's natural, primordial state, "inescapably a part of the human condition." And Christianity is no help because man's estrangement from God in guilt, despair and uncertainty can never be overcome. So Kierkegaard's vision of Chris-

---

72 *Postscript*, pp. 316, 156; (KW 12.1:354, 175); SV 10:55, 9:146; (7:307, 145).

tianity is nothing but a fascination with the horrific, a madness, a terror. Kierkegaard ends his life as he began it—a lost alienated ghost.[73] Such a

---

73 Josiah Thompson, *Kierkegaard*; for example, see pp. 84, 187, 200f. This distorted view of Kierkegaard's life and writings, in both its exaggerated (Thompson) and more scholarly forms (Taylor), has a basic reason and source. As noted later (following note 117 in chapter 6), this negative interpretation is shared by those who refuse to take seriously Kierkegaard's "second authorship" in which he explores and depicts the personal religious experience of the Christian faith, namely, from *Upbuilding Discourses in Various Spirits* (1846), through *Works of Love* and *Christian Discourses* (1847), to *The Sickness unto Death* and *Practice in Christianity* (1848). Rather, they concentrate on the earlier pseudonymous authorship and on late journal entries and the articles of the "attack on Christendom." As Taylor admits, "The most tortured expressions of such passionate world-negation are to be found in his late journal entries" (*Journeys*, p. 271, note 19). When I raised this point in a personal conversation with Josiah Thompson, he blandly admitted, "Those works [on Christian faith] simply did not interest me."
  Another prime example of this approach to the interpretation of Kierkegaard is found in Henning Fenger's *Kierkegaard, the Myths and Their Origins*. He says (p. xi), "I frankly confess that I am unable to follow Kierkegaard as he leaps out over a sea 70,000 fathoms deep." Rather, he is "fascinated by the young, the aesthetic [Kierkegaard]," and he is willing to "let others map the whole of the Kierkegaard continent." But then he does not let these "others" alone. He contends that "the theologians' nonchalant treatment of the source material" shuts their eyes to the fact that Kierkegaard's tortured life "led eventually to an absurd existentialism" which makes him "the Pied Piper of Hamelin, pulling everything along with him into destruction" (p. 214). This material, he argues, clearly indicates that Kierkegaard was "manic-depressive" (p. 68), "sexually warped" (p. 71), and an "algolagniac" (sado-masochist) (p. 210). Indeed, he has a section in which he explores the resemblances between Kierkegaard and the Marquis de Sade. "Both live in isolation, plagued by obsessions. ... Both ... must be regarded as persons who were unwell, tormented by a lack of human contact and loneliness. Both took revenge ... by dreaming and by making, in literature, the world different from what it was. Both dwelt in the borderline region where fiction and reality collide. ... They suffer from being the victims of their own strong imagination ... it was only in their fantasies that they succeeded in wholly realizing themselves." But they were utterly different in that "Kierkegaard never went beyond his fantasies. ... As an eroticist, Kierkegaard, like the Marquis de Sade, was bound to his imagination, but in contrast to the Marquis, he lived his erotic life at his desk, with pen in hand" (pp. 209–10). So for Fenger, Kierkegaard's whole life is nothing but "a work of art, ... a novel (in several volumes) or a play in several acts, where the main character improvises or writes his role as he goes along" (p. 211).
  Thompson, Taylor, and Fenger are prime examples of what happens when one chooses to ignore, or is unable to enter into, or perhaps is afraid to enter, the heartland of the "continent," the main act of the "play," that comprise the very real, concrete, historical life and personage that is Søren Kierkegaard. The rest of this (my) book succeeds, I believe, in showing that their portrayals of Kierkegaard's life and thought are clearly contradicted by materials from both the pseudonymous and the patently acknowledged Kierkegaardian literatures, in fact by materials that describe human potentiality only within the realm of the "universally human," that is, the realm that is limited to the aesthetic, ethical, and

misrepresentation is so gross that one is tempted to read it as sensationalist journalism, even though clearly not intended as such by the author. However, the assertions of Mark Taylor must be taken seriously because they are based on a very careful and scholarly reading of Kierkegaard and are shared by a number of other interpreters. He says that for Kierkegaard "the Absolute Paradox is not intrinsically rational but is inherently self contradictory and irreducibly absurd. ... Faith and reason ... are antithetical. ... The object of faith is an 'offense' to reason, the 'shipwreck' of reason, the 'crucifixion' of understanding." This interpretation is both accurate and yet misleading. Taylor's misreading is revealed when he adds, "Unlike Hegel, Kierkegaard does not distinguish reason and understanding. ... Hegel insists that Vernunft [reason] rationally mediates the opposites established and maintained by Verstand [understanding]."[74] Kierkegaard not only distinguishes between reason (*Forstand*) and understanding (*Forstaaelse*), but also between two different kinds of understanding.

He notes that "there is an old saying that to understand [*at forstaae*] and to understand are two things, and so they are." He of course recognizes that reason, as speculative logical conceptualization, attains a certain kind of understanding. But he also insists that "inwardness is an understanding; ... for a man to understand what he himself says is one thing, and to understand himself in what is said is something else."[75] Likewise, he insists that faith has its own peculiar kind of understanding, even though that understanding is not to be grasped by "reason" in the specific sense of abstract thought. For Christian faith, the teacher must

---

religious experience that is open to every human being, without drawing, that is, upon the unique and particular experience that is shaped by concrete, historical, Christian materials. And in the next volume on *Kierkegaard as Theologian*, it will be shown that Kierkegaard's central understanding of Christian faith does not end in a vision of terror and madness and despair but in a positive, liberating, and creative experience of loving forgiveness and renewal. And it will also be shown that Kierkegaard claimed this experience as his own, as the ultimate reality of his own person and life, in spite of his increasing sense of his life's being restricted by physical disability, social isolation, and financial ruin during the last few years of his life. His increasingly negative and iconoclastic statements about sexuality, marriage, and the breeding of children are not reflective of or rooted in his central vision and description of human existence in both its universally human and particularly Christian forms—despite the views to the contrary expressed by Julia Watkin in her article "The Logic of Søren Kierkegaard's Misogyny 1854–1855" *Kierkegaardiana* 15 (1991): 82–92.

74 Mark Taylor, *Journeys*, p. 137. See also Robert Widenman's article, "Kierkegaard's Terminology and English," *Kierkegaardiana* 7 (1968):113ff.

75 *The Concept of Anxiety*, pp. 126f.; (KW 8:142); SV 6:223; (4:408).

82   *My Self: A Task*

not only bring the truth to the learner but must also "give him the condition necessary for understanding it." In regard to this paradox of reconciliation, "reason [*Forstand*] certainly does not think it, could not itself discover it, and when it is announced cannot understand it." On this particular point, then, reason and the paradox "are in understanding [*Forstaaelse*] with each other; but this understanding is present only in the moment of passion [faith]." Faith certainly does not "understand" the paradox rationally any more than does reason, but it "comes to an understanding with the paradox." Faith is a "union" of the learner and the paradox, and in that union there comes a new kind of understanding.[76] But it is a totally different kind of understanding than reason seeks. Toward the end of his life Kierkegaard asks, "are you in understanding with God, do you think very earnestly and strive sincerely to understand—and this is God's eternally unchangeable will for you as for every human being, that one should strive thereafter—to strive sincerely to understand what God's will could be for you?"[77] There is an understanding with the heart and will as well as with the mind. One can understand "ethically" as well as conceptually.

The fundamental issue, however, is not the distinction between reason and understanding (which Kierkegaard certainly makes), but the nature of the unity and harmony which the human self seeks and needs between the opposites of his existence (finitude/infinitude, necessity/possibility, temporal/eternal). Taylor argues that Hegel, with his "new" logic, achieves this unity by an "integrative dialectic of internal rationality," so that "for Hegel, the structure of spirit is essentially self-referential negativity that binds together coimplicated opposites." But Kierkegaard, he says, sticks with the logical principles of contradiction and identity (Aristotle, Kant), and so rejects the capacity of reason to mediate the opposites, and thus ends tragically with mutually exclusive opposites and with the human individual torn in two and permanently isolated from one's self, one's neighbour, and one's God.[78] (Kierkegaard's knowledge and views of logic will be explored in chapter 5.)

---

76 *Philosophical Fragments*, pp. 17, 59, 72, see also pp. 46, 48, 55, 67; (KW 7:14, 47, 59, see also pp. 37, 39, 44f.); SV 6: 19, 47, 56, see also pp. 38, 39, 44, 52; (4:184, 214f., 224f., see also 204, 205, 211f., 220).

77 "The Unchangeableness of God," in *Edifying Discourses: A Selection*, ed. Paul L. Holmer, trans. David F. and Lillian M. Swenson (New York: Harper and Bros., 1958), p. 256; SV 19:258; (14:286f.).

78 Mark Taylor, *Journeys*, pp. 168ff.

Actually, Kierkegaard's understanding of the human self and spirit is not controlled by any system of logical principles but by his own analysis of the phenomena of his own experience, especially as that experience is impacted by the Christian religious experience. In describing that self-understanding, in both the images of the imagination and the conceptual categories of the mind, he found that the logical principles of both coimplication and contradiction were applicable to the structure and operation of the human self. For example, on the one hand, one's particular finitude is never captured and contained as such in the imagination and concepts of one's infinitude, nor are one's fantasies and ideas totally commensurable with the confines of the "necessities" of finitude. On the other hand, the authentic self knows itself to be *simultaneously* both finite and infinite, both necessary and possible. In spite of their qualitative contradiction as opposites, the two sides are mysteriously coimplicated in such a way that they are open to and need each other, and eventually find unity and harmony in that "third" called the self. So, as we have seen, Kierkegaard makes the flat statement that "the self is a synthesis, for which reason [*hvorfor*] the one is continuously its opposite."[79] Here we do not have a coincidence but certainly a coimplication of opposites.

The real issue is *how* this unity and harmony come into being. Taylor insists that Kierkegaard's "way," namely, freedom-in-faith, is illusory and impossible and lands the human individual in permanent despair. Before we look at Kierkegaard's notion of freedom, however, we must see precisely how he distinguishes objective reflection and subjective reflection, and thereby rejects the "way" of "internal rationality" as the moving power for the resolution of the human dichotomy. This distinction, which he elaborates in great detail in *Concluding Unscientific Postscript*, is his more sophisticated treatment of the difference between reason and faith as stated so enigmatically in *Philosophical Fragments*.

The distinction between objective and subjective reflection has as its background a general theory about "thinking." Contrary to those who accuse Kierkegaard of having no use for thinking and especially for reason and thus resorting totally to voluntarism and fideism, Kierkegaard actually spent his life's time and energies thinking. He had a profound interest in logic and in the rational coherence of the basic categories which he worked out. In the introductory book one of *Postscript*, he says, "All honour to speculation, all praise to everyone who in truth is occupied

---

79 *Sickness*, p. 163; (KW 19:30); SV 15:88; (11:143).

with it. To negate the value of speculation ... would be in my opinion to prostitute oneself, and would be especially fatuous of one most of whose life is dedicated to its service, and who admires the Greeks"—obviously describing himself.[80]

For Kierkegaard, the whole question of truth revolves around the issue of the relationship between thinking and being. Are they identical, or does one seek "correspondence"? If "being" is taken in the more concrete empirical sense of a living human individual, then thinking must be seen as an integral function of existence. "As existence has put together thinking and existing in such a way that the existing one is a thinking one, thus there are two media: abstraction and actuality." Even when one is turned inward subjectively, still one is, "as an existing one, essentially interested in one's own thinking, existing as one does in it." But at this point the existing individual faces a dilemma. Human thinking tends quite naturally and easily to form concepts by abstracting from actuality. And yet one seeks to "think in the medium of existence itself, where existence as the process-of-becoming tends to prevent the existing one from thinking, since actuality does not allow thinking, whereas the existing one is still a thinking one." Therefore, "to draw the conclusion that an existing one who actually exists does not think at all is an unwarranted misunderstanding. Certainly he thinks, but he thinks about everything in relation to himself, being infinitely interested in the fact of existing."[81]

So, for Kierkegaard, everyone who is the least bit self-conscious is involved in thinking. Anyone who has moved out of naïve immediacy with one's sensuous-social existence and has begun to reflect about that existence in the light of unrealized fantasies, possibilities, and idealities is engaged in thinking as a function of one's being. But that person also becomes aware of a certain dichotomy, of a kind of "otherness" in one's thinking in contrast with one's being. How does one handle this dichotomy? Can it be bridged? How? And what does one make of the fact that one's unique identity as subject or self waits for its definition at this intersection and emerges in the resolution of this dilemma?

According to Kierkegaard, human thinking works in two different ways at this juncture. He calls them "objective reflection" and "subjective

---

80 *Postscript*, p. 54; (KW 12.1:55–6); SV 9:51 (7:42).

81 Ibid; for material in this paragraph, the order of page references are: 169f., 278, 67, 280f.; (KW 12.1:189f., 314, 73, 316f.); SV 9:157f., 10:20, 9:63, 10:22f.; (7:157f., 269, 55, 271f.).

reflection."[82] Each produces a different kind of "truth," both of which are valid and useful within certain limits. The difficulty is this: whereas most participants in subjective reflection acknowledge the limited validity and usefulness of objective reflection, many participants in objective reflection deny the distinctiveness and unique validity of subjective reflection and seek to co-opt it as a phase or element within objective reflection and its truth.

Kierkegaard considered Hegel to be the chief proponent of objective reflection in his day, and saw the application of his System to be the total ruination of Christian faith. The accuracy and fairness of Kierkegaard's understanding and representation of Hegel's thought are certainly open to debate, but that debate need not concern us here.[83] What Kierkegaard deems "objective reflection" is a way of thinking and a method of grasping reality that is still very much alive in our own day. And his own depiction and defence of "subjective reflection" is still one of the most forceful presentations of an alternative way of thinking about and understanding human existence. Subjective reflection, let us remember, is the mode in which one arrives at full *self*-consciousness.

What, then, is "objective reflection"? Kierkegaard proposes three basic characteristics: (1) it assumes continuity, (2) it seeks generalities, (3) its attitude is disinterestedness.

(1) The basic assumption of this way of thinking can be expressed as follows. All reality is of a piece; there are no breaks or discontinuities. There are diversity and plurality but no firm boundaries or divisions. There are even oppositions and what may be called "negativities," but they are aspects of a larger whole, and are overcome and resolved by a process of reasonable mediation. Dualism is a false perspective. Hegel was right in denying Kant's *ding-an-sich* (thing-in-itself) as something beyond human knowledge, and was right in asserting that the structures of reality correspond to the structures of human understanding. In our more contemporary language, humans are intelligent beings living in an intelligible universe, and we must reject the radical opposition between nature and art, the natural and supernatural, nature and experience, the natural and transcendental, nature and man.

---

82 Ibid., p. 171; (KW 12.1:192); SV 9:159f.; (7:159).

83 Niels Thulstrup, *Kierkegaard's Relation to Hegel* is an example of defence of Kierkegaard's evaluation of Hegel. Mark Taylor, *Journeys to Selfhood: Hegel and Kierkegaard* is an example of defence of Hegel against Kierkegaard. The bibliography of treatments on both sides is extensive.

Kierkegaard insists that this kind of thinking works on the assumption that the objective-subjective distinction is transcended, ultimately obliterated (annulled), and that there is a basic underlying identity of being and thinking. In other words, the apparent difference between actuality and abstract concepts about it is always overcome by an inherent rational relationship. The magic phrase, says Kierkegaard, is "as long—until." So "every time a transition is needed, the opposite continues as long until it changes into [*slaaer over i*] its opposite."[84] He of course has Hegel in mind, when the latter says such things as "a consideration of everything that is, shows that *in its own self* everything is in its selfsameness different from itself and self-contradictory, and that in its difference, in its contradiction, it is self-identical, and is in its own self this movement of transition of one of these categories into the other, and for this reason, that each is in its own self the opposite of itself." This view is, as we have seen, what Mark Taylor calls Hegel's "integrative dialectic of internal rationality," or his "self-referential negativity that binds together coimplicated opposites."[85] Taylor argues persuasively that, in the light of Hegel's intense interest in nature, history, culture, and unique individuality, it is incorrect to accuse him of being a monist who identifies being and thinking. But it is certainly clear that such a view which asserts internal, rational coimplication of being and thinking also asserts the superiority of the power of thinking over all the complexities of being (nature, actual human existence) to the point of being able to comprehend them all within human conceptuality and to bring them all under rational control. This view is precisely what Kierkegaard takes exception to (as we shall see).

Kierkegaard recognizes that all thinking at the level of conscious reflection consists of abstraction from the concreteness of actuality. But he says there is a tendency in abstract thinking to move on to what he calls "pure thinking" (*rene Tænken*) which forgets or ignores its relation to that from which it abstracts. The object or content of "pure" thinking is thinking itself and the relationship among the abstract concepts it has formed. When this content is called "truth," then the strict identity of reality with rational speculation has occurred. Strangely for our ears,

---

84 *Postscript*. For Kierkegaard's discussion of this view and his attribution of it to Hegel, see pp. 172–3, 291–302; (KW 12.1:192–3, 327–38); SV 9:160f., 10:31–41; (7:160f., 251–93). For the quotation, see p. 301; (KW 12.1:337).

85 Mark Taylor, *Journeys*, p. 146 for quote from Hegel; pp. 168f. for his comment.

Kierkegaard calls this process "scientific" (*videnskabelig*, which also means "scholarly"). He says,

> Scientific [thinking] rises from the lower to the higher, and thinking becomes the highest. In the perspective of world-history, it [thinking] ascends from the lower to the higher; the stages of imagination and feeling are left behind; the stage of thinking as the highest is the ultimate. ... Science turns more and more away from the primitive impression of existence; there is nothing to perceive or experience; everything is finished, and the task of speculation is to pigeonhole, classify and methodically arrange the particular concepts.[86]

This is too neat even for the Newtonian world. But even in our post-Einsteinian world when a unified field theory is seriously in doubt, when we know that the universe speaks some languages we do not understand, when we always mean more than we can say, still there is a pervasive "naturalism" in philosophy and the sciences which holds onto faith in human intelligence or "reason." This means that whether one uses the categories of speculative logic, or those of quantum physics, or those of linguistic analysis, or those of psycho-neuro-biology, or those of scientific historiography, the basic perspective is the same: being (reality, actuality, nature) includes enormous diversity held together and pervaded by an overruling unitary system of "forces" or "relationships" or "qualities" or "processes," with no qualitative breaks or disjunctions. And this being includes human intelligence and rationality as integral to it and representative of the total system. Although agreeing with the truth of this perspective in most realms of being, Kierkegaard launched against it his assertion of one, absolute "either/or" which shatters the whole system and disqualifies it as *the* truth for human beings.

(2) This brings us to the second characteristic of objective reflection, namely, its search for and commitment to generalities as the ultimate truth. The concomitant of this perspective is that the particular, unique individual factor has only relative and temporary significance within the context of the whole—whether that "whole" is conceived as a system of abstract universals or as an ongoing material process that incorporates the universals (right-wing or left-wing Hegelianism).

Kierkegaard sees this kind of thinking essentially as a process of abstraction from what he calls "reality" (*Virkelighed*, that is, concrete actuality) or

---

86 *Postscript*, p. 278f., 307; (KW 12.1:313–15, 344); SV 10:20f., 46; (7:269–70, 298). For the quotation, see p. 307; (KW 12.1:344).

"existence" (that is, the particular, processive conditions of human life). The product of this thinking is "thought-determinants" (concepts) or "purely metaphysical determinants" which reveal "an immanence of cause and effect, ground and consequence." This product Kierkegaard likes to call "possibility." "Only by annulling reality can abstraction get hold of it, but to annul it is precisely to transform it into possibility." So "all knowledge of reality is possibility." This abstraction of possibility from reality can either "go before or come after" the reality. In other words, all so-called "objective" knowledge is either a "hypothesis" about ("going before") reality, or an "approximation" to ("coming after") reality. So abstract objective concepts comprise only a "possibility" of what reality *is*, in spite of their vaunted claim to provide "answers" which are universally "true."[87]

However, the constant temptation of this kind of "objective reflection," as we have already noted, is to go on to the stage of "pure thinking" which asserts that "possibility is higher than reality," to that thinking which is concerned with its own thoughts or concepts as ultimate reality. Thus, "The way of objective reflection," Kierkegaard says, "makes the subject [i.e., the particular individual] to be the accidental, and thereby makes existence to be the indifferent, the vanishing." Because abstract thinking seeks only the general and the universal, "it ignores the concrete, the temporal, the becoming of existence, the predicament of the existing individual arising from his being compounded of the eternal and the temporal situated in existence."[88]

The basic attitude of objective reflection, therefore, is what Kierkegaard calls "disinterestedness."

(3) He asks: who is doing all this abstract thinking of philosophy and science? And he answers: "a human being, an existing individual." In order to do this kind of thinking and to consider its product as the highest and ultimate truth, one must "forget ... this distinctive singularity [*Eiendommelighed*] of one's being," must forget "what it means that you and I, we, are human beings, each one for oneself." Abstract thinking turns everyone into an observer, a spectator (*Betragter*). Thus it even turns "subjectivity" itself and also "immortality" into abstract generalities. "Abstraction gives no heed to whether a particular [*enkelt*] existing human

---

[87] For the material in this paragraph, in the order of appearance, see ibid., pp. 181, 138, 279–82, 173, 68; (KW 12.1:203, 155, 314–17, 194, 73); SV 9:169, 129, 10:21–4, 9:161, 63; (7:169f., 128, 270–3, 161, 55f.).

[88] Ibid., pp. 173, 267; (KW 12.1:194, 301); SV 9:161, 10:9; (7:161, 257f.)

being is immortal, which precisely is the problem. It is disinterested [*interesselos*]."

The reason for this is clear. "Objective knowledge" for philosophy and science is not of the particular but of the general. "The requirement of abstraction is to become disinterested in order to get to know something." "Science organizes the elements of subjectivity into a knowledge of them, and this knowledge is the highest, and all knowledge is an annulment of, a withdrawal from existence." So "abstract thinking has the task of understanding the concrete abstractly."[89]

As we shall now see, Kierkegaard regards the entire project of "objective reflection"—with its stress on continuity, generalities, and disinterestedness—as gaining a kind of "knowledge" at the expense of losing the one thing of highest importance: the unique, particular subject or self. It is this kind of human intelligence which, in *Philosophical Fragments*, Kierkegaard calls "reason," the kind of rationality that is incapable of comprehending the individual self, its freedom and its life of faith. Although some of his language used in mounting his attack may sound dated and irrelevant to our present discussion of these issues, the general position and perspective he attacks is still very much alive.

In a recent review by W.V. Quine of some lectures by P.F. Strawson, we have a presentation of a thoroughgoing defence of analytic philosophy as a kind of naturalism. According to this perspective, "Our words ... and all our learning of them go back directly or indirectly to the association of utterances with concurrent sensory stimulation. ... We can say with the reductive naturalist that moral law has no objective support in nature, being merely a pattern of human response and behavior rooted in natural selection and moral training." The distinction between the mental and the physical "is just the relation between two sorts of descriptions. Each single, dated mental event or state is an event or state of the body and could in principle be described exhaustively in physiological language." One can grant that personal history is irreducible and indispensable, but one does not have to grant ontological status to its "mentalistic terms of motives, purposes, desires, beliefs, and the like." And certainly a tough-minded naturalist will "repudiate abstract objects of 'intentional' kind, [such as] thoughts, ideas, propositions, properties, as opposed to natural objects. ... Intentional objects can indeed be ban-

---

89 For the material quoted in the last two paragraphs, see in order ibid., pp. 109, 118, 268, 280, 311, 315; (KW 12.1:120, 133, 302, 316, 347–8, 352); SV 9:102–3, 110, 10:10, 22, 49, 53; (7:98–9, 107–8, 258–9, 271–2, 301, 305).

ished and good riddance; but the extensional abstract objects, numbers notably, remain to be reckoned with."[90]

Here is a contemporary philosophical position which exactly matches Kierkegaard's description of "objective reflection." It assumes the continuity of a single reality called "nature." The only objects granted ontological status are abstract mathematical formulations of the sciences. And it declares "good riddance" to all the mentalistic locutions and intentional objects of personal history as mere patterns of human behaviour not rooted in "nature." This is still probably the single strongest philosophical position in Western thought, and it pervades the thinking of millions of philosophically unsophisticated Westerners and is following Western technology into the East. Mark Taylor proposes a revised and updated Hegelianism as a philosophical alternative which will preserve concrete individuality in the context of a reality characterized by unitary rationality. But we will see below that the "self" so preserved is not the same self that Kierkegaard considers the only one worth preserving. And when one reads Taylor's quotation of what he calls Hegel's summary of the structure and development of the self, one can only be incredulous when he claims that such a view of things can be made meaningful and can become powerfully effective for the human race as it faces the enormous complexities of human existence at any time and place, but especially in light of the mad absurdities confronting us at the end of the twentieth century.[91]

We turn now, therefore, to Kierkegaard's proposed alternative to this kind of "objective" thinking, to what he calls "subjective" thinking or reflection. He makes four basic points about it: (1) it rejects abstraction, (2) it occurs in "inwardness," (3) it accepts isolation, (4) it requires indirect communication.

(1) We have already seen that Kierkegaard firmly rejects the identity of thinking and being, because all thinking involves some kind of abstraction from the rich diversity of being. To indicate this richness and concreteness of being, he prefers to call it "existence" (*Existents*) or "actuality" (*Virkelighed*, which may also be translated "reality" if the latter term is taken as including the empirical rather than just the ideal). And the irreducible form of human existence that must be accounted for is the individual. The common-sense, irrefutable assumption must be that

---

90 W.V. Quine, from a review of P.F. Strawson's *Skepticism and Naturalism: Some Varieties*, in *New York Review of Books*, 14 Feb. 1985, p. 32.
91 Mark Taylor, *Journeys*; see pp. 273–6.

"a particular [*enkelt*] existing human being is certainly not an idea; one's existence is surely something other than the conceptual-existence of an idea. ... Existence breaks apart the ideal identity of thinking and being. ... To be a particular human being never consists of a pure idea-existence. Only pure [i.e., abstract, general] humanity exists that way; that is to say, it does not exist at all. Existence always consists of the particular individual; the abstraction does not *exist.*"[92] And this is true no matter what kind of fancy "logic" one uses.

What is it about actual human existence that repels and refuses being caught and contained in a set of rationally formed and related concepts? With this question we must explore again and at a deeper level what was alluded to in chapter 1 under the topic "the self is a relation," and in chapter 2 in its entirety under the topic "my self: a synthesis of two." More particularly, this question brings us back to the assertion, at the beginning of chapter 2, that, for Kierkegaard, the primal duality of human existence is between the "outward" and the "inward." And it is precisely the outward or external dimension of the human being—one's bodilyness, finitude, and necessity—that makes that "existing," "actual" entity so impervious to being captured and contained as an "idea." (But in the next chapter we shall see that one's "outwardness" transforms one's "inwardness" so as to put it "in time" and "in process-of-becoming," and thus one's inwardness also becomes resistant and impervious to abstraction.)

Now we must ask again, with greater exactitude, what it is about this outward finitude that makes it so resistant. Let us remember Kierkegaard's key terms for distinguishing between inward and outward.[93] Inwardness is the realm of imagination, fantasy. Outwardness is the fortuitous/accidental (*Tilfældige*). My finitude is my body, my sensuousness and all its extended relationships: "that I am this particular being, born in this land, at this time, under all the multifarious influences of these changing circumstances," with "these capabilities, aptitudes, etc., in this concretion of relationships, etc."[94] To call this entire dimension of my being "fortuitous" is to say that I did not choose it; it just happened to me. I can and do modify it by what I choose to do with it, but *that* which I modify, *that* which I started existence with, I did not choose and cannot change.

---

92 *Postscript*, pp. 293f.; (KW 12.1:329–30); SV 10:33f.; (7:284–5).
93 See above the section on "The Essential Duality" in chapter 2.
94 *Journals*, 1587; III A 1; and *Sickness*, p. 201f.; (KW 19:68); SV 15:122; (11:179).

My Self: A Task

The importance of this character of human existence, for Kierkegaard, cannot be overstated. As already noted, he was convinced that he was in touch with one of the irreducible ineluctable dimensions of cosmic reality. And its importance for human selfhood, as we will spell out later, is that it serves as the badge and the guarantee of each human being's individuality, of one's being "something definite," being a unique "particular one" (*Enkelte*), over against and in eternal distinction from every other human being (and indeed, over against and in eternal distinction from the Creator of all).[95] Little wonder that Kierkegaard says (early in his career) that "I become conscious simultaneously in my eternal validity ... and in my fortuitous finitude [*tilfældige Endelighed*]." And (late in his career) he refers to one's "essential fortuitousness ... in which one is oneself for oneself."[96]

Kierkegaard (as an aesthetic scribe in part I of *Either/Or*) has another very revealing way of describing the role that the fortuitous-finitude of human existence plays in my becoming my self. He calls it the "occasion" (*Anledning*).[97] In italics, he says, "The occasion is a category of finitude." As the occasion, my finitude is not "ground or cause" but "as such is the unessential and fortuitous," the "fortuitous external circumstance." So my fortuitous finitude as occasion is inherently ambivalent. "The occasion is not positively productive but negatively productive. A creation is a production from nothing; the occasion however is the nothing which lets everything emerge. ... Therefore, not anything new comes with the occasion, but everything emerges with the occasion. ... Without the occasion nothing at all happens, and yet the occasion has no part at all in what does happen. ... The occasion is, then, in and for itself, nothing, and only something in relation to that which it gives rise to, and in relation to this is exactly nothing." What it is that is "in and for itself," which therefore is the "ground and cause" of what happens, we will consider in the next section on "inwardness" (and more fully in chapter 5 under "the self's possibility").

Our concern here is to be clear about the role that our fortuitous finitude plays as the indispensable occasion with which my self comes into

---

95 See *Postscript*, pp. 220f.; (KW 12.1:246); SV 9:206; (7:207). But in the next chapter we shall see that the self's definitive particularity is *inward*, is lodged in "the self's possibility" and its "inner necessity."

96 *Journals*, 1587; III A 1; and *Sickness*, p. 166; (KW 19:33); SV 15:91; (11:147).

97 Although I do not find any significant use of this term after *Either/Or*, compare his use of "situation" in late journal entries (see section on "Situation" in Hongs' *Journals*, also entries 4314, 4326, 4933). For "occasion" in this paragraph, see *Either/Or*, 1:231–6; (KW 3:233–8); SV 2:215–20; (1:207–12).

being. Kierkegaard claims that "the occasion is the ultimate category, the legitimate transition-category from the sphere of the idea to actuality. ... The whole of actuality can be completed [ready] in the idea, but without the occasion it never becomes actual. *The occasion is a category of finitude*, and it is impossible for immanent thinking to get hold of it; for that it is too paradoxical. ... That which comes out of the occasion is something entirely other than the occasion itself—which is an absurdity for all immanent thinking." He urges that "logic should consider this. It can become absorbed as much as it wants to in immanent thinking, or rush down from nothing into the most concrete form; but the occasion it never reaches, and therefore, never actuality." So, although the idea and the occasion, thinking and being, are never separated in human existence, although they "join here" in the sense that "the one always is its opposite," what brings and ties them together is not an immanent, logical or rational necessity. In order for the possibilities of imagination and thought to become actual, there must first be inwardness and the leap of freedom. My fortuitous finitude is of such a quality that it cannot be caught in the web of language and ideas.

The point here, therefore, is that my becoming my self is an event in which my unique particularity is established by the integral incorporation of my fortuitous finitude into my actual selfhood in such a way that it cannot be dropped out or set aside (annulled) in the transition movement from possibility to actuality. If such an "abstraction" takes place, then what is reached is only another form of possibility rather than actuality. The uniqueness of the individual is lost.

At the same time, to become and to preserve that unique individuality which is defined (in part) by one's "outwardness," one's particular fortuitous finitude, requires that individual, paradoxically, to turn *inward* and to engage in another kind of thinking, totally different from abstraction, namely, "subjective" thinking. The ground must be found "inward" in another kind of thinking which is capable of accomplishing the human task "to unify (synthesize) the accidental and the universal" (*Either/Or*), the task of becoming self-conscious and willing to be oneself as the unity of one's finite and infinite selves (*The Sickness unto Death*), the task of "becoming subjective" (*Postscript*).[98]

(2) To describe "subjective thinking" and "becoming subjective" involves an analysis of one of the most difficult and elusive aspects of

---

98 See the first two pages of this chapter.

Kierkegaard's thought. It is usually accomplished by saying that it is "inwardness"—as if that were a self-evident phenomenon. But the elusiveness does not lie in Kierkegaard's thought or language but in the phenomenon itself. His own description is therefore deliberately multiple, diverse and unsystematic. He is simply *pointing* to what he considers to be a fundamental aspect of universal human experience, and, in the end, one either emits the "ah-ha" of recognition of one's own experience of self or concludes that on this crucial point Kierkegaard is hopelessly obscure or downright mistaken, or both.

Let us recall again that, with this topic, we are approaching that one strange "place" or "event" or "act" where, Kierkegaard says, one "can speak, at one and the same time, about [one's] infinitude and finitude, and think these together in one instant," where one can "understand these extreme opposites together, and understand oneself existing in them"—a place and act which is "so dialectically difficult and yet so needful."[99] And this is precisely what *he* means by *self*-consciousness, that is, consciousness of self as that authentic "third" which is neither merely finitude nor merely infinitude but is a peculiar unity of both of them.

In order to "point" to this strange phenomenon, Kierkegaard uses two related terms for which there are no clear definitive translations. They are *Inderlighed* and *Inderliggjørelse*. The first is universally translated as "inwardness," the second usually as "inward transformation" or "development of inwardness." These translations obscure the point Kierkegaard is trying to make. All thinking and reflection are "inward." And Kierkegaard uses a variety of explicit terms to indicate this, such as *indvortes, indefter, inadvendt*, all meaning inward, inner, introspective. But when he says that subjective reflection is *Inderlighed*, he obviously means something more. The word basically means "fervour," "intensity," "heartfelt." So, when he says that, in order to distinguish it from objective reflection, he will "show subjective reflection's search back inward [*ind efter*] i *Inderlighed*," he obviously means "inward with fervent intensity."[100] Or when he says, "The *Inderlighed* of the immediate [i.e., non-religious] person is outwardness [*Udvorteshed*]; he has his dialectic outside of himself," he obviously means that the immediate person's "intensity" is *not* directed inward but is oriented outward.[101]

---

99 *Postscript*, pp. 156, 316; (KW 12.1:175, 354); SV 9:146, 10:55; (7:145, 307).
100 Ibid., p. 177; (KW 12.1:198–9); SV 9:165; (7:166).
101 *Journal*, 2116; VI B 98:77. This entry is a background note for *Postscript*, p. 451; (KW 12.1:505); SV 10:182; (7:439).

Coming to Consciousness 95

When one turns inward in reflection, therefore, one can choose to ignore one's own unique peculiarities (subjectivity) and search by rational abstraction for the universal patterns of human being and behaviour as illustrated in one's own life (objectivity). But reflection may turn in the other direction. "Subjective reflection turns inward [*indefter*] towards subjectivity, and wants to be of the truth in this *Inderliggjørelse*."[102] The latter term literally means a "fervent-doing" or rendering. So Kierkegaard is saying that one so involved with one's own subjectivity is a person "with an infinite passionate interest in an eternal blessedness"—for one's own being, of course. In this interest, "the subject is in its utmost endeavour, in its very extremity."[103] So both of these terms indicate that turning our attention inwardly toward one's self as unique subject cannot be done with cool disinterested rationality but involves us in strenuous, passionate, interested exertion of the mind and heart. "To think one thought in the direction of inwardness [*indefter*] away from all distraction, ... this is very strenuous." This "strenuous exertion" (*Anstrengelse*) is the only way to "self-deepening" (*Selvfordybelse*).

It is one thing to think in such a way that one's attentiveness is solely and constantly outward, in the direction of an object which is something external [*Udvortes*]. It is something else to be so turned inward in thinking so that constantly in every moment one becomes conscious him/herself, conscious of one's own condition [or state] during [*under*] thinking, or how it goes with one during thinking. But only this latter is essentially thinking, it is transparency. ... When one thinks only one thought, one has no outward object; one has an inward direction in self-deepening; one makes a discovery concerning one's own inner [*indre*] condition [or state].[104]

So subjective reflection is thinking with "fervent intensity" about oneself in one's inmost, hidden subjectivity, in the process of "strenuous self-deepening." Another way Kierkegaard has of making this point is to say that essential human knowledge does not "relate to something existent as its object. But it means that knowledge relates to the knower, who essentially is an existing one, and therefore all essential knowledge relates essentially to existence and to the fact of existing." On the contrary,

---

102 *Postscript*, p. 175; (KW 12.1:196); SV 9:163; (7:164).
103 Ibid., pp. 51f.; (KW 12.1:53); SV 9:48f.; (7:40).
104 *Works of Love*, pp. 217, 331f.; SV 12:222f., 343f.; (9:220f., 341f.).

"When the question of truth is asked objectively, one reflects objectively on truth as an object to which the knower relates. One does not reflect on the relation, but on the fact that this is the truth, the true to which one relates. If that to which one relates is the truth, the true, then the subject is in the truth. When the question of truth is asked subjectively, one reflects subjectively on the individual's relation; if only this 'how' of the relation is in truth, then the individual is in truth." Then Kierkegaard adds the hyberbole (which he admits in a footnote): "... the individual is in truth, even if he relates in this way to that-which-is-untruth." In other words, the ultimate and most important truth for a human being is not some universal truth lying out there in an objective universe but that truth as it relates to my existence, the question of how I relate to that truth. So Kierkegaard says, "For the existing one the fact of existing is one's highest interest, and one's interest in one's own existence is one's reality."[105]

How, then, does one go about this kind of reflection, which is "subjective," which by its intense fervour and strenuousness accomplishes a deepening of consciousness of self? How is this thinking different from "objective" rational analysis which produces abstract generalizations (in whose context the particularities of an individual must find their place and meaning)? How does one "think" so as to hang on to and to unite the contradictory opposites of one's fortuitous finitude and one's infinite capacity to picture and to conceptualize the possible? How can there be any such kind of thinking when, as Kierkegaard himself says, all thinking involves abstraction and produces only "possibilities," either before or after the fact, so that "all knowledge [*Viden*] about actuality is possibility"?[106]

There is, according to Kierkegaard, one kind of "knowing" (*vidende*) or "understanding" (*forstaae*) which escapes these strictures and does not produce abstract possibilities. It is the knowing and understanding of *one's own self*.

The only actuality about which an existing individual is more than cognitive [*vidende*] is one's own actuality, the fact that one exists. ... The only actuality there is for an existing [individual] is his/her own ethical [actuality]; all other actuality one has only knowldege about, but true knowledge is a translation into possi-

---

105 *Postscript*, pp. 177–8, 279; (KW 12.1:197–9, 314); SV 9:165f., 10:21; (7:165–6, 270).
106 Ibid., pp. 280f.; (KW 12.1:316); SV 10:22; (7:271–2).

bility. ... The ethical has to do with particular [*enkelte*] human beings, and surely to take note of each particular one [*Enkelt*]. ... The ethical grasps the particular individual and requires that she/he refrain from all observing, especially of the world and of humanity, because the ethical as the inward [*Indvortes*] cannot be observed by anyone who stands outside; it can be carried out only by the particular subject, who then can know [*vidende*] about what dwells within him/her, the only actuality that does not become a possibility by being known, and [which] cannot be known simply by being thought, since it is one's own actuality, which one knew as conceived [*tænkt*] actuality, that is, as possibility, before it became actuality.[107]

This conviction, that each individual human being has a way of turning inward to that mysterious core of one's being where finitude and infinitude meet, and to "know" and "understand" it as definitive of one's unique selfhood without ending in the abstractions of conceptual and linguistic formulations—this conviction is central and formative for all of Kierkegaard's thinking and writing. Without this working assumption, his entire phenomenological method collapses. This conviction is also the key to what he means by "inwardness" (*Inderlighed*).

This turning inward is a form of awareness and consciousness that does not work with or take the form of ideas *about* one's self, which can be expressed in clear, linguistic, conceptual definitions. The content of this consciousness is what Kierkegaard calls "concrete." By this he does not mean simply the outward tangible aspects of one's being. "To become oneself is to become concrete. But to become concrete is neither to become [merely] finite nor to become [merely] infinite, for that which is to become concrete is indeed a synthesis."[108] In other words, the self which comes to consciousness, or of which one becomes conscious, is neither the "infinite" or "negative" self that is projected as desirable possibility, nor the "immediate" self open to direct sensuous sensation. The actual concrete self occurs or dwells in that hidden private place or event where each side is open to and accepts the modification of the other. So the universal "human" with its ideal possibilities becomes (and is found only as) this unique particular individual who cannot be caught and "known" in the most elaborate set of abstract generalizations.

---

107 Ibid., pp. 280, 284; (KW 12.1:316, 320); SV 10:22, 26; (7:271, 275f.).
108 *Sickness*, p. 162; (KW 19:30); SV 15:87f.; (11:143).

So Kierkegaard will say, "The more concrete the content of consciousness is, the more concrete the understanding becomes. ... The most concrete content that consciousness can have is consciousness of itself, of the individual him/herself—not the pure self-consciousness, but the self-consciousness that is so concrete that no author, however rich in words and powerful of description, has ever been able to describe a single such [self-consciousness], although every single human being is such a one." And when one asks how this consciousness works so as to come to this kind of understanding which is beyond linguistic expression, he goes on to say, "This self-consciousness is not contemplation [objective inspection], for he who believes this has not understood himself, because he sees that meanwhile he himself is in-the-process-of-becoming [*i Vorden*] and consequently cannot be something completed for contemplation. This self-consciousness, therefore, is action, and this action is in turn inwardness."[109] But what kind of "action" is it that yields this deep inward consciousness of the concrete self?

Let us remember that what is required for penetration to that level of self-consciousness just described is indeed a certain kind of thinking or reflection which Kierkegaard calls "subjective." He says, "There is required, in order to be a subjective thinker, imagination, feeling, dialectic of existence-inwardness with passion. But first and last passion, because it is impossible, while existing, to think about existence without coming at it with passion, because this matter of existing is an immense contradiction, which the subjective thinker has not to abstract from but to remain in."[110] With the use of the words "feeling" (*Følelse*, that is, emotion) and "passion" (*Lidenskab*), Kierkegaard obviously means by "imagination" something quite other than the projection of possibilities. He is pointing to a capacity of the human mind, of human consciousness, which most humans neglect because of its difficulty, or which they deliberately ignore or sublimate because they instinctively fear the revelations and demands it may lead to (the negative aspect of angst). Or they escape this demand by yielding to the temptation to believe that "objective reflection" is the only truth, always moving away from one's particularity to ever higher and more inclusive generalities. In this approach to reality, "the stages of imagination and feeling have been left behind, and thinking as the highest stage is also the last. ... Science turns more and more away from the primitive impressions of existence;

---

109 *The Concept of Anxiety*, pp. 127f.; (KW 8:142); SV 6:223f.; (4:408f.).
110 *Postscript*, pp. 312f.; (KW 12.1:350); SV 15:87f.; (7:303).

one does not love, does not believe, does not act, but one knows what love, what faith is, and the task is simply to find their place in the system"[111] In "subjective reflection," Kierkegaard is inviting every individual human being to concentrate all of the sensitivities of one's consciousness intently and fervently toward that inward, hidden, most private centre of one's being: the place and event in which the "immense contradiction," the "qualitative disjunction," of opposites (finitude/infinitude, necessity/possibility, temporal/eternal), inherent in one's being, comes into view, and one beholds the manner of their interplay in their openness to and need of each other.

This "viewing" and "beholding," however, is not a cool, objective, disinterested observation or inspection which allows a rational analysis of the factors of the event and a description of it in general terms so that it can be given universal significance in the total scope of things. Indeed, the event is not so much "viewed" but participated in, not held in consciousness in the form of concepts and their complex linguistic formulas but in immediate intuitive "feeling," not felt with bodily senses but with "the passion of infinitude," of one's own infinitude. And this infinite, passionate, personal interest and concern is not aroused by contemplation of the eternity of abstract universals but consists in itself of the direct experience of the infinite, eternal significance of how *my* unique gestalt of infinite possibilities takes shape and concretion in *my* own peculiar, unique, particular gestalt of finitude. At this place, in this event, I am conscious of my "self," of who "I" am; I am conscious as "subject," and my "subjectivity" is known and understood as "the truth." And this understanding is not of an abstracted possibility but of a concrete actuality.

This event, experienced in my consciousness, is what Kierkegaard is pointing to when he says, "The culmination of inwardness in an existing subject is passion." This is so because "Only momentarily can the particular individual, while existing, be in the unity of infinitude and finitude, which is over and beyond existing. That moment is the instant of passion. ... So passion is the culmination of existence for an existing individual—and we are all of us existing individuals. In passion the existing subject is infinitized in the eternity of imagination [*Phantasi*], and yet at the same time one is very definitely [i.e., most specifically] oneself."[112] This arrival at the event of inward subjectivity " is the passion of infini-

---

111 Ibid., p. 307; (KW 12.1:344); SV 10:46; (7:298).
112 Ibid., pp. 176f.; (KW 12.1:197); SV 9:164f.; (7:164).

100   *My Self: A Task*

tude, and the passion of infinitude is itself the truth. But the passion of infinitude is precisely subjectivity, and so subjectivity is the truth. Objectively viewed there is no infinite decision. ... Only in subjectivity is there decision [*Afgjørelse*]. ... The *passion* of infinitude is the decision-making-factor [*Afgjørende*], not its *content*, because its content is precisely the self. In this way the subjective 'how' and subjectivity is the truth" (emphasis added).[113]

The importance of Kierkegaard's emphasis on "passion" cannot be overstated, because, as we have seen, it takes us to the very heart of what he means by "subjectivity" as consciousness of self, and what he means by saying that "subjectivity is truth." Three more aspects of passion, therefore, will be noted here (even though it will be analysed more fully under "the leap of decision" in chapter 6).

First, "passion" as described in *Postscript* is an elaboration of what Kierkegaard had earlier called "earnestness" (*Alvor*). Let us recall that "Earnestness means personhood [*Personlighed*] itself, and only an earnest individual-person [*Personlighed*] is an actual individual-person." This is the case because the proper object of earnestness is one's self, which "every human being has." So "Inwardness, certitude, is earnestness. ... Whenever inwardness is lacking, the spirit is finitized. Inwardness is therefore eternity or the constituent [determinant] of the eternal in a human being."[114]

Secondly, if my subjectivity is known and understood as the truth for me, then I have to live with the fact that objectively this truth appears as paradox, as the absurd. When truth is objectively known, it is something known and held in common with others. And it takes one of two forms; either that of the facts of sense impressions which can be checked and confirmed with those of others, or that of generalized concepts abstracted from the common experience of reality and whose formulation can be made public and agreed upon. But the uniqueness of my inward, passionate consciousness of that hidden point of meeting and unity of my finitude and infinitude can never be expressed and caught either in the terms of outward sense impressions, or in the form of universal abstract ideas and concepts. Thus, for these two forms of truth, the truth of my subjectivity must remain a matter of contradiction,

---

113 Ibid., p. 181; (KW 12.1:203); SV 9:169; (7:169–70).
114 *The Concept of Anxiety*, pp. 133f.; (KW 8:149–51); SV 6:229–31; (4:415–17). See also *Journals and Papers*, 2112, 2113, 2114; V B 65, 66, 227:5, which are background notes to *The Concept of Anxiety* and *Eighteen Upbuilding Discourses*.

paradox, absurdity. "Thus, objectively one has only uncertainty, but it is precisely this that intensifies the infinite passion of inwardness. And the truth is precisely this daring [risk] to choose the objectively uncertain with the passion of infinitude."[115]

Thirdly, subjectivity (self-consciousness) can relieve this passionate intensity only by escaping at times into the immediacy of sense experience or into the coolness of objective universal concepts. But subjectivity (selfhood) is lost if one stays in these realms too long. Subjectivity demands constant repetition of the moments of passionate, earnest consciousness of and participation in that inward hidden centre of one's being. In other words, subjectivity is never completed, never arrives at a result or goal in which one can rest. To be self in self-consciousness is always to be "on the way," to be "in-process-of-becoming" (*i Vorden*), "in the process of appropriation" (*i Tilegnelsens Proces*).[116]

Kierkegaard captures this view of human existence in one of the most radical and revealing passages in the entire corpus of his writings. In it, there is the phrase "God-relationship," which we have not explored yet. But in the context of our present topic (My Self: A Task), "God" should be understood in terms of what Kierkegaard calls "religiousness A." That is to say, "God-relationship" is to be understood as the universal human potentiality for being open to the awareness that the task of becoming one's self is the great concession and urgent demand of the "eternal," that is, it is a built-in dynamic of human existence that is present and operative in every time and place, and which cannot be ignored or got rid of, because it is a *given* of human existence. The passage, from *Works of Love*, reads as follows:

If it were not so, that the single human being, honourable, upright, respectable, God-fearing, can under the same circumstances do exactly the opposite to what another human being does, who is also honourable, upright, respectable, God-fearing—then the God-relationship would not essentially exist, not in its deepest meaning. If one could with unqualified validity judge every human being according to a universally given standard [rule, criterion: *Maalestok*], then the the God-relationship would essentially be abolished; then everything would turn outward [*ud efter*], fulfilling itself paganly in the life of the state or society; then to live would become much too easy, but also exceedingly empty; then spiritual-

---

115 *Postscript*, pp. 182–3; (KW 12.1:203); SV 9:169–70; (7:170).
116 Ibid., pp. 68, 72; see also 79, 170, 274; (KW 12.1:73 78; see also 86, 190, 308–9); SV 9:63, 67; see also 9:74, 158f., 10:15; (7:55, 59–60; see also 67, 158, 264–5).

struggle or self-deepening would be neither possible nor necessary, since the God-relationship develops in a human being precisely in and through this most intractable [difficult, tricky] clash of infinite disagreement [that is, the clash between a merely human conception of love and a God-related love].[117]

Kierkegaard is throwing down the gauntlet: you cannot have a free, responsible, unique self with ultimate eternal significance, and at the same time insist that the thinking and behaviour of every human being finally conform with a universal principle, standard, or criterion, whether the principle is imposed from without or is immanently necessitated.

With this analysis and depiction of the nature of subjective thinking as "inwardness" and "subjectivity," we have achieved the substantive clarification of "The Methodology of Consciousness," and thereby also of "Consciousness of My Self." But as indicated above, there are two other characteristics or implications of subjective thinking: namely, it accepts isolation, and it requires indirect communication. These will now be briefly commented on.

(3) It is often said that Kierkegaard's view of the self puts upon us the unbearable burden not only of constant intense endeavour to become self but also of total isolation and loneliness, separated from the company of the rest of the human community. Some go so far as to say that he rejects totally the social character of human existence. The latter charge is absurd and can be easily disproven by reference to numerous materials throughout the authorship.[118] We have already noted at several points that, for Kierkegaard, our "finitude" includes our placement in the whole temporal/spatial order of family, society, nation, and world-history, and that each one's peculiar, unique individuality is, at least in part, set by the pattern of one's unique share of these external givens. He was all too aware that most people spend their lives seeking happiness and success through adjusting to the expectations and demands of family and society. Everyone is inescapably social. And he himself agonizes in his journals and letters about his relations with his father, his siblings, and of course, to his dying day, with his one and only beloved, Regine. He expends the last energies of his life in seeking to

---

117 *Works of Love*, p. 217; SV 12:222f.; (9:220f.). For the definition of the "clash" see p. 218; SV 12:113; (9:109).

118 See e.g. Bruce H. Kirmmse, "Psychology and Society: The Social Falsification of the Self in *The Sickness unto Death*," in *Kierkegaard's Truth: The Disclosure of the Self*, pp. 167–92; see also his more recent *Kierkegaard in Golden Age Denmark*, part two; also Merold Westphal, *Kierkegaard's Critique of Reason and Society*.

reform a social institution, the church, whose hierarchy he considers to be apostate. Yet, to this dying day, he seeks the consolation of its Scriptures and its sacrament.

What does he mean, then, when he says (the year before he dies), "to become spirit is to become the particular individual [*den Enkelte*]; isolation is the *conditio sine qua non*, an indispensable condition"?[119] Clearly, he is reiterating his central thesis that at that critical juncture, when the individual faces the decision, deep within one's hidden subjectivity, whether or not to be and become one's own unique self, one is indeed "alone" and "isolated" in the sense that no one and nothing else can make that decision for him/her. The decision is not compelled or necessitated by a persuasive weight of historical evidence, or by a clear system of concepts and rational argument, or by one's own participation in a tradition, or by the forceful example and coercion of one's own immediate community of peers, or by the expectations and demands of the larger society in which one lives. All of these external conditions set the "occasion" and open up the "possibility" of the decision, but, at that juncture where the decision must be made, the individual is alone. As Kierkegaard puts it in an early statement (*Either/Or*), "When the soul is alone [*ene*] in all the world, then there appears before one ... the eternal power itself. ... And the *I* chooses itself, or rather, it receives itself."[120] This is the critical, decisive nature of the self as "freedom," which we will explore at length in the next several chapters.

Here, however, it must be stated clearly again, what has already been thoroughly clarified above, that this being "alone" and "isolated" at the critical point of decision does not at all mean that one withdraws from human society. Again and again throughout the authorship, including his normative statements about the "self" in *The Sickness unto Death*, Kierkegaard insists that this aloneness is hidden and gives no external sign. The person who lives as one before the eternal appears perfectly normal to others: one works, marries, and has children, fulfils one's social responsibilities, etc. So it is misleading for Mark Taylor to take, as indicating a total break with society, Kierkegaard's statement that "intercourse with God is in the deepest sense and unconditionally unsocial." The meaning of "unsocial" is clearly spelled out in the foregoing sentences, namely: when one stands before God, one must withdraw from "intercourse with the *many* with whom one has to do socially, convention-

---

119 *Journals*, 2074; XI^1 A 518.
120 *Either/Or*, 2:181; (KW 4:177); SV 3:166; (2:160).

ally without essential inwardness [*Inderlighed*], and with more or less indifference."[121] In other words, one's relationship with the eternal is not helped but prevented if one's consciousness is that of the merely "social and conventional," is outward, lacking all personal intensity and commitment (*Inderlighed*), and hence is "indifferent." In this sense of "social," one must be "unsocial" (in the "deepest sense") in one's decisive stand before the eternal.

On the other hand, Kierkegaard asserts again and again that "The one who has ethically chosen and found oneself possesses oneself as determined in one's whole concretion. ... The self that is the goal is not an abstract self, ... but a concrete self in living interaction with these definite surroundings, these conditons of life, this order of things." This Kierkegaard assumes as late as *The Sickness unto Death*, even though, after that, he would not agree with Judge William's addition: "The self which is the goal is not simply a personal self, but a social, a civic self."[122] Kierkegaard's lack of a sense of *spiritual* community will be commented on later when his concept of "love" is analysed theologically. But it is perfectly clear that his view of the spirit or self, as standing alone before the eternal, in no way cuts that self off from being tied into and living within the *human*, finite community. "Without wanting to deny the reality of the church or that Christianity affirms it," he simply wants to object to the thesis that the church is the creation of or a derivitive from "the sociality which belongs to human nature. ... Christianity is related to spirit—and sociality is related essentially to the soul-body synthesis. ... Christianity teaches that eternal life is not exactly social."[123] Furthermore, as is made abundantly clear in *Philosophical Fragments* and *The Book on Adler*, Kierkegaard clearly saw that there would be no succeeding generations of Christians if it were not for the empirical historical witness of Jesus' contemporaries, of the Scriptures, of church tradition and sacraments.

---

121 See "The Lillies of the Field and the Birds of the Air," in *Christian Discourses*, trans. by Walter Lowrie, p. 334; SV 14:146; (11:25). See Mark Taylor, *Journeys*, p. 180. So he is mistaken when he says that, for Kierkegaard, "spiritual individuality requires severing the umbilical cord of sociality," and that the spiritual pilgrim "remains a lonely wayfarer." He also distorts the meaning of the quote from "The Lillies of the Field" by mistranslating it as "intercourse with God is, in the deepest sense, absolutely non-social" (bracketing "in the deepest sense" with commas and omitting the "and." Also, "unsocial" is not the same as "non-social."

122 *Either/Or*, 2:266f.; (KW 4:262); SV 3:242; (2:235).

123 *Journals*, 4341; X^4 A 226.

(4) Finally, we must briefly state that subjective thinking, "subjectivity," "inwardness," involves one inevitably in indirect communication. This is a subject of such complexity in Kierkegaard that an adequate treatment would require an analysis of the entire corpus of his writings. So it is not treated comprehensively here but only in a few aspects which shed light on the consciousness of subjectivity and selfhood.

As already noted, subjective reflection turns in upon itself and so "it belongs to the subject and to none other." Only the subjective thinker himself knows what "moves within him." "In thinking, one thinks the universal, but as one existing in this thinking, as one acquiring it in one's inwardness, one becomes more and more subjectively isolated." Furthermore, the subjective thinker becomes aware that, in subjective reflection, one is involved in a continuing, never finished process, because one is thinking about oneself *concretely*; that is to say, one is trying to bring together in interplay and unity both one's vision of the universal human possibility of the infinite and one's awareness of being oneself in the specific unique particularity of one's own processive finitude.

Both of these aspects of subjective reflection and subjectivity become especially obvious and potently determinative when two persons wish to share or communicate their own self-consciousness with each other. One must first seek a "word" for expression or clarification of one's self-consciousness to and for oneself. Then one must find a "form" of expressing that "word" which is appropriate and truthful to the realities of the inwardness and incompleteness of one's self-consciousness, to the reality of the "immense contradiction" of existing at the meeting point of the infinite and the finite. The only form thus appropriate is one that is "ambiguous" (*svig*, i.e., duplicitous) and "indirect." "Just as the existing subjective thinker has freed herself through this doubleness, so the secret of communication consists precisely in freeing the other, and just for that reason one must not communicate directly."[124]

This duty to free one's auditor has infinite complications for communication. "If inwardness is the truth, ... then truth is appropriation by one's own efforts. ... If a teacher assumes that there is a direct relationship between himself and the learner, then his inwardness is not inwardness but an immediate outpouring, because the respect for the learner [which recognizes] that he is in himself inwardness is precisely the teacher's inwardness. ... The devout and silent understanding in accordance with which

---

124 For the material and quotes in the last two paragraphs, see *Postscript*, pp. 68–70; (KW 12.1:73–5); SV 9:202; (7:56–8).

the learner by herself appropriates what is to be learned, distancing herself from the teacher because she turns inward into herself, this is inwardness."[125] This respect for one's auditor requires careful attention to the form of communication.

> The subjective *thinker's form* ... of his communication is his *style*. His form must be as manifold as the opposites that he holds together. ... To the same degree that the subjective thinker is concrete, to the same degree his form must also be concretely dialectical. ... His form must first and last be related to existence. ... But existence-reality cannot be communicated, and the subjective thinker has her own actuality in her own ethical existence. If actuality is to be understood by a third party, it must be understood as possibility, and a communicator who is conscious of this, precisely in order to be oriented to existence, will see to it that his existence-communication, is in the form of possibility. A presentation in the form of possibility positions the recipient ... [with the problem of] existing therein. ... In the form of possibility, the presentation becomes a requirement [claim, demand].[126]

This form of communication means that one must accept one's isolation within one's own passionate inwardness, and that sharing this true subjectivity between two persons is always a chancy matter. "Absolute passion cannot be understood by a third party [i.e., third to me and my passion], and this holds for both one's relation to others and for their relation to him. In absolute passion the passionate one is in the extremity of his concrete subjectivity as a consequence of having reflected out of every relativity of outwardness. ... All understanding between one human being and another must always be in something tertiary, something abstract, which neither of them is. But in the absolute passion which is the very extremity of subjectivity, and in the inward 'how' of this passion, the individual is precisely at the farthest distance from this third thing."[127]

Thus the arrival at true self-consciousness, at the truth that subjectivity is the truth, does not by any means "cut the umbililcal cord of sociality," but when one is concerned with communicating this kind of truth, it does limit true human sociality to that limited number of relations in which this difficult art-form of communication can be and is practised.

---

125 Ibid., pp. 216f.; (KW 12.1:242); SV 9:202; (7:203–4).
126 Ibid., pp. 319–20; (KW 12.1:357–8); SV 10:57f.; (7:309–310).
127 Ibid., pp. 454–5; (KW 12.1:509); SV 10:185; (7:442–3).

The forces and powers of impersonal sociality of course continue to be exerted, but one does not come to authentic consciousness of self with others, or before the eternal, in and through those structures.

This brings us, then, to the end of our analysis and description of "subjective thinking" as "The Methodology of Consciousness." It has been lengthy because it has involved a preliminary clarification of what Kierkegaard actually means by the "self" and by "consciousness" of the self. His entire view of human existence stands or falls on the persuasiveness of this depiction of what it means to be a self. The description in this section is far from Kierkegaard's complete view, but it is at the heart of the matter (when one leaves out any consideration of the relation of his anthropology to his theology, as we are doing in this volume).

One essential element of his view remains, however: the self as freedom, which will be explored in the next several chapters. Transition to this topic requires a brief consideration of the fact that *consciousness* of self is not identical with *becoming* self.

4 The Limits of Consciousness

As already noted, subjectivity as a kind of thinking or knowing is still short of enactment of self. As Kierkegaard says, "For an existing individual the goal of movement is decision and repetition." So "actual subjectivity is not the knowing but is ethical existing subjectivity, because in knowing one is in the medium of possibility." But possibility is the content of objective reflection, whereas "the problem is decision and all decision resides in subjectivity." And if one seeks to resolve the problem objectively, "then subjectivity shirks something of the pain and crisis of decision."[128]

Sometimes Kierkegaard seems to equate the ethical with the passionate personal interestedness of the inwardness of subjectivity. But actually the ethical as decision, while occurring in inwardness, is an element or factor or movement in subjectivity which is to be distinguished from *consciousness* of the self as a task, no matter how profound and intense. "The transition from possibility to actuality is ... a movement. ... There is a pause, a leap."[129] So "The ethical is not merely a knowing [*Viden*]; it is

---

128 Ibid., pp. 277, 281, 115; (KW 12.1:312, 316, 129); SV 10:19, 22, 9:107; (7:268, 271–2, 104).
129 Ibid., p. 306; (KW 12.1:342); SV 10:45; (7:296).

also a doing [*Gjøren*] which relates to a knowing."[130] The ethical is "action" (*Handling*), but not simply as anticipated in thought, which is only the possibility. "When I think that I will do this or that, this thinking is not yet an action, and in all eternity is qualitatively different therefrom; but yet it is a possibility in which the interest of action and actuality is already reflected." Nevertheless, this action occurs in subjectvity. "Actuality is not the outward action, but an inwardness in which the individual annuls possibility and identifies oneself with the thought in order to exist in it. This is action. ... Actuality is interestedness by existing in it." So "The pathos of the ethical is to act. ... Ethically the highest pathos is that of interestedness, which is expressed in that I actively transform my whole existence in regard to the object of interest."[131]

What, then, is this "movement" which is a "leap"? What does this "decision" consist of, performed at that deepest most inward point of passionate interest? How does it comprise the complete transformation of one's actual existence? How does self-consciousness turn into self-becoming? Kierkegaard's answer is: *freedom*. And with and in "freedom," *My Self: A Task* is ultimately achieved—although never finished.

---

130 Ibid., p. 143; (KW 12.1:160); SV 9:134; (7:132).
131 Ibid., pp. 302–4, 349–50; (KW 12.1:339–40, 390); SV 10:41f., 85; (7:293–5, 338).

4

My Self: A Task
Part 2: Freedom: The Dialectical in Temporality/Eternity

THE RELEVANCE OF THE DYAD TEMPORAL/ETERNAL FOR THE SELF

It has been impossible, in this exposition of the "self" as a "task," to trace the emergence of self-consciousness without constant reference to the topic of freedom. At the very begining, it was said that the transition from possibility to actuality occurs only as the "leap" of freedom. But before freedom could be described, it was necessary to analyse its precursors: angst, reflection, and consciousness. And a brief preliminary summary of some aspects of freedom was required in order to clarify the nature of angst. Now those aspects must be explored and exposited in detail. Kierkegaard's understanding of "freedom" is the fulcrum on which everything else balances or around which everything else turns in his entire thought structure, in his total picture of the human being, society, world-history, nature, and God. It is the critical point in his substantive departure from Hegel. Its acceptance or rejection is the final test of the helpfulness of Kierkegaard for our own contemporary quest for the nature and meaning of human existence.

Freedom, Kierkegaard says, is in the end something simple. It is so simple that there is no way to explain it. Like sin, "freedom presupposes itself, and sin cannot be explained by anything antecedent to it, any more than can freedom. ... Freedom is infinite and arises out of nothing."[1] But freedom can be located in the process of human existence, and its antecedents and its products in that process can be described. Likewise, some aspects of the operation of freedom can be pointed to

---

[1] *The Concept of Anxiety*, p. 100; (KW 8:112); SV 6:197; (4:380f.).

with certain similes and analogies. In the following exploration of its location and operation in human existence (in this and the next four chapters), freedom will be considered under five topics: (1) freedom as the dialectic in the determinants temporality and eternity, (2) freedom as the dialectic in the determinants possibility and necessity, (3) the leap as freedom's form, (4) love as freedom's content, (5) the leap of love as indeterminate.

First, however, it must be acknowledged that this list of topics presents a significant shift both in order and content. Throughout the entire foregoing analysis and depiction of Kierkegaard's understanding of human existence and of the individual as self, there has been an almost total concentration on only two of the three dyads used in his normative definition of the self in the opening paragraph of *The Sickness unto Death*. And we have used them in the form in which they appear in the later section where they are described not in the light of self-consciousness but simply as basic, original "constituents of the synthesis," namely, as infinitude/finitude and possibility/necessity. This means we viewed possibility primarily in its relation to infinitude, and viewed necessity primarily in its relationship to finitude. And this procedure entailed no real analysis at all of the third dyad, temporal/eternal.

Out of the interaction between our finitude/necessity and infinitude/possibility, however, there emerges consciousness of a self who is other than the immediate self of the two, namely, a self which is a positive unity of the two. But mere consciousness of the "infinite possibility" of such a self does not automatically bring it into being. A "decision" and an "action" are required. As we shall see later, Climacus in *Postscript* had realized that this action requires openness to the religious and the movement of a kind of faith. But (as we will describe later) out of his sufferings in the Corsair affair, Kierkegaard came to the conviction that a wholly new exploration of the religious was required. And in that context he came to a new understanding of the importance of Haufniensis's exposition of time (in *The Concept of Anxiety*) according to which the future is the incognito of the presence of the eternal. So when Anti-Climacus in *Sickness* gives his formula for the human spirit or self, he follows the dyad "infinitude and finitude" with that of "the temporal and the eternal," and then is ready to say that the self is also a synthesis not of possibility/necessity but of "freedom and necessity." Indeed, he says later, "The self is freedom. But freedom is the dialectical in the determinants possibility and necessity."[2] This change of order and terminology signals a radical shift in the meanings of both possibility and necessity when applied to the self and its freedom.

KIERKEGAARD'S CONCEPT OF TIME

First, then, there must be a clarification of the nature of time and the temporal, and a preliminary and partial treatment of what Kierkegaard means by the "eternal." Then will follow (in the next chapter) a much more detailed and exact analysis of the dyad possibility/necessity than has been possible up to this point.

Awareness of the demand or requirement for decisive action comes only at the depth of "subjectivity," that is, at that point of inward passionate concern about the interplay and contradiction between one's inescapable finitude and one's unlimited possibilities. This point is the true locale of human "existence," of human "actuality." It can be "known" only by each individual for and by her/himself, through that peculiar kind of thinking that Kierkegaard calls "subjective reflection." "Abstract thinking," he says, "ignores the concrete, temporality, existence's becoming, the predicament of the existing [individual] arising from being compounded of [both] the eternal and the temporal, established in existence." Likewise, "When pure thought speaks of the immediate unity of reflection-in-self and reflection-in-other, and says that this immediate unity is annulled, something must then step in between the factors of the immediate unity. What is it? It is time. But time can be assigned no place within pure thought."[3]

So awareness of the demand for decisive action, for the exertion of "freedom," at the depth (or height) of self-consciousness evokes in the existing individual a new and strange comprehension of time. Kierkegaard (Haufniensis) argues that for most human beings, who live at the purely psychical/sensuous level of immediacy (with little or no sense, or a repressed sense, of responsible self), time consists only of an infinite succession of moments which are in a constant process of "passing by" (*Gaaen-forbi*). In this succession no moment is "present"; rather, the "present" is only an empty fleeting point between each moment of awareness. Thus there is no authentic sense of a past or a future to which

---

2 *Sickness*, p. 162; (KW 19:29); SV 15:87; (11:142).
3 *Postscript*, pp. 267, 278; (KW 12.1:301, 314); SV 10:9, 20; (7:257–8, 269).

one relates responsibly. In order to halt this rushing succession of moments, one usually "spatializes" them, that is, robs them of any temporal quality by defining the moments in terms of things that one can sense and preserve and arrange as the locus of one's being. And if a moment is not incarnated in a sensuous feeling of things in space, then it is empty.[4] And if we are dissatisfied with the sensible things and relations in our lives, we experience the "unhappy consciousness" of living either in memory or in hope of a more satisfying set of circumstances. Then our "present" is indeed empty. "The unhappy person is one who has one's ideal, the content of one's life, the fulness of one's consciousness, one's true being, in some manner outside of one's self. The unhappy one is always absent, never present to oneself. But obviously one can be absent either in past or in future time."[5]

On the contrary, a person who has come to full self-consciousness comes to an awareness of being dialectically related to time. And this relation enables one to have an authentic "present," in which one is "present to oneself." And this present enables one to make an authentic distinction between past and future. What then is this dialectic in respect to time, which is so different from time as an infinite progression of moments which must be spatialized in order to locate oneself at any particular moment?

Kierkegaard first works out his answer in terms of the "historical." In his later works (*Postscript, Sickness, Practice in Christianity,* and late journal entries), "historical," and especially "world-historical," become terms of opprobrium, identified with the impersonal forces of society which crush the uniqueness of the human individual. But in his earlier works (*Either/Or, Fragments, Concept of Anxiety*), he distinguishes between the historical "in the more concrete sense" of eyewitness reporting of empirical fact, and the historical "in the stricter sense which is dialectical with respect to time" where he has in mind the "coming-into-existence" of the unique, particular individual.[6]

He says that the past has happened, and *what* happened cannot be changed; its "thus" is immutable. But "its possible 'how' could have happened otherwise." Thus "the immutability of the past has been brought about by a change, by the change of coming-into-existence [*Tilblivelse*]. ... Coming-into-existence is the transformation of actuality by freedom.

---

4 *The Concept of Anxiety,* pp. 76–8; (KW 8:85f.); SV 6:174; (4:355f.).
5 *Either/Or,* 1:220–3; (KW 3:222–5); SV 2:204–7; (1:196–9).
6 *Philosophical Fragments,* pp. 73, 94; (KW 7:59, 76); SV 6:56, 70; (4:224, 239).

If the past had become necessary, then it would no longer belong to freedom. ... Freedom itself would be an illusion, and so would coming-into-existence." This means, then, that "the presence of the historical has coming-into-existence within it," and that one must approach the historical past, in spite of its appearance of necessity and immutability, with an "organ" which will sense the hidden actuality of that strange inner character of "coming-into-existence" (freedom). This organ for the historical is "wonder" or "faith."[7]

Wonder or faith is required when one regards the historical as not only being the product of impersonal social forces but as also containing the element of individual personal agency (freedom), because the latter element evokes a certain uncertainty about the historical past (including my own past), about "how" it happened and how it might have been different, even while one is very certain about "what" happened. "The past is understood only in this contradiction [*Modsigelse*] of certainty and uncertainty, which is the distinguishing mark of coming-into-existence and so also of the past." Therefore

> the historical cannot be immediately perceptible [to the senses] because it has the deceptiveness [*Svigagtighed*] of coming-into-existence within itself. The immediate impression of a natural phenomenon or of an event is not the impression of the historical, because *coming-into-existence* cannot be immediately perceived [by the senses] but only the [immediate] presence. ... The immediate sensation and the immediate cognition cannot deceive. Thereby it is manifest that the historical cannot become their object because the historical has within itself this deceptiveness which is [the deceptiveness] of coming-into-existence, ... a deceptiveness whereby that which is most certain is rendered dubious.[8]

This uncertainty about the past is equally characteristic of the future, because both the coming-into-existence that is still to happen in the future and the coming-into-existence that is embedded in the past have the characteristic of "possibility, out of which [neither] could emerge with necessity." In other words, the dialectic of certainty/uncertainty is rooted in the dialectical character of authentically human time: seeking

---

7 Ibid., pp. 94–6, 99–101; (KW 7:76–8, 80–2); SV 6:70f., 73f.; (4:239f., 243f.). "Wonder" is a translation of the Danish *Beundringen*, which literally means "admiration." But Kierkegaard uses it to translate the Greek word *thaumadzein* (wonder, amazement) from Plato and Aristotle. See *Journals*, 3284; III A 107.

8 The material of this paragraph and the next is from ibid., pp. 99–101; (KW 7:80–2); SV 6:73f.; (4:243–5).

to be present to oneself in a "present" between one's past and one's future. Only so does one have a "present" which is not an empty point between fleeting moments of time. Only so can one stop the infinite progression of moments in some other way than by spatializing them into things, namely, by coming to consciousness of one's past and of one's future, conscious that between them there is a qualitative opposition or contradiction in that one's past exists while one's future does not yet exist, and between them there is a pause, a break, a gap, and one is one's *self* precisely there: in the freedom of decision that effects the coming-into-existence of one's infinite, eternal, possible self.

Here at this juncture, at this point, one's finitude/infinitude, one's necessity/possibility, is thoroughly qualified by another dialectic: temporality/eternity. The eternal is indeed not a constituent element of the basic structure of the human being as a synthesis of two, but it is something that beckons to every human being from beyond oneself. At the point of full self-consciousness, at the crucial juncture between one's past and one's future, at the dread moment of the felt demand and task to *become* one's self, there is an openness, in the human awareness, to the possibility of an "eternal blessedness," the possibility that one's own unique existence can achieve or be given absolute significance, an openness to the certain conviction, against all apparent uncertainty, that the achievement of this significance is the ultimate, infinite, passionate, personal interest (and intended destiny) of every individual. This juncture, if freedom dares to choose, may also be called "the instant [moment]" (*Øieblikket*), which is "that ambiguity in which time and eternity touch each other, and herewith is posited the concept of *temporality*, where time constantly precludes [*afskærer*] eternity and eternity constantly pervades time. Only now does that division acquire its significance: the present time, the past time, the future time."9

THE RESULTANT NATURE OF FREEDOM

In the context of such a perspective, Kierkegaard isolates "freedom" as the definitive characteristic of the particular (*enkelt*) human being or self. "The self is composed of infinitude and finitude. But this synthesis

---

9 *The Concept of Anxiety*, p. 80; (KW 8:89); SV 6:177; (4:359). See pp. 73–83 for the full discussion of "the instant," which will be referred to later. But in the present quotation, to translate *afskære* as "intersects" (Lowrie and Thomte) is not supported by the essential meaning of the word, nor does it make sense in Kierkegaard's conception of time.

is a relation, and a relation which, even though derived, relates to itself, which is freedom. The self is freedom. But freedom is the dialectical [factor] in the determinants possibility and necessity."[10] Now we are able to see why Kierkegaard says, in the first paragraph of *Sickness*, that "the human being is a synthesis of infinitude and finitude, of the temporal and the eternal, of *freedom* and necessity," but when he "reflects abstractly on the constituents of which the self as a synthesis is composed" without respect to self-consciousness, he speaks of "*possibility* and necessity" [in section A. under "The Forms of This Sickness (Despair)"]. Obviously, he means that "possibility" and "freedom" are not identical. Freedom is an added (dialectical) factor in the interplay of possibility and necessity as opposites. Possibility becomes freedom only when the basic human duality of infinitude/finitude and possibility/necessity becomes pervaded and modified by the individual's experience of temporality/eternity. Only at this point of full self-consciousness does the demand and the task of the self as freedom come into view. Only at that point in space/time when a relation to the "eternal" evokes in an individual an awareness of the dialectic of certainty and uncertainty in the dialectic between one's past and one's future, and when one is aroused to a deep, inward, passionate, personal interest in achieving a harmony of the two as one's "present," only then does one "know" and "believe" that contemplation of infinite possibilities is not enough to effect a "transition" from possibility to actuality but that there is also required of a person an absolute decision, a choice, an action with all possible intensity of one's inward being. This decision, choice, action is "freedom."

This complicated and absolute interdependence of, on the one hand, the act of the self freely choosing to become itself and, on the other, the act or event of the self relating to the eternal is put most succinctly by Kierkegaard in the condensed, "geometric," formulaic language of the first page of *Sickness*: "The self is a relation which relates to itself. ... Such a relation which relates to itself, a self, must either have established itself, or have been established by an other. ... The self of a human being is such a derived, established relation, a relation which relates to itself, and in relating to itself relates to an other." In other words, the act of freely becoming oneself, through choosing to relate one's possibility and necessity, requires or involves a simultaneous choosing to relate one's being-in-time to the eternal.

10 *Sickness*, p. 162; (KW 19:29); SV 15:87; (11:142).

Kierkegaard could use this condensed language because he had already laid the ground work for understanding it in his earlier work *The Concept of Anxiety*. There his central point is:

> The synthesis of the temporal and the eternal is not another synthesis, but is the expression of the first synthesis, according to which the human being is a synthesis of soul and body, which is sustained by spirit. As soon as the spirit is posited, the instant is there. ... The synthesis of the psychical and the sensuous is to be posited by spirit, but the spirit is the eternal, and therefore actually exists only when the spirit posits the first synthesis along with [*tillige som*] the second synthesis of the temporal and the eternal.[11]

In summary, Kierkegaard is saying: out of reflection on the contrast between my given, irreversible finitude of sensuous and social conditioning, and my fantasies of my infinite desires as possibilities, I become conscious of another potential self wherein the desires of my dreams "come-into-existence" within the conditions of my finitude to form my actual concrete self. But then my consciousness of this self is filled with angst because I realize that the "movement" or "transition" to this potential self is not easy or inevitable, not "necessary." There is no set of physical conditions, or any set or system of logical reasons, or any irresistible psychic compulsion, which moves me automatically into this new state of being. Rather, I sense a pause, a break, a gap, between my "past" (what I already am) and my "future" (what I may become). And in that "instant," in that moment which is no longer empty but is an actual "present" held in suspension between my past and future, there comes a transcendent demand to risk the leap across that gap, a transcendent affirmation (against all apparent uncertainties) that in the decision to make that leap with all passionate inward concern lies the key to the ultimate meaning and "eternal blessedness" of human existence. My "angst" is the dialectical feeling/attitude of being overpowered with the allure and the longing to make that leap, and yet being frozen with fear of failing ("falling"). Only that demand-and-affirmation, which both invades me and yet transcends me, enables (but not compels) me to take the risk, to "believe," and so to find the "faith" required to be certain against all uncertainty. So faith is the third factor that unites the temporal and the eternal. And precisely and only there, at that point where

---

11 *The Concept of Anxiety*, pp. 76–9, 81; (KW 8:85–90); SV 6:173–8; (4:355–6of.). For quotations, see pp. 79, 81; (KW 8:88, 90); SV 6:176, 178; (358, 360).

Freedom: The Dialectical in Temporality/Eternity

the "synthesis" of my time (past-present-future) and of the eternal demand/affirmation occurs simultaneously with the "synthesis" of my finite necessity and my infinite fantasies of possibilities—only there does the authentic human "spirit" (self) come-into-existence as an unending, exciting process of adventure. So the self is "freedom," the freedom of that "instant" which is continuously repeated. Or, the self is that (double) "relation" (of finite-to-infinite and temporal-to-eternal) which "relates to itself" (chooses to be itself in that double relation). To say that "the self is freedom" is the same as to say that "the self is a relation which relates to itself."[12]

Thus we have "located" freedom. We have described its occasion as the self relating to its past and to its future. Freedom is to be found in the self's struggle to interrelate these two magnitudes of its being, instead of avoiding their pressures by escaping into a false "present" of spatialized sensuous immediacy. It is worthwhile to note one crucial implication of this location of freedom, before we go on to a description of what freedom does in relation to one's past and future and of how it does it.

The location of freedom reveals quite clearly that human freedom is limited, or as Kierkegaard puts it, it is "entangled" (*hildet*, a strange word meaning "snared" or "prejudiced"). In a key passage,[13] where he is discussing the nature of sexuality, Kierkegaard is pointing to two ways in which human freedom is limited or entangled. First, freedom is not to be confused with "the act of abstract *liberum arbitrium*," that is, with an arbitrary and unconditional freedom. Human freedom is limited, entangled, oriented in the sense that it is not freedom *from* (all restrictions and definitions of goals or objects), but is freedom *for* (that which is "good" and "true"). And what a person experiences, when freely choosing what is *not* good and true, is not freedom but the loss of freedom. This limitation that is inherent in freedom itself is rooted in and reflective of a second kind of limitation.

What is good and true for a particular human individual does not consist of, is not defined by, a set of universal objective principles which

---

12 It should be noted that this analysis of freedom (as located at the intersection of possibility/necessity and temporality/eternity) is only preliminary, only an outline whose content is to be explored in detail in what follows. The dialectic of possibility/necessity comprises the subject matter of the next chapter, and the role of the "eternal" (the religious) in the event of freedom will be developed in two places, first, in a preliminary way at the end of this chapter, and secondly, under the topics of "the unconditional" and "the religious" in the chapter on freedom as the leap.

13 *The Concept of Anxiety*, pp. 44f.; (KW 8:49); SV 6:142f.; (4:320).

are to be applied by all humans under all circumstances. As Kierkegaard puts it in *Either/Or* (and repeats in *Sickness*), "What then is this self of mine? ... It is the most abstract of all things, and yet at the same time it is the most concrete of all—it is freedom. ... This self contains within itself a rich concretion, a manifold of determinants and characteristics, in short, is the whole aesthetic self which is chosen ethically."[14] So one's freedom plays the absolutely crucial and determinative role in one's becoming oneself. But that freedom is constructed and oriented just *for* that particular purpose and telos. It is not absolute in being free *from* all limitations, and so being able to chose to be and become whatever one wishes or dreams.

Later on in this study, it will be shown that the purposiveness or orientation of human freedom imposes even other limitations upon it. But here we wish to explore in greater detail the limitations involved in choosing what one is and in choosing what one may become: one's past and one's future.

FREEDOM IN RELATION TO THE PAST

We have seen that the self as freedom occurs when the self comes to consciousness of the dialectic between one's past and future, when one no longer seeks to halt fleeting time by spatializing it into a false "present." Rather, the self is freedom when it seeks to interrelate its past and future, its specific finitude and its unrealized possibilities. In this event one's human "time" becomes "temporality" as one's past/future is seen in the light of "eternity," that is, is seen as possessing eternal significance, is given meaning and promise from beyond itself. So, Kierkegaard says, "There comes a moment in a human being's life when [one's] immediacy comes to a head, and the spirit [self] demands a higher form in which it would apprehend itself as spirit. As immediate spirit, a human being is bound up with the whole earthly life, and now the spirit would assemble itself out of this scatteredness and explain itself to itself; the personal-individuality would become conscious in its eternal validity [*Gyldighed*]." Or again, "It is an earnest and significant moment when for eternity one binds oneself to an eternal power, when one accepts oneself as that one whose memory time will never blot out, when in an eternal and unfailing sense becomes conscious as that one [which] one is."[15]

---

14 *Either/Or* 2:218, 227; (KW 4:214, 222f.); SV 3:199, 206; (2:192, 199).
15 Ibid., 2:193, 210; (KW 4:188f., 206); SV 3:177, 192; (2:170f., 185).

Such consciousness requires, first of all, a certain orientation and relation to one's past. To see one's past accumulated self as a dead burden, to be repressed and jettisoned and escaped, is to lose oneself. To want and to try to become something or someone new and different every day is not "freedom," but it is to be exiled from what is the authentic good and truth which one's self actually is. So the first task and delimitation of freedom is: to "choose oneself." For Kierkegaard, all freedom and becoming of self begins with this specific and concrete action. The orientation of freedom toward the unrealized possibilities of the future is empty and futile unless freedom has first chosen the self one already is, unless freedom has reached backward to the beginning and assembled together all the scattered pieces of the self and brought them forward to be accepted as one's authentic self in the living present.

So, Kierkegaard says (in his early formulations in *Either/Or*), "I return to my category. ... I return to the significance of choosing." What he essentially means by this action is described in a ninety-page section of the second part of *Either/Or*, and can be best summarized in a series of quotations.

That which stands out in my either/or, is the ethical. It is therefore not yet a question of the choice of something [in particular], it is not a question of the reality of that which is chosen, but the reality of choosing. This is the crucial thing. ... When all has become still around one, as solemn as a starlight night, when the soul comes to be alone in the whole world, then there appears before one, not a distinguished human being, but the eternal power itself. The heavens part, as it were, and the I chooses itself, or more correctly, receives itself. Then the soul has seen the highest, which no mortal eye can see and which never can be forgotten; then the personal-individuality receives the accolade of knighthood that ennobles it for an eternity. He does not become another [person] than he was before, but he becomes himself, the consciousness integrates, and he is himself. ... Even the poorest person is everything when she has chosen herself; for the great thing is not to be this or that but to be oneself, and every human-being can be this if she wills it.[16]

It is precisely in this "instant," when one's poor limited finitude is given the accent and the affirmation of the eternal, that one comes to understand the true significance of one's temporality, and one is ennabled to *choose* to *be* what one already is.

16 Ibid., 2:180f.; (KW 4:176f.); SV 3:166f.; (2:160f.).

It is precisely the beauty of temporality that the infinite spirit and the finite spirit are separated in it, and it is precisely the greatness of the finite spirit that temporality is assigned to it. Temporality ... exists for the sake of the human being and is the greatest of all the gifts of grace. The eternal dignity [*Værdighed*, worthiness] of a human being consists precisely in the fact that he can acquire a history. The divine element in her consists in the fact that she herself, if she will, can give to this history continuity, because this it acquires only when it is not the sum of what has taken place or has happened to me but is my own work, in such a way that even what has befallen me is transformed by me and translated from necessity to freedom.[17]

How does this transformation take place? First of all, this choosing, freely, to be oneself, this acceptance of all one's accumulated past, must not be done grudgingly, half-heartedly, selectively, partially, or relatively, i.e., with certain qualifications or conditions. The choosing must be done "absolutely." To choose absolutely is what it means to see one's self as having eternal significance, what it means to regard the gift of one's unique particular self with deep, inward, personal, passionate interest. It is to regard one's own self with ultimate wonder and faith, as possessing "eternal validity" against all appearances to the contrary. So then,

I choose the absolute, because I am myself the absolute; I posit the absolute, and I am myself the absolute; but in complete identity with this I may say: I choose the absolute that chooses me, I posit the absolute that posited me, because if I do not remember that this second expression is equally absolute, my category of choosing is untrue, because it is precisely the identity of both [propositions].

In this stark statement of a seemingly absolute logical contradiction, Kierkegaard is pointing to the existential reality of human experience that when I freely and gladly accept all that has befallen me and happened to me in the past as definitive of who I am, of my self, then this free acceptance ("choosing") completely transforms my relation to my past and the way it operates in my present active being, and, as we shall see, the way in which it operates in my relation to my future possibilities. And so he continues, "But what is it, then that I choose—is it this or that? No, because I choose absolutely, and I choose absolutely precisely by having chosen not to choose this or that. I choose the absolute, and what is the absolute? It is myself in my eternal validity [*Gyldighed*]. Something

17 Ibid., 2:254f.; (KW 4:250); SV 3:231; (2:224).

other than myself I can never choose as the absolute, for if I choose something else, I choose it as something finite and so do not choose it absolutely."[18]

However, secondly, it must be emphasized again that, in this transformation, "one chooses oneself and not another. This self that one thus chooses is infinitely concrete." What does Kierkegaard mean by "concrete"? As we have heard him say,

> When you choose yourself absolutely, you easily discover that this self is not an abstraction. ... This self contains in itself a rich concretion, a multiplicity of determinants and qualities; in short, it is the whole aesthetical self that is chosen ethically. ... Whoever chooses oneself ethically chooses oneself concretely as this specific individual, and achieves this concretion by the fact that this choice is identical with that repentance which ratifies the choice.[19]

So this first form of freedom (in relation to one's past), as the choosing of oneself, must be done absolutely and concretely. But in the last quotation, Kierkegaard added a third qualification of this act of freedom: it must be done "repentantly." This is a favourite theme that appears often in his writings (and we will explore it in greater detail in chapter 6). Here in *Either/Or* he says,

> A person discovers that the self he chooses has a boundless multiplicity in itself, inasmuch as it has a history, a history in which he acknowledges [or recognizes] identity with himself. ... He cannot relinquish anything of all this, not the most painful, not the hardest [to bear], and yet the expression for this struggle, for this acquisition is—repentance. He repents back into himself, back into the family, back into the race, until he finds himself in God. ... One holds onto repentance, for only in this way does one choose oneself.[20]

Later, he adds, "The truly concrete choice is that wherewith at the very same instant I choose myself out of the world, I choose myself back into the world. That is, when I repenting choose myself, I gather myself together in all my finite concretion, and when I have thus chosen myself out of finitude, I am in the most absolute continuity with it."[21]

18 For the last two paragraphs, see ibid., 2:217–19; (KW 4:213–15); SV 3:198–200ff.; (2:191–3).
19 Ibid., 2:226f., 255; (KW 4:222, 250f.); SV 3:206, 232; (2:199, 225).
20 Ibid., 2:220f.; (KW 4:216f.); SV 3:200f.; (2:193f.).
21 Ibid., 2:252f.; (KW 4:248); SV 3:229f.; (2:223).

My Self: A Task

Now we can see how choosing oneself "absolutely," "concretely," and "repentantly" works a qualitative transformation of one's self, precisely while one remains who one has always been. As already noted, Kierkegaard says that when one chooses one's self in this way, everything that has befallen and happened to a person is "transformed and translated from necessity to freedom." This means that "one remains oneself, quite the same as one was before, down to the least significant peculiarity [*Eiendommelighed*], and yet one becomes an other, because the choice permeates [pervades, suffuses] everything and transforms it. Thus one's finite personal-individuality is now infinitized in the choice, in which one infinitely chooses oneself." When one chooses as one's own everything one has been and is, this permeating choice transforms one's whole being because now

one assumes responsibility for all this. One does not hesitate as to whether or not one should include this particular thing [*det Enkelte*], because one knows that something much more important gets lost if one does not. In the moment of choice one is in the most complete isolation, because one withdraws from the surroundings; and yet at the same moment one is in absolute continuity, because one chooses oneself as product. And this choice is freedom's choice, so that when one chooses oneself as product one can just as well be said to produce oneself. Thus at the moment of choice, one is at the point of consummation, because one's personhood is consummating itself; and yet in the same moment one is exactly at the beginning, because one chooses oneself according to one's freedom. As product one is squeezed into the forms of actuality, [but] in the choice one makes oneself elastic, transforming all one's outwardness into inwardness. ... This concretion is the individual's actuality; but since one chooses it according to one's freedom, so one can also say that it is one's possibility, or ... that it is one's task. ... But the fact that the individual sees one's possibility as one's task expresses precisely one's sovereignty over oneself.[22]

Kierkegaard asserts that this experience of pervading all that one has ever been or done with the free choice of claiming it all for oneself, "assuming responsibility" for all of it, viewing it all not as a dead past under

---

22 Ibid., 2:227, 255f.; (KW 4:223, 250f.); SV 3:207, 232; (2:200, 225f.). By the time Kierkegaard writes *Postscript*, he does not like to speak of the self as "product" at all, because of his stress on the "process of coming-into-existence." But although in *Either/Or*, he had not worked out his concept of temporality as a dialectic of past/future as in *Fragments* and *The Concept of Anxiety*, or his concept of possibility as in *Postscript* and *Sickness*, yet he assumes and carries forward *Either/Or*'s concept of "choosing the self" in all the works that follow.

the dread hand of fate and necessity to be repressed and escaped, but viewing it as rich with infinite possibility—this experience is infinitely liberating and rewarding because it reveals that one's true identity (the self) lies in this central act of freedom; it reveals that all the forms of one's finite, concrete singularity are not an end but a beginning, a task. And it is precisely because of this centrality of the self as *task* that Kierkegaard makes "choosing oneself" to be the first crucial form of freedom. Certainly, "one who lives ethically has seen oneself, knows oneself, penetrates with his consciousness one's whole concretion." But the Greek ideal of γνωθι σεαυτον (know yourself) is not ultimate. "It cannot be the goal if it is not at the same time the beginning. The ethical individual knows himself, but this knowledge is not a mere contemplation (for with that the individual is determined by one's necessity), it is a reflection upon oneself which itself is an action, and therefore I have deliberately used the expression 'choose yourself' instead of 'know yourself.' When the individual knows herself, she is not finished."23

However, Kierkegaard injects one final cautionary note about the "entangled," limited, qualified nature of this freedom of choosing oneself. To choose oneself is not to create oneself. Here again (in *Either/Or*) Kierkegaard states his basic dialectic of freedom, which he later reformulates in more subtle terms in *Fragments* and *Sickness*.

The self which one chooses is infinitely concrete, for it is in fact oneself, and yet it is absolutely distinct from one's former self, because one has chosen it absolutely. This self did not previously exist, because it came into existence by means of the choice, and yet it did exist, because it was in fact 'oneself.' In this case choice performs the two dialectical movements simultaneously: that which is chosen does not exist and comes into existence by the choice; that which is chosen exists, otherwise it was not a choice. In other words, if what I chose did not exist but came into existence absolutely by the choice, then I did not choose, then I created. But I do not create myself, I choose myself.24

So freedom is "entangled" or "oriented" in that it must perform "two dialectical movements" simultaneously. On the one hand, I must acknowledge, gladly and without reservation, that I did not "posit" or create the original basic forms and contents of my self; these were given to me, along with many events and conditions that have befallen and happened

23 Ibid., 2:263; (KW 4:258); SV 3:239; (2:232).
24 Ibid., 2:219f.; (KW 4:215); SV 3:200; (2:193).

to me without any choice of mine involved. On the other hand, in freedom I must see and acknowledge, with fear and trembling, with courage and daring, with wonder and faith, that this finite necessary self may be completely transformed if I choose to assume responsiblity for it and make it my own, *my* self. All things become new and open. This choice confronts me as an enormous and frightening possibility and as the original element in the self-defining task of my existence. So, in one sense, my self is already there, but it will become an entirely new self if I choose it. Here, Kierkegaard says, is the absolute either/or which cannot be escaped or annulled: either I choose, or I do not choose. There can be no part way, no both/and, no easy mediation and transition by inherent logical necessity.[25]

If I do not choose myself in this sense, either I lose all self-consciousness by immersing my life in the finite forms of the world about me and within me, and having my actions determined by the external standards and customs of society and by blind drives and desires, or I forget and ignore my concrete self by being absorbed in dreams of being someone else. As Kierkegaard put it later in a more sophisticated analysis,

> In order to will in despair to be oneself, there must be consciousness of the infinite self. This infinite self, however, is really only the most abstract form, the most abstract possibility of the self, and it is this self one despairingly wills to be, detaching itself from every relation to the power which posited itself. ... By the aid of this infinite form the self despairingly wills to dispose of itself or to create itself, to make its self that self it wills to be, distinguishing in its concrete self what it will and what it will not accept. One's concrete self, or one's concretion, has in fact necessity and limitations, it is this perfectly definite thing, with these faculties, dispositions, etc., in this concretion of relationships, etc. But with the help of this infinite form, the negative self, one wills first to undertake to reconstruct the whole thing, in order to get out of it in this way a self such as one wants ...—and it is thus one wills to be oneself. ... One is not willing to put on one's self, or to see one's task in the self given her/him.[26]

In this situation, "what really is lacking is the power to obey, to submit to the necessary in oneself, to what may be called one's limit. Therefore the misfortune does not consist in the fact that such a self did not amount to anything in the world; no, the misfortune is that this person

---

25 Ibid., 2:179f.; (KW 4:175f.); SV 3:165f.; (2:159f.).
26 *Sickness*, pp. 201f.; (KW 19:68); SV 15:122f.; (11:179).

did not become aware [observant, attentive] of itself, aware that the self one is, is a perfectly definite something and thus the necessary."[27]

With these thoughts, Kierkegaard dissociates himself once and for all from that form of "existentialism" which argues that for human beings "existence precedes essence," that the individual is "free" to choose and to become whatever he wills, that one's past has no hold over him. Kierkegaard asserts a very real and irreducible freedom, but it is a deeply "entangled" freedom, entangled in its own given purpose and orientation, namely, for the self to choose to be and to become that self which it has been given to be, both in its past and its future. The struggle and the agony of this kind of freedom must be apparent to every human with any degree of self-awareness and self-consciousness. Have we not all, at times, especially in adolescence, dreamed and longed to be someone else, to escape the drastic limitations of our body, our family, our economic and class conditions, our native capacities, our social ineptness, limitations on our career possibilities, etc., etc.? The present author certainly did. Such dreams were dominant in my spirit and frustrated my work and my happiness into young adulthood—until one day, without being conscious of it, I began to accept my limitations. And when one of my colleagues entered my office, while I was idly swinging a tennis racket, and asked me, "Arnold, do you think you will ever amount to anything?" I replied without reflection, "That used to worry me a lot, but now I don't give a damn!" It became a sacramental moment for me, because I suddenly saw in a flash that I was happy to be who I was. And from then on, my future seemed to open up as a new beginning, with infinite possibilities. I had "chosen myself."

FREEDOM IN RELATION TO THE FUTURE

We have seen, therefore, that the first form of freedom is the choosing to be responsible for one's "past," that is, for one's entire accumulated self with its history. But that is not the definitive form of freedom, because if that is all that one chooses to do, one is not free. Choosing to *be* what one already *is* is not an end but a beginning. The self one chooses is not essentially a product but also an ongoing process. And choosing as a beginning faces the indeterminate future. The self as freedom is located precisely at the dialectical point between the "necessity" of one's past and the "possibility" of one's future. At this point, freedom faces a

---

[27] Ibid., p. 169; (KW 19:36); SV 15:94; (11:149).

very different task in choosing its future than it did in choosing its past. It is this task of choosing my future—in strict relation to my past—that Kierkegaard has in mind when he says, "The self is freedom." So, "freedom" is the self, in its duality of finitude/infinitude, as it acts to interrelate its past (necessity) and its future (possibility).

In the first main section of the previous chapter (on angst), we described what happens in human consciousness when the fantasies of one's infinitude take on the character of possibilities, namely, the experience of angst with its duality of sympathy and antipathy, of desire and fear. There it was noted that the experience of angst is the first intimation of freedom in its basic sense as an essential property of human nature, namely, as the sheer capacity of "being able" without any definition of what one is able to do. And it was also noted that "freedom" has a second meaning, namely, the act of choosing, both in the form of choosing to *be* what one *is* (one's past), and especially in the form of choosing to actualize one's possible self (one's future).[28] Now we must give a preliminary description of Kierkegaard's concept of possibility, not in its initial operation in a human's "being able," but in its definitive form in the human task of choosing one's future. In this latter context, Kierkegaard says, "Possibility is the heaviest of all categories."[29] His reasons for this assertion must be spelled out in detail because they will carry us to the heart of Kierkegaard's view of the source and meaning of human freedom. (An even fuller treatment of "possibility" will appear in the next chapter on "Freedom as the Dialectical in the Determinants Possibility and Necessity.")

First of all, Kierkegaard stresses that "possibility" has to do with one's as yet undetermined future. We have heard him say that one's past also has a certain character of being "possible" in the sense that one may or may not choose to identify one's self with it and claim responsibility for it. There is also a certain indeterminateness about the past in the hidden "how" of its coming into being; that is to say, what is now one's past "necessity" was once only one of several possibilities which had to be chosen in one's hidden inwardness or subjectivity. Still again, my past may fill me with angst because elements in it loom as "possibilities" which I may reluctantly repeat.

Nevertheless, possibility essentially and most significantly has to do with one's future. "The possible corresponds exactly to the future. For

---

28 See above the sections on angst in chapter 3.
29 *The Concept of Anxiety*, p. 140; (KW 8:156); SV 6:235; (4:422).

freedom, the possible is the future. For time, the future is the possible." Genuine angst is engendered not by one's past but by the demand of one's future for decision and choice.

The one who is educated by angst is educated by possibility, and only the one who is educated by possibility is educated according to one's infinitude. Possibility is therefore the heaviest of all categories. ... In possibility all things are equally possible, and whoever has been truly brought up by possibility has grasped the terrible as well as the joyful. ... Only in this way can possibility be educative, because finitude and finite relations, in which an individual is assigned a place, ... educate only finitely. ... In order that an individual may be educated absolutely and infinitely by possibility, he must be honest toward possibility and have faith. By faith I understand ... the inner (*indre*) certainty that anticipates infinitude. ... If an individual defrauds possibility by which he is educated, he never arrives at faith.[30]

If, therefore, "the self is freedom" as the self faces the task of choosing to enact one's future possibility, one must also say that the self is its "future" as it seeks to integrate its chosen possibilities into its accumulated past. "For freedom, the possible is the future." But when the choosing self gets this sense of its time as future, it comes to a dialectical sense of temporality, standing at the juncture of its future *and* its past and seeking to combine them in a full and meaningful present. "The future signifies more than the present and the past, because the future is in a sense the whole of which the past is a part."[31] So "for time, the future is the possible." Without the future, one's past is dead necessity, and one's "present" is not temporal but purely spatial, consisting of an arrangement of finite things. But when one's future takes on the character of one's own authentic possibilities, concretely related to one's accumulated past, then one finds oneself located in the freedom to establish a full and meaningful present.

So "possibility" is a "heavy" category for Kierkegaard because it is one's future, whose free choice determines who one is: one's self. But possibility is the *heaviest* of all categories for quite a different but related reason. To be educated or formed absolutely by possibility, he says, one must not only be "honest" about it but must also "have faith." Why faith? Because facing possibility as one's *future* places one in a different

---

30 Ibid., pp. 82, 139ff.; (KW 8:91, 156f.); SV 6:179, 235f.; (4:361, 422f.).
31 Ibid., pp. 80f.; (KW 8:89f.); SV 6:177; (4:359).

(but related) duality or opposition from that of one's own finitude/infinitude or necessity/possibility. Now I find myself in the dialectic of time, in the duality or opposition between the temporal and the eternal. The possibilities of my infinitude are *mine* and become constituent elements of my actuality as I posit my self in their unification with my finitude/necessity. But when these possibilities reveal themselves, not as inherent inevitable necessities of my actuality, but as something "future" beyond the gap of my decision and choice, then a profound uncertainty and doubt intrudes about the relation between my future and my past. And in order "constantly in certainty to abolish ... the uncertainty involved in coming-into-existence," I must "believe in possibility," I must have faith that I am supported, from beyond my own limits, in my very limited struggle freely to become myself. I must believe in the "eternal validity" of that struggle. The eternal must pervade my time.[32]

The experience of possibility, therefore, is the weightiest, most important event in my existence because, if I face it honestly and follow its leading all the way, it proves to be the opening to the awareness of the reality and presence of the "eternal" invading my time. For Kierkegaard, the human individual never achieves the fulfilment of selfhood until one arrives at the synthesis of the temporal and the eternal. So when one's possibility points one to the future, then "the future is in a sense the whole of which the past is a part" because "the future is the incognito in which the eternal, as incommensurable with time, nevertheless would preserve its association [*Omgængelse*, tractability] with time."[33]

FREEDOM AND THE ETERNAL

It is thus proper to say that "the eternal" is truly the heaviest category for understanding human existence. To speak of the eternal marks the transition from one sphere or dimension of human existence to another, from what Kierkegaard labels the "ethical" to what he calls the "religious." Two points must be remembered concerning his view of the "spheres." First, the aesthetic, ethical, and religious spheres are not mutually exclusive but are overlapping and progressively inclusive, so that the ethical catches up and carries forward the aesthetic, and the reli-

---

32 For these ideas and language, see *Fragments*, p. 101; (KW 7:81); SV 6:74; (4:245); *Sickness*, pp. 171f.; (KW 19:38f.); SV 15:95f.; (11:151f.); *The Concept of Anxiety*, p. 80 as in previous note.
33 *The Concept of Anxiety*, p. 80; (KW 8:89); SV 6:177; (4:359).

gious includes and assumes both the aesthetic and the ethical. Secondly, the "religious" in this context refers to a dimension of human existence that is universally open to human experience, no matter what the conditions, time or place (religiousness A). It does not refer to the particular historically conditioned religious experience of Christianity or of any other religion (religiousness B).

To speak of the eternal, then, points to an element of transcendence which every human being encounters (consciously or unconsciously) in the process of seeking to become truly and wholly one's self. And the first incognito of its presence is one's consciousness of the future as the demand for choice and decision in regards to possibilities that one is able to actualize. As already noted, the third factor which forms the unity of one's finitude and infinitude is the self, and this self-achievement occurs when one chooses absolutely, with infinite inward passion, to accept one's given and accumulated finitude as a dimension of one's identity, and chooses to stamp upon that finitude the character of one's inward infinite possibility. "But one is also *a synthesis of the temporal and the eternal*. ... As for the latter synthesis, it is immediately striking that it is formed in another way than the first. ... In this case, where is the third [factor]?"[34] Again, Kierkegaard's answer is: faith.[35] In other words, to choose a future possibility is risky. It requires one to transcend, to go beyond and outside of the security of the concrete actuality of what one already *is*. What one already is does indeed limit and confine but does not *determine* what one will become—*unless* one fails (refuses) to make this second choice. Will one dare to risk this second choice of one's future indeterminate possibility? Or will one be content, out of fear of failure to make the right choice, to let the conditions (both inward and outward) of one's actuality determine (necessitate) what one will become?

At this juncture lies freedom, and so "the self is freedom." But whence comes the faith for the daring? Is "faith" not just another manifestation of one's own self-determination? Why call this choice "religious" as distinct from one's "ethical" choice to identify one's self with what one already is? Are not the possibilities of one's "future" already inherent in what one is and has been? And will not these possibilities emerge natu-

---

34 Ibid., p. 76; (KW 8:85); SV 6:173; (4:355).
35 This answer is given indirectly in chapter v of *The Concept of Anxiety*, which is a kind of a postscript, since this book was purported to be only a "psychological" study. But this answer is given directly in that work's companion volume, *Philosophical Fragments*; see pp. 59f., 67, 73, 101; (KW 7:47f, 54, 59, 81f.); SV 6:47, 52, 56, 74; (4:214f., 220, 224f., 244f.).

rally and inevitably without the agony of choosing and the fear of failing? If so, says Kierkegaard, freedom is an illusion, and there is no self. But if I am "honest" about the way possibilities appear as "future," they do not appear as inevitable. Rather, they evoke a profound sense of angst in which I am both allured and repelled, I both desire and fear them. I am in the presence of something that "transcends" me, not in the sense of being totally foreign and outside of my being and experience, but in the sense of being a condition or qualification of my existence that is not simply "mine," that is more than "me," that is a given of all human existence. And it invades and pervades my particular existence precisely in the "instant" when I sense and acknowledge that my freedom to choose my possible future is both a concession and a demand from that enveloping condition of my existence that both transcends and pervades my own particular existence.

In other words, my angst, as evoked by the sense of my possible self as future, makes me aware of existing in a dual relationship: on the one hand, to that possible self whom I am free to actualize or bring-into-existence, and on the other hand, to a condition which sets limits to that freedom and holds the power of retribution or reprisal if I overstep those limits. But now this transcendent condition is seen not as an alien and inimical force but as friendly and helpful, because it is from this second relation that the faith and courage come to enact my possibility as *future*, the courage not only to *be* myself but also to *become* myself. This courage, to dare and to risk the actualization of my possibilities, requires not only that I believe in my freedom to be able to do so but also that I believe in a structure or dynamic of reality that makes possible my openness to possibility and that encourages me in my risk-taking by guaranteeing my self's continuing significance and meaning in the ultimate scheme of things.

My freedom, to be and especially to become myself, therefore, is not an illusion grounded in "mere" human subjectivity. Rather, my freedom, as an expression of the authentic actuality of my subjectivity, discovers itself to be in a relation with and in response to a corresponding dynamic that transcends all human individuality, an infinite force that—with a "freedom" of its own—sustains, enables, and conditions my own limited freedom. And it is the discovery of this relationship that enables the courage to dare and to risk the choice and decision to act, to "leap" into that "future" that now becomes real "present" in which one can dwell and be one's self. Kierkegaard tries to capture the complexity and elusiveness of this hidden inward relationship, and yet to express the phenomenological force of its givenness, in the following passage (with his usual dense and abstruse language): "Just as (in the previous chapter) the spirit, when it is about to be posited in the synthesis, or, more correctly, when it is about to posit the synthesis as the spirit's (freedom's) possibility in the individuality, expresses itself as angst, so here again the future is the eternal's (freedom's) possibility in the individuality [expressed] as angst."[36] So the freedom of the human spirit to posit the synthesis, and the freedom of the eternal to manifest possibility as future, meet and correspond with each other in the moment of angst (that is, the moment of "fear and trembling").

It should be noted that "freedom" is a common attribute or common-ground of the human self and the transcendent condition of human existence. But freedom takes a different form for each party. For the human individual, freedom is "possibility" as the synthesis of one's finitude and infinitude; for the transcendent condition (the eternal), freedom is "possibility" as the future, demanding the synthesis of the individual's past and future, which is the incognito of the synthesis of the temporal and the eternal. As already noted (several times), my freedom as "being able" to accomplish the synthesis of my infinitude (imagined possibilities) with my finitude (particular psychic-physical conditions) actually occurs only with the simultaneous accomplishment of the synthesis of my accumulated past with my possibilities seen as future—the freedom and courage for which do not lie inherently and necessarily within my own self but come to me and are offered to me from the transcendent condition of my existence. So I come to see that "possibility" and "freedom" are structures or functions (dynamics) that transcend me. I see that my freedom in the face of possibility-as-future is not an illusion, not a chance variation, not an individual or species peculiarity that is lost in the flow of universal necessary principles and forces. Rather, my freedom is an expression of and is supported by a universal dynamic of all reality which conditions all human existence. Again: it is from this vision and conviction that there flows the courage I need to embrace the future as mine, and to incorporate it into my actuality.

What are we to call this universal structure or dynamic which is clearly transcendent to human existence and the human individual, and yet is so amenable, tractable, companionable (*omgængelig*) with human nature that the individual self is so structured and functions in such a way as to be open to and glad to receive that dynamic as it seeks to invade and

---

36 *The Concept of Anxiety*, p. 81; (KW 8:91); SV 6:178f.; (4:361).

pervade human existence? It is such a unique dimension and experience in human existence that Kierkegaard calls it "religious" as something more than the "ethical," which refers to the innate powers of understanding and self-determination of the human individual. So, as we have seen, Kierkegaard denominates this universal dynamic and transcendent condition "the eternal." And he does not hesitate to refer to the eternal as "God." Again, we must stress that here we are considering "religion" and "God" only under the rubric of religiousness A. Therefore, we are staying within the strictures of "Kierkegaard the Humanist" and using "religious" and "God" to refer only to structures and dynamics of the human world that are universally open to human experience and description. The analysis and the description of these structures, therefore, fall under the classification of psychology and philosophy rather than theology. It is obvious that Kierkegaard uses his theologically acquired insights to inform his psychological and philosophical analyses and reflections, and yet he does not require that one shares his theology in order to share the insights of his reflections.

It is important for us to be clear about Kierkegaard's use of "the eternal" and "God" in this context, because only so can we be clear about both the ultimate significance and the definite limits of human freedom, and so be able, in the chapter on the "leap" of freedom, to describe the extremity of freedom in its relation to the eternal. In that context there will also be given a more detailed depiction of religiousness A and its experience of the eternal, as well as of the way that that experience functions in freedom as act.

Kierkegaard does not hesitate to speak of "the eternal in the human being," and to say that one cannot get rid of it, just as "one cannot get rid of ... one's self." But he also says that one can "lose the eternal and one's self."[37] So he is asserting that, while there is an inherent and indestructible capacity for relationship with the eternal in every human being, the actual relationship may be broken or "lost." As already noted, the first and essential form (or incognito) of this innate capacity for the eternal is the human sense of the possible as "future." This equivalency is also indicated when Kierkegaard says that the eternal is what "releases one from despair" and so is "one's salvation," and yet also says, "possibility is the only salvation."[38] In other words, Kierkegaard sees "possibility" not only as the amorphous nothing which evokes profound angst in the

---

37 *Sickness*, pp. 150, 195; (KW 19:17, 62); SV 15:76, 117; (11:131, 174).
38 Ibid., pp. 194n, 172; (KW 19:61, 38); SV 15:116, 96; (11:173, 151).

Freedom: The Dialectical in Temporality/Eternity

human breast (see the section on angst in the previous chapter), but, more decisively, "possibility" as the name for that dynamic in the human universe which awakens the consciousness of the demand that one choose to enact one's authentic possible (future) self within the confines of one's already-existing self, that dynamic which also enables the courage so to choose.

So, the eternal, or "God," is: *possibility*. In *Postscript*, Kierkegaard speaks briefly of "the possiblity-relation, which every existing individual has with God," as the "life's force in the ethical. ... And the possibility-relation, which is the enthusiasm of the ethicist in his joy over God, is God's freedom, which when properly understood never in all eternity becomes immanence" (immanence, in this context, being the principle of the world-historical).[39] But it is in *The Sickness unto Death* that he makes the transcendent character of "possibility" absolutely clear. He says that "sometimes the ingenuity of human imagination is sufficient to procure possibility, but finally, when we are required to *believe*, then only this helps: that for God all things are possible." The use of the phrase "for God" is Kierkegaard's way of indicating that "possibility" transcends or is something more than that very significant and perfectly legitimate realm of human imagination that he calls "infinitude." He has just been making the point that the infinite possibilities of human imagination, operating by itself and on its own, can be ultimately deceptive in ignoring human finitude and necessity. Then "in possibility all things are possible. Therefore, in possibility one can run wild," in craving and desiring, or in melancholy fantasies with their mixture of hope and fear (angst). But when one comes to realize that the wild fantasies of one's imagination are not really possible, when "a human being is brought to this extremity so that there is no possibility," when "one understands that, humanly speaking, one's destruction is the most certain thing of all," then one comes to see that "all-things-are-possible" is not a condition rooted in one's own merely individual human existence, but is a condition that, like air, surrounds and transcends one's whole being. "Possibility is the only saving thing. [Given] possibility, then the despairing person breathes again, revives again, because without possibility a human being seems unable to breathe." So everything "depends solely on whether one obtains possibility, that is, whether one will believe. ... This is the dialectic of believing. ... To understand that humanly it is

---

[39] *Postscript*, pp. 139–140; (KW 12.1:156–7); SV 9:130; (7:128–9).

one's destruction and nevertheless to believe in possibility is to believe." This is what it means to say that "for God" all things are possible.[40]

It is in this postulation of "possibility" as an ontological/phenomenological structure of reality that Kierkegaard comes to his clearest explication of what he means by the "religious" and by "God" within the context of religiousness A (as aspects of reality to which human awareness and experience are universally open). In a passage immediately following the above quotations, he finally states this thesis in one of his so-called "algebraic" formulas.

> To lack possibility means either that everything has become necessary for a person or that everything has become trivial. ... The self of the determinist cannot breathe, because it is impossible to breathe necessity exclusively, because that would utterly suffocate a person's self. ... The fatalist has no God, or what amounts to the same thing, his God is necessity. Since for God all things are possible, so God is this: all things are possible. ... To pray is also to breathe, and possibility is for the self what oxygen is for breathing. ... [So] for prayer there must be a God, [that is, there must be both] a self—*and* possibility, or a self and possibility in the pregnant sense, because God is this: that all things are possible, or, that all things are possible is: God. Only the one whose being has been so shaken that she/he has become spirit by understanding that all things are possible, only that one has anything to do with God [emphasis added].[41]

So it is clear that "God," "religious," and "prayer" are theological terms used by Kierkegaard to express or to point to the actuality and the absolute and ultimate significance of "possibility" as a universal and inescapable condition (structure, dynamic) of human existence, and to signify that human well-being (in becoming one's self) involves a positive relation with that "possibility" (which relation he calls "believing").

In the light of this explication and depiction of the "eternal," we now can see both the ultimate significance and the definite limits of human freedom in relation to possibility as "future." My "freedom" finds its enablement and its fulfilment in my willingness to "believe" in that possibility, contrary to all the dictates of sense data and rational logic. So, I "become spirit [my self] by understanding that all things are possible."

---

40 *Sickness*, p. 170ff.; (KW 19:37ff.); SV 15:94ff.; (11:150ff.).

41 Ibid, pp. 173f.; (KW 19:40); SV 15:97; (11:152f.). Both the translation (in part) and the punctuation in this quote are mine, in order to make Kierkegaard's meaning starkly clear.

And this peculiar kind of understanding I must call "believing," and I must confess that my capacity to believe comes as much from the condition-of-possibility as it does from my own willingness. And this relationship with the eternal consists of an incipient form of faith: "the contradiction between the infinite passion of inwardness and objective uncertainty."[42]

In this context we must recall a point that has been made several times above, that not only is my freedom "entangled" by the faith-relation to the eternal, but also this freedom for possibility-as-future is entangled in the fact that it is truly "my" freedom only if I choose future possibilities that are capable of being integrated with my "past," that is, with my whole, accumulated, specific, finite, existent self. Otherwise, I would be choosing to create and to become an *other* self or person. The "future" self I choose must be in harmony with, a potentiality of, within the limits of the finitude/necessity of my "past" self. So the limitation imposed on my freedom, by its need to be in a happy relation with the possibility-condition (the "eternal") that transcends it, coordinates with and requires the limitation imposed by my finitude/necessity.

However, although this point has been made repeatedly, the exact way in which "possibility" and "necessity" are *interrelated* in the "actuality" of a single, particular, human individual (*den Enkelte*) has not been defined. So before we can go on to Kierkegaard's definitive qualification of freedom as "the leap," we must explore one more, and extremely complex, characteristic of the dialectical function of freedom in its task of interrelating and harmonizing the self's past and future. And this will involve a qualitatively different examination of "possibility" and "necessity" from what was accomplished in chapter 2, where they were described primarily at the pre-conscious level in which the dialectic of freedom is not yet operative. Therefore, the question which Kierkegaard raises in *The Sickness unto Death* was not yet faced, namely, how does the necessity of the self define it more exactly (see note 50 in chapter 2)? And even the development of the concepts of possibility and necessity in the section just completed (on temporality/eternity) has assumed a simplistic identity of possibility with "the future" and of necessity with "my finitude." But now that the categories of subjectivity and subjective reflection have

---

42 *Postscript*, pp. 182; (KW 12.1:204); SV 9:170; (7:170). Climacus also gives a definition of faith in *Fragments*, but that is clearly a Christian definition of faith and will be commented on when we distinguish between Religiousness A and B [see *Fragments*, pp. 72–3; (KW 7:59); SV 6:56; (4:224)].

been brought into play (in chapter 3) and the dialectic of the temporal vis-à-vis the eternal has been seen to modify the nature of freedom, we are prepared to explore the more profound and complex nature and operation of possibility and necessity in the human self as Kierkegaard came to understand them in *Sickness*.

5

My Self: A Task
Part 3: Freedom: The Dialectical in Possibility/Necessity

INTRODUCTION

"The self is composed of infinitude and finitude. But this synthesis is a relation which, even though it is derived, relates to itself, which is freedom. The self is freedom. But *freedom is the dialectical [factor?] in the determinants possibility and necessity*" (emphasis added).[1]

What is Kierkegaard saying about freedom in this formulation? Clearly, he is rejecting the idea that human "freedom" is nothing more than the immanent, inferential, necessary working out of the inherent potentialities of one's given finitude. And, as already noted above, freedom is something more, something *other* than the openness of human imaginative infinitude to being possible. Freedom is not a determinant or quality. It is something that happens, it is an event, or as Kierkegaard likes to say, it is "sudden." It is the act of the relation (of two) relating to itself. And it is not a smooth, easy transition from one state of being to another. "All coming-into-existence [*Tilblivelse*] is a suffering [*Liden*]."[2] (We will ask "why" later.)

But in what sense is this act and event of freedom "dialectical"? In the sense that we have been exploring up to this point, namely, it occurs in-between, it consists of bringing into unity two opposing contradictory movements.

To become oneself is to become concrete. But to become concrete is neither to be [simply] finite nor to be [simply] infinite, because that which is going to be-

---

1 *Sickness*, p. 162; (KW 19:29); SV 15:87; (11:142).
2 *Fragments*, p. 91; (KW 7:74); SV 6:68; (4:237).

come concrete is precisely a synthesis. The development must therefore consist in infinitely moving away from oneself in the infinitizing of the self, and in infinitely coming back to oneself in the finitizing [of oneself]. ... So, while it is *furthest away* from itself in being most infinitized in intention and resolve, it is in the same instant *nearest* itself in accomplishing the infinitely little things of the deeds which can be accomplished this very day, this very hour, this very moment.[3]

So my freedom, my self, is defined in its very essence by my capacity to construct in my imagination my future possibilities, my possible self, but only in so far as these possibilities consist of those little definite things I am *able* to do and in actuality *do* here and now, only as they can be and *are* brought back out of pure fantasy and within the finite confines of my actual concrete self. Hence the self as *freedom* is the dialectical. The self indeed embraces its infinitude by the power of imagination and is not itself without it. The self indeed embraces its finitude with all of its unique particularity and is not itself without it. But the self is neither simply one or the other, nor the immediate undifferentiated unity of the two. The self as freedom is the conscious, deliberate, passionate, interested bringing of the two into interplay and into intentional unity. And this act is continuous and never completed. The self-as-a-whole is this concrete processive event. The self-as-freedom is the dialectical in this ongoing interplay of its infinitude and its finitude.

Kierkegaard, however, makes a similar but much more complex point in the use of another set of his favourite terms (as used in *The Sickness unto Death*). He says,

Just as finitude is the limiting aspect in relation to infinitude, so necessity in relation to possibility is that which restrains. ... The self, *kata dynamin* [potentially], is just as possible as [it is] necessary; because it is indeed itself, but it must also become itself. Inasmuch as it is itself, it is [the] necessary, and inasmuch as it must become itself, it is a possibility. Now if possibility outruns necessity, then the self runs away from itself in possibility, and it has no necessity to which it must return. ... This self becomes an abstract possiblity. ... The instant something appears to be possible, a new possibility appears, until these phantasmagoria follow so rapidly upon one another that it seems as if all things were possible, and this is exactly the final moment in which the individual himself becomes entirely a mirage. What the self now lacks is indeed actuality, and in ordinary lan-

---

3 *Sickness*, pp. 162f., 165; (KW 19:30, 32); SV 15:87, 89; (11:143, 145).

guage, too, we say that a human-being has become unreal. However, closer scrutiny reveals that what one actually lacks is necessity. The case is not as philosophers explain: that necessity is the unity of possibility and actuality—no, actuality is the unity of possibility and necessity. When a self runs wild in possibility, ... what is missing is the genuine ability to obey, to submit to the necessity in one's self, to what may be called one's boundary [limitation]. Therefore, the tragedy is not that such a self did not amount to something in the world; no, the tragedy is that one did not become aware of oneself, aware that the self one is is a very definite something and thus the necessary.[4]

So, again we conclude, the self-as-freedom is the dialectical in this ongoing interplay and intentional unification of the self's possibility and its necessity.

This passage has been quoted at length, however (and we shall return to it repeatedly throughout the next one hundred pages), because it raises a major issue in the interpretation of Kierkegaard which must be faced and resolved before we can come to final clarification of what "freedom" exactly *is*, that is, what Kierkegaard means by the "leap." The issue can be posed by asking Kierkegaard the following question: what is the relation of "possibility" to "necessity" in the process of possibility's coming-into-existence, in its becoming actuality? It seems that we get two different answers from the "editorial" Kierkegaard.[5] As Climacus (*Fragments*), he says that no possibility, by becoming actual, ever becomes necessary. So he rejects the (Hegelian) assertion that "necessity is the unity [*Eenhed*] of possibility and actuality."[6] As Anti-Climacus (*Sickness*), as we have just seen above, he says that what the infinitude of possibility really lacks and needs is precisely necessity. And so he comes to a conclusion not arrived at by Climacus, that (contra Hegel) "actuality is the unity of possibility and necessity."

Obviously, these are two very different statements, but do they contradict each other? What has happened between *Fragments* and *Sickness*? This problem in interpretation has been discussed in the secondary literature for at least the last thirty years. A few years ago an excellent summary of this discussion and the diverse answers proposed was given by

---

4 Ibid., pp. 168–170; (KW 19:35f.); SV 15:93f.; (11:148f.).
5 Kierkegaard admits to having "edited" (*Udgivet*) the works of Climacus and of Anti-Climacus.
6 *Fragments*, pp. 91f.; (KW 7:74); SV 6:68; (4:237f.).

Poul Lübcke, along with his own alternative proposal.[7] We agree with Lübcke that while there is an obvious shift in terminology, the different uses of "possibility" and "necessity" can be harmonized by interpreting them in the context of logical categories. His use of the categories of modal logic is very helpful and suggestive, but here some broader perspectives of contemporary logic will be used in order to interpret the significance of Kierkegaard's extension of the meaning of "possibility" so as to apply it to the "eternal," and his inclusion of "necessity" as an integral factor in human existential actuality while rejecting Hegel's assertion that "necessity is the unity of possibility and actuality."

To make these points adequately requires some knowledge of Kierkegaard's own familiarity with logic (Aristotelian, Kantian, Hegelian, and that of his contemporaries), and also requires reference to recent developments in the field of logic during the nineteenth and twentieth centuries. So before this direct application of logical principles can be made to Kierkegaard's use of the modal categories "possibility" and "necessity," it will be helpful to see briefly how these categories came to his attention in his studies, and then to survey extensively the development of his own exposition of the concept "possibility" from *Either/Or* through *The Sickness unto Death*. Only then can we understand what happened to his concept "necessity" in this development.

In order to clarify the character of freedom by exploring it as "the dialectical [factor] in the determinants possibility and necessity," it must, first of all, be noted that these determinants are always discussed by Kierkegaard (from *Fragments* on) in relation to a third one: actuality (*Virkelighed*). From early in his university days (eleven years altogether!), Kierkegaard's mind seemed to have an instinctive recognition of those terms and concepts which he would use later for the elucidation of his own view of things, and would seize them and store them away for future reference. So while listening to H. L. Martensen lecture during the

---

[7] Poul Lübcke, "Modalität und Zeit bei Kierkegaard und Heidegger," pp. 114–34. The treatments of the problem summarized by him are those of J. Sløk, *Die Anthropologie Kierkegaards*, p. 36; M. Theunissen, *Der Begriff Ernst bei Søren Kierkegaard*, p. 49; J. Holl, *Kierkegaards Konzeption des Selbst*, p. 126. A later treatment can be found in Alastair Hannay, *Kierkegaard*, p. 143. Sløk says there is no contradiction in terminology, but Kierkegaard is writing from different perspectives and toward different purposes. Theunissen finds a substantive change and contradiction, accountable by a development in Kierkegaard's thinking. Holl sees the differences as a sign of structural difficulty in Kierkegaard's works due to the operation, at different times, of conflicting modes of thought: dualism, subjective monism, objective monism. Hannay sees it as a critical shift (in Kierkegaard's thinking) from regarding necessity as a "logical constraint" to regarding it as a "situational" limitation on free choice.

winter semester of 1838–39 on "the history of the newer philosophies from Kant to Hegel," he made in his notes a very careful table of Kant's twelve categories in which Martensen (apparently) simplified those of modality as: possibility, actuality, necessity. (Martensen also seems to have given Kant's famous dictum in reverse; Kierkegaard quotes it as: "intuition without concept is empty, concept without intuition is blind," whereas Kant says, "Gedanken ohne Inhalt sind leer, Anschauungen ohne Begriffe sind blind.")

He also heard and noted (with italics) this condensed summary of Hegel: "All opposites merge in a dialectically mediated unity, which is *actuality*. Thus one can understand Hegel's statement that '*Actuality is the rational*,' so that immediacy in and for itself is not the rational, nor is everything that happens, because everything that happens does not have the essential in it. Actuality is simply the marriage of the inner with the outer, so that actuality is the substantial, substance, it is negation of the negation, it is necessity, wherein all the determinants of finitude are contained."[8]

That such statements as these supplied Kierkegaard with much food for thought is evident in his reaction to the famous lectures of Schelling in Berlin in the autumn of 1841 (where he had fled after breaking his engagement with Regine). He tells his journal:

I am so happy to have heard Schelling's second lecture—indescribably. ... The embryonic child of thought leapt for joy within me as in Elizabeth, when he mentioned the word "actuality" in connection with the relation of philosophy to actuality. ... This one word recalled all my philosophical pains and sufferings.

In the notes he took on this lecture, he records Schelling as saying:

Everything actual is double sided: *quid sit* (what it is), *quod sit* (that it is). Therefore philosophy can stand in a double relation to it; one can have a concept without knowledge [*Erkjendelse*] (a concept is expressed by *quid sit*, but from that it does not follow that I know: *quod sit*), but not knowledge without the concept.[9]

---

8 *Papirer*, vol. XII, p. 286 on Kant; p. 325 on Hegel. Kant's dictum is found in his *Gesammelte Schriften* (Berlin: Druck und Verlag von Georg Reimer, 1911), vol. IV, *Kritik der reinen Vernumft* (1st ed.), p. 48. (i.e., in his Transcendental Logic, Introduction, Section I: Of Logic in General). I first heard it, in a graduate philosophy seminar, in this form: Concepts without percepts are empty; percepts without concepts are blind.

9 *Journals*, 5535; III A 179; the quote from the notes is from *Papirer* XIII, pp. 254f.

However, his enchantment with Schelling soon waned. He quit attending the lectures and turned to the task of finishing his feverish writing of *Either/Or.* Here he expresses his disappointment by saying, "What the philosophers say about actuality is often as disappointing as a sign you see in a shop window, which reads: Pressing Done Here. If you brought your clothes to be pressed, you would be fooled; for the sign is simply for sale."[10] So the problem of how actuality is related to possibility and necessity had certainly been planted in his mind as a major issue for him, but he had not found a resolution as yet. So, in *Either/Or* he does not tackle the problem, but is content to play with the dialectic of possible/actual in relation to Marie Beaumarchais's broken engagement. But in that connection he does make the pregnant assertion, "The actual is higher than the possible," and this becomes a central conviction and theme throughout his authorship.[11]

The year after finishing *Either/Or* (i.e. 1843), however, he began reading Tennemann's history of philosophy, some books by the German philosopher Friedrich Adolf Trendelenburg on Aristotle and logic, and some of Aristotle's own writings. He becomes excited about Aristotle's concept of κινησις (*kinesis*) as descriptive of the transition from possibility to actuality, because he understands it to be a movement and "change" (Tennemann's translation) which is not merely logical or rational. So he likes Tennemann's assertion that "κινησις is difficult to define because it belongs neither to possibility nor to actuality, is more than possibility and less than actuality."[12] Behind this concept of κινησις is Aristotle's insistence on an absolute distinction between potentiality and actuality, which he accused the Megarians of denying. William and Martha Kneale comment, "In spite of its strangeness, this thesis is natural enough among Eleatics, since, as Aristotle goes on to say, it is equivalent in effect to a denial of motion or change of any kind. But if it were correct, the modal words 'possible' and 'necessary' would both alike be superfluous," and amount to a denial of the "Aristotelian theory of real potentiality. ... To Aristotle it would appear to be a denial of the distinction between the possible and the actual."[13] Although Kierkegaard nowhere comments on this particular point in Aristotle, it is clearly his intuition that Aristotle's κινησις is qualitatively different from Hegel's

10 *Either/Or*, 1:31; (KW 3:32); SV 2:34; (1:16).
11 Ibid., 1:178f.; (KW 3:180); SV 2:167; (1:157).
12 *Journals*, 258; IV C 47; 259; IV C 48; 260; IV C 80; 261; IV C 87.
13 William and Martha Kneale, *The Development of Logic*, p. 117.

"mediation" (*Vermittlung*), and that it makes room for that pause, break, gap between possibility and actuality where the leap of freedom takes place, where the human being becomes unique, particular, choosing, responsible, believing self.

Kierkegaard was significantly helped in his development of an alternative to Hegel's view of actuality by his reading Trendelenburg. As he was reading Tennemann, he also began early in 1843 to read Trendelenburg's *Erläuterungen zu den Elementen der aristotelischen Logic*, and in January of 1844 (while writing *Fragments* and *Concept of Anxiety*) he began reading Trendelenburg's chief work *Logische Untersuchungen* (*Logical Investigations*). Kierkegaard must have been excited when he read, in the very first chapter of his first edition of the latter book, "No category touches more deeply the essence of thinking than modality, according to which judgment [*Urteile*] is presented as the judgment of actuality, possibility, and necessity." And later in the book he found a whole chapter on "*Die modalen Kategorien*" (ch. XI of first edition), in which, among many other ideas, he would run across Trendelenburg's distinction between "the actuality of the possible" and "the possibility of the actual." The former has to do with "*what* is possible," the latter with "*how* something is possible," the former with the "result," the latter with the "process." And the latter he calls "the inner possibility," which is precisely what Kierkegaard struggles to analyse and clarify.[14] But, as will be shown later, Kierkegaard finally describes possibility (in *Sickness*) in very different terms from those used by Trendelenburg.

A year later (1845) while he is writing *Postscript*, Kierkegaard writes in a background note for that book, "Very likely what our age needs most to illuminate the relationship between logic and ontology is an examination of the concepts: possibility, actuality and necessity. ... Good comments are to be found in Trendelenburg's *Logische Untersuchungen*."[15] One would think that Kierkegaard would have attempted this examination of these concepts and their implications for the relation of logic and ontology in *Postscript*, and perhaps would have used directly those "good comments" from Trendelenburg. But, as will be shown below, he does not. For one thing, Kierkegaard is not ready to make this

---

14 A. Trendelenburg, *Logische Untersuchungen* (1st ed. Berlin 1840; 3rd ed. Leipzig: Verlag von S. Hirzel, 1870), 3rd ed., 1:27, 2:191. In the 2nd ed. (1862) and the 3rd ed. (1870), Trendelenburg added three chapters: a first on "Logic and metaphysics as fundamental science," a middle one on "Purpose (*Zweck*) and Will" which would have interested Kierkegaard, and a final one on "Idealism and Realism."

15 *Journals*, 199; VI B 54:21.

clarification of the concepts, but neither is he inclined to take over perspectives of others unchanged; rather, he borrows terms and concepts, redefines them, and puts them together in new combinations in order to explore and to depict his own unique vision of human, existential actuality.

As already noted, he complains that Trendelenburg draws most of his examples from mathematics and the natural sciences and almost none from ethics.[16] So he must have been greatly dissatisfied with Trendelenburg's "reconciliation of freedom and necessity" by using Aristotle's concept of first and final cause (God) as determinative of the efficient cause (human will): "Creative freedom does not operate groundless out of itself; but in service and as a tool of a divine purpose, freedom is merged, as it were, with necessity [*geht die Freiheit wie in die Notwendigkeit auf*] and can be expressed in terms of external coercion: 'I can do nothing else' [Luther]. One's own development is self-limitation. And the fixed limitation is necessity."[17] In fact, Kierkegaard may have this passage in mind (although he is directly criticizing a sermon of Luther) when he writes in his journal (of 1850), "If I step forth witnessing as Luther himself did, witnessing against the pope, this is voluntary; he could, indeed, have refrained from doing it. To declare that he could not do otherwise is quite correct, but it is a sham if he in this way makes the prompting of the spirit identical with external necessity."[18]

Later Trendelenburg adds (in the second edition) a chapter on "Purpose [*Zweck*] and Will" to his earlier chapters on "Purpose" and "The Categories [derived] from Purpose," because his first treatment made human existence sound, he says, like a machine manipulated by "the finger of God." But even in his new analysis of human will, and even with his acknowledgment that "First of all with the concept of purpose in the living being does the genuine sense of the self make its appearance," he still describes human will as just a more complicated example of the "inner purpose" that operates in the chemical formation of crystals, the flow of water down hill, the assimilation of inorganic matter by plants, the instincts of animals, and the operation of a machine to accomplish a task—all set in motion by the First Cause and impelled to keep moving by the pull of the Final Cause.[19] This is hardly a descrip-

---

16 Ibid., 2352; V C 12 (1844).
17 Trendelenburg, *Logische Untersuchungen*, 3rd ed., 2:209.
18 *Journals*, 4950; X³ A 43.
19 Trendelenburg, *Logische Untersuchungen*, 3rd ed., 2:95–97.

tion of "necessity" in relation to human freedom as found in *The Sickness unto Death*, or of the sovereignty of God's love in all of Kierkegaard's writings, where he mounts a persistent attack on the concept of divine determinism. So, although Kierkegaard did not see this second edition, and in spite of his lavish praise of Trendelenburg for the help he did receive from him, Kierkegaard still had to find his own formulation of the nature of possibility and necessity, and their relation to actuality, because, he concludes, "Trendelenburg does not seem to be at all aware of the leap."[20]

We turn, therefore, to an extensive and detailed analysis of his formulation of the dialectic of possibility and necessity, from its first expression in *Philosophical Fragments* to its final form in *The Sickness unto Death*. After a few introductory remarks, this analysis will progress through the following topics on possibility: (1) Possibility as Future in *Fragments* and *The Concept of Anxiety*; (2) The New Perspective on Possibility in *Postscript*; (3) Possibility in *The Sickness unto Death*; then the following topics on necessity: (1) Necessity in *Either/Or*, *Fragments* and *Postscript*; (2) Change in the Concept of Necessity; (3) New Formulation of Necessity in *Sickness*; (4) Resolution of the Conflict between *Fragments* and *Sickness*.

MAJOR FORMULATIONS ON POSSIBILITY BY KIERKEGAARD

It must first of all be noted that the concept "possibility" was more central to Kierkegaard's concerns than the concept "necessity." Therefore, in all his writings from *Fragments* to *Sickness* he spends much more time analysing the nature of possibility than that of necessity. There is also a continuity in his treatment of possibility, even though there are significant elaborations and additions in *Postscript* and *Sickness*. On the other hand, in *Sickness* a totally new and positive concept of necessity emerges, and a more complex and lengthy analysis will be required to understand this very important shift in Kierkegaard's thinking.

From the university lectures of Martensen and from his reading of Tennemann and Trendelenburg, Kierkegaard certainly knew that "possibility" and "necessity" have been major points of discussion and definition for logicians since Aristotle. And it was just this discussion that convinced him that the "necessity" of speculative (Hegelian) logic and of

20 *Journals*, 2341; V A 74 (1844).

formal deductive (mathematical) logic lies in a world apart from the event of the coming-into-existence of "possibility" by human choice. However, in the new Aristotelianism which Trendelenburg formulated (in mathematical, scientific terms) in opposition to Hegelian philosophy, Kierkegaard found stimulus for his own thinking in Trendelenburg's idea of an "inner possibility" and his "positive concept" of necessity.

1 Possibility as "Future" in Fragments *and* The Concept of Anxiety

Briefly but clearly, Kerkegaard first makes his initial insight, the association of the possible with the future, in *Fragments*. He is making the point that the change involved in anything coming-into-existence is a change from possibility to actuality, and that "All coming-into-existence [*Tilblivelse*] occurs in [*ved*] freedom, not of [*af*] necessity." In this connection he takes Aristotle to task for working with two meanings of "possible" in the attempt to clarify the relation of "possible" and "necessary."[21] Aristotle laid the foundation for formal modal logic by asserting that "possible" may be defined in terms of "necessary" simply with the help of negation. Hence in our contemporary logic, to say that a certain proposition is "possible" is simply an abbreviation for saying that it is "not-necessarily-not."[22] Or as William and Martha Kneale put it, "possible" simply means "not impossible," or "it is not necessary that-not-P."[23] Aristotle, however, complicated and confused this simple definition by also insisting "that 'It is possible that-P' and 'It is contingent that-P' mutually entail each other." In other words, when we say something is "possible," we are not only asserting rational coherence of statements but also indicating the involvement and operation of contingent conditions. The Kneales agree with Kierkegaard that this is a confusing and contradictory definition of "possible," but for opposite reasons. They say that this confusion derived from Aristotle's metaphysical assumption that "the distinction between the necessary and the impossible on the one hand and the merely factual on the other is of fundamental importance," and thus he ended up with "an unnecessarily difficult definition of possibility." The Kneales insist that the only proper meaning of "possible" is the formal logical one: "not impossible," and this means that the "neces-

21 *Philosophical Fragments*, pp. 92f.; (KW 7:74f.); SV 6:68f.; (4:237f.).
22 W.H. Newton-Smith, *Logic: An Introductory Course*, pp. 205f.
23 For a full analysis of Aristotle's formulations, see William and Martha Kneale, *The Development of Logic*, pp. 82-86. Following quotations are from these pages unless otherwise noted.

sary" is also "possible," and the "possible" is "necessary." And so they urge that we use the term "contingent" to designate Aristotle's other concept of "possible" as the "neither impossible nor necessary."

Kierkegaard, on the other hand, suggests just the opposite procedure for correcting Aristotle. He asserts that the latter's "mistake is to begin with the thesis that everything necessary is possible." But, Kierkegaard insists, "the possible cannot be predicated of the necessary," because the possible is oriented toward becoming actuality. Becoming actual is "the change of coming-into-existence [*Tilblivelse*]," and human "existence" includes the contingent and fortuitous, the occasional, because it is a synthesis of the infinite and the finite. In other words, the *kind* of "possibility" which Kierkegaard chooses as definitive is closer to Aristotle's second definition of it as having to do with the "contingent" than to the Kneales' choice of the first definition as having to do with the "necessary". As we have noted several times, the contingent or fortuitous (*tilfældig*) dimension of human existence is a ruling category throughout Kierkegaard's authorship. And this dimension was shown (from *Either/ Or*) to provide the "occasion" (*Anledning*) apart from which "nothing at all happens." This does not mean that the possible *is* the contingent (as will be shown at length from materials in *Sickness*), but human possibility "exists" only in relation to the contingent occasions of human finitude.

In other words, for Kierkegaard (here in *Fragments*) the authentically "possible" has nothing to do with what is metaphysically, logically, scientifically, or historically "necessary." Therefore, "the doctrine of true and false propositions (Epicurus) confuses the issue here, since it reflects on essence, not on being, with the result that nothing is achieved along that path with regard to defining the *future*" (emphasis added). The possible, as a characteristic of human existence, is oriented toward the *future*, toward coming-into-existence, and "All coming into existence occurs in [*ved*] freedom, not of [*af*] necessity." So, he concludes, "The actual [of human existence] is no more necessary than the possible."[24] Obviously, "necessity" is here conceived strictly in terms of that necessity involved in logical identity, natural law, or historical causation, and so Kierkegaard cannot allow *this* "necessity" to qualify *this* "possibility" in any way (a view which is radically modified in *The Sickness unto Death*, when another kind of "necessity" is considered).

In *The Concept of Anxiety* (published as a companion to *Fragments*), there is a much more thorough elaboration of this equation of the pos-

24 *Philosophical Fragments*, pp. 92f.; (KW 7:74f.); SV 6:68f.; (4:237f.).

sible with the future (in his disquisition on "time" and "temporality" at the beginning of chapter III). We need not summarize this material again (see section on Kierkegaard's concept of time in chapter 4), but simply emphasize that Kierkegaard's treatment of "possibility" (in *Fragments* and *Anxiety*) manifests a rigid insistence that the only "possibility" he is interested in is that which qualifies, is a determinant of, human existence. Therefore, the "possible" must come to terms with the contingent, fortuitous location of an individual in a certain "space," in a complex set of "situations" and "occasions," and with the fact that the individual *either* may drift with the currents of these situations and allow oneself to be shaped (determined) by them, *or* may become a "freely acting cause" in their midst by becoming conscious of alternative ways in which one's "infinite possibility" may relate to these contingent conditions in an indeterminate future, thus "being able" (free) to choose who (the self) one is to "become" and be responsible for. The opposition between this contingent and fortuitous character of one's finitude and the creative possibilities of one's infinitude fills one with angst in the "pause" before the "leap" by which alone the possible becomes actual (this "opposition" is also revised and restated in *Sickness*, as will be shown below).

(Kierkegaard makes another important point about possibility in *Fragments* when he says, "All coming-into-existence is a *suffering*," because "the possible ... manifests itself as nothing in the moment it becomes actual, because possibility is *annihilated* by [becoming] actuality.[25]" But since this point is picked up and modified in *Sickness*, it will be summarized in that context below.)

However, during the year following the publication of these companion books, Kierkegaard continued to read more of Trendelenburg and Aristotle, and he was forced to face some new questions about "possibility" as he came to write his book on "logical problems," *Concluding Unscientific Postscript*.

2 *New Perspective in* Postscript

A primary question for which Kierkegaard seeks an answer in *Postscript* is this: *how* does the transition from possibility to actuality take place? It is not enough just to answer: "in freedom." What actually goes on in the thinking and consciousness of a human being just before the "leap"? Both contingent possibility and logical possibility are still merely "possi-

25 Ibid., p. 91; (KW 7:74); SV 6:68; (4:237).

ble." Kierkegaard's readings in logic have shown him that simply to say something is "possible" does not distinguish it qualitatively from the products of abstractive thinking in the sciences, or the products of pure deductive thinking in logic. As noted above (see section on objective reflection in chapter 3), he recognizes that all thinking produces nothing but possibilities by abstraction, either before or after actuality, and so "all knowledge about reality is possibility." Even the attempt to communicate one's own selfhood or to grasp that of another is to traffic in possibilities.

So, here in *Postscript*, he has come to admit, implicitly at least, two kinds of possibility. There are the abstract generalities of science and philosophy which, as possibilities, are universally true, and are rationally coherent, and thus "necessary." Then there are the particular possibilities of unique particular individuals which become real not by the individual's thinking them or even by intending to realize them but only by doing them, so that they lose their character as "possible" and become "actual." In the latter case, no matter how fully and exactly the possibilities are conceived, they are still only "conceived reality" and therefore possibility. But, for Kierkegaard, there is one crucial difference between these two kinds of possibility. For science and philosophy (as metaphysics), the system of exactly and coherently *conceived* realities is "higher" than the world of actual particularities because the actual is simply there to be known, to be caught in conceived generalities (possibilities), and the particular example is ephemeral while the generality is universal and always true. But for the individual human being, the conceived possibility is not an end in itself but a goal to be actualized in one's own actuality; so the actual is "higher" than the possible.[26]

This second kind of possibility, as that of the particular, human, existing individual, takes on, therefore, a peculiar quality in its being lower than the actuality of the concrete self. This possibility must serve the actuality of the concrete self. The only relevant, and in a sense real, possibilities are those that are already "present" as potentialities in the concrete self in its particular time and place (situation) (see "Interlude" in *Fragments*). So the first prerequisite for the transition from this possibility into its actuality is that the concrete self become *conscious* of itself (described in chapter 3 in the section "Consciousness of My Self"). For this task, Kierkegaard says, the self must employ another kind of thinking which he calls "subjective reflection," the only kind of knowing and

---

26 *Postscript*, pp. 284–5; (KW 12.1:320-1); SV 10:26; (7:275–6).

understanding that does not turn its object into mere possibility (see section in chapter 3).

In *Postscript*, therefore, Kierkegaard picks up from where he left off in *Fragments* and *Anxiety* but takes his analysis of possibility two steps further. As in those two works, here also he says that "the transition from possibility to actuality is ... a κίνησις, a movement [change]." And this movement in human existence (as opposed to the movement in logic) involves *time*. "This cannot be expressed or understood in the language of abstraction; for in the sphere of the abstract, movement cannot have assigned to it either time or space which presuppose movement or are presupposed by it. Here then there is a pause and a leap. ... When existence gives to movement *time*, ... the leap manifests itself in the only way it can: either that it must come, or that it has been" (emphasis added).[27] Therefore, "where everything is in-process-of-becoming [*i Vorden*], ... where *eternity* is related as *futurity* to the one-in-process-of-becoming [*den Vordende*], there the absolute disjunction belongs. When I put eternity and becoming together, I do not get rest, but futurity."[28] So in *Postscript*, Kierkegaard clearly assumes that that "possibility" which is a determinant of human existence is constituent to the fact that human being as such is temporal, oriented toward one's future, paused before a breach (*Brud*) demanding a leap (*Spring*) as the only way to bring possibility into actuality.

However, as just noted, *Postscript* does not aim to explore this temporal character of human possibility. Rather, it emphasizes that "the possible" is still merely *possible*. Or in Aristotelian terms, while the possible is certainly "not impossible," yet "neither is it necessary," and so it is "contingent." But contingent upon *what*? It is in pursuing this question that Kierkegaard (Climacus) takes his analysis of possibility two steps further in *Postscript*: (1) as just noted, the precondition for the leap of freedom (by which possibility becomes actuality) is "subjectivity," or "consciousness of self"; but (2) true subjectivity (i.e., becoming "a relation which relates to itself") requires a relating to the "eternal" (described briefly above in section on "Freedom and the Eternal"). Since the latter point will be explored further in the next chapter, there is just one more point to be made about *Postscript*'s depiction of how a human being comes to subjectivity—which will serve as a transition to an analysis of how possibility is treated in *The Sickness unto Death*.

---

27 Ibid., p. 306; (KW 12.1:342); SV 10:46; (7:296–7).
28 Ibid., p. 272; (KW 12.1:307); SV 10:14; (7:263).

We have already seen that, for Kierkegaard, the key to the attainment of subjectivity or consciousness of self is passional "inwardness" (*Inderlighed* and *Inderliggjørelse*). But in this connection he uses some other language (concerning how one turns "inward") which (perhaps) he has not thought through very clearly but which reappears in *Sickness* with great clarity. As previously noted, "passion" is a prime requisite for achieving the unity of one's finitude and infinitude in the self as the "positive third." Only in passionate inwardness is one able to overcome the "tremendous contradiction" which is inherent in being an existing individual and in becoming a self. "Objective reflection" achieves this unity only in abstraction, only in idea, not in the actuality of the "qualitative disjunction" of human existence. But in describing how "passion" achieves this unity of self-consciousness, Kierkegaard uses some other terms that lead to confusion. He says, "In order to be a subjective thinker, there is required imagination [*Phantasie*], feeling, dialectic of existence-inwardness with passion. But first and last passion, because it is impossible, while existing, to think about existence without coming [at it] with passion, because this matter of existing is an immense contradiction, which the subjective thinker has not to abstract from but to remain in."[29]

His addition of imagination and feeling to passion, as the requisites of "subjective thinking," is very problematic in light of the clear definition of the role of imagination in the exploration of possibility according to *Sickness*. This addition is not an isolated, offhand reference, because in the context of the above quotation, he bemoans several times the fact that the scientific frame of mind leaves behind "the stages of imagination and feeling," and so "turns more and more away from a primitive impression of existence." He argues that "in existence all factors are present simultaneously. In respect to existence, thinking is not higher than imagination and feeling, but coordinate." So, while "the subjective thinker ... has the intellectual passion to hold firm the qualitative disjunction" (that belongs to existence), still "the subjective thinker in addition has aesthetic passion and ethical passion, by which concretion is acquired." This confluence and coordination of all the dimensions of a human being means that "the subjective thinker is aesthetic enough to give his life aesthetic content, ethical enough to regulate it, dialectical enough in thinking to master it."[30]

29 Ibid., pp. 312–13; (KW 12.1:350); SV 10:87–8; (7:303).
30 Ibid., in order: pp. 307–8, 310, 313, 314; (KW 12.1:344–5, 346–7, 350, 351); SV 10:46–7, 48–9, 52; (7:298–9, 300–1, 304).

It would appear that, here in *Postscript*, Kierkegaard is using "imagination" to refer to that "aesthetic feeling" (Kant? Schleiermacher?) by which one sinks back and down below the level of conceptual analysis and formation to a level of consciousness where one is sensitive to a "primitive impression" of one's life which gives that life "aesthetic content." So imagination, in this sense, is not primarily concerned with future, unrealized possibility. Yet, in a much earlier passage in *Postscript*, Kierkegaard says that "in passion" the two sides of human existential being are held together: "In passion the existing subject is infinitized in the eternity of imagination, and yet at the same time is most specifically himself [*sig selv*]."[31] In the latter usage of "imagination," he is anticipating the very clear and restricted meaning given to it two years later in *Sickness*.

3 Possibility in The Sickness unto Death

In *Sickness* (which this study takes as normative for Kierkegaard's thought), the author appears to be primarily interested in analysing one particular—indeed, *the*—crucial form of human "sickness": despair, the failure of a human being to become self. But in every section of the book, there is either stated explicitly or suggested implicitly the "formula" for the complete eradication of this sickness unto death, the prescription for health unto life. The very opening section concludes with it: "in relating to itself, and in willing to be itself, the self rests transparently in the power that established it." So again, as in *Postscript*, Kierkegaard is concerned to analyse and to describe, even more closely, that transition, that event in and by which the task faced by every human individual is accomplished: to become one's self, by bringing one's possible self into actuality.

As in *Fragments*, the transition is a movement of freedom; indeed, "the self is freedom."[32] And the new perspective of *Postscript* is also carried forward. He speaks of that despair that comes from "not willing to be oneself," and says that such a one has "no infinite consciousness of the self," and so fails to make "a total break with immediacy" because "one does not have the self-reflection or ethical reflection for that." Rather, such a one "turns away completely from the inward [*ind efter*] way along which one should have advanced in order truly to become a self"; one

---

31 Ibid., p. 176; (KW 12.1:197); SV 9:164; (7:164).
32 *Sickness*, p. 162; (KW 19:29); SV 15:87; (11:142).

fails to use and thus loses "the little bit of passion, feeling, imagination, the little bit of inwardness [*Inderlighed*] one had."[33]

However, in *Sickness* a significant new step is taken in its more developed concept of imagination and the role it plays in relation to possibility. As a result, there emerges a more closely defined concept of possibility, and (as will be shown later in this chapter) a radical shift in the type and scope of necessity (in comparison with the view in *Fragments*).

As noted above, imagination in *Postscript* is primarily associated with that kind of "feeling" which is a passionate, personal, interested inwardness. This passionate inwardness, as a form of thinking or reflection, enables one to grasp one's own selfhood with an intuitive immediacy which avoids the mode of abstraction that is characteristic of all other thinking. The result is a self-consciousness in which the opposition and disjunction of thought and being, of objective and subjective, are overcome in the unification of thought-passion, aesthetic passion, and ethical passion. This "subjectivity" is truth because in it the individual chooses to be what one already is (potentially) in one's true self.

To "become" one's self, however, involves one in *time*, in facing the future, in enacting one's "possibility" not simply as a potentiality already present in one's current actuality (not "possibility" merely as the "not impossible"), but also as one's infinite "possibility" in relation to a future, indeterminate, contingent, finite, variable (the "neither impossible nor necessary"). This latter "possibility" holds the promise, therefore, of a qualitative change in one's actuality, which also opens up new ranges of possibilities. If, as in *Postscript*, this latter possibility of the unique, particular individual (*den Enkelte*) is "lower" than one's actuality, in the sense that its ultimate significance does not lie in its being possible but in its becoming actual (its coming-into-existence), then how does the individual explore and envision one's own peculiar possibility? By the time he writes *Sickness*, Kierkegaard sees that it is not adequate to answer this question simply with: through subjectivity or self-consciousness. *Before* the leap of choosing a particular future possibility, another step is required. And Kierkegaard defines this step in an expanded role of the imagination in which imagination is distinguished from "feeling."

He gives a general definition or characterization of imagination by saying that it "is the medium for the process-of-infinitizing [*Uendeliggjørende*]." As such, it is a mode of thinking or reflection, which takes as

---

[33] Ibid., pp. 184, 188, 189, 192; (KW 19:50, 55f., 59); SV 15:106, 111, 114; (11:162f., 167f., 171).

its task the exploration of *anything* in its ideality, unrestricted by consideration of finite conditions or particularity. So, "imagination is infinitizing reflection." As such, "it is not [just] any capacity, as the other capacities, ... it is the capacity *instar omnium* [equivalent to all—in importance]." So Kierkegaard shows how it can be applied to any capacity such as feeling, thinking, willing, and he asserts (in accord with J.G. Fichte) that "even in relation to knowledge, imagination is the source of the categories." So "imagination is the possibility of any and all reflection."[34]

Kierkegaard does not attempt to explain how imagination differs from other types of reflection, or how it relates to his distinction (in *Postscript*) between objective and subjective reflection. His primary concern in *Sickness* is not the formulation of a general theory of imagination but a description of how it operates in the process of an individual's coming-into-existence as self.

---

34 Ibid., pp. 163f.; (KW 19:30f.); SV 15:88f.; (11:144f.). Recently much attention has been given to Kierkegaard's concept of imagination. Two works especially have come to my attention. David J. Gouwens published *Kierkegaard's Dialectic of the Imagination* in 1989. Although insightful on many issues, it does not relate imagination to the nature of the leap and of will, which are the special concerns of this present treatment of the self. Directly relevant to my themes is the later work of M. Jaimie Ferreira, *Transforming Vision* (1991), which unfortunately was published after the completion of this present work. There is much in Ferreira's treatment with which my own is in deep accord; for example, her exposition of the "leap" as assuming both continuity and discontinuity, both activity and passivity; also her argument that a *purely* volitionalist interpretation of Kierkegaard's concept of "will" is mistaken (although I give different reasons). She also provides an extensive analysis of the ways in which imagination and the passion of the leap are related in Kierkegaard's thought—an aspect which I occasionally refer to in passing but do not explore in detail.

There is, however, one emphasis in her interpretation of imagination (in Kierkegaard) that makes me uneasy and that I would like to explore with her. Ferreira says: "the transforming choice [of infinitizing the self] ... is constituted by [imaginative exploration]," so "it is imaginative vision, rather than deliberate decision, which is said to effect change" (p.83); "deliberate decision can be said to play a role in the acquisition of faith ... but what occurs at the moment of acceptance is not a volition but rather a shift in perspective, an engagement or surrender, which is an achievement of imagination" (p.126). Kierkegaard has a much more complex view of "willing" and therefore of "decision" than Ferreira seems to recognize. So when he says that the Socratic definition of sin as ignorance "lacks a dialectical determinant appropriate to the transition from having understood something to doing it," Kierkegaard does not say that what is lacking is imagination but rather "willing," and then proceeds to give a very subtle and complex analysis of the failure of willing as self-deception (*Sickness*, KW 19:93ff.). Imagination plays a decisive role in the transition, but it is prior to the leap and interacts with other elements of the self, and this interaction as a whole makes the leap.

The self, as it is posited or established (*er sat*), both is and is not (as in *Fragments*). "Every moment that a self exists, it is in a process-of-becoming [*i Vorden*], for the self *kata dynamin* [in potentiality] does not actually exist, is simply that which ought to come-into-existence [*blive til*]." "Insofar as it [the self] must become itself, it is a possibility." And it is precisely the function of imagination to explore and to depict this possibility. "Inasmuch as the self, as a synthesis of finitude and infinitude, is established, is *kata dynamin*, in order to become [itself], it reflects in the medium of imagination, and thereby the infinite possibility appears [or, is manifested]." "The self is reflection, and imagination is reflection, is the self's re-presentation [*Gjengivelse*] of the self, which is the self's possibility. Imagination is the possibility of all reflection; and the intensity of this medium is the possibility of the intensity of the self."[35] (One must keep in mind that, in his usage of "reflection" [*Reflexion*], Kierkegaard often plays on its dual meaning: reproduction of an image, or consideration of or thinking about an idea.)

So the product of this peculiar kind of reflection called "imagination" is a picture or rendition, to one's conscious self, of one's self in its "infinite possibility." To explain what he means by this kind of "possibility," Kierkegaard uses some other language. He says that this "infinite self is really only the most abstract form, the most abstract possibility of the self," and that this "infinite form" of the self is only "the negative self" or the "hypothetical self." As we shall see presently, this product of the imagination can be and often is misused by the individual in the attempt to become one's self. Nevertheless, this depiction of the infinite self has an indispensable and positive role to play in this attempt. By means of this kind of self-consciousness, "with this certain degree of reflection begins the act of discrimination wherein the self becomes aware of itself as essentially distinct from the environment and external-world [*Udvortesheden*] and [their] influence upon it. ... Now the self, with a certain degree of reflection, is willing to take on the self." It gains "a dim idea that there may even be something eternal in the self." So this "consciousness of a self that is won by infinite abstraction from every externality" produces a "naked abstract self which, compared with immediacy's fully dressed self, is the first form of infinite self," and—even more important—serves as "the advancing impetus in the whole process by which a self infinitely takes on its actual self with its difficulties and advantages."[36]

---

35 Ibid., pp. 163.f, 168; (KW 19: 30f. 35); SV 15:88f., 93; (11:144f., 148).
36 Ibid., pp. 202f., 188; (KW 19:68f., 54f.); SV 15:122f., 110f.; (11:179f., 166f.).

In this language there are several important points about the nature of that "possibility" envisioned by the imagination in contrast to the "possibility" available to rational conceptual thinking (what he calls, in *Postscript*, "objective reflection"). (a) This naked, abstract, negative, hypothetical self is only the *first* form of the infinite self. At this stage the self is incomplete. The possible self is not the goal in itself. (b) But at this stage of envisioned possibility something crucial takes place: the self becomes aware that there is something "eternal" about itself, and therefore every self has a quality that distinguishes it from, that makes it transcendent to, its accidental, fortuitous externalities. (c) Nevertheless, this awareness, this vision, as a *first* stage, then serves as the impelling force that motivates a *process* in which this naked abstract self takes on, clothes itself with, precisely its unique fortuitous finitude and so becomes its *actual* self. The self "sees its task in that self given to him/her."[37]

The question remains: how does this vision serve as such an "advancing impetus"? What is there about this vision of the imagination that impels the self to seek a reconciliation, a harmonization, a unity of that "absolute disjunction" between one's infinitude of possibility and one's very particular, unique, finite concretion? Kierkegaard had worked out a partial answer the previous year in *Works of Love*, and certainly assumes it here in *Sickness*.[38] As already noted, *Works of Love* is an unusual volume in that it takes the form of edifying discourses on some biblical texts, but it contains "some Christian reflections." And one of the central issues concerning which Kierkegaard reflects therein is: what comprises "the universal-human" (*det Almene-Menneskelige*), what is "common for all [humans], the eternal likeness, ... the equality of eternity"; *and*, how is that related to the unique individuality (*Eiendommelighed*), to the distinctions which mark off each human being from every other human being?[39]

The abstract, naked, infinite self which one seeks to picture by the power of imagination is the locus of (even though not identical with) this quality of the "universal-human" which one shares equally and in common with every other human being, and which every other human being shares equally with oneself (with me). This quality is the ground for the "something eternal in the self" that I become aware of. Kierke-

---

37 Ibid., p. 202; (KW 19:68); SV 15:123; (11:179).

38 He composed *Works of Love* in January–August 1847 and published it 29 September 1847. He composed *The Sickness unto Death* in January–May of 1848 but published it 30 July 1849. A very different answer will appear in the next chapter when we consider The Leap as a Passionate Transition.

39 *Works of Love*, pp. 330, 96, 252; SV 12:342, 90, 259f.; (9:340, 87, 257f.).

gaard explores this dimension in the context of describing what it means to "love your neighbour as yourself" (in part one, section II of *Works*). And his point is that this love of neighbour and of self is not based on the distinctions that make each of us different and unique but upon the vision that, from the perspective of the "eternal," every individual is the "same," that is, is equal in worth and dignity. From this perspective, "differences hang loosely about the individual," and "then there steadily shines in every individual that essential other, that which is common to all humans." Whether one is looking at a sovereign king or at a wretched beggar, one ignores the externalities and regards only "the inner glory, the equality of glory" which is common to both, but which "the outer garments conceal."[40]

Whatever role "the eternal" itself may play in the origin and sustenance of this vision (which will be explored later), I become aware of my own sharing in that universal equality when, by the power of that peculiar kind of reflection called "imagination," I project that picture of myself as abstracted from all my external particularities and as composed of "infinite possibility." It is as one becomes conscious of the task of *becoming* one's unique "self's possibility" that one begins to gain the vision and the conviction of one's self as equal in dignity and worth with every other human being. But, as will become clear below, the "self's possibility" is not identical with or limited to this quality of the universal-human.

Kierkegaard, however, stresses that this abstract self is only a "hypothetical" self yet to be actualized; it is a "negative" self in the sense that it is, as such, not yet completed in its concreteness, and therefore it does not know the fluid uncertainty of existence. And this characteristic of "possibility" as applied to the human self must never be forgotten or neglected; hence it is "lower" than, is prior to, actuality. Otherwise, imagination (as already noted above), however indispensable in the process of becoming oneself, may actually hinder and keep the process from fulfilment. Kierkegaard distinguishes between imagination (*Phantasie*) and the fantastic (*det Phantastiske*), the latter being the misuse of the former. "The fantastic," he says, "is in general that which leads a human being out into the infinite in such a way that it only leads one away from oneself and thereby prevents one from coming back to oneself." "If possibility outruns necessity so that the self runs away from itself in possibility, it has no necessity to which it must return. ... Thus possibility seems

40 Ibid., pp. 96f.; SV 12:90; (9:87).

greater and greater to the self; more and more becomes possible because nothing becomes actual. Eventually everything seems possible, but this is exactly the point at which the abyss swallows up the self."[41]

Thus, the abstract naked self of the imagination is only the *first* form of the infinite self. "To become oneself"—it must be repeated—"is to become concrete. But to become concrete is neither to become [remain] finite nor to become [remain] infinite, for that which is to become concrete is a synthesis." And this dialectic means that, in the synthesis, "the one constantly is its opposite."[42] In other words, the self cannot be infinite (in an authentic way) without simultaneously being finite. In *Works of Love* Kierkegaard makes this point very clearly. In the early part of the book, as just quoted above, one is encouraged to concentrate on the universal-human, on the inner likeness and equality which every one shares from the eternal perspective. So we are to regard individual differences as a "disguise" hanging loosely about eternal likeness, and we are to concentrate on "eternal growth, which grows away from distinctions."[43]

Later in the book, however, he stresses the importance of these differences. He says, "With what infinite love nature, or God in nature [religiousness A], encompasses all the differences which have life and being! ... What love! First, it makes no distinctions, none whatsoever. Then next, just like the first, it differentiates infinitely in loving the differences." And with the help of this love, everyone "becomes one's own-unique-individuality [*Eiendommelige*]." In other words, being universally human and equal in infinite dignity is inseparable from being absolutely unique in finite differentiation. And the "source and origin of all individuality [*Eiendommelighed*]" does not lie in human imagination or will, but comes from beyond all that is human, as a gift. "If one has the courage to be oneself *before God*, then one has authentic-individuality." In other words, if I believe that both my equality and my uniqueness are "loved," are given and supported by an essential and universal dynamic or structure of existence, then I am "before God"; that is to say, I know that "individuality is not mine but is God's gift by which he gives me being, yes, gives everything, gives being to everything." Then I know that "to have individuality is to believe in the individuality of every other single [person]." This conviction is grounded in the faith that "he who cre-

---

41 *Sickness*, pp. 163f., 169; (KW 19:30f., 35f.); SV 15:88f., 93; (11:144, 149).
42 Ibid., pp. 162f.; (KW 19:30); SV 15:87f; (11:143).
43 *Works of Love*, p. 96; SV 12:90; (9:87).

ated out of nothing nevertheless creates individuality, so that creation over against him shall not be nothing."[44]

It is clear that Kierkegaard means to say two things in this analysis. On the one hand, to participate only in the universal-human alone, by itself, amounts to nothing for the individual as individual. If that participation were the be-all and end-all, the individual as such would be nothing; his/her unique, distinctive identity (*Enkelte, Eiendommelige*) would possess no ultimate significance in itself, would eventually be erased and lost in the ongoing process of life, and would be noted only for its contribution to human society and knowledge as a corporate, continuing whole. On the other hand, the unique particularities that define the concrete individual have no ground in themselves as such to guarantee infinite worth and eternal dignity. By themselves they are ephemeral, contingent accidents, soon to be swallowed up in the shifting patterns on the flowing stream of physical-historical phenomena. They are granted ultimate dignity and continuing worth only as the universal-human inheres, that is to say, only as the universal likeness and eternal equality of every individual is seen (believed) to be given and sustained by the transcendent structures of human existence. This is not a new idea for Kierkegaard but one which he had worked out at the very beginning of his authorship in *Either/Or*: "This is the secret which the individual life has with itself, that it is simultaneously an individual life and also the universal. ... One makes oneself the universal human-being not by taking off one's concretion, for then one becomes nothing, but by putting it on and permeating it with the universal. The universal human-being is not a phantom, but every human-being is the universal human-being; that is to say, every human-being is assigned the way by which she/he becomes the universal human-being."[45]

This event in which the individual becomes simultaneously the universal and the particular is certainly what Kierkegaard is (in part) pointing to when, in *Sickness*, he says that the infinite abstract self depicted in the imagination serves as "the advancing impetus in the whole process by which a self infinitely takes on its actual self with its difficulties and advantages." But this formulation raises a serious question or dilemma concerning the meaning of "possibility" as applied to the human self. It

---

44 Ibid., 252f.; SV 12:259–61; (9:257–9). This formulation in *Works* is not new for Kierkegaard. A form of it can be found as early as *Either/Or*, 2:254f; (KW 4:250-1); SV 3:231; (2:224). And another in *Postscript*, pp. 320–1, 220–1; (KW 12.1:358–9, 246–7); SV 10:58–9; 9:206; (7:310–11, 207–8).

45 *Either/Or*, 2:260; (KW 4:255f.); SV 3:236; (2:229).

was stated above that Kierkegaard maintains a continuity in his concept of possibility from *Fragments* through *Sickness*. And this is true in respect to two basic theses: possibility is future; and possibility becomes actuality only in freedom, never of necessity. But the new formulation in *Sickness* about the function of the imagination might seem to indicate that the "self's possibility" depicted in the imagination is limited to the self's "infinite possibility" or "infinite form" which is the "negative" and "hypothetical" self. So the question or dilemma arises: does "possibility" refer to, is "possibility" a quality of, (a) only the potential selfhood which is inherent in every human being? Or, does "possibility" also refer to and consist of a quality that inheres in (b) those indeterminate, fortuitous, contingent conditions which serve as the occasion for the individual self's acquisition of its unique particularity in actuality?

Or is there a third option: does the "possible self" pictured in imagination consist of (c) something *more* than the universal potentiality of selfhood, but, as yet, something *less* than the concrete actual self? And does something of one's uniqueness (*Eiendommelighed*) also inhere in this (intermediate) possible self, as well as in the unique particularity of one's finite differentiations as incorporated into the concrete actual self? Another way of putting this third option is to suggest that my "finitude," my "specificity" (*Bestemthed*), refers not only to the unique particularity of the more or less extrinsic qualities that my specific place, time, heredity, family and social setting have imparted to me as a physical/psychic entity. Rather my "finitude" may also refer to the unique particularity of those intrinsic qualities of my inward subjective self which define who I am essentially and about whose accumulation and format I have had some choice and determination. They are "mine" not in the same sense as those extrinsic qualities which have been given to me and with which I am stuck, like it or not. Rather, these intrinsic qualities are "mine," indeed are "me," because I have had a determinative role in shaping them.

Kierkegaard nowhere directly raises or answers these questions. But they must be resolved if we are to clarify the meaning of his assertion that "freedom [self] is the dialectical in the determinants possibility and necessity." The difficulty partly lies in the fact that in *The Sickness unto Death*, his last major (and normative) philosophical/theological work, Kierkegaard, with a new burst of insight that produced (he says) new "crucial categories," explores "possibility" in greater complexity than before, and quite deliberately expounds a new formulation of "necessity." So these questions can now serve as the occasion to state in summary form Kierkegaard's final formulation of the nature of possibility as possibility occurs in the domain of human selfhood.

The answers to our questions are not too far below the surface of these formulations in *Sickness*. When the "self's possibility" comes into existence, becomes actuality, that self is "concrete." And "that which is to become concrete is a synthesis" of the finite and the infinite. In this dialectical situation, "the one constantly is its opposite."[46] In other words, for Kierkegaard there are never two distinct, separable entities, the finite self and the infinite self, which somehow have to be beaten or melted together into a synthesis. In their original state, they constitute a synthesis. The "self" which becomes conscious in subjective reflection and is depicted in imagination is already and essentially an indissoluble duality-in-unity. So the function of imagination, as described in *Sickness*, is to make a distinction within an entity (the self) where there is no division. As just noted above, this kind of reflection is an "act of discrimination wherein the self becomes aware of itself as essentially distinct from the environment and external-world [*Udvortesheden*] and [their] influence upon it," and "one's imagination discovers a possibility that, *if it eventuated* [took place], would thus become the break with immediacy" (emphasis added).[47]

However, it should be noted, the consciousness of self as essentially distinct (in possibility) involves and requires a simultaneous awareness of the unique and extended finitude in which that self is incarnated (its "concretion") and apart from which it is not itself. And hence the imagination, which foresees (pre-pictures) a possibility for the self that breaks with its current immediacy, must be ready for and attentive to the unique specific conditions required for the concretion of that possibility, which will ensure that the possibility becomes the self's actuality and thus not remain a disembodied, irrelevant, despairing dream and fantasy (*Det Phantastiske*). Or, as is probably the case in most instances, it will be a particular situation, with its specific conditions and demands, that will challenge the "self's possibility" to decide and to choose the one most appropriate possibility that is offered in its imagination.

Kierkegaard makes this point in a dense and rather awkwardly phrased passage. He is describing how imagination can slip over into the fantastic in a human being's feeling, knowing, and willing, and thus the self "moves further and further away from its self." In this case, "will-

---

46 *Sickness*, pp. 162f.; (KW 19:30); SV 15:88; (11:143).
47 Ibid., p. 188; (KW 19:54); SV 15:110; (11:166f.).

ing does not constantly become to the same degree concrete as abstract." Now one expects Kierkegaard to describe the self in this state of fantasized willing, but, following the simple connector *saa* (so, then, such), he actually describes the self when it *is* "to the same degree concrete as abstract": "then [in the latter case] the more it is infinitized in intention and resolve, the more and more [it] becomes itself simultaneously [*ganske naeverende og samtidig*] in the little things of the task that can be accomplished at once; thus, while being infinitized, it comes back in the strongest sense to its self; thus while *farthest* from its self, when it is most infinitized in intention and resolve, it is in the same instant *nearest* its self in accomplishing the infinitely little things of the work which can be accomplished this very day, this very hour, this very minute."[48] In other words, imagination properly employed is not divorced from simultaneous consciousness of and concern for the concrete self.

If this analysis is correct, then, for Kierkegaard, the task of the self's conscious reflection, as engaged in the infinitizing activity of its imagination, does not end with grasping the naked, abstract, "infinite form" of the self. Its final task does not lie in imagination's dispersal in the exploration of feeling, knowing, willing separately, but is achieved in picturing the possible self in its wholeness, its unity, its concreteness, its actuality. This view of imagination builds on the characterization developed earlier in chapter 2 above (at notes 38–43), that is, imagination (as directed toward the human self) works with images rather than with concepts and thus is better able to project the richness and complexity of concrete actuality of the self than are abstract concepts and categories. Images must use the language of sense, and yet as formed in subjective reflection they take on figurative, analogical, symbolic power, and so can capture the nature of the human individual as spirit, as self, and can move the self, serving as an "advancing impetus" and driving force in the process of becoming one's self.

For example, in my imagination I may picture myself as "generous," but this "naked possibility" of my "infinite form" is immediately clothed by my imagination in some concrete act of giving to someone in need, or in my commitment to a program for the poor such as social security. And this "clothed" possibility will serve as the impetus to move me actually to give some money to the next beggar on the street, or to vote for increase in my taxes to support social security (although, as we will see

---

48 Ibid., pp. 164f.; (KW 19:31f.); SV 15:89; (11:145).

later, Kierkegaard does stress the qualitative difference and distance between picturing an act in the imagination, in the abstract, and actually doing it).

This analysis resolves the questions, raised in options (a) and (b) posed above, by suggesting that the "possibility" of self pictured by the imagination involves both, but lies somewhere *in between* (a) the universally human *potential* for selfhood *and* (b) the unique, contingent, fortuitous, extrinsic conditions in which a particular individual is "concrete." This third option suggests that this analysis holds some deeper implications for the nature of "possibility" as applied to the self, and that those implications mark an advance in Kierkegaard's concept of possibility in *Sickness* as compared with previous formulations.

To speak of the self's "possibility" is certainly to speak of the self as oriented toward its future, a future that is marked with uncertainty, that demands courage and risk, that requires faith in the eternal in order to have the daring to step into it. And the movement of transition from the present (with its past) into that future, or, in other language, the act of bringing that possible future self into the actuality of the present self (with its past), is an act of freedom: a decision, a choice, a "leap." As we have seen, these are themes that have been present since the writing of *Fragments* and *The Concept of Anxiety*. Now, however, three new insights about the "self's possiblity" emerge (and they will explicate our third option posed above): (a) what it means to *become* one's possible self, and what the relation between "possibility" and "becoming" is; (b) what happens to possibility when it becomes actuality; and (c) a more rigorous delimitation of possibility by what Kierkegaard now is willing to call one's "necessity" (which will carry us into the last major topic of this chapter as outlined above on p. 145).

(a) As noted several times before, Kierkegaard says that "the self κατα δυναμιν [as established in potentiality] is just as much possible as necessary, because it certainly is itself, yet it must become itself. Insofar as it is itself, it is [the] necessary, and insofar as it must become itself, it is a possibility." So "possibility and necessity are equally essential for becoming." But "the self κατα δυναμιν does not actually exist, is simply that which ought to come into existence [*skal blive til*]." And this "becoming" is integral to being a self. "In every moment it exists, a self is in-the-process-of-becoming [*i Vorden*]. ... Insofar as the self is not becoming itself, it is not itself."[49]

---

[49] Ibid., pp. 168, 163; (KW 19:35, 30); SV 15:92f., 88; (11:148, 143).

What then is this "becoming" of the self's "possibility"? Is it simply the present actual self's being transformed through its inescapable participation in new and different finite contingent circumstances as they press upon and get incorporated into the self's actuality? This process, which happens to everyone, does not measure up to Kierkegaard's language of choosing one's future in freedom. Then does "becoming" simply consist of the self's seeking, quite rationally, to enact a plan, to pursue a goal, to implement a purpose by selecting and reshaping the finite conditions that are appropriate? This view seems to accord with the language of *Fragments* in its talk about "coming-into-existence" and "freedom." *Works of Love* adds to the notion of "becoming" by seeing it as the event in which the universally human is incorporated into the particular distinctive differences of the unique individual, and these "differences" have generally been taken in the foregoing as meaning the unique set of extrinsic, finite, contingent conditions of each person's life. But *The Sickness unto Death* suggests another possible reading of all this language about differences, particular unique individuality, and coming-into-existence. And this reading will clarify Kierkegaard's final formulation of the meaning of "possibility."

First, it is clear that Kierkegaard distinguishes between the self as κατα δυναμιν and the self as "existing." The former refers, in part, to the way in which every human being, physically-psychically [literally: soulishly-bodily], is put together basically in the same way. "Every human being is a psychical/physical synthesis naturally fitted [*anlagt*] to be spirit. This is the construction."[50] But no individual, as one originally finds oneself in *existence*, is as yet spirit or self. Selfhood, κατα δυναμιν, is a given built-in *potentiality* which may or may not emerge or be achieved. But as an "existing one," every individual becomes aware (more or less) of now living in the "immense contradition" or opposition of thinking/being, infinitude/finitude, possibility/actuality, future/past, knowing/doing. The self as what one *is* potentially has the quality of "necessity" (to be explored later). But seen as what one ought to *become*, it has the quality of "possibility."

So the *existing* self, as distinguished from the self κατα δυναμιν, is the becoming self. The precondition of becoming self is the self as possibility. If the self simply *is*, there is no possibility, no future, no freedom, no becoming (coming-into-existence). So becoming is choosing (I choose,

---

50 Ibid., p. 176; (KW 19:43); SV 15:100; (11:156).

therefore I am; knowing is not enough by itself);[51] becoming is freedom; becoming is the self. So becoming is the passage, transition, movement of what already *is*, as a given *potentiality*, into the state of concreteness, of being actual.

Thus far, this event of "becoming" sounds the same as the description of "coming-into-existence" in *Fragments*. Insofar as the given self must come-into-existence, it is "possibility," and the transition does not occur of necessity but in freedom. But there is a subtle shift in the meanings or referents of these basic terms. In *Fragments*, the "necessary" does not refer to the potential self, whereas in *Sickness* it does. In *Fragments*, the "necessary" points to a quality inherent in logical inference or rational co-implication, or in the chain of physical causation. "So the only thing that cannot come into existence [*blive til*] is the necessary, because the necessary *is*."[52] But in *Sickness* another kind of "necessity" is operating (to be described later in this chapter), as is clear from the fact it is seen as a quality of the potential self. This self does not exist but is "naturally fitted" to come into existence, to become. And this structural potentiality has built into it the demand, claim, requirement to become. It has the quality of *skal*: obligation, must, ought. So when *Sickness* says of the self κατα δυναμιν, "Insofar as it [the self] is itself, it is [the] necessary," the reference is (in part) to the self's *givenness*, but this "necessary" self also has the quality of a demand and obligation to "become," which directly implies that this same self has the character of being "possibility." As we shall see, the necessity involved is of a different kind from that referred to in *Fragments*. But our concern here is to see the implications for the nature of possibility.

Secondly, therefore, we must ask the question: if both the given potentiality of selfhood, and the particular contingent conditions in which the self is actualized, are seen as limiting factors (*Begrændsende*) that restrain (*holde igjen*) one's infinite possibility,[53] then we must ask in what does "possibility" consist? In all former characterizations of possibility (in this present work) it was assumed that "possibility" referred backwards to one's given but unrealized potentiality and forwards to the accidentality and indeterminateness of the unique particular conditions of each individual's existence. Now, in *Sickness*, "possibility" does not refer to either one, but points to something *in between* them. And clearly this

---

51 *Either/Or*, 2:263; (KW 4:259); SV 3:239; (2:232).
52 *Philosophical Fragments*, p. 91; (KW 7:74); SV 6:68; (4:237).
53 *Sickness*, p. 168; (KW 19:35); SV 15:93; (11:148).

"possibility" is not identical with the event of becoming; rather, it is its presupposition. What then is the referent for this use of "possibility" by Kierkegaard?

As already suggested, the "self's possibility" in this sense is something more than the given potentiality of selfhood which is shared in universally and equally by every human individual. Yet it is something less than, something prior to and "lower" than, the event in which possibility "becomes" concrete actuality. As this something more, my "self" does not subsist in that pure ideality of the undifferentiated, universal, human essence wherein all human beings are alike. With the help of the reflective analysis of my imagination I may *believe*, before the eternal, that I possess this infinite dignity and worth, but I *exist* indissolubly within the complex matrix of my extended finitude, which presents itself to my consciousness as an "immense opposition" to my "self's possibility." So, obviously, this possible self is less than the actual self which has, in the event of becoming, come to terms with its finitude and overcome the opposition between the two.

So again: of and in what does the self's *possibility* consist? What is the object of *self*-consciousness when my subjective reflection and imagination produce an awareness of my self as "possibility"? Using again the passage already quoted above, Kierkegaard asserts that, when I turn with personal, passionate, interested intensity to "see" or to bring to consciousness my most inward, private, hidden self, this kind of reflection is an "act of discrimination wherein the self becomes aware of itself as essentially distinct from the environment and external-world and [their] influence upon it."[54] I become aware of my self as infinite possibility, abstracted and naked, distinguishable (even though not separable) from all the specifics of my outward, observable "history." But is this abstract, naked, negative, hypothetical infinite-self absolutely empty and barren of any distinguishing characteristics?

On the contrary, Kierkegaard sees this "self's possibility"—come to full consciousness through the imagination of subjective reflection—as the locus, the holder, the preserver, the effective continuity of the self's definitive uniqueness as individual human spirit or self (*Enkelte, Eiendommelige*). Here in my "self's possibility" lies that essential gestalt[55] of both

54 Ibid., p. 188; (KW 19:55f.); SV 15:111; (11:167f.).
55 In the sense of the definition given in Merriam Webster's *Third International Dictionary of the English Language Unabridged* (1968) (except I would substitute "entities" in place of "phenomena"): "a structure or configuration of ... psychological phenomena so integrated as to constitute a functional unity with properties not derivable from its parts in summation."

inherited and acquired characteristics which, in their continuing, integrated, functional unity, define who I *am* in potentiality and possibility (but always in relation to both my present finite conditions and my future contingent conditions). In my most inward hidden self I am that gestalt of capacities, inclinations, dispositions, tastes, temperament, humour, insights, attitudes, values, ideals, intentions, commitments, beliefs, etc., and of locations on spectrums such as tough/soft, phlegmatic/excitable, patient/impatient, sensitive/insensitive, stable/unstable, etc. That gestalt is my self's possibility, which I am called upon, in full self-consciousness, to heed and to "obey" when faced with the choice of *becoming* my self here and now in the "present" and "at the spot." But that abstracted, naked, infinite self (my self's possibility)—although never "existing" in and by itself, and held in "being" only in reflective imagination—is the presupposition and prerequisite of that choosing and becoming in actuality. This integrated configuration and functional unity define who I am, so that if this gestalt dissolves, or if it ceases to inform my self-awareness and to find expression in my behaviour and relationships, then I lose my identity, and *I* cease to exist.

This meaning of "possibility" can best be illustrated and clarified by some examples in which this concept of the self is assumed by Kierkegaard. The first one has been referred to above as "one of the most radical and revealing passages in the entire corpus of his writings." He is making the point that what defines being "human" does not lie only in "the universally human" (*det Almene-Menneskelige*) but also in the fact that "within the race every individual [*Enkelt*] is the essentially different or unique [*Eiendommelige*]." And then he depicts and thus defines this individual uniqueness not by referring to one's external, finite, contingent characteristics and conditions but by asserting that

the single human being [who is] honourable, upright, respectable, God-fearing, can under the same circumstances do exactly the opposite to what another human being does, who is also honourable, upright, respectable, God-fearing. ... If one could with unqualified truthfulness judge every human being according to an established universal standard (*Maalestok*: rule, criterion), ... everything would turn outward, fulfilling itself in the life of the state or society; then to live would become too easy, but also exceedingly empty; then neither spiritual struggle nor the deepening of self would be either possible or necessary.[56]

---

56 *Works of Love*, p. 217; SV 12:222f.; (9:220f.).

What is the source of this "doing exactly the opposite"? Clearly not the "conditions" or external situation, because they are the same (in this hypothetical case). And clearly not the "universally human," because that is the same for every human being. So the source and locale of this individual uniqueness lies *in between*, in the hidden, private, passionate, personal subjectivity of that individual. This subjectivity (*Postscript*), this "self's possibility" (*Sickness*)—that comes to *self*-consciousness by the power of imaginative reflection—is the precondition and prerequisite of the choosing and the becoming in which I, in my essential infinite possibility, become actuality in the conditions of my unique, accidental, contingent finitude. And it is precisely the gestalt of that subjectivity, with its integrated functional unity, that is the locus and source of my particularity (*Enkelt*) and uniqueness (*Eiendommelige*) as self, or, we might say, the source of my "finitude" of spirit and specificity of person.

Another example of how Kierkegaard makes this point (already explored above) is his view of the "fortuitous external circumstance" as the "occasion." On the one hand, "the occasion is the ultimate category, the legitimate transition category from the sphere of the idea to actuality. ... The whole of actuality can be completed [ready] in the idea, but without the occasion it never becomes actual. *The occasion is a category of finitude*." So "everything emerges with the occasion. ... Without the occasion nothing at all happens." On the other hand, "The occasion is not positively productive but negatively productive. A creation is a production out of nothing. ... Therefore, not anything new comes with the occasion. ... The occasion has no part at all in what does happen. ... The occasion is, then, in and for itself, nothing, and [is] something only in relation to that which it gives rise to, and in relation to this [it] is exactly nothing." So "that which comes out of the occasion is something entirely other than the occasion itself," and has its "ground or cause" elsewhere.[57]

As suggested above, the source, ground or cause of the something "new" and "entirely other," that becomes actual with the occasion, is the inwardness of subjectivity and the leap of freedom in choosing. Now, in the language of *The Sickness unto Death*, the source is the self as possibility, the self as that inner gestalt which has being and continuity in and of itself insofar as it is distinguished in consciousness by the power of reflective imagination, even while being inseparable from that same self's unique particularity of contingent fortuitous finitude (past, present, future). In this passage in *Either/Or*, Kierkegaard makes it eminently clear that the "new" is not, on the one hand, the product of the "logic" of

---

57 *Either/Or*, 1:231–6; (KW 3:233–8); SV 2:215–20; (1:207–12).

"immanent thinking" which moves by the necessity of some universal spirit or selfhood; nor, on the other hand, is it the product of the causal force of external, finite, contingent circumstances. He obviously is pointing to a source *in between* these two, i.e. what he comes to call "subjectivity" in *Postscript*, and what he depicts as the "self's possibility" in *Sickness*.

How the transition or movement from possibility to actuality takes place, what actually happens in that gap, will be considered in the next chapter on freedom as the leap. But another helpful example of what Kierkegaard means by the self's "possibility" is found in a comment of his (in *Postscript*) on the distinction between thought and action. This distinction may be made, he says, by assigning "thought" to the realm of possibility and "action" to the realm of subjectivity. But he admits that there is a thin or vague (literally, "light" and "easy"—*let*) borderline between the two.

Thus when I think that I will do this or that, this thought is not yet an action, ... but yet it is a possibility in which the interest of action and actuality already reflects itself. Also, the disinterestedness and objectivity thereof [thought] begin to be disturbed, because responsibility and actuality seek to lay hold of it [the thought]. ... Actuality is not the outward action, but an inwardness [*Indvorteshed*] in which the individual cancels out [*ophæver*] the possibility and identifies with the thought so as to exist in it. This is the action.

In other words, possibility as disinterested objective concept is the farthest remove from action. But when one takes a passionate, inward, subjective interest in regard to possibility, so that one decides to "exist therein," then the thin line between possibility and actuality has been crossed. "Between possibility and actuality there is perhaps no difference at all [i.e. in content]; in form there is always an essential one. Actuality is interestedness in existing therein." So Kierkegaard says, as an example, "The external element in Luther's action consists of stepping forward at the Diet of Worms, but from the instant he existed in willing it with all the passionate decision of his subjectivity, ... then he had acted."[58]

The implication of this passage in *Postscript* is that one can speak authentically of the "self's possibility" only if two kinds of possibility have been overcome and left behind: first, the objective possibility of pure concept, which claims to be truth in itself and is abstracted from any interest in its applicability to personal, particular, individual existence;

58 *Postscript*, pp. 302, 304; (KW 12.1:339, 340–1); SV 10:42, 43; (7:293, 295).

and secondly, the possibility of the fantastic, when one is content to live in dreams which move further and further out and away from one's finite, particular uniqueness as an individual distinct from every other human being. "Possibility" which is authentically the *self's* is indeed abstract, naked, infinite in the sense that, while being conscious and pictured in imaginative reflection, it still has not been enacted and (to use one of Kierkegaard's favourite images) "clothed" within the confines of one's given and accumulated concreteness, including the "occasion" now demanding action. Nevertheless, this inner abstract gestalt of my self's "possibility," if it is to be authentically me or mine, must turn and bend itself willingly, interestedly, passionately toward the new "future" concrescences of my self that *now* open up within the ever-shifting patterns of my extended finitude, and I must *choose* to *become* myself within them in the shape and form which is consonant with who I am in the gestalt of my self's possibility. Otherwise my concrete self will be coerced and determined and shaped solely by purely external physical and social forces, and by psychological conditions that are "below" or "external" to my conscious and responsible self.

Does this view of the "self's possibility" (described in the last ten pages as the unique gestalt of pure infinite qualities located *in between* the universal, given potentialities of "the human," and, the particular, finite, fortuitous conditions of the individual) answer to the self-consciousness of the normative (average, standard, normal) human person? The present author would illustrate the validity of this view in the following way (and please allow the first person). The one person I know best, besides myself, is the one with whom I have had a constant and intimate relationship for sixty years. For roughly the first half of those sixty years, she played and fulfilled admirably the dutiful role of wife and mother: entertaining students and colleagues of her husband, giving total devotion to the care and nurture of our two beloved sons, continuing to be a faithful and loving daughter to her aging parents, doing her stint as Sunday school teacher, Cub Scout den mother, PTA drudge, etc., etc. I assumed that I knew who she was through-and-through, and loved her dearly. Then, quite suddenly, as our two sons became teenagers and no longer wanted her close attention, there appeared a series of startling emanations from her hidden interior being, revelations of secret qualities or potentialities ("possibilities") of which I had had no intimation and of whose existence I had never dreamed.

The first breakout (that I noticed; were their earlier ones?) was triggered by her reading a *Time* magazine cover story about Nelson Glueck, the pioneer archaeologist of the remains of ancient Near Eastern cultures. To my total amazement, she became absorbed, for several years, with the study of the archaeology and ancient history of the Near Eastern and Mediterranean cultures. She eventually filled a bookcase with books, monographs, and articles about every site from Ur of the Chaldees to the Roman theatres in southern France and Spain, as well as studies of many side items such as the treasures of Sutton Woo. And this interest profoundly affected our life, because every summer became a trek to visit the sites throughout Greece (including a scary drive up the disappearing trail on the western slopes of the Peloponnesian mountains in order to get to the Temple of Bassae); to wander among the lonely ruins of Priene, Miletos, and Didyma as well as Ephesus; to hire a taxi to drive us up the Bekaa Valley, through guard posts of armed soldiers, in order to view the towering columns of Baalbek; in lonely and cold December to find a guide in Shiraz to take us through the splendours of Persepolis and then to dare to drive on through vast empty spaces, with visions of distant long-abandoned caravansarai, to Parsargadae, there to climb up the steep steps and view the empty cubicle of Cyrus's tomb; and on Christmas day, during a forced stayover in Imman, to have the unexpected thrill of being guided through Jerash by the son of a workman who helped dig it all out; and then on to Egypt, to spend two weeks floating down the Nile on a boat from Asswan to Cairo, getting off to visit all the ancient sites of the pharaohs with the help of both an Egyptian and an English archaeologist; and on and on and on. And all this and much more *only* because of a hidden secret "possibility" treasured in the interior life and being of my wife and finally brought to light by her reading about Nelson Glueck! What was (or is) the form or character of that original, naked, abstract "possibility" which gave birth to all this? Surely nothing so specific as "interest in archaeology." Could she even put a name to it, some pregnant but vague metaphor for longing-for-the-mysterious unknown? Probably not.

And a number of other startling breakouts followed (which I will only list). The claim of women's lib, that women get great satisfaction out of organizing a business venture and bringing it to successful fruition without any help from men, came home to me when she and a friend brought into being and managed a thrift shop over a period of eight years which is still producing tens of thousands of dollars in support of a school—and she was the one I kidded about not being able to balance the check book! And in her role as co-manager, she had to make annual verbal reports to a large women's organization, and suddenly I discovered that this very private person who shrank from public speaking had a startling talent for picturesque and humorous speech. During this period she also took a few classes in water colour painting and produced a picture that I still proudly hang on our walls among some very professional originals. Then later I discovered that she was secretly writing poetry, which I demanded to read and which is filled with moving insights and whimsical impressions of everyday scenes of nature and humanity—all in highly disciplined sparse language. My wife a poet?

I could go on with other illustrations (which she would not want me to narrate). But the point is this: over the last thirty-five years, I have come to see that the other human being whom you know most intimately remains a fathomless well of mysterious unknown depths and complexity. The closer you come to the other one's mystery, and the more the other one reveals of that mystery, the more clearly you come to see that there are even vaster regions and depths of the other's interior being which remain unknown and in large measure unknowable. You come to realize that just as there are great stretches of your own interior being which you have never shared with anyone, much of which you could not find the medium for sharing even if you wanted to, just so it is true of every other human being. As Kierkegaard says, "To have unique-self-identity-which-belongs-to-you-alone [*Eiendommelighed*] is to believe in such identity of every other [individual]."[59] It is precisely this identity which he points to when he speaks of the "self's possibility."

(b) Now the above illustrations (from *Works of Love, Either/Or, Postscript*) of what Kierkegaard means by "the self's possibility" lead to consideration of the second new insight about possibility in *Sickness* (see above p. 163), namely, what happens to possibility when it becomes actuality. Granted, that "I" am my "self's possibility" as that inner subjective gestalt which is the carrier and continuity of my abstract and yet unique identity as a human being, and which is the prerequisite and precondition of all becoming-my-self in actuality. Nevertheless, that gestalt is truly *my* self's "possibility" only if and when I choose to *exist* as such *within* the particular finite conditions which present themselves as an occasion or situation which is "future" to me in the sense that it demands decision here and now. Otherwise, that gestalt is only fantasy, the fantastic. So, the question now is: granted I do choose to enact my self's possibility within this occasion or situation, what change takes place in and to my "possibility" when it becomes my "actuality"? In the authorship, Kierke-

---

59 *Works of Love*, p. 253; SV 12:261; (9:259).

gaard has two different ways of getting at this question. One asks the further question (with which this entire section on possibility/necessity began): does possibility become necessity in actuality? (This will be pursued as the last topic of this section.) The other way is as follows.

As already noted, Climacus, in *Fragments*, says that when possibility becomes actuality, there is always a suffering: "The suffering of actuality ... is this: that the possible (not only the possible which will be excluded but also the possible which will be embraced) reveals itself as nothing [*Intet*] in the instant it becomes actual, because in [becoming] actuality, possibility is *annihilated*" (*tilintetgjort*, literally: "made-into-nothing"). But in *The Sickness unto Death*, Anti-Climacus comments, "Admittedly, thinkers say that actuality is annihilated possibility, but that is not entirely true; it is the completed, the efficacious possibility. ... Actuality in relation to possibility is a corroboration."[60]

Between these two statements there is a significant shift of perspective on the nature of "possibility," not by contradiction but by addition. Anti-Climacus does not say that Climacus's view is untrue but that it is not the whole truth. Climacus is making a point that is one of Kierkegaard's constant themes (contra Hegel), namely, that possibility does not pass over into actuality smoothly, easily, rationally, of necessity. Rather, this movement (κινησις) consists of an act of freedom, and this act brings with it a suffering and agony which is something more than that caused by the uncertainty of the outcome (the original basic angst, experienced as one moves out of innocent immediacy, and which is evoked by the "nothingness of the not-being" of that which may come-into-existence, by the fact that "possibility" both "is" and "is-not"). There is an additional kind of uncertainty inherent in coming-into-existence when one has achieved a measure of self-consciousness and reflection, and this uncertainty is an additional source of freedom's pain and anguish. This second kind of uncertainty is evoked by: "the annihilated possibility, which also is the annihilation of every other possibility."[61]

What then is the pain and suffering involved in this "annihilation" of possibility? First of all, what had been a glittering ideality of my infinitude must now "abandon" (*forlade*, "leave behind") its non-being when it comes-into-existence within the limits of my finitude; it simply ceases to be "possibility," and therefore I am no longer "free" in regard to that

---

60 *Philosophical Fragments*, p. 91; (KW 7:74); SV 6:68; (4:237); *Sickness*, p. 148; (KW 19:15); SV 15:75; (11:129f.).
61 *Philosophical Fragments*, p. 101; (KW 7:81); SV 6:74; (4:245).

option. But even worse, I have also eliminated all the other possibilities which I might have chosen instead of this particular one within the limits of this specific set of finite conditions. So I am filled with pain and anguish because I am not certain that this particular option is what I want, is what is "the good" for me. How can I bear closing off all other possibilities? Should I not put off my decision while I contemplate my infinitude of possibilities? Behind the question, "Do I really want to do this?" is the deeper existential question, "Do I really want to *be* this?" because in choosing what to do, I am shaping and delimiting what and who I am in actuality, and perhaps also reshaping that inner gestalt of my "self's possibility."

Anti-Climacus in no way denies that this delimitation of my "possibility" takes place in its becoming my "actuality." In fact, he intensifies this point in his redefinition of "necessity" (as will be shown soon below). But he sees this movement and change not so much in its negative aspects of "annihilation" and loss, but in its positive aspects of completion, consummation, fulfilment of my self-as-possibility. Behind this shift of evaluation lies a shift in "location" of the "self's possibility." In *Fragments* and *Concept of Anxiety*, either the "possible" self is the ideal given essence which is "nothing" in that it has not come-into-existence, or the "possible" is the "future," whose enactment in the concrete situation has yet to be chosen, to be dared. But in *Postscript* and *Works of Love*, the self's possibility becomes interiorized in subjectivity, and in *Sickness* it is located *in between* ideal potentiality and future enactment, a self which comes to consciousness in reflective imagination. This self's possibility, if it can escape pure fantasy and can believe in itself, knows itself to be "naturally fitted," "structured," "intended" for the task of becoming itself or clothing itself within the fortuitous conditions and situations that confront it here and now. And thus becoming actuality is not an anguishing loss and annihilation but a completion, a consummation, a fulfilment.

At this point it must be emphasized that my "actuality" or "concreteness" as self is not identical with my finitude ("finitude" taken in its most inclusive sense as my brain in all its complex functions, my whole body and its physiology, my external observable history, my immediate environment, the entire complex of my personal, familial, social, economic, political relationships, etc.). My "actuality" includes all that; all of that is, indeed, "necessary" to my actuality. But my self in its actuality also includes, is a peculiar synthesis or unity of, that finitude *and* the infinitude of my "possibility." My actuality is my finitude as it is indwelt, informed, shaped, qualified (in a hidden, invisible, unobservable way) by that unique gestalt of "possibility" which is definitive of who I am in my continuity as a self with ultimate dignity and worth. What is "peculiar" about this unity is that, in it, my infinite possibility and my finite necessity are "annihilated" and "abandoned" only in their independence of each other or in the dominance of one over the other. In this unity each finds its consummation and fulfilment in being operatively present in harmony with the other, and thus they comprise a whole which includes them and yet is something new and different from each in isolation. In this unity of actuality each is transformed: my infinite possibility accepts the limits of my finitude, and my finitude is shaped, formed, and given direction by the indwelling of my infinite possibility. This unity is not a mere extant synthesis or relation, but is a true emergent "third," a dynamic processive event in which "the relation relates to itself," and hence is "spirit," is "self."

Here again Kierkegaard would want to stress: "actuality is the unity of possibility and necessity," although what he means by necessity in *Sickness* is much more complicated than mere finitude (as we shall see). But he would also want to stress that this "actuality" of the self is not the product of initiative from either side, that is, from possibility as such or from the requirement to be concrete. Nor does it result from any natural inevitable progression immanent within their interface with each other. "*Freedom* is the dialectical in the determinants possibility and necessity." In the instant of encounter between my self's possibility and the demand to be concrete, there is tension, and a pause, a gap. And it is bridged and reconciled only in freedom as a "leap" (yet to be analysed). So one might say that "actuality" is *enacted* freedom. Hence my freedom, in regard to this particular occasion of enactment of possibility, might be said to have been "annihilated," but equally said to have been fulfilled. I am free not just to *be* free as a thing in itself, or to be free *from* all delimitation and self-definition, but to be free *for* becoming myself in actuality. "The self is freedom."[62]

The nature and crucial importance of this consummation and fulfilment of my self (my freedom) in "actuality" was stated very explicitly by Kierkegaard in several late journal entries made (from August to November 1849) as reflections on how differently the disciples regarded Jesus' death before it happened (possibility) and after it happened (actuality). He says, "The situation must be present. ... There is a distinction between understanding in possibility (an understanding which is

62 *Sickness*, pp. 169, 162; (KW 19:36, 29); SV 15:93f., 87; (11:149, 142).

always misunderstanding) and understanding in actuality. ... It is impossible to become spirit [self] in 'possibility.' Only when it [a self-sacrificing plan] becomes actuality ... is one born again to understand truly what he had somewhat understood from the beginning, yet in such a way that misunderstanding slumbered within. Then the spirit [self] becomes integrated as spirit. ... The spirit is now in essential pure unity with itself."

Later he explains this misunderstanding in possibility. "The fact is that when I understand something in possibility, I remain essentially unchanged, I remain in the old ways [or, the old man], and make use of my imagination; when it becomes actuality, then it is I who am changed. ... When it is a matter of understanding in possibility, I have strenuously to exert all my imagination; when it is a matter of understanding the same thing in actuality, I am spared all exertion in regard to my imagination; actuality is placed very close to me." The trouble with imagination in the realm of possibility is that "Imagination constantly wants to foreshorten and to slip in another picture," that is, a picture of the desirable end without any depiction of the hard and agonizing process of enactment of possibility within the stubborn factuality of my finitude. Thus in coming-into-existence, in becoming actuality, the self's possibility is changed, and I come to a self-understanding which is never to be had by the most intense exertion of imagination in the realm of possibility.[63]

How profoundly and pragmatically Kierkegaard believed this qualitative distinction between knowing something in the imagination of possibility and knowing the same thing in and through its enactment in actuality finds its best expression in *Works of Love*. Although there is no word, no deed, which unconditionally demonstrates and proves "love," yet there is no authentic love without the deed.[64] "It is quite conceivable that an inspired, eloquent, distinguished person could in the upperclass circles advocate love to one's neighbour, but when it came to a little piece of actuality, he would be unable to subject his mind obediently to the view he had victoriously championed. But to champion an opposite viewpoint from within and behind the partitions of distinction, a viewpoint which ... will take the distinctions away, means nevertheless the maintenance of the distinctions." So scholars and rich men will enthusiastically advocate the equality of all humans within their own elevated and secure environment, but then "in a refined and cowardly

---

63 *Journals*, 4326, 3346, 3345; X¹ A 417, X² A 202, X² A 114.
64 *Works of Love*, p. 30; SV 12:18f.; (9:16).

manner would avoid contact with actuality's opposition to distinctions." So "it is one thing to let ideas strive with ideas; it is one thing to battle and be victorious in a dispute; it is something else to be victorious over one's own mind when one battles in the actuality of life. ... The measure of a man's fundamental disposition is this: how far is what he understands from what he does, how great is the distance between his understanding and his action?"⁶⁵

One question remains, however, concerning the relation of the self's possibility to the self's actuality. Does the progressive actualization of the self entail the gradual elimination of the self's possibility? Does the opposition and tension between the two finally fade away so that a person can relax and just *be* oneself? For Kierkegaard, such an eventuality would mean the utter loss of self. He was aware of this danger as he wrote the journal entries just quoted. Granted the absoluteness of the demand for the actualization of my possibility, nevertheless, he says, "now the question is whether I can preserve myself; ... actuality is placed very close to me, all too close; it has, as it were, swallowed me, and the question now is whether I can rescue myself from it" (3346).

What then is this "self" that is in danger of being swallowed by, that needs to be preserved and rescued from, one's own actuality? What else than my "self's possibility," which is differentiated from all of one's externality and is the prerequisite of all becoming. "The self is freedom," and as long as the self "exists," the self is in the process of becoming. This must mean, then, that the transformation of the self's possibility that takes place in its actualization is absorbed back into that inner gestalt of subjectivity wherein the self knows its own continuity as distinct from all of its involvement in the contingent conditions and situations of its finitude. And by this inner growth and transformation, the imagination is directed to ever new possibilities of enactment in future situations. If the self's becoming actuality is the essential task and ultimate desideratum of human existence, and if the self's identity, its essential dignity and worth, lies in this becoming as a continuing process, then the continuing health and functioning of the self's inward, subjective "possibility" is absolutely prerequisite for the essential task of being a human being. "Possibility is the only saving thing." The outcome "depends solely upon whether one obtains possibility."⁶⁶

---

65 Ibid., pp. 86–8; SV 12:79-81; (9:76–9).
66 *Sickness*, p. 172; (KW 19:38f.); SV 15:96; (11:151).

MAJOR FORMULATIONS ON NECESSITY BY KIERKEGAARD

Thus concludes the summary of the development of Kierkegaard's concept of "possibility" from *Fragments* through *The Sickness unto Death* and some journal entries of 1849. Some reference to his concept of "necessity" has been unavoidable, because the two compose an indissoluble dialectic (wherein freedom dwells), so that one cannot be defined without reference to the other. But now we proceed to a similar summary of the development of his concept of necessity (as indicated in the outline of this chapter on p. ooo above). Thus we will be able finally to answer the question that first evoked a treatment of the entire problem of Kierkegaard's "logic," namely, what happened to Kierkegaard's thinking about "necessity" between *Fragments* and *Sickness* (p. ooo above).

1 Necessity in Either/Or, Fragments, *and* Postscript

It may be true (as commented above p. 145) that the concept of possibility is more central to Kierkegaard's concerns than that of necessity. Yet, it was the spectre of "necessity" that constantly haunted his thinking and proved the more difficult for him to come to terms with. Necessity appeared as the demon in Hegel's System of (so-called) Logic which Kierkegaard fought to contravene, and which was the foil against which he sharpened his own set of categories and concepts. Necessity appeared as the overruling power and unifying force in the systems of nature and the world-historical (*Verdenshistoriske*). Necessity appeared as the false "god" of those fatalists who sink into despair and lose self because they believe that "everything has become necessary" instead of "everything is possible."[67] It was only after the shock of *The Corsair* incident, with its consequent spiritual deepening and his finding "a new string in my instrument," that he came to a vision of an entirely different and positive kind of necessity. This pilgrimage of mind and spirit is as important to trace as the developments in his understanding of possibility.

Kierkegaard's first familiarity with the concepts of possibility and necessity came from his lectures and readings at the university. As previously mentioned, his notes from the lectures of H.L. Martensen (1838–39) show that the professor summarized Kant's categories of modality as possibility, actuality, necessity. Kierkegaard immediately puts these ideas to work as reflected in a journal entry of July 1840: in the sphere of

---

67 Ibid., p. 173; (KW 19:40); SV 15:97; (11:152f.).

knowledge, "we can say that the finite spirit is as it is, the unity of necessity and freedom, ... and thus it is also the unity of consequence [*Resultat*] and striving"[68] (an insight that carries right through to the definition of the self in *The Sickness unto Death*). At the very same time, he began to write his master's dissertation on *The Concept of Irony*, and in a comment on some ideas attributed to Socrates by Xenophon, he says that "a much more Socratic insight into human nature and essence" would obtain "were Socrates to bring the human being into collision not with chance [*Tilfældighed*] but with necessity. For it [is] indeed possible that hailstones might beat down the farmer's crops; but [the fact] that there would be no germinating force in the ground if the deity did not will it (in spite of every human operation) is yet a much deeper negation. The one is a conception of possibility as possibility, the other an attempt to exhibit actuality as hypothetical possibility."[69] Here Kierkegaard makes the subtle distinction between possibility as a determinant of merely fortuitous external conditions (hailstones), and a possibility inherent in actuality (power of germination) as a kind of necessity. This idea of an inner possibility as a kind of necessity does not reappear until *Sickness*.

These are, however, stray and incidental comments on necessity, no matter how brilliant and insightful. Kierkegaard's first direct and systematic formulation concerning necessity comes, a year later, within the guise of Judge William's dissertation on "The Balance between the Esthetic and the Ethical in the Development of Personhood" (*Either/Or, II*). He is considering the mediation of opposites by (Hegelian) philosophy. "Philosophy," he says, "turns toward the past, toward the totality of experienced world-history (*Verdenshistorie*)," whereas "action is essentially future tense." But philosophic mediation annuls the principle of contradiction, and thus each passes over into the other to form a "higher unity." This applies not only to past and future but likewise to "the two spheres ... of thought and freedom." For authentic freedom, however, "the contradiction does exist, because the [one] excludes the [other]," because "as truly as there is a time to come, so truly there is an Either/Or," a choice either to stay with the past or to move in freedom into a new future.[70]

Therefore, "The spheres with which philosophy properly has to deal, the spheres proper to thought, are logic, nature, and history. Here ne-

---

68 *Journals*, 2274; III A 5.
69 *The Concept of Irony* (Blooomington: Indiana University Press 1968), p. 58n; (KW 2:21n); SV 1:79f.; (13:116f.).
70 *Either/Or*, 2:174-8; (KW 4:170-3); SV 3:160-3; (2:155-7).

cessity rules, and therefore mediation has its validity." Obviously, the "necessity" that Judge William has in mind is that which is revealed or discovered by human thinking as it analyses thought itself and its ways of arriving at "truth" (logic), as it analyses all the structures and processes of nature and formulates its observations into universal laws (nature, science), as it analyses the macro movements in human social existence and discovers regularities that negate the continuing significance of individual persons and events (history).[71] For him, it is the same *kind* of necessity that is evidenced in each of these cases.

Judge William recognizes that "with history there is a difficulty, for here, it is said, freedom prevails." But, he continues, if history is properly interpreted, the difficulty is resolved. Granted, "The individual acts, but this action enters into the order of things that maintains the whole of existence. ... [T]his higher order of things that digests, so to speak, the free actions and works them together in its eternal laws is necessity, and this necessity is the movement in world-history." This means that "[P]hilosophy has nothing at all to do with what could be called the inner deed [*Gjerning*], but the inner deed is the true life of freedom. Philosophy considers the external deed, yet in turn it does not see this as isolated but sees it as assimilated into and transformed in the the world-historical process. This process is the proper subject for philosophy, and it considers this under the determinant of necessity."[72] Of course, Judge William's main concern is not with the subject of necessity but with the fact that "the whole personality is not involved in the movement" of abstract thought and its necessity; or with the fact that the person who lives purely aesthetically "develops with necessity, not in freedom; no metamorphosis takes place in him, no infinite eternal movement."[73]

As we shall see, this view of "history" as strictly the realm of necessity is modified in *Fragments*. Yet, the general position that logic, nature and *world*-history are the spheres where "necessity rules," and therefore are foreign and inimical to the inner sphere of individual subjectivity whence ethical decision and free action derive, is maintained throughout the three-year period of the authorship from *Either/Or* (1842) through *Philosophical Fragments* (1844), *The Concept of Anxiety* (1844),

---

71 Ibid., p. 178; (KW 4:174); SV 3:164; (2:158).

72 Idem. In their KW vol. 4, the Hongs give several interesting quotes from Hegel's works concerning the relation of freedom to historical necessity (n.29, pp. 485f.). But at the time of *Either/Or* Kierkegaard had not read these passages because in 1842 he was still dependent on secondary sources for his knowledge of Hegel.

73 Ibid., pp. 216, 229; (KW 4:212, 225); SV 3:197, 209; (2:190, 201).

Stages on Life's Way (1844-45), and *Concluding Unscientific Postscript* (1845). But in *Either/Or* no attempt is made to analyse the essential character of necessity, except by its opposition and contradiction to the individual's "choosing" in "freedom." In the rest of these works (except for *Stages*) Kierkegaard undertakes to describe what it is about logic, nature (science), and world-history that makes them qualitatively distinct from and at enmity with individual subjectivity. But the first clear and direct definition of necessity appears in the "Interlude" in *Fragments*, and it is illustrated in all three fields (logic, nature, and history). This characterization of necessity has been tangentially discussed already, but the focus was mainly on possibility.

For our purpose here, the key statements (in *Fragments*) for the field of "logic" are these: "The only thing that cannot come into existence is the necessary, because the necessary *is*. ... [N]ecessity ... is not a qualification [*Bestemmelse*] of being but of essence, since the essence of the necessary is to be. ... All coming into existence occurs in [*ved*] freedom, not of [*af*] necessity. No coming-into-existence [*Tilblivende*] comes into existence by way of a ground, but everything by way of a cause. Every cause ends in a freely-effecting [*fritvirkende*] cause."[74] Two references will help to clarify what kind of "logical" necessity Kierkegaard has in mind in this passage.

First, in analysing the relation of human understanding (reason) to the absolute paradox (also in *Fragments*), Kierkegaard discusses the proofs of God's existence as illustrated in Spinoza's argument that God's "essence involves existence."[75]

He [Spinoza] explains *perfectio* by *realitas*, *esse*. Consequently, the more perfect the thing is, the more it *is*; but its perfection is that it has more *esse* in itself, which means that the more it is, the more it is. So much for the tautology. But what is lacking here is a distinction between factual [*faktisk*] being and ideal [*ideel*] being. ... With regard to factual being, to speak of more or less being is meaningless. ... Factual being is indifferent to the differentiation of all essence-determinants. ... *But as soon as I speak ideally about being, I am speaking no longer about being, but about essence.* The necessary has the highest ideality, therefore it is.

74 *Fragments*, pp. 91-3; (KW 7:74f.); SV 6:68f.; (4:237-9).
75 Ibid., pp. 51nf.; (KW 7:41nf.); SV 6:41nf.; (4:208nf.). For this passage do not read David Swenson's translation, not even in Howard Hong's revised translation of 1962, which leaves Swenson's seriously flawed translation standing. In their own translation in KW, vol. 7 (1985), the Hongs make the necessary corrections.

But this being is its essence, whereby it expressly cannot become dialectical in the determinants of factual being, because it is.

It is clear, then, that when Kierkegaard says that "the necessary *is*," and that "necessity ... is not a qualification of being but of essence," he is speaking of that necessity that obtains in the realm of ideas totally abstracted from existential (factual) being with its determinants of space and time. As long as one is dealing purely with the interrelationship of ideas, then (as he says in *Either/Or*) the necessity of the logical coimplication of "mediation" (Hegel) is valid. But the "existence" which is essentially "involved" in "essence" is that of *ideal* (abstract) being, and hence its "necessity" does not embrace or function in the transition (the relationship) between possibility and the *factual* being of actuality. Furthermore, it should be noted that the coherence of *ideas* and their "necessary" coimplication that make up Hegel's "logic" is not identical with the coherence and "necessity" that bind together the premises and conclusions of twentieth-century propositional and predicate logics. This difference explains why Hegel's logic is generally viewed as metaphysics, and hence is not discussed or included in the field of twentieth-century logic.

Secondly, Kierkegaard adds (in the "Interlude") quite a different quality to this necessity when he says that "All coming-into-existence occurs in freedom, not of necessity. No coming-into-existence comes into existence by way of a ground, but everything by way of a cause. Every cause ends in a freely-effecting cause." His use of the concepts of "ground" and "cause" derives from an entirely different perspective on the kind of necessity (involved in these comments) from that found in Hegel. In an extensive note (*Fragments*, KW 7:301f.) the Hongs suggest that Kierkegaard's use of the concept "ground" directly reflects its exposition in Hegel's own *Logic*. But this is questionable for several reasons.

It appears that Kierkegaard never read extensively in Hegel's own writings.[76] His university lectures and readings during the late 1830s gave him a thorough acquaintance with Hegel's chief ideas, both from pro-Hegelians such as J.L. Heiberg and H.C. Martensen and from anti-Hegelians such as Poul Møller and F.C. Sibbern. Then during his stay in Berlin (October 1841 to March 1842), he heard the lectures of two prominent Hegelians, Philip Marheineke and Karl Werder, and ac-

---

[76] For a further elaboration of what follows, see my monograph on *Trendelenburg's Influence on Kierkegaard's Modal Categories*, especially the opening section on "Kierkegaard's Knowledge of Logic."

Freedom: The Dialectical in Possibility/Necessity 183

quired the latter's book, *Logik, als Commentar und Ergänzgung zu Hegels Wissenschaft der Logik*. Obviously, Kierkegaard developed a negative view of Hegel's philosophy from the start, as is evidenced by his earliest comments in his journals (June 1836 onward).

At the same time, he was finding philosophic support for his own perspectives from very careful reading of the many-volumed *Geschichte der Philosophie* by W.G. Tennemann. He had already read much of Plato, but Tennemann attracted him to Descartes, Leibniz, and especially Aristotle. So during 1843 and 1844, he proceeded to acquire some forty-two volumes of Aristotle's works and secondary studies about him. And Niels Thulstrup maintains that "[o]nly after Kierkegaard had read Aristotle, the history of ancient philosophy, Descartes, and Leibniz, did he concentrate his attention on Hegel's logic," and that during this period, Kierkegaard's own "concept of logic has now become dominated by that of Aristotle."[77]

It must also be noted that from the beginning of his study of Aristotle, his primary guide in interpretation was the very influential German philosopher of his own day, Friederich Adolf Trendelenburg. Kierkegaard acquired his two works on Aristotle's logic in February of 1843, and five other volumes of his writings shortly thereafter. From this philosopher he quickly gained not only his major criticisms of Hegel's system (from his *Die logische Frage in Hegel's System*), but also a clarification of many of his own ideas. So he confides to his journal, "There is no modern philosopher from whom I have profited so much as from Trendelenburg. ... [N]ow that I have read him, how much more lucid and clear everything is to me. My relation to him is very special."[78]

The point to this excursus on Aristotle and Trendelenburg is that Kierkegaard's comments on "ground" and "cause" in the "Interlude" of *Fragments* clearly reflect the Aristotelian views of Trendelenburg rather than those of Hegel. Kierkegaard had purchased Trendelenburg's major work, *Logische Untersuchungen*, in January of 1844, and was avidly reading it while writing *Fragments* and *The Concept of Anxiety* during March–May of that year. References to it (and other works by Trendelenburg) are sprinkled throughout the journals and papers for that year. In a background note for the Introduction to *The Concept of Anxiety*,

---

77 Niels Thulstrup, *Kierkegaard's Relation to Hegel*, pp. 296, 294.
78 *Journals*, 5978; VIII^1 A 18. For a summary of Trendelenburg's critique of Hegel's logic, see Gershon G. Rosenstock, *F.A. Trendelenburg: Forerunner of John Dewey*, pp. 19–27. A translation of his *Die Logische Frage in Hegels System* may be found in *The Journal of Speculative Philosophy*, 5 (1871), 349–59; 6 (1872), 82–93, 163–75, 350–61.

Kierkegaard evidences the presence of Trendelenburg in his thoughts at that time by remarking, "Should anyone want further explication of the unwarranted use of the negative in logic, I simply refer him to Adolf Trendelenburg's *Die logische Frage in Hegel's System, zwei Streitsschriften, Berlin 1843*. Trendelenburg is well schooled in Greek philosophy and is unimpressed by humbug."[79]

The way in which Trendelenburg defines "ground" and "cause" and interrelates them is clearly what Kierkegaard has in mind in the "Interlude," whereas in the quotations from Hegel (in Hongs' note on "ground" for *Fragments*) there is much talk of ground and how existence is bound to it by necessity, but there is no mention of cause. Trendelenburg says,

The effecting cause [*wirkende Ursache*, the direct equivalent of Kierkegaard's *virkende Aarsag* in *Fragments*] and the purpose, which are the determinative conditions of the thing [*Dinge*], can be known; if they are known, then they designate *ground* in regard to what is conceived therefrom. ... The cause becomes ground if it is grasped universally; and the universal is the characteristic by which the concept is imbued through [the process of] thinking. The cause, as the thing [*Sache*], is a particular and is related ... to a particular fact [*Thatsache*]. ... The same cause appears as ground if it is abstracted [*erhoben*] into the universal and is accordingly placed under the law of organic life. ... In the ground, the blind linking of the forwardpressing causes and effects is transformed into a necessity-of-thought [*gedachte Notwendigkeit*]. The purpose, which originates in the mind, combines more easily with the concept of ground; and is called "ground" when it is conceived as determinative of other [things].

Then Trendelenburg refers approvingly to the use of Aristotle's "causes" (*materialis, formalis, efficiens, finalis*) to explain the "causality of things-that-have-being [*Seienden*]." Thus, "in this way it has been shown that form and matter are dependent on the effecting cause of the movement, and when the purpose has emerged, all three are governed by the purpose."[80]

---

79 See *Journals*, 2341, V A 74; 1941, V A 75; 3300, V A 98; 5742, V C 11; 2352, V C 12. The quotation from a background note for *The Concept of Anxiety* is from *Papirer*, V B 49:6; a translation is in *The Concept of Anxiety*, KW 8:181.

80 Friedrich Adolf Trendelenburg, *Logische Untersuchungen*, 3rd ed., vol. 2, pp. 179f. For an extended study of Trendelenburg's concepts of ground, possibility, necessity, and actuality, and of their influence on and relationship to Kierkegaard's own concepts, see my monograph referred to in note 76 above. See also G.G. Rosenstock, *F.A. Trendelenburg*, chapter 5 on Trendelenburg "As a Pioneer in Naturalism."

Kierkegaard liked this analysis of the relation of being and thinking *up to a point*. He liked Trendelenburg's empiricism, which gives relatively independent status to particular things (*Sache*) that cannot be reduced to thoughts, and that comprise "the factual" as providing "the fixed signals for the inner constructing mind." Trendelenburg also gives extensive analysis of the importance and irreducible character of the "accidental" (*das Zufällige*: fortuitous, contingent), which, along with the factual or particular, plays such an important role in Kierkegaard's categories. But in the end, it is not only Hegel's but more particularly Trendelenburg's "ground" that Kierkegaard rejects as the explanatory factor in the event of "coming-into-existence." Trendelenburg may distinguish between ground and cause, between the necessary and the accidental, between being and thinking. But finally he views thinking as having the capacity for—indeed, the task and duty of—"penetrating" the factual and "conquering" the accidental until it "disappears in the same measure as knowledge advances, and the necessity of the part enlarges to the necessity of the whole." In this way, "the blind linking of forward-pressing causes and effects are transformed into a necessity-of-thought." So freedom may appear to have common cause with accident, acknowledging the indeterminacy of the contingent. But true freedom seeks to escape that "sinister realm." "Freedom and accident ... are set in opposition in their true senses. Freedom, when it follows its [own] definition, wills to unite itself with reason and accordingly with necessity."[81]

In summary, then, the "ground" that Kierkegaard rejects is the conceptual unity of cause and effect in the service of the mind's "purpose," a unity discovered by reason's analysis of the factual, and formulated into universal laws as the "higher necessity" that unifies all things. Obviously, this "ground" and its "necessity" are something more than those operative in Hegel's metaphysical logic, or those operative in the propositional and predicate logics of the twentieth century.[82] And in the end

---

81 Ibid., 2:216f.

82 Hence Swenson's translation of the passage in *Fragments* is at best ambiguous when he inserts the word "logical" into Kierkegaard's text, to make it read, "Nothing comes into existence by virtue of a [logical] ground." And so also Johannes Sløk's comment on this passage is questionable when he says, "'Ground' designates here the logical, that is, timeless, not successively-determined coherence of *concepts*, in contrast to which 'cause' is an empirical concept which designates the historical, temporally and successively determined dependence between one *event* and another. That an occurrence in nature must realize a certain possibility is not identical with a necessity in the logical sense." See *Die Anthropologie Kierkegaards*, p. 38. Trendelenburg's "logic" embraces both of Sløk's kinds of necessity, what he calls the "logical" and the "empirical." Again, see my monograph for further exposition of this point.

Kierkegaard had to reject Trendelenburg's Aristotelian organicism because its overruling universal "purpose" does not allow for that gap or breach (*Brud*) before which the human mind and spirit must pause (*standse*) and make a free decision and choice, which is like a leap (*Spring*). So as he is writing *Fragments*, Kierkegaard takes Trendelenburg to task (in the journals) because he "resorts all too frequently to examples from mathematics and the natural sciences. Regrettably one finds almost no examples of the ethical in logic, which ... serves to support my theory of the leap, which is essentially at home in the realm of freedom." And, "Trendelenburg does not seem to be at all aware of the leap."[83] Kierkegaard's essential disagreement with Trendelenburg is evidenced in his change of the latter's "effecting cause" (*wirkende Ursache*) to "*freely*-effecting cause" (*fritvirkende Aarsag*).

This discussion of Trendelenburg's influence on Kierkegaard's interpretation of "logical" necessity serves as a transition to the second "sphere" where "necessity rules" according to Judge William, viz. "nature" (see note 71 above). In *Fragments* there are only a few incidental references to nature, as something to be distinguished from the historical. At the beginning of his studies Kierkegaard had a sympathetic interest in the researches of the natural sciences, and, as indicated in *Either/Or*, accepted the fact that "necessity" rules in the field of natural law. But he assumed that the sciences would acknowledge the limitation of their truth to the sphere of the physical, and would not intrude into the psychical and spiritual.[84]

But as he read more of Trendelenburg, he saw that the latter conceived of freedom as being "rational" and hence left no room for ethical freedom but absorbed it into the necessity of universal laws. And in November 1846, Kierkegaard purchased a book that obviously intrigued him, Carl G. Carus's *Psyche: zur Entwicklungsgeschichte der Seele* [Psyche: The History of the Evolution of the Soul]. He promptly read it and made some twenty critical remarks (in his journal) about its attempt to explain human consciousness in the terms of physics and physiology. In this he saw the danger that "all of ethics becomes illusory, and ethics in the race is treated statistically by averages or is calculated as one calculates vibrations in laws of nature." Hence physiology claims to "explain

---

83 *Journals*, 2352; VC 12; 2341; VA 74.
84 See the Hongs' extended note on this matter in *Journals*, vol. 3, pp. 829f.

the criminal, that the whole thing was a natural necessity." This view means the end of wonder, ethics, and belief.[85]

This critique of the natural sciences does not appear in *Fragments*, but Kierkegaard's representation of "nature" lays the foundation for it. He says, "nature is too abstract to be, in the stricter sense of the word, dialectical with respect to time. Nature's imperfection is that it does not have a history" (in the sense of being dialectical). "Nature as spatial determination exists only immediately. Something that is dialectical with respect to time has an intrinsic duplexity [*Dobbelthed*, doubleness], so that after having been present it can endure as a past, ... and as something bygone it has actuality, for it is certain and trustworthy that it occurred. But that it occurred is, in turn, precisely its uncertainty." Therefore, "[b]ecause the historical intrinsically has the *deceptiveness* [*Svigagtighed*] of coming-into-existence, it cannot be sensed immediately. The immediate impression of a natural phenomenon or of an event is not the impression of the historical, for the *coming-into-existence* cannot be sensed immediately."[86]

Thus the "necessity" that inheres in the sphere of nature consists of the direct and immediate relation and the unbroken continuity of things. This relation is open to immediate sense experience and to cognition (by rational conceptualization). Since "immediate sensation and immediate cognition cannot deceive," there is in these relations no element of the deceptiveness that is involved in all coming-into-existence, i.e., in the movement from possibility to actuality by means of human choices made from among several alternatives that lie in the future. So the immediate experiences of sense and the direct formulation of rational (scientific) concepts grasp only the direct necessary relations "of a natural phenomenon or of an event," and cannot discern that "in any [teleological] progress ... there is in each moment a pause (here wonder stands *in pausa* and waits for the coming-into-existence), which is the pause of coming-into-existence and the pause of possibility precisely because the *telos* is outside." In the case of coming-into-existence, "[t]he occurrence can be known immediately but not that it has occurred, not even that it is in the process of occurring. ... The deceptiveness of the occurrence is that it has

---

85 *Journals*, 2807; VII¹ A 182; 2809; VII¹ A 186. The importance of this topic to Kierkegaard is evidenced by the fact that his notes in response to Carus's book run in his journal from VII¹ A 182 to 200, interrupting a line of thought about God's omnipotence (181) and the fact that God is never an object to human consciousness because God is subject (201). Most of these notes are translated in Hongs' *Journals and Papers*, 2806–24.

86 *Fragments*, pp. 94, 97f., 100; (KW 7:76, 79, 81); SV 6:70, 72, 74; (4:239, 242, 244).

occurred, and therein lies the transition from nothing, from non-being, and from the multiple possible 'how.' Immediate sense [perception] and cognition do not have any intimation of the uncertainty with which belief approaches its object, but neither [do they have intimation of] the certitude that extricates [belief] from the incertitude."[87]

As noted, these statements about the kind of necessity involved in the sphere of nature are worked out by Kierkegaard by contrasting nature with history. But, obviously, in *Fragments*, he is talking about a kind of history very different from that sphere of the world-historical process where, according to Judge William in *Either/Or*, necessity also rules. In fact, in *Postscript* Kierkegaard goes further and says flatly, "The trustworthiness of sense [perception] is a deception. ... The trustworthiness claimed by a knowledge of the historical is also a mere deception, insofar as it claims to be the trustworthiness of actuality."[88]

So, in *Fragments*, he distinguishes between "the historical in the more concrete sense" (or "the directly, literally historical") as consisting of an historical eyewitness's account of the particular historical circumstances, and "the historical in the stricter sense, which is dialectical with respect to time" and consists of that coming-into-existence which is a fact of "history" (in time and place) and yet is not observable directly by sense or cognition but is "known" only by belief.[89] In other words, Climacus rejects Judge William's notions and insists that the sphere of history (in the stricter sense) does indeed include "the free actions of free individuals," and that such free actions are *not* woven back into the "necessity" of the "eternal laws" of "the order of things." So, he says, "The more special historical coming-into-existence comes into existence by a relatively freely-effecting cause [*fritvirkende Aarsag*], which in turn points to an absolutely freely-effecting cause."[90]

For Climacus, therefore, both in *Fragments* and in *Postscript*, the eternal necessary laws, discerned by human rational analysis of both the structures of nature and the macro movements of the world-historical process, do not annul or set aside or swallow up (*aufheben* in German, *ophæve* in Danish) that peculiar event that is dialectical in respect to time in that, on the one hand, it is an observable fact of history and yet, on the other, it hides within it an unobservable pause before a breach

---

87 Ibid., pp. 100f.; (KW 7:80–2); SV 6:74f.; (4:244f.).
88 *Postscript*, p. 280; (KW 12.1:316); SV 10:22; (7:271).
89 *Fragments*, pp. 73, 94, 108; (KW 7:59, 76, 87); SV 6:56, 70, 79f.; (4:225, 240, 250f.).
90 Ibid., p. 94; (KW 7:76); SV 6:70; (4:240).

which cannot be bridged by either logical or physical force but only by the leap of freedom which is enabled purely by the courage to believe—against all evidence to the contrary. In *Fragments*, he spells this out by analysing the dialectic of past and future from the perspective of the event of coming-into-existence by means of the freely effecting cause.

Climacus admits that what has happened cannot, in a certain sense, be undone or changed. But, he asks, "Is this unchangeableness the unchangeableness of necessity?" No!—because the historical in the concrete sense (open to immediate sense and cognition) contains, hidden within it, the "more special historical coming-into-existence ... by way of ... an absolutely freely effecting cause." Hence the "actual 'thus and so' " of the past is unchangeable, but "its possible 'how' could ... have been different."

In other words, the certainty that the past has actually occurred is balanced by an "uncertainty regarding it in the same sense as there is uncertainty regarding the future, the possibility ... out of which it could not possibly *come forth* with necessity. ... [W]herever coming into existence is involved (which is indeed involved in the past), there the uncertainty (which is the uncertainty of coming into existence) of the most certain coming into existence can express itself only in this passion" ("the passionate sense of coming into existence, that is, wonder"). Kierkegaard sees here an absolute either/or. "If the past had become necessary, ... it would follow that the future would also be necessary. If necessity could supervene at one single point, then we could no longer speak of the past and the future. ... If the past had become necessary, then it could not belong to freedom, ... and freedom itself would be an illusion."[91]

Thus, Kierkegaard acknowledges that a kind of necessity rules in the rational coherence of ideas, and also in chains of cause and effect in physical nature, and this necessity can be formulated into universal laws. Indeed, this necessity rules even in the macro movements of history when "world-history" is viewed "in purely metaphysical determinants" and hence "speculatively as the immanence of cause and effect, ground and consequent," and thus as excluding "what makes an action ethically the individual's," i.e., "intention" (*Hensigt*).[92] But he insists that human history includes and is shaped by the hidden, inward, intentional resolve and decision of individuals, and that such resolve and decision occur only with the leap of courage and freedom.

---

91 Ibid., pp. 95–9; (KW 7:76–80); SV 6:70–3; (4:240–4).
92 *Postscript*, pp. 138–9; (KW 12.1:155); SV 9:129; (7:127–8).

This concept of necessity clearly continues to be operative to the end of *Concluding Unscientific Postscript.* The language changes. In this book, intended to be his treatment of "logical problems,"[93] Kierkegaard rarely mentions "logic" as such but speaks constantly of it as that "abstract speculative thinking" and "objective reflection" which, by its very nature, is incapable of capturing and including the actuality of existing human individuals and their ethical-religious actions. He also speaks frequently of the world-historical as teaching much about the world but nothing about one's individual self because of its objectifying concern, which changes the ethical into the non-ethical.[94] Hence, his concept of necessity remains the same as in *Philosophical Fragments.* In *Postscript*, he explores and expands the role of the accidental or contingent (*Tilfældighed*) in the historical event of coming-into-existence through the leap of freedom, to the point of saying, "It is precisely through coming into existence [*bliver til*], becoming historical, that [everything] has its element of contingency, because contingency is precisely one factor in all coming-into-existence [*Tilblivelse*]." But at the same spot, he vehemently denies "the necessity of the historical," and quotes *Fragments* to the effect that "nothing comes into existence by necessity, because coming-into-existence and necessity contradict each other."[95]

It is clear, then, that from *Either/Or* through *Postscript* Kierkegaard sees all kinds of necessity (logical, natural, historical) as inimical to, contradictory of, excluded from the inner, passionate, interested subjectivity (spirit, self) which is decisive in the ethical-religious existence of the individual. So in *Fragments* he says, "Necessity stands entirely by itself." And he repeats this in *Postscript* (with a direct reference to *Fragments*): "Necessity must be dealt with by itself," which immediately follows his assertion that "Subjectivty is truth; subjectivity is actuality."[96] So, as noted before, here in *Fragments* he denies Hegel's thesis that "necessity [is] a unity of possibility and actuality," but he is not ready to say (as he does in *The Sickness unto Death*) that "actuality is a unity of possibility and necessity."[97] The actuality of the human being, as ethical-religious being, lies in subjectivity.

---

93 See Hongs' *Søren Kierkegaard's Journals and Papers*, vol. 5, p. 530, notes 1204, 1211.
94 For example, see *Postscript*, pp. 75f., 88–90, 121–23, 134–42; (KW 12.1:80–2, 96–8, 135–8, 149–159); SV 9:70f., 82–4, 112–14, 124–32; (7:62f., 76–8, 110–12, 122–31).
95 Ibid., p. 90; (KW 12.1:98); SV 9:84; (7:78).
96 *Fragments* p. 92; (KW 7:74); SV 6:69; (4:238); *Postscript* p. 306; SV 10:45; (7:297).
97 *Sickness*, p. 169; (KW 19:36); SV 15:94; (11:149).

2 The Change in the Concept of Necessity after Postscript

What, then, happened to Kierkegaard's own *self*-consciousness between his finishing of *Postscript* in December of 1845 and his composition of *Sickness* during the first six months of 1848, so that in the latter he delineates a kind of necessity that plays a positive role in the becoming of the self, and that becomes an integral dimension of the self's actuality?

Externally, the simple answer is: the *Corsair* affair. The origin and sequential steps in this momentous and complex event in Kierkegaard's life have been reconstructed with great thoroughness and perspicacity by Howard and Edna Hong, along with all the relevant materials, in vol. XIII of *Kierkegaard's Writings*. They rightly conclude that "the most important consequence was wholly unexpected and unintended: the second phase of Kierkegaard's authorship."[98] But what is relevant for our subject of Kierkegaard's concept of necessity is the inward transformation of his own self-understanding, because this transformation centres on a new and profound sense of the role played by God's "governance" (*Styrelse*) in uniquely *Christian* believing and acting—and the suffering involved therein (see note 99 below). That these concerns are major influences in the shaping of the "second phase" of the authorship must be made clear.

The derisive and degrading attack on Kierkegaard in the *Corsair* occurred during the first six months of 1846. This coincided with the publication of *Concluding Unscientific Postscript* at the end of February. And he makes his first "Report" on the attack in a journal entry of March 9th. He says that he must keep calm and remain silent, not violating his own principle of indirect communication ("double reflection" in *Postscript*). He must remain faithful to his "existence-idea," so that it becomes "elevating and ennobling" to himself "in the religious sense." He sees that, in the whole event, "something more eventuates which is not due to me but to Governance," something he will "understand far better afterwards." But the affair is far from over, and little does he anticipate what will eventuate. He dogmatically declares "my activity as an author is finished," and wishes "I could make myself become a pastor."[99]

---

98 Page xiii in *The Corsair Affair*, edited and translated by Howard V. Hong and Edna H. Hong (Princeton: Princeton University Press, 1982). See especially the "Historical Introduction."

99 *Journals*, 5887; VII¹ A 98.

The important point is that, from this moment on, he increasingly sees the hand of God's providential governance in all the events of the closing years of his life (as is evidenced by the increasing reflection about it in both his journals and writings).[100] During the remainder of 1846, the *Corsair*'s defamation and ridicule penetrated all levels of Copenhagen's populace, and as the derision from the people in the streets and in society became more virulent, Kierkegaard poured out his heart in a series of his "talks," eventually collected and published (13 March 1847) under the title *Upbuilding Discourses in Various Spirits*. Their central focus, especially in "An Occasional Discourse" ("On the Occasion of a Confession") and in "Gospel of Sufferings," is an exploration of how Christian faith enables one to accept joyfully the sufferings which come when one seeks to be obedient to the conditions imposed by God's governance. And even the charming meditations on "What We Learn from the Lilies of the Fields and from the Birds of the Air" conclude with a solemn discourse on the fact that what we learn from them is this: "no one can serve two masters," and we must "seek first the kingdom of God and his righteousness." It is in these contemplations that there first emerges, for Kierkegaard, a new and positive view of "necessity."

The discourse subtitled "On the Occasion of a Confession" centres on one thesis—"purity of heart is to will one thing" (James 4:8)—and the large middle section explores the thesis that to will one thing truly is to will the good truly. And this section ends with a meditation on "If a human being would will the good truly, then that person must be willing to suffer all for the good." Kierkegaard is trying to fathom the mystery behind the fact that, just at the pinnacle of his career as an author, when he has decided to end that career and wishes to retire to a humble parish in the countryside, he is cast down from that pinnacle in disgrace, and made to suffer derision and ostracism even from those who had admired him.

---

100 E.g., see the increasingly numerous references to *Styrelse* in following journal entries, in Niels Jørgen Cappelørn's Index to *Søren Kierkegaards Papirer*. But for conclusive evidence of this decisive shift, see Alastair McKinnon's fascinating monograph, "Dating Kierkegaard's Battles with Fate" (Det Kongelige Danske Videnskabernes Selskab, Historisk-filosofiske Meddelelser 52:3; København, Kommissionær: Munksgaard, 1986). His study is strictly statistical, but it demonstrates that the first significant "cut" occurs, both in the journals and the works, precisely in the materials that I use below to clarify the psychological and theological content of Kierkegaard's new emphasis on Governance. See especially pp. 12, 18.

Freedom: The Dialectical in Possibility/Necessity

In a way, he had invited this event by his rebuff of Goldschmidt and his attack on P.L. Møller. But the scale and intensity and vicious tone of their reaction was beyond all his expectations. And as noted above, the cataclysmic significance of the event for his life convinces him that it was not the product of an unfortunate and accidental complex of circumstances that he could have and should have avoided. Rather, he is shocked into the awareness that the event had its roots in Governance, and that he is being called by Governance to seek out the implications for a radical change in his life. *Why* these sufferings? Why, like Abraham, is one called to abandon one's "essential wish" in life and to become an "essential sufferer" by journeying into a strange land and to dwell among strangers?

He does not yet know the answer to these questions, but one thing becomes clear. The event is no meaningless accident. Rather,

> Another [S.K. himself] comes perhaps by another way but to the same place. Silently, the governing [*styrende*] necessity leads him onward. Severe and earnest, not cruel, for it is never that, duty comes behind and brings up the rear of the procession. But the path is not the path of the wish. Now he halts for a moment, even the two severe guides are touched by his suffering: look, there a side path branches off; "goodby, thou wish of my youth, thou friendly place, where I had hoped to be able to build and to dwell with my wish!" So they move on; the governing necessity silently in advance, duty severe and earnest comes behind, not cruel, because duty is never that.[101]

Clearly, in this passage Kierkegaard depicts his sufferings as a way by which Governance is "leading" (*føre*, guiding, conducting) him away from the "friendly place" where he had been dwelling, and by which a sense of severe and earnest (but not cruel) duty is pushing him (like Abraham) onto a path of pilgrimage toward a strange and unknown destiny. And in the guiding, demanding, compelling character of his situation, he sees the hand of the Eternal. "When the sufferer actually takes his sufferings to heart, then he receives help from the Eternal toward his decision. Because to take one's sufferings to heart is to be weaned from the temporal order [*Timelighed*], ... in order to find rest in the blessed trustworthiness of the Eternal." He must learn "to let go of the-things-of-this-world [*Timelighed*]" and seek the purity of heart that wills one thing,

---

101 *Upbuilding Discourses in Various Spirits*, "Part One: An Occasional Discourse" (D.V. Steere translation, *Purity of Heart*), pp. 152–3; (KW 15:102–3); SV 11:96; (8:199).

because "it is double-mindedness when the sufferer uses his strength to conceal the pain instead of letting himself be healed by the Eternal."[102] And the governing force of this set of circumstances, which he obviously views as calling him to do and to suffer for the Good, he does not hesitate to call "necessity."

Do, then, these circumstances and their "necessity" conflict with and rob him of his freedom? Quite to the contrary, *this* kind of necessity demands and evokes, indeed, requires his free, voluntary response and participation. A few pages later (after the last quotation), Kierkegaard asks a question. "One thing remains to be discussed before leaving the matter of sufferings: can one be said to *will* suffering"—that is, "will," not "in the sense of desire" but "in the noble sense of freedom"? His answer is yes, and he distinguishes between two modes of voluntary suffering. On the one hand, will may take the form of *courage* which "chooses the burdensome way of a higher calling" and thus "freely wills suffering" because one must face "a treacherous opposition within oneself … in league with the opposition without."

On the other hand, Kierkegaard is more interested in the case when will takes the form of *patience*, which bears sufferings that are not knowingly accepted as part of freely choosing a "higher calling" but that come unexpectedly as the inescapable accompaniment of conditions imposed on one from without (and he loves the play on words, in the Danish, which indicates that "patience" [*Taalmod*] includes but is something more than "courage" [Mod]). Obviously, his own sufferings that resulted from the *Corsair* affair were of this kind. And he sees that he must not rebel and cry out against these sufferings because they play a part in "the good" which he is to serve. So, he must bear them with "patience," which he defines as "that courage which voluntarily accepts sufferings which cannot be avoided," which "are forced on one."

But what difference does patience make in the actual condition of the sufferer? It heals and saves the person. "There is in the sufferer herself a treacherous resistance [to suffering?] which is in league with [one's] horror of inevitability, and together they seek to crush her," and "[i]f the compulsion of necessity presses upon a soul which neither possesses nor wills to possess the resilience-power of freedom, then the soul becomes cowed [oppressed]." On the contrary, patience, which has the courage to accept voluntarily unavoidable sufferings, "precisely thereby finds itself free in the midst of unavoidable sufferings. Thus patience performs

---

102 Ibid., pp. 166–8; (KW 15:113–15); SV 11:105–7; (8:208–10).

... an even greater miracle than courage." Indeed, "patience makes itself free in unavoidable suffering." This is so because "[t]he outward impossibility of being able to set oneself free *from* suffering does not hinder the inner possibility of actually being able to set oneself free *in* suffering" (emphasis added). Indeed, in this kind of suffering, "necessity is the compulsion; but one cannot be compelled into patience. ... Patience is the counterpressure of resilience, whereby the one who is coerced is set free within the coercion."

How does such patience heal and save? Is not one who adopts this kind of attitude simply "making a virtue out of necessity"? Kierkegaard replies,

Undeniably, one is making a virtue out of necessity; that is just the secret. ... One brings a determinant of freedom (virtue) out of that which is determined as necessity. And it is precisely therein that the healing power of the decision for the Eternal resides: that the sufferer may freely accept the compulsory suffering. ... It is salvation by the decision of the eternal that the sufferer, while the coercion of necessity seeks to squeeze [collapse?] the heart, *opens* oneself for the eternal, and eternally acquiesces in *willing* to suffer all. ... When a human being dares to declare: "I am eternity's free citizen," then necessity cannot imprison her except in—voluntary confinement.[103]

Therefore, our conclusion is: the unexpected sufferings imposed on Kierkegaard as a result of the *Corsair* affair, imposed with a sense of inevitable, unavoidable, and inescapable *necessity*, lead him to a comprehension of a kind of "necessity" that does not conflict with or negate his freedom. On the contrary, in these "upbuilding talks" with himself while the affair is in process, he comes to see these events as the instrumentality used by a loving, even though severe and earnest, providential Governance to compel him to face some critical decisions about his life and future, decisions that are forced upon him by the "necessity" of his sufferings, but decisions whose outcome is not determined by that necessity. On the contrary, the necessity of the unavoidable sufferings simply provides the occasion that demands and evokes his own heartfelt "determinant of freedom" to "open himself to the eternal," and thus to experience "the healing power of the decision of the eternal" by which he is

---

103 Ibid. For all of the quotes in the last four paragraphs see pp. 171–5; (KW 15:117–20); SV 11:109–111; (8:212–14).

enabled to "acquiesce eternally to suffer all." *This* necessity becomes an integral dimension of his own actuality.

What concrete form did this free acquiescence take? Shortly after he completes these "upbuilding discourses," Kierkegaard makes several revealing entries in his journal during January of 1847.[104] He praises God for "all the assaults of rabble barbarism" that have come upon him, because "now I have gained time to learn inwardly." And what has he learned? First, that his idyllic and religious motivations for wishing to become a rural pastor were "a melancholy idea," which he now firmly rejects. Secondly, that "now I stand resolved on the spot in a way I never have been," that is, on the spot of being an author. He is convinced that he is "not suited for the tasks of a rural pastor," but that "as far as my intelligence, talents, skills, and mental constitution are concerned, there can be no doubt that I am rightly constructed in every way" for the task of being an author. Indeed, his unique and particular authorship must now take a new form in the light of the fact that "the literary, social, and political situation requires an *extraordinaire* [*Extraordinair*]." And he is confronted by the haunting idea that "the question now is ... whether there is anyone in the kingdom suitable to be that except me."

Thus, Kierkegaard's experience of "patience" in the *Corsair* affair reveals to him still another kind of "necessity," to which he is called to acquiesce, than the necessity of the unexpected and unavoidable sufferings forced upon him by "the assaults of rabble barbarism." His "inward learning," by which he assures himself that he is to continue to be an author, takes the form of the conviction that "to continue along this road is not something of-my-own-working [*Selvgjort*], for it was my calling, my whole *habitus* [nature] calculated in view of such [a road]." He admits that "[o]nly when I am writing" is it possible that "I forget all the disagreeable things in life, all the sufferings; then I am at home with my thoughts and am happy."

Yet now, with his new authorship, he knows that he will invite the "persecutions of the aristocrats and the insults of the rabble." But he can do no other, because his "becoming an author is not self-chosen; on the contrary it is by virtue of my whole individuality and its deepest need [urge, demand]." He is convinced that "an urge like this, so plentiful, so

---

104 The quotes in following paragraphs are from *Journals*, 5961, 5962, 5966; VII[1] A 221, 222, 229. These are dated 20–24 January 1847, as he was finishing *The Book on Adler*, and they reflect his analysis of Adler's claim of divine guidance and of being called as an *extraordinaire*.

inexhaustible, which after continuing day after day for five or six years still surges just as copiously, must certainly be a calling from God." So he prays, "God, give me your blessing and assistance, and above all spiritual assurance ... against the doubts that arise within me. ... Once again I must steer into the open sea ['out in 70,000 fathoms'], live in grace and out of grace, utterly in God's power [*Vold*, which has the connotation of violence]. ... At every moment it takes faith."

In these passages Kierkegaard does not use the word "necessity," but, just as he felt the force of an outer necessity in his unavoidable sufferings, so here he feels the force of an inner necessity in the structure of his whole unique being, with its demand and urging to fulfil a certain "calling" in these particular circumstances at this particular time and place. And just as the outer necessity left room for and required the freedom of his patient acquiescence, so this inner necessity leaves room for and requires the response of his joyful acceptance of this calling, indeed, requires the response of faith that will carry him out "into the open sea." Clearly, this outer necessity that can be transformed into freedom through patience, and this inner necessity which is a qualification of his definitive "individuality" and requires risky choosing, comprise a kind of necessity that is qualitatively different from the necessity involved in logic, nature, and history as described from *Either/Or* through *Postscript*. But an analysis of its specific characteristics will await its description in *The Sickness unto Death*.

Two years later (1849), after the prodigious outpourings in the authorship of 1847–48, Kierkegaard has an even clearer view of the positive significance of the *Corsair* event and of the new kind of necessity it brought into his life. Again (in his journal) he affirms that he intended to stop writing with the *Concluding Postscript*, "[b]ut what happens, I get involved with all that rabble persecution, and that was the very thing that made me remain on the spot." But actually it was not the persecution as such but its awakening him to the conviction that "Christianly, the only question is that of obedience." "Thus Governance itself has kept me in the harness," with the result that "1848 was the year of my richest productivity." Governance, however, did not produce simply a quantitative continuation of the authorship but also a qualitative change in substance. "I have become," he says, "an author in an entirely different sense, for originally I thought of being an author as an escape ... from going to the country as a pastor. But has not my situation already changed in that *qua* author I have begun to work for the religious." And why? "It was the tension of actuality which put a new string in my instrument, *forced* me to publish even more" (emphasis added; the word is *tvang*, compel, coerce, the same word he used in *Upbuilding Discourses* to speak of "the compulsion of necessity").[105]

In this reflection Kierkegaard expresses, for the first time, the insight that there may be a kind of compulsion (necessity) as an integral dimension of his own "actuality," that is, in the total unity of his "individuality" (unique personhood or selfhood), and that this kind of necessity may play a positive role as the occasion and medium of God's providential governance. He gives a more specific characterization of the content of this governance in another journal entry later that same year (1849).[106]

The entry is entitled "An Accounting with Respect to My Move Against the Corsair." He says that the whole affair, his attack and the resulting vilification and ostracism, "has become my own education and development." Again he says that "[a]s author I have got a new string in my instrument, have been enabled to hit notes I never would have dreamed of otherwise." And the result is: "I have achieved 'actuality' in a stricter sense." He describes the specific content of this stricter meaning of actuality in this way: "If I had not taken this step, the *double* danger [*fare*, hazard, trouble] connected with the [essentially] Christian would have totally escaped me; thus I could have continued to conceive the [essentially] Christian in terms of the difficulty [*Vanskelighed*] of inwardness."

The formulation of this "double-danger" had come to his consciousness as (in 1847) he composed another set of discourses (*Works of Love*) shortly after finishing *Upbuilding Discourses in Various Spirits*. He warns that Christian preachers and teachers, almost universally, wax eloquent about "Christian self-renunciation" which "makes one's life so strenuous inwardly" because of the demands of "faith, love and humility." This is the first danger or difficulty. But there is a final or ultimate (*sidste*) hazard or "difficulty" (*Vanskelighed*) which they never mention, and thereby totally distort Christianity and deceive their hearers. The preachers lead one to believe that Christian self-renunciation will win the respect and admiration of others, whereas just the opposite is true: "it will go hard with you in the world." Indeed, the Christian must be prepared to "submit to being abominated almost as a criminal, scorned and ridiculed." It is a total mistake and distortion when people represent "the world's opposition as an accidental relation to Christianity." Rather, "the world's

---

105 Ibid., 6356; X^1 A 138.
106 Ibid., 6548; X^2 A 251.

Freedom: The Dialectical in Possibility/Necessity 199

opposition stands in an *essential* relation to the inwardness of Christianity." So, "[w]hat Christianity calls self-renunciation involves precisely and essentially a *double-danger.*"[107]

Here again, neither in the journal entry nor in *Works of Love* does Kierkegaard mention the concept "necessity." But it is clear that when he speaks of the "essential relationship" between "the inwardness of Christianity" and "the world's opposition" (in the form of scorn and ridicule), he is recalling the essential relationship between the outward "compulsion of necessity" in his sufferings from the *Corsair* incident and the emergence of his inward Christian "patience" in which he became free and gained the courage to acquiesce to and thus to be victorious over his sufferings. If a Christian truly practises the inwardness of self-renunciation, then she *necessarily* invokes the world's opposition, scorn, and ridicule. Likewise, he comes to see the same "essential relationship" between his sufferings and his being "called" and "compelled" by God to resume his authorship, and in a new religious vein.

Indeed, in a journal entry of 1848,[108] he applies this notion of the "double-danger" or difficulty of being a Christian directly to this major shift in his authorship. He gives an even clearer definition of the doubleness of the difficulty. "First, all the suffering of inwardness involved in becoming a Christian, the losing of reason and being crucified on the paradox.—This is the issue *Concluding Postscript* presents as ideally as possible. Then [secondly], the danger of the Christian's having to live in the world of secularity and expressing in it that he is a Christian. Here belongs all the later productivity, which will culminate in what I have ready and which could be published under the title: *Collected Works of Consummation*" (by which he means *The Sickness unto Death, Practice in Christianity*, which he was still writing, and *Armed Neutrality*).[109]

Obviously, Kierkegaard considers *Postscript*'s ideal presentation of the thesis "Truth is subjectivity" to be radically deficient in what is essentially Christian. In *Point of View* he insists that *Postscript* is not merely an aesthetic work, but neither is it properly religious. In *Postscript* he speaks much of the absolute need that inward ethical decision be enacted in the process of individual existence, in actuality. But there he had not learned—what finds expression in all the newly religious authorship that follows—that living out one's faith-conviction in the outward secu-

107 *Works of Love*, pp. 185–8; SV 12:185–8; (9:182–5).
108 *Journals*, 493; IX A 414.
109 See ibid., 493; IX A 414.

lar world is bound, with the "compulsion of necessity," to evoke virulent opposition, scorn, and ridicule, in short, sufferings. And the "inward learning" that came with these sufferings also revealed to him an inward necessity, namely, the demand of his "whole individuality and its deepest need [urge]" as the "calling of God" to initiate the new religious authorship.

This comprehension of his own experience was, for Kierkegaard, the seed out of which grew the formulation of the concept of a kind of necessity qualitatively different from any he had known before, different from the "necessity" involved in logic, nature, or history, yet a "necessity" which is an integral dimension of and function within the unity of the actuality of the authentic human self. This formulation was one of the new "notes" that he "never would have dreamed of" except for the *Corsair* affair and his phenomenological analysis of its implications for his own religious self-consciousness. It found expression not only in *Upbuilding Discourses in Various Spirits* (1846) but also in *Christian Discourses* (1847) whose composition overlapped with the beginning of *The Sickness unto Death* (1848). For example, "Joyful Notes in the Strife of Suffering" ends with the thesis that "Misfortune is good fortune." And "Thoughts which Wound from Behind" contains the thesis that "It is blessed nevertheless—to suffer derision in a good cause."[110] While writing these discourses, Kierkegaard projected another similar series entitled *Some Joyful Thoughts*, with four parts: (1) Tribulation yields steadfastness, (2) Steadfastness yields experience [i.e. understanding], (3) Experience yields hope, (4) Hope does not shame.[111]

3 The New Formulation on Necessity in Sickness

Kierkegaard's continued and seemingly exaggerated (one is tempted to say obsessive) absorption with the meaning of his sufferings stemming from the *Corsair* affair served as the occasion, nevertheless, in *The Sickness unto Death*, for a quite abstract, technical, and highly sophisticated formulation of his insights into a new (for him) kind of necessity. He turns from religious meditations on the personal meaning of his own inner experience of sufferings and of God's calling, to an abstract analysis of the role "necessity" plays in the operational structure of the self in the process of "becoming" oneself. So he can now speak of "freedom" as

---

110 See *Christian Discourses*, translated by Walter Lowrie, and SV 13.
111 *Journals*, 2198; VIII[1] A 360.

Freedom: The Dialectical in Possibility/Necessity

"the dialectical in the determinants possibility and necessity." We must now take a close look at that formulation.

Kierkegaard explores what he calls "the self's necessity" in close dialectical relation with what he calls "the self's possibility."[112] However, before we can clarify what he has in mind as the self's "necessity," we must first distinguish three characteristics (determinants) of the self (as depicted in *Sickness*) which might easily be identified as kinds of "necessity" but to which he does not apply this designation.

First, he draws a direct parallel between the self's necessity and the self's finitude. "Just as finitude is the limiting aspect in relation to infinitude, so necessity, in relation to possibility, is that which restrains [*holder igjen*, i.e., holds back]."[113] As has been shown repeatedly above, finitude is seen as an integral dimension of the self; without it one cannot become and remain oneself. In general it is the self in its external particularity. It comprehends one's brain, body, and sensuousness, but also one's environmental conditions and social relationships, one's definite location in space and time. It is only in this dimension that the self is "concrete" and "actual." And throughout the entire authorship, Kierkegaard stresses that, whatever the self is in its infinitude and possibility, the self becomes itself in actuality only when it enacts its infinite possibility within the confines of the totality of its particular finitude.

The clear implication of such a view is that one's finitude is "necessary" for and in the process of one's becoming oneself. And, as we have heard in some of his edifying discourses, Kierkegaard does not hesitate to view the external events of the *Corsair* affair, and the sufferings they imposed on him, as "the compulsion of necessity," both in the sense that they befell him unexpectedly and unwanted, and in the sense that there is an "essential relation" between Christian self-renunciation and the world's opposition and scorn. He also comes to regard the whole event as manifesting a "governing necessity" by which God leads and pushes him into a new and creative phase of his authorship.

On the other hand, it is just as clear that this kind of necessity does not imply that one's finitude *causes* one's becoming self, that one becomes oneself "of necessity." In other words, the self's necessity that is involved in "freedom" (in one's freely becoming oneself) is something

---

112 For "the self's necessity," see *Sickness*, pp. 170, 188; (KW 19:37, 54); SV 15:94, 110; (11:150, 167). For "the self's possibility," see ibid., p. 164 and (by implication) p. 168; (KW 19:31, 35); SV 15:89, 93; (11:144, 148).
113 Ibid., p. 168; (KW 19:35); SV 15:93; (11:148).

quite different from the compulsions which derive from one's finitude. And therefore in *Sickness*, Kierkegaard distinguishes between necessity and finitude, and between the *way* in which necessity "holds back" possibility in contrast with the way in which finitude "limits" infinitude (this "way" will be spelled out below).

The second characteristic of the self that operates with a kind of necessity is not a particular attribute or characteristic, but the total *structure* of the individual, which is universally present in every human being. Kierkegaard describes it as follows: "Every human being is a psychical-physical synthesis naturally fitted [*anlagt*, predisposed] to be spirit; this is the construction." And again, "every human being is fitted [*anlagt*] to be a self, determined so as to become him/herself." Indeed, "to have a self, to be a self, is the greatest, the infinite concession granted to [every] human being, but it is also eternity's claim upon him/her." In fact, this construction and predisposition may be called "the eternal in the human being," because it is something one "cannot get rid of. ... A human being cannot get rid of the relation that relates to itself any more than [one can get rid of] one's self, which, after all, is one and the same thing, since the self is the relation to oneself." No matter how hard one tries, "one cannot throw it away once and for all, ... no, never in all eternity; ... nothing is more impossible."[114]

Here, surely, Kierkegaard accepts logic's dictum that the not-possible (the "impossible") is the necessary, but in quite a different sense from what obtains in logic. It is "necessary" that this fundamental structure and predisposition, this concession and claim of the eternal, be present and consciously operative if this particular thing or being is to be "human." Indeed, this structure does make its claim inevitably and irresistibly, so that "necessarily" a human being cannot avoid or get rid of this structure and its claim. Yet, this structure and its claim do not operate in such a way that it causes or naturally necessitates its implementation and fulfilment, nor is the fulfilment logically entailed in the structure. The self's necessity that is involved in one's "freely" *becoming* one's self is quite different from what makes this structure's claim to be inevitable and irresistible. So in *Sickness* Kierkegaard does not apply the word "necessity" to the structure as such.

The third determinant of the self which might easily be judged to involve a kind of necessity is asserted by Kierkegaard in the opening para-

---

114 Ibid., pp. 176, 166, 154, 150; (KW 19:43, 33, 21, 17); SV 15:100, 91, 80, 76; (11:156, 146, 135, 130).

graphs of *The Sickness unto Death*, and it certainly serves as the ground and background for his entire exposition of the dialectic of possibility/ necessity in the self. To put it succinctly, the self is "derived." That is to say, while the self essentially is "a relation which relates to itself," yet it has not "established [*sat*] itself," but has been given being or "been established by an *other*" (emphasis added), and stands in "complete dependence" on this other. The self is dependent on the other not only for its origin, composition, and structure, but also in the sense that "the self cannot come to or be in equilibrium and rest by itself, but only, while relating to itself, by relating to that which has established the entire relation." Later he reasserts this point and clearly identifies "the other": "The self is the conscious synthesis of infinitude and finitude, which relates to itself, whose task is to become itself, which can be done only through the relationship to God."[115]

Again, it must be emphasized that the "necessity" involved in this dependent relationship does not compromise and is external to the freedom involved in the essential act of "the relation relating to itself." The "other" (however conceived or defined) in no way causes or necessitates this act, nor is the act related to the other by the necessity of logical entailment. Indeed, Kierkegaard says that the event in which "the relation relates to itself" is made possible only by the fact that "God, who constituted the human being to be a relation, lets it go out of his hand, so to speak."[116] Hence this relation of dependence is not what Kierkegaard has in mind when, in *Sickness*, he speaks of that dialectic of possibility/ necessity which is inherent to the event of the self becoming itself in freedom.

What kind of necessity is it, then, that appears to be *internal* to the event of the self becoming itself, when Kierkegaard says, "The self is freedom. But freedom is the dialectical in the determinants possibility and necessity"? Obviously, it is something other than the compulsions and the limits that derive from one's finitude, or from one's given structure, or from one's dependence on the "other" which gives or establishes the structure.

Kierkegaard provides an extremely subtle analysis of this necessity in his depiction of the self as κατα δυναμιν, under the topic "Possibility's Despair Is to Lack Necessity." As already noted, he can clarify the nature of "the self's necessity" only in its relationship with "the self's possibility."

---

115 Ibid., pp. 146f., 162; (KW 19:13f., 29f.); SV 15:73f., 87; (11:128, 142).
116 Ibid., p. 149; (KW 19:16); SV 15:75; (11:130).

Indeed, "for [the task of] becoming (and the self must certainly become itself), possibility and necessity are equally essential. Just as infinitude and finitude *belong to* the self, so also do possibility and necessity" (emphasis added). So also, as one's finitude "delimits" the extremity of one's infinitude, so necessity "holds back" possibility as it is tempted to wonder off into the fantastic. But in the latter comparison lies a significant difference between how finitude "delimits" and how necessity "holds back."[117]

On the one hand, "finitude" refers to external conditions in which this particular self, in its infinitude, is embroiled and with which it stands in an unbreakable synthesis. There is "a dialectic inherent in the self, whereby the one [element] constantly *is* its opposite."[118] In other words, the self, that one is "naturally fitted" and "determined" to become, includes all of one's "finitude," one's outward aesthetic, sensuous, physical, bodily dimensions, as well as the complex of physical and social relationships or conditions, within which one must exist in one's infinitude. And this relation means that one must explore one's infinitude by the power of imagination in such a way that the self does not "lead a fantasized existence in abstract infinitizing or in abstract isolation, continually lacking itself, from which it only moves further and further away." Rather, one's infinite self of the imagination must happily give way to and live within the boundaries and limits of one's very particular finitude. The self must "dare to be itself in its essential contingency [*Tilfældighed*] ... in which one is himself for himself."[119]

On the other hand, as has been indicated several times before, to view the self in terms of the polarity of possibility/necessity is to add a qualitatively new dimension over and above the polarity of infinitude/finitude. Infinitude is a more or less static concept, referring to a state of being in human existence in which one may happily reside in one's fantasy-world as an end in itself. Possibility is a dynamic concept, containing an implicit call for action. Possibility points to the future, to what does not yet exist in actuality, and therefore involves one in decision, choice, the leap, which require courage. Kierkegaard puts it this way: the self is indeed a synthesis of finitude and infinitude, but this synthesis is also "a relation, ... which, even though it is derived, relates to itself, which is freedom. The self is freedom. But freedom is the dialectical in the deter-

---

117 Ibid., p. 168; (KW 19:35); SV 15:93; (11:148).
118 Ibid., p. 163; (KW 19:30); SV 15:88; (11:143).
119 Ibid., pp. 165f.; (KW 19:32f.); SV 15:90f.; (11:145ff.).

minants possibility and necessity."[120] So the earlier view of necessity simply as the restrictive, limiting character of finitude is now radically altered in *Sickness*, even more so than the revision of possibility. The way that the self's necessity "holds back" the self's possiblity is now qualitatively different from the way one's finitude sets limits for one's infinitude, especially when one considers that this necessity plays a positive role in the event of "freedom," which is the self. What, then, does this necessity consist of, where is it located, and how does it operate?

The answer lies in Kierkegaard's careful exposition of the nature of the self κατα δυναμιν.[121] The Greek phrase literally means: according to (as concerns, in terms of) a thing's ability, capacity, power. Kierkegaard equates it with the character of the self as *sat* (from *sætte*), i.e., the self as composed or set up or posited as a postulate or a potentiality, something that exists in a state of potency with the capacity for developing into a state of actuality. It is then the "primitive construction" of every human being in that every one is "naturally fitted to be a self, determined [in such a way as] to become oneself," but not this structure simply as a universal but as it occurs in *this* particular individual, as a unique instance of the universal.

So Kierkegaard says, "the self κατα δυναμιν does not exist actually, is simply that which ought to come into existence [*skal blive til*]." On the other hand, "a self, every moment it exists, is in the-process-of-becoming [*i Vorden*]. ... Insofar as the self is not becoming itself [*ikke vorder sig selv*], it is not itself." Because of its strange state of *being* yet *not existing*, this potential self possesses some paradoxical characteristics. "The self κατα δυναμιν is just as much possible as necessary, because it certainly is itself, yet it must become itself [*skal vorder sig selv*]. Insofar as it is itself, it is [the] necessary, and insofar as it must become itself, it is a possibility." So, "possibility and necessity are equally essential for becoming (and the self must [*skal*] freely become itself)." They both "belong" to the self.

Here Kierkegaard is contrasting "isness" and "existence" as qualities of the self. The self κατα δυναμιν "is" (*er*), in its pure potentiality. But it does "not exist" in actuality (*er ikke virkeligt til*). In its pure "isness," he calls it the "necessary." As qualified by the demand to "come-into-existence," he calls it "a possibility." But then he adds the paradox: in pure potentiality the self *is*, yet if it is not *becoming* itself, it *is not* itself. Kierkegaard had formulated this conundrum early on in *Either/Or*. In speaking

---

120 Ibid., p. 163; (KW 19:29); SV 15:87; (11:142).
121 Ibid., pp. 163, 168ff.; (KW 19:30, 35ff.); SV 15:88, 93f.; (11:143, 148ff.).

about choosing "my self," he says, "What I choose, I do not posit [*sætter*], for if it were not posited I could not choose it, and yet if I did not posit it by choosing it then I could not choose it. It is [*er*], for if it were not I could not choose it; it is not, for it first becomes [*bliver*] through my choosing it."[122] But here he does not speak of possibility and necessity.

In *Philosophical Fragments* he again anticipates the formulation in *Sickness*, and applies the terms possibility and necessity, but between the two a radical shift has occurred. A brief statement of this shift has been given earlier in this section on possibility/necessity (at note 50), but a more detailed analysis is required here in order to clarify Kierkegaard's concept of necessity. As in *Sickness*, so also in *Fragments* "the necessary is." And "coming-into-existence" is a change from non-being into being. Yet, "this non-being ... must also be [*være til*]," and "such a being that nevertheless is a non-being is possibility." On the other hand, in *Fragments* Climacus cannot (as Anti-Climacus does in *Sickness*) assert that there is a kind of necessity inherent in this non-being that "is" (even though it does not yet "exist"), because in *Fragments* he asserts that "the only thing that cannot come into existence is the necessary."[123] Obviously, there has been a qualitative change in the *kind* of necessity that Kierkegaard is talking about. To get at this shift and change, a further analysis of the self κατα δυναμιν is required.

In the highly formularized statements in *Sickness*, Kierkegaard is ascribing two different attributes or dimensions to the self κατα δυναμιν, which he could not do in *Fragments*. On the one hand, this self is pure potentiality, abstracted from and naked of any and all *extrinsic* finite particularity, uninvolved in any process of change and actualization. On the other hand, this abstract pure potentiality has, at the same time, the quality of being "possible" or "a possibility," because built into the very given structure of such selfhood is the insistent and ineradicable demand or command: you shall (*skal*: must, ought, have the task to) *become* your self, by enacting your potentiality in "existence," that is, within the conditions of your unique finite particularity. As already indicated, Kierkegaard denominates these two attributes or dimensions of the self κατα δυναμιν as "the self's necessity" and "the self's possibility."[124] Let us

---

122 *Either/Or*, 2:217f.; (KW 4:213f.); SV 3:198f.; (2:192).
123 *Philosophical Fragments*, p. 91f.; (KW 7:74f.); SV 6:68f.; (4:237).
124 Again, for "the self's necessity," see *Sickness*, pp. 170, 188; (KW 19:37, 54); SV 15:94, 110; (11:150, 167). For "the self's possibility," see ibid., pp. 164, (and by implication) 168; (KW 19:31, 35); SV 15:89, 93; (11:144, 148).

look more closely at this distinction in order to clarify the kind of necessity inherent in selfhood.

We have already analysed what Kierkegaard means by the self's possibility. It consists (it was proposed) in that essential gestalt of both inherited and acquired characteristics (capacities, inclinations, dispositions, attitudes, values, ideals, beliefs, etc.) which, in their continuing, integrated, functional unity, define who that individual *is* (at note 55 in this chapter). The self, in this dimension of its being κατα δυναμιν, is (as we heard earlier) that "naked abstract self which ... is the first form of the infinite self." And it may be called the "hypothetical self" and the "negative self" insofar as it has not yet become involved in becoming actualized as the concrete self. But this gestalt is properly called the self's possibility only if and insofar as it is consciously and intentionally oriented toward becoming actual here and now in response to situations demanding action. So (it was said above) the self's possibility lies *in between* the given structure of the universally "human" ("naturally fitted to be a self"), and its actualization or concrescence within the particular finitude of the unique individual. It is something more than the former, something less than the latter.

Now, however, this view of the self's *possibility* will be significantly modified when it is related specifically to Kierkegaard's view of the self's *necessity* in the same passages of *The Sickness unto Death*.

First it must be noted that both possibility and necessity can operate in the self in either a positive or a negative way. Each operates positively when functioning in dialectical relation with the other, that is, when "the relation [of the two] relates to itself," because this mode of operation comprises the self becoming itself in freedom. Each operates negatively when attempting to function without regard of the other, that is, in immediacy, without being in dialectical opposition to the other, or in Kierkegaard's language, when "the two relate to the relation and in the relation to the relation," because this mode of operation prevents the self from becoming itself and lands the self in despair. It is very important to Kierkegaard to analyse and to understand how each determinant has the capacity to ignore the other, that is, to be ignorant and unconscious of the other in immediacy, because the occurrence of this "misrelation" comprises the capacity of the self to make this fundamental mistake and hence to *fail* at the task of becoming itself. Without the capacity for failure there is no capacity for freedom (as will be exposited at length in regard to indeterminacy in chapter 8). Or as Kierkegaard puts it, "the opposite of freedom is guilt," not "necessity."[125] Hence his most profound analysis and depiction of freedom and faith occur in the context of his treatment of despair in *The Sickness unto Death*. (This failure will be analysed in part in chapter 8 as "self-deception," but can be fully interpreted only as "sin" by "Kierkegaard as Thelogian.")

However, this failure can be described simply (for our present purpose). On the one hand, possibility in the self can function in a very negative way as what Kierkegaard calls "the fantastic," when "the self runs away from itself in possibility. ... This self becomes an abstract possibility; it flounders in possibility until it is exhausted," lost in a series of "phantasmagoria" in which "the individual himself becomes entirely a mirage." Or even worse, in defiance the self uses "this infinite self, ... the most abstract form, the most abstract possibility of the self" as the instrument by which "to be master of itself, or to recreate itself, ... to determine what one will have or not have in one's concrete self."[126] On the other hand, the self's possibility, as the "naked abstract self" which is "won by infinite abstraction from every externality," can be seen as playing a positive and essential role in "the act of differentiation wherein the self becomes aware of itself as essentially distinct from the environment," and hence serves as "the advancing impetus in the whole process by which a self becomes responsible for its actual self."[127]

The same is true of necessity in the self. On the one hand, there is a kind of necessity that can function in the self as a negative force that frustrates the task of becoming oneself. "To lack possibility means ... that everything has become necessary for a person. ... The determinist, the fatalist, is in despair and as one in despair has lost one's self, because for this individual everything has become necessity. ... The fatalist is in despair, has lost God and thus one's self. ... The fatalist has no God, or what amounts to the same thing, one's God is necessity." This condition signifies failure at the critical point, because "Personhood is a synthesis of possibility and necessity."[128] What, then, on the other hand, is the "necessity" that is "essential" and "belongs" to authentic personhood, that inheres in the self become actuality, and that plays a positive role in freedom defined as "the dialectical in the determinants possibility and necessity"? In answering this question we will finally be able to resolve

---

125 *The Concept of Anxiety*, p. 97; (KW 8:108); SV 6:194; (4:377).
126 *Sickness*, pp. 169, 201; (KW 19:35f., 68); SV 15:93, 122; (11:149, 179).
127 Ibid., p. 188; (KW 19:54f.); SV 15:110f.; (11:166f.).
128 Ibid., p. 173; (KW 19:40); SV 15:97; (11:152f.).

the dilemma of the apparent contradiction between the concept of necessity in *Fragments* and that in *Sickness*, the dilemma with which we began this entire section on "Freedom as the Dialectical in the Determinants: Possibility and Necessity" (at note 50 above). Let us look carefully at Kierkegaard's very precise definition of *this* kind of necessity.

This necessity is a determinant of the potential self (κατα δυναμιν), which is also simultaneously "just as possible as [it is] necessary."[129] Each determinant is to be understood not as a thing in itself or by itself, but only in its dialectical interplay with the other. This potential self both already "is" and, at the same time, knows the demand that "it must become itself." So there are not two different selves, the necessary and the possible. Rather, the one single potential self has a double-sided self-awareness; it both "is" and "must become," and hence is qualified dialectically as both "necessary" and "possible." That is to say, the potential self is *authentically* "necessary" only when what it *is* is oriented toward becoming, and is *authentically* "possible" only when what it desires and chooses to become is qualified by what it is.

However, this dialectical interplay within the consciousness of the potential self may or may not occur (or as Kierkegaard repeatedly puts it, it occurs "in freedom, not of necessity"). The potential self, "in order to become [itself], reflects in the medium of imagination, and thereby the infinite possibility becomes manifest." But here is the point of crisis, and of danger. The potential self may "run wild in possibility" and hence "run away from itself." The self loses itself "because this self fantastically reflect[s] itself in possibility," but "the mirror of possibility ... does not tell the truth," because "in the possibility of itself the self is still far from or is only half of itself." What is missing is the double-sided self-awareness. "What one actually lacks is necessity," or "aware[ness] that the self one is is a wholly definite something [*et ganske bestemt Noget*], and thus the necessary." And "what is missing is essentially the power to obey, to submit to the necessity in one's self, to what may be called one's boundary." So, "the question is how this self's necessity defines it more specifically," how one can "take possibility back into necessity" and "find one's way back to one's self."

The specific question is: *what kind* of necessity is this to which one must submit one's possibility (as depicted in the medium of imagina-

---

129 The material in this paragraph and the next is taken from the section entitled "Possibility's Despair Is to Lack Necessity," ibid., pp. 168–70; (KW 19:35–7); SV 15:93f.; (11:148–50).

tion), and which thereby qualifies what the self will be in its actualization? In another passage Kierkegaard gives a kind of an answer.[130] He is again depicting the dangers that lie in the "consciousness of an infinite self, ... the most abstract possibility of the self," when "the self in despair wants to be master of itself or to recreate itself," that is, a person "does not want to put on one's self, does not want to see one's task in the self given to him/her," thus "severing the self from any relation to a power that has established it." But in this context Kierkegaard also provides a picture of the positive normative self. "One's concrete self ... certainly has necessity and boundaries, is this totally definite being [*dette ganske Bestemte*; cf. similar phrase in paragraph above], with these natural capacities, predispositions, etc., in this concretion of relationships [or: conditions]."

What, then, are these capacities, predispositions, and relationships which of "necessity" must be observed as "boundaries" *if* one is to become one's actual concrete self? They certainly include those relations which he has described as qualities of one's *extrinsic* finitude, but they clearly include also those *intrinsic* qualities, that essential gestalt, of one's unique subjectivity (see above pp. 160 and 166f.). So Kierkegaard goes on to say, "no derived self [i.e., established by an other], by reconsidering itself, can give itself more than that self is—it remains itself from first to last; in [its] self-redoubling it becomes neither more nor less than itself." He is clearly talking about a very inward, subjective, reflective process. By the act of "reconsidering oneself" he has clearly in mind the turning of consciousness toward one's "infinite self," toward "the most abstract form, the most abstract possibility of the self," what may also be called "the negative self" and "hypothetical self."[131] And in the journals he explains that "every self-reduplication still does not contain anything more than this self contains," that this "turning inward in self-reduplication ... is purely human."[132]

It is this self, composed of given "capacities, predispositions, etc.," that *is* and *remains* the self, that *defines* the self. It is the potential self as thus determined that sets a "boundary" within the sphere of one's infinite possibilities of the imagination, beyond which boundary the self cannot "run wild" without "working itself into the very opposite; it really becomes no self," because then "there is nothing steadfast; at no mo-

---

130 Ibid., pp. 201–3; (KW 19:67–9); SV 15:122f.; (11:179f.).
131 Idem.
132 *Journals*, 1793, X³ A 670; 3660, X² A 116; 188, X² A 396.

ment is the self steadfast, that is, eternally steadfast." In its consciousness of being "given" in its most inward abstract capacities, predispositions, etc., the potential self (κατα δυναμιν) is "the necessary"; that is to say, the potential self as thus determined is "necessary" in the sense of being what the potential self determined as "possibility" (oriented toward becoming itself) must "obey" and "submit to," must "find its way back to," must use to "define it[self] more specifically," *if* the potential-self-as-possibility is to become its true self in actuality. Then, indeed, "actuality" will be "the unity of possibility and necessity."[133]

Again, it must be emphasized, Kierkegaard is not indicating two distinct selves (necessary and possible), or even two subdivisions within the self, which oppose, conflict, and war with each other for dominance. Rather, he is depicting one potential self (κατα δυναμιν) with a double-sided or double-dimensioned or bipolar dialectical self-consciousness. Within this self-consciousness there constantly is an opposition and tension as one dimension or facet is tempted to ignore or actively to suppress the other. This analysis now requires a significant refinement of our previous definition of the self's possibility (as indicated above, pp. 160–2, and pages at note 55). We had previously identified the self's possibility with that abstract, infinite, naked, negative self which consists in an essential gestalt of inner dispositions and attitudes functioning as a continuing integrated unity in a particular, unique individual, *but* (we added) only insofar as this gestalt is oriented toward becoming actual here and now. Hence, we had located this self's possibility as lying between the structure of the universally "human" and the concrete actualization of the self within the particular finitude of the unique individual.

Now, after a detailed analysis of the self's necessity as defined in *Sickness*, it becomes clear that Kierkegaard makes a distinction *within* what

---

133 This paragraph is a pastiche of phrases from *Sickness* on pp. 164–5, 168–170; (KW 19:31–2, 35–7); SV 15:89–90, 93–4; (11:144–6. 148–50). The same view of the "self's necessity" is clearly implied in the context of the other occurrence of this phrase: ibid., pp. 187f.; (54f.); 110f.; (166f.). There "the self's necessity" is identified with "the composition [*Sammensætning*: makeup] of the self" in which some "difficulty" is discovered which "requires a total break with immediacy." What is being referred to is not the universal structure of the "human," or even the total structure of the particular individual. It designates what is discovered in the self when the self "with a certain degree of reflection begins the act of differentiation whereby the self becomes aware of itself as essentially distinct from the environment and external-world and from their influence upon it." What results from this action is that "a self ... is won by infinite abstraction from every externality, this naked abstract self, ... the first form of the infinite self." This is clearly the potential abstract self that is "necessary" to "obey."

we had called the self's possibility, namely, between, on the one hand, the essential gestalt conscious of itself as an abstract, infinite, naked, negative potentiality of what a particular self *is* in itself, and, on the other hand, the essential gestalt conscious of itself as this potentiality under a call, command, demand that it must *become* itself and therefore a potentiality oriented toward actuality. The first he calls the self's necessity, the second he calls the self's possibility. Hence the self's possibility is located in between the unique abstract potentiality of this particular individual (not the "universally human"), and, the concrete actualization of that potentiality here and now. This location and peculiar state of the self's possibility will be of great importance when we come, in the next chapter, to analyse the nature of the "leap" in its relation to what contemporary philosophy of action calls "intentionality."

It is of prime importance to establish unequivocally that what Kierkegaard (in *Sickness*) means by the self's necessity (as well as the self's possibility) is not a quality of the self's extrinsic finitude and its involvement in the accidental and contingent, but is a quality that is operative in the inward domain of the self's coherent gestalt of attitudes, predispositions, etc. (which, as has been suggested earlier, could be called one's intrinsic finitude). In the passage we have been considering, where he describes at length the attempt of the self to use its infinite, abstract, negative form to master and recreate itself, he makes the pregnant comment that this "negative form of the self exercises a *loosening* power as well as a *binding* power" (emphasis added).[134] In this context he is exemplifying its self-destroying loosening power when the self "does not want to see its given self as its task," but seeks to become a totally new and "other" self.

On the other hand, in his original reference to the self's necessity,[135] he is clearly speaking of the binding power of the infinite, abstract, negative self. He is considering the problem of the self "running wild in possibility" and thus "running away from itself." What is needed, he says, is for the self "to become aware of itself, aware that the self one is [i.e., *kata dynamin*, potentially] is a very definite something," not some universal "humanness" to be shaped any which way. In other words, the potential self in its abstract infinite form is comprised of a set of certain definite "capabilities and predispostions" (what we today would call attitudes, beliefs, values, etc.), with a definite functioning unity or gestalt. What is

---

134 Ibid., pp. 203; (KW 19:69); SV 15:123; (11:180).
135 Ibid., pp. 169f.; (KW 19:36f.); SV 15:93f.; (11:149f.).

needed is not for the self to deny or subvert the creative projection of the self's possibility in one's imagination, because then one would cease to be a self or person and become merely a thing. What is needed is for the self gladly "to obey, to submit to" the *determinateness* of one's infinite abstract potentiality, as "the necessity in one's self," as a "boundary" or "borderline" within one's potential self (κατα δυναμιν) beyond which one's imagination must not seek to explore other possible selves, because the latter use of the imagination amounts to a refusal to become the unique self one is "given" to be (what is meant by "given" will be commented on directly).

This event of choosing (to submit one's possibilities-for-enactment to the "binding power" of the determinate character of what one is in one's essential gestalt) is the event of the self becoming itself in freedom. So, "the self is freedom," because "freedom is the dialectical in the determinants possibility and necessity." Kierkegaard makes this point even more clearly in various journal entries, both as a general principle and as illustrated in his own life's experience.

The key entry (often quoted above) is a late one (1851) in a series about Augustine. Kierkegaard is arguing that "abstract freedom-of-choice [*Valgfrihed*] (liberum arbitrium) is a delusion," because one assumes that one has this "abstract possibility" as a continuous option throughout life. He asserts, "it is very true and very much a part of experience, what Augustine says of true freedom (distinguished from freedom-of-choice), namely, that a human being has the most compelling sense of freedom when, with completely decisive resolve, one stamps upon one's action that inner necessity which excludes the thought of any other possibility. Then the 'agony' of freedom-of-choice or choice comes to an end."[136] Clearly, the "necessity" which delimits "possibility" does not come from external conditions of one's finitude but from one's "inner" sense and judgment of what is "right" for *one's own unique self* to do in that particular situation.

Two entries from the previous year (1850) explicate this point.[137] In the one, he is arguing that when "the spirit drives us" or "impels" us, "it is still the voluntary [*Frivillige*]." So "if I step forth witnessing as Luther himself did, ... this is voluntary; he could indeed have refrained from doing it. To declare that he could not do otherwise is quite correct, but it is a sham if he in this way makes the impelling of the spirit identical

---

136 *Journals*, 1268, 1269; X⁴ A 175, 177.
137 Ibid., 4950, X³ A 43; 1261, X² A 428.

with external necessity." So what is the "inner necessity" that determines the act and yet does not rob it of being voluntary? In the other entry, he contends that in each situation, a human being comes to see, to judge, to know that there is "the one thing needful" (*det ene Fornødne*, i.e., necessary, requisite), which is "the right thing" (*det Rigtige*). So as to "the content [*Inhold*] of freedom ... there must be no *choice*." And yet one must *choose* the one thing "necessary," and this choosing is "the form-determinant [*Form-Bestemmelse*] in freedom." (This distinction between the form of freedom and the content of freedom will be explored in the next two chapters.) "Consequently, the very fact that there is no *choice* signifies the tremendous passion or intensity with which one *chooses*." So, "freedom really *is* only when, in the same moment [that] ... it *is* (freedom-of-choice), it hastens with infinite speed to bind itself unconditionally in the choice of submission [i.e., to the one thing necessary], the choice whose truth is that there can be no question of any choice."

Clearly, the one thing necessary in a particular situation is not dictated by the external conditions of that situation, although they are certainly taken into consideration by the choosing subject. Rather, the one thing necessary is evaluated and determined (i.e., judged) within that subject, and done so in the light of that subject's gestalt of attitudes, predispositions, values, beliefs, etc., that is, in the light of who that subject *is*. In most cases, the *content* of freedom, "the right thing," the one thing "necessitated" by the subject's gestalt in *this* situation, is clear; there is no choice. But whether the subject will heed this "boundary line" within its imagined possibilities, and whether the subject will choose to follow "the right thing," hangs in the balance. It depends on whether, at the instant of insight and judgment, the subject freely "binds itself *unconditionally*" in "obeying and submitting to the necessity in one's self."

The key word is: *unconditionally*. It means that the only "necessity" (the conditional) involved in this event consists of who (what) one *is* in oneself. (As will be noted just below, "what one *is* in oneself" includes the God-relationship and its "governance." The religious dimension of the self will be fully explored in the next chapter.) The subject certainly considers the external conditions, but they do not dictate or necessitate one's decision as to what is the "right thing." The decision is, in this sense, "unconditional." Kierkegaard, in a later journal entry (1852), puts it this way, "As far as venturing everything is concerned, I have no 'Why?' at all; that which determines me is simply and solely the unconditional; I must do it, I cannot do otherwise. ... In the unconditional all teleology vanishes. ... Only when every 'Why?' vanishes in the night of the unconditioned and becomes silent in the silence of the unconditioned, only then can a human being venture everything; if he glimpses one 'Why?', ... he sees 1000 'Whys'—then watch out, he will never venture a thing but will become a professor of the 1000 'Whys' " (can't you hear Kierkegaard chortling!).[138] Here Kierkegaard is illustrating again the point of that key passage in *Works of Love* where he says that two human beings, both equally "honourable, upright, respectable, God-fearing, can under the same circumstances do exactly the opposite," because we cannot "judge every human being according to an established universal standard." If the latter obtained, then "the God-relationship would essentially be abolished; then everything would turn outward, fulfilling itself in political or social life. ... Then neither spiritual-struggle nor self-deepening would be either possible or required."[139]

This principle, that the "necessity," in the definition of freedom as "the dialectical in the determinants possibility and necessity," consists of the "binding power" of the infinite, abstract, negative gestalt of the inner self is also illustrated in numerous journal entries about Kierkegaard's own personal self-understanding that grew out of his sufferings from the *Corsair* affair. Indeed, it is argued above (pp. 192–200) that the formulation of this principle derived (phenomenologically) from his own personal experiences. Hence, when Kierkegaard declares that, through the *Corsair* affair, "Governance kept me in the harness" (that is, in the discipline of a new authorship), he is not alluding to a compulsion or necessitation from irresistible external conditions. Indeed, he does say, "it was the tension of actuality which put a new string in my instrument, forced me to publish even more." But in the same entry he says, "Christianly, the only question is that of obedience." And the word for "obedience" (*Lydighed*) is the same as when (in *Sickness*) he speaks of "obeying [*lyde*] ... the necessity in one's self." And the word "forced" (*tvang*) is the same word he uses in *Upbuilding Discourses* in speaking of the "compulsion of necessity."

In other words, his experience of "governance" is (as we have seen) an inward one in which he comes to see that his "intelligence, talents, skills and mental constitution," his "whole *habitus*," his "whole individuality and its deepest urge" are "constructed" and "designed" in such a way as to comprise "a calling from God" to continue his authorship. And

138 Ibid., 4901, x⁴ A 613.
139 *Works of Love*, p. 217; SV 12:222f.; (9:210f.).

in this inward awareness, Governance is far from being an irresistible compulsion; it must be seen, acknowledged, accepted, and enacted by one's self. It evokes rather than overrides one's free response.

This interpretation also fits his general characterization of Governance. He says, "The understanding of my life as an author and of my self was ... a gift of Governance. ... Governance has helped me do the right thing." So, "Governance is indeed everywhere present and thus in one sense is the closest of all. But in another sense it is infinitely far away. That is—it refuses to intervene forcibly, it omnipotently constrains its own omnipotence." The way Governance intervenes is this: "Governance ... relates everyone's collisions to one's capacities. The collisions of my life—very likely because I have been granted unusual capacities—... have led me to recognize at once my identity, my personal peculiarities; and thus I can correlate the nature of my collisions with my uniqueness of spirit/mind [*min Aands Eiendommelighed*]." Governance works this way because "God is not, in the external palpable sense, a power who, face to face with me, asserts his rights. His will is proclaimed to me [indirectly] ... in his Word. ... [W]hat is thus broadly articulated in his Word is realized first of all in action on the part of the individual through a more particular understanding of his whole concretion—the more particular understanding I have in and through myself." "With the help of God's governance everything becomes more and more inward."[140]

There is one more penultimate question about this self's necessity. Kierkegaard says, "the self one is is a very definite something and thus the necessary." Does, then, the makeup of this determinateness of the infinite, abstract, negative gestalt of the potential self never change? We have heard Kierkegaard say that, when considering one's infinite possibility of the self through the medium of the imagination, one must submit to the necessity in one's self, that is, one must "want to put on one's self," must "want to see one's task in the self *given* to him/her" (emphasis added). And this is so because "no derived self, by reconsidering itself [*at see pa sig selv*], can give itself more than that self is—it remains itself from first to last; in self-reduplication it becomes neither more nor less than itself."[141]

---

140 *Journals*, in order of appearance: 6511, X^2 A 106; 1450, XI^2 A 170; 6385, XA 260; 1273, X^5 A 13; 2640, IX A 126. These entries are dated from 1848 to 1854.
141 *Sickness*, p. 202; (KW 19:68f.); SV 15:123; (11:179f.).

The question, then (that Kierkegaard seems nowhere to consider directly), is this: does not the self (abstracted and distinct from all externalities, which one "remains from first to last") grow and develop and get transformed in the process? This question was considered at length above, but before the nature of the self's necessity had been clarified. Now we must intensify the question by asking: when Kierkegaard says that this self, which one is "naturally fitted" to become, has been "established [*sat*] by an other," that it has been "given [*givne*]" to be "put on" and to be "clothed" in one's finitude and thus become "actual" and "concrete," does he mean that the "self's possibility" has been determined at conception as to its content and structure, and that it "becomes neither more nor less" no matter what the self experiences throughout life? Then, does such a given self operate as "the necessary" in the sense that it contains potentially within it everything that will unfold in the actual historical life of that self? Does this necessary self, then, bind the self-as-possibility and the self-as-actuality together with a kind of necessity that removes any qualitative distinction between them, so that the possible is the actual, and the actual is the possible (as Hegel said)?

Obviously, such a conclusion cannot be Kierkegaard's meaning, and this on two counts. First, it can be shown that Kierkegaard does assume that the self develops and changes in the process of becoming in actuality (concretely) what it already "is" potentially in possibility, and that this development and change include transformations in the content, emphasis, balance, and functioning of the self as abstract possibility. Therefore, the quality of the self's potentiality as the "necessary" is open-ended, even while being "a very definite [determinate] something." Secondly, the mode or way in which this determinateness of the self's possibility limits and determines the process of the self's becoming is not "the necessary" in the sense of formal logical inference, or of rational coimplication, or of psychic/social/physical causation. Therefore the "necessity" involved in Kierkegaard's becoming of the self is of a different order or kind. Let us look at these two points in some detail, because they will clear the way for a final characterization of Kierkegaard's definitive concept of necessity in *The Sickness unto Death* (as distinct from that concept in *Philosophical Fragments*).

First, then, how does change take place in the self's possibility, and of what does the change consist? The potential self (κατα δυναμιν)—as it *is* a "very definite something" and therefore "the necessary"—has been variously described above by Kierkegaard as consisting of one's capacities, predispositions, and concretion of relationships, one's intelligence, talents, skills, mental constitution, one's whole *habitus* and individuality, one's identity, personal peculiarities, and the uniqueness that belongs to a particular individual spirit. This self-in-potentiality has been depicted above as an inner gestalt which consists not only of essential given characteristics and dispositions but also of certain acquired basic values, beliefs, attitudes which operate in the gestalt more or less unconsciously and without question, and yet are also called into play when the self is making "infinite" decisions and choices.

Kierkegaard includes given characteristics, etc., explicitly, but basic values, etc., only by implication. Certainly one's "whole identity," one's "uniqueness of spirit," which operates as an integrated, unitary configuration in the judgment of what is "the one thing needful" in a particular situation, includes one's basic commitment to certain values and beliefs; that is to say, it includes the ethical, willing, choosing self. In asserting that this self-in-potentiality (the necessary) is explored "in the medium of the imagination" in order to depict "the infinite possibility" of the self, Kierkegaard is directly implying that the abstract, potential (necessary) self includes the sphere of the ethical and hence values, etc., because he explicitly says that in this "rendition of the self as the self's possibility," "the imagination is related to feeling, knowing, and willing." In other words, "willing" is a dimension of the self-in-potentiality, and as such it is not an empty contentless capacity. Rather, when willing is functioning properly, then "the more it is infinitized [in imagination] in intention and resolve, the more and more it simultaneously becomes itself in the little things of the task which can be accomplished at once; thus while being infinitized it comes back in the strongest sense to itself."[142] So the ethical, with its ruling values and beliefs, is an operative dimension or facet of that self-in-potentiality functioning as the "necessary."

This inclusion of the ethical in the self's potentiality is so important that some supporting evidence must be given (i.e., from Kierkegaard). And the relevant passages (from the journals and *Works of Love*) have already been analysed above (at notes 62 and 63 in this chapter). There we heard that "understanding [something] in possibility ... is always a misunderstanding" in comparison with "understanding [something] in actuality." This is so because one explores possibility only in imagination, and "it is impossible to become spirit [self] in imagination." So

---

142 *Sickness*, pp. 168, 163–5; (KW 19:35, 30–2); SV 15:93, 88–9; (11:148, 144–5).

"when I understand something [merely] in possibility, I remain essentially unchanged, I remain in [my] old person [*det Gamle*]." But when this possibility "becomes actuality, then it is I who am changed," and "then the spirit [self] becomes integrated as spirit."

In other words, the new and true self-understanding that is achieved when one's possibility is enacted in actuality involves the whole self. As Kierkegaard says in *Works of Love*, it is easy to advocate equality of all classes of human beings, and to profess love for every "neighbour" who is in misery, when one remains at a distance behind "the partitions of distinction." But "at a distance one's neighbour is [only] a figment-of-the-imagination [*Inbildning*]," because "what makes the difference is whether we understand at a distance—then we do not act accordingly—or close at hand—then we do act accordingly and 'cannot do otherwise.'" This distance between "what one understands and what one does" is the true "measure of what fundamental disposition [*Sindelag*] resides in a human being."[143] So the "*I* who am changed" by the new self-understanding that comes when I pass from imagination to actuality includes my ethical judgments as expressive of my "fundamental disposition."

We must conclude, therefore, that the self's most abstract gestalt of potentiality, and its kind of inherent "necessity," include and involve not only given capacities and dispositions but also acquired *essential* values and beliefs; and this latter dimension of the gestalt comes to new "understanding in actuality," and thereby grows and is reshaped through experience. I, as my essential self, do *not* "remain essentially unchanged" or "remain in [my] old person." So the language of Kierkegaard about the self as "given" and as "remain[ing] itself from first to last" must refer to the fact that at any given point in the process of becoming itself, the self is "given" as a "very definite something," and is such in continuity with what it has been "from first to last," and it cannot transform this given self simply by "reconsidering" itself in the imagination. And, most important, the "necessity" that is characteristic of the gestalt is therefore consonant with—indeed, is participant in—the process of the self's coming-into-existence, and in such a way as to evoke and require rather than to override and dissolve freedom, *and* in such a way as to leave open the possibility that the single, human, individual potential-self may *fail* to come-into-existence, to achieve fulfilment in actuality. So what *kind* of necessity is this?

143 *Works of Love*, pp. 86–9; sv 12:79–82; (9:76–80).

This question brings us to the second point raised a few pages above. Clearly, whatever Kierkegaard means by this necessity, he does not accept Hegel's formulation. It is precisely in the context of his attempt to explain how and why one must "submit to the necessity in one's self" that he also flatly rejects what he understands to be the Hegelian thesis that "necessity is unity of possibility and actuality," and asserts: "No! actuality is unity [oneness] of possibility and necessity."[144] And while Mark Taylor argues that Kierkegaard "attributes to Hegel a much stronger necessitarian position than Hegel intended to affirm," Taylor's own explication of Hegel's view makes Kierkegaard's point (*negatively*) with more precision than does Kierkegaard himself.[145]

Taylor says, "Hegel uses the term *actuality* (*Wirklichkeit*) to define the rational unity-within-distinction of reality and ideality. ... [A]ctuality and possibility are coimplicates whose inextricable unity constitutes necessity. It seems self-evident that the actual is possible. ... Actuality, therefore, must be implicitly identical with possibility. ... Hegel insists that not only is actuality in itself possibility, but real [as distinct from formal] possibility in itself is actuality. ... The spiritual unity of possibility and actuality eventuates in necessity." And from this analysis comes Hegel's final conclusion (as summarized by Taylor): "implicitly, necessity is freedom. Alternately phrased, 'freedom reveals itself as the *truth of necessity.*' ... Oppositions necessarily bound in a relationship of coimplication are, in fact, free." So what kind of necessity is this? "From Hegel's perspective, freedom is necessity *rationally* comprehended. ... [P]ossibility and actuality join in necessity, which is freedom" (emphasis added).[146]

Clearly, in his formulation ("actuality is unity of possibility and necessity") Kierkegaard is using each of the major terms (to describe human personal existence) with meanings totally different from Hegel's usage. Possibility and actuality cannot be "coimplicates whose unity is necessity," because the transition from one to the other is achieved only by a leap of free decision and is not necessitated by their coimplication, as is evidenced by human *failure* to make the transition. As we will see (in in the sections on self-deception in chapter 8), Kierkegaard vigorously asserts that just because a person knows rationally which specific "actuality" is implied (coimplicated), that is, is demanded by a certain "possibility," does not mean that that person will do it. So actuality can-

---

144 *Sickness*, p. 169; (19:36); 15:93f.; (11:149).
145 Mark C. Taylor, *Journeys to Selfhood*, p. 126, n.76.
146 Ibid., pp. 155–8.

not be a "rational unity-within-distinction" because free decision is ethical (and religious), not simply rational. And hence the "necessity" that freedom heeds cannot be (purely) "rationally comprehended." So, again, what is the kind of "necessity" that Kierkegaard ascribes to the self in its potentiality and possibility?

4 Resolution of the Conflict between Fragments *and* Sickness

We are now ready (at last!) to address the question which initiated this long section on "Freedom as the Dialectical in the Determinants: Possibility and Necessity," namely: what happened to Kierkegaard's concepts of possibility and necessity between *Philosophical Fragments* and *The Sickness unto Death*? The general answer that has emerged is this: his concept of possibility became much more complex and sophisticated, while he made a significant shift in the *kind* of necessity under consideration.

It was also emphasized, at the beginning of this section, that Kierkegaard knew full well that, in bringing these concepts to bear on his interpretation of the self, he was getting entangled in the field of logic.[147] So it will now be appropriate and helpful to use some developments in recent logic to help clarify the *kind* of necessity that Kierkegaard, in *Sickness*, attributes to the self in the process of becoming oneself, in contrast with the necessity which he, in *Fragments*, rejects as irrelevant to this process.

Contemporary logic has been extended in several ways beyond the confines of formal mathematical logic that dominated the field in the early decades of this century. (The implications for Kierkegaard's concept of freedom will be spelled out more fully in chapters 6 and 8.) Many logicians now treat aspects of thought and argument which are relevant to Kierkegaard's concept of the self. For example, we find interest in diverse applications of "necessary" and "possible"; in highly controversial "conditional propositions" ("if ... then") whose truth depends on an undefined connection between antecedent ("if ...") and consequent ("... then"); in so-called "attitudinal propositions" which express matters of belief, desire, value, etc. The last example will be very helpful in clarifying what Kierkegaard means by the "leap" in the next chapter. The first two are more relevant to the concept of necessity.

---

147 As noted before, his knowledge of logic is spelled out in the opening section of my monograph, *Trendelenburg's Influence on Kierkegaard's Modal Categories*.

The most important consideration in understanding "necessity" is the recognition that there are several different kinds of necessity and possibility in the usage of general (natural) language, while formal logic deals only with rational entailment of different elements in purely (so-called) "analytic" propositions, which are considered "necessarily true" if they are "logically true." One analysis discerns the following kinds of necessity: logical (formal) necessity (when a given system of logic ensures that a proposition will be true); epistemic necessity (given what we already know, a proposition must be true; this includes "physical necessity"); moral necessity (when a person is "at fault unless he sees to it that a proposition is or becomes true"); temporal necessity (when a proposition is true at all times).[148]

Obviously, Kierkegaard's necessity falls under the classification of "moral," although what he means by "the inner necessity"—which excludes "the thought of an other possibility" and which one must "stamp upon one's actions" with "completely decisive resolve"—is something quite different from "the moral code" mentioned in the context of the above analysis. But the key question is this: what form does a propositional statement take when it expresses moral necessity, and how does it differ from a proposition that expresses "logical" or "epistemic" necessity?

It is proposed here that the necessity which Kierkegaard describes, as inherently operative in the self's potentiality in relation to the self's possibility, would be expressed in what today's logic calls "conditional" propositions. As just noted, a conditional is a statement that includes *two* propositions usually introduced by "if ... , then ... ," and the two are called antecedent and consequent. But the problem is that the "truth" of the total conditional statement is not determined by the truth of the two propositions but by the "connection" between the antecedent and the consequent. This connection is not obvious or clear because it varies qualitatively according to the kind of dependency relationship between the two propositions and so according to the kind of "necessity" involved in this dependency.

For example, the relationship may be purely that of formal logical entailment which satisfies the necessity involved in the principles of bivalence (true or false) and of contraposition (if P then Q, if not-Q then

---

148 James D. McCawley, *Everything That Linguists Have Always Wanted to Know about Logic—But Were Ashamed to Ask*, pp. 273f. He also argues that there is a type of possibility corresponding to each type of necessity (p. 279f.).

not-P). But the dependency (necessity) implied by the use of conditionals in most ordinary language is not of this type, but may be that which is assumed in making promises, in giving advice as to what to expect under certain circumstances of daily existence, in ascribing accountability for human actions or for the results of actions, and (be it noted) in scientific formulations of what will happen under certain physical conditions ("laws" of nature). In some of these relationships there is involved dependency between facts, events, states, etc. expressed in each of the propositions. And the relationship is complicated even further by so-called "maxims of cooperation" that are assumed in all interaction between persons, especially in speech acts (maxims concerning quantity of what is asserted, quality of grounds for assertion, relevance to subject at hand, manner of expression).

However, for understanding the kind of necessity involved in the relation between the self's potentiality and the self's possibility (in the event of the enactment of that possibility in actuality), it is most important to note one more complexity in the field of conditionals: the distinction between indicative conditionals (If Bill's plane left at 2:00, he's in Pittsburgh by now) and counterfactual conditionals (If Solti had been conducting, I would have gone to the concert). Both types usually assume that "the antecedent is temporally and/or causally and/or epistemologically prior to the consequent." But they are qualitatively different in that for the indicative conditional, the connection is "between partial knowledge of a state of affairs ... and more complete knowledge," while for the counterfactual conditional, the connection "involves the relationship between the real world and alternative worlds."[149] And when one begins to formulate one's intentions or to evaluate human behaviour (my own or another's) in terms of alternative worlds, factors come into play that go beyond matters of fact and the structures of formal logic, and these factors include so-called "world-creating" predicates such as believing, thinking, intending, wanting, etc., in other words, propositional attitudes. So here is the point at which modal logic's concern with "possibility" and "necessity," and conditional logic's concern with "if ... , then. ...", and philosophy of action's concern with a "logic" of human "freedom" and "responsibility" all come together and interpenetrate each other.

---

149 Ibid., pp. 315ff.

SUMMARY OF ANALYSIS OF THE DIALECTICAL IN THE DETERMINANTS POSSIBILITY AND NECESSITY

We come now, therefore, to the conclusion of the analysis of the dialectic of possibility and necessity that began some one hundred pages above. Our conclusions are: (1) Kierkegaard is dealing with possibility/necessity as operative in the domain or sphere of the moral (the ethical/religious); (2) the logic of the moral domain (as depicted by Kierkegaard) requires that propositions be stated only in the conditional form; (3) the conditional propositions (used to describe Kierkegaard's notions of possibility/necessity in the ethical/religious domain) will never be indicative but always counterfactual, and therefore always have to do with alternative worlds projected in imagination and expressive of a particular individual's thinking, believing, desiring, intending, etc. These conclusions may be illustrated, from the entire foregoing analysis of Kierkegaard's concept of the self, as follows.

First, the human self is depicted throughout the authorship as being essentially ethical, as inescapably, integrally involved in *choosing*, choosing to *be* and to *become* oneself (or *not* to be and to become). Furthermore, the self can be successful in this choosing only if the self relates itself to the eternal, to the power which established it in the first place. So, although Kierkegaard recognizes that "possibility" and "necessity" have legitimate meanings in the spheres of philosophy, natural science, and history, he argues that they have quite different meanings in the sphere of *his* "category," namely, the individual human being (*Individ*), not as a universal but as a unique particular individual (*Enkelte*). In choosing, one faces a discontinuity, a "gap" between one's past and one's future (possibility), between what one is in possibility and what one is to become in actuality, and no rational, physical or social force can compel (necessitate) that transition. It requires a decision and a leap. And one may (everyone does) *fail.*

Secondly, the indeterminacy of this transition can be expressed only in *conditional* propositions because the transition involves the complex interdependency and interaction of several very different states of affairs and domains.[150] On the one hand, the transition involves the physical (temporal/spatial) domain of the individual's "finitude" as setting

---

[150] The terms "state of affairs" and "domain" are used loosely here to fit the purposes of the analysis. Even in more strict logical discourse, their meanings have some fluidity. See McCawley, *Everything*, pp. 62–9, 161f., 170–5, 274.

the "necessary" conditions or situation within which one's possibility is to be enacted. On the other hand, it involves the inner psychic (intentional) domain of the individual's gestalt of values, beliefs, etc. from which derives the *quality* of what is possible for this particular individual (the *moral* imperative or "law" always emerges from an inner consciousness of the unique self; it never appears as a universal standard or norm imposed as a coercive external force). So the state of affairs in which the transition takes place involves the interdependency (necessary connection) and interaction of these two domains. But this state is even more complex, because, as we have seen above, it is grounded on and presumes two other states, namely, that every human being is "naturally fitted" to be and become a self, and that one can succeed in becoming one's self only by relating positively with the eternal (the power which established the self).

These three interrelated states and domains may be described in indicative conditionals which express what will happen when a certain set of conditions obtains (as in the natural sciences). For example, if I accept my finitude as the locus for enacting my possibilities, then I am able to be become myself in actuality. And, if I am naturally fitted to be and become a self, then I am a "human" being (this could be a proposition of formal logic because the antecedent is implicated in the consequent by definition). And, if I relate to the eternal, then I am able to achieve the positive unity of my infinitude and finitude in actuality. But these statements are not true indicative conditionals (as in science), because they do not describe what *will* happen (necessarily), but what *may* happen. In each case, there is an element of uncertainty. Neither one's finitude, nor one's given structure, nor even one's relation to the eternal guarantees (necessarily *causes*) the transition from possibility to actuality (even though the necessity of each *for* the transition obtains independently of the individual's choice).

So, thirdly, the kind of necessity that connects the domains and states involved in the becoming of one's self requires the use of counterfactual conditionals. For example, if I would become in actuality what I am in possibility, then I must be willing to enact that possibility within the confines of my finitude. And, if I would become a genuinely human being, then I must not try to ignore or get rid of what I am naturally fitted to be. And, if I would achieve a positive unity of my possibility and my finitude, then I must also simultaneously relate to the eternal. In each case, the alternative world (of my becoming myself in actuality) is connected (by the ethical necessity of my choosing) with a real world (my finitude, my given structure, the eternal). In all three of these cases, the "real" world is a condition of my being that is, in differing ways, *external* to the domain of my "choosing," and yet each condition is "necessary" for my choosing to become my self. But, as demonstrated above, the "necessity" of these three external conditions *for* choosing is not the same kind of "necessity" that is involved *in* choosing. The former is "epistemic" while the latter is "moral" necessity.

So, as noted above, the critical kind of necessity that Kierkegaard is concerned about in *Sickness* is qualitatively different from these three instances. It is a necessity that is operative *internally*, in the transition of "freedom" (choosing), that Kierkegaard has in mind when he speaks of freedom as "the dialectical in the determinants possibility and necessity," or when he says "actuality is unity of possibility and necessity." This necessity resides in that peculiar state of affairs where there is interdependency between two domains both of which are *interior* to the individual's self-consciousness, two domains so closely related that it is difficult to distinguish them, because they are two *what?*—dimensions? aspects? moments? elements?—of a single state, that is, of what Kierkegaard calls the self κατα δυναμιν, the self as a single entity with a twofold bipolar self-consciousness.

The self in this state is "just as possible as [it is] necessary." On the one hand, this self is aware of itself as the necessary, that is, as a given determinate gestalt of basic capacities, dispositions, values, beliefs, attitudes, etc. abstracted from any particular finite concretion (what logic calls "essential properties" which "an individual must have if it is to retain its identity," in contrast to "accidental properties" which "an individual could acquire or lose without changing its identity").[151] On the other hand, this same self-conscious self, "in order to become [itself], reflects in the medium of imagination, and thereby [its] infinite possibility becomes manifest," and hence this self is aware of itself as the possible.

In what sense is this self, as given determinate gestalt, "necessary" in the self's state as κατα δυναμιν? Not in the deterministic sense of causing or necessitating the self's possibility which emerges in the process of the self's seeking to respond to the demand that it ("must") become itself in actuality. This self (as the possible), reflecting in the medium of imagination, *may* or *may not* relate to and pay attention to itself as given, determinate, abstract gestalt. At this juncture the self may "run wild in possibility" and never return to the self it is "given" to become. In order

---

151 Ibid.; see pp. 174 (including note 2), 288.

to become its true self ("and the self must [*skal*][152] freely become itself"), the imagined infinite possibility of the self *must* "obey" and "submit to the necessity in one's self, to what may be called one's boundary."

This kind of necessity, like the other three above, can be expressed, and hence understood, not in indicative conditional propositions but only in counterfactual conditionals, because this necessity also inheres in the interdependency or connection between a real world and alternative worlds. The alternative worlds under consideration here consist of the projections or depictions of the self's possibilities as explored in imagination. In *Sickness*, Kierkegaard is trying to express how these alternative worlds are related "necessarily" to the real world, that is, to the world that already *is*. But the real world that he has in mind here is not the world of the self's finitude, or the universal structure of the human, or the self's relation to the eternal, all of which are indeed necessary in order for the self's possibility to become actuality. Rather, here Kierkegaard has in mind the real world of the self that the self already *is* in potentiality (*kata dynamin*) *within* itself, the self as that abstract gestalt of capabilities, dispositions, values, beliefs, etc. (even though "the self κατα δυναμιν does not actually exist"). This "real" world of the self is Kierkegaard's concern because "the self one is [κατα δυναμιν] is a very definite something and thus the necessary," while, on the contrary, "in the possibility of itself the self is still far from or is only half itself. Therefore, the question is how this self's necessity defines it more specifically."[153] In other words, the question is *not* how the self's possibility is oriented and related *forward* towards the *external* worlds of one's finitude, one's structure, one's social being, but rather how the self's possibility is oriented and related *inward* toward the *internal* world of a gestalt of those "essential properties" which define one's very identity (of course, in relationship with the "eternal" as immanent to oneself).

Let us try, then, to express and thus explain this kind of necessity in the form of two counterfactual conditionals. Negatively put: if the self should run wild in fantasy while imagining its possibilities, and give no heed to "the very definite something" (the determinateness) of its po-

---

152 Kierkegaard invariably uses the Danish verb *skulle* to express the "necessity" involved in becoming oneself, and in the seventeen variant shades of meaning given for this word by Vinterberg and Bodelsen, not one carries the sense of necessity involved in logical inference or in physical causation expressive of "natural law." Rather, all but one express moral, ethical, or social obligation or intention which may or may not be followed, that hangs on decision and choice.

153 *Sickness*, pp. 163, 169f.; (KW 19:30, 36f.); SV 15:88, 94; (11:143, 149f.).

tential self as a boundary to its possibilities, then instead of becoming itself, it "works itself into the very opposite, it really becomes no self."[154] Positively put: if a self would become itself, become the "very definite something" it is "given" in potentiality to become, then, in exploring its possibilities in imagination, the self's possibility must willingly and gladly "submit" to being limited by and conformed to the determinateness of that inner abstract gestalt which defines who and what the self *is* in its continuing identity.

The "necessity" that makes a "connection" or "interdependency" between the antecedent and consequent of these conditional propositions obviously is not that of formal logic, or of rational coimplication, or of physical causation, or of social conditioning. Rather (to repeat), in traditional language, the connection is moral or ethical, in the sense that I decide decisively to do the "right thing," the "one thing needful," i.e., the thing I judge and "know" to be in accord with, to be "necessitated" by, my essential beliefs, values, and convictions. Or in the language of contemporary philosophy of action, the connection is intentional, in the sense that my intention is formed in accord with (is "caused" by) my essential values, desires, and beliefs, and then I act accordingly. In both of these languages, the "necessity" involved in the connection is the assumption that I "must" be "true" to my "self." Obviously, both languages assume an element of indeterminacy in the connection, because both leave room for the possibility of failure.

So when Kierkegaard says that freedom occurs when one acts in accord with "that inner necessity which excludes consideration of any other possibility,"[155] what he means by "inner necessity" is what is demanded by what one essentially *is*, what is "necessary" in order to become (in actuality) one's authentic self. Or as he puts it in *Works of Love*, "One has authentic-individuality [*Eiendommelighed*] if one has courage to be oneself before God." And he defines this courage "to be oneself before God" as "courage for this godpleasing daring" which is a paradoxical mixture of "humility and pride [*Stolthed*, arrogance]."[156] In other words, freedom (acting voluntarily) is always dialectical: a risky, daring venture (the possible), in which one listens submissively only to the voice of one's own heart of hearts, to the core of one's being (the necessary), which is believed to be endowed with absolute dignity and worth

---

154 Ibid., p. 202; (KW 19:69); SV 15:123; (11:180).
155 *Journals*, 1269, X^4 A 177.
156 *Works of Love*, p. 253; SV 12:260; (9:258f.).

(the eternal), and which therefore is to be asserted with pride and arrogance (i.e., unconditionally) against all odds, against all other voices. Then one knows what it means to be bound by an "inner necessity," to which one says, "I can do no other." Kierkegaard's necessity is an ethical/religious necessity which demands, enables, and evokes one's own voluntary response.

An example may help. I have a basic essential belief in and commitment to racial equality. So, if I am confronted with pressure to participate in an act of racial prejudice, then I become *my* self in that situation only by refusing to participate, or, better yet, by openly condemning the act, i.e., by excluding consideration of any other possibility than what is "necessitated" by my essential identity. But this act of excluding consideration of any other possibility assumes an awarenesss in my imagination of at least two "alternative worlds" as possibilities, and the act I commit is determined *either* by conforming, "with completely decisive resolve," my possibilities to my belief, *or* by shutting my ears to that inner voice and allowing my action to conform to, and hence to be determined by, the external pressure of my social peers. The delicacy and complexity at the point of juncture between the alternatives of this either/or will be analysed in detail in the next chapter on the "leap," but Kierkegaard captures it in a memorable line: "renunciation within possibility is still a coveting."[157]

In following the "or" option, Kierkegaard would say that I am not becoming *my* self, indeed, am becoming *no* self. "Instead of taking the possibility back into necessity [i.e., instead of acknowledging who and what I essentially am], [I] chase after possibility [i.e., consider more pleasant alternatives]—and at last cannot find [my] way back to [my]self."[158] On the other hand, if I follow the "either" option, Kierkegaard would say that I manifest the fact that, "with a certain degree of reflection, [there] begins the act of discrimination wherein [my] self becomes aware of itself as essentially distinct from [my] environment and the external-world and [from] their influence upon it." And now, in this situation, "my self ... wills to be responsible for itself," even though I have "come up against some difficulty" because of "the way [my] self is put together" (*Selvets Sammensætning*), i.e., "the self's necessity." I have become aware of "something eternal in [my] self," and therefore "the difficulty ... requires a total break with immediacy." I have become conscious of my self

---

157 *The Concept of Anxiety*, p. 98; (KW 8:109); SV 6:195; (4:378).
158 *Sickness*, p. 170; (KW 19:37); SV 15:94; (11:150).

as "a self that is won by infinite abstraction from every externality, a naked abstract self, which ... is the first form of the infinite self and the advancing impetus in the whole process by which [my] self infinitely becomes responsible for its actual self with all its difficulties and advantages."[159] In other words, I have "the courage to be myself before [the eternal]."

Now we understand why Kierkegaard says that "*freedom* is the dialectical in the determinants possibility and necessity." As has been repeatedly said before, this kind of necessity which characterizes ethical or intentional decision and action, this demand that one *must* submit one's possibilities to be shaped and infused with the determinateness of the "given" potential self, does not obliterate voluntary decision and choice. Indeed, this act of voluntary submission defines freedom, *is* freedom. This act is "the dialectical" because it occurs in the interplay between my consideration of possible (alternate) worlds and my awareness of the demands made by who I essentially *am*. Now we understand what he means by saying that concrete actualization of one's self is "unity of possibility and necessity." And hence, contrary to what he said in *Fragments*, the necessary, i.e. what is necessitated of me if I am to become my self, has now given shape and direction to the projection of my self's possibility, and in that way the necessary has "come-into-existence," has been actualized, and is a "determinant" in the event of my freedom itself.

Now, at last, the final question about freedom must be asked: how does freedom occur? How does one "decide" to do the "one thing needful?" How does one "submit to" that "inner necessity" of one's essential self? Or negatively, how does one ignore it, and either "run wild in possibility" as the fantastic, or submit to the external compulsions of one's environment, or to the internal compulsions of one's desires, and thus become "unfree"? Is this even a proper question? Or are freedom and its failure (sin) ineffable surds beyond any further analysis? In *The Concept of Anxiety* Kierkegaard seems to take the latter position: "sin presupposes itself, just as freedom [presupposes itself], and [sin] cannot be explained by anything antecedent to it, [anymore than can freedom]."[160] And he had laid the groundwork for this position in *Either/Or* where he says, "The good is because I will it, and otherwise it is not at all. This is the expression of freedom, and the same is also the case with

---

159 Ibid., p. 188; (KW 19:54f.); SV 15:110f.; (11:166f.).
160 *The Concept of Anxiety*, p. 100; (KW 8:112); SV 6:197; (4:380f.).

evil—it is only inasmuch as I will it. ... The good is the being-in-and-for-itself, posited by the being-in-and-for-itself, and this is freedom."[161]

However, the fact that freedom cannot be explained by anything *antecedent* to it does not exclude analysis of the inner structure and process of that very complex event in which occurs the formation of voluntary decision and choice, the formation of intentionality. At the heart of this formation occurs what Kierkegaard calls the "leap" (*Spring*).

---

161 *Either/Or*, 2:228; (KW 4:224); SV 3:208; (2:201).

6

My Self: A Task
Part 4: The Leap as Freedom's Form

Throughout the entire foregoing text, the words "free" and "voluntary" have been used as if they indicate a simple, self-evident and irreducible act (or event) of "deciding" and "choosing." Certainly Kierkegaard assumes and believes in such an event when he says that "the self is freedom." While writing *Works of Love* (1847), he confides to his journal, "That which has made my life so strenuous but also full of discoveries is that I ... have had to choose decision infinitely. ... In the decisions of the spirit, one can make up one's mind freely. ... To 'be compelled' is the only help in finite matters—freedom's choice [is] the only salvation in the infinite matters." And near the end of his life (1854), he comes to believe that involvement in Christian suffering occurs only by "freedom [*det Fri*], the voluntary [*det Frivillige*], self-determination [*Selvbestemmelsen*], ... because here it is left to the individual himself [*En selv*] whether one will or will not."[1]

However, this seemingly simplistic view of freedom is hardly that of Kierkegaard. The preceeding 150 pages of exposition of the dialectic of freedom could be taken as commentary on one of his most enigmatic statements: "freedom is not free in itself, but entangled [*hildet*], not in necessity, but in itself."[2] We have seen that freedom is entangled in itself because it occurs at the juncture between the self's past and future, because it requires an agonized turning from the temporal to the eternal, because it must comprehend and unify both the self's finitude

---

1 *Journals*, 1253; VIII[1] A 178; 1275; XI[1] A 24.
2 *The Concept of Anxiety*, p. 45; (KW 12.1:323, 199); (KW 8:49); SV 6:143; (4:320).

and its infinitude, because in its very essence freedom consists in the dialectical between the self's necessity (in a totally new sense) and the self's possibility. But given all these determinants, delimitations, and entanglements of freedom, Kierkegaard nevertheless contends that, in the definitive moment of freedom as an event, there is an irreducible element of indeterminacy: the leap.

In this present chapter we will analyse the leap as Kierkegaard's depiction of freedom's *form*. For Climacus (in *Postscript*) the question of form is the question of *how* one comes to the truth, rather than the question of *what* the truth is. Climacus is centrally concerned to make clear that truth for human individual existence is "subjectivity," that is, inward, personal, passionate, interested decision about matters of infinite, essential, eternal significance. So he says, "The how of the truth is precisely the truth." We have even heard him engage in hyperbole by saying, "When one raises the question of truth objectively, then one reflects about truth as an object to which the cognizer relates. ... When one raises the question of truth subjectively, then one reflects subjectively on the *relationship* of the individual [to the truth]; if only the *how* of this relationship is in truth, then the individual is in truth, even if the individual thus relates to untruth."[3]

In the context of his "second" authorship, Kierkegaard comes to be equally concerned with the *content* of the truth and so with the content of the truly free act. So, after the completion of his major works (by 1850), he confides to his journal (as we have also noted), "There is something in relation to which there must and, by definition, can not be any choice, and yet there is a choice. Therefore, just the fact that there is not any *choice* expresses the tremendous passion or intensity with which one *chooses*." So, "freedom-of-choice [*Valgfrihed*] is only a form-determinant of freedom, and the accentuation of freedom-of-choice is exactly the forfeiture of freedom. The content of freedom is decisive for freedom to such an extent that the very truth of freedom-of-choice is: there must be no choice, provided there yet is a choice."[4] Hence, in the next chapter we will turn to the topic of Love as Freedom's Content. But whenever in the second authorship Kierkegaard speaks of freedom, he assumes the indeterminacy of the leap.

---

3 *Postscript*, pp. 287, 178; (KW 12.1:323, 199); SV 10:28, 9:166; (7:278, 166).
4 *Journals*, 1261; X⁴ A 428.

THE ISSUE OF DETERMINISM/INDETERMINISM

The word "indeterminacy" calls into play a long and hoary debate which, from ancient times, ranges through discussions in and between the fields of religion, philosophy, the natural sciences, and psychology. The issues involved in the debate can best be clarified, first of all, not in the language of Kierkegaard but in that of recent philosophy of action, and this clarification will in turn help us to interpret what Kierkegaard really means by freedom, and by the "leap" at the heart of freedom. So we will give here a brief summary of some of the relevant ideas from philosophy of action as illustrated in the writings of Donald Davidson.

Traditionally, the proponents of free will and free choice have rejected out of hand any form of determinism, because the two appear to be mutually exclusive. Especially in the twentieth century, when some proponents of "scientific" explanation contend that it is the only and the wholly adequate explanation of whatever happens, a closed deterministic system of physical causes (reduced to laws) seems to make freedom to be an illusion. So proponents of freedom often insist that a free act is *sui generis*, and hence is not "caused." A free act, they say, is an act of pure "will," a decision and choice that cannot be traced to or explained by any "cause." Does this mean that every choice, to be free, must start from scratch, *de novo*, out of nothing? Does existence precede essence, so that each individual creates and forms his/her own essence as one goes through life (Sartre)? But would not this view make free choice to be arbitrary, capricious, and whimsical? Would not such a view deny any continuity and therefore any identity to the chooser?

Recent philosophy of action contends that the opposition of determinism (as causation) to freedom is a false dichotomy. So Donald Davidson, one of the leading expositors of that philosophy, contends that Hobbes, Locke, Hume, Moore, Schlick, Ayer, Stevenson, and a host of others have succeeded in "remov[ing] the confusions that can make determinism seem to frustrate freedom" (EAE 63).[5] The four main points

---

5 We will use the views of Donald Davidson as the primary representation of philosophy of action because he has written on a wider range of aspects of this philosophy than most. We will use four sources for his views: his own collection of *Essays on Actions and Events*; his "Responses" in *Essays on Davidson: Action and Events*, ed. Bruce Vermazen and Merrill B. Hintikka; his essay on "Paradoxes of Irrationality" in *Philosophical Essays on Freud*, ed. R. Wolheim and J. Hopkins; his essay on "Deception and Division" in *Action and Events: Perspectives on the Philosophy of Donald Davidson*, ed. E. LePore and B.P. McLaughlin. References to these sources will be indicated in the text by EAE, EOD, POI, DAD, plus page number(s).

in the way Davidson himself reconciles determinism and freedom are as follows.

(1) A free act is a caused act, because the "causality" derives from within the agent him/herself, rather than from events (outside the agent) whose consequences for other events can be formulated into "laws." But not all acts performed by an agent are free; only those that are "intentional" qualify as free (EAE 63–5, 79–81).

(2) An intentional act is one "caused" by the agent's own "attitudes," that is, in general by one's "desires" and "beliefs," which include one's fears, hopes, wishes, urges, promptings, holding, knowing, perceiving, noticing, deciding, willing, moral views (felt duties and obligations), aesthetic principles, economic prejudices, social conventions, goals, values, purposes—in short, anything from one's "permanent character traits" to one's "most passing fancy." But the *kind* of cause, involved in the relation between one's attitudes and one's act, that makes the act "intentional" is not ordinary event causality as stated in a law of physics. In agent causality, even one's own inner desires/beliefs do not cause the agent to act. Rather, as "agent," one acts *because of* what one values the most and what one believes is possible. There is a difference between saying, "Desire caused him to do it," and, "Desire was the cause of his doing it." Only the latter kind of action may be called "intentional" and therefore "free." And this analysis makes clear what is meant by saying that "freedom to act is a causal power of the agent," and "explain[s] the possibility of autonomous action in a world of causality" (EAE 73–9).

(3) However, to say that one chooses to act because of one's desires/beliefs is too simple. The interplay between one's usually conflicting desires, values, commitments, etc. and one's often unclear beliefs about what is actually possible in one's concrete "world" is very complex. Before one can *act*, and act *intentionally*, one must come to a *specific* intention or disposition to act, which sets aside or rules out every other possible way of acting. And at the heart of this complex process of coming to hold a specific intention (the state of intending) lies an event of *evaluation* (EAE 70–101; EOD 199–202).

Davidson states that this event occurs as follows (in "the common calculus of decision under uncertainty"): "actual choices and decisions are governed by ... the value an agent puts on a contemplated action"; in turn, this value "depends on the values he places on the various ways he thinks the world may turn out to be, given the action. ... [T]he weighted sum of the desirabilities of the outcomes of the *chosen* course of action is greater than the weighted sum of the outcomes of *any* of the alternatives" (emphasis added) (EOD 199). Thus Davidson "identifie[s] intentions [and the"state of intending"] with certain 'all-out' or unconditional evaluative attitudes" (EOD 212, 220). And he concludes, "Only if an agent values one line of action *more highly* than any alternative does he act intentionally" (emphasis added)(EOD 200).

The question must be asked, however, does the weighting of the sum of desirabilities occur automatically (of necessity)? Does "the unconditional evaluative attitude" just pop out of the interplay within the "coherent pattern" of one's desires/beliefs by the application of the "common calculus of decision under uncertainty"? Is "evaluating" infallible, always arriving at one, and only one, clear and certain answer? Obviously not. The various scenarios for "the way the world may turn out to be" are obviously filled with uncertainties because of the unpredictability of and our limited knowledge about the contingent conditions of the "world" out there. But an even more disturbing element in the process of evaluating consists of conflict that often obtains among the different alternative worlds projected by different conflicting congeries of desire and by different conflicting value systems which exist and operate within the psyche of the same individual. In the face of such conflicts, how does one come to an "unconditional evaluative attitude," that is, to a clear-cut intention or decision? Or, in common parlance, how do I make up my mind what to do?

Davidson forcibly rejects the notion that the decisive factor is some "mysterious act of the will or special attitude or episode of willing," which amounts to "an embarrassing entity that has to be added to the world's furniture" (EAE 87f.). Willing in this sense would be simply that arbitrary, capricious, uncaused kind of freedom already rejected in favour of an action that is "free" because it is caused by one's own pro attitudes and beliefs. But he admits that he is left with two very complicated and perhaps irresolvable problems. He contends that the state of intending, of coming to an unconditional evaluative attitude, is distinct from both the desires/beliefs that precede it and the action that follows it. So, first, there is the problem of how the action emerges from the intention. And secondly, there is the problem of how to explain the fact that, in the situation of conflicting values and beliefs, the agent may have come to a clear judgment or attitude (intention) as to what is best to do, and yet either fail to enact it or intentionally choose to enact a less preferable alternative ("weakness of will" or *akrasia*).

Davidson resolves the first problem in a general way as follows. A "person" is defined by "a coherent and plausible pattern in his [her] attitudes and actions" (EAE 221). And there is a rough kind of law or rule that when the person's pattern of attitudes balances off conflicting values and comes to a clear intention, and when conditions of time, place, etc. are suitable to the held intention, then "an agent will perform an action with a certain intention" (EAE 76). This is the plausible, reasonable, rational expectation. So one can say that the intention plus certain conditions "cause" the action, in the sense that it is "reasonable" for the agent to decide to enact his intention when the conditions are propitious. But what of the second problem: why does one not always enact the intention projected by one's pattern of attitudes, and sometimes deliberately perform an act contrary to that intention?

Davidson addressed this question early on in his essay "How Is Weakness of Will Possible" (1970), and returned to the problem in later and much more complex and sophisticated analyses in "Paradoxes of Irrationality" (c. 1981) and "Deception and Division" (c. 1984). But his answer is the same: such an action is inexplicable, is an irrational surd. In the first essay he says, "the agent has no reason ... for not letting his better reason for not doing [the less preferred alternative] prevail. ... [T]he actor cannot understand himself: he recognizes, in his own intentional behavior, something essentially surd" (EAE 41f.). In the last essay he says that the agent takes the "irrational step" of "drawing the boundary that keeps the inconsistent beliefs apart" in order to "avoid accepting what the requirement [of total evidence] counsels. But this cannot be a *reason* for neglecting the requirement. Nothing can be viewed as a good reason for failing to reason according to one's best standards of rationality" (DAD 148).

These answers to the two problems have significant implications for the nature of freedom, and they will be stated eventually. But first we must note some language Davidson uses to describe that crucial central moment or point at which the agent shifts in his/her intention. This will help in defining more closely what it means to "evaluate" alternative possibilities and thus come to one dominant intention (unconditional evaluative attitude) which one then enacts. Certainly at this point we do not observe or assume an unencumbered, arbitrary, uncaused act of "willing." Rather, Davidson says that, in the case of irrational akratic behaviour, the person "seeks evidence for the falsity of the proposition [one does not like], or disregards the evidence for its truth." Or at an even less active level, there occurs "an intentional directing of attention away from the evidence in favor of p" (DAD 139, 145). In fact, one could assume nothing more than a gradual, semiconscious *withdrawal* of attention from the alternative with the greater weight of desirability.

This event of directing or withdrawing one's *attention* is the final, irreducible and unanalysable factor that makes an act intentional or "free," and makes the actor "responsible." So Davidson says that in self-deception "the person ... must have played a part in bringing it about. ... [W]eakness of warrant is self-induced (one *did* it)." Indeed, "self-deception requires intervention by the agent. ... It is hard to say what the relation must be between the motive someone has who deceives himself and the specific alteration in belief he works in himself. ... Of course the relation is not accidental. ... The self-deceiver must intend the 'deception'" (DAD 142, 144). So the agent cannot excuse himself by claiming that his better judgment was simply overpowered by the superior "motivational strength" of his lower-level motives. At this pivotal decisive juncture, however blurred and dim to one's consciousness, one's *evaluative attention* ("attention" defined as selective awareness and as focusing consciousness to produce greater vividness and clarity of certain of its contents relative to others) *turns* (not "is turned") in one direction or the other.

(4) This point brings us to a final emphasis in philosophy of action concerning indeterminacy. As just noted, Davidson admits that he cannot specify the "relation" between the "motive" for one's self-deception and "the specific alteration in belief." For example, *how* does my desire to play tennis produce the belief that I do not need to attend a crucial committee meeting? Or *how* does one account for the fact that I fully intend to fix the broken screen door this afternoon, and *either* I do it, *or* I let the afternoon slip by without doing it? Or *how* does a developing friendship with a black associate at work persuade me that my former racial prejudice has no warrant and that I must abandon it? How can one say that all of these relations of intention and action are "caused" by my mental attitudes, and yet say that all the actions are intentional and hence voluntary and "free"? Even the "turning" of one's "evaluative attention" is not an arbitrary, unrelated, capricious act or event, but is somehow related to and expressive of that "coherent and plausible pattern of attitudes" which defines who an individual person *is*. "We make sense of particular beliefs only as they cohere with other beliefs, with preferences, with intentions, hopes, fears, expectations, and the rest" (EAE 233f., 221f.). Even the violations and the improvements of that pattern are judged and interpreted in terms of that pattern.

Davidson admits that his extensive analyses of intending, akrasia, and self-deception do not provide a definitional reduction of intentional action which explains *how* intentions and their enactment take shape in a way that makes them free of all external coercion and natural physical causation. But he argues that his analysis does provide adequate grounds for an ontological reduction which "is enough to answer many puzzles about the relation between the mind and the body, and to explain the possibility of autonomous action in a world of causality" (EAE 88). The three main points of his argument can be stated briefly as follows.

First, "mental events" must be distinguished from other purely physical events, because perceiving, desiring, thinking, hoping, believing, and especially intending "resist capture in the nomological net of physical theory" (EAE 208). The physical has laws that explain change by "other changes and conditions physically described," while the mental is understood by reference "to the background of reasons, beliefs and intentions of the individual," whose causal power cannot be reduced to strict laws. "There cannot be tight connections between the realms [of the physical and the mental] if each is to retain allegiance to its proper source of evidence" (EAE 222f.). So when we seek to describe the interactions of persons with their environment, "what emerge are not the strict quantitative laws embedded in sophisticated theory that we confidently expect in physics." This is so because "When we attribute a belief, a desire, a goal, an intention or a meaning to an agent, we necessarily operate within a system of concepts in part determined by the structure of beliefs and desires of the agent himself. ... [T]his feature has no counterpart in the world of physics" (EAE 230f.). Hence, "Psychological concepts have an autonomy relative to the physical," because "psychological events and states often have causes that have no natural psychological descriptions," namely, "an irreducible *normative* element in all attributions of attitude" (EAE 240f.). Because of this element we are confronted with "the nomological irreducibility of the mental" (EAE 222).

Secondly, however, this view does not assume a body/mind dualism, but may be described as "anomolous monism." It is "monism, because it holds that psychological events are physical events." But it is "anomolous, because it insists that events do not fall under strict laws when described in psychological terms," that is, "mental phenomena can [not] be given purely physical explanations" (EAE 214, 231).

Thirdly, this distinctiveness of mental phenomena within the realm of physical phenomena clearly implies and assumes that human intentional behaviour is characterized essentially by a certain indeterminacy that makes it unpredictable in the manner of purely physical phenomena. As noted above, intentional behaviour is "explained" by reference to "attitudes" such as "a desire, value, purpose, goal, or aim the person had, and a belief connecting the desire with the action to be explained." But "we cannot turn this mode of explanation into something more like a science." Such an attempt has been proposed "by substitut[ing] for desires and beliefs more directly observable events. ... But a theory of action inspired by this idea has no chance of explaining complex behavior unless it succeeds in inferring or constructing the patterns of thought and emotions of the agent" (EAE 231, 233f.).

A corollary of this indeterminacy of intentional action in the area of explanation is the unpredictability of that action. Predictability would require "a quantitative calculus that brings all relevant beliefs and desires into the picture," and would require "a theory that deals directly with the relations between actions, and treats wants and thoughts as theoretical constructs." But such a calculus or theory "has no predictive power at all unless it is assumed that beliefs and values do not change over time," whereas it is obvious that "merely making choices (with no reward or feedback) alters future choices" (EAE 233–6). Therefore, "[s]ince psychological phenomena do not constitute a closed system, this amounts to saying that they are not, even in theory, amenable to precise prediction or subsumption under deterministic laws. The limit thus placed on the social sciences is set not by nature, but by us when we decide to view [human beings] as rational agents with goals and purposes, and as subject to moral evaluation" (EAE 239).

So: in the operation of values and beliefs in voluntary actions, we are faced with "the indeterminacy that results from the absence of a clear line between the analytic and the synthetic. A theory to explain a person's verbal and other behavior requires the assignment of propositional content to his sentences and attitudes. But where theory constrains us to draw a sharp line, only a shaded area is indicated by the evidence. Within this area there is ... no matter of fact. We draw the line as best we can" in the light of "normative considerations (among others)" (EOD 245). This kind of indeterminacy requires the assumption, then, that intentions/dispositions and their corresponding actions are not caused, in any direct and deterministic way, by anything outside (i.e., except) the infinitely complex and unanalysable interplay of all the diverse mental attitudes which comprise that "coherent [and sometimes incoherent] pattern" which defines who "I" am, at the heart of which interplay is an ineffable and irreducible element and moment of evaluation.

The interplay is unique in each instance of decision, and the evaluative attention yields comparative weightings of alternatives in a process so subtle and complex that it defies direct observation and description, even by the one within whom it occurs. And the outcome is unpredictable no matter how often the agent faces similar situations demanding choice (intention) and action. And, most notably, whenever someone (as agent) completes an *intentional* action, even though it be an *akratic* action, that person cannot escape the sense that he/she *chose* to do it *voluntarily*, of his/her own "free will," and therefore accepts responsibility for that action—even though that person cannot begin to describe *how* she/he came to that intention (decision, choice), or *how* the action emerged ("rationally" or "akraticly") from the intention (decision). So Kierkegaard, near the end of his life (1852), after the completion of his formal authorship and before his decision to launch his "attack" on Christendom, muses as follows: "The fact that I do not make myself more comfortable and am not looking for financial security could be called pride, arrogance [probably by his brother, the Bishop]. Is it that? Well, who knows himself in this way?" Then he proceeds to say that "I think" and "it seems to me" that he is following "something higher ... constantly moving within me" when he decides not to take a rural parish but to stay with his calling to be a writer.[6] Clearly, in this decision he has that "most compelling sense of freedom" which comes when one obeys one's own "inner necessity."[7]

Without using this exposition of intentional action, in twentieth-century philosophy of action, as a procrustean bed, let us proceed to see how it may help to clarify Kierkegaard's own analysis of the process in which a free action takes place.

Kierkegaard's earliest reflections about freedom (1834) occur in a refutation of predestination as a "thoroughgoing abortion."[8] But his

---

6 *Journals*, 6805; X^4 A 559.

7 See comments in text above at notes 180 and 181 in chapter 5.

8 *Journals*, 1230; 1231; 3542–6; I A 5, 7, 10, 19, 20, 22, 43. These reflections were stimulated by his hearing H.N. Clausen's lectures on dogmatics (1833–34) in which Clausen commented on the doctrine of predestination as treated in Augustine, Calvin, and the Lutheran creeds and confessions (see *Papirer*, XII, pp. 118–23).

earliest references to "leap" are not connected with freedom. Rather, he speaks of the "despairing leap" into Christianity which some people made in early times, or of the marvellous illogical leaps of "ingenuity" that characterized the poetry and folk songs of the Middle Ages. He does make one technical application of the idea when, in analysing the origin of modern philosophy (in *Johannes Climacus*), he says the origin involved a "severance," that is, "a consequence by which the opposite results from something. This is ordinarily called a leap."[9]

How, then, did he come just a year later (1844) to what he calls "my theory of the leap"? Alastair McKinnon has initiated one of his thorough (and revealing) computer-analyses of Kierkegaard's usage of "leap" (in its relation to "faith") throughout the *Samlede Værker*, and he has provided a list of some fifty words that occur frequently in its context. He believes that a study of the term as related to these words "should give one a better feel for the range, use and focus of the concept."[10] Some of these contextual words will be brought to bear in the following analysis, but first it should be noted that certain external readings were helping Kierkegaard in the formulation of his "theory."

ORIGIN AND DEVELOPMENT OF THE CONCEPT
OF THE LEAP

During the years 1841–42 his assiduous reading of W. G. Tennemann's *Geschichte der Philosophie* led him to a profound interest in Aristotle, whose works he began to collect and read. And he found (as noted in the previous chapter) a highly valued guide to Aristotle's thought in F.A. Trendelenburg, whose two books on Aristotle's logic he acquired in February of 1843. Then in 1843, while reading J.G. Jacobi's *Sämmtliche Werke*, he learned about Lessing's use of the word "leap." He had been reading Lessing since his university days (especially in regard to literary theory), but now turned to his essay *Über den Beweis des Geistes und der*

---

[9] *Johannes Climacus, or De omnibus dubitandum est*, p. 122; (KW 7:138); *Papier*, IV B 1, p. 121 (1842–43).

[10] From a personal letter to me dated 28 February 1989. He also generously provided me with a preliminary "map" showing the frequency of use and the period of composition in the twenty-one books where the term and its variants appear. Since then (as noted) he has used this study in connection with a paper on "Kierkegaard and 'the Leap of Faith.'" The latter paper has appeared in *Kierkegaardiana* 16 (1993):107–25.

Kraft (in his *Sämmliche Schriften*) and gained stimulus for new insights for a more sophisticated concept of the leap.[11]

The fruits of this reading, for his concepts of freedom and the leap, first appear in his search for some kind of "transition" (*Overgang*) (between thinking and being, between possibility and actuality) other than Hegel's "mediation." "Hegel," he says, "has never done justice to transition's-category."[12] He first discovered (while making a series of notes from his reading of Tennemann in 1843) that the transition he was looking for has the characteristic of being "passionate" (*pathetisk*). Contrary to Descartes, he says, the transition from thought to action in freedom "is a *passionate* transition, not [simply] dialectical, for dialectically nothing can be derived." This transition is a matter of will, "because [the transition] to the infinite, which consists in pathos, takes only courage."[13]

Then even more significantly (as noted in chapter 5), he was led to Aristotle's concept of κινησις which Tennemann translates as "change." This, Kierkegaard says, "is of the utmost importance." Why? Because he sees that the movement involved does not occur merely within thought

---

11 See Niels Thulstrup, *Kierkegaard's Relation to Hegel*, pp. 316f. In *Postscript* Johannes Climacus tells us that he had "read" *Fear and Trembling* before he read Lessing on the leap, and does not really learn very much from Lessing. But he also makes the enigmatic remark that, "Whether Johannes de silentio had become attentive to the leap by reading Lessing, or not, I leave undecided," suggesting that Kierkegaard had read both Jacobi and Lessing's essay before writing *Fear and Trembling*, and clearly before writing *Fragments* and *The Concept of Anxiety*. In any case, his reading of Lessing obviously stimulated him to develop his own more complicated concept in *Postscript*, which we will summarize below. For the books of Tennemann, Trendelenburg, Lessing, and Jacobi which were in Kierkegaard's library, see *Auktionsprotokol over Søren Kierkegaards Bogsamling*, pp. 57, 95, 96. And for his earliest references to Lessing, see his notes in *Journals*, 5085; 5120; 5158; I C 53, 72, 100 (1835–36). For the references to *Postscript* in this note, see pp. 96f.; (KW 12 1·105-6); SV 9:90-1; (7:85-6).

12 *Journals*, 260; IV C 80 (1842–43). Kierkegaard had been concerned about the nature of the "transition's-category" since his university days, when (1838) he composed a satirical "drama" ("A heroic-patriotic-cosmopolitan-philanthropic-fatalistic Drama") entitled "The Conflict between the Old and New Soap- cellars (*Säbekielder*, or *Säbekälder*, a soap-storeroom)." In it a philosopher named Herr von Springgaasen (Jumping-Jack) comments on how the idea of transition's-category is well illustrated in Hegel's use of a speculative rational system as the commencement of world-history (*Papirer*, II B 21, p. 303; see Kierkegaard's Writings, vol. 1, *Early Polemical Writings*, edited and translated by Julia Watkin, p 122.

13 *Journals*, 2339; IV C 12. Hong translates *pathetisk* as "pathos-filled" to distinguish it from *lidenskabelig*. But in *Postscript* we will see that they mean the same thing for Kierkegaard.

and language. Something more is going on, because the change "is more than possibility and less than actuality." There are changes of quantity, quality, and place. And thus he arrives at the crucial question: "can there occur a transition from a quantitative determinant to a qualitative [determinant] without a leap? And does not the whole of life rest in that?"[14] With the notions of passion and leap Kierkegaard had the initial building blocks for his own unique delineation of freedom as *event* (act), and hence as something more than a state (of being).

These reflections make their first appearance in the authorship in *Fear and Trembling*, which he was writing at the same time (1843) he was making the above notes from Tennemann. In a draft for *The Concept of Anxiety* he claims that in *Fear and Trembling* "the necessity of 'the leap' is emphasized numerous times both as dialectical and as passionate, which is the substance of the leap."[15] This is an exaggeration, because the leap as such is mentioned in only three passages, and his analysis of it is still at a simplistic level. But he does, in a way, assume throughout the book what he says about the leap early on, by making one very interesting and important point: he distinguishes carefully and sharply between "the leap" and "faith," and sees them in a dialectical unity. And hence whenever he talks about faith (the ubiquitous subject of *Fear and Trembling*), he assumes the leap.

Kierkegaard (i.e., Johannes de Silentio) distinguishes between two distinct movements. First, there is the "movement of infinity," which is "the leap whereby I cross over into infinity." Secondly, there is "the movement of faith" which "must continually be made by virtue of [*i Kraft af*] the absurd." Since this distinction is assumed but expressed in complex variations in the extended treatment of the leap in *Postscript*, it will be helpful to spell it out here in order for us to understand the description of how the two movements are intertwined in *Postscript*.

The leap into infinity is called for when "the whole substance of one's life" is concentrated into a single love or desire, but the conditions of "reality" confront this "ideality" with the cry: "impossibility." Then "the slaves of the finite, the frogs in the swamp of life, scream: That kind of love is foolishness." And when one's own thoughts examine the conditions of life and come to the same conclusion ("impossibility"), should one "forget it all"? No! "Only the lower natures forget themselves and become something new." Rather, at this moment of crisis, if one remains

---

14 Ibid., 2339; IV C 12; 261, IV C 87.
15 Ibid., 2343; V B 49:14.

true to "the substance of one's life," then "one becomes very quiet, one dismisses [those thoughts], *one becomes solitary* [*ene*], and then one undertakes the movement [of infinity]" (emphasis added).[16]

What then is the character of this movement? It is not "reflection" which promises "mediation" of the conflict between ideality and reality (*Idealitet, Realitet*), and which "in Hegel is supposed to explain everything." Such "mediation is a chimera." Rather, "Every movement of infinity is carried out through passion. ... This is the continual leap in existence that explains the movement." And where does this passionate leap *up*, away from the limitations of the finite, land one? What is the "infinite?" The central passion and "whole substance" of one's life "become[s] ... the expression of an eternal love, ... transfigured into a love of the eternal being, which indeed denie[s] the fulfilment but ... reconcile[s] ... in the eternal consciousness of its validity in an eternal form that no actuality can take away." So one "makes the impossibility possible by expressing it spiritually, but one expresses it spiritually by renouncing it. The desire ... is now turned inward, but it is not therefore lost, nor is it forgotten." One becomes "sufficient unto oneself, ... and precisely this proves that one has made the movement infinitely." So one gains the "resilience" of "infinite resignation." I "make the infinite movement in order to find myself and gain rest in myself," because "only in infinite resignation do I become my self unambiguously in my eternal validity," or, "what I gain in resignation is my eternal consciousness."[17]

This state of infinite resignation is certainly better than simply submitting to and living in the merely finite determinants of existence, with no consciousness of one's eternal validity. But for Kierkegaard it is not an end in itself, but simply a stage in preparation for a second movement. To try to reside in the ideality of the infinite would be, he says, like a ballet dancer who conceives and practises his leaps as purely upward movements, with no thought that he must also come down. But the art of

16 For quotations in this and the previous paragraph, see *Fear and Trembling*, pp. 47, 52–4; (KW 6:36, 41–3); SV 5:35, 39–40; (3:87, 92–4). I am indebted to Alastair McKinnon for first pointing out to me (in October 1986) that the phrase "leap of faith" does not occur in the Kierkegaard corpus. Thus his paper on this topic, referred to above in note 10, is of great importance. Following up on his lead, I have become increasingly convinced that to use the phrase "leap of faith" seriously misrepresents Kierkegaard's understanding of both "leap" and "faith," especially when the reference is to Christian faith. The materials presented here in the text give part of the reason, but more explicit treatments will be found below in this chapter in the section on "The Breach in Religiousness A," and also in chapter 8 in the section on "The Second Breach: the Self vs. the Eternal." See especially note 5 in chapter 8.

17 Ibid., pp. 52–5, 46, 57; (KW 6:42–4, 35, 46); SV 5:40–2, 3; (3:92–5, 86, 96).

coming down into a certain stance is qualitatively different from the art of leaping up. So we come to the second part of what Kierkegaard calls the "double-movement" or the "dialectic of faith."[18]

First, the two movements are distinct and separate. The leap into infinity and resignation comes first, and (for Abraham) this is a "stage" which "pass[es] from his view." Then "he actually goes further and comes to faith." So the two must not be confused, as if "faith is needed in order to renounce everything." Indeed, "the act of resignation does not require faith," but is "a purely philosophical movement that I venture to make when it is demanded and can discipline myself to make. ... I make this movement all by myself. ... It takes a purely human courage to renounce the whole temporal realm in order to gain eternity."

Faith, however, is in a dialectical relation with the first movement of the leap into infinite resignation. On the one hand, it is always the case that "faith has resignation prior to itself," and hence "anyone who has not made this movement does not have faith, for only in resignation do I become conscious of my eternal validity, and only then can one speak of grasping existence by virtue of faith." On the other hand, the leap does not land one in faith, nor is faith in any sense a leap that *I* accomplish, "all by myself." What, then, does the movement of faith accomplish, and how does it happen?

In contrast to the leap that makes the movements of infinity, "faith makes the opposite movement: ... it makes the movements of finitude." Whereas the leap into infinity is accomplished by grasping the eternal in its purely ideal state and renouncing its realization in actuality, faith "goes further" by coming down from the leap so that it "does not lose the finite but gains it whole and intact," and "the whole earthly figure one presents is a new creation." In other words, "[b]y faith I do not renounce anything; on the contrary by faith I receive everything." And in contrast with the purely human courage it takes to renounce the whole temporal realm, "it takes a paradox and humble courage to grasp the whole temporal realm ... and this courage is of faith."[19]

But *how* does this happen? What is the secret power of faith that transcends the leap of infinitude into one's eternal consciousness, so that the impossible now becomes possible, not just in the ideality of infinity but in actuality? Kierkegaard's repeated answer is that faith works "by virtue of the absurd" (and the word translated "virtue" is literally

18 Ibid., pp. 51f., 46f.; (KW 6:41, 36); SV 5:39, 34f.; (3:91f., 87).
19 Ibid., pp. 48, 51f., 59; (KW 6:37f., 40f., 48f.); SV 5:36, 39, 46; (3:88f., 91, 97).

"power" or "energy": *Kraft*). And what is the "absurd," or "the paradox of existence," and whence comes its power? The paradox is this: first, one refuses to submit dumbly to the impossibility of one's aspirations as a matter of fate, and asserts their eternal validity by the leap into infinite consciousness, even while admitting that, "humanly speaking," one's "understanding" (*Forstand*) accepts their impossibility.

Then, only when this first movement has been made, only then does the possibility of a second totally different movement appear; only when "in infinite resignation ... I become conscious of my eternal validity ... can one speak of grasping existence by virtue of faith." Why? Because "my eternal consciousness is my love of God," and hence in this moment another possibility comes into view: my reflecting on myself may shift to reflecting on God, "for he who loves God without faith reflects upon himself; he who loves God in faith reflects upon God." So the question whether one can move beyond the state of infinite resignation cannot be resolved by a "purely philosophical movement" or by "purely human courage;" it "is a matter between oneself and the eternal being, who is the object of faith."

So "the marvellous happens." In reflecting on God, one comes to see and to believe that "for God all things are possible." This is the absurdity which human understanding cannot grasp. In this new relation with God, in this new kind of love of God, clearly "faith is no aesthetic emotion but something far higher; it is not the spontaneous inclination of the heart but the paradox of existence." In this instant, "the whole earthly figure one presents is a new creation by virtue of the absurd. One resigned everything infinitely, and then one grasped everything again by virtue of the absurd." So "it takes a paradox [impossible/possible] and humble courage to grasp the whole temporal realm by virtue of the absurd, and this courage is of faith." This courage, then, is not something I do "all by myself" (like the leap). Indeed, "by my own strength I cannot get the least little thing that belongs to finitude, for I continually use my strength in resigning everything." This courage comes when "my love of God conquer[s] within me." Then "by faith I receive everything."[20]

---

20 Ibid.; quotes in last two paragraphs will be found in the following pages but not in this order: pp. 48, 51f., 57–9, 62; (KW 6:37, 40f., 46–9, 51); SV 5:35, 39, 44–6, 48; (3:88, 91, 96–9, 101). This concept of faith is spelled out more exactly a year later in *Philosophical Fragments*, and even more fully in *Postscript* and *Sickness*. But even from this material in *Fear and Trembling*, it should be clear that faith is a relationship with God in which one *lives*, and therefore faith is not a leap which one *does* "all by oneself." The nature of faith will be dealt with further under the leap as religious.

It is critical to note at this point that Kierkegaard himself acknowledges that the notions of leap, faith, absurd, and paradox as Johannes de Silentio expounds them here in *Fear and Trembling* are only incipient and rather blurred concepts compared with their development two years later by Climacus in *Postscript*. Here the leap into infinity is primarily a leap out of a purely aesthetic existence into an ethical one, and yet it secures an "eternal" consciousness and validity which is religious, because "my eternal consciousness is my love of God." Furthermore, here the "object of faith" is not the eternal-in-time (Jesus) but is simply "the eternal being." Here it is a faith "by virtue of the absurd," whereas in *Postscript* "faith believes the absurd," and this, Kierkegaard says, is a very different concept of the absurd. So here Johannes de Silentio describes only the faith of Abraham ("the formal definition of faith" as in religiousness A), which imparts courage immanently when "my love of God [the eternal being] conquer[s] within me." Hence "the content of [this] faith cannot be Christian, that Jesus Christ has come into existence" (religiousness B).[21]

This fragmentary and precursory character of these notions in *Fear and Trembling* is commented on by Climacus in his retrospective "A Glance at a Contemporary Effort in Danish Literature" (in *Postscript*). He has been discussing *Either/Or, Repetition,* and *Fear and Trembling,* and says, "In none of these pseudonymous writings had sin been brought out." And this means they are not fully and adequately religious, because "Sin is a decisive expression for the religious existence." So in another comment on the religious at the general level of edification (i.e., of religiousness A), he points out that in five edifying discourses written at the same time as the latter two works (1843), Magister Kierkegaard attempts "to see how much one can attain in the upbuilding in a purely philosophical [manner]." And in a footnote he explains "the philosophical" as being the poetic "delineation of states of mind with a psychological colouring" with "the *principal* aim of transferring everything over into the upbuilding."[22]

---

21 See *Journals,* 10, 11, 12; x^6 B 79, 80, 81. In these entries made in 1850, Kierkegaard clearly says that "there is a difference between the absurd in *Fear and Trembling* and the paradox in *Concluding Unscientific Postscript,*" and that in *Postscript* "there are more precise qualifications which Johannes Climacus gives to make sure that the absurd as such is not the absurd in the ordinary sense." Indeed, "The absurd is a category, and the most developed thinking is required to define the Christian absurd accurately and with conceptual correctness."

22 *Postscript* pp. 239, 229f.; (KW 12.1:267–8, 256–7); SV 9:224, 214–15; (7:227, 216–17).

However, in spite of this fuzziness of concepts, it is important to note that the clear distinction between the leap and faith as developed in *Fear and Trembling* is maintained throughout the the rest of the Kierkegaardian corpus (even though in different language), and that nowhere can he discuss faith without involving the question of the leap because of their dialectical relation as described in *Fear and Trembling* (even though he never speaks of a "leap of faith"). The next year (1844) Kierkegaard addressed the notion of the leap directly in a much more sophisticated fashion, and he recorded this thinking in a series of journal entries. He used his new insights extensively in *The Concept of Anxiety* (1844), and developed them even further in *Postscript* (1845). All of these materials, plus some later journal entries and passages from *Sickness*, will be presented topically (rather than chronologically) in order to obtain a unified picture of what Kierkegaard means by "the leap" in freedom-as-event. In this chapter, this picture will concentrate on five topics: (1) the variety of leaps, (2) the leap as μεταβασις εις αλλο γενος ("passing [from one] into another genus [class, kind]," in English transliteration, *metabasis eis allo genos*), (3) the leap as concerned with the infinite/eternal, (4) the leap as a passionate (*pathetisk*) transition, (5) the leap as transition from the ethical to the religious.

THE VARIETY OF LEAPS

Kierkegaard begins by asking again the question he came to the previous year, "How does a new quality emerge from a continuous quantitative determinant?" And again his answer is, "with a leap." But he recognizes that there are different kinds of change and transition, and so also "a qualitative difference between leaps." The diversity is apparent when one speaks of a "leap" as occurring in transitions such as: water turning to ice, understanding an author, the Bible as a human book becoming the Word of God, a good person becoming evil, the paradox of the eternal entering time, the transition from aesthetics to ethics and from ethics to religion, proving the existence of God from a demonstration, emergence of sin-consciousness, drawing an inference from induction and analogy, moving from eudaemonism to a sense of duty.[23]

From this analysis Kierkegaard becomes very clear about the kind of leap that he is interested in. "My theory of the leap," he says, "is essen-

---

23 *Journals*, 2345; 2349; V C 1, 7 (1844).

tially at home in the realm of freedom."[24] We have gone through an extensive analysis of the conditions or locale of freedom, i.e., the individual's relation to past, future, eternity, possibility, necessity. But now Kierkegaard addresses the question of how freedom actually occurs, as event. His answer: as a "leap." And we turn first to what Johannes de Silentio calls the leap into infinity, that is, the leap from the aesthetic sphere *to* the ethical sphere, or the leap *of* the ethical.

The main source of Kierkegaard's thinking on this subject will be *Postscript*. But a word of warning must be sounded. *Postscript* is a pastiche of widely diverse perspectives on a number of distinct even though interrelated subjects. Hence, what follows, on the topic of the "leap," seeks a clarity and consistency that may not have existed even in Kierkegaard's mind.

We proceed, then, to an analysis of that particular kind of leap that "is at home in the realm of freedom," the ethical leap of action in time/space in contrast to the leap of insight and understanding involved in objective reflection.

THE LEAP AS μετάβασις εις αλλο γενος

Kierkegaard indicates the most general character of the leap (involved in freedom) by categorizing it as a μεταβασις εις αλλο γενος. In *Postscript* and in a late journal entry, he makes a direct equation of the leap with the "passing." He is rejecting the presence of a "direct [*ligefrem*] transition" from rational and historical evidence to the truths of ethics and religion. To reach the latter, there must always be a "μεταβασις εις αλλο γενος, a leap."[25] Kierkegaard's use of this Aristotelian concept had been suggested to him by his reading of G.E. Lessing's essay *Über den Beweis des Geistes und der Kraft* (probably sometime in 1843).[26] The importance of this phrase to Kierkegaard is evidenced by his continuous use of it from its first appearance in *Fragments*, to its decisive application in *Postscript*, to an unexpected usage in *Practice in Christianity*, to two late journal en-

---

24 Ibid, 2352; V C 12.
25 *Postscript*, p. 90; SV 9:84; (KW 12.1:98); (7:78); *Journals*, 2358; X¹ A 361 (1849).
26 See note 11 above. He clearly had read it before his writing of *Philosophical Fragments* and *The Concept of Anxiety* from March through May of 1844, as evidenced by his references to Lessing in these two works and by the first appearance of this phrase in *Fragments* p. 90; (7:73); SV 6:68; (4:236). Direct mention of Lessing's essay, however, does not appear until *Postscript*, p. 88; (KW 12.1:95–6); SV 9:82; (7:76). In his essay, Lessing is discussing the conflict between the truths of faith and the truths of historical evidence. He says that the truths

tries of 1849 and 1854.[27] It has several implications for what Kierkegaard means by the leap.

The basic point of this characterization of the leap concerns the degree of indirectness or discontinuity in the qualitative transition achieved by the leap of "free" decision and action, in contrast with the supposedly direct unbroken line of rational, scientific, or historical demonstration in what Kierkegaard calls a "quantitative" or "dialectical" or "necessary" transition. In *Postscript* Kierkegaard is expounding the thesis that "a logical system can be produced, but there cannot be produced any system of existence." He launches a satiric attack on the Hegelian contention that a purely logical system "begins with the immediate, and therefore [is] presuppositionless [*forudsætningsløst*], and therefore absolute; that is: the beginning of the System is the absolute beginning." Kierkegaard objects that this supposed immediate beginning "*is itself reached through reflection,*" and reflection is infinite, and

---

of faith (that Christ raised a man from the dead, that he himself was resurrected from the dead, that he was the Son of God, that the Son is of the same essence as God) are "truths of one and the same class, following one another quite naturally." But "with historical truth [one] leaps across into a wholly other class of truths," which "demand that I should reform all my metaphysical and moral concepts, because I cannot support the resurrection of Christ with any believable witness," and hence "I am required to alter all my basic ideas of the essence of the Godhead." Then he adds, "if that is not a μεταβασις εις αλλο γενος, then I do not know what else Aristotle meant by this designation." See G.E. Lessing, *Schriften II*, vol. 3, pp. 310f.

The passage in Aristotle from which Lessing derived the phrase is to be found in his *Organon: Analytica Posteriora*, book 1, chs. 6, 7. For translation, see *The Basic Works of Aristotle*, ed. Richard McKeon, pp. 119–22. In chapter 6 Aristotle is saying that, in order to attain "reasoned knowledge" or "demonstrations which produce scientific knowledge," one must construct syllogisms which use only the "essential attributes" of the subjects, and the subjects must all be of the same genus. Then in chapter 7 he says, "It follows that we cannot in demonstrating pass from one genus to another (μεταβασις εις αλλο γενος)." As examples, he says, "We cannot prove geometrical truths by arithmetic," and "Geometry ... cannot show that the straight line is the most beautiful of lines or the contrary of the circle; for these qualities do not belong to lines in virtue of their peculiar genus, but through some property which it shares with other genera."

27 These passages will appear in the following text except for the journal entry of 1854: *Journals*, 615; XI² A 263. Here Kierkegaard is reflecting on the fact that a radical collision with one's contemporaries often ends in catastrophe, obviously referring to his attack on Christendom. And if one consciously arranges this catastrophe, then "this consciousness is ... the really Christian concept of being sacrificed, a voluntary sacrifice. ... Catastrophe is the real μεταβασις εις αλλο γενος."

cannot be used to stop itself in order to procure an absolute presuppositionless beginning.[28]

What, then, will bring reflection to a halt or pause (*Standsning*) before a break or breach (*Brud*) or pit (*Grav*), so that a new beginning and a new quality may emerge? Only "something other [than reflection, that is], and this other is something wholly other than the logical," namely, "a resolve [*Beslutning*]," or "a decision [*Afgjørelse*]" (indeed, "the leap is the category of decision"). Here Kierkegaard brings into play several key ideas for the explication of the leap, and they are all intertwined. A leap as a resolve or decision is qualitatively different from a rational inference from other ideas or factual evidence, because the latter is an abstraction from the concrete individual circumstances of human existence. The leap of decision is called for, because the individual faces the demand for "transition from possibility to actuality, ... α κίνησις, a movement. This cannot be expressed or understood in the language of abstraction, because the latter cannot give to movement either time or space, which presuppose [movement] or are presupposed by it. ... In abstract thinking there is no breach, but neither is there a transition. ... But when existence provides time in the movement, and I reflect it, then the leap makes its appearance as only it can: either that it must come, or that it has already been."[29]

Does Kierkegaard mean, then, that the leap of decision, to enact a certain possibility within the given conditions of a particular time and place, is an absolute presuppositionless beginning? Does he then regard the "freedom" (involved in this decision) to be arbitrary and without the qualification of any conditions? We have seen again and again that such is not the case. And here, in his explication of the event of freedom as a "leap," he makes the point again through a very fine distinction. He has just said that a new beginning can occur only when reflection is halted by a resolve. Then he adds, "Only when the beginning, at which reflection stops, is a decisive-breach [*Gjennembrud*], so that the absolute beginning breaks out [*bryder frem*] through the infinite continuous reflection, only then is the beginning presuppositionless. On the contrary, if it is a breach [*Brud*] whereby reflection is interrupted [*afbrydes*], in order that the beginning may emerge, then the beginning is not absolute, since it has occurred by a μετάβασις εις αλλο γενος" (i.e., by a

---

28 *Postscript*, pp. 99–102; (KW 12.1:109–12); SV 9:93–6; (7:88–91).

29 Ibid., pp. 103, 91, 306; (KW 12.1:113, 99, 342); SV 9:97, 85; SV 10:45; (7:92, 79, 296–7).

leap). So, he concludes, "instead of talking or dreaming about an absolute beginning," let's "talk about a leap."[30]

Hence, with the distinction between "breaking out" (*bryde frem*) of reflection and "interrupting" (*afbryde*) reflection, Kierkegaard makes the crucial point that the leap (as μεταβασις εις αλλο γενος) is only an interruption of reflection, and therefore is not an absolute beginning: "if a resolve is required, then presuppositionlessness [*Forudsætningsløshed*] is renounced." And he repeats the same point in a late journal entry (1849): in "the qualitative leap ... there is no direct transition, ... but everywhere a μεταβασις εις αλλο γενος, a leap, whereby I interrupt [*bryder ... af*] the whole progression of reason [*Raisonement*] and define a qualitative newness, but a [newness] αλλο γενος."[31] In other words, the newness of an αλλο γενος is not absolute or presuppositionless.

His example in the journal entry makes this point clearly. He says that there is a qualitative leap from "reading the Bible as an ordinary human book" to "taking it as God's word, as Holy Scripture." There is no direct transition, and yet there is both continuity and discontinuity. The human book is a presupposition to the hearing of God's word, but something else has intervened so as to transform the human words into an αλλο γενος. There remains the continuity of "language," but now this "family" (taxometrically speaking) is subdivided into two "genera," because the "newness" of the language of God makes it qualitatively different from (even while using the same words of) the purely human language. As Kierkegaard puts it in the opening paragraph of part II of *Works of Love*, "One in whom the spirit is awakened ... remains in the language [of the visible world], except that his language is figurative [*overført*]. Figurative language is not a brand new language," but "[j]ust as spirit is invisible, so also is its language a secret, ... is the quiet whispering secret of the figurative—[audible] to the one who has ears."

This conclusion in *Postscript*, however, that the leap has presuppositions and does not initiate an *absolutely* new beginning, seems to contradict flatly the assertions about the leap in *The Concept of Anxiety*. As we have already heard, in *Anxiety* Haufniensis asserts that freedom, and its failure in sin, "cannot be explained by anything antecedent. ... Freedom is infinite and arises out of nothing. Therefore, to want to say that a human being sins necessarily is to want to lay out the curve [*Cirkel*] of the leap into a straight line." So a new quality can never arise out of a

---

30 Ibid., pp. 103, 105; (KW 12.1:113, 115); SV 9:97–8; (7:92, 94).
31 Ibid., p. 103; (KW 12.1:113); SV 9:97; (7:92); *Journals*, 2358; X¹ A 361.

continuous quantitative determination; rather, it "appears with the leap, with the suddenness of the enigmatic." "The determinants of approximation ... cannot bring forth the leap." So it is repeatedly said, "sin, like freedom, presupposes itself."[32]

On the other hand, one of the central assertions in *The Concept of Anxiety* is that "freedom is not free in itself but entangled, not by necessity, but in itself." And the entire book is a psychological exploration of how "angst" serves as a "middle term" that is required in the transition from possibility to actuality, how angst sets the last stage of approximation before the leap (even though "it no more explains the qualitative leap than it can justify it ethically"). Indeed, he calls the work of angst a "predisposition" and "presupposition" of the leap. Even in the state of innocence, the individual becomes aware of a "complex of presentiments" which reinforce each other in "reflectiveness," and as they "come nearer and nearer to the individual," they "communicate vigorously with the ignorance of innocence." Of course, in innocence they are merely a "predisposition" (*Prædisponer*) which is as yet an undefined "nothing." But "when by the qualitative leap one becomes guilty," then this reflective complex of presentiments "is the presupposition [*Forudsætning*] by which one goes beyond himself, because sin presupposes itself."[33]

What Kierkegaard seems to be saying in this tortured language is something like this. Freedom, as the event in which an individual chooses to enact a possibility, certainly has its presuppositions apart from which no choice occurs and hence no transition from possibility to actuality. But even if one has a complete knowledge of that "complex of presentiments," there is no way to infer with certainty what action will be taken by the agent, or indeed to demonstrate that there is a hidden, "straight," unbroken line of causal necessitation from presuppositions to action. Rather, in the transition in between, there is a "movement" or "change" (κινησις) that is something *more* than contemplated abstract possibilities, and yet something *less* than the actuality of their enactment.[34] This movement is required because a *particular* state of actuality in human existence is qualitatively different (an αλλο γενος) from the whole set of its presuppositions and possibilities. The coherence of the actuality with its possibility is not achieved by logical infer-

---

32 *The Concept of Anxiety*, in the order of appearance, pp. 100, 27f., 54, 100; (KW 8:112, 30, 60, 112); SV 6; 197, 126, 152, 197; (4:380f., 302, 331, 380).

33 Ibid., pp. 45, 55; (KW 8:49, 61f.); SV 6: 143, 153; (4:320, 332).

34 *Journals*, 258; IV C 47.

ence or rational deduction, or by simple continuity in physical causal process. Rather, in the enactment of that *kind* of possibility which is achieved through the human individual as agent, there occurs a pause (*Standsning*), and a break or breach (*Brud*) opens up before the agent. It is not an absolute break that demands an absolutely fresh beginning *ex nihilo*, but more an interruption that still has the conditional presence of presuppositions and predispositions and a set of fairly clear possibilities restricted by what the finite conditions will allow.

This rejection of the concept of a pure, abstract, presuppositionless freedom appeared early in Kierkegaard's thinking in the form of his critique of the notion of *liberum arbitrium*, and this critique continues in journal entries throughout the authorship. In Latin, *arbitrium* is the making of a judgment after listening to conflicting witnesses, and so a *liberum* judgment is one made without the presupposition of witnesses; it is to decide "arbitrarily" and unconditionally what one wants to do, to decide for oneself what is "good." In an early journal entry (1840), he remarks (contra Hegel), "That philosophy must begin with a presupposition [*Forudsætning*] ought not to be regarded as a *defect* but as a *blessing*," and the same is true with freedom, which should not be conceived as "contentless *arbitrium*." Rather, in "positive freedom ... we also find a presupposition, because this *liberum arbitrium* is never really found, but world-existence itself has already provided it."[35]

This point is repeated in *Either/Or* (1842), but is elaborated in *The Concept of Anxiety* (1844). "To maintain that freedom begins as *liberum arbitrium* (which is found nowhere, cf. Leibniz) that can choose good just as well as evil inevitably makes every explanation impossible. To speak of good and evil as the objects of freedom finitizes both freedom and the concepts of good and evil. Freedom is infinite and arises out of nothing." And in a draft for this passage, he comments that the very notion of *liberum arbitrium* "is basically an abrogation of freedom," because "freedom means to be capable. Good and evil exist nowhere outside freedom, since this very distinction comes into existence through freedom."[36] In other words, "positive" freedom consists of ultimate commitment to "infinite" or ideal good(s). To be free means to be *able* to choose the good; freedom is the enactment of the good. Not to choose the good is not freedom but "evil," unfreedom. So the "good" is the pre-

---

35 Ibid., 1240; III A 48.
36 *Either/Or*, 2:178; (KW 4:173f.); SV 3:163; (2:157); *The Concept of Anxiety*, p. 100; (KW 8:112); SV 6:197; (4:380f.); *Journals*, 1249; V B 56:2 (or KW 8:200f.).

supposition of freedom, is that which makes "explanation" possible. And "evil" is not a preexistent alternative, but what freedom brings into existence when it fails to choose the good.

Thus in later journal entries (in 1849 and 1851), Kierkegaard says that the notion of "a blank and bare *liberum arbitrium* is a chimera," and that "abstract freedom of choice [*liberum arbitrium*] is a delusion [*Indbilding*], as if a human being at every moment of his life stood continually in this abstract possibility." Rather, freedom is "an historical condition," and "so it is with the will" which "has ... a continually progressive history." So, even though freedom "arises out of nothing," yet it is conditional. In a key journal entry of 1850 (which we have used before), he says that in each situation where a truly significant (i.e., an "infinite") decision is to be made, it becomes apparent that there is only "one thing needful ... in such a way that there must be no question of any choice" (that is, as to *what* should be done). And yet, "the very fact that there is no *choice* expresses the tremendous passion or intensity with which one *chooses*" (here Kierkegaard uses the Danish word *Intensitet*, but note: "intensity" is the literal meaning of *Inderlighed*, which is regularly translated into English as "inwardness"). In other words, coming to judge or to "see," and to acknowledge and hence to "know," what *is* the "one thing needful" (the "good"), is not the act of freedom, but is the presupposition and precondition of freedom. But *knowing* what is the right and good thing to do does not guarantee that one will do it. To *do* the good requires a passionate, intense, inward resolve or decision to identify one's being and existence with that good. In this sense freedom is "infinite" and "arises from nothing."[37]

Now, all that has been brought out in this second point on the leap (as a μεταβασις εις αλλο γενος, and hence as comprising a breach or discontinuity which nevertheless occurs only within the conditions of certain presuppositions) is essentially the same point that our contemporary philosophy of action makes by saying that a free action is a "caused" action. That is to say, behind the act of an "agent" is a causality that is essentially different from rational inference and physical determination. An agent forms or arrives at an intention *because of* the interplay of one's desires (values) and beliefs (Kierkegaard's "self's possibility"). These are psychic phenomena which are also physical, but are not reducible to laws because of their "normative" element for which there is no parallel in purely physical phenomena (Kierkegaard's

---

37 *Journals*, 1260; x^2 A 243; 1268; x^4 A 175; 1261; x^2 A 428.

"breach"). This "normative element" means that an intention consists in an "all-out or unconditional evaluative attitude," that is, the "agent values one line of action more highly than any alternative" (Kierkegaard's "one thing needful" or the "good"). The action that emerges from an intention is therefore "voluntary" because it originates from within the agent. Yet this action is not arbitrary and capricious (uncaused) because it expresses who the agent is as "a coherent plausible pattern [of] attitudes" (Kierkegaard's inner gestalt of "the self's possibility" operating as "the self's necessity").

However, all this analysis is concerned purely with isolating what Kierkegaard calls "the *content* of freedom" about which there is no choice. It does not yet isolate "the *form*-determinant of freedom," that is, the *leap* as "freedom-of-choice" (*Valgfrihed*), choosing to *do* (to "exist in") the one thing needful. He considers the content to be absolutely "decisive for freedom," so that "emphasizing freedom-of-choice as such" [i.e. by itself] means the forfeiture of freedom.[38] So we have spent considerable time describing Kierkegaard's concepts of "the self's possibility" and "the self's necessity" as the presuppositions of freedom in order to understand freedom as the dialectical factor or event in the interplay of possibility and necessity.

Nevertheless, Kierkegaard takes the problem of how the action itself emerges from the self's possibility/necessity (the "state of intending") much more seriously than does Davidson. Having come to "an unconditional evaluative attitude," that is, to a clear conviction as to the "one thing needful," the agent still, according to Kierkegaard, faces a breach or gap. And that breach now opens up into an infinite chasm, because what is required of him/her is not a process of cool consistent reasoning or of efficient knowledgeable marshalling of physical evidence and resources. What is demanded, what is absolutely requisite is: a choice, a decision, a resolve. And Kierkegaard contends that the most adequate metaphor for this event is that of "a leap" as a "passionate transition."

Whence does this "passion" come? Or in the language of philosophy of action, whence comes the "motivational strength" to overcome lethargy ("weakness of will"), to conquer other conflicting desires and values? Or in Kierkegaard's terms, whence comes the "courage" to enact the "one thing needful" in the face of fear of the uncertainty of outcome, or of fear of opposition and criticism from external social forces and structures? An initial answer to this question can be gained through

---

38 Ibid., 1261; X^2 A 428.

a closer delineation of *which* possibilities of the human self authentic "freedom" has to do with. Thus far we have spoken of the "self's possibility" as consisting of a gestalt of undifferentiated capacities, inclinations, dispositions, tastes, attitudes, values, ideals, beliefs, etc. With such a definition, "freedom" could have to do with anything from the decision to wear either a red or a blue tie or dress, to the decision to take a stand on abortion in accord with one's inmost convictions in the face of opposition from spouse, friends, and one's employer. But for Kierkegaard freedom has to do with a very restricted area of decision-making, and the delineation of this area will help clarify why a "passionate transition" is involved. He designates this area succinctly when he says, "In the decisions of the spirit one can make up one's mind [*beslutte sig ud*] freely, but in relation to finitude (for example, physical well-being) one actually must be compelled. Finite decisions are in a certain sense too trifling for one to come at [them] in terms of the infinite. ... To 'be compelled' is the only help in [matters of] finitude—freedom's choice is the only salvation in [matters of] infinitude."[39]

So let us explore in more detail what he means by the area of the infinite in one's possibilities, and the peculiar nature of decision-making (of the "leap") in this realm.

THE LEAP AS CONCERNED WITH THE INFINITE/ETERNAL

We have already heard from *Fear and Trembling* (see material from note 17 above) that one makes "the movement of infinity" by turning to "a love of the eternal being" which conveys "the eternal consciousness of [one's] validity in an eternal form that no actuality can take away." This consciousness enables one to serve "ideality" with "the whole substance of one's life," and to ignore the cries of "Impossible!" from "the slaves of the finite." Thus in "infinite resignation" I gain "my eternal validity" and "my eternal consciousness." Here, this movement is identified as the leap, and is clearly distinguished from the second "movement of faith ... by virtue of the absurd."

In *The Sickness unto Death*, no mention is made of the leap, but the movement of infinity is described: "With [a] certain degree of reflection per se [*Reflexion i sig*] begins the act of discrimination wherein the self becomes aware of itself as essentially distinct from the environment and external-world and [from] their influence upon it." This reflection and

---

[39] Ibid, 1253; VIII¹ A 178.

its awareness "[help] one to understand that there is much one can lose without losing the self." Indeed, it imparts "a dim idea that there may even be something eternal in the self." And if one has adequate "self-reflection or ethical reflection," then one gains that "consciousness of a self ... which is the first form of the infinite self and the advancing impetus in the whole process by which a self infinitely becomes responsible for its actual self with all its difficulties and advantages."[40]

In other words, freedom as resolve or decision has to do with those possibilities of the self which have the character of being the infinite or "something eternal *in* the *self*" (emphasis added). It does not have to do with what "one can lose without losing the self," that is, with those matters of limited, temporary, relative, peripheral, non-essential significance. These words in *Sickness* are obviously reminiscent of the treatment (in *Either/Or*) of Jesus' words, "What would it profit a person if one gained the whole world but damaged one's own soul?"[41] Kierkegaard, eccentrically but typically, suggests that we reverse the question, that is, how much of one's "world" can one lose without doing damage to one's "soul" or self? His answer: "all the finite qualifications that I possess in my immediacy" (such as "my wealth, my honour in the eyes of others, my intellectual capacity"). And since my self is undamaged by losing them all, I am "indifferent toward them." And Kierkegaard immediately shows that this negative possibility of doing damage not externally but to "a person's innermost being" has as its positive alternative the act in which "you choose yourself absolutely," that is, in "freedom." And "thus one's finite personality is now made infinite in the choice, in which one infinitely chooses oneself."

In Judge William's same "letter" in *Either/Or*, the same point is made even more explicit a little later in another terminology. He says, "The ethical individual ... distinguishes between the essential and the accidental [*Tilfældige*]. Everything that is posited in one's freedom belongs to one essentially, however accidental it may seem to be; everything that is not [posited in one's freedom] is accidental to one, however essential it may seem to be." So "essentially only that belongs to me which I ethically take on as a task," that for which I assume personal re-

---

40 *Sickness*, p. 188; (KW 19:54f.); SV 15:110f.; (11:166f.).

41 *Either/Or*, 2:224ff.; (KW 4:220ff.); SV 3:204ff.; (2:197ff.). See Mt. 16:26; Lk. 9:25. It is interesting that the English translation (RSV) takes one meaning of ζημιoω, viz. to lose or forfeit, while the Danish translation uses its other meaning, viz. to damage. Also, it is clear that Kierkegaard is reading the Mathean passage which uses the word "soul" (ψυχη), whereas the Lukan passage speaks of losing or forfeiting "oneself" (εαυτον).

sponsibility. And this way of making the distinction makes it clear that a particular individual cannot be sorted out into elements that are essential or accidental as such. Rather, "this whole distinction is an illusion," because "to a certain degree the person who lives ethically cancels the distinction between the accidental and the essential, because one takes responsibility for all of oneself as equally essential; but it comes back again, for after one has done that, one makes a distinction, but in such a manner that one takes an essential responsibility for excluding what he excludes as accidental."[42]

In other words, when, in the context of this perspective, one says that "freedom is the dialectic in the determinants possibility and necessity," one means that freedom in the particular individual consists in choosing to enact and to take responsibility for those possibilities which are consistent with one's essential being, what one cannot "lose" or deny without losing or denying who and what one *is* in one's "innermost being." Likewise, my freedom consists in taking an essential responsibility for excluding certain possibilities as accidental or incidental in my innermost makeup as a self, so that "If I refuse to take it on, then my having refused it essentially belongs to me."[43]

This concept of what is "essential" in being a human individual or self is picked up by Kierkegaard and carried forward throughout the rest of the authorship. In *Postscript* he makes the distinction between essential and accidental cognition (*Erkjenden*). "All essential cognition concerns existence, or only cognition whose relation to existence is essential is essential cognition. That cognition which does not, inwardly in the reflection of inwardness, concern existence is, essentially viewed, accidental cognition; its degree and scope are essentially viewed as indifferent." This relation to existence "means that cognition relates to the one who is perceiving, who is essentially one who exists. ... Only ethical and ethical-religious cognition is therefore essential cognition." In other words, coming to perceive and to understand abstract universal concepts about the world in general is not essential to being and becoming a human individual self. Rather coming to perceive and to understand what *I* the perceiver ought to do in this specific situation in space and time is what is essential. All other cognition is an indifferent matter for that "freedom" which defines who I essentially am.

---

42 Ibid., 2:264f; (KW 4:260f.); SV 3:240f.; (2:233f.).
43 Idem.

Here Kierkegaard has arrived at his identification of the essential (for the human self) with something profoundly inward. So a few pages later he asserts, "When subjectivity, inwardness is the truth, then truth is determined objectively as paradox. ... The paradox is the objective uncertainty, which is the expression for the passion of inwardness, which precisely is the truth. ... The eternal essential truth, that is, that which relates essentially to an existing one by being essentially concerned with the fact of existing, is the paradox, all other knowledge being accidental, indifferent in its degree and scope."[44]

But what is this inward, subjective, eternal, essential truth, and what does it have to do with the mode of human existence in space/time? In his next major work, *Works of Love*, Kierkegaard contrasts the "eternal growth" of the individual toward the "essentially other," which all humans have in common and equally, with the external "distinctions," which are indifferent. But then he turns around and stresses the absolute unique individuality (*Eiendommelighed*) that inheres in each human person and that is given and guaranteed by God. In *Sickness* he speaks of a person becoming "mature in an essential consciousness of the self." Later he identifies this with a sense of "continuity with regard to one's consciousness of oneself," and then adds that "eternity is the essential continuity and demands this of a person, or that one be conscious as spirit and have faith."[45]

Clearly in both *Works of Love* and *Sickness* he is developing what he calls in *Postscript* the "ethical-religious" aspect of self-conciousness, and doing so from a specifically Christian perspective. So in *Works* he describes in detail how the essential equality of all human beings and the qualitative uniqueness of each individual will be affirmed and established *only* in the triadic relationship of self-sacrificial non-preferential love. And in *Sickness* he asserts, in multiple variations, that the self can escape despair and achieve eternal continuity in self-consciousness (spirit) *only* through faith in All-things-are-possible (God). In the next chapter we will explore at length how the relationship with eternal "love," and hence with all-things-are-possible, transforms human existence and human relationships even at the pre-Christian level of religiousness A. But let us now summarize what we have thus far heard

---

[44] *Postscript*, pp. 176f., 183; (KW 12.1:197–8, 204–5); SV 9:164–5, 170–1; (7:165, 171).

[45] *Works of Love*, pp. 96f., 252f.; SV 12:89f., 259ff.; (9:87f., 257ff.); *Sickness*, pp. 193, 236; (KW 19:59, 105); SV 15:115, 156; (11:171, 215).

Kierkegaard saying on the leap from possibility to actuality, and then use some more terminology from *Postscript* for its clarification.

"Freedom" as enactment of possibilities is limited by Kierkegaard to the making of those decisions that bring into play what is "infinite" and "eternal" in one's innermost being as an individual living in space and time. ("Bring into play" here means "are caused by" in the sense of "are done *because of*.") The infinite/eternal "*in* the self" consists of that more or less unified *core* (gestalt) of capacities, inclinations, dispositions, tastes, attitudes, values, beliefs, ideals, etc. in so far as that core determines what is "essential" to a particular self, what one cannot lose or deny or ignore without losing or denying or ignoring *who* one *is*. And the test of what is truly essential in a self is not what one ideally or abstractly thinks or feels or hopes or says about one's self. Rather, those determinants are truly essential which a person "exists in," those which "inwardly in the reflection of inwardness concern existence," that is, those which come to grips with what this particular person should do in one particular situation in space/time.

This understanding of the essential infinite self is precisely what is caught in Kierkegaard's formula in *Sickness*, "freedom is the dialectical in the determinants possibility and necessity." As exposited in detail above, the "self's necessity" consists of those abstract infinite qualities of the "self's possibility" which set the limit to what one may seek to do in actuality if one is to be faithful to and is to become who one is or who one has been "given" to be as a "very definite something and thus the necessary." So he says, "When a self runs wild in possibility, ... [w]hat is missing is essentially the power to obey, to submit to the necessity in one's self, to what may be called one's boundary."[46]

This delineation of the "infinite," as those possibilities which "freedom" has to do with, receives one further specification in *Postscript* when it describes the "leap into the infinite" as the individual's having "a relation to an eternal blessedness" (not "happiness").[47] As has been pointed out above on several occasions, whenever Kierkegaard speaks of the "eternal," he has reference to something qualitatively distinct from the dimension of the "infinite" in the human self, indeed, something transcendent to the self even when he speaks of the eternal as

---

46 *Sickness*, pp. 163, 169; (KW 19:29, 36); SV 15:87, 94; (11:142, 149).

47 "Blessedness" is used instead of Swenson's "happiness" because the latter term is usually taken to mean a superficial sensuous/social contentment or pleasure. We will deal later with how Kierkegaard conceived of the content and character of this blessedness, and how his idea differs from the superficial idea of happiness.

being something "in" the consciousness of the self. In other words, whenever he speaks of the eternal, he is talking about the transition from the ethical sphere to the ethical-religious sphere.

But as we will see later, Kierkegaard argues that this latter sphere in its initial form (religiousness A) is still one of immanence. That is to say, the awareness of being related to something that is "other" than (transcendent to) one's self, and yet is *absolutely* essential to and needed by one's self (is a qualitative either/or, a life or death matter)—this awareness does not arise out of reference to and stimulus by "something outside oneself" (*Noget uden for sig selv*). Rather, this sphere or level of self-consciousness is an awareness that "the relation to an eternal blessedness is not conditioned by anything," but that the self is involved in "the dialectical interiorization [*Inderliggjørelse*] of the relation," or in "the dialectical deepening of interiorization."[48]

If, then, freedom is one's involvement in determining one's actual existence in accord with what one essentially is in one's inner gestalt of attitudes, dispositions, values, beliefs, etc., what does it mean to say that this involvement is qualified by one's "relation to an eternal blessedness"? How does this qualification specify more exactly how that gestalt comes to bear on that leap from possibility to actuality? And, secondly, how does this qualification reveal the source of the motivating power of that "completely decisive resolve" to "stamp upon one's action that inner necessity which excludes the thought of another possibility"?

A key to this language about an "eternal blessedness" is found in a very late journal entry (August of 1854). Kierkegaard says, "A decision of eternity in time is the most intensive intensity, the most intensive leap." By this "decision" he means "something eternal being decided in time." And by "time" he means *now*, a decision that must not, cannot, be put off, because "no one can know if one will be alive the next hour"; so "this anxious uneasiness [in the face of death] leads naturally to a decision of eternity."[49] In other words, one's ultimate, essential, absolute "blessedness" or well-being is being decided here and now. How does this happen?

"In relation to an eternal blessedness as the absolute good, passion [*Pathos*] denotes not words but the fact that this idea transforms the ex-

---

48 *Postscript*, pp. 494, see also 498; (KW 12.1:556, 560–1); SV 10:225, 229; (7:485, 488–9). The meaning and nature of "interiorization" will be treated in the next section below.

49 *Journals*, 4806; A XI¹ 329.

isting one, indeed, one's whole existence." So "the passion, corresponding adequately to an eternal blessedness, is the transformation by which the existing-one, while existing, alters everything in one's existence in respect to that highest good." But this "everything" must be qualified. There are "insignificant matters" in the planning of one's life, which are subject to chance and change. For example, one may fall in love and marry or may not; one may be rich but then become poor; and so forth. And so "one changes his existence in the moment of choice." But such conditions are "relative ends," and they "cannot, without irrationality, transform one's existence absolutely." And those who expend their "worldly wisdom" on such matters are not "existentially expressing [their] relationship to the absolute good."[50]

Certainly, one does not cease being or living as finite, because "existence is composed of infinitude and finitude, so the existing one is infinite and finite." But, even while living within the demands of eating, working, marrying, having children, etc., "If for an individual an eternal blessedness is one's highest good, then that means that the factors of one's finitude must once and for all be renounced in respect to the eternal blessedness." It is not sufficient to say that one wants "a good living, a pretty wife, health, a social position," and, oh yes! "also an eternal blessedness." This "*at the same time* to *wish* an eternal blessedness is double nonsense." This blessedness is not just one more present on the Christmas tree, nor is it simply a *wish*: "an eternal blessedness essentially relates to existing essentially."[51]

So Kierkegaard adds to the distinction between essential and accidental the distinction between absolute and relative ends. Even a relative end (τέλος) such as energetically making money is able to transform a human life, but only relatively. "All relative willing [*Villen*] is recognizable as willing something for the sake of something else, but the highest τέλος must be willed for its own sake." So one's highest end is never a particular "something," but is that which one considers to be an end in itself, that which is "absolute" and "eternal" at the core of one's being, for which the particular thing only serves as an occasion for expression.[52] For example, if I give food to the starving children of the Sudan, I do so not simply to assuage their hunger for a day, but to enable them

---

50 *Postscript*, 347–9n; (KW 12.1:387–9); SV 10:82–4; (7:336–8).
51 Ibid., pp. 350–1; (KW 12.1:391–2); SV 10:85–6; (7:339–40).
52 Ibid., pp. 353–4; (KW 12.1:393–5); SV 10:88–9; (7:341–2), for this paragraph and the next.

to have the freedom to develop as unique human beings, which is my absolute value or concern, an end in itself.

This service of one's absolute τέλος involves a rigid discipline. If one expresses one's eternal blessedness "existentially in existence," this requires that "one allows resignation to examine one's entire immediacy with all its yearnings and desires. And if one finds a single tenacious spot of resistance, then one has no relation to an eternal blessedness." This examination means that "the individual must not have one's life in immediacy," and resignation means that one must be ready to accept "whatever befalls one in life." There can be no "mediation" (Hegel) which finally unifies and harmonizes our relative desires and our absolute commitment to what we believe to be "eternal." And it should be noted that "this existential passion [*Pathos*] is the poor-person's passion, ... because every human being can act within him/herself."

It is important to note that Kierkegaard's distinctions between "essential" and "accidental" (and hence between "absolute" and "relative") as determinative of the identity of an individual person may appear to be antiquated from several twentieth-century perspectives; for example, the perspective of a relativistic psychology that treats the ego as a set of interacting structures and capacities or as an organization of functions, rather than as an integral personality or centred personal agent; or the perspective of philosophy of deconstruction for which the individual is only a temporary swirl or pattern in a social language-event composed of a flowing everchanging stream of "traces," rather than an authentic individuated selfhood; or the perspective of physics that conceives of ultimate and lasting reality as composed of certain physical relationships which can be reduced to numbers and signs in a formula. But as pointed out above, there is a more open and inclusive kind of contemporary logic that argues that the concept of essential and accidental properties has a long and noteworthy tradition and needs to be revived in the twentieth century "if a useful notion of 'state of affairs' is to be developed," or if one is to be able to "identify the individuals of one world with the individuals of another world" (see notes 148 and 149 in chapter 5). Also, several current schools of psychotherapy are now finding it therapeutic and therefore intellectually defensible to assume and to appeal to a "responsible self," and the distinction between the physical and the mental is again up for debate and redefinition.

To summarize: the "most intensive leap," that is, the leap of freedom, occurs as a "decision in time" (*Afgjørelse i Tid*) about one thing and one thing only: one's "eternal blessedness." That is to say, honest-to-goodness "freedom" for Kierkegaard, that which deserves such a noble name, occurs only when one faces a choice, here and now, which requires a passionate resolve or decision that calls into play those absolute ultimate values, ideals, convictions, beliefs, etc. which are definitive of who one *is*, which one cannot lose or deny without losing or denying one's very self, which alone is of infinite and eternal dignity and worth. And every such decision involves one in a risky, daring "leap," because one's inner subjective certitude as to what is the "highest good" in this situation is *always* accompanied by public objective uncertainty as to the grounds and the results of this decision. To demand certainty means the end of freedom and responsibility. "To risk [to venture] is the correlate of uncertainty; as soon as certainty is there, [all] risking ceases."[53]

There are many matters and situations which publicly or historically seem to be of the greatest importance, which yet may not engage one's self at this definitive level of freedom, because the self judges them to be matters of indifference (although such a judgment itself must be "free" most intensely). On the other hand, what may appear publicly to be a matter of no importance may engage a particular individual inwardly and subjectively in the most intense struggle in "deciding something in time" that is of "eternal" or absolute significance for that person. Perhaps the most vivid image for this event is suggested by Kierkegaard's analysis of the nature of "time" in *The Concept of Anxiety*. In ordinary time, he says, the present moment is an empty blip between a fleeting past and a yet-to-come future. But when the self in freedom achieves the synthesis of the sensuous and the psychical, there also must occur the synthesis of the temporal and the eternal, and then the present moment becomes full. Full of what? He calls this moment "the fullness of time," but "the fullness of time is the moment as the eternal, and yet this eternal is also the future and the past."[54] The image is this: instead of trying to forget my past and living in hope of a new future, I reach backward with one arm and bring forward into the present all of my past (I "choose" it), and I reach forward with the other arm and bring (enact) now into the present my immediately future possibility, and my present moment is full, full of the harmony and unity of both my most pedestrian finitude *and* my absolute eternal infinitude. My most abstract ideal possibility has become my inner necessity by coming-into-existence. The eternal is *now*, is "the fullness of time."

53 Ibid., p. 380; (KW 12.1:424); SV 10:114; (7:368).
54 *The Concept of Anxiety*, p. 81; (KW 8:90); SV 6:178; (4:360).

Does this conceptuality of "eternal blessedness" answer our question as to what explains the "leap," the transition from intention to act, from the self's "possibility" to the self's "actuality"? It explains "what" happens but not the "how." Two questions still remain. Why does Kierkegaard say that this decision or transition must be "passionate"? And why does he say that it must be "religious"? We have asked several times, whence the passion for the leap? Now we turn directly to the first question as our fourth topic (see p. 249 above).

THE LEAP AS A PASSIONATE TRANSITION

Early on (1843), Kierkegaard confides to his journal, "What I wish in a human being is ... ευκαταφορια εις παθος [*eukataphoria eis pathos*]," that is, "a disposition to being deeply affected." We have already heard him say (in the same year) in *Fear and Trembling* that "every movement of infinity is carried out through passion [*Lidenskab*]. ... This is the continual leap in existence"; and we have heard his journal comment that in *Fear and Trembling* "the necessity of 'the leap' is emphasized ... with respect ... to pathos which is the substance of the leap" ("substance" [*Gehalt*] in the sense of what makes the leap a leap).[55] So he wants his pervasive appeal to *Lidenskab* (especially in *Postscript*) to be interpreted in terms of the Greek concept of παθος (*pathos*) as one's being deeply affected by or about something, as having passionate feelings about something, even to the point of being willing to suffer for it, because (for Kierkegaard) it has infinite value and significance. (So here Kierkegaard's adjective *pathetisk* has been regularly translated "passionate," although the Hongs use "passion-filled" in order to distinguish it from the usual Danish word for "passionate," *lidenskabelig*.)

This kind of passion is central to Kierkegaard's concern because he sees it as required in the appropriation of the truth of "subjective reflection" as opposed to the dispassionate accumulation or learning of the truths of "objective reflection." The latter truth consists of results of inquiry in the form of empirical facts and abstract generalizations that can be directly transmitted to the learner. But when "inwardness is the truth" in subjective reflection, "the desire to communicate results is an unnatural transition [*Overgang*] between one human being and another,

---

55 *Journals*, 4512; IV A 44; 2343; V B 49:14; *Fear and Trembling*, p. 53; (KW 6:42); SV 5:40; (3:93).

inasmuch as every human being is spirit, and the truth is precisely the self-activity of appropriation, which a result prevents."[56]

In other words, the truth that is relevant for me as spirit or self is appropriated by me only through my own inward evaluation and decision in the light of that essential core of absolute values, beliefs, convictions, etc. (my "infinite self" or "self's possibility") which define who I am as a unique person, and which must be "obeyed" for the sake of my "eternal blessedness." And this evaluation/decision requires "passion" in the sense of "courage" to "believe" in it because no external facts or abstract reasoning can determine or guarantee the evaluation/decision for me. So for me as subject, as person, as self, "the objective uncertainty, held fast in appropriation by means of the most passionate inwardness, is the truth, the highest truth there is for an existing-one." It is this character of this kind of truth that prevents it from being directly expressible and communicable. So "pathos is inwardness" only when it is "pathos in the form of opposition" between truth that can be directly expressed and communicated and the truth of subjectivity that cannot. And it is "especially in ethical capability [*Kunnen*, being able] and religious [capability]" that "the transition is passionate [*pathetisk*]," and this passionate transition is "the leap."[57]

Another way Kierkegaard has of making this point is by distinguishing among aesthetic, ethical, and religious pathos (i.e., of religiousness A). Later we will see how he makes a sharp distinction between the ethical and religiousness A, but in regard to pathos he describes them in the same terms. Aesthetic passion "expresses itself in words" and moves one "to lose oneself in the idea." Actuality is merely "the occasion" from which to derive the idea. So the idea caught in words is "higher" than actuality. For "existential pathos" (both ethical and religious), "the idea is related in a transforming way to the existence of the individual," and therefore "the deed is the highest pathos," rather than the word. So, "Ethically the highest pathos is interestedness, which is expressed by the fact that I actively transform the whole of my existence in relation to the object of interest." Likewise, the pathos of religiousness A, having

56 *Postscript*, pp. 216–17; (KW 12.1:242); SV 9:202; (7:203f.).

57 *Postscript*, pp. 182, 217; (KW 12.1:203, 242); SV 9:169–70, 202; (7:170, 204); *Journals*, 653; VIII[2] B 85:5. See also 2339; IV C 12: "A passionate [*pathetisk*] transition can be achieved by every one if he wills it, because [the transition] to the infinite, which consists in pathos, takes only courage." And 3129; VIII[1] A 92: "What our age needs is *pathos*, ... the passionate [*Lidenskab*] and the passion-filled (*Pathetiske*) in order to get, if possible, a beneficial passion-filled breeze blowing. The tragedy of our age is reason and reflection."

"passed through the ethical and preserved it in itself, ... consists not in singing and hymning and composing verses, but just in existing." However, its "object" is "an eternal blessedness," and "The pathos, corresponding adequately to an eternal blessedness, is the transformation by which the existing-one, while existing, alters everything in his existence in respect to that highest good."[58] So, note, "eternal blessedness" does not have to do with "pie in the sky when I die," but with the incarnation of a transcendental ideal ("highest good") into the conditions and events of my "existence" here and now.

In other words, for Kierkegaard, when I face that kind of judgment, decision, and choice which cannot be arrived at by cool objective marshalling of facts and rational inference and generalization, but which requires that I turn inward to that essential gestalt of basic values, beliefs, commitments, etc. which define who I am, then the decisive factor, in the leap into the αλλο γενος of the truth valued most highly in my "subjectivity," is "infinite, personal, impassioned (*i Lidenskab*) interestedness."[59] The key to the nature of "freedom" and "the voluntary" as *event* lies in this passion. It provides the driving force of that "inner necessity" which is mine alone, which derives from nothing outside my core identity, and which is the decisive criterion for which of my variety of often conflicting values, beliefs, and commitments are definitive of who I am, definitive of the truth of my subjectivity, that is to say, decisive for which of them are essential and absolute for me in this particular situation here and now. In other words, as subject or self, I *am* that interrelated complex of values, ideals, beliefs, etc. to which I give ultimate, absolute, and *passionate* commitment, and in which I am personally passionately interested: "The culmination [*Høieste*] of inwardness in an existing subject is passion."[60]

Why is passionate interestedness the culmination of the inwardness of subjectivity? Because there in my most intense self-consciousness, I face the ultimate question: where does "truth" lie for me when I face this kind of decision? I find no help from that truth offered by objective universals about the structures of physical or historical or social or psychological nature. And so I turn to that kind of truth that calls into play my ultimate values, ideals, beliefs, etc. But has not the human race, after

---

58 *Postscript*, pp. 347–50; (KW 12.1:387–391); SV 10:82–5; (7:335–9).

59 Ibid., p. 30 and, for variations of the formula, pp. 28, 33, 35, 51, 52; (KW 12.1:29 and 27, 33, 34, 52, 53); SV 9:29 and 27, 32, 33, 48, 49; (7:18 and 16, 21, 23, 39, 40).

60 Ibid., p. 177; (KW 12.1:199); SV 9:165; (7:166).

millennia of experience with making ethical decisions, been able to distil objective, public, external, universal criteria which are adequate for determining what is "good" for each ethical situation and dilemma faced by a human individual?

In a dozen different ways, we have heard Kierkegaard answer this question with a resounding "NO!" For him, to assume that such external criteria can answer a specific ethical dilemma faced by a particular individual at a concrete time and place amounts to a denial and obliteration of the ethical, indeed, of the very reality of the unique individual human self and of the freedom that is definitive of selfhood. At the crucial juncture of resolve/decision by the individual, the "truth" of the "good" is determined by one's turning inward, not outward, by being intensely subjective, not objective, by determining the "good" in terms of one's own unique self, not in terms of a universal, by finally becoming passionately interested in and committed to doing that one thing needful demanded by one's "inner necessity," not engaging in cool calculation of relative probabilities. And again the question: why or whence this passion?

The answer (at its first level) is two-sided.[61] Basically, I become passionate in my resolve when I sense that this free resolve, determined strictly in accord with my most inward subjectivity, entails essentially my "eternal blessedness." In other language, my ultimate and absolute dignity and worth as a unique individual is assured to me, is established and conserved in my self-consciousness, only in, by, with my decision to act thus, as dictated by my own subjectivity. This moment, when I contemplate in totally subjective reflection the one thing needful now demanded of me, is filled with fear and trembling, because I sense that my infinite (absolute) and eternal (ultimate) blessedness (significance) as a person hangs in the balance, indeed, may be lost. No moment of self-consciousness holds greater or more intense pathos.

This moment is passionate (*pathetisk*) for another reason. The more strictly inward or subjective the resolve is, the less objectively will it be supported by external public evidence and opinion. In fact, Kierkegaard argues that action out of such resolve will most certainly evoke disagreement and opposition. And the agent of such action, still at the moment of decision, will anticipate such opposition, and one's certitude

---

[61] A second answer will be presented in the next major section of this chapter when we see that the leap of freedom must finally involve a religious dimension.

of resolve will always be accompanied by an equal uncertainty as to the results. And the leap of absolute certitude in the context of inevitable uncertainty demands passionate courage.

These two sources of passion in the moment of decision are not unrelated, but merge. Thus: for me to resolve to act decisively out of my own subjectivity requires that I believe passionately enough in the dignity and worth of my own inward definitive selfhood so as to act in accord with it in the face of objective uncertainty and opposition. So Kierkegaard says, "Decision is rooted in subjectivity, essentially in [one's] passion, and maximally in infinite, interested, personal passion concerning one's eternal blessedness." And again, "In infinite passionate interest concerning one's eternal blessedness, subjectivity is [engaged] in its most extreme exertion, at its zenith."[62] Yet, in all the foregoing analysis of the sources of that passion which motivates the leap of freedom that enacts one's possibility within actuality, the central question is not answered: how does this "passionate interestedness" comes about? Is it simply a given of psychic-social conditioning, or is it a voluntary movement within one's subjectivity? If this passionate interestedness is indeed the key to the nature of the leap of freedom as event, then this question must be faced.

Let us use the language of contemporary philosophy of action to help in the clarification of what the question is all about. In its terms, Kierkegaard seems to be saying that the "leap" of free action occurs in my coming to hold an intention which expresses (is "caused" by) that coherent pattern of values and beliefs ("reasons" or "attitudes") which define who I am. But this intention must take the form of more than recognizing the desirability of something; it must comprise an "all-out or unconditional evaluative attitude" so that "an agent values one line of action more highly than any other." Davidson, however, admits that this analysis "leaves [open] the question what the relation between the intention and the action is," that is, what *moves* the agent from intention to enactment of intention. He speaks of "a resolve or a commitment" as something additional to an intention, but when he analyses this transition, he only speaks of a rough kind of law to the effect that "whenever certain conditions are satisfied, an agent will perform an action with a certain intention." That is to say, if the conditions of time and place and other relationships are suitable to the intention, then the intention

---

62 *Postscript*, pp. 35, 52; (KW 12.1:34, 53); SV 9:33, 49; (7:23, 40).

makes the action "plausible" or "rational," and "an agent will perform" the action—*if,* of course, the agent is being "reasonable" (EOD 221, EAE 76, 100).

At this point Kierkegaard insists that the element of a resolve or a commitment is something other than being plausible or reasonable. Indeed, as we have heard, a resolve (*Beslutning*) is the only thing that can bring the rational process of reflection to a halt, because it is a qualitatively different kind of mental state or event from being plausible or reasonable.[63] Resolve consists in or accomplishes a transition into a totally αλλο γενος, whereas being plausible or reasonable involves no halt and breach but simply elicits an action that is in continuity and consistency with the already-formed intention. When Kierkegaard says that "a human being has the most compelling sense of freedom when, with completely decisive resolve, one stamps upon one's action that inner necessity which excludes the thought of any other possibility," this "completely decisive resolve" is exactly what he means by a "leap" from possibility to actuality, motivated by an infinite, inward, personal, passionate interestedness.[64] And he would argue that no "law" of plausibility or reasonableness can account for this transition from intention to action.

Davidson comes closer to an appreciation of Kierkegaard's added element of passionate interestedness when he says that the "judgment" or "disposition" or "evaluative attitude" which precedes and leads to action must be "all-out" and "unconditional." The latter designation is a very powerful word whether used in the field of logic, or physics, or ethics, or religion. But Davidson gives us very little indication of what he means by "unconditional" as he applies it to intentional action, except as a means of distinguishing intentions from "prima-facie judgments" which merely express that a certain kind of action is desirable in a general way. Of which "conditions" is an evaluative attitude free, when it takes the form of an intention to act? It would seem that it is free of other alternative and perhaps conflicting prima-facie judgments; that is to say, one selects or yields to one course of action, and excludes any other possible one(s) from consideration. So Davidson describes in some detail how "the common calculus of decision under

---

63 Ibid., p. 103; (KW 12.1:114); SV 9:97; (7:92).
64 *Journals,* 1269; X⁴ A 177.

uncertainty" takes place, namely, by a careful balancing of what one's various desires and values dictate, and by one's best judgments (beliefs) about how a certain action would work out in the actual world (EAE 98–101, 221; EOD 199f.). But he recognizes that in spite of coming to such an all-out judgment or disposition, "a present intention does not need to be anything like a resolve or commitment." So this distinction between a prima-facie liking and an unconditional intention does not explain how alternatives are excluded when there is a sharp conflict between two prima-facie judgments or dispositions, or between an "all-things-considered" judgment and an alternative compelling desire; nor does it explain the move from an unconditional disposition (intention) to its enactment.

Kierkegaard came late in life (the 1850s) to his own notion of "the unconditioned" (*Det Ubetingede*),[65] and we have already briefly noted its importance in reference to his concept of necessity (see notes 137, 138 in chapter 5). In contrast to Davidson, he sees it as located at a different place in the "calculus of decision under uncertainty," and therefore as playing a very different role in the process. He identifies the unconditioned with "being-in-and-for-itself" (*Iogforsigværende*), as the essential characteristic of "being human." This state consists in "sheer transparent subjectivity," so that when one asks how one should love, or obey, or believe, or venture out, the answer is: unconditionally. That is to say, one must act as being-in-and-for-itself, which can occur only for "that which infinitely subjectively has its subjectivity infinitely in its power [*Magt*] as subjectivity." So deciding/acting out of one's own sheer, undiluted, unshadowed ("transparent") subjectivity means that one's resolve is not determined by "a relationship to environment, a relationship to an other." One's motivation does not derive from "reasons" (*Raisonements*), or "knowledge of grounds" (*Grunde*), or "guarantees," or "probability" arrived at by "shrewd calculation." One does not ask "Why?" or "For what purpose [*Hensigt*]?" Rather, "every 'Why' vanishes in the night of the unconditioned and becomes silent in the silence of the unconditioned." For such a one, "no teleological consideration can induce one actually to venture everything. ... In the unconditioned all teleology vanishes." So when I risk and venture everything, "I have no 'Why' at all; that

---

[65] See the entries given in Hongs' *Journals* under the headings "The Unconditioned" (nos. 4893–4919) and "Venture, Risk" (nos. 4927–45).

which determines me is simply and solely the unconditional; I must do it, I cannot do otherwise."[66]

Admittedly, in all these late journal entries Kierkegaard is expositing the unconditional as a perspective on life gained uniquely in and through Christian faith. And he has to admit that not even the person of Christian faith is "able unconditionally to express the unconditioned," because no one stands in an immediate relationship to God. Hence even Christians must rely on "grace" when they try to act in accord with the unconditioned, and so inevitably experience collisions with their environment.[67] But Kierkegaard has explored the element of the unconditional in human decision-making in broader more psychological terms in his earlier (1846) *Upbuilding Discourses in Various Spirits* (in the Part One, entitled "On the Occasion of a Confession"). Let us turn to that exposition.

In the journal entries on "the unconditional" and on "venture" (see these headings in Hongs' *Journals*), he repeatedly asserts that most people may acknowledge certain unconditional claims on their lives, but they respond to them by saying, "Well, yes, but up to a point,' or to a certain degree.'" So they live their lives according to common sense, the relative and the mediocre, and the absolute good becomes an illusion.[68]

---

66 *Journals*, 1449, XI^2 A 133; 536, X^4 A 581; 4901, X^4 A 613. It is tempting to explore at this point Kierkegaard's usage of "being-in-and-for-itself" (along with his use of "being-for-itself") throughout the authorship, and to compare it with Sartre's distinction between "being-in-itself" (*être-en-soi*) and "being-for-itself" (*être-pour-soi*). It is my conclusion that Kierkegaard does not make a sharp and consistent distinction in his varied use of alternative forms of this phrase (for example, beginning in *The Concept of Irony* and going through the authorship and into late journal entries, we find *i og for sig selv, I og for sig værende, i-og-for-sig-værende, i og for sig, for sig værende, for sig, i sig*, and all of them, especially the last two, are often used in a non-technical sense). So I do not find supportable the particular distinction between "in himself" and "for itself" that the Hongs claim to find in the opening pages of *The Sickness unto Death*. And it is certainly misleading to suggest that it would be enlightening to compare this usage with that of Sartre in *Being and Nothingness* (see their translation of *Sickness*, KW 19:14 at note 6, and pp. 174–5). Moreover, I believe that it will be more appropriate to consider Kierkegaard's usage when we come to his Christian theology (especially his concepts of God and creation) in the light of this statement in *Christian Discourses*: "There is only one who totally knows himself, who in and for himself (*i og for sig selv*) knows what he himself is, that is God," and therefore a human being can be her/himself "only by being in the One who is in and for himself." And in this passage Kierkegaard is clearly talking about how a human being "becomes a Christian" by being "before God" [*Christian Discourses*, p. 43, SV 13:44; (10:45); note: Walter Lowrie's translation is incomplete].

67 Ibid., 2898, X^5 A 96; 4933, X^3 A 470.

68 For example, ibid., 4901, X^4 A 613; 4911, X^1 A 516; 4918, XI^2 A 205; 4933, X^3 A 470.

These phrases in the journals are a direct allusion to the exposition of "double-mindedness" in the discourse (on Confession) where it says, "The fundamental expression for all double-mindedness in relation to the good is this: that it only wills it to a certain degree" (*til en vis Grad*, the same words as in the journal entries on the unconditional). And against this double-mindedness of wanting the good but not really willing it, Kierkegaard projects his profound analysis of what it means "to will one thing." And point after point anticipates his exposition of the unconditional six to eight years later.

First, willing one thing requires that one turns away from the "busyness" of life, away from the "mass of connections, stimuli and hindrances" that come at one from the external environment, because "double-mindedness dwells in busyness." One "must have chosen the unseen, chosen that which is inward," and thus "win a deeper knowledge of oneself." Only in this way does one have "*time or tranquillity for gaining the transparency*, which is needed for understanding oneself in willing one thing." Do I truthfully will one thing? One's life must first "win that transparency which is a condition for being able to put the question to oneself, and for being able to answer it."[69]

What does Kierkegaard mean by "transparency" (*Gjennemsigtighed*)— as a prerequisite to willing one thing at the core of free resolve and decision? It is a term to which he gave special meaning in *Either/Or* and which he continued to use throughout the works and the journals to the year of his death. Literally the Danish word means to "see through" and is translated as "trans-parent" (Latin meaning to "show through"). But for Kierkegaard it means to see thoroughly, wholly, clearly, steadily who and what one is as a concrete self or subject.

In *Either/Or* he says that transparency does not consist in "choosing oneself abstractly," as if "abstractions are transparent" instead of being "the dim, the misty." Rather transparency consists in "choosing oneself ethically," because only in this choice "one ... has taken on oneself, has put on oneself, has totally interpenetrated oneself so that [one's] every movement is accompanied by consciousness of responsibility for oneself." So "becoming transparent to oneself" requires that "one become conscious of oneself so thoroughly that no accidental element escapes

---

69 *Upbuilding Discourses in Various Spirits*, "Part One: An Occasional Discourse" (*Purity of Heart*), pp. 104, 108, 183; (KW 15:64, 67, 126–7); SV 11:63, 66, 116–17; (8:167, 169–70, 219).

him/her," so that the person "sees in [this concretion] its task."[70] And the same meaning appears in late journal entries (of 1854) where he says that becoming a person means that "one is so illuminated that he cannot hide from himself, ... as if he were transparent." So "pure transparency" means that "one's original subjectivity" has been "wholly penetrated" without any "residue"—even though he admits that no human being ever achieves such an ideal.[71]

If one succeeds in thus turning inward and penetrating wholly one's essential subjectivity and becoming purely conscious of and transparent to oneself, then the stage is set for one's willing one thing, that is, obeying the unconditional. A sure sign of this success is that, at the moment of decision, one does not turn outward to listen to and regard "the many"—the many alternatives proposed by the many of the mass in society. One must turn a deaf ear to all "comparison." "Where there are many, there is externality and comparison, and indulgence, and excuse and evasion. ... In eternity there is no collective failure. In eternity each individual ... will be interrogated as an individual, alone by oneself as individual and about the particulars in one's life."[72]

So, granted that one turns inward and becomes transparent to oneself, yet it must be asked: how does one escape from this comparison, with its excuses and evasions? Kierkegaard answers that, in place of the mind (*Sind*, disposition, temperament, mentality) that is divided and torn in two directions, one must achieve a "collected" or "centred" (*samlet*) mentality "which has collected itself from every diversion, from every relationship, in order to centre on its relationship to itself as the unique individual [*den Enkelte*], who is responsible before God." In this way one is delivered from "every comparison which tempts one either ... to despondency ... or to pride." And how does one achieve this centring of one's mentality? Does it come as a simple, straightforward, rational conclusion? No. Just as Kierkegaard says (in the context of Christian faith) that obedience to the unconditional requires the help of divine "grace,"

---

70 *Either/Or*, pp. 2:252, 258; (KW 4:248, 253); SV 3:229, 234; (2:222, 227f.). For other expositions of "transparency" in the works see: *Stages*, pp. 376, 388; (KW 11:414, 427–8); SV 8:213, 225; (6:386, 399); *Postscript*, p. 228; (KW 12.1:255); SV 9:213; (7:215); *Works of Love*, pp. 331f.; SV 12:344; (9:342); *Sickness*, pp. 147, 182, 262; (KW 19:14, 49, 131); SV 15:74, 105, 180; (11:128, 161, 241).

71 *Journals*, 3224, 4384; XI² A 107, 132. For other occurrences in *Journals* see: 1050, VIII¹ A 320; 3105, X³ A 542; 3228, XI¹ A 402; 4434, VII¹ B 192:12.

72 *Upbuilding Discourses in Various Spirits*, "Part One: An Occasional Discourse" (*Purity of Heart*), pp. 211–12; (KW 15:148–9); SV 11:135; (8:237).

The Leap as Freedom's Form 277

so here he pictures the achievement of willing one thing by the centred mentality as occurring in the context of the act of "confession" by the individual who is "responsible before God." Or, as he puts it more in the language of religiousness A, "repentance and remorse belong to the eternal in a human being."[73]

It must be noted once more that mention of the "eternal" by Kierkegaard is a signal that he has entered the sphere of religiousness A, but the relevance of this shift for the topic of freedom as event will be dealt with in the next section of this chapter. Here "confession" as an aspect of universal human "consciousness of the eternal" will be explored phenomenologically as the directly experienced context required for the emergence of "transparent subjectivity" in the "centred mentality" that is able to "will one thing" unconditionally. This exploration will be one more step in the clarification of how and why the passionate transition from possibility to actuality, from intention to act, is a free voluntary "leap."

For Kierkegaard, "confession" can be experienced by anyone because "Over every human being's wandering through life there watches a providence [*Forsyn*], which provides everyone with two guides: the one calls forward, the other calls backward." Obviously, this sense of "calling" is not restricted to Christian faith, but is inherent in being a "human-being" (*Menneske*). But how does it lead to confession? This double call does not lead the wanderer into confusion and irresolution, because the two calls "are in eternal understanding with each other, because the one calls forward to the good, the other calls back from the evil." And the wanderer must listen to both in order "to know where he is on the way." The one calls "forward to something new, something novel—but also away from the experience." The other (repentance) "laboriously gathers up the experience."[74]

---

73 Ibid., pp. 215f., 41; (KW 15:151–2, 15); SV 11:138, 21f.; (8:240, 126).

74 Ibid., pp. 39f.; (KW 15:13–14); SV 11:21; (8:125f.). This sense of "repentance" as a backward movement is not expressed in or derived from either the Danish or English words, both of which basically mean "to be sorry for." The backward movement, however, is clearly present in the Greek word, μετανοια (*metanoia*), which means a "reversal" or "reconsideration." And Kierkegaard knew his Greek well. This meaning of the Greek is derived from one of the two Hebrew words used in the Old Testament for the verb "to repent," namely, from שׁוּב (*shub*), meaning "to turn back"; the other, נחם (*nacham*), means "to be sorry." But, as usual, Kierkegaard takes a word and an idea and develops his own peculiar meanings.

So confession with its repentance and remorse is the more urgent and has priority. But not in the sense of being sorrowful and sad, but in *Either/Or*'s sense of "choosing oneself," choosing to be all that one has cumulatively and concretely become throughout one's life up to this point, so "repentance is one's love for one's self" (see above in chapter 4 the section entitled "Freedom in Relation to the Past"). Just as Judge William says, "choosing oneself is identical with repenting oneself," so in his discourse on confession, Kierkegaard says that in confession before the all-knowing eternal one, the person seeks "the repose of contemplation in unity with oneself," and thus the person confessing "gets to know something about oneself that one did not know before. ... The prayer does not change God, but it changes the one who prays. ... Much that you are able to avoid in darkness, you first get to know by letting an all-knowing one become knowledgeable thereof."[75]

But in the discourse (written four years after *Either/Or*) Kierkegaard adds a new element to repentance. The guiding voice that calls one "backward," to open, honest, silent contemplation of all that one has been and done and become, does so with "the seriousness [*Alvor*] of eternity." In the stillness "it calls for earnestness [*Alvor*]" and "wishes to be understood." What is to be understood is not simply the need to see one's self transparently and to accept what one is wholly, before stepping "forward" into the new and the novel. What is to be understood is that the "time" of repentance is not "temporal" in the sense of an hour which I may take now and then out of the busyness of my week. The time of repentance is "the eleventh hour"; it must occur "at once" (*strax*). "Repentance shall have its time in the sense of freedom with the stamp of eternity." Too often human beings, young and old, "count on having a long time at their disposal" to straighten things out, "but repentance and remorse know that time is to be circumvented [*omgaa*] in fear and trembling."[76] Why?

Seeing what is the one thing needful, what is demanded, in this situation by one's inner sense of the absolute unconditional good, places one in and at the unique moment of possibility that can and will never be repeated, namely, the moment of resolve to enact that one and only possibility here and *now*, "at once," in spite of all one's "repented" (admitted and accepted) fallibilities, weaknesses, failures, and in the face of irresolvable uncertainty of the outcome (aggravated by others' criticism and opposition). And this "moment" fills you with fear and trembling not

75 Ibid., pp. 47, 51; (KW 15:19, 22–3); SV 11:26, 28f.; (8:130, 132).
76 Ibid., pp. 49f., 41–3; (KW 15:21, 15–16); SV 11:28, 22f. (8:131–2, 126–7).

because of the judgment of your peers (you have withdrawn from all "comparison"), but because of the "stress of the eternal," that is, because in this "moment" there hangs in the balance whether or not your act will express your eternal dignity and worth as a unique individual person, all by yourself and alone, whether or not your act will receive the affirmation and benediction of "the eternal within you," of what is ultimate and absolute and unconditional for you.

So, in a sense, you are not alone, even though you alone make the decision. As suggested above, Kierkegaard's depiction of the occurrence of willing one thing in the context of confession before God (the eternal in you) is analogous to his assertion of the need of grace to choose the unconditional. In *Sickness* he repeatedly links "repentance and grace" as the common foes of "despair over sin." And in *Postscript* he clearly assigns the act of repentance to "the ethical-religious sphere" as distinct from the "higher" sphere of religiousness B (Christian faith).[77] And in spite of the fact that Johannes Climacus takes *Either/Or* to task for not being "religiously oriented" and hence neglecting "the need for divine assistance," actually there is one passage in which Judge William depicts repentance rather well within the ethical-religious categories of *Postscript*.

We have already heard him say that "choosing oneself is identical with repenting oneself." It is "repenting" in his sense of moving "backward," "discovering that the self one chooses has boundless multiplicity within itself inasmuch as it has a history," and realizing that "one can give up nothing of all this, not the most painful, not the hardest," because this "possession ... is one's blessedness." So "one repents back into oneself, ... until one finds oneself in God," because "only in this way can one choose oneself absolutely." Then he adds a further, and in this context, a rather peculiar qualification to repentance. He says that the word "repentance" is "the only expression in language" for "the love of God," that is, "the love of the absolute." So one is not alone in that "moment" of the crucial eleventh hour when one must "at once" or not at all "will one thing," choose "the one thing needful" infinitely, absolutely, unconditionally. This repenting back into oneself is itself to "love [the absolute] absolutely out of my innermost being." And (as in *Postscript*) "only when I choose myself as guilty do I absolutely choose myself." So "oneself is, so to speak, outside one, and it has to be acquired, and repentance is one's love for it, because one chooses it absolutely from the hand of the eternal God." In other words, "As soon as I love freely and love God, then I re-

---

77 *Sickness*, pp. 240f.; (KW 19:109f.); SV 15:160; (11:219f.); *Postscript*, pp. 463, 230; (KW 12.1:519, 257-8); SV 10:194; (7:453); SV 9:215; (7:218).

pent." And the only basis of the fact that "the expression of my love of God is repentance" is this: "that [God] has loved me first."[78]

What phenomena of human self-consciousness does all this language describe? "God" means that: the coming to consciousness of an all-out unconditional judgment (conviction) that *one thing only* is demanded in this particular situation (in the light, that is, of my ultimate, infinite, abstract gestalt), contrary to any objective proof and against much external advice, hence requiring courage and passion if I am to remain true to myself and choose to be myself in spite of all my frailties and failures. So "God" means that: this state of intention so to act is enabled by the condition that I simultaneously have a sense that the values, beliefs, the "good" which I "obey" in coming to this decision/intention have a being of their own that transcends my own personal individual commitment to them and hence assert themselves as the absolute, the eternal, the unconditional in their own right, and that they affirm and bless my commitment and thus evoke my "love" and devotion toward them, thus making possible (but not necessary) my obedience of them here and now.

So I am not alone. My deepest, innermost, uniquely individual self-conscious gestalt comes to a borderline of itself where it touches on and is touched by something universal and eternal, as *in* and yet *other than* my self, and I know my self to be affirmed, supported, and encouraged ("loved me first") by this absolute (the eternal) to will-and-do the one thing needful with a pure heart, i.e., absolutely and unconditonally, in the face of all the undoubted relativity and fallibility of my being and knowledge and commitment. To make such a "leap" I must sense the extremity and singularity of the moment: once-and-for-all, now-or-never, win-it-or-lose-it; and the "it" is the ultimate, absolute, eternal dignity and worth of me, my self ("it" is my "salvation," my "eternal blessedness").

This sense or awareness can come only in one form, with one essential quality: the extremity of angst and passion and earnestness: fear and trembling; the instant when all comparison with and consideration of alternatives has come to an end, when *here* (no other conditions) and *now* (no other time) *either* I do it, *or* I do not and never will do it. If, in this moment, there is no anxious passionate earnestness, then there is no freedom, no "completely decisive resolve," but only a cool distant calculation which does not involve one's own absolute convictions and commitments, one's self, and hence consists only of a smooth uninterrupted transition to a rational inference and conclusion, dictated (necessitated) by considerations external to my self. No wonder that the

---

78 *Either/Or*, pp. 2:220f.; (KW 4:216f.); SV 3:200f.; (2:193f.).

moment of freedom to choose, of decision, of resolve not only *what* to do but *whether* to do it, must be characterized as a "passionate transition."

Is this what Kierkegaard really means? Obviously, this analysis of why the leap of freedom is "passionate" has brought us within the confines of our second question (see p. 267 above): why is the leap or transition also "religious"?—and so to our fifth topic on the leap in general (see p. 249 above): the leap as transition from the ethical to the religious. We cannot know why the leap is "passionate" without knowing why it is "religious." And it is this latter question, of the religious source and empowerment of the passion, which holds the clue to our central question about freedom, namely: is that passionate interestedness, which motivates the leap of freedom, simply a product of psychic-social conditioning, or is it a voluntary movement within one's subjectivity? Or if the question is pushed on into the religious sphere, does that divine providence, which sets the conditions of universal humanity by providing the two "guides" for our wanderings through life, determine how each of us will respond and therefore fatalistically ordain our ends?

Let us remember that we are considering how Kierkegaard the "humanist" answers these questions. Therefore, in search for his answers, it is only fair, as well as needful, that we look more fully at his depiction of the possibilities and limits of the sphere of religiousness A. But let it meanwhile be noted that it is precisely in the context of his delineation of "repentance" in his discourse "On the Occasion of a Confession" that he first proposes that the human being's failure to know oneself and to choose to become oneself in passionate interestedness is to be traced finally not to ignorance but to self-deception.[79] And, as we shall see, this concept will be a key tool in the discovery and explication of indeterminacy in Kierkegaard's concept of freedom.

THE LEAP AS TRANSITION FROM ETHICAL TO RELIGIOUS

From what has thus far been said about freedom as event, we come to the clear but (for many) disturbing conclusion that, for Kierkegaard, authentic human freedom is not a (merely) ethical phenomenon but an ethical-religious one. It is imperative, therefore, to penetrate what

---

79 *Upbuilding Discourses in Various Spirits*, "Part One: An Occasional Discourse" (*Purity of Heart*), pp. 52, 55; (KW 15:23, 25); SV 11:29, 31; (8:133, 135). The term occurs in earlier works, but not in this specific sense. See listings for *Selvbedrag* and related words in McKinnon's *Kierkegaard Indices*, vol. 2, *Fundamental Polyglot Konkordans*, and vol. 3, *Index Verborum*.

Kierkegaard means by "the religious," because we are engaged in the attempt to isolate the "passionate transition" (that characterizes the event of freedom as the "leap") as a movement that is totally within the capacities of every human being, and that therefore is distinct from and prior to that particular and uniquely Christian movement of faith by virtue of the absurd and as "believing the absurd."

The question that hangs in the air, and which haunts this entire investigation of Kierkegaard's concept of the self, is this: does Kierkegaard finally arrive at the view that authentic freedom is possible only in and by that faith relationship with God which occurs "by virtue of the absurd," that is, by encounter with the Eternal-in-time in the historical figure of Jesus? Are "free" human beings, then, limited to those few (if any) Christian believers who escape the communal ritualistic spirit of mass religion and who achieve the pure unconditionality of isolated individual loyalty to Christ's demand (imitation of Christ's pattern) of total self-sacrificing suffering love? In other words, does Kierkegaard's "humanist" depiction of the lone individual coming to self-consciousness through angst and subjective reflection, arriving at a vision of the absolute good through the dialectic of the self's possibility and necessity, and finally, with the help of the immanent eternal, achieving centred transparent subjectivity so as to make the leap of freedom (with fear and trembling) into the actuality of the concrete self here and now—does, then, this magnificent structure with its glittering heights and fathomless depths come crashing down into the dust and mist of a beautiful but hopeless illusion? Does then the "second authorship," centred on the universality of despair (*Sickness*) and the absolute requirement of "the imitation of Christ" (*Practice in Christianity*), negate and annul all the brilliant achievements of the "first authorship" up through *Postscript*? Were then Martin Heidegger and Jean-Paul Sartre well advised to ignore Kierkegaard the theologian and to rescue bits and scraps from Kierkegaard the humanist in order to construct new and self-sufficient depictions of the human condition, including freedom? Or are others even better advised when they junk the whole of Kierkegaard and return to Hegel as the only adequate prophet and philosopher for a twentieth-century humanism? Or does Kierkegaard depict the general "religious" dimension of his humanism as enabling a measure of authentic freedom by which the individual is able to achieve significant self-actualization? And are there materials to be found in the post-*Postscript* authorship, especially in the discourses and *The Sickness unto Death*, which may legitimately be used in support of such a depiction? Let us see.

In the last and lengthy major section of *Postscript*, Kierkegaard (Climacus) makes a sharp distinction between a universal dimension of religiousness (*Religieusitet*) inherent in and open to every human individual, and the unique historically particular religiousness of Christian faith. He first spends 150 pages analysing religiousness A under the topic of "The Passionate" (*Det Pathetiske*), and then only 27 pages on religiousness B as "The Dialectical" (*Det Dialektiske*) because, he says, he has already dealt with the latter in *Philosophical Fragments*. And in between these two is a brief section entitled "Parenthetical Clause between A and B," explaining the difference.[80] His basic points (for our purposes here) are that religiousness A is "not specifically Christian" and "has only human nature in its universality as its presupposition," and that it must be present before awareness of the dialectic of religiousness B is possible. What, then, is present in religiousness A that makes it a "stage" or "sphere" (an αλλο γενος) qualitatively beyond the ethical, that may clarify what happens when one hears and obeys another "voice"? Religiousness A has already been described above in general terms in the section "Freedom and the Eternal" in chapter 4, but now needs more specific definition.

First a preliminary note. What Kierkegaard has in mind by "religiousness" in the form of A does not necessarily involve god-language, although he usually uses it. In *Fear and Trembling* we heard him say that "my eternal consciousness is my love of God," and so "he who loves God

---

80 *Postscript*, pp. 493–8; (KW 12.1:555–61); SV 10:224–30; (7:484–90). In spite of the clear distinction drawn between A and B, Kierkegaard's analyses and descriptions of the two in *Postscript* are often confusing. He admits that the description of A "is sometimes a confused tumultuous pathos, composed of all sorts of things, aesthetics, ethics, religiousness A, and Christianity, and hence is sometimes self-contradictory" (but he adds, "By me religiousness A has never been called Christian"). This confusion is intensified by one of his basic theses about the stages or spheres, namely, that the characteristics of each stage are carried forward and subsumed in the following stage, and hence all the characteristics of the aesthetic, ethical, and ethico-religious spheres are present and operative in the sphere of religiousness B. So at various times he ascribes to both religiousness A and religiousness B: isolation or aloneness, passion of the infinite, passion of inwardness, relationship with one's eternal blessedness, the human being as eternal, subjectivity as truth, affirmation of an objective uncertainty, the factor of decision, and even the elements of "paradox" and "faith." Caution must therefore be used to determine which sphere a particular passage is describing, because the only sure insignia of religiousness B are references to the *absolute* paradox and to "the absurd," i.e., to human encounter with the presence of the eternal in time, in history. And passages which include these references to the absolute paradox and the absurd must be carefully picked apart in order to discern which are elements of the first movement or leap into the infinite/eternal, and which are elements of the second movement of faith by virtue of the absurd.

without faith reflects upon himself; he who loves God in faith reflects upon God." In other words, there is a certain kind of self-reflection that is "religious" in the sense that it not only consists of a leap into one's infinitude but also leads one to an awareness of one's "eternal consciousness" and "eternal validity." The "religious" is an awareness of an affirmation of one's significance (as a unique individual) that comes from beyond (transcends) one's own relative belief and courage, that is rooted in an "eternity" which touches one at the depth or height of one's inward self-consciousness. He makes the same point in a much more sophisticated way in *Postscript*:

> Religiousness A is the dialectic of interiorization [*Inderliggjørelse*]; it is the relationship to an eternal blessedness which is not conditioned by something [else], but is the dialectical interiorization of the relationship, and so is conditioned only by the interiorization, which is dialectical. Religiousness B, on the contrary, ... makes conditions in such a way that the conditions are not [merely] the dialectical deepening of the interiorization, but are a definite something which more closely determines [defines, identifies] the eternal blessedness, not because it defines more closely the individual's appropriation of it, but more closely defines the eternal blessedness itself (whereas in A the only closer definition is the closer definition of interiorization).[81]

So he contrasts the "dialectic of interiorization [*Inderliggjørelse*]"[82] of religiousness A with the "paradoxical dialectic" of B. By the former, he means the tension and struggle involved in the individual's attempt to relate to one's "eternal blessedness" (one's eternal dignity and validity) by transforming one's existence through a decision to "die away from

---

81 Ibid., p. 494; (KW 12.1:556); SV 10:225; (7:485).

82 Exactly what Kierkegaard had in mind by the word *Inderliggjørelse* has caused his translators some consternation. David Swenson (or Walter Lowrie?) in *Postscript* used several different phrases: "inward transformation," "realization of inwardness," "actualization of inwardness," "intensification of inwardness." Howard Hong in *Journals and Papers* generally settled for "inward deepening," but in one case (no. 3981) chose "interiorization." The present study goes with the last suggestion for two reasons. First, it corresponds with Lowrie's and Hong's translations of two correlative terms: "infinitization" for *Uendeliggjørelse*, and "finitizing" for *Endeliggjørelse* [*Sickness*, p. 163; (KW 19:30); SV 15:88; (11:143)]. Secondly, in the text that follows, it is shown that this translation fits Kierkegaard's own definition of it in *Postscript*, even though the Danish adjective *inderlig* does not mean "inward" but "fervent, intense, intimate." "Inwardness" has become the accepted translation of *Inderlighed*, but as indicated in our text at this point, Kierkegaard means an inwardness of a particular kind, namely, "subjectivity."

[the life of] immediacy while still remaining in the finite" and to become nothing (impotent) before the eternal so as to make room for the eternal at the heart of one's being—that is, inwardly in one's "subjectivity." Hence, this dialectic of interiorization finds expression in the tension between one's objective uncertainty and one's attempt to hold that uncertainty as absolute truth by the most passionate, inward, personal interestedness and seriousness. By the latter dialectic (paradoxical), he means the tension and interplay between, on the one hand, one's eternal consciousness and validity held in inwardness, and, on the other, one's awareness of the absurdity that the eternal is within one's spatial/temporal existence outside of oneself, and that one is in need of it in order to achieve and to maintain one's eternal validity as defined more closely in Jesus Christ.[83] So what occurs by means of religiousness A's "leap ... into infinity" is the deepening and the closer definition of the individual's "interiorization" as being open to and in touch with the eternal as *immanent*.

Kierkegaard clearly defines what he means by this obscure compounded word (*Inderliggjørelse*) by indicating that the "dialectical reflection" of religiousness A consists of what earlier in *Postscript* he spent considerable time defining as "subjective reflection." He says, "Subjective reflection turns inward [*indefter*] towards subjectivity, and chooses [*vil*] to be the truth in this interiorization."[84] In other words, the leap, which is the act or event of freedom, is identical with coming to the "religious" conviction (judgment) that "subjectivity is truth," *and* with the "religious" decision to live and to act according to that truth in a specific situation, in spite of the fact that no objective certainty is available. So the word "God" in the parlance of religiousness A signifies this "eternal consciousness" or "interiorization."

How, then, does the dialectic of interiorization (with its emergent awareness that one's consciousness of the self's validity is accented with the eternal and has an inherent potentiality for "eternal blessedness") go beyond the purely "ethical" and become a new and distinctive sphere in human existence (even while bringing the ethical forward as an integral element of the religious)?

---

83 For these characterizations of the two dialectics, see *Postscript*, pp. 187, 412–14, 494, 497–8; (KW 12.1:209, 460–63, 556, 560–1); SV 9:174; (7:175–6); SV 10:144–6, 225, 229–30; (7:400–3, 485, 488–9); also see the summary statement of the initial, the essential, and the decisive expressions of "existential passion" at the beginning of the section on each of these topic in part II, chapter IV of *Postscript*.

84 Ibid., p. 175; (KW 12.1:196); SV 9:163; (7:164).

The glory and truth and "revelation" of the ethicist, Climacus says, lies in one's having attained a certain measure of inwardness, "enough to lay hold of the ethical with infinite passion, duty and the eternal validity of the universal." And through it one experiences that edification which "produces the necessary adequate terror [*Forfærdelse*]," because "in the moment of despair one had, with the passion of infinitude, chosen oneself out of the *terror* of possessing oneself, one's life and actuality in the aesthetic dream, in melancholy, in hiddenness." So throughout *Postscript* Climacus stresses the nobility of the ethical as a qualitative leap beyond the aesthetic into a totally αλλο γενος of human existence, a stage that must be experienced and preserved personally, inwardly, and passionately before there can be any question of experiencing the "religious."

In the religious, however, the ethicist experiences the terror as "a new determinant of inwardness, ... a higher sphere" in which "the ethical ... is now the hindering element, and that which helps the individual to a higher revelation beyond the ethical is something else." Indeed, "the ethical becomes the temptation," because now "the ethicist is striving against the aesthetic," but "also against the religious, ... against the decisive form of a higher standpoint."[85] So Climacus takes to task the "ethicist" in *Either/Or* for a fraudulent deception (*en Mislighed*). There it is argued that "the ethical self should be found immanently in [its] despair, that the individual wins himself by standing fast in despair." But Climacus insists that this view is fraudulent because "When I despair, I use myself in order to despair, and so I indeed can by myself despair of everything, but when I do this, I do not by myself come back." That is to say, in the language of *Lilies*, I can indeed by myself come to the awareness that all my old voices have not led me to the truth, but I cannot myself produce the new and saving voice.

Climacus concedes that the ethicist has cleverly "used a determinant of freedom, [viz.] to choose oneself, which seems to remove the difficulty. ... But this does not help." If *Either/Or* had been clear about its own deception, "the book would have had to be religiously constructed" or oriented, because "in the moment of decision" when the individual would choose to be him/herself, "the individual needs divine assistance." If one arrives at this point with "an understanding of the existence-relationship between the aesthetic and the ethical," and does so "with passion and inwardness," then "one will doubtless become aware

---

85 Ibid., pp. 231, 262; (KW 12.1:258–9, 295); SV 9:216, 247; (7:218, 252).

of the religious—and the *leap*."[86] But what is it that one becomes aware of at the extremity of the ethical, that fills one with a terror that is "a new determinant of inwardness," that points to the need of "divine assistance"?

Kierkegaard uses several different terminologies in answering this question, but what they all describe is this: at the extremity of the ethical, every human person experiences the fact that one is not able to enact unconditionally the unconditional demand of the absolute good. He states the case quite bluntly in *Postscript*: "The ethical is present in every moment with its infinite demand, but the individual is not capable of realizing it. This impotence of the individual ... consists in the fact that the individual finds oneself in precisely the opposite state of what the ethical demands, so that, far from being able to begin, every moment one remains in this state, one is prevented more and more from being able to begin. The [individual] relates to actuality not as possibility, but as impossibility."[87]

In this pregnant passage (and its context) Kierkegaard is asserting with decisive force his view that for the fulfilment of human individual selfhood, the aesthetic and the ethical in and by themselves are inadequate and impotent, that inherent in the authentic human subject is the capability for and openness to the "religious" in addition to the aesthetic and the ethical. In the context he is speaking of "the teleological suspension of the ethical," and flatly asserts that "this terrifying release from [the demand] to perform the ethical, the individual's heterogeneity with the ethical, this suspension from the ethical is *sin*, as the state [*Tilstand*] of the human being." Note: Kierkegaard is speaking of sin as a state of being, not as an act (although he has analysed and depicted the act of sin in great detail in *The Concept of Anxiety*). What is wrong is not (in this perspective) something I have done, but something lacking in the mode or state in which I am trying to live. I am in an aesthetic-ethical state merely, rather than in an aesthetic-ethical-religious state. "The impotence of the individual," Kierkegaard says, "must not be understood as the incompleteness of one's persistent striving toward the attainment of an ideal," as if I could achieve the fulfilment of the ethical ideal on my own, if I just strive a little harder and longer. "In such a case no suspension is posited"; that is to say, there is no recognition that the

---

86 Ibid., pp. 230–1; (KW 12.1:257–8); SV 9:215f.; (7:217–18).
87 Ibid., pp. 238–9; (KW 12.1:266–7); SV 9:223; (7:226).

ethical itself, by itself, is impotent to accomplish what the ethical demands.

A direct inference of this position is that the sense of ethical demand has its origin not in some humanly devised and formulated system of ethical absolutes taken as definitive of the authentically human, and therefore realizable by adequate and earnest human endeavour. Rather, the ethical demand comes from a source beyond the human individual; that is, it asserts a quality of being-eternal in and of itself, a quality that requires a relation to itself-as-source for the fulfilment of its demand. So in the entire forgoing exposition of Kierkegaard's concept of the self, we have seen several times that "freedom" (the capacity to fulfil the ethical demand) does indeed require the self to exist in the dialectic of possibility/necessity/actuality, but also that this dialectic is not the wholly adequate condition for freedom: the self must also and simultaneously come to consciousness in the dialectic of temporal/eternal.

We heard this, for example, in the language of *The Concept of Anxiety*. The *whole* self is comprised of two interdependent and yet quite distinct syntheses: the synthesis of the finite and the infinite, achieved in the "third" dimension called "spirit" (self); and the synthesis of the temporal (self) and the eternal (god), achieved in the "third" relationship called "faith." And the realization of the first synthesis requires the realization of the second. So, as Climacus says, if one faces the task of enacting the ethical ideal with only the dialectic of possibility/actuality, one is confronted with impossibility. Or in the language of *The Sickness unto Death*, the term "possibility" on the one hand indicates the "self's possibility" as the infinite/eternal dimension of the individual as such; on the other hand it points to an awareness that one's own self as possibility is affirmed by a structure or dynamic of reality which may be called "all-things-are-possible," or "God," and hence "possibility is the only salvation [*Frelsende*]."

Hence the ethical as the eternal has two distinct and yet inseparable aspects. On the one hand, it is definitive of who one *is* and of what one ought to become, and hence is immanent to one's own being (the purely ethical). On the other hand, it has the quality of being a demand, and hence of having the capacity to judge, and, most remarkably, of having the power to move and enable (but not to compel) one to believe (the ethical-religious). In other words, in the general "religious" awareness of the individual human being, the infinite/eternal has both the quality of kinship with and the quality of transcendence to the individual self.

Admittedly, the passage in *Postscript* that expounds the teleological suspension of the ethical does so on the assumption of Christian faith, but the application is broader. And *Postscript* makes the same points, with more elaborate detail, in its exposition of religiousness A. We will follow its outline as given under the title "The Passionate" (*Det Pathetiske*), which describes religiousness A in its initial expression, its essential expression, and its decisive expression.

Basically, a human being has the experience of being "religious" whenever the object of one's passionate interestedness is nothing less than one's "eternal blessedness [*Salighed*]," and in such a way that one's interest is "ethical," that is to say, is "expressed by the fact that I actively transform my whole existence commensurate with the object of [my] interest." In other words, to be "religious" means to concentrate my whole conscious, active, concrete being on what is ultimate, absolute, essential in the definition of who I am, on what I cannot lose without losing my self; and to do this in such a way that I open every secret hidden corner of my entire life to its light, to its demand, to its judgment. In this moment I become aware that my ultimate beatitude is at stake, that my infinite eternal dignity and integrity hang in the balance. The shining of this light, the voice of this demand, come with the authority of the "eternal," come from what has the power to give my existence ultimate and everlasting significance (blessedness).[88]

What is the immediate effect? How do I "actively transform my whole existence"? The existing human being "is composed of [both] infinitude and finitude," but "if an eternal blessedness is one's highest good, ... the elements of finitude are once and for all actively reduced to what must be given up," because "the absolute τέλος cannot be put on a level with other things [*tages med*]." And "the fact that resignation examines [one's] immediacy means that the individual must not have one's life in it." Of course, "the individual does not cease to be a human being, nor does one divest oneself of the manifold composite garment of finitude. ... In immediacy the individual is rooted in finitude; but when resignation is convinced that the individual has acquired the absolute direction toward the absolute τέλος, all is changed, the roots are severed. One lives in finitude, but one does not have one's life in it."[89]

---

88 Ibid., p. 350; (KW 12.1:391); SV 10:85f.; (7:339).
89 Ibid., pp. 350, 352, 354, 367; (KW 12.1:391, 393, 395, 410); SV 10:85f., 87, 89, 101f.; (7:339, 341, 342-3, 355-6).

But why is this experience, which is clearly ethical, also described as being religious, above and beyond the merely ethical? Because this resignation, this giving up of life's elements of finitude, in favour of an absolute telos, involves making an "absolute distinction" and a "passionate decision." The distinction is between the absolute telos of one's life and the relative ends of one's life. And the passionate decision of resignation is to allow no mediation between them. Rather, this absolute distinction "makes space" for the absolute telos and thus "gets rid of the vulgar mob of relative ends in order that the person making the distinction absolutely can relate to the absolute." So "the maximum task is simultaneously to be able to relate absolutely to the absolute τελος and [to relate] relatively to the relative [ends], or always to have the absolute τελος with oneself [hos sig]." And there Climacus discerns the religious dimension: the one who relates absolutely to the absolute telos "*ipso facto* also [relates] to God" (Kierkegaard uses *eo ipso*). In other words, in becoming aware of the absolute *distinction* between absolute and relative ends, one also becomes aware of an "absolute *difference*" between one's self and the absolute telos, in that the telos demands to become the arbiter of one's existence. So this awareness may be called a "God-relationship." In this way the religious sphere includes but transcends the ethical sphere.[90]

At this point we face a critical problem in Kierkegaard's depiction of the possibilities and limits of self-realization within the sphere of religiousness A, that is, in religious awareness that "has only human nature in its universality as its presupposition." We have asserted several times that, in the awareness of religiousness A, the "eternal" and one's relationship to an "eternal blessedness" as "absolute telos" manifest the quality of a kind of transcendence toward the subject. The problem is this: does this kind of transcendence comprise what Kierkegaard calls a "breach" (*Brud*), a qualitative disjunction? The answer is critical, because if, in religiousness A, there is no such breach, then there is no leap. And if no leap, then no freedom. And if no freedom, then no self. In *Postscript* we get two different answers to our question.

On the one hand, when he is distinguishing between religiousness A and B toward the end of *Postscript*, Climacus clearly and repeatedly says that religiousness A is one of immanence, e.g., "Inasmuch as the upbuilding is an essential predicate of all religiousness, so religiousness A will have its upbuilding [element]. ... The upbuilding in the sphere of religiousness A is immanence." This means that awareness of a God-relation-

90 Ibid., pp. 366–371; (KW 12.1:409–14); SV 10:100–5; (7:355–9).

ship emerges at the height or depth of one's own most intense, inward, passionate, interested subjectivity. As we have heard, he allows a kind of dialectic in A but it is "the dialectical deepening of the interiorization" of one's "relationship to an eternal blessedness." But this dialectic does not comprise an authentic breach "in the relationship between an existing-one and the eternal, because the eternal embraces the existing-one on all sides, and therefore the disrelationship [*Misforhold*] remains within immanence. If the breach is to be constituted, the eternal must be conditioned as a temporal thing, as in time, as historical, by means of which the existing-one and the eternal-in-time get eternity between them." So, "in the paradoxical religiousness [i.e., B] the eternal is [present] at a definite place, and this is precisely the breach of immanence."[91]

Climacus's use of "disrelationship" is significant because Anti-Climacus picks it up and uses it (in *Sickness*) as the definitive quality of the state of despair. In the same passage Climacus has come to the point (which we will deal with directly) that the decisive expression for religiousness A as "the passionate" is a consciousness of guilt. And he comments that although the essential consciousness of guilt absorbs one as deeply as possible into existence, at the same time it "is the expression for the fact that the existing-one relates to an eternal blessedness," but it does so "by expressing the disrelationship" that one stands in toward one's eternal blessedness. In other words, as he says throughout *Postscript*, "the positive is perceptible [*kjendelig*, identifiable, recognizable] in the negative." As a result, "the existing-one cannot get hold of the relationship [to an eternal blessedness], because the disrelationship constantly stands in between as token for the relationship." Or to put it another way, "the identity of the subject is such that [its] guilt does not make the subject into an other, which is the mark for the breach."[92]

This material seems to give a definitive answer to our question: in religiousness A no breach "as such," so no leap, no freedom, and no actualization of the "self's possiblity," and hence nothing but disrelationship in guilt (despair). On the other hand, there is another set of materials in *Postscript* that yields a different picture. Granted, religiousness A does not produce a "breach *with* [*med*] immanence," otherwise it would not be an experience open to "human nature in its universality." But when Climacus speaks of a "disrelationship *within* immanence," he implies a kind of

---

91 Ibid., pp. 497, 474, 506; (KW 12.1:560, 532, 571); SV 10:229, 205, 238; (7:488–9, 464–5, 498).

92 Ibid., pp. 473f.; (KW 12.1:531–2); SV 10:204f.; (7:463–5).

breach, which requires a form of decision (leap), which in turn achieves a level of self-actualization. So this kind of breach is of key importance for understanding the positive possibilities of religiousness A, but this breach and these possibilities must first be set within the context of the "essential" and "decisive" expressions of religiousness A—to which we now turn.

We have seen that the initial expression of "the existential pathos" consists, first, of the discernment of the radical distinction between the relative ends of one's sensuous-social existence and one's relation to the absolute telos of an eternal blessedness, and, secondly, of the transformation of one's whole existence by the active and decisive renunciation of all finite satisfactions in favour of the demands of the absolute telos. These two qualities determine this pathos to be "religious," that is, to be a transition to a sphere beyond (but including) the aesthetic and the ethical. The essential and decisive expressions of religiousness A can be stated more briefly.

If one truly and "absolutely" determines to renounce finite satisfactions and to transform one's existence in tune with absolute blessedness, then (says Climacus) one is essentially involved in suffering. Not in the sense of some misfortune that befalls you externally, or even as hardships that you voluntarily assume. Rather, "religious suffering" is inward, where one is alone with the eternal and its demand. "This suffering concerns the fact that one is separated from one's happiness [*Glæde*], but it also signifies one's relation [to it], so that being without suffering signifies that one is not religious." In other words, in being finite, being in immediacy, "the individual really is absolutely [absorbed] in relative ends," but if at the same time one relates to the absolute telos of eternal blessedness, then one is inescapably involved in "the suffering which is a dying-away from immediacy."

Again, why is this suffering called "religious"? Because at the core of this profoundly inward struggle and conflict is the awareness "that the individual is capable of absolutely nothing, but is nothing before God, because here once more the God-relationship is perceptible in the negative, and self-annihilation is the essential form of the God-relationship. ... Religiously the task is to comprehend that one is nothing before God, or that [one] is absolutely nothing and thereby before God. And one requires to have this not-to-be-able constantly before oneself, and when it disappears, religiousness disappears."[93]

---

[93] For the last two paragraphs see ibid., pp. 406, 412; (KW 12.1:453, 460–1); SV 10:138, 144; (7:394, 401).

So the essential quality of this religious existential pathos is that of a sense of human impotence to accomplish *on one's own* the demand to commit oneself absolutely to the absolute telos, to that which alone imparts eternal significance and dignity to one's being-in-existence. Does this sense of impotence, then, mean that one inevitably ends in despair? Is "disrelationship" the final state of all human striving to achieve the ideal of self-actualization? By no means! Not if this essential expression leads to the decisive or "highest" expression of existential pathos in the form of awareness of one's "totality of guilt." What does Climacus mean by the experience of total guilt?

The awareness of impotence before the absolute telos (suffering) comes decisively not in the sphere of abstract reflection about self and ideals but as one is plunged most deeply into one's finite existence in space/time. So one is tempted "to shove the guilt [of one's impotence and failure] away from oneself onto existence, or onto the one who placed him/her in existence, and so be without guilt." But such a mentality would indicate that one is still thinking in purely outward aesthetic terms, whereas if one has come to the sense of impotence by turning profoundly inward and by relating there to the absolute telos of one's eternal blessedness, then one measures oneself by "eternity's essence-criterion" (*Evighedens Væsens-Bestemmelse*), rather than having a merely "comparative guilt-consciousness" which "has its criterion [*Maalestok*] outside of itself." Thus, "in as much as the conception of God is present, the determinant of guilt changes into a qualitative one," and one is not essentially concerned about particular cases. "The one who is [in this way] totally guilty can very well be innocent in the particular case."[94]

It would seem, then, that consciousness of guilt has nothing to do with the wrongness of particular external acts but refers to an inward subjective awareness of one's being in a state of qualitative separation from what grants eternal blessedness to one's existence as a unique particular individual self. So "guilt" does not indicate an act or state of rebellion. To the contrary, in this case as in all of religiousness A, the positive is perceptible in the negative. Climacus makes this point vividly in his comparison of religiousness A and B. "In religiousness A an eternal blessedness is a single thing, and the passionate [relation to it] becomes the dialectical factor in the dialectic of interiorization. ... In proportion as the existing individual expresses the existential pathos

---

94 Ibid., pp. 470, 473; (KW 12.1:528, 531); SV 10: 201, 204; (7:461, 463).

(resignation—suffering—the totality of guilt-consciousness), to the same degree his passionate relation to an eternal blessedness increases."

Then he comments that religiousness A has its own peculiar form of edification (upbuilding) "whenever the God-relationship is found by the existing-one in the inwardness of subjectivity." And precisely

> the totality of guilt-consciousness is the most edifying element in religiousness A. The edifying element in the sphere of religiousness A is immanence, is the annihilation in which the individual puts oneself out of the way in order to find God, since it is precisely the individual himself who is the hindrance. Here also the edifying element is quite rightly perceptible in the negative, in the self-annihilation which finds the God-relationship in itself, which by its very suffering sinks down into the God-relationship, finds its ground in it, because God is the foundation [*i Grunden*] only when everything that is in the way is cleared away, every finite thing and first and foremost the individual herself in her finitude, in her claim of rights against God. ... In the ethical-religious sphere the individual himself is the place, when the individual has annihilated himself.[95]

Later we will inquire into what this upbuilding consists of, how far it achieves some measure of self-actualization. But the above characterization of the totality of guilt-consciousness obviously stresses its positive upbuilding power and function at the height and depth of one's inward subjective awareness of a relationship to an eternal blessedness, to that which assures one's own eternal dignity and significance. So Climacus says that every human being must learn to turn inward and to achieve "the relationship of silence with the ideal, ... seeking in silence the criterion which is in one's innermost being." This turning is possible because "in every human being there is and can and must be this mutual understanding with the ideal which demands all and comforts only in annihilation before God." And thus Climacus concludes that "the eternal recollection of guilt [which occurs] in hidden inwardness comprises in no way despair." Indeed, "the eternal recollection signifies the relationship to an eternal blessedness, ... [and] always is sufficient to prevent the plunge of despair."[96]

The same depiction of the awareness of the eternal at the height of the religion of immanence is also made by Anti-Climacus in *Sickness*, but in very different language. In this language (as previously indicated), he

---

95 Ibid., pp. 497–8; (KW 12.1:560–1); SV 10:229; (7:488–9).
96 Ibid., pp. 487–8, 492–3; (KW 12.1:548, 554); SV 10:218–19, 224; (7:477–8, 484).

The Leap as Freedom's Form

says, "God is this: that all things are possible" (or as Kierkegaard's Danish has it, "every thing is possible").[97] But coming to the awareness that my self as possibility is related to and dependent on a transcendent condition of possibility is always preceded by a negative experience, namely, "one understands that, humanly speaking, one's destruction [*Undergang*] is the most certain thing of all." So everything "depends solely on whether one obtains possibility, that is, whether one will believe." And "this is the dialectic of believing. ... To understand that humanly it is one's destruction, and nevertheless to believe in possibility, this is to believe." Indeed, "only the one whose being has been so shaken that one has become spirit by understanding that all things are possible, only that one has anything to do with God."[98]

In other words, the "saving" relationship to "possibility" as a transcendent phenomenological structure or dynamic of reality does not consist of an abstract conceptual perception. It is a "believing" relationship at the heart of which is a dialectic: on the one hand, there is the human inward self at the point of utter impotence and lostness ("destruction"), and on the other side there is "nevertheless" the reality of "all-things-are-possible." And the relationship, the "transition," which unites the two is the inward, earnest, personal, passionate interestedness of believing, of faith, and therefore the relationship is "religious."

The critical question about this material from *Sickness* is whether it can properly be appropriated to describe religiousness A, and therefore taken as descriptive of that relationship with the eternal through the dialectic of interiorization at the depth of subjectivity, or whether it is strictly "theological" in the Christian sense, and therefore descriptive strictly of that faith which is a relationship with the "paradox" and the "absurdity" of the historical presence of the eternal-in-time in the figure of Jesus. It is the thesis of this interpretation of Kierkegaard that the concept of God as "all-things-are-possible" falls within the scope of that

---

97 The Hongs properly use "with God everything is possible" for Kierkegaard's *for Gud er Alt muligt*. And Kierkegaard's Danish Bible contains that translation of the Greek in Mark 10:27, *Alt er muligt for God* (*Bibelen eller den hellige Skrift, Udgivet af Chr. H. Kalkar, Kjøbenhavn*, 1847; see *Auktionsprotokol over Søren Kierkegaards Bogsamling, Hovedsamling* nos. 8–10, p. 8). However, in the Greek, παντα δυνατα παρα το θεο, the παντα can only be the nominative plural and therefore must be translated "all things." And that is what I use because that is what is familiar to English readers of either the King James or the Revised Standard Versions. It is interesting to note that another Danish translation used the plural, "*Alle Ting ere mulige for Gud*" (in *N. T. ved Kong Frederik den Siettes, Kiøbenhavn*, 1841, *Trykt paa de Kongelige Baisenhuses Forlag*), but this version was not in Kierkegaard's library.

98 *Sickness*, pp. 170–4; (KW 19:37-40); SV 15:94-7; (11:150-3).

religiousness which has "only human nature in its universality as its assumption."[99] There is clear and persuasive evidence for this thesis.

First, it should be noted that this description of "God" occurs in that section of *Sickness* where Anti-Climacus analyses despair "without regard to its being conscious or not, consequently only with regard to the contituents of the synthesis," that is, not in the context of any particular religious experience. Thus in the entire section entitled "Necessity's Despair Is to Lack Possibility" there is not the slightest reference to faith as encompassing the "paradox" or as operating "by virtue of the absurd." On the contrary, the language is explicitly that used by Climacus in his description of religiousness A.

Anti-Climacus begins by noting that the fact that "with God all things are possible ... is eternally true and consequently true at every moment. This is indeed a generally recognized truth, which is commonly expressed in this way, but the [critical] decision occurs only when the human individual [*Mennesket*] is brought to one's extremity, such that humanly speaking there is no possibility." So, confronting this crisis which is common to most human beings, what generally happens at the point of decision? Again Anti-Climacus gives us an observation about the generic human being. "Whether a human being is helped miraculously depends essentially upon the degree of passion of the understanding whereby one has understood that help was impossible, and next upon how honest one is toward the power which nevertheless did help her/him." Anti-Climacus admits that "ordinarily [but not exclusively] humans do neither the one nor the other; they cry out that help is impossible without once straining their understanding to find help, and afterward they ungratefully lie." So at this level of religiousness, the possibility of help from "a power" beyond oneself, yet immanent to the human spirit, lies open to every human being. But to be so open requires passion and honesty—"honesty" in the sense of not deliberately deceiving ("lying" to) oneself about one's own limitations and about the real presence of help from beyond oneself.

Then Anti-Climacus comes to his central formulation of his point. "Personhood [*Personlighed*]," he says, "is a synthesis of possibility and

---

99 In fact, it is my thesis that the entirety of part one of *Sickness* describes the state of the self prior to the experience of Christian faith (I am indebted to Niels Jørgen Cappelørn for first making this observation to me, although I do not hold him responsible for the use I make of it here). On the other hand, I reserve the analysis and description of despair in part one of *Sickness* for treatment under the heading of "Kierkegaard as Theologian," the reasons for which will be given later.

necessity." So "there must be ... a self and possibility in the pregnant sense, because god is this: that all things are possible." And by direct entailment, "Anyone who does not have a god [i.e., possibility] does not have a self, either." In other words, only that human being can become a self or person who passionately recognizes and honestly acknowledges that one's own inherent character as possibility is open to and dependent upon empowerment from a structure of the reality (in which one moves and has being) whose definitive quality may be described as all-things-are-possible. This structure appears and asserts itself (at the depth of one's self-consciousness and subjectivity) as a dynamic, as a "power," as "a god." Hence, striving for and achieving some measure of self-actualization, i.e., "becoming oneself," is essentially, inherently, inescapably, universally "religious." And Anti-Climacus's use of language about "the power" and "a god" is a clear indication that he is describing universal human experience in the sphere of religiousness A.[100]

Now we are ready to return to the issue raised above: if this self-annihilation before God and the qualitative inward experience of guilt, as the decisive expression of one's passionate relationship to an eternal blessedness, has a positive result rather than ending in despair, and if therefore one does not end in a disrelationship (the definitive quality of despair), then Climacus must assume some kind of breach and some kind of leap of freedom *within* the immanence of universal humanity. Let us now explore the nature of that breach and that leap, in order to determine the form and level of self-actualization that is possible within religiousness which has "only human nature in its universality as its assumption."

We have noted repeatedly that we cannot speak of freedom until the self has come to a certain pause or stop, and faces a qualitative breach or gap. The breach is brought to light by an interruption in the continuity of "objective reflection," in the flow of rational inference and deduction, or of the abstraction of principles from empirical observations, when objective reflection proves to be impotent to resolve the problem of ethical choice and action in time/space. What is demanded is not an absolutely new beginning, but a transition to a qualitatively different sphere, a μεταβασις εις αλλο γενος, where a new mode of procedure is required. But before we see in more detail what this new mode consists of, the negative nature of the breach must be emphasized.

---

100 For the last two paragraphs, see *Sickness*, pp. 171-4; (KW 19:38-40); SV 15:95-7; (11:151-3).

We have just heard Climacus assert that the existential pathos involved in the transition from the ethical sphere to the religious is "negative" in that it requires suffering, self-annihilation, and guilt. For this purpose we will have to draw on diverse materials from both the acknowledged and pseudonymous writings, and therefore will refer indiscriminantly to the single author "Kierkegaard." But first it must be absolutely clear that in *Postscript* he does recognize the presence of a radical breach in the transition from the ethical sphere to that of religiousness A.

The key passage occurs in the chapter entitled "Truth Is Subjectivity," and we have seen that when *Postscript* says that "Religiousness A is the dialectic of interiorization," it is tying religiousness A to the discovery that "subjectivity is truth," because "subjective reflection turns inward towards subjectivity, and chooses to be the truth in this interiorization." In this key passage Kierkegaard is asserting that, although God is everywhere in creation, God is not there directly (*ligefremt*), and therefore a direct (i.e., an aesthetic, outward) relationship with God is not a "true" relationship. "Only when the particular [*enkelte*] individual turns inward into oneself (hence only in the inwardness of self-activity [*Selvvirksomhedens*]), does one become aware and capable of seeing God. The direct relationship to God is precisely paganism, and only when the breach [*Brud*] occurs, only then can one speak of a true God-relationship. But this breach is precisely the principal [*første*] act of inwardness in the direction of the determination that truth is inwardness. ... This breach is precisely the breakthrough of [or, accomplished in] inwardness, the act effected-by-oneself [*Selvvirksomhedens*], the principal determinant of the fact that truth is inwardness."[101]

The breach here described is certainly not that between religiousness A and Christian faith, because the latter is faced by the paradox of the eternal-in-time, whereas the former has its "relationship to an eternal blessedness" merely by means of "the dialectical deepening of interiorization." Here the breach in question is that which occurs within religiousness A when it ceases to look for God outwardly and directly, and turns inward by one's own self-activity and discovers that truth is inwardness or subjectivity. Now we are ready to describe in more detail what Kierkegaard sees as happening when one becomes aware of and is able to "see God" with the immanent experience of subjectivity.

---

101 *Postscript*, p. 218; (KW 12.1:293-4); SV 9:203; (7:204-5).

One of the primary things he does is to characterize the halt and the breach in religiousness A as the experience of utter "isolation." We have already heard in *Fear and Trembling* that when the "knight" is confronted with the world's (and his own reason's) judgment that his ideal love and hope are totally impossible, he rejects the temptation to become a "slave of the finite" and hence forget "the whole substance" of his life. Rather, in this moment of crisis, "one becomes very quiet, one dismisses [those thoughts], one becomes solitary [*ene*]." *Postscript* picks up on this point and asserts that "the leap ... cannot be taught or communicated directly precisely because it is an act of isolation, since it is left to the individual [*Enkelte*] to resolve [*beslutte sig*: decide, make up one's mind]" whether to accept what cannot be thought. In other words, "the leap is the category of decision [*Afgjørelse*]."[102] But one's resolve or decision assumes or involves that one "breaks with reason [*Forstand*] and thinking and immanence," that one is alone and isolated, because the leap of decision is not something that can be learned from or communicated by an other. "Every human being is spirit, and truth [comes] precisely as appropriation by one's own self-activity," when one "turns within oneself." So, "the category of transition is a breach of immanence, is a leap," and (as just noted) "this breach is the principal act of inwardness in the direction of the determination that truth is inwardness." But note: the "immanence" referred to here is both that of immediacy which assumes a direct outward relationship with the truth, as well as that immanence of the ethical which assumes that the individual is able to accomplish eternal blessedness on one's own; so the breach described here still occurs within the immanence of religiousness A.[103]

Hence, while Kierkegaard says that "the leap is the category of decision" (i.e. the leap *is* decision), he also says that "the leap ... is isolation's act"; that is to say, the leap occurs only when an individual encounters a break or breach which has the character of a kind of isolation. What kind?

As just noted, in the particular γενος or sphere of being and experience here called a "breach," one is alone and isolated in two ways. One continues to think, to reason, and to consult one's immediate feelings, but their conclusions do not comprise an act in space/time. One is deserted by these usually dependable sources of truth, and left to draw upon a qualitatively different resource: something called "resolve" or

---

102 Ibid., pp. 92, 91; (KW 12.1:100, 99); SV 9:86, 85; (7:80, 79).
103 Ibid., in order of appearance: pp. 505, 217, 262, 218; (KW 12.1:569, 242, 295, 243); SV 10: 237; SV 9:202, 248, 203; (7:496, 203-4, 253, 205).

"decision." But, secondly, one is also left alone in that no one else can make up your mind for you, no matter how wise their advice or how strong their example. One must inwardly "appropriate" (*sig tilegne*), by one's own self-activity (*Selvvirksomhed*), the truth in and for this particular situation.[104] But if all one's usual means for determining the truth do not apply in this new sphere or γενος, to what resource does one turn at this critical juncture in order to make up one's own mind, in order to come to a "completely decisive resolve" which comprises the leap of freedom?

For Kierkegaard this is the moment of "fear and trembling." All avenues to the truth that one ordinarily depends on have come to a halt, a stop, a pause (*Standsning*), and one enters a vast breach or chasm (*Brud*) between one's "self's possibility" and self's actuality. He clearly describes this event as happening within the "initial expression" of religiousness A: "The individual becomes infinitized only by the venture [risk]. ... By the venture he himself becomes an other. ... And when he has risked it, he is no longer the same. Thus appropriate space is gained for the *discrimen* [distinctive mark] of the transition, an intervening yawning chasm [*Dyb*] suitable as the scene for the passion of infinitude, a gulf [*Svælg*] which understanding [or reason: *Forstand*] cannot go over either forward or backward."[105]

The stopping before this chasm fills one with fear and trembling because, he says, it is like the halt of death that comes to every human being at the end of a life lived in being "constantly on the go and never stopping, in the medium of ceaselessness (temporality, the merely quantified, etc.)." Or this halting is "comparable to a fish's being taken out of water and having to breathe in the air." So in this halt a human being "shudders at this other element," because one senses that the breach one enters is not empty, but that "an enormous power resides in 'the stop,'" and its power is limitless. To be confronted immanently by "the limitless, the infinite, the eternal-as-standing-still [*Stillestaaen*] within the halt is just like dying."[106]

---

104 Ibid., pp. 182, 217, 327-8; (KW 12.1:203, 242, 365); SV 9:169-70, 202, 10:64; (7:170, 203-4, 316).

105 Ibid., p. 379; (KW 12.1:423-4); SV 10:113; (7:367).

106 *Journals*, 4798; X³ A 47 (1850). *Stillestaaen* literally means static or stationary, even stagnant. But here Kierkegaard has in mind the opposite of what he calls the "deceptiveness" or "illusiveness" (*Svigagtighed*) of the eternal coming into existence in time [see e.g. *Philosophical Fragments*, p. 100; (KW 7:81); SV 6:74; (4:244f.); or *Postscript*, p. 218; (KW 12.1:243); SV 9:203; (7:205)]. Here he is saying that in the halt/breach, one encounters the absolute in an undeniable manner, as when one faces death inescapably.

But this "death" of all one's natural resources to get at the truth, this experience of the radical stop and breach, is not purely negative. Indeed, its intended and proper function is positive. In his edifying discourse "An Occasional Discourse" (from *Upbuilding Discourses in Various Spirits*), Kierkegaard says that it is an ultimate experience which calls for "a collected [centred] mentality [disposition] ... that has collected itself from every distraction, from every relationship, in order to centre upon its relation to itself as the individual [*Enkelte*] who is responsible before God," and "responsible for every relation in which one normally stands [*er*]." So the individual must "at a specific time come to a decisive stop." But the important thing is this: "the stopping is not indolent repose. The stop is also movement; it is the inward movement of the heart; it is self-deepening in inwardness."[107] In other words, at the stop and in this chasm or breach, the new mode or αλλο γενος that one enters is no longer simply the ethical but is the new sphere of the religious, that is, the ethical-religious sphere of religiousness A.

How does "God" appear in the breach, in the "isolation" that one experiences as the facing of "death"? How is the positive perceived in this most profound negative? Let us look first at Kierkegaard's use of the notion of "silence" as the setting in which the individual accomplishes this leap into the religious.

Kierkegaard liked the saying of Savanarola, "The father of prayer is silence, its mother [is] solitude," and the Pythagorean instruction that "character training begins with silence."[108] In his analysis of this silence, he uses god-language, but as will be shown below, it should be read in terms of ethico-religiousness A rather than in the more restrictive theological sense of religiousness B.

The "death" we experience in the halt and the breach need not plunge us into despair before the enormous power of the infinite and the eternal. Rather than railing against this power that has brought about the "death" of all our own grand powers to command the truth, Kierkegaard counsels, "From the lilies and the birds as teachers let us learn silence, or learn to be silent. ... You shall in the deepest sense make yourself nothing, become nothing ... , learn to be silent. In this silence is the beginning," because this silence is the "fear-of-God" (*Gudsfrygt*) and "the beginning of wisdom." "In this silence the many thoughts

---

107 *Upbuilding Discourses in Various Spirits*, "Part One: An Occasional Discourse" (D.V. Steere translation, *Purity of Heart*), pp. 215-217; (KW 15:152-3); SV 11: 138-9; (8:240-1).
108 *Journals*, 3460; X⁴ A 281 (1851); 2324; X² A 235; 2334; XI² A 128.

of wish and desire fall dumb out of godly fear [*forstummer gudfrygtigt*]. ... Only in such fear and trembling can a human being talk with God." But this is difficult because "much fear and trembling makes the voice [*at Talen*] fall dumb in silence."

Yet this silence, this dumbness, is the beginning of wisdom because in the silence two things may happen. First one may hear a voice, and then one may obey. When one has stoppped one's ears to all the voices of "truth" to which one ordinarily listens, when one no longer seeks "to hear oneself speak," then one becomes "the opposite of a speaker, one becomes a hearer," one *listens* for another voice. So this silence is: "to wait until one ... hears God." Here there is fear and trembling because you are "alone in the whole world, you ... are alone in the environment of the solemn silence, so alone that every doubt, and every objection, and every excuse, and every evasion, and every question, in short, every voice, is reduced to silence in your own inward [self], every voice, that is, every voice but God's, which around you and within you talks to you by means of the silence." And this kind of "silence" (i.e., listening) is "the first condition for being able to obey," because this kind of listening to God is the same as loving God, and loving God is the same as obeying God. "When all around you is solemn silence, and when there is silence within you, then do you sense, and sense with the force of infinitude, the truth of the saying 'you shall love the Lord your God, and [God] only shall you serve', and you sense that it is *you*, you who shall love God, you, you alone in the whole world."[109]

Clearly in this analysis of what happens in the pause and breach (which the self encounters as it attempts the transition from the self's possibility to the self's fulfilment in actuality), a totally new and quite mysterious factor has emerged, something beyond the purely ethical clarification of "the one thing needful" and beyond the self's sense of duty to do it. If I enter this "silence," if I sense and perceive that all my previous voices of truth have fallen silent, if I—with fear and trembling—wait to hear a qualitatively new voice, then I have "leaped" (made a transition) into an αλλο γενος or new sphere of being: the religious, or more accurately, the ethico-religious sphere of religiousness A. Kierkegaard is making the flat assertion that the highest and purest of ethical visions of the Good, and the strongest most intense ethical determination to do the Good, are impotent by *themselves* to effect the transi-

---

109 *The Lilies of the Field and the Birds of the Air*, in *Christian Discourses*, pp. 322f., 336; sv 14:135f., 148; (11:14f., 27f.).

tion from the glittering possibility to its concrete incarnation in actuality, or in today's language, from the very best intention to concrete action in existence (space/time).

In other words, he is pointing to a boundary line that looms up at the ultimate edge of every human consciousness as it follows the lure and excitement of becoming one's own true self in freedom: the desperate need for a voice of affirmation and encouragement from beyond the limits of one's own strength and conviction, from beyond all human wisdom and power to define truth; a voice that speaks with the accents of the original ground and source of one's very existence, a voice that says with absolute authority, "all things are possible." Kierkegaard is saying to every human being: stop your ears to all the voices of this finite world, listen to the silence in all fear and trembling, and the voice will come. And with it, the strength and courage to "obey" the demands of one's most inward, uniquely individual and personal vision of the Good.

Admittedly, the foregoing analysis of silence is drawn from a work at the pinnacle of Kierkegaard's theological authorship, *The Lilies in the Field and the Birds under the Heavens*, which was written the year after *Practice in Christianity*. But the same thoughts on silence appear early in Kierkegaard's thinking and clearly refer to general human religiousness. For example, in a journal entry of 1843 he says, "Every human being who knows how to keep [silent] becomes a divine child, because in silence there is concentration on one's divine origin; one who speaks remains a human being." And in the same year, he writes in *Fear and Trembling*, "silence is divinity's mutual understanding with the single individual [*den Enkelte*]." Moreover, in the passage in *Lilies* it is notable that Kierkegaard speaks only of "hearing" and "obeying" the new voice, rather than of the theological "believing by virtue of the absurd." He explicitly says, "by being obedient oneself, one can learn obedience from oneself." And the God he speaks of is the one "who is your creator and sustainer, in whom you live and move and have your being [*lever, røres og er*]," rather than the redeemer God incarnate.[110] So the voice one listens for comes from a boundary line and an abyss at the outermost edge of universal-individual human consciousness, a kind of eternity tangentially touching human temporality. As Kierkegaard explicitly says, "The upbuilding [element] in the sphere of religiousness A is [that] of immanence."[111]

---

110 *Journals*, 3978; IV A 28; *Fear and Trembling*, p. 97; (KW 6:88); SV 5:80; (3:136); *Lilies*, pp. 335f.; SV 14:147f.; (11:26f.).
111 *Postscript*, pp. 497–8; (KW 12.1:560–1); SV 10:229; (7:489).

This language is decisive for Kierkegaard's depiction of what he calls "human nature in its universality" within religiousness A (or of what we are calling his "humanist" depiction of the self with "the merely human self" as its criterion, rather than "the theological self").[112] This language is crucial because it depicts a "halt" and a "breach" and therefore a "leap" *within* the total and ultimate self-consciousness of "the merely human self." It assumes that within the consciousness of universal human nature or the merely human self there is possible a kind of God-consciousness and God-relationship, indeed, that such a consciousness is normal and natural for every human being.

Or to put it in non-theological language: one may become aware of the need to relate to a structure, or better, to a dynamic of reality that is both immanent and transcendent to one's deepest, most inward, private, personal, individual focus or gestalt of what gives one's self its essential integrity, dignity, and everlasting worth. What one needs is: first, affirmation of one's discernment of and commitment to the difference between what is essential and absolute for maintaining one's self identity, and what is relative, unimportant, and dispensable; and, secondly, en-courage-ment to venture and to risk all in order to transform one's entire existence by living concretely in accord with what one knows is the essential, the absolute at the core and at the height of one's being. But this affirmation and this encouragement are received or "heard" only when the single lone individual turns away from all the outward voices and turns inward in isolation, and there becomes silent and enters that silence that takes the shape and has the force of "death," death of the self-sufficient self in the experience of resignation, self-annihilation, and the totality of guilt-consciousness; and in the silence this self "listens" for the "voice" that says, "all things are possible." In other words, in this listening, the self has made the daring leap of freedom, the "completely decisive resolve," to "wait" before the eternal. And the eternal imparts itself in the relationship of "love" (faith).

Finally, the exact nature of this leap (from the ethical to the religious), both its possibilities and limitations, will become clearer by (once more) showing how the breach, the leap, and the believing (faith) involved in religiousness A are quite distinct from what happens in religiousness B (Christian faith).

The chasm or gulf within religiousness A certainly is not the same as the breach (*Brud*) experienced when one is confronted with the "ab-

---

112 *Sickness*, p. 210; (KW 19:79); SV 15:133; (11:191).

surd" claim of the eternal-in-time in the historical figure of Jesus. Hence the believing or faith involved in this "venture" is not the same as the faith that is involved in the experience of the presence of the eternal in an historical event, in the life of a particular human being. But this chasm or gulf is characterized as "religious" and as involving a believing for which one must make the venture of, have the daring for, the risky leap from the ethical sphere to the religious sphere.

Climacus's analysis in *Postscript* provides a basic and essential clarification. He states in direct language that he uses the term "faith" in two qualitatively different senses when speaking of (A) the general religious capability for a God-relationship in universal humanity, and, in contrast, when speaking of (B) the faith-relationship with God as encountered in the historical event of Jesus Christ. He takes Socrates as exemplifying A because "Socratic ignorance is an analogue to the determinant: the absurd," and "Socratic inwardness in existing is an analogue to faith." So "[w]hen Socrates believed that God is, he held fast the objective uncertainty with the whole passion of inwardness, and faith precisely consists in this contradiction, in this risk." In religiousness A, "[i]f I wish to preserve myself in faith I must constantly take care that I hold fast the objective uncertainty, that I, in objective uncertainty, am over seventy thousand fathoms of water, and yet believe." In religiousness B, however, "it is otherwise. Instead of the objective uncertainty, here is the certainty that objectively viewed it is the absurd, and this absurdity held fast in the passion of inwardness is faith." And "the absurd" we are talking about is this: "that the eternal truth has come into existence in time, that God has come into existence, was born, has grown up, etc.; has come into existence just like [every other] individual human being, not to be distinguished from any other human being."[113]

The difference, however, between "an objective uncertainty held fast with the whole passion of inwardness" and "the absurd held fast in the passion of inwardness" does not clearly specify the difference between the two kinds of faiths. The role of the immanent eternal in A and the role of the transcendent God in B are two qualitatively different events. In A the closer definition and achievement of "faith" as a healing, freeing event is dependent on the initiative of the individual's ever more inward self-activity, the work of what Climacus calls "a dialectical deepening of interiorization" in relation to one's awareness of the

---

113 *Postscript*, pp. 183–4, 188, 182, 188; (KW 12.1:205, 210, 204, 210); SV 9:171, 175, 170, 175; (7:171, 176, 170, 176).

"voice" of the immanent other. So in *Postscript* "faith" consists, rather ambiguously, of the believer's being open to the the eternal *and* of the eternal's coming in as the source of affirmation and encouragement, all held together by the act of "believing." On the other hand, in B the closer definition and achievement comes from the individual's voluntary turning of one's attention and openness ever more intensely to the objective external presence of the eternal (in the historical event of the life of Jesus Christ) and then voluntarily waiting upon and receiving the initiative of that presence.

So in A the relationship of faith is totally immanent to one's own spiritual depths, and the otherness of the immanent eternal is difficult to maintain and is always clouded with uncertainty and doubt, which require both enormous concentration of mind/spirit and courage of heart to keep them in check. But in B the relationship of faith is quite different. One listens to a voice that concretely defines ever more closely the very content of what it means to possess "eternal blessedness." And this voice does not come from within oneself; rather, one must "relate to something outside oneself in order to find upbuilding. ... The paradoxical upbuilding therefore corresponds to the determinant of God in time as particular human-being."[114] So, although Climacus does not explicitly say so in *Postscript*, "faith" in religiousness B (Christianity) is a much more complex relationship to something outside and objective to the believer, even while requiring personal appropriation in profoundly subjective, passionate conviction and devotion.

This view of Christian faith had been given a formulation by Climacus in his earlier work, *Philosophical Fragments*, and is picked up and developed explicitly in Kierkegaard's second (Christian) authorship, in his acknowledged discourses from *Works of Love* onward and in the writings of Anti-Climacus. In chapter 1 of *Fragments*, Climacus sets out to explore an "experimental" alternative to Socrates' approach to the Truth (his retreating back into eternity through reflection). Climacus proposes that the teacher must both bring the truth with him to give to the learner and also provide the learner with the "condition" required to understand it. In chapter II he depicts the teacher as the king or the God who assumes the guise of a humble beggar to come down into the finite world of the maiden (learner) whom the God wishes to woo. In chapter

---

114 Ibid., pp. 494, 498; (KW 12.1:556. 561); SV 10:225, 229–30; (7:485, 489). For another treatment of this ambiguity in a different context, see the section on "The Second Breach" in chapter 8.

III he casts the relationship into the abstract terms of the contradiction between the paradox (of what is described in chapters I and II) and human reason or understanding. He says that the paradox becomes "absolute" when the teacher (the God) not only "negatively, brings out the absolute difference of sin," but also "positively, wills to annul the absolute difference in the absolute equality." And twice he says we shall have to search for the name of that "happy passion" in which the two come to an understanding.

In chapter IV Climacus asks, "How does the learner come to an understanding with this paradox?" His answer: in that "happy passion" which "we shall call *faith*." And he gives a very exact definition of faith: "... when the understanding [or reason: *Forstand*] steps aside and the paradox gives itself; and the third [something] in which this occurs (because it does not occur in the understanding, which is discharged, or in the paradox which gives itself—consequently in something) is that happy passion to which we shall now give a name, ... *faith*." In other words, faith in religiousness B (Christianity) is not simply something I do, *my* believing. Nor is faith simply something God does, the eternal's graceful immanent coming and empowering. Rather, faith is a *relationship* in which there is a happy meeting, the resolution of a collision of opposites to which each makes a necessary (though unequal) contribution. The learner must *willingly* listen to the truth as defined by the teacher; the beloved must *freely* accept the difficult love offered by the king/God who comes in the puzzling garb of a humble equal. But it is the omnipotent lover/teacher who condescends to take the initiative to come and who thereby provides the only condition in which their happy union is possible.[115]

This character of the meeting between God-in-Jesus-Christ and sinful humanity lost in despair is obviously qualitatively different from the God-relationship available to every human being through the "interiorization" described by Climacus. And Kierkegaard summarizes the gist of this view (as explicated in his overtly Christian writings) in a "loose paper" and a journal entry late in his life (1854).[116] "In the New Testament," he says, "faith is not an intellectual but an ethical determinant; it signifies the relationship of personal-individuality [*Personlighed*] between God and the human-being." Or even more exactly, "Faith is the expres-

---

115 *Fragments*, pp. 17, 59, 73; (KW 7:14, 47, 59); SV 6:19, 46f., 56; (4:184, 214, 224).

116 *Journals*, 1154, XI² A 380; 180, XI¹ A 237. With this sense of "faith" in mind, the phrase "leap of faith" is totally erroneous and misleading.

sion [term] for: the relationship of personal-individuality to personal-individuality." So "The concept *faith* [emphasis added] lies in the purely personal relationship between God as personal-individuality and the believing-one [*Troende*] as personal-individuality *in existence.*" So faith is something other, something more than my willingness to believe. Here is repeated the formula found in *Fragments*: faith, in its essential concept, does not reside either *in me* or *in God,* but is that very special mutual relationship in which two individualities relate to each other in accordance with their both being personal—in spite of the infinite qualitative difference that distinguishes them in other ways.

In these journal entries Kierkegaard also provides us with a definition of what he means by "personal-individuality" or "personal." It is not comprised of a set of "axioms" or of "immediate accessibility." Rather it is a "curving-into-oneself, a *clausum* [enclosed place], an αδυτον [sanctuary], a μυστηριον [secret]; personal-individuality is: the 'in-there' [*derinde*]." This essential hiddenness of the personal being means that he/she is accessible only indirectly, so that one personal being "must relate believingly" to another personal being. So even when two such personal beings passionately love each other, "it can never come to more than the fact that the one believes that the other loves him or her." And this "believing" is "against reason," and grasps what "one cannot see." Here, then, Kierkegaard makes the fine distinction between, on the one hand, faith as a "relationship" or state of being, as a "third something," in which two personal beings exist and live in devotion to each other, and on the other hand, faith as "believing," as a "determinant" and an "ethical" act of each party to the relationship. In other words, even at the depth of the *Christian* faith relationship, the element of human decision (the ethical, the voluntary, the leap) still plays a role.

When we come to consider Kierkegaard as theologian, we will have to explore many ramifications of this analysis of faith (is the human spirit also "hidden" from Holy Spirit? does God therefore also "believe" in the human person? is divine grace irresistible or does "the possibility of offence" mean that, even under the power of Christian grace, believing is voluntary? what is the relation of faith to love? etc.). But our present consideration of the nature of faith in religiousness B certainly makes clear that faith in religiousness A is so profoundly a matter of "immanence," of pure "subjectivity" and "interiorization," that the two kinds of faith comprise two qualitatively distinct spheres, and that the leap from religiousness A to B is qualitatively different from the leap from the ethical to religiousness A.

Specifically, in its faith-relationship to the eternal, religiousness A is weak in two regards (in contrast to religiousness B). First, the eternal (the divine) does not appear on the horizon of human consciousness as if on its own initiative and as making its own claim. Rather, the human spirit on its own initiative (even though providentially coerced by failures and tragedies) searches for the eternal, discovers it, listens to it, submits to it, and uses it. Secondly, when the eternal is discovered and listened to (immanently and subjectively), the eternal does not unequivocally specify what human "eternal blessedness" actually consists of, and therefore "love" as the religious ethic for human relations is usually not clearly defined, but is left as a contradictory confusion of self-interest and self-sacrifice. Or to put it from the human perspective, when the human spirit listens to the eternal within one's own consciousness, that spirit does not universally hear the same thing, or at least its interpretation and description of what it hears have resulted in a proliferation of seemingly diverse ethical ideals and systems. And each system has its own idea as to what adequate actualization of the ideal consists of. Some ethicists see flat contradiction between and among the systems. Others are impressed with their underlying unanimity. So, in what now follows, we must be careful not to overstate either the clarity or the force of the content of the ethical-religious sphere that is open to universal humanity, that is, in Kierkegaard's view.

Nevertheless, we must now seek to answer directly the question posed several times already: in what way and how far does the "transformation of one's entire existence" occur within religiousness A? Or to use the figure of speech suggested above: in what accents does the voice (in the silence) speak? Does "all-things-are-possible" tell me just *what* things are "desirable" and "good" for me, my self, to do? Do I receive an answer when I ask, "What *is* it that pleases God?" And does this transformation take place here and now in actuality? Or does it remain a fond hope for some future beyond the end of temporal earthly existence, while my life of "faith" here and now ends in resignation and despair?

In spite of all his language about resignation, suffering, impotence, guilt, and despair, it is a serious and crucial misreading of Kierkegaard to assume that these very real aspects of human consciousness in the ethical-religious sphere of existence mean the total failure of the self to achieve any measure of authentic freedom and actualization. This negative conclusion has received a strong statement and agile defence in Mark Taylor's *Journeys to Selfhood: Hegel & Kierkegaard*. He accepts the implication of Hegel's position that the coincidentia oppositorum definitive of Kierkegaard's notion of spirit leaves contraries unreconciled, creating the fragmentation characteristic of spiritlessness. ... Kierkegaard differentiates but cannot reintegrate opposites. ... Self is set against other, subject against object, existence against essence, finitude against infinitude, reality against ideality, actuality against possibility, freedom against necessity, individuality against universality, self against society, time against eternity, man against God. ... The project of faith is destined to fail. ... The journey to meet the alien God carries the wayfarer farther and farther from human community until at last self is completely isolated from other. ... Kierkegaardian faith is a revival of Jewish positivity in which a servile subject is completely obedient to an omnipotent Lord and Master. ... Kierkegaard's interpretation of authentic selfhood negates itself in the very effort to affirm itself, and necessarily passes over into its opposite—Hegelian spirit.[117]

Every one of these characterizations of Kierkegaard's thought (contained in these four pages of Taylor's "Prefatory Conclusion") has already been demonstrated in the foregoing to be a gross, even ludicrous, misreading and misrepresentation. Clearly the believer in Kierkegaard's religion (A or B) is not a "servile subject" precisely because this God does not use omnipotence to be "Lord and Master," but uses omnipotence to make the believer "independent," free and responsible, because only so can God and believer be united in the equality of love. Omnipotence provides all the "help" required for this consummation without turning the human self into an automaton.

It is significant that in these four pages Taylor first quotes the "absolute" statements from *Fear and Trembling* and then demolishes them with contradictions from *Attack on Christendom*, and admits in a footnote (as noted previously) that "the most tortured expressions of such passionate world-negation are to be found in late journal entries." There are no references to *Postscript, Upbuilding Discourses in Various Spirits, Works of Love, The Sickness unto Death, Practice in Christianity,* and *The Lily of the Field and the Bird of the Air.* Such neglect of the core of Kierkegaard's thought is at least a mistaken if not an irresponsible methodology. When one considers Kierkegaard's own characterization of *Sickness* in his journals, there are good reasons for taking *Sickness* as normative for Kierkegaard's thought, and good reasons for not taking the pessimism of late journal entries and *Attack* as representing the definitive position and valid conclusion of the entire Kierkegaardian corpus.

117 Taylor, *Journeys*, pp. 269–72.

How far, then, can the self go in becoming itself in actuality within the limits of religiousness A? That such a "becoming" occurs there can be no doubt. "In the religiousness of immanence ... the individual's relationship to the eternal determines that, through the dialectic of interiorization, he transforms his existence in accordance with this relation. ... Religiousness A makes the fact of existing as strenuous as possible, ... but does not base the relationship to an eternal blessedness upon one's existing, but has the relationship to an eternal blessedness as the basis for the transformation of existence." So what eventuates is not just a deepening of one's inward commitment to the absolute or eternal, but also a transformation of one's entire "existence" which includes one's concrete finitude.[118]

Does this mean then that one's obedience to one's absolute telos is observable and evident in the finite external act, and therefore subject to evaluation by an objective norm? As we have heard, the consummation of the ethical is not in words or intentions but in acts. The constant emphasis of *Works of Love* is that love of neighbour is not an intention but a "work" or "deed." So in his "Little Sketch" of "The ethical and ethical-religious Dialectic of Communication" (written the same year as *Works* but never published), Kierkegaard stresses again and again that the ethical occurs only "in the situation of actuality," that in "achieving actuality" one must "live and learn on the street."[119]

Nevertheless, Climacus flatly states that "Actuality is not the external act." Certainly, it is not merely a conceived intention as a disinterested objective possibility. Rather, "Actuality is ... an inwardness [*Indvorteshed*] in which the individual annuls [mere] possibility and identifies with the thought in order to exist therein. This is action." In this case, "thinking ... is a possibility in which the interest of actuality and action is already reflected," indeed "actuality and responsibility want to have a firm grip on it." So later when he asks, "What is it that pleases God?", he simply answers, "true religiousness is hidden inwardness," whose "absolute passion cannot be understood by a third party," because "in absolute passion the passionate one is in the extremity of its concrete subjectivity as a consequence of having reflected out of every relativity of outwardness."[120]

---

118 *Postscript*, p. 508–9; (KW 12.1:574); SV 10:240–1; (7:500).
119 *Journals*, 649:28, 653:18; VIII² B 81:28, 85:18.
120 *Postscript*, pp. 302–3, 452, 454; (KW 12.1:339, 506, 508–9); SV 10:42, 183, 185; (7:293, 440, 442).

Here, however, we face a serious dilemma. When it is asked, "What is it that pleases God?", that is, "What happens when one actualizes one's absolute telos, or obeys the 'voice' of the eternal that speaks in the 'silence' of one's consciousness of 'not-being-able?'", it is not enough simply to say that one acts with "passion" and "inwardness." It is not even enough to answer the question in the language of *Sickness*, that is, it pleases God or the eternal when the individual acts concretely in accord with that gestalt of essential values, convictions, beliefs, ideals, etc. which define who that person is, stamping on one's action, with decisive resolve, that inner necessity that excludes consideration of any other possibility. The dilemma is this: what if my most inward, passionate, essential gestalt has as its dominant quality the lust for power and control over others; or even worse, what if my consciousness of "eternal blessedness" comes to me in acts of sadistic torture (mental or physical) of others?

Is there really no criterion of the "good" or of "blessedness" which transcends and hence objectively judges the individual when he/she listens to that "voice" at the height/depth of one's subjectivity? Let us reconsider the two passages with which we began this chapter. What does Climacus mean when he says, "When one raises the question of truth objectively, then one reflects about truth as an object, to which the cognizer relates. ... If that to which one relates is simply the truth or the true, then the subject is [considered to be] in the truth. When one raises the question of truth subjectively, then one reflects subjectively on the *relationship* of the individual [to the truth]; if only the 'how' of this relationship is in truth, then the individual is in truth, even if one thus relates to [something that is] untruth" (emphasis added). Or he makes the point even more clearly a little later: "Objectively the emphasis is on *what* is said [or done], subjectively the emphasis is on *how* it is said [or done]. ... Ethically-religiously the emphasis is on 'how'. ... At its maximum this 'how' is the passion of infinitude, and the passion of infinitude is the very truth. But the passion of infinitude is precisely subjectivity, and thus subjectivity is the truth. ... The passion of infinitude is the deciding factor, not its content, because its content is precisely the self [*den selv*]."[121]

Does Climacus really mean that one is doing the "good" and "true" thing if only one is doing it with all one's passion of the infinite, even if one is a slaver, or is grinding down the poor for one's own enrichment?

---

[121] Ibid., pp. 178, 181; (KW 12.1:199, 202–3); SV 9:166, 169; (7:166, 169–70).

Does he make no distinction as to "what" the "content" of a "good" and "true" act may be? Apparently, Kierkegaard never addresses this question directly (at least in all the materials of the authorship surveyed for this present study). But it is the thesis here that in Climacus's concepts of subjectivity and of religiousness A, in Kierkegaard's own depiction of confession before the eternal in his discourse "On the Occasion of a Confession," and in Anti-Climacus's concept of the self as the dialectical in the determinants of possibility/necessity, there lies a clear and firm assumption that answers our question. To put it succinctly: in subjectivity and religiousness (as exposited above) the self in freedom relates to the infinite/eternal (and hence to itself) in such a way that the good and true "one-thing-needful" in the present concrete situation becomes clear as to its *content*, and either one does it with the "passion of infinitude," with the "whole heart," with "completely decisive resolve," or one fails to do it.

As already noted, in a late journal entry (1850, and from the perspective of Christianity or religiousness B) Kierkegaard specifically reverses Climacus's view of the role of the "content" or the "what" of ethical-religious truth, even while retaining his stress on the indispensability of the "how" of subjectvity (the passion of infinitude). In this passage (which we have used several times previously) Kierkegaard says that there can be no choice as to *what* is "the one thing needful," even though the individual as "spirit" (self) must still choose it. Then he adds, "freedom-of-choice [*Valgfrihed*] is only a *form*-determinant of freedom, and ... emphasizing freedom-of-choice as such is the forfeiture of freedom. The *content* of freedom is decisive for freedom" (emphasis added).[122]

In other words, both the *content* of the one-thing-needful and the *decision* to do it are essential constituents in the event of "freedom." Climacus, as we have just heard, insists that in religiousness A the relationship to an eternal blessedness is not derived from one's existence; rather, the transformation of one's existence derives from one's relationship to an eternal blessedness. Then he adds, "From the individual's relation to the eternal, there results the 'how' of one's existence, not the converse, and thereby infinitely more comes out [of the relationship] than was put in."[123] It is our thesis here that this "infinitely more" includes not only the "how" but also a determination of the "content" of "the one thing needful" even within religiousness A, and even though one's own

---

122 *Journals*, 1261; X² A 428.
123 *Postscript*, p. 509; (KW 12.1:544); SV 10:241; (7:500).

unique definitive gestalt of one's self's possibility plays a critical role in determining this content. In other words, the infinite, the eternal, the absolute telos to which the universal human spirit is open "speaks" to each unique individual self about the "good" and the "true," but the particular way in which that good is enacted is determined by the response of the unique individual self, reacting with passionate conviction in one's own particular situation here and now.

The point is this: there is of course "content" in what a person does. The content of a human decision and act is not given or determined "objectively," i.e. by a purely physical condition or a purely rational conception or idea or a socially imposed standard of "dos" and "don'ts." Rather, the content derives from the fact that the human self (who makes the decision and performs the act) is composed of and exists dialectically in the unity of infinite/finite, possible/necessary, eternal/temporal. The infinite/eternal (in its peculiar state of immanence/transcendence) defines the content of *what* should be done, but only as possibility. The individual person as existing (in time/space) must enact this possibility within the conditions of one's own finitude at a particular time/place. These conditions further define (restrict) the content by giving it concreteness. But the transition from possibility to actuality is not automatic or inevitable, not easy and natural, not accomplished objectively and logically. Possibility, even as intention, is not yet "truth" for a self, because *becoming* self concretely is the truth. So the transition must be accomplished. The question is "How?" The answer: by the "*passion of the infinite*," that is, in subjectivity. Again: "Objectively [i.e., conceptually, logically] viewed there is no infinite decision. ... Decision occurs only in subjectivity. ... The passion of infinitude, not its content, is the deciding-thing [*Afgjørende*], because its content is precisely the self" (i.e. the synthesis of infinite/finite, possible/necessary, eternal/temporal). "In this way the subjective 'how' and subjectivity are the truth."[124]

In other words, there certainly is a content to the one-thing-needful. But the content may be clearly defined and known and acknowledged in and by the self's consciousness of what is "spoken" to him/her by the infinite/eternal at the height/depth of the self-conscious gestalt of the self's possibility, by consciousness of what is demanded by one's own absolute telos or eternal blessedness, and *yet* that content is still only a possibility which the self may or may not enact. This content is not yet

---

124 Ibid., p. 181; (KW 12.1:203); SV 9:169; (7:169–170).

"truth" for her/him because the self has not yet made the infinite passionate decision to *exist* in it; one has not yet chosen to transform one's entire existence in conformity with it. Although the content is absolutely requisite and decisive in setting the stage for the good and the true, it is not the deciding factor in its enactment. So, as noted before, Climacus can indulge in the hyperbole of saying that "If only the 'how' of this relationship is in truth, then the individual is in truth, even if one thus relates to [a content that is] untruth," because "it is only for the sake of clarifying [the essential truth] as ... subjectivity that this contradiction is set up."[125]

Kierkegaard never directly or in a summary fashion describes the "infinitely more" that comes out of the relationship with the eternal, but he provides a rich and indisputable indication of its reality and character in diverse pictures and definitions. So Kierkegaard does not maintain in the authorship as a whole one of the major distinctions Climacus makes (in *Postscript*) between religiousness A and B. As noted above, Climacus says that in religiousness A "the relationship to an eternal blessedness is not conditioned [*betinget*] by any *thing* [i.e., historical, factual], ... and so is conditioned only by the interiorization which is dialectical"; hence its "only closer definition is the closer definition of interiorization." On the contrary, "religiousness B [Christianity] ... sets conditions in such a way that the conditions are ... a definite something which more closely defines the eternal blessedness [itself], ... not simply ... the individual's appropriation of it."[126] It is the thesis here, as already stated, that even in *Postscript* and more clearly yet in other writings there is given a closer definition of the "content" of one's "eternal blessedness" within the immanence of that experience of the eternal which comes when an individual makes the transition from the aesthetic sphere to the spheres of the ethical and the ethical-religious (as in religiousness A).

It is requisite for our understanding of Kierkegaard's concept of the self as "freedom" to look at the pictures and to summarize the definitions which provide this closer definition. And we must ask these pictures and definitions: do the infinite/eternal, the absolute telos, one's eternal blessedness, as they speak to the self about the content of the good and the true, express themselves in a universal pattern that is authoritative for all human individuals, every place and every time? If so, does this pattern take the form of an objective standard expressed as a

---

125 Ibid., pp. 178 and 178n.; (KW 12.1:199); SV 9:166; (7:166).
126 Ibid., p. 494; (KW 12.1:556); SV 10:225; (7:485).

set of rules or list of virtues? If not, what is the form of this pattern, and how does it emerge? Let us begin with the definitions already elaborated above.

Putting it in summary fashion, what happens to me when I open myself to the infinite and the eternal, to my absolute telos and eternal blessedness, to my self's possibility and the necessity of obeying its specificity, to confession before the all-knowing one and to the "god" who is "all-things-are-possible"—what happens is this: I become absorbed in what is essential and qualitative, and become indifferent to what is accidental, contingent, quantitative; I experience a dying away from the easy unreflective life of immediacy, and find myself engaged in the struggle to appropriate the hidden truth of inwardness which can be possessed only in the certainty/uncertainty of faith; I find the meaning of my existence as a human being centred in personal, inward, infinite, passionate, interested subjectivity and know that such subjectivity is lost when I focus my being on and in the objectivity of rational, disinterested universals in the form of abstract concepts; I feel compelled to reject my self-sufficiency, to acknowledge the totality of guilt-consciousness and to undergo self-annihilation; I come to believe in my infinite dignity as an individual, in the possibility of my eternal blessedness, and to see clearly the ephemerality of temporal possessions and pleasures; I become willing to risk commitment to absolute ends even though it means the loss and sacrifice of relative ends.

Are these grand generalizations and their rich complex terminologies really nothing more than statements of the *formal* reality of what it means to be free, without a hint of what the concrete *content* of a free act might or must be? Or do they have very specific implications for the behaviour of anyone who confesses them? Does Kierkegaard's whole philosophy of self-actualization come down finally to nothing more than Polonius's pompous, shallow advice to Laertes, "This above all: to thine own self be true, / And it must follow, as the night the day, / Thou canst not then be false to any man," advice on the same level as "Neither a borrower nor a lender be"?[127] Does one's "eternal blessedness" really amount to nothing more than the cheap eudaemonism of "be happy!", or at best a philosophy of enlightened self-interest?

We have translated Kierkegaard's *evige Salighed* as "eternal blessedness" rather than "eternal happiness" to indicate that he does not advocate an undefined vague eudaemonism. Now this thesis must be substantiated

---

[127] William Shakespeare, *Hamlet*, act I, sc. III.

by clarifying the content of freedom as "eternal blessedness." "Happiness" has been a markedly ambiguous idea ever since Aristotle's exposition of ευδαιμονια (*eudaimonia*) in his *Nicomachean Ethics*. For example, an acrimonious debate emerged (in 1989) about the meaning of Joseph Campbell's prescription for happiness, "Follow your bliss." There were accusations that he "sanctions selfishness on a colossal scale," and that his vague contentless description of happiness allowed him to harbour anti-Semitic and anti-black sentiments.[128]

These are the issues that must be faced in any evaluation of Kierkegaard's depiction of the human self's becoming itself in relation to one's "absolute telos" and one's "eternal blessedness." The point has been repeatedly made that for Kierkegaard each stage or sphere carries along and includes the previous one(s) within itself. Hence the religious sphere is always ethical, and he makes this point in *Postscript* by formally denominating religiousness A as the "ethical-religious" sphere, which he says is important because "ethically accentuating existing ... hinders the existing one in abstractly remaining within immanence."[129] In other words, becoming open to the religious resource, with its encouragement and its new "revelations" about the human condition, does not relieve the individual from making ethical decisions and from performing ethical actions. Quite the opposite, because the religious resource is precisely what demands and enables one to *become* one's ideal, infinite, potential self in *actuality*. And Kierkegaard does not hesitate to describe these ethical enactments in very specific language.

One of the clearest examples is Climacus's description of what it means to relate to one's absolute telos (eternal blessedness). He is saying that if one relates thus *passionately*, then it "consists in expressing this existentially in existence." Such a relationship is not simply giving evidence *about* it, but consists in "transforming one's own existence into a testimony to it." The relationship is actual "only when one allows resignation to examine one's entire immediacy" in such a way that one realizes that "the individual must not have one's life in [immediacy],"

---

128 See Brendan Gill's original attack on Campbell in the *New York Review of Books*, 28 September 1989, pp. 16–19, and the exchange of letters in response in the issue of 9 November 1989, pp. 57–61. Gill not only accuses Campbell of presenting (in the TV series "Joseph Campbell and the Power of Myth") a superficial concept of bliss or happiness, but also insists that this view of bliss fostered and sanctioned a certain social-political position which found expression in forms of fascism and racism in Campbell's life, and which even encouraged an other-worldly spirituality in league with a crass materialism.

129 *Postscript*, p. 507; (KW 12.1:572–3); SV 10:239; (7:499).

because one sees "what can happen in one's life" if one lives in sheer immediacy. And what does happen?

Someone who is situated with a wife and children in a good living, cozily indoors, and is a councillor of justice, a "serious man" who nevertheless wants to do something for his eternal happiness, provided the duties of his office and his wife and children permit it, an enthusiast who, by Jove, is not afraid of spending ten rix-dollars on it, may say, "Well, all right, go ahead with this inspection business, but when, as quickly as possible, it is over, then we will come to mediation, won't we?" [130]

What's wrong with mediation in "ethical and ethical-religious matters"? Of course mediation is inescapable when one "relates ... relatively to relative [ends]." But "Mediation wants to make existence easier for the existing-one by leaving out an absolute relationship to an absolute τελος [*telos*]." On the other hand, mediation does not absolve one from "the agonizing self-contradiction of worldly passion [which] results from the fact that the individual relates *absolutely* to a relative τελος [*telos*]," such as "making a prudent business transaction, a profitable speculation in the stock-market, instead of a daring risk" for the sake of an absolute end. But, Climacus maintains, "to relate absolutely to that which is relative is the most common form of madness." And then he becomes very specific about the manifestations of this kind of madness: "vanity, avarice, envy."[131]

In other words, the transformation of one's existence that comes with relating absolutely to an absolute telos has very specific "content," namely, the elimination of these manifestations. In one of his *Upbuilding Discourses in Various Spirits* (written the year after *Postscript*), Kierkegaard makes the same point but expands the language. He says that when one "has forgotten the eternal," one is subject to a "deceptive ignorance" about what really is present and operative within one's existence. And then he gives another very specific list of manifestations of the lack of relationship to the eternal: "hate, anger, vengeance, despondency, depression, despair, fear of the future, trust in the world, faith in oneself, pride that mixes in even with sympathy, envy that mixes in even with friendship."[132]

---

130 Ibid., pp. 353–4; (KW 12.1:394–5); SV 10:889f.; (7:342).
131 Ibid., pp. 377–9; (KW 12.1:421–3); SV 10:111-113; (7:366–7).
132 *Upbuilding Discourses in Various Spirits*, "Part One: An Occasional Discourse" (*Purity of Heart*), pp. 51–2; (KW 15:23); SV 11:29; (8:133).

What, then, is the positive content of the free act which occurs when one relates to "an eternal blessedness," when one relates absolutely to one's absolute telos? What is the positive that is implied by this list of negative traits or dispositions? Why do we not find anywhere in the authorship a list of virtues in contrast to this list of vices (sins)? This question takes us to the heart of what comprises the "goodness" of that "self" which "is freedom." And to answer this question requires us to draw upon some materials from the authorship which up to this point have not been dealt with directly or at length.

First, it will be helpful to look at the very general point of Kierkegaard's distinction between goodness and virtue. This distinction is important because when he speaks of "virtue" he is using it in its Aristotelian sense rather than in one modern sense of a moral action in conformity to a standard of right imposed by an external authority. The difference between goodness and virtue came to him early on in his reading of Aristotle (i.e., from February 1843 onward). He finds that Aristotle distinguishes between moral and intellectual virtues and considers intellectual contemplation (of the unchanging truths of science and philosophical wisdom) as "the highest happiness [*Lyksalighed*]." Of course he disagrees with the latter view but excuses Aristotle because he "has not understood the self deeply enough" since he "has not perceived spirit as a [human] determinant." On the other hand, he says that Aristotle is entirely right in maintaining that the virtue of the "middle-way" applies only to "the so-called moral virtues," because the latter do battle only in the field of inclination and disinclination rather than in that of good and evil.[133] How does Kierkegaard understand this latter distinction between inclination/disinclination and good/evil?

Kierkegaard reads Aristotle as holding that "the moral virtues have to do only with the irrational part of the soul." Why? How? Kierkegaard obviously has in mind Aristotle's division of the human soul into the rational and the irrational, and his definition of the "moral" task as the bringing of (irrational) human desires and appetites under the control of reason, rather than leaving them to operate irrationally on their own. How is this task accomplished? It must be noted that virtue is distinct from the free act, because, Kierkegaard notes, "The free act is the discrete; virtue is the continuous. [Aristotle] therefore says most profoundly that free action lies totally within a human being's power; virtue

---

133 *Journals*, 3292; IV C 25; 3892; IV C 26; 892; IV C 16.

does not, except with respect to the beginning, because it is a competence (continuity)."[134]

In other words, moral virtue for Aristotle is an inbred disposition or character that prompts one to make the right (rational) choices, that is, always to choose the mean between two extremes (e. g., courage, between timidity and foolhardiness, or liberality, between avarice and prodigality). Such character is the product of the development of natural gifts through moral education. So it involves one's whole life including the social/political provision of a good standard of material existence, stable family life, a good education, and including one's personal possession of health, intelligence, charm, beauty, etc. So virtue (αρετη, *arete*) is whatever provides humans with the "good life" or "well-being," and ευδαιμονια (*eudaimonia*) is that general state of well-being, not just a psychological feeling of being "happy."

Kierkegaard recognizes the operative validity of this view of virtue and sees that it has a role to play in the ethical life as commonly practised. So in his "Little Sketch" of the ethical dialectic of communication, he says, "In regard to the ethical and the ethical-religious, the genuine communication and instruction is *education* or *upbringing*. By upbringing one becomes that which one is essentially regarded to be (a horse, if it is trained and the trainer has good sense, becomes precisely a horse). Upbringing begins with regarding the one who must be brought up as being κατα δυναμιν [potentially] that which he ought to become, and, by regarding him from this point of view, one brings it out of him. One *brings it up*; consequently, it is there."

Certainly this kind of "upbringing" can develop dispositions that favour one's well-being and can root out inclinations that work against it. So we have heard Kierkegaard admit that it often takes "long, long continuous effort ... to get rid of a habit, even if one ever so earnestly has made a resolution." Indeed, when "one is fighting against things beyond one's control," then the fight "at first ... for a time elicits rather than removes them, until finally one gradually becomes victorious in a long, long drawn-out battle." Hence "in relation to finitude (for example,

---

[134] Ibid., 893; IV C 16; obviously *Discrete* in the Danish should not be translated "discreet" (as by Hong) but "discrete" in contrast to "continuous" (the Danish word is used in both senses). The same point shows up again a year later in *Fragments* where Kierkegaard quotes (paraphrases) Aristotle as saying (in *Nicomachean Ethics*, III, 5, 1114a), "The depraved person and the virtuous person presumably do not have power over their moral condition, but in the beginning they did have the power to become one or the other" (p. 21) (KW 7:17); SV 6:21; (4:186).

physical well-being) one actually must be compelled," because "finite decisions are in a certain sense too light for one to come at them from infinitude. ... To 'be compelled' is the only help in finite affairs."[135]

But Kierkegaard contends that the upbringing aimed at by ethical and ethical-religious communication is not the evocation of virtuous dispositions or competencies which provide continuous control of one's behaviour. Rather, ethical upbringing consists of the demand for and the encouragement of "discrete" free acts which "lie totally within a human being's power." Ethical upbringing results not in the "aesthetic capability [*Kunnen*, i.e., "being able"] ... of competence," but in "oughtness-capability" (*Skullen-Kunne*), i.e., being able to do what one *ought*, which is a free voluntary act rather than one determined by an inbred disposition. It is a free act because "in ethical capability and religious [capability] the transition is passionate [*pathetisk*]" and therefore involves "the leap." In this distinction between virtue and the free act Kierkegaard goes to the heart of what it means to be a self, the heart of what he calls "the problem of what it is to be a human being, of whether you and I [each] really is a human being," because "The voluntary [*Det Frivillige*] is the precise form for qualitatively being spirit."[136]

Kierkegaard further differentiates his view of human "goodness" and "blessedness" from that of Aristotle in his "decisive definition" arrived at in *Sickness*: "the opposite of sin [and despair] is not virtue but faith."[137] In other words, what goes wrong in an individual struggling to become self is not made right by the inculcation of right dispositions which produce well-being. Rather, release and fulfilment come only with the individual inward struggle to believe that one's absolute telos is true and meaningful because one believes that all-things-are-possible—and believes this in the face of objective uncertainty and discouragement. Kierkegaard notes that "πιστις [*pistis*, faith] in the classical Greek means the conviction ... which relates to probability," whereas "Christianity ... relates πιστις to the improbable." So for both Plato and Aristotle "faith is a concept that belongs in the sphere of the intellectual," whereas "Christianly, faith is at home in the existential [*Existentielle*]."[138]

---

135 For quotations in the last two paragraphs, see *Journals*, 650:12, VIII^2; 1260, X^2 243; 1253, VIII^1 178.
136 Ibid., 653:4, 5, 10; 657, pp. 304, 307; VIII^2 B 85:3, 85:8, 89, pp. 186, 189; 1258, X^2 A 159.
137 *Sickness*, p. 213; (KW 19:82); SV 15:136; (11:194); see also same statement on pp. 1255; (KW 19:49, 124); SV 15:105, 173; (11:161, 234).
138 *Journals*, 7; X^2 A 354; 180; XI^1 A 237.

Then Kierkegaard gives an explication of this existential kind of faith (which we have looked at before above at note 116) that broadens it beyond a merely Christian phenomenon, and makes it applicable to the ethical-religious sphere. "Faith," he says, "is the expression for the relationship of personal-individuality [*Personlighed*] to personal-individuality" (and in this late journal entry of 1854 the Danish *Personlighed* clearly is used in Webster's first meaning of "personality" as "the quality or state of being a person," which is equivalent to Kierkegaard's meaning of "self." So in *Sickness* the Hongs choose the term "personhood" as a translation).[139] And the faith-relationship spoken of is twofold. On the one hand, "Personhood [being-a-person or self] is not a sum of propositions nor is it something immediately accessible; being-a-person consists in a curving inwardly into oneself, a *clausum* [enclosed place], an αδυτον [*aduton*, sanctuary], a μυστηριον [*musterion*, secret]; personhood consists of this 'in-there,' ... the in-there which one, him/herself being-a-person, must relate to believingly. Between personhood and personhood no other relationship is possible."

So, on the other hand, this believing relationship must prevail not only in one's relationship to oneself but also in the relationship between any two entities which possess the quality of personhood. For the "two most passionate lovers who ever lived," their love "can never come to more than the fact that the one *believes* that the other loves him or her" (emphasis added). Likewise, "In the purely personal relationship between God as personhood, and the believer as personhood *in existence*, lies the concept 'faith,'" because "faith is oriented toward will, personhood, not toward intellectuality."[140]

Now the question remains: if the good act, the one thing needful in a particular situation, is not determined by inbred habitual virtue, but consists of an act that is "totally within the power of the human being" and so performed "willingly" at each "discrete" moment of decision, and that issues from one's most inward, uniquely personal, passionate believing (in the face of objective uncertainty), then how does the agent determine the *positive content* of the one and only good and right possibility in this situation? If the agent does not rely on his virtue (in the sense of the application either of a rational principle [the golden mean] or of a

---

139 *Sickness*, p. 173; (KW 19:40); SV 15:97; (11:152).

140 *Journals*, 180; XI[1] A 237. Another very suggestive way that Kierkegaard differentiates his position from that of Aristotle and the ancient Greeks appears in his differentiation between the ancient and the modern sense of the "tragic." See *Either/Or*, 1:137–47; (KW 3:139–49); SV 2:129–38; (1:117–27).

set of universal principles), then how does the agent's "believing" relationship with one's neighbour and with the eternal operate so as to enable the agent to "perceive" (*erkende*) and to "choose" the one thing needful, the absolute good? Or, what does it mean that "faith is oriented toward will"?

First, Kierkegaard contends that ethical choosing in conjunction with religious believing activates and fulfils a "higher nature" of human being, as distinguished from a "lower nature." Secondly, he uses one single term (concept, category) to designate the positive and definitive quality of the active relationship which religious believing and ethical choosing establishes, namely, the quality of love. Let us now proceed to explore these two concepts (but primarily the latter) as a way of getting at the content of the free and good act.

7

My Self: A Task
Part 5: Love as Freedom's Content

We will proceed first to see how Kierkegaard distinguishes the "higher nature" of the human individual as the vicinage of freedom, and we will need then to demonstrate that the only *positive* definition of the content of the higher life and hence of "freedom" is provided by his concept of love.

The distinction between lower and higher natures is especially important because it sets the location of and directs our attention to the functioning of what Kierkegaard calls "the will" or the act of "willing."[1] In this crucial passage in *Sickness* he is taking to task what he calls the Socratic definition of sin as ignorance, which presumes that if one understands what is right, then "it would quickly induce one to do it." He says that this definition is defective because "it lacks a dialectical determinant appropriate to the transition from having understood [*forstaaet*] something to doing it," namely, the element of "willing." And he accuses the Greek way of thinking of "not having the courage to declare that a person knowingly does wrong, knows what is right and does the wrong."

In order to maintain and to explain the reality of freedom and the voluntary, is Kierkegaard, then, resorting to what Donald Davidson calls some "mysterious act of the will or special attitude or episode of willing," which amounts to "an embarrassing entity that has to be added to the world's furniture," in other words, willing as an arbitrary, capricious,

---

1 *Sickness*, pp. 224f.; (KW 19:93f.); SV 15:145–7; (11:204f.). Kierkegaard uses the substantive "the will" (*Villien*, which in today's Danish is *Viljen*), but the Hongs certainly represent Kierkegaard's thinking correctly by translating it "willing," since "will" is not a thing or entity for him but an event or action taking place in a dialectical relationship. The same is true of *Erkjende* and *Erkjendelse*, although I think "perceiving" or "apprehending" is closer to Kierkegaard's meaning than the Hongs' "knowing" and "comprehension."

uncaused choosing (see the summary of Davidson's position at the beginning of chapter 6)? We have gone to great lengths to reject this accusation by showing how Kierkegaard agrees with Davidson's contention that a free act is still a "caused" act, not caused in a deterministic sense, but certainly performed "because" of who the agent is and how the agent, within him/herself, comes to decision and action. But we did note that although Davidson develops a very subtle and complex analysis of how a human being comes freely to intentionality, he provides an inadequate account of how the agent moves from intention to action. So in our next and concluding chapter, we must show finally just what Kierkegaard means by "willing" in relation to self-deception, and then proceed to see whether his analysis provides an adequate account of how one moves *freely* from intention to action, i. e., indeterminately. But for our present purposes we will limit our analysis to what is meant by "higher" and "lower" natures, and how "love" defines the content of an act by one's "higher" nature.

DISTINCTION BETWEEN HIGHER AND LOWER NATURES

Unsurprisingly, he specifically designates the "higher nature" as the human being's capacity for and openness to "ethical and ethical-religious perceiving [*Erkjende*: apprehending, cognition]" of "what is right" (*det Rette*), or, in the language of *Postscript*, of one's "absolute good" or "eternal blessedness." And he says that this perception unavoidably leads one to the crisis of arriving at "decisions and conclusions." On the other hand, what Kierkegaard attributes to the "lower nature" may come as a surprise. He does not mean simply the determinant of "sensuousness" or what he occasionally calls the "animal determinant"—although he everywhere assumes that these are qualifications of human nature as such. Rather, in *Sickness* he specifically categorizes as "lower" the entire realm of "aesthetic and metaphysical perceiving" which human beings are constantly pursuing and whose discoveries and insights were regarded (Kierkegaard felt in his day) as ultimate truth. Certainly, at this realm's lowest level of aesthetic taste and sensibility in desires, "truth" and "goodness" are reduced to a matter of "pleasant or unpleasant."[2] But

---

[2] *Journals*, 4483; XI¹ A 475. This is an entry from late 1854, and manifests Kierkegaard's general pessimism of those years: "Humankind is a synthesis, a composite of the lower and the higher, and from birth on it is almost completely in the power of the lower. The pleasant—and the unpleasant—are what determine it, and it remains just about that way throughout life for most human beings."

Kierkegaard's central concern and object of attack is the claim of the System (Hegel's) to have attained the highest and indeed the final truth by means of the abstract, objective, disinterested speculation of metaphysical thinking in and for itself, as an end in itself.

That this is the issue in the use of this language in *Sickness* is clear from the fact that the language derives from *Postscript*. The central problem that Climacus attacks, in order to clear the way for the last main section on religiousness, is the question: which is "higher," possibility or actuality? His answer: "Poetically and intellectually possibility is higher in comparison with actuality, the aesthetic and the intellectual being disinterested." But "ethically regarded actuality is higher than possibility." The former view produces the cataclysmic result that "[i]t is decisively concluded that thinking is the highest [stage]." Hence, "scientifically everything rises from the lower to the higher, and so thinking becomes the highest [stage]," and "as the highest it is the last."[3]

From this perspective "the individual is regarded as related to the development of the human spirit as an animal-specimen to its species, as if development of spirit were something that one generation could bequeath to another; and as if it were the generation that is determined as spirit and not the individuals." On the contrary (Climacus argues),

> Development of spirit is self-activity [something the individual self does]; the spiritually developed individual takes his development with him in death. ... Ethics concentrates on the individual, and ethically understood the task of every individual is to become a whole human being, just as it is the ethical presupposition that everyone is born in the state of being able to become that. ... In existence the abstract scientific definition of being human is something that may be higher than being a particular [*enkelt*] existing human being, or perhaps something lower; but in any case, there is in existence nothing but the particular human being. As regards existence, it will not do to unify the differences in terms of thinking, because the advancing method does not fit or correspond with existing *qua* human being. ... As regards existence, thinking is by no means higher than imagination and feeling, but is coordinate.[4]

It should be clear, then, that Kierkegaard in no way denies the reality and inescapable functioning of the social and "scientific" approaches to human existence. Human beings certainly are social animals, and much

---

[3] *Postscript*, pp. 282, 284, 307; (KW 12.1:318, 320, 344); SV 10:24f., 46; (7:273, 275, 298).
[4] Ibid., pp. 308–10; (KW 12.1:345-7); SV 10:47-9; (7:299–300).

of their activity is explainable as determined by and as examples of those aspects or dimensions of human nature. So he says, "sociality [*det Sociale*] is related essentially to the mind-body synthesis,"[5] that is, to the "lower" nature of the human being where individuals use their instincts and intelligence to adapt to the problems and demands of surviving and living "pleasantly" as members of a group (family, community, state, species). At this level there is no attempt by the mind-body relation ("infinite/finite") to "relate to itself," that is, become conscious of itself as unique "self" ("spirit") and as possessing the capacity for self-determination, that is, freedom. And yet it is precisely this capacity of human beings that defines what it is to be a *human* animal.

Hence (as stated in the *Postscript* passage above), although selfhood or spirituality is a universal potentiality of human nature, it is acquired or actualized ("developed") only in and by the individual and cannot be inherited, no matter what the social environment. The actualized self is not related to its generation and society as "the animal specimen to its species." So Kierkegaard says, "'the crowd' is an animal qualification," and "eternal life is simply not social." Hence "community [*Samfund*] cannot be deduced from 'spirit,'" and the church's notion of "congregation" (*Menighed*) is nothing more than "an accommodation, a concession in consideration of how little we are [spirit] or can endure being spirit."[6]

Kierkegaard's attack on the (supposedly) scientific notion that the individual is only an example or specimen of the species also finds expression in his persistent attack on the notion of the "crowd" versus the individual throughout the authorship.[7] To subsume the individual within the mass or crowd, for the individual to submit to and to lose oneself in a larger social unit of any kind, is seen by Kierkegaard as the loss of essential human existence as such. Of course, his major attack on the crowd

---

5 *Journals*, 4341; X⁴ A 226.
6 Idem.
7 Our treatment of Kierkegaard's evaluation of the social/political dimension of human existence will be reserved for the second (theological) part of this study of his concept of the self. This delay will allow the consideration of his clearly theological materials along with his philosophical materials in a concluding critique of the strengths and weaknesses of his anthropological ontology, coming as it will immediately following a summary presentation of his theological concepts of faith and love.

In the meantime, those with a special interest in the topic should read the thorough and perceptive account of Kierkegaard's own social-political setting and of the social-political concerns expressed throughout his authorship in Bruce Kirmmse's *Kierkegaard in Golden Age Denmark*. See also the expositions of "Kierkegaard's Politics" and "Kierkegaard's Sociology" in Merold Westphal's *Kierkegaard's Critique of Reason and Society*. Westphal makes innovative use of the materials in Kierkegaard's *Two Ages (A Literary Review)*.

mentality is to be found in *Two Ages (A Literary Review)*, which in turn is based on *The Concept of Anxiety*, where he insists that every human being is the original Adam/Eve as regards the experience of "subjective angst" in response to the demand that one become spirit (self) in freedom, even while recognizing that we all experience the "objective angst" involved in the burden of inherited instincts and social conditioning.

Perhaps, however, this view of mass humanity receives its most vivid expression in some satiric and yet sympathetic pictures in *Sickness*. He restates his general thesis that "every human being is an individual human being and is to become conscious of being an individual human being. If human beings are first permitted to run together in what Aristotle calls the animal category—the crowd—then this abstraction ... comes to be regarded as something; then it does not take long before this abstraction becomes God." And in three different passages he gives similar pictures of the dire consequences of the failure to become one's authentic self. They show that each of the various forms of this failure (i.e., forms of despair) finds expression in and is compensated for by the individual's losing oneself in the sociality of the crowd.

The first instance is that of the person who lives in the despair of a fantasyland. "But to become fantastic in this way ... does not mean ... that a person cannot go on living fairly well, ... and it may not be detected that in a deeper sense he lacks a self. ... The greatest hazard of all, losing the self, can occur very quietly in the world, as if it were nothing at all. No other loss can occur so quietly; any other loss—an arm, a leg, five dollars, a wife—is sure to be noticed." The second instance is that of the person who weakly gives up in the struggle to become one's unique self, and settles for the life of immediacy where rules the dialectic of the pleasant and the unpleasant, of good luck, bad luck, fate. "The whole question of the self becomes a kind of false door with nothing behind it in the background of his soul." He forgets it and "finds it almost ludicrous, especially when he is together with other competent and dynamic men who have an aptitude for real life. Charming! He has been happily married now for several years, as it says in novels, a dynamic and enterprising man, a father and citizen, perhaps even an important man; ... his conduct is based on respect of persons or on the way others regard one, and others judge according to one's social position." The third instance is that of a person who has retained a sharp sense and even love of one's self as unique and distinct, but keeps this awareness in the back of one's soul behind "a carefully closed door." Yet "outwardly he looks every bit 'a real man.' He is a university graduate, husband, father, a competent public office holder, a respectable father, pleasant company, very gentle to his wife, solicitude personified to his children." He longs for solitude, to be with one's self, but he never admits it, because most people "need the soothing lullaby of social life in order to be able to eat, drink, sleep, fall in love, etc. ... [I]n the constant sociality of our day we shrink from solitude to the point that no use of it is known other than as a punishment for criminals."[8]

Let us remember that we are seeking guidance as to what is the content of the good act, of one's eternal blessedness. And by specifying what Kierkegaard means by the "lower" nature of human life and activity, it is hoped that he will indicate, at least by inference, what is the content of the "higher." This detailed depiction of those two aspects of human existence lived on its lower level (the metaphysical/scientific and the aesthetic/social) at least helps us to be as vivid as possible about the location or occasion of the battle of what Kierkegaard calls "willing" the good, and thereby to take one more step in its "closer definition."

He sees the fragile consciousness of my self (as potentiality and task) as under constant attack, subject to powerful absorbing allurement and insidious temptation from both aspects. On the one hand, with their overpowering grandeur and constancy, the abstract universalities of philosophy and the sciences press their claim to be *ultimate truth*. On the other hand, with its imperious undeniable demands, the concrete immediacy of the whole complex morass of my sensuousness pushes its claim to be *life itself* (sensuousness as my body, including all its relationships both social and physical out to the ends of the universe, that sensuousness in which our consciousness has its origins and from which there is not a single instant of escape, until it, and with it my consciousness, dies). And the struggle of my self-conscious self for fulfilment is infinitely complicated by the fact that universals/laws are indeed a kind of truth which I cannot deny or ignore in my becoming self, and that sensate and sentient physicality provides the indispensable occasion and situation for the actualization of self. So I-in-my-self-consciousness stand, I exist, I live at the intersection of, in the interaction between, on the one hand, these two overpowering undeniable magnitudes, and on the other, an awareness which I cannot cast away or get rid of, namely that to have a self, to be a self, is both eternity's greatest and infinite *concession* to me, and also eternity's *claim* (inescapable requirement) upon me.[9]

---

8 *Sickness*, pp. 249, 165, 189f., 197; (KW 19:117f., 32f., 56, 63f.); SV 15:167, 90, 111f., 118f.; (11:227, 146, 168, 175).

9 Ibid., p. 154; (KW 19:21); SV 15:80; (11:135).

"WILLING" LOCATED BETWEEN THE TWO

But we have to ask again: does this location and description of the situation of willing help define the content of the act which occurs when willing obeys the individual's higher nature, that is, when the self wills to do the one thing needful as defined by the self's ethical and ethical-religious perception of the good? Our answer is still nothing more than a definition by negation. The good act, in which the unique and individual self becomes itself and achieves eternal blessedness through its ethical and religious commitment, clearly is not sensuous apprehension of the beautiful in its ideal possibility or the achievement of the pleasant in psycho-physical immediacy with one's socio-physical environment. Nor, on the other hand, is the good act simply the comprehension of philosophical and/or scientific universals into which the individual is absorbed, and eventually lost, as nothing more than an ephemeral example of the universal. Anyone who finds fulfilment, or locates one's ultimate truth, in these (very real) dimensions of human existence loses one's self rather than finds it. Such a one has given unconditional commitment to relative ends and conditional commitment to absolute ends, and therefore such a one lives in "madness." And the manifestations of this madness can be specified: vanity, avarice, envy, pride, hate, anger, vengeance, despair, fear of the future (see notes 125 and 126 in chapter 6).

So the exploration of Kierkegaard's distinction between the higher and lower natures of the human individual has defined more closely the *locus* of goodness and blessedness, but not its positive content. Is there no way to specify the quality of that act which one performs unconditionally in obedience to one's ethical awareness and vision of the absolute demand of the eternal (of "all-things-are-possible"), no way to qualify it in such a way that one's "inner necessity" not only determines the "how" but also commands the "what" of the act? What is the quality that motivates that act and defines the resulting relationship of the self with itself, with others, with the eternal, that relationship which evokes and imparts infinite dignity and worth ("eternal blessedness") to the one who acts in this way?

LOVE AS CONTENT OF FREEDOM

Kierkegaard finds only one word with which to point to this quality: love. But as with such terms or concepts as angst, despair, repentance, self, and faith, he gives to "love" his own peculiar, complicated but revealing definition and description.

Love as Freedom's Content 331

There are no significant anticipations of the treatment of this concept as contained in *Works of Love*. But *Works* clearly makes two references to earlier materials on the content of goodness. First, we have already noted (in chapter 1) that early on (in *Fragments*) Kierkegaard draws an analogy between the passion of love (which unites the divine and the human in equality) and the passion of faith (which reconciles the contradiction between reason and the absolute paradox). In fact, this analogy can be interpreted as meaning that "faith" and "love" are two ways of describing the same ethical-religious relationship. And this identification is important for our present question about how to specify the essential content or quality of the good act. If the opposite of sin (goodness) is not virtue but faith, then we can also say that goodness is essentially love. And, as we shall see, this relationship of faith and love means that there is no authentic loving that is not grounded in believing, and no authentic believing that does not find expression in loving.

This relationship is assumed throughout *Works of Love*. The very first topic is "Love's Hidden Life," in which it is asserted that there is no word or deed which as such "unconditionally demonstrates love." This is so because love has its origin in a "hidden place ... in a human being's most-inward-depths [*Inderste*]," a "place you cannot see." Therefore, "one must believe in love. ... This is the first and last thing to be said about love if one is know what love is." In the middle of the book is a section on "Love Believes All Things," and therefore "Love is the very opposite of mistrust." And in its "Conclusion" Kierkegaard says that the secret of the power of love was expressed by Jesus when he said to the centurion, "Be it unto you as you believed" (Mt. 8:13). So "it is eternally certain that it will happen to you as you believe." Only if you love, will you know love from the eternal. And two years after *Works of Love* he makes this relationship explicit in a journal entry. He says that faith (like love) cannot be seen, and so we cannot be sure a person has it. "But faith shall be perceived [recognized] in love. ... Because love ... is love's-deed [*Gjerning*]."[10]

Secondly, the definition-by-negation of that goodness that is determined by the self's "inner necessity" (as noted above) is repeated in *Works*, only now the positive content or quality of that goodness is desig-

---

10 *Works of Love*, pp. 30, 26, 32, 216, 346f.; SV 12:18f., 14, 21, 221, 360; (9:16f., 12f., 19f., 219, 358f.); *Journals*, 2423; X[1] 489. This interpretation of Jesus' words to the centurion is picked up and used again in *Sickness*, where these words are taken as the Christian alternative to Descartes's *cogito ergo sum* [p. 224; (KW 19:93); SV 15:146; (11:204)].

nated as "love." Kierkegaard is interpreting the claim that "Love Hopes All Things."[11] He is saying that the lover believes in "the possibility of the good" for every other human being, no matter how wretched the other's present condition. Hope is integral to love; so the lover cannot despair of or give up on the most wretched of human beings.

If one despairs of others, it is proof that one is in despair him/herself. "It must be because one is not a lover," because one is weighed down by worldliness, earthly passions, shrewdness, anger, envy, malice, cowardly fearful small-mindedness.

When all these ... are in a human being ... then love is not present. [And] if there is less love in a person, there is also less of the eternal; but if there is less of the eternal, there is also less possibility, less readiness [*Sands*] for possibility (because possibility emerges from the fact that the eternal in time arouses [*berører*] the eternal in a human being; if there is nothing eternal in the human being, the arousing by the eternal is futile, and there is no possibility). ... The lover on the contrary hopes all things; nothing [in the other] ... taints his/her hope or falsifies possibility. Every morning, yes, every moment, she/he renews hope and enlivens possiblity.

In this passage it is clear that Kierkegaard is proposing a positive content or quality of the act(s) in which one relates absolutely to one's absolute telos or eternal blessedness, in which one becomes in actuality one's infinite, ideal "self's possibility" as defined by one's "inner necessity"—in contrast to the purely negative definition of that act in *Postscript* and in the discourse "On the Occasion of a Confessional." This quality which specifies the content is "love." And it is very significant and noteworthy that he posits an essential interrelationship among love, the eternal, and possibility, because "possibility" and "the eternal" have proved to be key concepts throughout this entire study of Kierkegaard's understanding of "my self." And his uses of these terms here are especially significant because they are a marked step beyond *Postscript* and anticipate their use in *Sickness*.

"The eternal" here refers both to a kind of orientation that lodges in the human being, as well as to a transcendent reality which enters human "time" in order to "touch" and thus arouse the eternal in the human

---

11 1 Cor. 13:7. Again, Kierkegaard's singular *Alt* should be translated "all things" in accord with the Greek παντα (*panta*). The following quotations are from *Works of Love*, pp. 239–41; SV 12:245–8; (9:243–6).

being. It is this being touched by the eternal that opens up and enables the fulfilment of "possibility" in the human being's actuality. And the possibility grasped in the understanding of the lover is "that at every moment the possibility of the good exists for [every] other human being." This is the case, because for the lover, "if possibility is kept pure, all things are possible [*er Alt muligt*]."[12] Here Kierkegaard has taken the phrase "all things" from "love hopes all things" and uses it to qualify "possibility," obviously an anticipation and source of the use of the identical Danish words when, in *Sickness*, he says, "God is: all things are possible [*Alt er muligt*]."[13] "Love," then, is the best key we have to the definitive quality and content of that act in which the self relates to its absolute telos and eternal blessedness, in which the "self's possibility" becomes actualized in accord with the "self's [inner] necessity." What unique meaning, then, does Kierkegaard impart to this word, which has become in our day such an empty cliché whose meaninglessness is celebrated in numerous novels and movies?

Before we answer this question, we must again face a question already raised several times. Granted, *Works of Love* is our only source for an exposition of Kierkegaard's concept of love. But he himself labels it as "Some Christian Reflections in the Form of Discourses." How then can its materials be applied to our question: how far, according to Kierkegaard, can the human self go in becoming itself in actuality within the limits of religiousness A? With this question we must recognize that we stand at that borderline where Kierkegaard the humanist takes his first declared step into the sphere of religiousness B, into his new authorship, into his new calling as Kierkegaard the theologian (a step taken in the months just prior to writing *Works*, in the third part of *Upbuilding Discourses in Various Spirits*, entitled "Gospel of Suffering. Christian Discourses"). And yet, we propose, there are in *Works* several perspectives which make some of Kierkegaard's reflections on love applicable and relevant to the individual who is struggling to become self within the limits of religiousness A.

Without doubt or question, Kierkegaard considers love—"spiritually understood" as "duty"—to be one of the unique contributions of Christian faith. In regard to the imperative, "You *shall* love," he says that we must "humbly confess with the wonder of faith that such a command did not spring up in any human heart." He asks us to ponder what the

---

12 Ibid., pp. 239f.; SV 12:245–7; (9:243f.).
13 *Sickness*, pp. 173f.; (KW 19:40); SV 15:97; (11:153).

human condition "would have been if Christianity had not come into the world. What courage it takes to say for the first time, 'You *shall* love,' or, more correctly, what divine authority it takes in order, with these words, to turn upside down the concepts and ideas of the natural human being! For there at the boundary where human speech halts and courage fails, there revelation breaks forth with divine creativeness and proclaims what is not difficult to understand in the sense of profundity or human parallels, but which still did not rise up in any human heart."

He draws the same sharp line when he insists that

> Secular or merely human reflection recognizes many kinds of love. ... With Christianity the opposite is the case. It recognizes only one kind of love, spiritual love. ... Merely human reflection conceives of love *either* simply as something purely spontaneous such as instinctual urge, inclination (sensuous love, ... friendship), ... *or* as something which ought to be aspired to and attained because reason perceives that to be loved and favoured, as well as to have people one loves and favours, is an earthly good. All this is really no concern of Christianity. ... Christianity lets all this have its validity and significance externally, but at the same time by its doctrine of love, ... it would have the change of infinity take place in inwardness [*Indvortes*].[14]

It must be noted, however, that the line drawn here by Kierkegaard is between the peculiarly and uniquely Christian experience of God's love and the perception of love derived from "the secular or merely human reflection" of what he repeatedly calls "the natural human being [*det naturlige Menneske*]." There is no reference to the intermediate sphere of religiousness A; indeed, after *Postscript* the distinction between religiousness A and B is not referred to again in the authorship or in the journals.[15] And yet we have drawn on both the discourses (*Purity of Heart*) and the pseudonymous authorship (*Sickness*) for depictions of the possibilities of ethical-religious experience that is universal and that does not depend on specifically Christian orientation.

In other words, the person depicted as "the natural human being" in *Works of Love* lives merely at the "lower" levels of aesthetic and metaphysical (and perhaps ethical) perception and values, and does not dwell in the same sphere as the individual led by "providence" into the experience

---

14 *Works of Love*, pp. 40f., 144; SV 12:29f., 140f.; (9:27f., 137f.).

15 At least in all the occurrences of *Religieusitet* listed by McKinnon in the *Kierkegaard Indices*, or by Cappelørn in the *Index* to the *Papirer*.

of "confession" before the "eternal" (*Purity of Heart*), or the one who enters into the "silence" where one undergoes "self-annihilation" and "totality of guilt" in order to "make room for God" (*Postscript*). There are similar materials in *Works of Love* which may serve as resources for characterizing the possibilities of "spiritual love" in universal human nature, and which therefore designate the content and quality of self-actualization in the "good" acts of a human being with only the resources of religiousness A available. Let us look at these materials.[16]

Kierkegaard argues that "the need for love" is "deeply grounded in the nature [*Væsen*, essence] of the human being." Indeed, this need is built into the very structure of the species at its origin. This fact is captured in the observation made at the very beginning, "It is not good for the human being[17] to be alone" (Gen. 2:18). And this need is immediately satisfied through the male/female distinction, in which something is both "taken" and "given ... for the sake of company [*Selskab*]— because love [*Kjerlighed*] and companionship [*Samlivet*] first take something from the human being before it gives."

So it is not strange that "throughout all time everyone who thought deeply concerning the nature of the human being has recognized in humanity this need for company. How often this has been said and repeated again and again, how often has one cried woe over the solitary person or portrayed the pain and misery of loneliness." But here, as

---

16 So the interpretation of *Works* presented here does not agree with the argument of Alastair Hannay when he says, "*Works of Love* ... , like *Purity of Heart*, is addressed to the converted. So ... we should not expect to find any attempt to justify the Christian way of life as such. In fact the aim of the work, again like *Purity of Heart*, is not 'discursive' in the philosophical sense at all, but explicatory" (in *Kierkegaard*, in the series *The Arguments of the Philosophers*, p. 243). First of all, Hannay seems unaware of the fact that an upbuilding discourse may be (as the Hongs note) either "in the more universal categories of the religious or the more specifically Christian categories" (Introduction to their translation of *Works of Love*, p. 11). Hannay also ignores Kierkegaard's own distinction between "upbuilding discourses" and "reflections" (*Overveielser*) (see *Journals* 641; VIII¹ A 923).

17 As usual, I am translating *Menneske* as the generic "human-being" in order to distinguish it from the Danish for male or man, *Mand*, and to avoid the traditional English use of "man" for the generic human race. Kierkegaard uses the Danish words that make the gender distinction in the very next sentence: *Qvinde* for "woman" and *Mand* for "man." This same distinction is in the Hebrew that lies behind Kierkegaard's quotation from Genesis. Hebrew for "the human being" is אדם (*adam*), which has always been translated "man," and became the proper name for the first "man." But in the corresponding passage in the first account of creation in the first chapter of Genesis, the generic term is first used and then the gender distinction is made: "God created the human being (אדם) in his own image, ... male (זכר, *zakar*) and female (נקבה, *neqebah*) he created them" (Gen. 1:27).

everywhere, Kierkegaard is insistent that this need is not fulfilled in the individual's becoming a member of "the crowd" (*Mængde*). In fact, the "life-together" (*Samlivet*) experienced "in the busy teeming crowd ... is both too much and too little," it is "corrupting, boisterous, bewildering." And the only cure "is to learn all over again the most important thing, to understand oneself in one's longing for company [*Selskab*]." It is for this understanding of oneself that this longing "belongs *essentially* to being a human being."[18] So the love-relationship which finds expression in the "companionship" of one individual with another has the unique characteristic and demand that neither individual loses one's identity—as happens in the crowd—but finds it. This quality comprises the "ethic" of love, and we will explore it in detail a little later.

But this ethic derives from and is dependent upon another characteristic of love. Love, Kierkegaard says, is the essential "content" and quality not only of the relationship that ought to obtain between one human being and an other, but also of the relationship between the human being and its source or origin. Obviously, the human race did not choose and establish its own definitive characteristics. We have seen that Kierkegaard does not hesitate to call this origin "a god," and we have heard him define this origin as a structure or dynamic of reality best described as "all-things-are-possible." But his most general term, and one that pervades the total authorship from the beginning to the end (including the journals) is "the eternal." All of these terms point to what Kierkegaard calls the "religious" dimension of human experience, and it is this dimension alone which is both the ground and the fulfilment of the human being as "self." If this dimension is denied or ignored or rejected, then the human individual will not be regarded as a self who possesses infinite dignity and significance. Rather, the individual will be regarded as nothing more than one temporary ephemeral example of a purely physical phenomenon called the human species, which itself is a temporary ephemeral example of biological life on a minor planet in a very unstable sun-system in a minor galaxy of the universe. And what is "eternal" in this universe can be summarized in a mathematical formula about energy in time/space.

18 For the last two paragraphs, *Works of Love*, pp. 153f.; SV 12:150; (9:147f.). I think it is misleading for the Hongs to use "community" and "society" to translate *Selskab* and *Samlivet*. For "community" Kierkegaard regularly uses *Samfund*, and for "society" he uses *Societet*, and he is suspicious of both of these forms of corporate human existence because they both tend to take on the negative character of a "crowd" in which the individual seeks or is invited to lose one's selfhood.

Against the latter conclusion of abstract objective reflection, we have seen Kierkegaard mount a massive and complex analysis and description of another dimension of reality which is "observed" through passionate, personal, interested, concrete, existential, subjective reflection directed inward to the domain of the human individual self, where the self is "touched" or "brushed" by the eternal. This domain he calls "the life of the spirit." And here in *Works of Love* he comes to a formulation about the eternal that is unique in his authorship. He is remarking that "the temporal and the eternal are heterogeneous," but that there is one medium in which they are brought into touch with each other. "What is it that connects and unites [*forbinder*] the temporal and the eternal? What is it other than love!" And this precisely means that love "is before all things and remains when all things are gone." Indeed, "love is the origin [*Ophav*, source, beginning] of all things, and spiritually understood love is the deepest ground of the life of the spirit. This foundation, spiritually understood, is incorporated into every human being in whom love abides."

Then Kierkegaard resorts to theological language. He argues that this foundation of love, which is laid down as potentiality in every human being, cannot be "implanted" by one human being "into the heart of another human being. ... No, this is a more-than-human relationship, a relationship unthinkable between human being and human being. ... It is God the creator who must implant love in each human being, God who is love itself."[19] In other words, if I really come to understand myself in my universal human need for love and in my longing for companionship, then I will come to a deeply inward point of awareness where my temporality and finitude are touched by the eternal and the infinite. I become aware that what binds me and another human being together has its origin and sustenance in what binds me and the infinite eternal together. And when I call these two bonds or relationships by the name "love," then I do not mean that kind of love which is "a matter of instinct and inclination, or a matter of feeling, or a matter of rational-calculation."[20]

What kind of love, then, is Kierkegaard talking about? What more specifically can be said about this unique relationship which is the eternal and original source and dynamic of all things, which is implanted as

---

19 Ibid., pp. 24, 205; SV 12:12, 209f.; (9:10, 207f.). The last phrase reads literally, "he who himself is love."

20 Ibid., p. 143; SV 12:140; (9:137).

the definitive potentiality in every human being, which is to be actualized in one's relationship with the eternal, with other human beings, and with one's self, and whose actualization comprises the fulfilment of one's absolute telos and one's eternal blessedness? Let us remember that just as Kierkegaard says here in *Works of Love* that *love* is the unity of the temporal and the eternal, so in *Sickness* (a year later) he says that the *self* is the synthesis of the temporal and the eternal. And just as he says here that "god" is "love," so there he says that "god" is "all-things-are-possible." And just as he says here that the absolute good act in every situation is "love's deed," so there he says that the potential self "becomes itself" (the absolute demand placed on every self) when the "self's possibility" submits to the "self's [inward] necessity."

What is being proposed here, then, is that just as the parable (analogy) of love in chapter II of *Fragments* provides a more human content to the meaning of the absolute paradox stated in chapters I and III, so the analysis of love and the description of its works in *Works of Love* provide the definitive clue as to the actual human content of the enactment of the self's possibility in accord with the demands of the self's absolute telos and eternal blessedness (*Postscript*) or in accord with "faith" in "all-things-are-possible" (*Sickness*).

Before we proceed to Kierkegaard's specification of this kind of love, however, we must ask once again whether these specifications are seen by him as operative within the limits of religiousness A, or whether they are operative only on the assumption of a stance within Christian faith. We have heard that this specific kind of love is the source of all things, that this love has been planted or structured into the very ground of every human life, and that it finds expression in the human being's universal sense of need for companionship. But the question remains: when, within religiousness A, an individual follows the lead of providence into confession of one's limitations and failures, when one in silence before the eternal dies away from immediacy and suffers total guilt consciousness and self-annihilation (impotence) in order to make room for god, does the "god" who (which) comes to fill that void speak in the accents of the kind of love that Christianity proclaims as the ultimate reality?

Alastair Hannay raises this question at the very end of his stimulating book on Kierkegaard as philosopher. He is discussing the conditions required of a philosopher who wants to "embrace Kierkegaard as a colleague." And he admits that one must finally ask whether the philosopher must be a Christian. "Indeed," he says, "Kierkegaard did regard Christianity as the only non-pagan life-view that appealed to the individual as such." Nevertheless, Hannay contends that "his basic commitment ... is to the principle that reality is a meaningful structured whole in which human life (for Kierkegaard each individual human life) plays a significant part."[21]

This is clearly too neat and reductionist a summary of Kierkegaard's basic commitment, but it makes a valid point in the light of the vast amount of material we have been able to adduce from his total writings to describe the emergence of human self-consciousness from its experience of angst, into an awareness of its basic bipolarity, and on into an increasingly complex and subtle consciousness of being essentially qualified as a synthesis of the temporal and eternal, of possibility and necessity, and as a process of movement from the aesthetic to the ethical, and from the ethical to the religious—all of this as taking place in a "meaningful structured whole" without the presupposition of concrete historical encounter with the Christian view of life or without the presupposition of being enclosed within the Christian faith experience.

The present author, for one, contends that everything that Kierkegaard ever wrote was permeated by the fact that his own inner spiritual existence and his emerging collection of concepts and categories were informed and shaped by the impact of Christianity, from his earliest days spent with his father and on throughout his university years and into his life as an author. Not one work or even one word is free of that influence. And yet his early romance with Plato (Socrates) and his later admiration of and indebtedness to Aristotle revealed to him the "reality of a meaningful structured whole" as grasped by those completely outside the impact of Christianity. So he was freed to find numerous parallels and analogies of Christian truth in so-called "pagan" thinkers. And he gladly accepted the help of Trendelenburg (an avowed Aristotelian) in finding those parallels.

It is legitimate, therefore, at least to look at each of Kierkegaard's specifications of the nature of what he calls "Christian" and "spiritual" love and ask if it is applicable to the possibilities of human awareness and human action within the confines of religiousness A. Let us remember that we are still looking for a way to clarify how an ethical-religious human being decides the "what" of the absolute good act, as well as the "how," and that this question is being pursued as part of the larger question (still unanswered) as to how the self as agent moves from knowing what is right to doing it, that is, from intention to action.

21 Hannay, *Kierkegaard*, p. 335.

We will look at five ways in which Kierkegaard specifies the kind of love that is the source and dynamic of all things and that lies at the foundation of authentic human existence: (1) the object of love is every other human being, because every human being is eternally equal; (2) love therefore is unconditional and does battle with preferential love; (3) unconditional love is possible only when God is a third term in one's relation with an other human being, because this makes love a duty, a matter of conscience; (4) such love is possible only because love toward an other presupposes love in the other; (5) such love transforms one's whole life when, and only when, expressed in and through concrete *works* of love. Each of these specifications will be treated here only in terms of its relevance for our present topic(s); later, when considering Kierkegaard as theologian, each will have to be exposited also theologically, because each acquires additional qualifications when perceived from within the Christian faith-relationship with God, or as Kierkegaard puts it, when "Christianly accented."

Admittedly, this line of differentiation is subtle and difficult to maintain, as was blandly admitted by Kierkegaard in a rather curious and uncharacteristic remark. Just after noting that it required "revelation ... with divine creativity" to say for the first time, "You *shall* love," he says, "This really is not difficult to understand, once it has been said, and it wants only to be understood in order to be performed."[22] This ease of understanding this particular unique Christian revelation and the ease of carrying it out in action are assumed by Kierkegaard because, as just noted before this remark, he recognizes that there are "human parallels" of this kind of love, but more fundamentally because he believes (as noted above) that this kind of love has been structured into the very nature of humanity as such at its origin. So the occurrence of the "human parallels" and of this understanding and performance of "Christian" love even by a "merely natural human being" ought not to surprise the Christian.[23]

---

22 *Works of Love*, p. 41; SV 12:30; (9:28).

23 In the late 1930s a Chinese philosopher who had converted to Christianity was a popular speaker at Christian conferences in the United States. I now forget his name, but I once heard him tell how he had studied all the Asian philosophies and religions, and in them had heard "god" or the "gods" described in every conceivable way with every conceivable attribute. But the first time he heard a Christian missionary speak in China he was absolutely shocked and astounded to hear the missionary say, "God is love," because this he had never heard or read before. And suddenly he knew in his heart that he had heard the truth, and that therefore Jesus must be the prophet of truth.

This position, however, leaves us with a very tricky problem: how to distinguish between, on the one hand, human parallels that are wholly independent of Christian influence and on the other expressions of Christian love that are indirectly and unconsciously derivative of the Christian formulation? For example, some of Kierkegaard's own basic notions about the human self have floated free of their source in his writings (and in his own Christian faith) and have taken root and come to fruition in the literatures of other-than-Christian cultures, without the slightest consciousness on the part of the users that these notions are not "original" but have been borrowed. This problem complicates our task of deciding what notions of love in *Works of Love* are possible within religiousness A, but we will try to be faithful to Kierkegaard's own perspectives on this matter (although in some instances Kierkegaard himself may not be consciously making the distinction).

The five specifications noted above are interdependent, so there is no ideal order in which to consider them. But we must note that all of them assume and are trying to draw a basic distinction between two kinds or classifications of love. The most general terms for them are "unconditional" and "preferential." Loving unconditionally is the state of the human spirit or self which enables one to perceive what one's absolute telos or inner necessity demands that one do in each particular situation; it defines the "what" or content of the "good" act; at the same time it is the only source of the inner passionate concern or interestedness which enables one to risk the uncertain and unknown and to *do* what one knows is the one-thing-needful here and now. So in the following, the term "love" means this state of the human spirit, unless otherwise indicated. And everything said about it represents Kierkegaard's depiction of it, unless otherwise indicated.

THE OBJECT OF LOVE

We will start with the (seemingly) simple assertion that "To love ... means, while remaining within the earthly distinctions alloted to one, essentially to will to exist equally for every human being without exception [*ubetinget*]." And the phrase "every human being" does not mean that abstraction called "the human race" which can be loved at a distance, but designates "those we can see," the particular "neighbour" who is "close at hand." "The object of love should be sought and found" not in a "dream-world" but "among actual human beings," and one's task is to "love them as they are," in "earnestness and truth."[24]

One possessed of love is able to show concern for and to give help to the specific individual that one sees at hand, because, no matter how crippled and deformed the other's essential humanity may be, or how buried under layers of temporal distinctions, love "wills that differences shall hang loosely about the individual. ... [T]hen there steadily shines in every individual that essential other, that which is common to all, the eternal likeness, the equality." And "this expectant solemnity ... is renewed every day by the eternal and by the equality of the eternal; ... this would be the reflection of the eternal." So "in being king, beggar, scholar, rich man, poor man, male, female, etc., ... we are therein precisely different. But in being neighbour we are all unconditionally [*ubetinget*] like each other. Distinction is temporality's confusing element which marks every human being as different, but neighbour is eternity's mark—on every human being."[25]

Obviously, this basic attitude and approach to every individual whom we encounter means that we ignore the external characteristics of each individual that strike us as differentiating, some of which we like and some we do not like. "Loving" in this sense means that, as stated in some rather famous words, "We hold ... that all men are created equal, that they are endowed ... with certain unalienable rights." But Kierkegaard recognizes that I as an individual am naturally inclined to be attracted to those individuals who have some distinctive characteristics which are particularly attractive to me. Therefore, it has to be acknowledged that there is a kind of battle going on in every human heart between two kinds of love.

UNCONDITIONAL LOVE VERSUS PREFERENTIAL LOVE

On the one hand there is the love which embraces *everyone* unconditionally and does so *equally*. On the other hand there is the love that embraces only *some* (perhaps just *one*) and does so *preferentially*. The first is a form of self-denial. The second is a form of self-love. In the first, the object of love is the individual in his eternal dignity and worth and (as we will soon see) in his absolute uniqueness as self or person, "not excluding a single one" whether rich or poor, mighty or weak, male or female,

---

24 *Works of Love*, pp. 92, 88, 159, 163; SV 12:86, 81, 156, 161; (9:83, 79, 154, 158f.).
25 Ibid., pp. 96f.; SV 12:90; (9:87f.).

black or white, etc. In the second, the object of love is various, a beloved (sensuously), friends, family, but in each case love is, in principle, selective on the basis of mutual attractiveness. In the first, "Self-denial casts out all preference [*Forkjerlighed*] just as it casts out all self-love."²⁶

Kierkegaard uses a variety of terms to designate each of these two forms of love, but for our purposes here let us chose two neutral ones (rejecting such harsh ones as "Christian" and "pagan"). On the one hand, there is "spiritual" love, not at all in the sense of non-physical or other-worldly but as the concern for another individual as "spirit" or self. For the other, we will speak of "preferential" love. It might be objected that it is strange and rather forced to use the word "love" to refer to concern for another human being as a self. But one has only to consult a Greek dictionary to find that φιλο- (*philo-*, love of-) is compounded with many things other than persons, for example φιλο-εργος (love of work), φιλο-κερης (love of gain), and even the abstract φιλοσοφια (love of wisdom). Kierkegaard agrees that to make the universal human individual self the object of love is a radical step, and that it requires a unique definition or redefinition of "love."

To make vividly clear what he means by spiritual love, Kierkegaard first of all accuses all other forms of love (preferential and selective) of being manifestations of self-love. He argues that in preferential forms of love one is being shaped and directed by "natural determinants (instinct-inclination)" which operate to bring self-satisfaction and hence serve "self-love." In self-love one can distinguish between the "I" which loves and the "self" which one loves ("I" love "myself"), between what can be called "the first I" and "the other I" (or "the other self"). So in sensuous/romantic love and in friendship-love, what one loves is the satisfaction of one's own inclinations which the "other" provides. One is not actually loving the truly *other*. Rather, "Love and friendship are the highest pitch of self-feeling, the I intoxicated with the other I." So no matter how passionate and boundless is one's devotion to the other as

---

26 Ibid., p. 67; SV 12:59; (9:57). It should be noted that Kierkegaard had available in the Danish language two different nouns for love, *Elskov* for passionate erotic love, and *Kjerlighed* (or *Kærlighed* in today's Danish) for charity or non-erotic affection. But he had only one verb, *elske*, which he had to use for both kinds of love. As usual, Kierkegaard loads these two nouns with conceptual freight which they do not suggest by themselves, and his usage of them throughout the authorship does not abide rigorously by the distinction made in *Works of Love*. So he should not be held responsible for Anders Nygren's rigid distinction between *eros* and *agape*.

beloved or friend, "[a]t the peak of love and friendship the two actually become one self, one I."[27]

In other words, in such relationships the so-called "other" is only a projection of one's own inclinations and desires, which find satisfaction in certain qualities of the other one. The lover romantically proclaims that the two have become one in "love," but actually the lover has possessed and absorbed the beloved into unity and identity with his/her own self. The lover therefore ignores, is not interested in, and actively suppresses those qualities in the other which do not match and reciprocate his/her own and which distinguish the other as different and unique. And such a lover shuts out from the circle of love and friendship any and every one who insists on asserting contradictory qualities. So "two friends love one another on the basis of likeness in customs, character, occupation, education, etc., consequently on the basis of the likeness by which they are different from other human beings."[28] Such love, therefore, is a matter of disposition and inclination; it manifests itself in predilection, preference, partiality; it is spontaneous/immediate and pleasure-seeking, and hence selfish and self-seeking.

In sharp absolute dichotomy with the self-love of preferential love, spiritual love is self-denying, it "seeks not its own." Rather, it refuses to judge others in terms of their differences, that is, in terms of how these differences will or will not satisfy one's own desires and preferences. Spiritual love concentrates on how each other one possesses "the equality of the eternal." This love sees each individual as unique "spirit" or self, each with his/her own eternal dignity and worth. So, "[s]piritual love takes away from myself all natural determinants and all self-love. Therefore love for my neighbour cannot make me one with the neighbour in a combined self. Love to one's neighbour is love between two eternal essences [*Væsener,* natures], each determined unto [*for*] itself as spirit. Love to one's neighbour is spiritual love, but two spirits can never become one self in a selfish sense." When, in sensuous love or friendship, two become one self, "neither of them has him/herself attained the spiritual qualification 'self,' neither of them has yet learned to love him/herself christianly [i.e., spiritually]. ... Only in love to one's neighbour is the self, which loves, purely spiritually determined as spirit, and one's neighbour [is] purely spiritually determined."[29]

27 Ibid., pp. 66–8; SV 12:58–60; (9:56–8).
28 Ibid., p. 69; SV 12:60f.; (9:58).
29 Idem.

Serious questions must be raised about this sharp dichotomy and mutual exclusivity which Kierkegaard seems to allege between preferential and spiritual love. For example, does he seriously contend that "natural human beings" exemplify the former and that "Christians" exemplify the latter? Indeed, can any individual cases be found which fully and perfectly embody either kind of love? We suggest that he does not mean either of these conclusions, but is trying to clarify the distinction between the two by stating them in hyperbole as extreme types. He everywhere denies that even the most profoundly Christian self ever achieves perfect spirituality. And we will see that even within *Works of Love* he offers modifications of his radical strictures on "natural" love as purely preferential love.

The central question can be put this way: does Kierkegaard allow for some kind of integration of or at least interrelationship between the two kinds of love? Alastair Hannay has stated the issue sharply. He argues that the assertion that all natural love is nothing but self-love is the grossest exaggeration, and so "to many the conclusion that no natural forms of love have ethical value will be morally repugnant." And in regard to Kierkegaard's contention (above) that one becomes qualified as "spirit" only in "love of one's neighbour," he remarks, "if this means that in undergoing the transition from *eros* to *agape* one has to drop not only the bonds of sensory gratification but also ties of friendly sympathy, conventional morality will surely be outraged." Such a conclusion "is a totally inhuman suggestion."[30]

Kierkegaard withdraws from these two extreme positions. He himself has to ask, "Yet surely [sensuous] love and friendship do love the beloved and the friend according to their unique individuality [*Eiendommelighed*]? Yes, it is true." In other words, these forms of preferential love need not be purely love of one's own self and its gratifications; rather, they are capable of breaking out of self-centred consciousness and becoming sympathetically aware of the truly unique otherness of the other, whether friend or beloved. Yet, he warns, this ability is limited, because "they can give up everything for the individuality of the other" with one exception. They cannot give up friendship or the love-relationship itself,

---

30 Hannay, *Kierkegaard*, pp. 263f. Hannay also gives very probing analyses of the notions of "preferential" and "self-regarding" as applied by Kierkegaard to natural love, and makes helpful comparisons between Kant's notion of "practical" love and Kierkegaard's "spiritual" love. His entire chapter on "Love of One's Neighbor" is worthy of careful study. In what follows I suggest the use of other materials in *Works of Love* in an attempt to resolve the issues he raises.

even when this is precisely the sacrifice required for the well-being of the other. This sacrifice, Kierkegaard argues, is possible only through the capacity of spiritual love for total self-denial out of concern for the other (Regine?).[31]

As for the possibilities of a positive interrelationship or union of preferential love and spiritual love, Kierkegaard makes a more positive statement. As noted repeatedly above, the unity of the self is a key emphasis of Kierkegaard and a major contribution to twentieth-century psychology's rejection of the dualism of body/soul. As we have seen, the self is a *synthesis* of finitude and infinitude, and never simply one or the other. Indeed, it is precisely this built-in inclusive polarity that makes self-consciousness and freedom possible. Kierkegaard also emphasizes again and again that as the self moves through the four "stages" or "spheres" of the aesthetic, the ethical, religiousness A, and religiousness B, the self does not leave behind the previous stage(s) but brings along and includes them.

So, early in *Works of Love* Kierkegaard notes that

> in other times ... it was supposed that Christianity had nothing to do with [sensuous] love because it is based on spontaneous inclination [*Drift*]. It was thought that Christianity, which as spirit has posited a split between flesh and spirit, detested love as sensuousness. But this was a misunderstanding, a case of exaggerated spirituality. ... No, precisely because Christianity in truth is spirit, it therefore understands by the sensuous something other than what is simply called the sensual. ... There is no supposition of any conflict between spirit and flesh, unless there is a rebellious spirit on the side of flesh, with which the spirit then struggles.[32]

We have also heard Climacus (*Postscript*) insist that the relationship to one's "eternal blessedness," which one attains through the self-annihilation and guilt consciousness of religiousness A, demands the transformation of one's entire existence. And Kierkegaard makes the same point about spiritual love in *Works*, except that instead of using the language of "eternal blessedness," he speaks of the "God-relationship" (which we will directly explore further). He says that it is "by a strange misunderstanding" that it is usually conceded that you need God's help

---

31 *Works of Love*, p. 255; SV 12:262; (9:26of.).

32 Ibid., p. 65; SV 12:56f.; (9:54f.). Danish uses the same word for "sensuous" and "sensual" (*Sandselige*), but the distinction made in English is clearly intended in this passage.

to love your neighbour, who is often a stranger, or even your enemy, or at least "the least lovable object," but that it is usually assumed that the God-relationship "should not penetrate every relationship," especially sensuous love and friendship where one "can best help oneself." Just the opposite is true. "The teaching about love to one's neighbour was ... designed precisely for this very thing, for transforming [sensuous] love and friendship." So he maintains that the command, "You shall love your neighbour, ... will teach every human being how one ought to love oneself, likewise will it also teach [sensuous] love and friendship what genuine love is." So Kierkegaard admonishes his readers, "in loving yourself preserve love to neighbour, in [sensuous] love and friendship preserve love to neighbour. ... Love your beloved faithfully and tenderly, but let love to neighbour be the sanctifying [element] in your covenant of union with God; love your friend honestly and devotedly, but let love to neighbour be what you learn from each other in the intimacy of friendship with God!"[33]

For example, "The [spouse] shall first and foremost be your neighbour. The fact that he/she is your [spouse] is then a narrower definition of your particular relationship to each other, but that which is the eternal, underlying reality must also undergird every expression of the particular." To be sure, one must admit that "one's [spouse] is loved differently from the friend, and the friend differently from the neighbour, but this is not an essential distinction, because the fundamental equality lies in the determinant 'neighbour.' It is with 'the neighbour' just as it is with the determinant 'the human being.' Every one of us is a human being, and at the same time is distinct, particular. But being a human being is the fundamental qualification."[34]

In other words, Kierkegaard does not see spiritual love and preferential love to be mutually exclusive. So when Hannay expostulates, "Surely

---

33 Ibid., pp. 117, 73f.; sv 12:112, 65f.; (9:121, 73f.).

34 Ibid., pp. 141f.; sv 12:138f.; (9:135f.) I replace Kierkegaard's "wife" with "spouse" to soften the male chauvinism of his culture which he reflected in many of his writings. In theory he was perfectly clear that men and women are equal in their humanity, as this passage specifically states. He is even clearer in *The Concept of Anxiety*, where he says that Christianity suspends the erotic, not because it is sinful "but as indifferent, because in spirit there is no difference between man and woman" [p. 63; (KW 8:70); sv 6:161; (4:340)]. I agree with Kierkegaard that in terms of essential dignity and worth and capacity as persons, men and women are equal. But I disagree that the erotic becomes a matter of indifference between men and women when they become "spiritual," that is, become fulfilled as "self." My view (here and as expanded on the next few pages) is in agreement with an analysis of this subject by Sylvia I. Walsh in her brief but excellent interpretation of *Works of Love*: "Forming

one should allow that 'neighbours' *can* also be friends, perhaps even loved ones, even erotically loved ones,"[35] Kierkegaard would say, "Yes, of course! But if you want to preserve and deepen your love of friends and loved ones, be sure that you first (or, also) love them as 'neighbours,'" because without this dimension every other love is only "a mutual and enchanting illusion of love."[36] For Kierkegaard, every form of preferential love becomes enriched and is given a secure basis if it is permeated by and grounded on that "spiritual" love which consists of respect and concern for both the fundamental humanity and the unique individuality of the other person(s). On the one hand, relationships based on sensuous attraction, on commonality of social or cultural or ethical values, on friendship, and even on family devotion are, as Kierkegaard says, a matter of lucky (fortuitous, accidental) contingency; the passions of these forms of "love" can wax and wane and even turn to jealousy and hatred and alienation. So they need the grounding and strength of spiritual love also. On the other hand, Kierkegaard fails to acknowledge that the individual who is capable of great spiritual love toward a countless number of "neighbours" in need, but who has never known any form of the commonality in preferential love, surely has missed one of the truly wondrous possibilities of human existence. But how could Kierkegaard deny this point when he had the experience of his lifelong love for Regine and his friendship with Emil Boesen who (almost alone) stayed with him to death?

Yet it is not clear that Kierkegaard would agree with the latter thesis, at least in the closing years of his life. As he lost hope in any reconciliation with Regine, as his physical and financial conditions worsened, as the derision from what he called the "rabble" continued, and as his attack on

---

the Heart: The Role of Love in Kierkegaard's Thought," in *The Grammar of the Heart*, ed. Richard H. Bell, pp. 239–41. But her further argument on pp. 243ff. using Kierkegaard's concept of "the second immediacy" I think is beside the point because by this concept Kierkegaard is clearly talking only about the possibilities of Christian love and faith. On the matter of natural human ability to love others in self-forgetfulness, see also the section below on "Reduplication and the Triad." My general position there is also in agreement with that of Sylvia Walsh. On pp. 246–8, she notes (but does not develop) certain "weaknesses" in Kierkegaard's interpretation of love. So she asserts that "our human need to *be* loved as well as to love" is "not adequately addressed by Kierkegaard," and notes that "surely reciprocity would be the ideal in Christian love, even if it cannot be demanded."

35 Hannay, *Kierkegaard*, p. 264.
36 *Works of Love*, p. 113; SV 12:107; (9:104).

Christendom alienated family and friends, his pessimism about all human relationships of love intensified. While writing *Works of Love* he confides to his journal that he is convinced that God's calling for his life lies strictly in his task of writing, and that this means that he will never have the security of a permanent position or the "comfort of wife and children." Nevertheless, "I will never disparage this happiness" (of marriage). But seven years later, in the year before he died, he levels a savage attack on marriage as nothing more than "tolerated fornication," and declares that sexuality and the having of children "is the culmination of human egotism. ... Consequently God wants the single state because he wants to be loved." Indeed, "The human is the relative, the mediocre. ... To love God is, then, impossible without hating what is human"—even though this "Christian hatred of human beings is anything but ... misanthropy ...; it is loving them in the idea, ultimately wishing them well."[37]

One wonders if Kierkegaard might have avoided these bitter formulations on sexuality if he had married Regine and sought to work out an understanding in accord with his idea of spiritual love within that relationship rather than insisting that it be a prerequisite of marriage. One wonders if Kierkegaard might have come to see that the universal "wretchedness and abjectness of human beings" is not the only truth of the human condition if he had indeed finally become pastor of a small rural parish. In the intimacy of the relationship of pastor and people, he would have discovered again and again examples of simple, unpretentious, unknown, self-sacrificing "works of love" among family members, friends, and neighbours. As a community leader, he would have witnessed, in times of catastrophe in hurricanes, famines, and earthquakes, countless deeds of self-forgetting compassion and generosity toward total strangers, with no thought of acknowledgment or recompense.

He also would have heard words from many simple (even "pagan") voices expressing in essence the conviction that he attributes to the Apostle of love: "to love human beings is still the only thing worth living for; without this love you really do not live; to love human beings is also the only salutary [*salige*] consolation for both time and eternity [literally: here and hereafter]."[38] If, after being married to Regine and serving as a pastor, Kierkegaard had in retirement written *Practice in Christianity*, it might have been a very different book, with something of

---

37 *Journals*, 5962, VII¹ A 222; 2629, XI² A 238; 2625, XI² A 160; 6902, XI¹ A 445.
38 *Journals*, 6902, XI¹ 445; *Works of Love*, p. 344; SV 12:357; (9:355).

the rich and compassionate humanity that one finds in the writings of Dietrich Bonhoeffer.

But then he probably would not have had the time of isolation required to write *The Sickness unto Death*, and that would have been a critical loss, not worth the gain (for him, at least, and a great loss for us). Anyway, as we have seen, Kierkegaard came to see quite clearly that the psyche shaped by his particular "providence" was not destined for marriage and parish, but for the loneliness of his study and for his incomparable formulation of the relevance of the "impossible possibility" of the Christian ethic.[39] And one who has been a pastor must wonder if he could have harnessed his genius to serve the needs of parishioners. Let us do the best we can with what Kierkegaard's providence provided.

So it is our thesis that these late views of humanity and its loves are not at all what we find in Kierkegaard's thinking in its normative form, as in *Works of Love* and *The Sickness unto Death*. In *Works* we find two essential ideas that radically qualify his idea of spiritual love and preserve it from the pessimism of these late journal entries. First, he insists that for a healthy love relationship between or among humans, the eternal ("God") must be present as a "middle determinant" (*Mellembestemmelse*, middle condition or stipulation), forming a triadic relationship. In other words, spiritual love is inherently "religious." Secondly, we must ask whether his understanding of love allows not only for the unilateral self-denying love that is expressed and given to one's neighbour as "the least lovable object," but also for a mutuality in which love is received from and shared with the other. For this topic we will look at Kierkegaard's thesis that "the lover presupposes that love is in the heart of the other human being."

LOVE'S TRIAD

Time and time again in this study of Kierkegaard's concept of the self, we have come to a point in his thinking where human consciousness discovers a boundary line in ethical sensitivity and aspiration. And to describe what lies beyond that boundary line he finds it necessary to resort to religious language and concepts. At these points he speaks of "silence," of "confession," of "self-annihilation" and "totality of guilt," of "the teleological suspension of the ethical," of "all things are possible."

---

39 See Reinhold Niebuhr, *An Interpretation of Christian Ethics*, pp. 109f.

In all of these languages the primary emphasis is on the singular relationship of the human heart and spirit to "the eternal," to "the absolute," to "God." Now, in *Works of Love*, he provides a distinct alternative by uniting the ethical and the religious, by interrelating one's acts toward other human beings and one's relationship with God. Thus he provides a conceptuality to illustrate what he has maintained all along, namely, that the spiritual includes the physical and the psychological dimensions of the human being, that the religious sphere catches up and brings along the aesthetic and the ethical spheres.

First we must ask whether this kind of presence of God or the eternal is limited to that provided in and by the peculiarly Christian faith-relationship. We have already looked at several ways (in *Works of Love*) in which Kierkegaard speaks of the possibilities of spiritual love in universal human nature. There are similar materials about the triadic or "threefold" (*Tredobbelt*) relationship "among humanbeing-God-humanbeing."[40]

The key treatment of love, for our purposes, occurs in the chapter entitled "Love Seeks Not Its Own" (part two, chapter IV). The main theme is that spiritual love eliminates the distinction *mine* and *yours*, even as it intensifies the distinction *you* and *I*. This is so, "because without *you* and *I* there is no love, and with *mine* and *yours* there is no love." The appearance of this kind of love, Kierkegaard maintains, upsets the whole natural order of normal human relations and expectations, just as revolution, war, earthquake, or any other terrible misfortune upsets the "justice" of the social order which has the task of maintaining the proper division between "mine" and "yours." The result is confusion and change. And he maintains that "love is a revolution, the most profound of all."[41]

He starts the chapter with a clearly Christian-inspired exposition of this kind of love. God is love, and God has created human beings in God's own image, so that they may become like God, become perfect as God is perfect. Christ also was love, and came into the world to become

---

40 For this specific language, see *Works of Love*, pp. 112f., 124; SV 12:107, 120; (9:104, 117).

41 Ibid., p. 248; SV 12:255; (9:253f.). The social-political implications of doing away with the distinction between "mine" and "yours" are not explored by Kierkegaard, because he sees this being accomplished only inwardly by the (rare) individual, and presupposes a faith-relationship with God. But it would be interesting to ask how social and political structures would be affected by any serious even though partial commitment to such a perspective.

the prototype of love in order to enable all human beings to become love also. As we shall see, Kierkegaard repeatedly exposits the uniquely Christian concept of God as creator, as the one who creates "out of nothing." And he makes a direct reference to his exposition of sin (in *The Concept of Anxiety*) when he describes here the human effort to define the moral law without reference to God; this attempt, he says, amounts to mutiny and rebellion against God, and the rebellion has its beginning in "dizziness."[42]

The clear presence and operation of these Christian perspectives, however, does not mean that Kierkegaard argues that one must be a Christian in order to be aware of and to be able to practise spiritual love, even though he repeatedly asserts that "There really is a strife between what the world and what God understand by love." In a number of subtle ways, he lays the groundwork for what might be called an "anthropological ontology" which leaves open the possibility of manifestations or intimations, of parallels or analogies or parables, of Christian spiritual love in "the natural human being." Here again we find ourselves at the borderline where there are overlappings of Kierkegaard as humanist and Kierkegaard as theologian. What we are trying to ascertain, in theological language, is how far Kierkegaard allows for a "natural revelation" derived from God's presence and work in "creation," and what powers human beings still have to read that revelation in creation in spite of the ravages of "sin."

To answer these questions adequately we should first have a full exposition of Kierkegaard's understanding of "creation" and "sin," but since his perspectives on these topics are uniquely Christian and therefore theological, we have reserved their treatment for the second part of this study of Kierkegaard's concept of the self: Kierkegaard the Theologian (see chapters on "My Self: A Gift" and "My Self: A Failure"). Kierkegaard would agree, we believe, that becoming a theologian does not mean that one ceases to be a humanist, just as becoming spiritual does not mean that one ceases to be physical, rational, and ethical. Just as in Christian faith one remains *simul justus et peccator*, so also as theologian one remains *simul Christianus et paganus*.

Let us look first at the very careful formulation of the ontology of love and its application to human relationships in the chapter "Love Seeks Not Its Own" and related passages.

---

42 Ibid., pp. 121f.; sv 12:117f.; (9:113f.). See *The Concept of Anxiety*, pp. 55f.; (kw 8:61f.); sv 6:152f.; (4:331f.).

"God" *is* love. Love seeks love. But not in the human sense that one seeks to become loved oneself. Authentic love is self-sacrificial in that it consists precisely in helping the other human being to seek "God," that is, love itself. We call love "God" because love alone is able to seek love and able itself to become the object of love, yet without seeking its own. "When a human being seeks to become the object for another person's love, he/she deliberately and falsely seeks his/her own," that is, does not sacrifice one's self for the other. This is the case because "no human being *is love*." Therefore, "the only true object of a human being's love is '*love*,' which is God, which therefore in a deeper sense is not an object at all, since it [what a person loves] is itself love." So we call love "God."[43]

Admittedly, Kierkegaard's language here has been twisted a little, but for the purpose of showing that what he really wants to say is not that "God is love," but that "love is God"—just as a year later in *Sickness* he explains that to say that "God is that all-things-are-possible" really means "that all-things-are-possible is God."[44] So in *Works of Love* he explicitly says that what we mean by "God" is not an object, not another individual, locatable thing in the universe. Rather, what we mean by "God" is a dynamic that conditions the entire universe of "things" (analogous to the curve of space or the second law of thermodynamics), a dynamic that is the source and ultimate explanation of how things work, present before and operative in the "big bang" that started all things, and therefore in a sense transcendent to while being immanent and present in all things.[45] So, just as Kierkegaard says in *Sickness* that "possibility" conditions all things, so here he is saying that "love" does also. But, it should be noted, he has in mind a certain "set" or "domain" of things in which the dynamic of "possibility" and "love" is operative, namely, human beings as self-conscious beings active in relationship with each other. And as we shall see directly, these two qualities or characteristics of the dynamic called "God" are profoundly interrelated in self-conscious human relationships, because "love" gives "possibility" its ethical character and explains what it means to be a human "self" in "freedom" (which in turn

---

43 *Works of Love*, p. 247; SV 12:254; (9:252f.).

44 *Sickness*, p. 173f.; (KW 19:40); SV 15:97; (11:153). The Hongs make this point by using this translation: "the being of God means that everything is possible, or that everything is possible means the being of God."

45 Paul Tillich makes this same point by saying that God is "personal" in the sense that "he carries within himself the ontological power of personality," but this does not mean that God is "*a* person." *Systematic Theology, Volume I*, pp. 244f.

explains what it means to call the Ultimate Dynamic of the universe "free" and "personal").

What then does it mean to say that to love another human being consists in helping the other one to seek love itself ("God")? A little later in the same chapter ("Love Seeks Not Its Own"), Kierkegaard gives an answer which he does not attribute to Christian revelation but sees as manifest to all human beings universally. "Let us for a moment consider nature," he says. "With what infinite love does nature, or God in nature, embrace all the diversity which has life and being [*Tilvær*]." It is as if the most insignificant and plain-looking little flower "has said to love: let me be something for myself, some property-that-belongs-to-me-alone [*Eiendommeligt*]. And then love helped it to become its own-distinctive-individual-characteristic [*Eiendommelige*]. ... So it is also in the relationship of love between human-being and human-being; only this true love loves every human being according to her/his unique-individuality [*Eiendommelighed*]." Consider the most insignificant person with the most modest gifts: "if one has had courage to be oneself before God, then one has one's authentic-individuality [*Eiendommelighed*]."[46]

But what does it mean, "*before God* to be oneself—for the emphasis rests on 'before God,' since this is the beginning and source of all unique-individuality"? Here Kierkegaard is assuming a formulation which he has made and used frequently in the foregoing pages of *Works of Love*: "God" as the "middle-determinant" (*Mellembestemmelse*) or the "third-party" (*Trediemand*) in the authentic love relationship between one human being and another. Love is always "a relationship between: humanbeing—God—humanbeing, ... God is the middle-determinant." This means that "to love God is in truth to love oneself; to help another human being to love God is to love another human being; to be helped by another human being to love God is to be loved." So "one dare not belong to anyone in love unless in the same love one belongs to God."[47]

Then Kierkegaard reformulates this relationship to express his ontology of love. "The love relationship is in essence [*hører til*] the threefold [*Tredobbelte*] [relationship]: the lover, the beloved, love; but love is God. Therefore, to love another human being is to help him/her to love God, and to be loved is to be helped." Or more precisely: "no humanbeing is love. ... Yet love is everywhere present where there is a lover." This is so because love is not just "a relationship between two," but "also

46 *Works of Love*, pp. 252f.; SV 12:259f.; (9:257–9).
47 Ibid., pp. 112f.; SV 12:107; (9:104f.).

a relationship among three. First there is the lover; next the one or those who are the objects [of love]; but for the third, there is present love itself."[48]

What, then, does this universal dynamic called "love" consist in? What does it do, that it should be given the ultimate ascription of power and the unconditional accolade of homage: God? What does it mean to "have courage to be oneself" *before God (Love)*? Kierkegaard gives this answer (again in the chapter "Love Seeks Not Its Own").

To have unique-individuality is to believe in the unique-individuality of every other [human-being]; because unique individuality is not mine, but is the gift of God, by which [God] gives me being [*at være*], and [God] indeed gives all things, and gives all things being. This is precisely the inscrutable richness of goodness in the goodness of God, that [God], the *almighty*, yet gives in such a way that the receiver obtains unique-individuality, that [God], who creates out of nothing, yet creates unique-individuality so that creation standing opposite to [God] does not become nothing, although it is taken from nothing and is nothing, yet becomes unique-individuality.[49] [Now, reread this passage, substituting the word "love" in place of each instance of the word "God."]

What Kierkegaard is saying is this: in order for me to regard my self as unique individual, with honour, respect, and concern (love), I must also *believe in* the unique individuality of every other person and grant to that individuality the same honour, respect, and concern (love). But the ground and source for such regard (for my self) and belief (in the selfhood of others) is not to be found in shared empirical evidence, or in the deliverances of sciences such as anthropology and psychology, or even in a philosophical construction of a universal ethic. Rather, I must become aware of and must believe in an origination and source of such love that transcends humanity as such. I must have acquired an awareness that my conscious existence as unique self is not of my own making, or simply an inheritance from my parents and my species, or derived simply from the conditioning of family, tribe, and nation. Rather it derives

---

48 Ibid., pp. 124, 280; SV 12:120, 289; (9:117, 287f.).

49 Ibid., p. 253; SV 12:261; (9:259). We have noted before the precursors of this concept and its language. First, in the idea that temporality does not exist for God's sake but is "the greatest of all the gifts of grace" for humanity's sake, separating the infinite spirit and the finite spirit and thus giving the human being the opportunity of freedom, in *Either/Or*, 2:254f.; (KW 4:250); SV 3:231; (2:224). And then the very language of *Works of Love* is found in *Postscript*, pp. 220; (KW 12.1:246); SV 9:206; (207).

from and therefore has kinship with the ultimate dynamics of the universe. As Kierkegaard puts it, "we can be like God only in loving," because "the kinship between human-being and human-being ... is secured by every individual's equal kinship with and relationship to God. ..."[50]

In other words, there is a dynamic or operating structure inherent in the universe (as we know it) which is reflected or expressed in the peculiarity of self-consciousness in the human individual. Awareness of this source or reference of human self-consciousness is what Kierkegaard calls the inherent "religious" quality or dimension of human self-consciousness. So he asks, "spiritually understood, what are the ground and foundation of the life of the spirit, which shall bear the building? It is precisely love; love is the origin [the beginning point] of all things, and spiritually understood love is the deepest ground of the life of the spirit. Spiritually understood, the foundation is laid [*lagt*] in every individual in whom love is."[51] Here it must be remembered that "spirit" and "self" are synonyms. Hence Kierkegaard is here anticipating his formulations in *Sickness* where he says, "Every human being is a psychical-sensuous synthesis naturally-fitted [*anlagt*] for the purpose of being spirit; this is the building." And again, "Every individual is primitively [and] naturally-fitted [*anlagt*] as a self, destined to become a self."[52]

One can call the source or origin of this primitive and natural foundation "the eternal" or "God" or any other word that indicates that the source is transcendent to humanity as such, and is not just another "object" in the universe, but is a dynamic that conditions everything in the universe. In calling this dynamic "the almighty creator" who "creates out of nothing," Kierkegaard is clearly using the language of Christian theology. But in giving the name "Love" to this universal dynamic, Kierkegaard is appealing to a ground of awareness that is open to every human being, namely, the possibility of coming to "know" another human being in such a way that one must acknowledge that the other one lives and exists as a focused centre of selfhood and self-consciousness just as unique, private, (mostly) hidden, mysterious, and self-determining as one's own self. And from this singular "knowing," one feels the ethical-religious *demand* to extrapolate the mystery of this truly *other* selfhood to every single individual of the human race, whether family and friend, or

---

50 *Works of Love*, pp. 74, 80; SV 12:66, 72; (9:64, 70). At the end of the second passage I have omitted the phrase "in Christ," but will comment on this matter directly.
51 Ibid., pp. 204f.; SV 12:209; (9:207).
52 *Sickness*, pp. 176, 166; (KW 19:43, 33); SV 15:100, 91; (11:156, 146).

stranger passed on the street and seen in myriad numbers in football stadium and airport, or the rich and powerful public figures of government, business, sports, and entertainment, or the convict sitting on death row, or "foreigner" and "enemy" seen en masse on nightly television news, shouting and shaking fists, or naked and dying of starvation. But this extrapolation is a matter of "believing" that "love is the origin of all things," that love (as regard and concern for the equal and eternal dignity and worth of every individual) has ontological status, and the believing is enabled and sustained by my own consciousness of kinship with and relationship to the eternal transcendent reality of love itself.

Kierkegaard makes the same point in another language, when he says that this kind of love is a matter of duty and conscience. "As soon as love, in its relationship to its object, does not in this relationship relate just as much to itself, ... then it has the law of its existence outside of itself and hence is dependent, in a corruptible, earthly, temporal sense. But love which has undergone the transformation of the eternal by becoming duty, and which loves because it *shall* [must, ought] love, that love is independent, it has the law of its existence in the very relationship of love to the eternal."[53] On the contrary, that preferential, immediate, spontaneous love which is motivated by feelings and inclinations induced by its object is obviously dependent on that object. Therefore, it is subject to change and can lose its ardour, joy, and power; indeed, it can change into its opposite, into hate and jealousy.[54]

Love as duty to obey inward eternal love itself, therefore, is the source of freedom. This kind of love is "eternally secured against every change, eternally made free in blessed independence, eternally and happily secured against despair," because it is "consciously grounded on the eternal." In other words, the source of that regard and concern (love) with which I act toward everyone and anyone in need is my own inward knowledge/belief that the other one possesses the same dignity and worth as a unique individual self as I do, and that this dignity and worth are derived not from me but from the eternal origin of all being, the ultimate dynamic of the universe, which is love itself. So no matter who the person in need is, no matter what is his/her condition or position, no matter what the time and place, I am "free" to love because the law of love is always eternally present with me.[55]

---

53 *Works of Love*, pp. 52f.; SV 12:43; (9:41).
54 Ibid., pp. 41, 49f.; SV 12:30, 39–41; (9:29, 37–9).
55 Ibid., pp. 44, 46; SV 12:34, 36; (9:32, 34).

Hence, "Duty makes a human being dependent and in the same instant eternally independent. ... One often thinks that freedom exists and that it is law which binds freedom. But it is just the opposite; without law freedom does not exist at all, and it is law which gives freedom." Or one can say that "Love is a matter of conscience and thus is not a matter of impulse and inclination," because "to relate to God is precisely to have conscience. ... The relationship between the individual and God, the God-relationship, is conscience."[56] In other words, when the source of loving is one's own relationship with eternal love itself, then one is indeed "dependent" on and in that relationship as the "law" of one's existence; one is "bound" by one's conscience. At the same time, one is independent (in one's loving) as regards all externals of time, place, condition, and lack of attractiveness of the object of one's love. So one is "free" in two ways. One is free of the need for desire and inclination toward the object of love. But one is also free in one's relationship to eternal love itself. The "demand" of eternal love is not that of instinct or habit or psychological-physical compulsion. The relationship of "believing" in eternal love does not obliterate the distinction between the eternal reality and the temporal self. The "religious" relationship does not drop out the ethical but intensifies it. The "law" of "thou shalt love" is not satisfied by cool rational calculation of enlightened self-interest. Rather, when one hears the voice of the eternal "thou shalt," the individual enters the place of "fear and trembling" because one must summon the courage of the most passionate, infinite, inward, personal, earnest interestedness in order to risk everything in the self-denying act of love which runs counter to all external evidence of expediency and common sense and social expectation. As we have heard Kierkegaard say, a decision made in time about something eternal "is the most intensive intensity, the most intensive leap," the ultimate and truest act of freedom.[57]

This entire view of love (as duty and a matter of conscience because "love itself" [God] must always be the middle-determinant in every love relationship between one human being and another) leaves us with a curious problem. Throughout *Works of Love* Kierkegaard constantly asserts that this kind of loving essentially involves self-forgetting, self-renunciation, and self-sacrifice. Furthermore, I the lover cannot expect

---

56 Ibid., pp. 53, 143; SV 12:43, 140; (9:42, 137). As noted before, Kierkegaard had previously formulated this concept of duty in *Either/Or*, 2:258–61; (KW 4:254–6); SV 3:234–7 (2:228–30).

57 *Journals*, 4806, XI¹ 329.

to be loved in return by either the neighbour or the world in general. In fact, I can only expect to be hated. But the curious problem is this: if every human being needs to be loved, first, in order to believe in his/her own eternal dignity and worth, and then, in order to become oneself in actuality, do I not need to receive love as well as give love? Is there not some kind of reciprocity and mutuality in authentically loving oneself and loving the other human being "before God," that is, in the presence of and in relation to the eternal dynamic of love itself?

Kierkegaard gives his own kind of answer to this question in his principle of "like for like" (*Lige for Lige*), particularly in one application of that principle in his proposition that "love presupposes love in the other," but also in a brief but profound exposition of how the phenomenon of "reduplication" (*Fordoblelse*) occurs when the eternal enters the temporal. And so we come to the fourth way in which Kierkegaard specifies the kind of love that lies at the foundation of authentic human existence.

LOVE PRESUPPOSES LOVE

Let us begin with the simple but profound proposition that whenever I, moved by spiritual love, approach a "neighbour" who may very well be "the least lovable object," I nevertheless "presuppose that love is present," that is, I "presuppose that love is in the heart of the other human being." As we have previously heard, "love is the deepest ground of the life of the spirit. ... The foundation is laid in every human being in whom love is." And this presupposition is crucially important, because on this "foundation" alone am I able to "entice forth the good," to "love-up love." And "to love it forth is to upbuild," to build "from the ground up, insofar as one lovingly presupposes it as fundamental [*i Grund*]," that is, "love [is able] to upbuild by presupposing that love is present." Indeed, "among all the relationships in the world there is no relationship where there is such a like-for-like, where that which comes forth so exactly corresponds to what had been presupposed."[58]

So this principle of like-for-like means that there is an essential built-in reciprocity in the love relationship between human beings. "Love ... is known and recognized by the love in an other. Like is known only by like. Only the one who abides in love can recognize love, just as one's love is to be recognized." Let us retranslate this sentence, substituting

---

58 *Works of Love*, pp. 204–7; SV 12:209–12; (9:207–10).

for the word "love" what Kierkegaard is really talking about. "My belief in and concern for the eternal dignity and worth of the unique identity of each individual ... is known and recognized by the other person because that same belief and concern resides fundamentally in him/her. Like is known only by like. Only if I so believe and am thus concerned am I able to recognize this belief and concern in others, just as my belief and concern can only thus be recognized." In other words, love is able to penetrate the accumulated accretions of all forms of alienation, hatred, and fear between human beings, and able to see, behind and below all unlovableness, that essential, eternally-given, unique identity as self which all human beings possess equally. This work of love is necessary, because "alas, love is never completely present in another human being." And the first purely human and unloving response is to seek to remove the flaw or frailty, to tear down as preliminary to building up. But true love "hides the multiplicity of sins." It refuses to discover or to concentrate on what is wrong but seeks to "hide" (forgive) it. "The lover understands that the possibility of good exists at every moment for the other human being." That is the ground on which love builds up.[59]

Now another like-for-like appears. Not only is there a reciprocity between what love presupposes and what love is able to elicit from the other, but there is also a reciprocity between what the lover is able to do for the other and what happens to the lover him/herself. And this is true negatively as well as positively.

Negatively, "To give up the other human being as hopelessly lost ... is proof that oneself is not a lover and consequently is indeed in despair. ... One who has given up one's love for the other is the loser. ... That person has ceased to be loving. ... Here again is the eternal's like-for-like: to despair over another human being is to be in despair oneself." So when one regards another as hopeless, doomed to downfall and perdition, one is reflecting the state of one's own mind and heart, namely, the state of "worldliness, the earthly passions of the unloving mind, ... heavy, sluggish, slack, dispirited, dejected." One may defend such an attitude as shrewdness, "presuming to have an elemental knowledge of the shabby side of existence." But actually it derives from a suppressed anger and envy, a "cowardly fearful small-mindedness." These are a sure sign that "love is not present." And "if there is less love in a [person], there is also

---

[59] Ibid., pp. 33, 207f., 239 and part II, chapter V, on "Love Hides the Multiplicity of Sins"; SV 12: 22, 212, 245; (9:20, 210, 243).

less of the eternal; ... if there is nothing eternal in a human being, the movement of the eternal is in vain and there is no possibility."[60]

Positively, just the opposite is the case. For example, "worldly intelligence thinks that one can very well hope for oneself without hoping for others. ... Worldly intelligence does not discern that love is by no means a third by itself but is the middle-determinant: without love, no hope for oneself; with love, hope for all others. To the degree that one hopes for oneself, to that same degree one hopes for others, because to that degree one is loving." And likewise the reverse: "to the degree that one hopes for others, precisely to the same degree one hopes for oneself, because this is the infinitely exact, eternal like-for-like, which is for all eternity."[61]

In this way, "Love builds up by presupposing that love is present." And in this relationship there is reciprocity. Kierkegaard encourages us to consider how this happens not only in our approach to others but also in the approach of others toward and to ourselves. "If any human being ever talked to you in this way, or acted toward you in this way, so that you really felt yourself built up thereby, then it was because you quite vividly perceived how he/she presupposed love to be in you." So "love" means not only that you "presuppose love in others," but also that "to be loving is precisely to assume, to presuppose that other human beings are loving."[62]

Does this assumption that others are also loving negate Kierkegaard's assertion that a loving person cannot expect the object of one's love necessarily to return one's love, indeed that such love evokes hatred from the world? No, because it is not necessarily, in fact rarely, the person to whom you show love who serves as the occasion for the awakening of love within you by the power of eternal love itself. In other words, the reciprocity or mutuality of love does not manifest itself in the emergence of a "congregation" or "communion" of lovers who affirm and support each other in and by doing works of love toward each other, a community wherein one can expect to be loved in return for loving, a community which excludes all who do not share in their reciprocal love. Indeed, for Kierkegaard this group-love is the most vicious kind of delusion. "What the world honours and loves under the name of love is the solidarity of self-love. This solidarity ... demands that one shall sacrifice

---

60 Ibid., pp. 239–41; SV 12:245–8; (9:243–6).
61 Ibid., 243, 239; SV 12:250, 245; (9:247f., 243).
62 Ibid., pp. 210f.; SV 12:215f.; (9:213f.).

the God-relationship in order to unite in a worldly way with the solidarity which locks God out."[63]

Here is the nub and the crux of the question as to how "love" determines the *content* of the "good" act which is demanded by the "absolute telos," by one's "eternal blessedness," the content of the "one thing needful" demanded by one's "inner necessity" as one stands before "all-things-are-possible," coming to a decision about something eternal within time, thus making "the most intensive leap." In other words, my loving an other who is in need of love is not motivated or caused or to be explained by the enlightened self-interest of my expectation to be loved or to get love in return.

Rather, my obedience to the "law" of love, to my "conscience," where in utter silence and self-annihilation I hear the voice saying, "THOU SHALT LOVE," is not motivated by a quid pro quo. I do not lose my life *in order* to gain it. Rather, my obedience, my "work of love" for a needy "neighbour," occurs voluntarily in the most inward agony as I, in fear and trembling, have the courage to believe and affirm that such love is "God," is the ultimate dynamic of reality, against all appearances and convictions of "this world" to the contrary; I have the courage to believe that "love" is present as a transcendent middle-determinant that is the source of the dignity and worth of every human being. "This is a more-than-human relationship, a relationship that is unthinkable between human-being and human-being; in this sense [merely] human love cannot build up. It is God, the creator, who must implant love in each human-being, God who is love itself."[64]

When one believes and trusts in the presence of this transcendent source and guarantor of individual dignity and worth, as the eternal dynamic of all existence, then one is enabled to have that courage which goes out as concern and affirmation of the unique individuality of whatever person one meets, and one is delivered from that constant ordinary human concern, "What is there in this for me?" It is true that the eternal like-for-like guarantees that "in the moment one saves the other, one saves oneself from death." But "love alone never thinks about the latter, about saving oneself, about acquiring confidence itself. The loving person only thinks lovingly about giving confidence and saving an other from death."[65]

---

63 Ibid., p. 123; SV 12:119; (9:115f.).
64 Ibid., p. 205; SV 12:210; (9:208).
65 Ibid., p. 262; SV 12:270; (9:268).

How, then, does the eternal like-for-like work, so that I too know and receive the power of love to affirm and call forth (build up) my own infinite dignity and worth? Well, says Kierkegaard, "the one who lovingly forgets him/herself, ... truly, such a one is not forgotten. There is the one who thinks of him/her: God in heaven; or, love thinks of her/him. God is love, and when a human-being out of love forgets him/herself, how could God then forget him/her? No, while the lover forgets him/herself and thinks of the other human-being, God thinks of the lover." So "the lover who forgets about him/herself, is remembered by love. ... And in this way it comes about that the lover receives what she/he gives."[66]

Within this explication of how love works, Kierkegaard supports his argument by a sophisticated application of his principle of "reduplication" (*Fordoblelse*), and thereby develops and deepens his ontology of love. He says, "Note the reduplication here: what the lover ... gives, this he/she ... receives. ... One receives precisely by giving, and receives exactly the same [thing] that one gives."[67] This dynamic of loving does not operate, as we have seen, in a merely human-to-human relationship but only when the middle determinant creates the triadic relationship of lover-love-beloved. That is to say, it is the transcendent ("divine") dynamic of love itself that effects this like-for-like. And the presence and operation of this dynamic of reduplication in human relationships is based upon and is an expression of the essential nature of "the eternal" in contrast to "the temporal."

The temporal, Kierkegaard says, is characterized by having the three modes of past, present, future. And therefore it never exists wholly or completely in actuality, or wholly in any one of these modes. Rather, "the temporal vanishes in time." This is so because, as Haufniensis puts it in *The Concept of Anxiety* (and as was spelled out at the beginning of chapter 4), time as infinite succession never gets a real foothold in the flow, since, in purely human time, what is future simply flips immediately into what is past. Thus "no moment is a present"; the present is simply "something infinitely contentless, which again is the infinite vanishing," except as "spatialized" and defined by things. In this kind of time, "One does not get the past by itself but in a simple continuity [*sim-*

---

66 Idem. But this act of affirmation by Love-itself presupposes that the lover has previously discovered and entered into a "religious" relationship with the eternal and thereby has already known love from God in the form of affirmation of his/her infinite dignity and worth. This apparent circularity and the conundrum it presents will be explored below in the section on "Reduplication and the Triad."

67 Ibid., p. 261; SV 12:269; (9:267).

pel Continuitet] with the future. ... The future is not by itself but in a simple continuity with the present." This whole dilemma of human time gets resolved only when time is invaded by the eternal, because the eternal breaks this simple continuity, it annuls the succession, it brings a present that is "infinitely contentful," because the eternal not only stops the flow but "also is [i.e., embraces] the future and the past."[68] But how does the eternal disrupt this "simple continuity" that characterizes the ordinary human sense of time? Precisely by that which is its essential nature: its inherent dynamic of "reduplication."

"Reduplication" as a specific concept first appears in *Postscript*, and then significant applications occur in several later works.[69] In *Postscript* there is first the idea of the "doubleness" (*Dobbelthed*) involved in the "double-reflection" (*Dobbelt-Reflexion*) which, Climacus says, "is implicit in the very idea of communication," that is, in what he calls "indirect communication" that is required when one self attempts to share its own inward, passionately and earnestly held truth with another self.[70] But this doubleness is actually just a specific case of the more general principle of "reduplication" which he develops later. And, as we shall see, both of these ideas are examples of and are rooted in Kierkegaard's fundamental belief in the essential and ineradicable duality or polarity that is operative not only in human existence (as a synthesis of infinite/finite) but also within the essential unity of the eternal.[71] Kierkegaard's concept and

---

68 *The Concept of Anxiety*, pp. 76f., 81; (KW 8:85f., 90); SV 6:174f., 178; (4:355f., 360).

69 See the listing under *Fordoblelse* in Alastair McKinnon's *Fundamental Polyglot Konkordans* (*The Kierkegaard Indices*, vol. 2). Especially significant are the uses in *Works of Love*, two different *Christian Discourses*, *Practice in Christianity*, and *The Point of View for My Work as an Author*. There are numerous occurrences in the journals but only incidentally; yet it is interesting that in late entries *Reduplication* replaces *Fordoblelse*. One wonders where Kierkegaard got this old English word, whose roots are in late Latin, but the word is not in German or French. It is clear that "reduplication" is what Kierkegaard means; so the Hongs' use of "redoubling" is misleading.

70 *Postscript*, pp. 67–74; (KW 12.1:72–80); SV 9:63–9; (7:55–61); the quotation is on p. 68n.; (KW 12.1:73n) SV 9:63; (7:56). In these pages Swenson (or Lowrie) improperly translates *Dobbelthed* several times as "reduplication." This first detailed analysis of indirect communication by Kierkegaard was, of course, expanded two years later (1847) in his unpublished notes for lectures ("A Little Sketch") on "The Dialectic of Ethical and Ethical-Religious Communication" (*Journals*, 648–57; VIII[2] 79–89). And the concept was specifically applied a year later (1848) to the nature of the faith relationship between the believer and the God-Man (*Practice in Christianity*, pp. 132–44; SV 16:129–39; [12:124–34]).

71 See chapter 2 above, especially the opening pages, on this topic of Kierkegaard's view of dualism.

theory of communication is extremely complex and outside the scope of the present study, but his notion of reduplication is integral to his understanding of the human self and its fulfilment in "love."

In another passage in *Postscript*, Climacus is trying to establish the nature of "truth" for the existing individual human being, and distinguishes between an empirical and an idealistic definition of the "accord" between "being" (*Væren*) and "thought" (*Tænken*). For the human being, truth is obviously empirical because the human exists concretely in time/space and therefore is always in the process of becoming, with no conclusion and likewise no clearly established beginning. But for more idealistic or abstract reflection, "thought and being signify one and the same thing, and the accord ... is simply an abstract identity with itself," so "the formula is a tautology." In this kind of reflection, "truth" is, first, that which is caught in the clear and consistent conception or thought. Then, secondly, reflection adds "being" to the "thought" by saying that "the truth *is*, that is, truth is a reduplication." So even in this abstract understanding of truth there is maintained a distinction within the identity of thought and being: [truth's] being is the abstract form of truth," and therefore "truth is not something single [*Enkelt*] but, in an entirely abstract sense, a reduplication, which is nevertheless cancelled at the very same moment."[72]

Let us now see how Kierkegaard applies this concept of reduplication to understanding the fact (as noted above) that what the lover gives, the lover also receives. Here too (in *Works of Love*) he, like Climacus, compares the temporal and the eternal.[73] The temporal is caught in the inescapable incompleteness of past-present-future, but "the eternal *is*." Of course, what Kierkegaard here means by the temporal is the human being caught in "the infinite succession of time" with its "contentless present." This human being certainly has "many diverse qualities [*Egenskaber*]," and they have a certain unity in that together they define what a person is as a "temporal object." But the trouble is that "as the temporal vanishes in time, it also exists merely in its qualities." And this state means that "a temporal object never has reduplication in itself." In other words, a human being is living in pure immediacy or identity with one's present batch of qualities, wherever they come from. There is no dialectical consciousness or act of discrimination wherein (in the lan-

---

72 *Postscript*, pp. 169f.; (KW 12.1:189–90); SV 9:157–8; (7:157–8).
73 For the following see *Works of Love*, p. 261; SV 12:269; (9:267).

guage of *Sickness*) "the self becomes aware of itself as essentially distinct from the environment and the external world and [their] influence upon it."

In contrast with this human being caught in time is the eternal. The eternal *is* in quite a different state, not the state of immediacy. "The eternal *is* not merely in its qualities, but *is* in itself in its qualities; it does not merely *have* qualities, but *is* in itself as simultaneously [*idet*] it has qualities" (emphasis added). In other words, within the eternal there is a dialectic between its being "in itself" and its being "in its qualities," but in such a way that the one form of being is never without the other; that is to say, the eternal *is* in both at one and the same time by means of a dynamic of reduplication of itself (in later works and journal entries, Kierkegaard often refers to reduplication as "dialectical").[74]

The dynamic of reduplication in the eternal, however, is different from the reduplication that occurs in the abstract identity of being and thought (as described in *Postscript*). The truth as captured in the latter excludes any relationship with or any inclusion of the qualities which define human individual existence. That truth is objective, abstract, universal, and disinterested, whereas the truth of human existence is subjective, concrete, individual, and passionately interested. The reduplication involved in the identity of thought and being allows for no real otherness, no distance between what is and what is possible, and therefore it allows no real freedom. On the other hand, Kierkegaard argues, the eternal (God), while being absolutely and qualitatively different from and transcendent to human existence in time/space, yet at the same time both is capable of and passionately desires a profound and continuing relationship with individual human beings existing in time/space.

Nowhere has this been expressed more clearly in the authorship than in *The Concept of Anxiety*. Haufniensis defines "the moment" as "that ambiguity wherein time and eternity touch each other, and with this the concept *temporality* is posited, when time constantly excludes [*afskærer*] eternity and eternity constantly pervades time." Or, as he puts it a few sentences later, "the future is the incognito in which the eternal, as incommensurable [*incommensurabelt*] with time, yet desires to preserve its

---

[74] For example, see *Journals*, 3746, IX A 486; 6593, X^2 A 560; *Practice in Christianity*, p. 142; (KW 20:143); SV 16:138; (12:133).

companionable intercourse [*Omgængelse*] with time."[75] This positive and concerned presence of the eternal in and with the conscious human self imparts the conviction that the unique self has eternal dignity and worth, and that the self has been given the task of becoming itself. So in *Sickness*, Anti-Climacus does not hesitate to speak of "something eternal in the self," even in the despairing self which has not succeeded in becoming itself and thus, in a sense, has lost the eternal. But this despairing self in its estrangement has two options in relating to the eternal which still encourages it to become itself. The self, with the conception of the self derived from the eternal, can determine to become that self directly, that is, by itself, on its own determining de novo what it wants to become without regard to what it *is* concretely in itself, that is, in *defiance* of the eternal. Or it can, "with the help of the eternal ... have courage to lose itself in order to win itself," to bring into actuality that self it has been given to be in possibility. This second option is "the thoroughfare to faith."[76]

Here, in our passage in *Works of Love*, this power of the eternal to help the self to become itself voluntarily is described perhaps even better than in *Sickness*, because here Kierkegaard uses the triadic concept of the love relationship in conjunction with the concept of reduplication. When the relationship with the eternal is described as "love" rather than "faith," then my relationship to the "other" is never just a singular relationship with the eternal (God) but is always a double relationship both with the eternal and with neighbour. Thus, Kierkegaard says, "when the eternal is in a human being, then the eternal is reduplicated in that person, so that, every moment it is in that person, it is in that person in a double manner: in an outward direction, and in an inward direction back into itself [i.e., into the eternal], but in such a way that this [double movement] is one and the same; because otherwise it is not reduplication."

Now Kierkegaard is able to say: "So it is with love. What love does, it is *that*; what love is, *that* it does—and in one and the same instant" (em-

---

[75] *The Concept of Anxiety*, p. 80; (KW 8:89); SV 6:177; (4:359). Walter Lowrie and Reidar Thomte translate *afskærer* as "intersect," but it clearly means to "cut off, bar, preclude," indicating what is called in the second quotation "incommensurability." Likewise, they both translate *Omgængelse* with neutral terms, "relation" and "association," while the word and its cognate, *Omgængelighed*, have a very positive sense of "sociability" and "intercourse" and "communion."

[76] *Sickness*, pp. 201f.; (KW 19:67f.); SV 15:122; (11:178f.). See also pp. 185, 188, 195; (KW 19:51, 55, 62); SV 15:108, 111, 117; (11:163, 167, 174).

phasis added). So when love "goes out of itself (in the outward direction), simultaneously it is in itself (in the inward direction); and in the same moment it is in itself, it therewith goes out of itself, in such a way that this going outward and this returning, this returning and this going outward, are simultaneously the one and the same." In going outward to the one who is in need of love, the self forgets (denies, annihilates) itself in pure obedience to the law of love in its conscience. But, as we have heard, the lover who forgets him/herself in going out to the other person "is not forgotten. ... Love thinks of him/her." That is to say, love goes back into itself in reduplicating for the lover what the lover has given away. "The lover who forgets him/herself is remembered by love. ... In this way love is always reduplicated in itself."[77]

So when the eternal is present as love in the self-consciousness of a human being, there is automatically reduplicated within that human being the dialectic of inward/outward that is integral to the eternal itself. And this dialectic delivers the human being from existing merely and immediately in one's qualities in-and-for-oneself. Kierkegaard says that being knowledgeable or wise may be a quality "being-for-itself" (*forsigværende*), which one does not or even cannot share with others. But not love. "If one should think that he/she were loving, but also that all others were not loving, ... here is a contradiction in terms [*i selve Tanken*], because to be loving is precisely to assume or presuppose that other human beings are loving. Love is not a quality being-for-itself, but a quality by which or in which you are for others."[78]

For a human being, however, this dialectic always involves one in a threefold relationship. As we have seen, being related to an other as one to be loved in and for his/her self, as one possessing infinite dignity and worth, requires the presence of a middle-determinant, love itself as an eternal dynamic. This eternal dynamic manifests itself as the absolute command of conscience, "Thou shalt love." And if and when I "stand before" this command as the dynamic of the eternal, with the courage of openness and honesty and hence "in fear and trembling," then two things happen, two things as "one and the same thing." First, I am enabled voluntarily to "deny" ("annihilate") my own self, actually to "forget" my own self's needs, desires, and happiness, because the total focus of my attention and my passionate interested concern has been turned outward toward the nearest human being(s) in need, the concrete indi-

---

77 *Works of Love*, pp. 261f.; SV 12:269f.; (9:267f.).
78 Ibid., p. 211; SV 12:216; (9:214).

vidual(s) whom I can see, and I choose to do immediately here and now what I am able to do for the other(s). So the "content" of "the one thing needful," of the absolute good of infinite demand in time, is determined by: (1) what the other person needs for the fulfilment of his/her own unique God-given unique selfhood, (2) what *I*, in my own unique selfhood, am able to do here and now, (3) my turning of my attention to the other's cry for help (silent or shouted), with all my most inward, infinite, passionate, personal, earnest interestedness and hence with decisive resolve to stamp upon my action "that inner necessity which excludes the thought of any other possibility." Then the second thing happens, namely, a reduplication of this outward movement in an inward direction, i.e., within and toward myself. The turning of my attention outward operates as both an expression and a reaffirmation of my knowing and believing that I too am the object of concern and encouragement (love) from the eternal dynamic that sets the conditions and possibilities of all human existence. In other words, a person who, by "losing" oneself, acts so as to honour and encourage the unique identity of another human being discovers that, as a result (a reduplication), one "finds" oneself, i.e., one comes to a realization of and belief in one's own infinite dignity and worth. This event is not something one worked for or aimed at or even expected. Rather, this event "happens"; it comes not from the dialectic between the two human beings involved in the love relationship, but from a "middle-determinant" or "third-party" in the relationship, namely, love itself.[79]

One final comment on this vision (theory) of love. The last point in the previous paragraph raises a conundrum which Kierkegaard does not directly acknowledge or discuss, but certainly implies. In the triadic (*Tredobbelte*) relationship of love, love-itself (God) is not the only middle-determinant (*Mellembestemmelse*) or third-party (*Tredieman*) that must be present to the relationship of the other two. Each point of the triangle is required for the maintenance of the relationship between the other two. So Kierkegaard says, "As soon as a love-relationship does not lead me to God, and as soon as I in a love-relationship do not lead the other human being to God, this love ... is not true love. ... God in this way not

---

[79] For Kierkegaard's specifically Christian formulation of the concept of reduplication see *Christian Discourses*, pp. 43, 215f.; SV 13:44, 197f.; (10:45, 208f.); and *Practice in Christianity*, pp. 142, 159, 201; (KW 20:143, 159, 205); SV 16:138, 155, 192f.; (12:133, 149, 189). These passages stress that being before God in reduplication does not destroy one's freedom but establishes it. So Christ's "drawing" human beings to himself by his divine love actually "establishes a choice." So "a self is reduplication, is freedom."

only becomes the third-party in every relationship of love but essentially becomes the only loved object, so that it is not the husband who is the wife's beloved, but it is God, and it is the wife who is helped by the husband to love God, and conversely, and so on."[80]

There are two difficulties with this passage, one merely linguistic, the other substantive. The latter is our concern here, but the first must be clarified before we proceed.

Kierkegaard is using "love" in two different senses when he says that every true "love-relationship" must lead the other person to "love God," and hence it is misleading if not mistaken to say that God "becomes the only loved object." "Loving" my neighbour means something quite different from "loving" God. Kierkegaard has gone to great lengths to show that "loving" my neighbour means to honour and respect every other human being as possessing equal uniqueness in dignity and worth, and thus "loving" my neighbour means to sacrifice passionately my own self-concern in order to help every other person to find his or her own unique identity as a gift and demand from the eternal dynamic of love-itself (God). Obviously, when I say that I "love" God, I do not mean that I want to help God find God's unique identity. Rather, I mean that I have come to know and to believe, with awe and wonder and "fear and trembling," and with grateful acquiescence, that there is an eternal dynamic at the heart of reality which has given me being and my own individual personal identity, and which constantly seeks to demand and to evoke that possibility into actuality, which (whom) therefore I must call "love-itself." In other words, to "love God" really means to know and to believe that "Love is God" and that "love-itself loves me." So it is proper and true that my neighbour is the object of my love, even though that love is derivative of and dependent on God (love-itself) as the object of my love. This clarification of terminology now helps us state the substantive difficulty.

The sticking point is indicated in the passage by the words "and conversely, and so on," which mean: "and on around the triangle." The implication of this interpretation, which Kierkegaard himself does not make explicit, is this: love-itself (God) is not present and related to one human being *except* in conjunction with the presence of another human being who manifests love to the first human being. In other words, no human being has a love relationship which is one-on-one with the

---

80 For this language and the quotation, see again *Works of Love*, p. 124; SV 12:120; (9:116f.).

eternal dynamic of love-itself, no matter how inward, spiritual, subjective, personal, and private that relationship may be. Granted, it is the task of each human being not to become the object of the other's love in the same sense that God is the object, because "no human being *is love*," that is, the ultimate source and guarantor of another's infinite dignity and worth; so granted it is the task of every lover to lead the other to love of the eternal (see note 43 above).

The conundrum can be stated as follows. It is clear that I cannot help an other to love the eternal unless I myself already know what it is to love and to be loved by the eternal. But how can I know that—if the triadic relationship holds—unless I have already been helped by an other who already knows what it is to love and be loved by the eternal? How does it all get started?

Kierkegaard as theologian has a direct answer to this question: the eternal takes the initiative by entering time in the God-man, Jesus Christ, and thus encounters human beings with the startling demand, "Thou shalt love," based on the startling presupposition that "love presupposes love in the other." But, as humanist, Kierkegaard does not have this answer available. And as humanist (as well as theologian) he wants to acknowledge that love is fundamental to human nature as such, and that consciousness of it is not lost even in the depth of despair.

For example, he faces the same dilemma when he raises the question as to how we humans decide "What is the law's demand of a human being?" The usual answer is "Well, human beings are going to decide this." But "Which human beings?" We do not trust any single person to make the decision. So, "is the agreement of a crowd of human beings, a certain number of votes, sufficient for this decision? How great a number?" And "if a purely human determination of what the law demands is the law's demand, ... how then can the individual come to begin to act ...? For in order to begin to act the individual must first find out from 'the others' what the law's demand is; but every one of these others must, each as an individual, find this out from 'the others'. ... The determinant 'the others' becomes fanciful, and the fancifully sought determination of what is the law's demand becomes a false alarm."

Kierkegaard's resolution for this dilemma is, of course, to bring in God as the middle-determinant. And this is possible because the human race has two simultaneous "courses" or "movements" (*Gang*) of existence. The primary one is its "existence in God," the secondary one is "actual existence." And it is by and from its primary existence that "every individual gets to know the law's demand from God," including the law of love. So it is the duty of every individual "unconditionally to obey and to hold fast to the God-relationship and the God-demand, thereby expressing for one's own part that God exists and is the only master. ... Only then is there strength and meaning and truth and actuality in existence."

Theoretically it would seem that everyone would then hear the one and the same command, and that we could learn it from each other. But what God demands, what the law of love demands, is related strictly to the unique individuality of each person, and to the particularity of the situation one faces, and to the unique individuality of the other one who needs to be loved. Therefore, "God, for the sake of certitude and equitableness and responsibility, wants every individual to get to know the law's demand from [God]. ... Thus it is also with the law of love. There is strength and truth and firmness in existence when we all, each one individually, get to know from God what is the demand according to which we have to direct our lives."[81]

How does this example help to resolve the dilemma that emerges from the triadic relationship of love? Kierkegaard proposes that the ethical problem, as to what is the "right" and "good" thing to do, requires a religious resolution, which comes not in the form of revealed laws that can be objectively stated and objectively applied, but in the form of an answer that comes inwardly and privately in the strenuous spiritual struggle of the individual who stands consciously in the presence of the eternal dynamic of the absolute telos. And ultimately, at the depth of such spiritual struggle, one comes to know that the absolute good speaks in the accents of love. Then we, each of us individually, will come to know "the demand according to which we have to direct our lives," and so to know in each situation *what* is the "content" of the "one thing needful," and so to acquire that courage which will resolve the final dilemma of *how* to do what we know in our hearts is the "truth."

---

81 All of the quotations since the last endnote are from ibid., pp. 120–2; SV 12:115–18; (9:111–14). But for the statement in the last paragraph that what God demands is related strictly to the unique individuality and situation of each person, see p. 217; SV 12:222f.; (9:220f.). Here is the key passage we have referred to several times as the most radical ethical statement Kierkegaard has made in all of his writings, namely, that two individuals, both of whom are "honourable, upright, respectable, God-fearing, can under the same state of affairs do just the opposite." Otherwise, "the God-relationship would not essentially exist, not in its deepest sense." And then "everything would turn outward, fulfilling itself in the life of the state or society." Then life would indeed become very easy, "but also exceedingly empty; then neither strenuous [spiritual] exertion nor self-deepening would be possible or required."

Kierkegaard (Climacus) believes that human nature as such retains the capacity for what he calls religiousness A: (1) the initial capacity for resignation of immediate ends in favour of a direction toward an absolute telos or absolute ends; (2) the essential capacity for the suffering involved in dying away from immediacy at a purely aesthetic/rational level; (3) the decisive capacity for "total guilt consciousness" which negatively takes the form of ethical impotence and self-denial, and which positively takes the form of self-annihilation in order to make room for the eternal (God) within one's consciousness, which means that one is conscious of being "decisively changed, ... becoming conscious by putting guilt together with the relationship to an eternal blessedness," and thus guilt-consciousness brings not only resentment (*Nagende*) but also alleviation (*Lindrende*) "because it is an expression of freedom ... in the ethical-religious sphere, where ... freedom is distinguished by guilt, not directly distinguished aesthetically, [rather] freedom distinguished by freedom."[82] And, as we have seen above, in *Works of Love* Kierkegaard proposes that this universal human religious capacity and the universal human need for love are so fundamental to human nature itself that the human being's basic religious capacity is able to take the form of the conscious perception that the eternal dynamic of all being has the essential quality of love. Therefore, those individuals who do not shut themselves off from their higher nature in order to live in the "basement" of immediacy and of merely outward determinants of conceptual abstractions or socially dictated patterns of behaviour are able to point each other toward the eternal itself in its dynamic of love, and so encourage each other to listen to and to follow the demands of that dynamic in all of their human relationships. And individuals who succeed in doing so will in the end also experience the return of that love toward themselves, by the power of reduplication issuing from eternal love-it-self.

Thus the conundrum of circularity as posed above gets resolved. "How does it all get started" is explained by the universal human resource of religious love which is built into the fundamental structure of human nature. Granted, that love may be experienced initially in the form of the self-centred gratification that comes from a mother's devotion to her child (which is so often lacking), and granted, it may soon seek to work through the sexual drive (which is universally deformed). Yet that love does get universally manifested in affirming and stimulating expressions

---

82 *Postscript*, p. 475; (KW 12.1:534); SV 10:206; (7:466).

among a host of individuals throughout the world and throughout history. And these expressions constantly give rise to a multitude of formulations in the stories, myths, literatures, philosophies, and religions of the great tribes of the human race. And although all of these expressions have their limitations and go through phases of corruption, still enough of the original truth and purity of the reality gets through in order to create mutually inspiring and supporting examples and occasions of that love, and these serve to strengthen and to keep alive the human perception of and belief in the eternal dynamic of that love. These expressions comprise the legitimacy of Climacus's characterization of religiousness A.

It should also be remembered that Climacus insists that a human being must experience the validity of this kind of universal ethical-religious truth (religiousness A) prior to and as a groundwork for sharing in the particularity of Christian faith (religiousness B). And neither Anti-Climacus in *Sickness* and *Practice in Christianity*, nor Kierkegaard in his late discourses, ever retracts this assumption.

Kierkegaard refuses to acknowledge that individuals who experience such ethical-religious truth might want to collect in some kind of group in order to encourage and learn from each other. This is what he says "the world" does. "If in self-love a human being wants to stick together with some other self-loving people, especially with many other self-loving people, then the world calls it love. Further the world cannot go in defining what love is, because it has neither God nor neighbour as a middle-determinant." So "a generous, sacrificial, magnanimous *human* love, which is not yet Christian love, is ridiculed by the world as foolishness" (emphasis added).[83] In this way Kierkegaard does insist that there are those individuals who, out of the resources of the human spirit as such (with its immanent inward awareness of a point of stopping in silence and awe and fear and trembling before the mystery of the eternal other), are capable of a self-denying, outgoing love that has both the eternal (God) and neighbour as middle-determinants, forming the essential triangle of true love.

This phenomenon of self-forgetting sacrificial love (that goes out to all those in need) is more profoundly present and operative in human nature, and finds much more varied expression in concrete acts, than Kierkegaard could ever have known or even suspected within the confines of his provincial setting and the limited scope of his personal social

---

83 *Works of Love*, pp. 123f.; SV 12:119; (9:115f.).

relationships. Before the end of his own century there emerged groups of individuals who risked their fortunes and their very lives in their dedication to bring slavery to an end, or to bring relief to the victims of the industrial revolution. And in the twentieth century, all of its "horrors of history" (Eliade) have been matched step by step with "works of love" whose agents have been dedicated to bringing justice to all racial and ethnic minorities, to branding as a delusion the belief that war and militarism can solve the political and social conflicts of the world, to bringing food for the bodies and enlightenment to the minds of the physically and mentally oppressed peoples of the planet, to inventing and projecting a new way of living that will reverse the destruction of our natural environment before the earth becomes uninhabitable for the human race and other species, and above all to lifting up the vision of the whole human race living in unity and harmony on our spaceship Earth.

And the tens of thousands who have performed these works of love have been propelled by what Kierkegaard has described as the ethical/religious consciousness of the human spirit, even though many of them would not use either the term "ethical" or the term "religious" to describe their own motivation. They would more likely speak in Kierkegaard's language of the recognition of the absolute dignity and worth of every human being without exception, the language of a "love" that "presupposes love" in *every* other human being, no matter of what race, ethnic group, nationality, or economic class. Recently, the present author asked one such doer of works of love whether the people she worked with had any religious motivation. She answered, "Some do, some don't. Personally I don't." Then what did motivate her? "It started with simply seeing the devastation brought to the lives of innocent people by the Viet Nam war, and its total uselessness. And many persons who, individually or in groups, now visit third world countries are converted [her word] simply by seeing the misery in which people live, especially when they see that these people are working as hard as they can twelve to fifteen hours a day merely to survive. Then these individuals simply and directly know that they have to forget themselves and help." In other words, she sees at work in these individuals the truth of Kierkegaard's insistence on the reality of the voice of conscience issuing the great "Thou shalt love!" This fundamental attitude, of immediate unquestioning obedience to the voice of conscience, has recently reoccurred in numerous unrelated instances of tens of thousands of people being moved by simple human compassion to sacrifice their time, talents, money, and comfort in order to help those whose lives have been devasted by hurricanes, floods, earthquakes, droughts, and war.

The one thing that Kierkegaard had not experienced and did not perceive in such manifestations of love (laid at the ground of every human spirit) was that the individuals so motivated have repeatedly found it natural and helpful to "stick together" in loosely organized societies or communities. Perhaps Kierkegaard's judgment that any form of group-religion is a form of "group-selfishness" was shaped by his suspicions of what he saw as the inward-directed, pietistic, and mystical emphasis of the "communal" Christian faith practised among the Grundvigians of his day. But in our day many have found some kind of association to be helpful as means of learning from and encouraging each other, as means for propagating the "faith" and for "converting" more individuals to this way of life, and as means for bringing pressure for reform of complex social, economic, and political structures which work, sometimes unwittingly, for the oppression and even destruction of the fundamental dignity and worth of individuals. Such associations and their "movements" would do well to listen to Kierkegaard's warnings about the dangers of the self-deification of the *we*, and of the demonic possibilities of the loss of individuality in any "mass" or "crowd" or "herd."[84] But these warnings must not be allowed to negate the very positive possibilities of human association of like-minded individuals when these individuals in their corporate existence remain absolutely committed to the "love" which affirms the ultimate and infinite dignity and worth of every single individual, and which guards against every tendency to submerge, lose, and even destroy the individual for the good of the group.

This optimistic view of the universal possibilities of love in the human species gets severely questioned by Kierkegaard as he explores more fully the universality of sin and despair, that is, in his new "Christian" authorship under the pseudonym of Anti-Climacus. As we look at how Kierkegaard the Christian theologian exposits these concepts, we will have to ask if his views of love as humanist survive or are amended or are rejected. And we will seek to discover how he understands the unique content and the peculiar function of the specifically Christian experience of the love of God in Jesus Christ.

These reflections bring us to our fifth and last specification of the nature of love according to Kierkegaard.

---

84 See chapters 3 and 4 in Merold Westphal's *Kierkegaard's Critique of Reason and Society*.

WORKS OF LOVE TRANSFORM HUMAN EXISTENCE

The penultimate question about Kierkegaard's concept of love is this: how far and in what ways does an ethical/religious love transform human existence *concretely*? (The ultimate question is: are the "works of love" free?—which we will take up as our concluding chapter on the indeterminacy or freedom in the leap of love.) Hence we are finally ready to give a direct answer to the question: what are the concrete works of love? Can they be specified?

As we have seen, Kierkegaard refuses to suggest any list of specific virtues which could be used as an objective measure of obedience to the absolute good or to the principle of love. Indeed, he (Climacus) goes so far as to assert in *Postscript* that the "actuality" of a good deed "is not the external action but an inwardness [*Indvorteshed*] in which the individual abolishes possibility and identifies with the thought in such a way as to exist therein. This is action." So, "Actuality is interestedness in existing therein" (i.e., in the "content" of the thought). Luther's actual act was not in standing before the Diet of Worms but was already performed "from the moment he existed in willing [it] with the passionate decision of his entire subjectivity."[85]

Later, however (as we have seen above), in *Works of Love*, *Practice in Christianity*, and journal entries about "the situation" (dated 1848–54), Kierkegaard comes to stress more and more the concrete conditions or situation as integral to and the fulfilment of "the action." In the journal entries he says such things as "It is the situation ... which reveals whether one's protestations of the truth within are [one's] character." And, there is "a distinction between understanding in possibility ... and understanding in actuality. It is impossible to become spirit in 'possiblity.' ... The situation must be present." And, the situation is always a spot at which one is "shot out into the infinite," where one "ventures out into water 70,000 fathoms deep. This is the situation."[86] This stress is important to Kierkegaard because it is only in the enactment of a faithful or loving intention within the conditions of the actual situation that the actor experiences inescapable suffering that comes from inevitable

---

85 *Postscript*, pp. 302, 304; (KW 12.1:339, 341); SV 10:42–3; (7:293, 295). The Hongs are mistaken in identifying the meaning of this passage with Kierkegaard's later insistence on the importance of "the situation." They correctly say that the emphasis here is on "beliefful action," but Kierkegaard has something more in mind in "the situation." (See Hongs' comment in their note 498 in *Journals* entry 1880; x³ A 454.)

86 *Journals*, 4314; x⁴ A 608; 4326, x¹ A 417; 1142; x⁴ A 114.

collision with the "world's" opposition. In other words, the object of human love is not the neighbour we imagine in intention but "the human beings we see," the nearest concrete individual who cries out in need.

Hence Kierkegaard reminds us that "in this little book we are constantly dealing only with the works of love, and therefore not with God's love but with human love. ... When in regard to human love we say that love abides, this [abiding] is readily seen to be a work [deed], or that it [the abiding] is not a quality of repose which love as such possesses, but a quality acquired in each moment, and also every moment it is acquired, it is again an active [*virksom*] deed." In other words, "one's love abides [only] in relationship to human beings."[87] So it is clear that works of love are not *merely* a matter of "willing [i.e., intending] with the passionate decision of one's entire subjectivity."

Certainly, a deed that is done without this passionate decision is not a work of love, but if the passionate loving decision or intention is not completed in an overt act "in relationship to [an other] human being" within the particular conditions or situation of an instant of space/time (here and now!), then no work of love has occurred. This does not mean that there are specific words or deeds which, if one simply does them, one "thereby unconditionally demonstrates love. It depends on *how* the deed is done." There are so-called good (loving) works such as contributing to charity, visiting the widow, clothing the naked, etc. But "one can perform [so-called] works of love in an unloving, even in a self-loving way, and when this is so, the works of love are nevertheless not the work of love." It is quite possible, "in preoccupation with *what* one does, to forget *how* one does it."[88]

While acknowledging this essential dialectic of inward/outward in the authentic work of love, yet it is our interest here to ask whether the "what" or content of love can be given any specification, whether Kierkegaard's spiritual love does make possible and encourage a "transformation of one's whole existence" in certain concrete forms and directions, or negatively, whether it discourages and even rules out certain forms of behaviour as failures of love. We have previously heard Kierkegaard castigate hate, envy, small-mindedness, lust, etc. as sure signs of the lack of love. In the passage just quoted he includes as positive expressions of love such things as giving money to the poor, visiting the bereaved and lonely, caring for the naked and starving. He has also

---

87 *Works of Love*, p. 280; sv 12:289; (9:287f.).
88 Ibid., p. 30; sv 12:18f.; (9:16f.).

strongly condemned every human relationship wherein one human person "loves" another human person in the sense of absorbing the other as an extension of one's own being, where the romantic notion of "becoming one" in love really means that one of the parties eliminates or sublimates any quality which differentiates him/her from the other party.

In *Works of Love*, however, Kierkegaard provides a more dramatic exposition of the content of love's works by mounting a fervent attack on certain examples of human failure in loving, especially failures to *do* what one knows (believes) and even confesses to be the good and loving "one thing needful" in a particular situation or set of circumstances. And then he goes on to suggest a basic principle that emerges in every single act of authentic love in relationship to other human beings. Let us look at the examples first.

In these examples Kierkegaard's formal principle is that one's true character, one's real beliefs and ultimate commitments, are not demonstrated in the battle of ideas against ideas but "when one battles in the actuality of life." There is an essential difference between "understanding at a distance" and understanding "close at hand" (*nærved*). "In a quiet hour's distance from all the confusion of life and the world, every human being understands what the highest is. ... [B]ut when confusion begins, understanding flees, or it reveals that this understanding was at a distance." The real test of what one stands for is this: "how far is it from what one understands to what one does, ... between understanding and action?" So a "distinguished person" may prefer to live in "stately seclusion," and likewise an "insignificant person" may choose "quiet obscurity," because it is easier and more comfortable when one "avoids opposition."[89]

In his examples of understanding that comes in and through action "close at hand," however, Kierkegaard becomes very specific. He contends that even those who do not praise God or Christianity are, on a purely humanistic basis, caused to "shudder" at the inhumanity of a classification of people according to caste. So he brands as "evil" (*Onde*) any attitude that encourages one human being to use the "distinctions of earthly life" to deny "kinship" with other human beings, even to the point of "presumptuously and insanely" contending that an other one "does not exist," i.e. as a human. And (quite in contrast with his own contemporaries who presented "Christian" arguments for slavery in

[89] Ibid., pp. 88, 93; SV 12:81, 86; (9:78f., 84).

America) he proclaims that, because Christianity has secured "the kinship of all human beings ... by every individual's equal kinship with and relationship to God in Christ," therefore "the times are past when the powerful and prominent alone were human beings, and the others [mere] serfs and slaves." Then he specifically adds, "This is owed to Christianity."

The fact that Kierkegaard, on both a humanitarian and Christian basis, spends seven or eight pages in a vehement condemnation of serfdom and slavery, and its aftermaths in Danish society, is interesting and significant in several respects, both personal and theoretical. On the personal side, he was only one generation out of serfdom on both his father's and mother's side. His father, Michael Pedersen Kierkegaard, was born in Jutland of peasant stock in 1756, and so was born into villeinage (*Stavnsbaand*). In the late seventeenth century the new landed nobility of counts and barons had been able to force the crown to concede to them the right to force peasants to occupy their estates and to demand free labour from their tenants, and these villeins were often abused by their masters, who used physical force in order to extract increased production. *Stavnsbaand* was not legally ended until 20 June 1788, and even then less than half of the Danish peasants had become freeholders by 1807.[90]

The bitter physical and mental anguish experienced in these conditions by Kierkegaard's father stayed with him to his dying day and stamped itself on the consciousness of the child Søren. Eight years after his father's death, just after finishing *Postscript* and resolving to fulfil his father's fervent desire that he qualify as a pastor, Kierkegaard confides this anguish to his journals (in 1846): "How horrifying the condition of the man, who once as a little boy, while tending sheep on the Jutland heath, suffering from extreme hardship, hunger and exhaustion, stood upon a hillock and cursed God—and the man was unable to forget it when he was eighty-two years old" (the age at which Kierkegaard's father died in 1838).[91] It seems clear that this anguish (his father's and his

---

90 See the article on "Denmark" in the 1972 edition of the *Encyclopædia Britannica*, vol. 7, pp. 243f. For a more thorough account of *stavnsbaand* and its gradual reform, see Bruce Kirmmse, *Kierkegaard in Golden Age Denmark*, the section on "The Peasant Reforms," pp. 12–21. Kirmmse shows that the liberal reform party that came to power in 1784 was motivated by a moralistic and utilitarian form of Christianity rather than pietism. They of course also had economic motives (see pp. 36–7).

91 *Journals*, 5874; VII[1] A 5. Read also 5873; VII[1] A 4, where he expresses his intention to quit writing and to become a pastor (which entry is dated 7 February 1846).

own) found expression again a year later in his impassioned attack on serfdom and slavery as the antithesis and denial of spiritual love.

The little boy was delivered from this physically and mentally depressing serfdom when he was twelve years old. A maternal uncle brought M.P. Kierkegaard to Copenhagen and employed him in the business of selling the wool that came from those same Jutland sheep. Ten years later he had his own company in the wholesale wool trade, in 1780 he expanded into foodstuffs, and in 1788 he received a royal patent to deal in Chinese and East India merchandise, as well as in sugar, coffee beans, etc. from the Danish West Indies.[92] This kind of trade was made possible in the mid-eighteenth century by French and English enterprises in Asia and America, when Denmark also acquired colonies in St Croix and St Thomas in the West Indies.[93] This latter development suggests another source for the passion of Søren Kierkegaard's attack on serfdom and slavery. The ships that brought his father's wares from the West Indies were, in all probability, engaging in the so-called "triangular slave trade." The ships left European ports loaded with liquor, firearms, cloth goods, and various trinkets to be exchanged for slaves on the west coast of Africa. Then the slaves were transported for sale in the colonies in the West Indies and the American continent. Finally, the ships were loaded with various staples from these areas for the homeward trip to Europe.[94] Hence Søren's inherited wealth, which gave him the freedom to remain unemployed and to write, was made possible at least indirectly by the enormous profits from one of the most vicious processes of enslavement ever practised in human history.

Was this in his mind, with a sense of guilt for living on such "dirty" money, when he wrote those passages in *Works of Love*? He must have been aware of the recent battles which brought an end to slavery. He could claim that "this is owed to Christianity," because of the work of the Société des Amis des Noirs founded in France in 1788, with the participation of Abbé Grégoire, and of the work of the Society for the Abolition of the Slave Trade founded in England in 1787, under the leadership of William Wilberforce and the Quakers. Their victories had been won only a few years before his birth, when the Convention of the French Revolution adopted in 1794 "the first enactment in history pro-

---

92 Walter Lowrie, *Kierkegaard*, pp. 19, 25.
93 *Encyclopædia Britannica*, vol. 7. pp. 243f.
94 The article on "Slavery" in *Encyclopædia Britannica*, vol. 20, pp. 634f.

hibiting slavery," and when the British Parliament adopted in 1811 a bill proclaiming slave trading to be a criminal offence.[95]

The point to this extended detour into biography and history is that Kierkegaard's use of the abolition of serfdom and slavery as a prime example of the concrete enactment and impact of spiritual (christian) love implies certain things about the ethical-religious consciousness and life of the individual, which things he does not seem to be aware of, or which he does not want to admit. (In the following pages we will use "christian" in lower case to indicate the nature of love rather than its origin.) He argues that "the one who loves one's neighbour is tranquil. One is made tranquil by being content with the earthly distinction alloted to him/her. ... One shall not covet what is one's neighbour's, ... nor the advantages granted him in life." So "Christianity has not wanted to storm forth to abolish distinctions, neither the distinction of prominence nor the distinction of insignificance, nor has it wanted in a worldly manner to make a worldly compromise between distinctions." All that neighbourly love desires is to acknowledge the "eternal likeness" and the "equality of the eternal" that resides in every individual in spite of all worldly distinctions.[96]

So in the very pages where he praises spiritual love (and Christianity) for playing a part in the abolition of serfdom and slavery, Kierkegaard warns that anyone of a more privileged class who loves members of the poor and lower classes as equals stands in "double danger." Such a one will be despised by one's peers and called a traitor and an egotist. On the other hand, the poor will reward such a one with mockery and insult because they see only the presumption of a do-gooder in the acts of love. Of course, "If one had sought to stand at the head of the humbler folk in a rebellion to trample down the differences of rank, then they could perhaps have honoured and loved such a one." But one moved by authentic love would not do this, because such a one would want only to express love's basic need—"to love one's neighbour," that is, as an individual.[97]

What Kierkegaard ignores is that villeinage on the soil of Jutland might well have survived into his own day if it had not been for the political activities of J.F. Struensee against the conservative landowners in the 1770s, and of C.D.F. Reventlow, who was the driving force of a government commission which finally freed the peasants in the 1780s. And

---

95 Ibid., pp. 637–9.
96 *Works of Love*, pp. 93, 96; SV 12:86, 90; (9:83, 87).
97 Ibid., p. 86; SV 12:79; (9:77).

both of these members of the aristocracy were moved by humanitarian reasons, derived from moralistic utilitarianism of the liberal reform movement, as well as possibly by religious beliefs. Likewise, slavery would not have ended when it did if the members of the societies in France, England, and later in America had not been politically active abolitionists, bringing the pressure of their individual consciences to bear upon the governing political entities of their respective countries. Kierkegaard seems to close his mind to the possibility—indeed, the actuality—that the political activities of abolitionists aimed at changing the legal structures of societies were often motivated precisely by that honour and concern for the eternal worth and dignity of every individual which he calls "love." Most of the abolitionists were not utopian idealists who fought in the name of some abstract concept of the perfect society. They were moved by compassion for those human individuals, seen with their own eyes, who were reduced to the status of tortured animals.

In some of the other examples Kierkegaard gives in the context of this same chapter in *Works of Love*, he seems to leave room for such action, or at least it is difficult to see how his language could lead to any other conclusion. He says that authentic love condemns a person's "haughtiness and pride" which conveys to others that "they do not exist for him." Love condemns that arrogance which "demands an expression of slavish subjection" from others. It condemns those who avoid contact, however genteelly, with those of lower class, because it is basically "inhuman and unchristian ... to want to deny one's relationship in the human race with all human beings, with absolutely every human-being." Any division of humans into separate classes is depravity for those of each and every class, because to "shrivel up in one's poverty" or to "wrap oneself in one's prominence" prevents one from being built up by love and in love.

Then Kierkegaard gives three examples of this kind of failure: (1) the eloquent distinguished person who advocates love to one's neighbour within the confines of his/her own upper-class circles, but cannot subject his/her intention to doing it in actuality, and thus maintains the barriers; (2) the scholar who "lectures enthusiastically on the doctrine of the equality of all human-beings" but only within the protective walls of academe; (3) the rich man who "makes every concession to the likeness of all human beings," but only in the company of other rich men. Against them all Kierkegaard throws the expression "To go with God," because "when one goes with God ... one is constrained to see, and to see in a unique way. When you go in company with God you need to see only one single person in misery, and you will not be able to escape what Christianity will have you understand, human likeness."[98]

Well, how do I affirm that others "exist" for me as individuals of eternal dignity? How do I implement my "relationship in the human race with all other human beings"? How do I bring my love of neighbour out from behind the distinctions of class "into actuality," and thus express concretely "the likeness of all human beings"? How do I "see one single person in misery" and do something that will reveal God's love for her/him? As we have seen, Kierkegaard's concept of the triadic structure of the love-relationship means that eternity's affirmation of a person's infinite dignity and worth comes to that person's consciousness only in, with, and through the act of love toward that person from another human being. So how does my obedience to the law of love define the "content" of my act of love?

Again, as we have stressed, "what" I do to point to and to affirm that other person's "eternal equality" depends upon the concrete conditions and situation of that person. And in one way, my act does seek to "remove" the distinctions which qualify that person. On the one hand, Jesus told the "rich young ruler" to sell all his possessions and give the proceeds to the poor. On the other hand, Jesus said that he had come to bring "good news to the poor, ... release to the captives, ... sight to the blind, ... liberty for those who are oppressed" (Lk. 4:18). As Kierkegaard says repeatedly, the demands of the equality of all humans can be as onerous and arduous for the poor and insignificant as for the rich and distinguished, because with the release from worldly distinctions and the assumption of eternal equality come freedom and responsibility.

But it is Kierkegaard himself who finally in *Sickness* defines the human self as a synthesis and concrete unity of the infinite *and* the finite, of the eternal *and* the temporal, of possibility *and* necessity. How then can he, in *Works of Love*, divorce the affirmation of a person's eternal equality in dignity and worth before God from a concern for the finite physical/social conditions that enable and are necessary for that person's actualization of his/her self's possibility? He does not really intend to do so, but he has a double worry. On the one hand, he sees how easy it is to be deceived into thinking that if you change the external conditions in which people live, you automatically change and bring to fulfilment

[98] Ibid., pp. 84–7; SV 12:77–80; (9:75–8).

their inward being as free and responsible persons (selves). He is convinced that this is not true, for either the rich or the poor. He says that we must not yield to "the presumptuous delusion that only the mighty and famous are the guilty ones, because if the poor and weak merely aspire defiantly for the superiority denied them in earthly existence instead of humbly aspiring for Christianity's blessed equality, this also damages the soul."[99]

On the other hand, Kierkegaard's social/political realism brings him very close to pessimism. He recognizes that there is "a well-intended secularity" which seeks "to bring about likeness among human-beings, to apportion the conditions of temporal existence equally, if possible, to all human-beings." It goes about defining this goal of one, ideal, temporal condition for all "with the aid of calculations and surveys," and "it rejoices when it succeeds in making temporal conditions similar for more and more." But in the end, Kierkegaard insists, even this well-intended worldliness "recognizes that its struggle is a pious wish, ... that its prospects are remote; if it rightly understood itself it would perceive that its vision will never be achieved in time, that even if this struggle were continued for millennia it would never attain its goal."[100]

The alternative to this futile struggle for secular equality, Kierkegaard proposes, is for everyone, whether poor or mighty, to "permeate his/her distinction with the sanctifying thought [*Tanke*] of christian equality," and thereby "lift oneself above the distinctions of earthly existence." Thus, in contrast to the ever-delayed utopia of social reform, "christianity is immediately at the goal, aided by the short-cut of the eternal: it allows all the distinctions to stand, but it teaches the equality of the eternal." So, "christianity will not take the distinction away, whether of aristocratic rank or of poverty," even though it "will not in partiality side with with any temporal distinction."[101]

What does all this mean concretely? Just what is a "work of love"? Is it nothing more than a "sanctifying thought," telling the neighbour in need to "go with God" and learn from God that everyone shares in the "equality of eternity"? Or does a work of love address the whole self of the single individual in misery, one's finite physical/social situation as well as one's eternal selfhood?

---

99 Ibid., p. 81; SV 12:74; (9:72).
100 Ibid., p. 82; SV 12:75; (9:73).
101 Ibid., pp. 82f., 81; SV 12:75, 74; (9:73, 72).

Let us suppose that Michael P. Kierkegaard, just after he had cursed God for his miserable plight at the age of twelve, had written his maternal uncle in Copenhagen, Niels Andersen Seding, appealing to the latter's "Christian love" for help. Michael would have been urgent in his request because he knew that if he stayed in Jutland just two more years, he would be bound to the estate as a villein for the next twenty-two years of his life. In that year of 1768 every peasant's son was still subject to villeinage from ages fourteen to thirty-six. Suppose the uncle anticipated what Søren Kierkegaard was later to write about christian love, and so he wrote Michael that Michael should not be concerned about living as a peasant/villein because christian love teaches that every individual shares alike in "the equality of the eternal." So Michael should turn inwardly to his God-relationship and learn from God that, whatever his status in this world, he possesses infinite dignity and worth. Then he would be able to "lift himself above the distinctions of earthly existence," and would not rebel against what life has allotted to him, because "one cannot live without the distinctions of earthly life which belong to each individual, whether by virtue of birth, position, circumstance, education, etc."[102]

Would that letter comprise a "work of love"? If the uncle had not brought Michael to Copenhagen, Michael might have been lucky and become a freehold farmer, but his son Søren would never have attended the university, or had the economic freedom to spend his life writing. If we were to interpret these words from *Works of Love* in this way, they would sound very much as if they issued from "a scholar ... lecturing enthusiastically on the doctrine of the equality of all human-beings" from within the caste distinctions of one who lives in the magnificent house on the Nytorv. But surely Kierkegaard would object to this reading of his words. The Kierkegaard who repeatedly and passionately proclaims in this book that "Serfdom's abominable era is past!" would not see the words of that supposed letter from the uncle as a "work of love." If God's love brought the end to serfdom and slavery, then God's love came concretely not only in the uncle's kindness toward Michael, but also in the courageous stand of persons like Struensee and Reventlow against their own aristocratic class, for the purpose of challenging the very moral and legal grounds of serfdom and for changing the social/political structure so that what Kierkegaard called the "equality of eternity" might not

---

102 Ibid., p. 81; SV 12:73; (9:71).

remain just a fond dream of possibility for the peasants, but become an actuality for them.

Kierkegaard must have known all this, because when he was eight years old (1821), his father made a large donation to the parish of Sæding in Jutland in memory of his uncle, N.A. Seding, who had delivered him from serfdom. And it is significant that the money was to be used to secure a good teacher for the school in Sæding, to help the needy pupils and to purchase suitable text-books.[103] Surely, when Søren later wrote that "love" brought serfdom to an end, he must have had in mind not only the kindness of N.A. Seding, but also the gift of his father to the school, as "works of love."

Of course, what was actualized in the closing decades of the eighteenth century was only the beginnings of a relative approximation of the ideal, but what would Kierkegaard think of the socialist equality of all citizens of Denmark today? Is it not strange that Kierkegaard derides the goal of "well-intended secularity" to make "temporal conditions similar for more and more," simply because this goal can only be a relative approximation of an impossible ideal of total equality? He always maintains that even the Christian life of faith is nothing more than a process of becoming, a series of acts in obedience to the absolute demands of the eternal but acts which never achieve the absolute concretely. The Christian life of faith is never, in existence, a finished product but only "on the way," and this is certainly also true of the life lived out of the faith of immanence in religiousness A. Kierkegaard would probably reply that the desire and drive for equality in the secular political sphere have relative justice and fairness as their highest principles, whereas the equality of eternity which has spiritual (christian) love as the third-party in every human relationship operates according to an absolute that abolishes completely the very distinction between "mine" and "yours" (see below). But Kierkegaard does not even consider the possibility that persons motivated by the same spiritual love may feel compelled to strive for relative increases in the equality of all human beings through political means, precisely in order in this way to open up the possibility of their coming to know the transformation of human existence by the truth and power of spiritual love.

Kierkegaard attempts to clarify the radicalness of this transformation, however, in one final characterization of the impact that living-in-accord-with-love has upon human relationships. Here we turn from

[103] Walter Lowrie, *Kierkegaard*, p. 21.

Kierkegaard's examples to his fundamental principle, from his personal involvement to his theoretical basis.

We have repeatedly stated that, for Kierkegaard, an evil act is whatever one does to deny, limit, corrupt, or crush the dignity and worth of any individual, to deny that that individual possesses eternal equality with every other human being, no matter what her or his natural talents and qualities may be, no matter what his or her social and economic status may be. Likewise, a good act is whatever affirms, encourages, evokes, and builds up another's dignity and equality. This sounds straightforward enough. Does it not simply mean "to each his own," each treating each other fairly?

No, says Kierkegaard. Before I can truly affirm the other in all his/her own unique identity, and in this way "love forth" and "upbuild" the other one as possessing equality before the eternal, I myself, in my self, must undergo a change. "Love is a transformation, the most remarkable of all." In fact, "Love is a revolution, the most profound of all." This revolution consists in a radical transformation in a human relationship, namely: in the event of my loving you, "there are a *you* and an *I*, and yet there are no *mine* and *yours*" (emphasis added). This is a transformation and revolution because "*mine* and *yours* (these pronouns of possession [*Eiendom*, i.e. property]) are in fact formed out of *you* and *I* and consequently are universally considered to be obligatory wherever there is *you* and *I*. And this holds true universally with one exception, with love, which is a revolution from the ground up. The deeper the revolution, the more completely does the distinction between mine and yours disappear, and the more perfect is love."[104]

In other words, Kierkegaard is not denying that there is an authentic, innate, built-in "mine." He goes on to speak of an "initial and continuing distinction between mine and yours hidden at the base [*i Grund*]," that is, in the fundamental structure of human nature as such. And a few pages later (as we have already noted), he uses another form of the term "property" (*Eiendom*) to designate the inviolable, God-given unique identity (*Eiendommelighed*) of every human individual, to designate the very "being" (*at være*) of the individual as such, the properties which define who I am, so that over against the eternal "the creature ... shall not be nothing." Indeed, on this basis, there is, there must be an authentic kind of *self*-love, that is, to honour and respect and treasure and freely to become what eternity has given each self to be and to be-

---

104 *Works of Love*, pp. 248f.; SV 12:255f.; (9:253f.).

come. So Kierkegaard says, "if one has had courage to be oneself [*sig selv*] before God, one has authentic-individuality [*Eiendommelighed*]." And again, "to love God is to love oneself in truth." This kind of self-love, Kierkegaard believes, is the clear assumption or implication of the biblical injunction, "You shall love your neighbour as [you love] yourself" (Lev. 19:18; Mt. 22:39).[105]

What, then, is the transformation and revolution that "loving" brings about in the self and yet without destroying or annihilating that individual identity? The one who is moved by eternal love, to compassion and concern for another human being in need, "does not love one's own unique-identity [*Eiendommelighed*], on the contrary loves each human being according to that one's unique-identity [*Eiendommelighed*]," and so "seeks ... not one's own" but "the other's own." And this outward revolutionary movement of love is made possible by an inward revolutionary transformation, namely: when I relate myself absolutely to the reality of eternal love itself, I am thereby enabled to forget or ignore the rightful demands of my own God-given selfhood when confronted by the needs of another human being. "Love's perfection consists essentially in the fact that it does not manifest the original and continuing distinction between mine and yours which it has hidden in its fundamental constitution [*i Grund*]. ... The deeper the revolution is, the more perfect is love."[106]

In other words, the "what" or content of the outward act of love, which meets the need of the other human being within the concrete conditions or situation in which the other exists, is inseparable from the "how" or motivation of the inward decision to "sacrifice" and "renounce" one's own legitimate self-concern (to keep it "hidden"). And this "decision" consists in concentrating one's attention wholly on the well-being of other human being in need, in response to eternity's command, "Thou shalt love!"—without any thought of return or reward, indeed, in readiness to risk derision and insult from "the world." Furthermore, this revolutionary transformation that takes place in the interior life and being of the lover has two other ramifications: in the lover's relationship with the beloved, and in the lover's relationship with eternal love-itself (god).

First, a strange thing happens when the lover succeeds in eliminating the category "mine" from any thought or consideration. Kierkegaard

---

105 Ibid., pp. 252f, 113; SV 12:259ff., 107; (9:257ff., 104).
106 Ibid., pp. 251f., 249; SV 12:259, 256; (9:257, 254).

says that "the distinction *mine* and *yours* is a relationship of antithesis [*Modsætning*], they exist only in and with each other; if the one distinction is totally eliminated, then the other is also totally deleted" (emphasis added). This means that if I sacrifice all thought of "mine" in order to go out to you in pure love, then you are enabled to believe in your own infinite dignity and worth as a gift from the eternal, and so your claim for "yours" at the expense of "mine" is also eliminated. In other words, in a relationship among humans where there is mutual respect and concern for the independent identity and infinite worth of each other, the intensity of self-awareness as "I" and "you" increases, but the natural claim for distinction and division between what is "mine" and "yours" diminishes and disappears because both parties recognize that individual identities are established and guaranteed only by a reality that transcends them both. As Kierkegaard says, "The true lover seeks not her/his own. He/she knows nothing about the demands of rigid rights, or of justice, or even of fairness"[107] (that is, demands for oneself, but what of demands for justice for others?).

Kierkegaard insists, however, that a human relationship in which the distinction between mine and yours diminishes and disappears is not normal or "natural" (in the sense of what we usually observe in the human situation). Or as he puts it, this kind of love never obtains in a purely human-to-human relationship. So we come to the second ramification of the interior transformation of self that has set aside its own legitimate self-interest. The operation of this kind of love is a sure sign of the presence of a "third-party" in the relationship, namely, of "love itself" (god). And the real and only "proof" of the presence and operation of transcendent love comes *after* (not before) an individual is moved by that love to renounce and sacrifice one's own self-interest out of compassion and concern for any human being one sees to be in need.

As we have spelled out in some detail above, this evidence of love's (god's) presence comes in the form of what Kierkegaard calls "reduplication," that is, in the fact that what the lover gives away is given back to him/her by love itself (god), which (who) remembers and cares for the lover even though the beloved and the world in general may actually resent and deride the sacrificial "work of love" on the part of the lover. Here in the passage on "mine" and "yours," Kierkegaard anticipates this notion in more specifically Christian language. He says that when "for

---

[107] Ibid., p. 251; SV 12:258; (9:256).

self-renouncing love the determinant 'mine' disappears completely, and the distinction 'mine' and 'yours' is totally annulled, ... then something wonderful [the miracle] happens, namely, heaven's blessing on self-renunciation's love: in the mysterious logic [*Forstand*] of blessedness, all-things are given to that one who had no 'mine' at all, that one who in self-renunciation made all of his to be yours. God is indeed all-things, and precisely by having nothing at all 'mine,' self-renunciation's love gains God and gains all-things." And then Kierkegaard adds the words that capture the mystery at the heart of Christian faith, "the one who loses his/her life [ψυχη] will gain it," which follows (not quoted here), "the one who seeks to gain his/her life will lose it" (Lk. 17:33).[108]

The "wonder" or miracle being described here is actually two-sided. On the one side, Kierkegaard is asserting his conviction that if I, with all my most inward, personal, infinite, passionate, earnest interestedness, believe in love as that ultimate dynamic of life that affirms and encourages every individual's unique identity as of eternal dignity and worth, then I am truly able (free) to set aside, renounce, sacrifice, forget my own self-interest and concern and am able to go out to an other human being to meet that person's need, with all my infinite, passionate, interested concern. This I am able to do, without even the tinge of a thought of, without having one eye on, a reward or recompense for myself. And then, on the other side, the miracle happens: in the wake of my performing such a "work of love," I, who had forgotten and denied my self, I come to a new and fresh and vivid perception of *my self*, to the most intense awareness and deepest sense of fulfilment of *my self* that I have ever had. By having negated and lost my self, I have thereby found out who I truly am, and have *become* who I truly am. Death is followed by new life.

Two questions insistently project themselves from such an assertion. First, does this revolutionary transformation at the core of a person's being actually occur? Is such selflessness, such a kind of love, a true possibility of human nature? Can even the power of a faith-relationship with the eternal overwhelm and transform every individual's basic self-centred concern for "one's own"? Is not every example of alleged loving self-sacrifice really a disguise for one's own self-satisfaction, and therefore a case of self-deception, or at best, a case of enlightened self-interest? Kierkegaard would reply: you will never learn the answer to these

---

108 Idem. The Greek behind the Danish and English translations is more complicated and subtle, but these translations make the main point that Kierkegaard is interested in.

questions through observation of others or by a process of rational analysis. You will learn the answer only in the doing.

The testimony of others, pro or con, can only serve as the occasion for you to turn inward in introspection of your own self-consciousness, and to listen in the silence for the voice of the eternal speaking in the accents of the absolute, saying, "You shall love your neighbour as your self!" Then when a "neighbour," a concrete specific individual whom you see with your own eyes, cries out for help, you are faced with the crisis of decision, you confront a "breach" across which only you, all by yourself, can "leap," without the help of inward habit or outward custom or rational argument or social pressure or force of law. And the issue hangs in the balance until *either* you "with completely decisive resolve ... stamp upon [your] action that inner necessity [of love] which excludes the thought of any other possibility," and you "decide something eternal in time, ... the most intensive leap"; *or* you delay and extend the moment of decision by considering a flood of qualifying conditions and alternative possibilities—and the moment is lost in the obscurity of indecision.[109]

In other words, the "deed of love" toward an other—out of concern for the need of that other and in renunciation of one's own self-concern, and enabled by one's belief in the reality of the dynamic of love-itself (god)—is the event of freedom in which the transition from intention to action is accomplished by one's own decision, the most intensive leap. So the possibility and actuality of such a "work of love" can be known only in the doing.

Climacus puts the issue succinctly, and Kierkegaard remains committed to this formulation throughout the authorship. Freedom, says Climacus, is the transition from possibility to actuality, "the transition from nothing, from non-being, and from the multiple possible 'how.'" Granted, "Immediate sensation and cognition cannot deceive," but "Immediate sense [perception] and cognition do not have any intimation of the unsureness with which belief approaches its object, but neither [do they have intimation of] the certitude that extricates [belief] from the incertitude." The Greek sceptics help us make this point, because "they doubted not by virtue of knowledge but by virtue of will. ... This implies that doubt can be terminated only in freedom, by an act of will." Likewise, "it is readily apparent that belief is not a knowledge [*Erkjendelse*] but an act of freedom, an expression of will. ... When belief resolves

---

109 *Journals*, 1269, X^4 A 177; 4806, XI^1 A 329.

to believe, it runs the risk that it was in error, but nevertheless it wills to believe. One never believes in any other way."[110]

But what kind of belief or faith was Kierkegaard assuming in *Works of Love* when he asserts that the decision to enact love toward another human being essentially involves belief in love-itself as the ultimate dynamic of human existence? That is our second question about his principle that love eliminates the distinction "mine" and "yours," the question about the miracle that "whoever loses one's life [in loving] will gain it." His language in this passage is clearly Christian. But we have shown that his language about "reduplication" in the eternal and in the event of love is philosophical rather than theological. The answer to our question is not clear. Are these two ramifications of self-renouncing love possibilities only for Christian faith, or are they also manifest in the lives of those restricted to religiousness A? It appears that Kierkegaard himself is standing here on the borderline between his thinking as humanist and his thinking as theologian, and he would probably have difficulty in answering this last question.

Joseph Campbell, in his conversations about myth and symbol (alluded to above), maintains that the readiness of humans to risk their very lives in the attempt to save others in dire circumstances is universal, manifest in all cultures and eras, expressed and encouraged by the ubiquitous myth and ritual of death/resurrection. Let us take Kierkegaard's own example of serfdom and slavery. Those who risked their reputations and fortunes in the fight for the abolition of slavery, both in Europe and in America, were hardly limited to Christians. American history is replete with verified stories of how innumerable people of diverse ethical/intellectual persuasions took part in the "underground railroad," working to smuggle runaway slaves out of the south, across the Mason-Dixon line to safe-houses in the north, and eventually to relocation in Canada. Often their very lives were in danger, let alone their public reputation and livelihood. They welcomed these individuals of another race into their homes, hid them and fed and clothed them, because they were moved by compassion when they saw human beings of equal dignity and worth being treated as or even worse than animals. The objects of their love were strangers, whom they had never seen before and would never see again. And there was no possible reward or recompense for their sacrifices—except the "aftertaste" of their own

---

110 *Fragments*, pp. 101–3; (KW 7:82f.); SV 6:75f.; (4:245–7).

sense of dignity and worth, the sense of their own fulfilment as human beings.

So, Kierkegaard can conclude: "Love is a transformation, the most remarkable of all. ... A person possessed by love is transformed, or becomes transformed." Why so remarkable? Because "*mine* and *yours* ... seem to be required wherever there are *you* and *I.*"[111] And his conclusion brings us to our conclusion about a question raised in the previous chapter, namely: how far can the self go in becoming itself in actuality within the limits of religiousness A? And this question quickly led to a more specific one: granted that the self is helped by the eternal to resolve the question of "how" to do the one-thing-needful, how then does this self, in becoming itself, decide "what" is the one-thing-needful? And we have seen how "love," as defined by Kierkegaard, is the answer to the questions about both the "how" and the "what" of the absolute good demanded by the eternal. The "how" is answered by the encouragement that comes from belief in love-itself as the ultimate dynamic of human existence. The "what" is answered by the specification of the concrete act that is required here and now in order to evoke and encourage and enable an other human being to live as the unique individual one is, with the sense of one's infinite dignity and worth.

Just how "concrete" is the specification of the one-thing-needful that emerges from the ultimate commitment to love-itself, from the relationship of love between two human beings, from the act of love of one human being toward another? First there is the negative answer. Love condemns and eliminates certain qualities from the human psyche and from their derivative actions and relationships, namely: envy, anger, lust, vanity, avarice, hate, vengeance, pride, despondency, despair, fear of the future, reliance on the world, etc. Secondly, love honours the independent identity of every other individual, and therefore prevents the absorption and loss of the individual into the life and being of an other, or into the conformity of the life of the crowd or mass. Thirdly, love distinguishes between what is essential and what is relative for the well-being and growth of the individual self. It asks, what can I lose (get along without) without doing damage to my self? Fourthly, in the loving realtionship the distinction between "mine"and "yours" fades and disappears for both the lover and the beloved, because the beloved experiences the fact that being-loved assumes the presence of love in him/herself. This experience then builds up love in and calls forth love from the one who is loved.

---

111 *Works of Love*, p. 248: SV 12:255f.; (9:254).

Hence the beloved also loses the sense of "mine" versus "yours." Nevertheless (fifthly), the one-thing-needful, that is the work of love, is never an abstract ideal or a pure intention or a right feeling. It is always incarnate in the finite material conditions of the other's specific situation, here at this place, now at this very moment, because, after all, the self is in essence a synthesis of the infinite *and* the finite, the eternal *and* the temporal.

So the good work of love does have "content," for the whole person or self, for both the self's psychic and sensuous dimensions. Yet the specific ingredients and shape of this content cannot be dictated or predetermined in accord with an objective and universal criterion, because it is determined in accord with "love" which in essence honours, considers, and calls into play the unique identity (*Eiendommelighed*) of both the lover and the beloved, which includes the unique conditions of the time and place of the act. Thus we come to a fresh, and final, understanding of what we have called Kierkegaard's most radical proposition in the entire authorship:

> [W]ithin the race every individual [*Enkelt*] is essentially different or unique [*Eiendommelige*]. ... If it were not so, that the one human being (honourable, upright, respectable, god-fearing) can under the same circumstances do just the opposite of what another human being does (also honourable, upright, respectable, god-fearing), then the god-relationship would not essentially exist, not in its deepest sense. If one could with unqualified validity judge every human being according to a universally given criterion, then the god-relationship would essentially be abolished; then everything would turn outward, being fulfilled in the life of the state or society; then living would become much too easy, but also exceedingly empty; then neither spiritual-struggle nor self-deepening would be either possible or necessary, because the god-relationship develops in a human being precisely in and through this most obdurate clash of disagreement [i.e., the clash between god-related love and merely human love].[112]

Many first-time readers of this statement are put off or even offended. How could two god-fearing individuals do opposite things when together they were confronted by the racial conflict in Selma during the 1960s? Well, they did. A group of friends of the same religious community decided to charter a bus to go to stand on the line with the blacks of Selma, but some of their friends chose not to go with them. Why? *Not*

---

112 Ibid., p, 217; SV 12:222f.; (9:220f.). For definition of the "clash" or "collision" mentioned, see ibid., p. 118; SV 12:113f.; (9:120f.), and *Journals*, 1880; X³ A 454.

because they had qualitatively different values or because they were weak and cowardly in their faith, but because the same faith and values moved them to feel hypocritical if they were to go to Selma, while at the same time neither they nor their friends were doing a thing for a small ghetto of blacks within a few miles from where they lived. Not that the ones who went on the bus were "wrong" and denying their faith. Those who went and those who stayed respected the free decision of each other as to what their common faith demanded of each individually. And they did the opposite. On the other hand, neither joined those whites in Selma who took cudgels to try to beat the blacks into submission. "Love" demanded that both, in their own ways, honour and defend the equal dignity of blacks and whites.

However, Kierkegaard assumes the operation of another fundamental source of opposite actions than simply the difference of opinion about how the particularities of a specific situation can best be met when viewed from the perspective of the same belief and conviction. The unique make-up of each "honourable, upright, respectable, god-fearing" individual also shapes and justifies how that individual will act in those "same circumstances." Everyone has unique elements in physical/biological structure, in psychic components and balance, in biographical experiences stored as memories, attitudes, values, dispositions, etc. And assuming that each of several individuals has the "courage to be oneself before God," and that each seeks earnestly to obey the command of love, yet each will enact that command in a different way precisely because of, as reflective of, the unique personal identity (*Eiendommelighed*) that each is.

This perspective on morality and the individual has recently received a strong and winsome statement by one of the founders of philosophy of action. In his book *Innocence and Experience*, Stuart Hampshire says that "a person's history, consciously and unconsciously remembered," twists one's imagination so that it is "starved at some points and over-developed at others." For one person "[c]ertain rhythms and shapes and landscapes are intensely significant," while those highly regarded by others are a matter of indifference. So, "[t]here is no reasonable requirement" that everyone should conform to "some imposed normality of concerns and interests." Indeed, "if one takes the standpoint of humanity as a whole, and not of the individual, there is no call for the repitition of a type, nor even of an ideally balanced human being."[113] Kierkegaard

---

113 Stuart Hampshire, *Innocence and Experience*; see the review by Alan Ryan in *The New York Review of Books*, 1 March 1990, pp. 34–7.

would want to argue with some of this, but I suspect that Hampshire's ultimate dynamic of "justice" comes very close to what Kierkegaard means by "love."

Now we must also recall that these questions (about the "how" and "what" of the good act in which the self becomes itself) were arrived at in the larger context of a search for understanding human freedom as event. We came to see that the event or act of freedom occurs in face of a "breach," and that it requires a "leap" to accomplish the "transition" across that breach, and that this leap is both "passionate" and "religious." But it was noted that one may be possessed of infinite passionate interestedness and of fervent religious belief in a general way, and yet one may not be moved to enact what one "knows" is the good and the right thing needful at this time and place. So we looked for a key to what happens in the transition in Kierkegaard's concept of love, with its five specifications.

Even then, however, we left open an ultimate question about freedom as event: are the works of love "free," that is, indeterminate? When I have turned away from all external norms and pressures and turned inward to become conscious of that gestalt of possibilities that defines my own unique selfhood, and then when I have listened in the silence of self-annihilation to the voice of the absolute speaking in the accents of eternal love, and then have turned my attention away from my own self out of compassion and concern for another human being in need, and when then I know with absolute clarity and conviction *what* is the one-thing-needful for this other particular person in these particular conditions, *then*: is the doing, the enactment of that one thing automatic and irresistible, or free and indeterminate? What does Climacus mean when he says that "belief is not [merely] a knowledge but an act of freedom, an expression of will"? Thus we come now to our final question about freedom as event, indeed, to our final interpretation of Anti-Climacus's words, "The self is freedom. But freedom is the dialectical in the determinants possibility and necessity."[114]

---

114 *Sickness*, p. 162; (KW 19:29); SV 15:87; (11:142).

8

My Self: A Task
Part 6: The Leap of Love Is Indeterminate

We turn again to take one last look at the enigma at the heart of Kierkegaard's entire conceptuality: the leap. In exploring the leap as the *form* of freedom, we hedged it in by delimiting it with a series of conditions so that the leap (and hence freedom) could not be understood as arbitrary and capricious. In exploring love as the *content* of freedom, we explored an ultimate and transcendent delimitation to which the leap must submit if it is to be authentically "free." But now the question arises whether the limits thus imposed leave any significant meaning to the terms "free" and "voluntary" as applied to human intentional actions. Is there any element of true indeterminacy?

It will help to clarify this final question and interpretation if we acknowledge that throughout our entire analysis of the leap there has been a confusion of tongues. There have been at least three different phenomena identified as "leaps," which occur in three different relationships, and which assume a different kind of breach in each of the relationships. And it now behooves us to make these distinctions clearly in order to isolate where authentic freedom lies, to clarify what freedom-as-event consists in.

Let us start with the three "breaches." (1) There is the breach of disparity, contradiction, opposition between, on the one hand, the self's possibility as existing within its finite conditions and in the immediacy of its unreflective acceptance of that existence, and on the other hand, the self's infinite ideality asserting itself as absolute telos, as one's eternal blessedness. (2) The self's possibility in its ideality experiences its impossibility, its impotence, the "death" of its self-sufficiency, in its relationship to the reality and power of all-things-are-possible (the eternal, God). So within the immanence of every individual's consciousness there may open up the breach between the self and the eternal as present within that consciousness. (3) Even having heard and heeded the voice of affirmation and encouragement from the eternal, the self's possibility still faces the absolute qualitative gap or difference between the purest and strongest possible intention and its actualization within the conditions of particular finitude.

For the resolution of the contradiction and conflict in each of these relationships a "transition" is called for. Kierkegaard insists that an authentic transition in human existence, in time/space, cannot be a "mediation" of opposites but is a κίνησις (*kinesis*), a movement involving the whole being of the existing individual. So a transition consists of something more than an abstract conceptual rationalization. A transition requires an infinite, personal, subjective, passionate interestedness in doing something, and it inherently has the quality of venture, risk, and uncertainty. Is it correct to call the transition in each of these relationships a "leap"? If so, does each of the three comprise what Kierkegaard calls the leap of freedom? Let us recollect and summarize what we have heard Kierkegaard saying about each of these three transitions. But as background we must remember Kierkegaard's most precise statements about the leap: "My theory of the leap ... is essentially at home in the sphere of freedom," and "The leap is the category of decision."[1]

In the first breach between a state of immediacy and a commitment to an absolute telos, the transition is clearly labelled a "leap" by Johannes de Silentio (in *Fear and Trembling*), and is described as such by Johannes Climacus (in *Postscript*) when he says that "with the passion of infinitude the ethicist had ... chosen himself out of the *terror* of having ... his actuality in aesthetic dreams." So in his journals Kierkegaard specifies that there is a leap from the aesthetic sphere to the ethical sphere.[2] We have heard this leap described variously as the qualitative shift from aesthetic external values to infinite inward values, from finite relative ends to eternal absolute ends. And this shift is accomplished by a "purely human courage" to make this decision and choice. Yet, this leap always ends in a purely inward "spiritual" commitment to and appreciation of these values because it ends in resignation to the impossibility of their actualization. So the leap into or the leap of the ethical brings the self to awareness of the second kind of breach.

---

1 *Journals*, 2352, V C 12; *Postscript*, p. 91; SV 9:85; (7:79).
2 *Postscript*, p. 231; (KW 12.1:258); SV 9:216; (7:218); *Journals* 2345, V C 1.

In this second breach between the death of one's self-sufficiency and the awareness of affirmation and encouragement from the eternal as "other," the transition also involves a "leap," because it consists in the passage from the ethical sphere to the religious sphere. But where and what is the leap of "decision" made in this transition? We have considered this question at some length previously (chapter 6, in the section on "The Breach in Religiousness A"), so here we will give only a brief summary. The question is pertinent because there is a double movement in this transition, a negative and a positive movement, in contrast to the simple straightforward, even though qualitative, choice or decision for the absolute telos in the first transition. Facing this second breach the ethical self at first feels a natural compulsion not only to "fight against the aesthetic" but "also against the religious." The self wishes to maintain itself as self-sufficient. Here the self is faced with a critical decision. Climacus says that if one has "understood the existence-relationship between the aesthetic and the ethical ... in passion and inwardness," then "one indeed becomes aware of the religious—and of *the leap*." And the decision is whether to acknowledge this awareness and to be open to it, or to turn away and to deny it.

Such a decision is indeed a "leap" because one goes from a sense and conviction of self-sufficiency in the ethical to the recognition that there is "something other" which "helps the individual to a higher revelation beyond the ethical." But the first form of this revelation is a negative one, in that one comes to see and acknowledge that "the ethical ... is now the hindrance," that one is faced with "the terror ... [of a] collision where the ethical becomes the temptation."[3]

We have seen this negative element appear in each of the several different descriptions of the experience of the "religious" in different parts of the Kierkegaardian corpus. In *Fear and Trembling* the leap into the infinite is accompanied by resignation of any hope to realize the infinite except in spiritual commitment. In the discourse on purity of heart, in order to avoid double-mindedness, one must turn inward and, in response to the voice of the eternal, first look backward in confession and repentance so as to see what is hidden in darkness. In *Postscript* ethical sensitivity finally ends with the sense of need for "divine help"

---

3 For this and the previous paragraph, *Postscript*, pp. 262, 231; (KW 12.1:295, 258–9); SV 9:247, 216; (7:252, 218).

because of the teleological suspension of the ethical. So religiousness A consists of giving up all finite things in favour of an eternal blessedness, of self-annihilation to make room for God, and of acceptance of one's totality of guilt-consciousness. In *Sickness* to believe in "all-things-are-possible" must be preceded by the awareness that on one's own one is faced by impossibility and one's sure destruction. In the discourses on purity of heart and the lilies, the religious experience is approached only by entering silence and a sense of the death of all one's previous resources.

In each of these descriptions "decision" takes its most subtle form, either in one's allowing one's awareness (attention) to focus and remain on an item of consciousness that threatens one's self-image to its very core, or in withdrawing one's awareness and turning away from this "truth" or "revelation." If one keeps one's attention focused, consciously and deliberately, on this "truth" with all of one's inward, personal, passionate interestedness, then one has indeed made a decision, a choice, and has "leaped" from one mode (γενος) of existence to another, from one "sphere" of understanding to another, from the ethical to the religious. And this leap is the first and negative, but absolutely critical, movement of the transition in the sense that it is the decision to accept the reality of one's impotence to realize the absolute telos, and to accept this "self-annihilation" in order to "make room for God," the decision to enter the realm of silence and to listen for and to a totally new and "other" voice. That is to say, one acknowledges one's need for the help of the eternal as "other," and focuses one's awareness and attention on the presence, the claim and the demand of "all-things-are-possible."

Only then comes the second, mysterious and positive movement in the transition, which takes the shape not of a clear-cut choice but of an openness and willingness to receive and hold fast the affirmation and encouragement from the side of the eternal, and thereby to possess the "humble courage" to believe that all-things-are-possible. This movement imparts positive form and dynamic to the new state (αλλο γενος) of the existing self, a state which is an immanent relationship in which the self and the immanent eternal interact in sympathy and harmony. In other words, the decision or leap in which one "annihilates" oneself or sets oneself aside to make room for God is followed by willingness to receive the movement of the eternal to fill that space. The decision to be absolutely silent and to listen is followed by the "speaking" of the eternal.

This relationship may be called "faith." But, as noted before, this relationship is an immanent possibility of every human being, and it is achieved simply by the courage and daring of the human subject. Hence it is "faith" in the sense of "believing" on the part of the human subject, in the Socratic sense of religiousness A (again see chapter 6, the section on "Faith as Healing the Breach").

This relationship of "believing" is what Climacus calls the "upbuilding" element in religiousness A. Now one is enabled to focus one's infinite, inward, personal, passionate interestedness on the eternal dignity and worth of one's self, even (or especially) against all objective uncertainty about one's eternal dignity and worth. And as we have heard Climacus say earlier, "the truth is precisely the daring [*Vovestykke*: risk, venture] to choose this objective uncertainty with the passion of infinitude," and this "definition of truth is a paraphrase [*Omskrivning*] for faith," because "[w]ithout risk [*Risico*] there is no faith." So in this faith-relationship of "interiorization" one may say that "the God-relationship is found by the existing-one," because "in the inwardness of subjectivity is the upbuilding which belongs to subjectivity."[4]

The key thing to note in this analysis of the second breach and the second transition is that the leap of decision involved in the negative movement (of impotence, listening, and self-annihilation) *precedes* faith. As noted before, "faith" (in religiousness A) is dialectical in that it always presupposes this leap, but faith consists not only of the leap as such, but of the leap *plus* the willingness to receive the encouragement from the eternal, the sustenance of all-things-are-possible. Faith is the state for which the leap of decision prepares the way. As Climacus says, the faith-relationship does indeed include "the daring to choose this objective uncertainty with the passion of infinitude," but faith also consists in the state of existing (actively living) in "the contradiction between the infinite passion of inwardness and objective uncertainty." So Kierkegaard repeatedly asserts that faith remains dialectical, because it is not a state of repose or a final, accomplished fulfilment, but is a continuing process of coming-into-being, always including the element of uncertainty. So the leap involved in faith must be "repeated" every day, every moment one remains an existing-one in time/space, and it must be accompanied (daily) by the opening of oneself to affirmation and encourage-

---

4 Ibid., pp. 181f., 497; (KW 12.1:203-4, 560); SV 9:169f, 10:229; (7:169f., 488f.).

ment from the eternal so that one can continue to believe that all-things-are-possible.[5]

This analysis, however, leaves a vital question unanswered. Does living in a faith-relationship with the immanent eternal, does hearing the word of affirmation and encouragement from all-things-are-possible, result directly and infallibly in the enactment of this particular self's possibility within the specific finite conditions of his/her existence? This question brings us to the third breach, the one between the self's clearly formed intention to do the one thing needful and the self's concrete act of doing it, and hence to the nature of the transition involved.

Climacus answers our question bluntly. He asks, "Having thought of some good that one intends [*vil*, wills, wants] to do, is it [the same as] having done it?" And he answers, "Not at all!" Then using the story of

---

[5] In a certain sense one could call this choosing (of self-annihilation in the presence of the eternal) the "leap of faith," because by this leap of decision, one takes the prerequisite step for opening the way for hearing the eternal's voice of affirmation and encouragement, which in turn enables one to believe in all-things-are-possible. But Kierkegaard never uses the phrase "leap of faith," because (I think) even in religiousness A he does not want to infer that the resources of the sphere of the religious are merely human (as in the sphere of the purely ethical). He wishes to preserve the element of "otherness" (a kind of transcendence) as characteristic of the eternal, so that the believing in all-things-are-possible is a kind of authentic God-relationship, even though in immanence at the depth (or height) of human subjectivity. Obviously, as noted before, it is clearly erroneous and misleading to speak of a leap of faith in the context of religiousness B, because as we have seen (text of chapter 6 at notes 113, 114, 115) the Christian concept of faith designates a qualitatively different relationship between God and the believer from that in religiousness A.

The most egregious attribution of this phrase to Kierkegaard occurs in (apparently) Swenson's mistaken and misleading translation of a passage in *Postscript*, p. 15; SV 9:15; (7:3). (Alastair McKinnon, in his article on "Kierkegaard and 'the Leap of Faith'" [see chapter 6, notes 10 and 16], asks who is responsible for this translation, since Swenson is clearly "suspicious" of it in his remarks on p. 163 of his *Something about Kierkegaard*.) In the "Introduction" of *Postscript*, Climacus is asserting that one must resist the temptation to replace faith with "certainty by substituting probablity and guarantee." Then Swenson's translation has Climacus saying that this temptation was rejected in the beginning "when he made the leap of faith, the qualitative transition from non-belief to belief." But Kierkegaard's Danish reads literally as follows: "when he himself initially made the leap's qualitative transition from unbeliever [*Ikke-Troende*] to believer [*Troende*]." Even if Climacus means that the decision to believe is a leap, the new God-relationship in "faith" includes more than the leap. As previously noted, the "qualitative transition" is not accomplished merely by the leap of human decision but requires and involves also the presence and initiative of the eternal.

the Good Samaritan, he says that the Levite might well have been thinking, while "still some distance from the unfortunate man that it would indeed be beautiful to help a sufferer." But "as he came nearer and nearer, then the difficulties became apparent, and he rode past. ... Consequently he did not act." Elsewhere he states categorically, "In relation to possibility the word is the highest pathos, in relation to actuality deed [*Gjerning*] is the highest pathos."[6] Thus he anticipates Kierkegaard's next major work (which is in his theological authorship), *Works of Love* (*Kjerlighedens Gjerninger*), in which (as we have seen) he repeatedly illustrates the thesis that merely to picture in the mind and to intend an act of love is no love at all; love is always a "work," an act. In other words, there is a leap of decision prior to the "religious" experience of faith, but there is also another and substantively different leap of decision that must follow and emerge from faith. So freedom as "event" does not refer to the experience of affirmation and encouragement from the eternal and the formation of a firm intention (although they are prerequisite). As we have heard Kierkegaard say, "true freedom" occurs "when with completely decisive resolve one stamps upon one's action that inner necessity which excludes the thought of any other possibility."[7]

This locating of the definitive event of freedom is supported by Climacus in *Postscript*. He says, "In the moment of passionate decision, where the way swings off from objective knowing, it seems as if the infinite decision were thereby completed. But at the same moment the existing-one is in temporality, and the subjective 'how' is transformed into a striving that is [indeed] impelled and repeatedly refreshed by the deciding passion of infinitude, but it is nevertheless a striving." And what is the striving? It is assumed that one has overcome the first difficulty of comprehending that one is not able to do anything on one's own, but now "there is the [second] difficulty: with God to be capable of [doing] it." In other words, after achieving the most profound faith-relationship with or through openness to the eternal (the God-relationship), there still remains something that the individual has to do by and for him/herself. As Climacus explicitly says, having comprehended the suffering of self-annihilation within the immanence of religiousness A, nevertheless religiousness A "by ethically accentuating the fact of existing, ... hinders the existing-one from abstractly remaining in immanence, or from

---

[6] *Postscript*, pp. 303, 349; (KW 12.1:339–40, 388–90); SV 10:42f., 84; (7:294, 337).
[7] *Journals*, 1269, X⁴ A 177.

becoming abstract by wishing to remain in immanence."[8] So the believing relationship with the eternal may be absolutely requisite for "helping" one to choose the one thing needful, but it only *helps*; it does not compel, it does not eliminate but affirms and requires the ethical freedom and responsibility of the individual, because the individual still faces the transition from the most passionate, committed, believing possibility to its actualization in the finite temporal realm of human existence.

This view of freedom is directly dependent on and expressive of Kierkegaard's consistent depiction of the essential relationship between the eternal (God) and the human person throughout the entire authorship, in both religiousness A and B. He makes the point most directly in his treatment of "Truth Is Subjectivity" in *Postscript*, where he is explicating the indirectness of all personal or spiritual communication between human beings. And then he says,

Not even God relates directly to the derived spirit. And this is the wonderful thing about creation, [that its purpose is] not to bring forth something that is nothing in relation to the creator, but to bring forth something that is something, and which in true worship [*Dyrkelse*] of God, can make use of this something in order to become by itself nothing before God. ... A direct relationship between spirit and spirit is unthinkable with respect to essential truth; if such a relationship is assumed, it actually means that one party has ceased to be spirit.

In other words, it is precisely in the God-relationship where the human self "by itself" must "make use of" its own given resources to "become" its self in relation to the transcendent source of its very being. It is in this very context that Climacus makes the point that "only when the breach has taken place, only then can there be any mention of a true God-relationship. But this breach is precisely the first act of inwardness in the direction of the stipulation [*Bestemmelse*] that truth is inwardness." And then he says flatly that this breach accomplished in inwardness is "the act of one's-own-effort" (*Selvvirksomhed*, perhaps "self initiative").[9]

This passage in *Postscript* is reminiscent of one in *Either/Or* and anticipates passages in *Works of Love* and in *Sickness*. In *Either/Or* Judge William

---

8 *Postscript*, pp. 182, 434–5, 507; (KW 12.1:203, 486, 572–3); SV 9:169; 10:166, 239; (7:170, 423, 499).

9 For the last two paragraphs, see ibid., pp. 220–1, 218; (KW 12.1:246–7, 243–4); SV 9:206, 203; (7:207–8, 205).

asks the question, "What is the meaning of temporality?" And he answers, "The particular beauty of temporality is that in it the infinite spirit and the finite spirit are separated, and it is the particular greatness of the finite spirit that temporality is assigned to it. Therefore, temporality does not exist, if I may dare speak this way, for the sake of God, ... but it exists for the sake of humankind and is the greatest of all the gifts of grace." This gift makes possible my "eternal dignity" because in temporality I may "achieve a history," not in its being "a summary of what has taken place or has happened to me, but [only when it is] my own deed [*Gjerning*] in such a way that even that which has happened to me is transformed and transferred from necessity to freedom."[10]

In *Works of Love* (as we have heard) Kierkegaard repeats the language of *Postscript*. He is saying that my unique individuality (*Eiendommelighed*) "is not mine but is God's gift by which [God] gives me being [*at være*]." It is the goodness of God that although "*almighty*, yet [God] gives in such a way that the receiver obtains unique individuality, that the one who creates out of nothing, yet creates unique individuality so that the creation over against [the creator] will not be nothing, although it is taken from nothing and is nothing, yet it will become unique individuality." In *Sickness* Anti-Climacus uses a graphic figure of speech to suggest the same thing. He is asking where despair came from and insists that the synthesis of finite/infinite, which comprises the human individual, was originally "in the proper relationship" as it came "from the hand of God." But then "God ... lets it go out of his hand, as it were, ... in as much as the relationship relates to itself." Or as he says a little later, "the self is ... a relation that, even though it is derived, relates to itself, which is freedom. The self is freedom." In other words, the "God-relationship" (in any form) never compromises the freedom and responsibility of the human individual who stands in that relationship. On the contrary, the God-relationship establishes, protects, assumes, evokes, and demands the exertion of human individual freedom.[11]

However, the God-relationship which is here under consideration is not that of creation or origin but that of "helping" the human individual to repair the damaged relationship (in each of its determinants: finite/

---

10 *Either/Or*, 2:254f.; (KW 4:250); SV 3:231; (2:224).

11 *Works of Love*, p. 253; SV 12:261; (9:259); *Sickness*, p. 149, 162; (KW 19:16, 29); SV 15:75, 87; (11:130, 142). In a draft of the latter passage, Kierkegaard puts our point even more clearly: "This relationship is spirit, self, and therein lies responsibility, under which is despair. ... God lets it go out of his hand. In this way the human being is self, and despair is possible" (*Papirer*, VIII^2 B 170:5).

infinite, necessity/possibility, temporal/eternal). Is the original distance between divine and human maintained, especially in the immanence of religiousness A, when the individual undergoes "self-annihilation" in order to "make room for God"? Or, as we have asked, does the divine infusion into the empty space, or in the language of religiousness B, does divine grace in the gift of faith, overwhelm the docile "believing" recipient by the power of love so that his/her obedient action flows naturally and inevitably from the God-relationship? As already indicated, Climacus (in *Postscript*) insists that even at the depth/height of the God-relationship there remains the final difficulty and striving: "with God to be able to do it."

This "difficulty," with its essential element of uncertainty as to the outcome, is depicted by Kierkegaard throughout his writings, from *Fragments* in 1844 to a late journal entry of 1854. In *Fragments* he expresses it in the stunning poetic "fairy story" of the omnipotent king who falls in love with the humble village maiden. The "difficulty" is that the sovereign could compel marriage in external obedience, but he understands that in that case he would lose her heart as her thoughts would be "lured into ... secret sorrow" as she remembered a village swain with whom she could have "loved ... in a position of equality," even though in a humble hut in obscurity. "Even if the girl were satisfied to become nothing, that would not satisfy the king," because the god-king wants to love and be loved in the only possible relationship for love, namely, equality. What if the beloved "became weary and lost her bold confidence! Oh, to sustain heaven and earth by an omnipotent 'Let there be' ...—how easy this would be compared with the possibility of the offence of the human race when out of love one became its saviour!" Thus "god is revealed in such a way as to bring about the most terrible decision." Will the learner, who is in untruth, believe, and learn to live in this relationship? This "situation of understanding—how terrifying, for it is indeed less terrifying to fall upon one's face when the mountains tremble at the voice of god than to sit with god as equals, and yet god's concern is precisely to sit this way."[12]

In *Fragments* Climacus recognizes that this story is only a poetic metaphor or analogy for the complexities of the (Christian) faith experience of the God-relationship. But two years later (1846) in a journal entry Kierkegaard provides a direct analysis of the omnipotence of God in relation to a human individual, and couches it in general rather than Christian religious terms. He says,

12 *Fragments*, pp. 32–43; (KW 7:26–35); SV 6:28–36; (4:195–202).

Only omnipotence can withdraw itself at the same time it gives itself away, and this relationship is the receiver's very independence [*Uafhængighed*, connotes autonomous, self-governing]. God's omnipotence is therefore [God's] goodness. Because God's goodness is to give [oneself] away completely, but in such a way that by omnipotently taking oneself back one makes the recipient independent. Omnipotence ... can give without giving up the least of its power, i.e., it can make [a being] independent. ... [So] omnipotence is not only able to create the most impressive of all—the whole visible world—but is able to create the most fragile of all things—a being independent of that omnipotence.

This view of omnipotence is the opposite of that one which "holds that it is greater and greater in proportion to its ability to compel and make dependent. ... The one to whom I owe absolutely everything has in fact made me independent."[13]

In two later journal entries (1849 and 1854) Kierkegaard describes how this independence or autonomy works in the Christian faith relationship to God, which description then certainly applies even more stringently to the "voice" and the "encouragement" that comes with the general God-consciousness of religiousness A. In the earlier one (written the year after *Sickness* and *Practice in Christianity*) he is commenting on the basic Christian doctrine that we are not saved by works but by God's grace through the gift of faith. But, he says, we must not understand this truth as meaning that "I am unable to do something myself with regard to becoming a believer," because then "we have election-by-grace in the fatalistic sense." Rather, "we must make a little concession," which is: the reality and irreducibility of "subjectivity." Finally the multiple levels of God's infinity and sovereignty "must at one point or another be halted at subjectivity. ... Subjectivity cannot be excluded, unless we want to have fatalism."[14]

In the later entry Kierkegaard is commenting on the saying of Jesus, "The gate is narrow and the way is hard that leads to life, and those who find it are few" (Mt. 7:14). He argues that by describing "the way" which we are called to follow as being "narrow," Jesus is directly implying "freedom, the voluntary, self-determination ... because here it is left to the individual him/herself [*En selv*] whether one will or will not," that is,

---

13 *Journals*, 1251, VII^1 A 181. He attributes this understanding of power to Socrates, and repeats *Postscript*'s view of the indirectness of the God-human as well of the human-human relationship.

14 Ibid., 4551, X^2 A 301.

whether one will or will not follow the "hard way" of obeying the demands of one's most inward, personal, infinite, passionate sense of the "one thing needful" in this particular situation in the light of the "voice" of the eternal absolute—in spite of the agonizing inner struggle to accept the "death" of all of one's other desires, hopes, and possibilities, in spite of one's total objective uncertainty as to what will eventuate, and in the face of certain opposition, trouble, and tribulation from without.[15]

In all of these passages in the writings of Kierkegaard from 1844 to 1854, there is the persistent and unequivocal insistence that, no matter how needful and powerful is the "help" that comes from the transcendent but immanent presence of the eternal (all-things-are-possible) at the depth/height of human self-consciousness, with each increase in the intensity of that help there is a corresponding increase in the angst and agony of a decision at the very core of one's most inward and definitive subjectivity: "will I, or will I not? here, in this situation, now, in this instant?" At this juncture lie the final breach and the definitive leap which provide the occasion and the occurrence of what Kierkegaard means by that "freedom" which is identical with being and becoming self, the only event that is worthy of that noble designation, freedom.

This insistence is perfectly in keeping with Kierkegaard's basic formulations of his concept of freedom. In *The Concept of Anxiety* he says that freedom in its simplicity and essence is a capacity structured into the given makeup of every human being. "Freedom's possibility is not being able [*at kunne*] to choose the good or the evil. ... The possibility is [simply] to *be able* [*at kunne*]." As we have seen in the earlier section entitled "Angst: the Birth-Pangs of Self-Consciousness" (chapter 3), this essential "being able" is originally without content or object because "only the possibility of being able is present as a higher form of ignorance, as a higher expression of angst, because in a higher sense it both is and is not, because in a higher sense one both loves it and flees from it." And the angst is there because one instinctively senses that one may or may not fulfil the promise of "being able."[16]

But this possibility comes to its flower and fulfilment in the essential task given to every human being: becoming one's self (again: not as an accomplished completed goal but as a lifelong ongoing process). So in *Sickness* Anti-Climacus can say "Freedom is the self," because when he

---

15 Ibid., 1274, 1275; XI¹ A 23, 24.
16 *The Concept of Anxiety*, pp. 40, 44; (KW 8:44f., 49); SV 6:138, 142; (4:315f., 320).

says that "the self is composed of infinitude and finitude," and that "freedom is the dialectical in the determinants possibility and necessity," he is saying that the self in actuality becomes itself only "concretely," that is, only when the infinite possibility of the self obeys the dual necessity of, first, acting in accord with its absolute telos (love), and second, incarnating that telos in the actual finite conditions and situation of that particular self's existence. Then it becomes true that "the self is a relation, which relates to itself, ... and in relating to itself relates to an other," that is, "relates to that which has established the entire relation" (the eternal, love-itself). Or to put it even more succinctly, for the human self "actuality is unity of possibility and necessity." Then it is true that "something eternal" has been "decided in time," and the self knows that this kind of decision "is the most intensive leap." Then, finally, the self "has the most powerful sense of freedom," because then "the human being ... with completely decisive resolve stamps upon her/his action that inner necessity which excludes the thought of any other possibility. Then ... the 'agony' of choice comes to an end."[17]

Granted, then: the passionate religious relationship with the eternal (as the ultimate dynamic of love) enables and encourages but does not compel the decisive leap across the final breach between, on the one hand, one's clear knowledge of and firm intention to do the one-thing-needful, and on the other hand, the enactment of that intention in actuality. Still, the question remains as to what happens in that "agony of choice" which leads to the enactment. If the transition is "an act of freedom, an expression of will," how then (as we asked at the beginning of chapter 6) can this act be "free" and "indeterminate" without being arbitrary, capricious, uncaused? If "willing" is the "field" of my most inward hidden being where the battle is joined, how can it be described? We must now return again to that crucial passage in *Sickness* where Anti-Climacus (Kierkegaard above and beyond himself) provides the most explicit and detailed analysis of the phenomenon of "willing" in the entire authorship.[18]

17 *Sickness*, pp. 146, 169; (KW 19:128, 149); SV 15:73, 94; (11:128, 149); *Journals*, 4806, XI¹ A 329; 1269, X⁴ A 177.

18 In the following pages, references to *Sickness* are from this passage until noted otherwise: pp. 224f.; (KW 19:93f.); SV 15:145–7; (11:204f.); see also the analysis of "higher" and "lower" natures at the beginning of chapter 7. For what follows, also reread the summary of the essential points in Donald Davidson's philosophy of action at the beginning of chapter 6.

Kierkegaard asserts that something called "willing" is the decisive element in the transition from understanding to doing; more particularly, from understanding what is the right and good thing one ought to do, to actually doing it. As previously noted (at the beginning of chapter 7), this willing is a struggle and battle because, Kierkegaard says, willing is "dialectical," that is, willing is located in between one's "higher" nature which ethically/religiously defines the "good" and one's "lower" nature which, as the aesthetic-metaphysical, diverts one's attention from that definition and delays and perhaps prevents the ethical-religious decision from being enacted. In the language of philosophy of action, "willing" does not have to do with the coming to a perception or "pure intention" of what is good and desirable in the light of the totality of one's essential values and beliefs in reference to a particular condition in one's life. This process of intending (perceiving the good) occurs in "the life of the spirit" prior to the event of willing. So, willing has to do with the coming to an "all-out" unconditional judgment that a specific action is now called for. Yet this settled judgment or disposition is not yet the act. "Willing" also includes that instant of self-consciousness in which I ask, "Will I do it, here and now?"

In this passage in *Sickness*, willing in itself might appear to be neutral, equally and sovereignly able to move in either direction. That would mean that human "freedom" is the ability to choose either good or evil (*liberum arbitrium*), or, even more radically, to determine what is good and what is evil. That is precisely what Kierkegaard denies. A human being indeed can "will" to follow either one's higher or one's lower nature, that is, can do the "rational" thing indicated by one's unconditional judgment in the light of the total evidence, or can do the "irrational" thing prompted by some limited but powerful desire. But for Kierkegaard the latter course is not freedom, is not *free* will, but the misuse or misdirection or failure of willing.

One is "free" in order to "will" the good, but this entails the alternative possibility of not willing it, or (as he says in *Sickness*) "being unwilling to understand [what is right], of not willing it." Truly *free* will, the voluntary, means one thing: willingly to choose to do the one thing needful, the one thing one knows (perceives) to be the good. Kierkegaard always assumes the formulation arrived at by Climacus in *Fragments*: "Inasmuch as [one] is in untruth but is that on one's own [*ved sig selv*], … one might seem to be free, for to be on one's own [*hos sig selv*] certainly is freedom. And yet one is indeed unfree and bound and shut out ["exiled" in Swenson], because to be free from the truth is indeed to be shut out, and to be shut out on one's own is indeed to be bound."[19]

So "willing" (whatever it means) does not indicate or designate a position of being in sovereign neutrality, able to define and to determine unconditionally by and for oneself what will be the "good," de novo, minute by minute and in each instance by itself. Rather, it designates the universal situation of every individual who has to "make up one's mind" on a matter of essential import. At this point one faces a situation of ambivalence (Kierkegaard's "dialectical"), being caught in the conflict and the crossfire between opposing and mutually exclusive alternatives, where one alternative is clearly or predominantly the option that is indicated by the application of one's highest and best values, commitments, etc. to the concrete situation as one sees and believes it to exist, but where other alternatives intrude into one's consciousness with various kinds of claims for consideration (one's sensuous desires, aesthetic preferences, intellectual interests, social pressures such as communal approbation and avoidance of conflict).

It is clear, then, that for Kierkegaard "willing" is not a separate faculty of the mind (although he seems to use this concept earlier in *Sickness* when he says that "a person can have fantastic feeling, knowing, and willing").[20] That is to say, willing is not something distinct from and independent of the self's "possibilities" (attitudes), or of the inner and outward "necessities" which impinge upon the passage of possibilities into actuality. Rather, here in *Sickness*, when Kierkegaard says that "willing appraises what is known," that "willing allows some time to elapse," that "knowing comes over to the side of willing," what he means by "willing" is the total conscious self engaged in subjective (ethical-religious) reflection in order to make up its mind, to come to "decisions and conclusions," not only about *what* to do but also *whether* to do it, here and now. In these decisions all dimensions of the self (finite/infinite, possible/necessary, temporal/eternal) are focused on and operative in this one matter. In the language of "On the Occasion of a Confession," the "mind ... collects itself from every distraction, ... from every comparison, ... in order to centre upon its relationship to itself as an individual, and in order precisely thus to become eternally responsi-

---

19 *Fragments*, p. 19; (KW 7:15); SV 6:20; (4:185).
20 *Sickness*, p. 163; (KW 19:30); SV 15:88; (11:144). In this passage "willing" is precisely the self being caught in the struggle to interrelate and synthesize the infinite and the finite dimensions of human existence.

ble for every relationship in which one ordinarily stands." One escapes "double-mindedness" and achieves "purity of heart" to "will one thing."[21]

So, in the journal entry where Kierkegaard describes what gives a person "the most powerful sense of freedom" (note 17 above), he distinguishes three elements: excluding, resolving, stamping. And freedom as event, the leap, is comprised of or occurs as the unity of all three. Each element must be present and modify the other two in order for the event to occur. The stamping of one's action presupposes that one has excluded all but one possibility, and that this exclusion (coming to an unconditional judgment or intention) is carried over into the action (into an αλλο γενος) "with completely decisive resolve." And it is precisely this complexity of the leap that keeps it from being a pure *liberum arbitrium* (Kierkegaard) or an "embarrassing entity ... added to the world's furniture" (Davidson), that keeps it from being an arbitrary, capricious, "uncaused" choice. Yet it is free, indeterminate, because the resolve and "courage" to act are not necessitated or automatically produced by anything extraneous (atomic structure, chemical process, DNA, psycho-physical desires and drives, social conditioning, ideologies, logic, etc.) to the unconditional judgment of one's intention in interplay with one's evaluation (beliefs) about what is possible within the finite situation where the act is called for. The resolve is "mine," and I claim and accept "responsibility" for it. And the total conditions of each occasion of my resolve are unique, and the outcome on each occasion is unpredictable beforehand and is inexplicable after the fact—except in terms of the unique elements of my subjectivity (including my faith-relationship with the eternal) which combine to form my resolve in relation to each particular occasion.

Some would still argue that the resolve or decision (that carries the intention into action) is directly "caused" by the combination of those elements, about which and about whose interaction I have only partial consciousness and hence little or no choice. So, they would say, Kierkegaard's "most powerful sense of freedom" is an illusion. But there is one point of reflective consciousness in the process of coming to a decision where the sense of indeterminate choice remains vivid and whose resolution is not open to direct causal analysis and explanation. This is the point where a human individual consciousness is confronted with a

---

21 *Upbuilding Discourses in Various Spirits*, "Part One: An Occasional Discourse" (*Purity of Heart*), pp. 104–5, 215–16; (KW 15:64–5, 152); SV 11:63–4, 138; (8:167–8:240).

clear conflict between mutually exclusive but equally attractive possibilities of action.

In the journal entry on freedom (note 17 above), the language of the phrase "excludes the thought of any other possibility" does not hint at or divulge what Kierkegaard here calls "the agony of choosing," but that agony centres precisely in this event. These cool words mean to point to that crucial inward spiritual struggle and striving of the self (in its most intense self-consciousness) to focus its attention solely and purely on the one thing (possibility) that is dictated by the self's "inner necessity" (re-read pages in chapter 5 that include notes 128–37); or (in the language of *Postscript*) the struggle to focus on the self's "absolute telos" and "eternal blessedness"; or (in the language of *Works of Love*) in response to the command "you shall love your neighbour as yourself," the struggle to renounce one's own self-interest and to concentrate one's whole passionate concern on the need of the other person. But this positive act of focusing is a struggle of uncertain (indeterminate) outcome because it is always accompanied by and hence cannot avoid the concomitant negative act of the self's struggle to shut its "ears" to the clamouring voices of other insistent possibilities or interests or concerns which oppose or seek to modify that "one thing" that the self perceives as the ultimate right and good thing in a particular situation.

The latter voices may assume the tone of sweet reasonableness in simply asking for some assurances that the "supposed" good will really work, and asking for a little delay in order to have time to investigate the issue and to compare this good with other alternatives. Or the voices may come with the passion and unqualified claim of sexual desire, or of lust for power, or of envy and hate, and thus set the stage for the self's (will's) intense "agony of choice." As noted above, philosophy of action describes this event as "the common calculus of decision under uncertainty." The agent chooses one alternative in the light of "values he places on the various ways he thinks the world may turn out to be, given the action. ... The weighted sum of the desirabilities of the outcomes of the chosen course of action is greater than the weighted sum of the outcomes of any of the alternatives." But Davidson admits that there is one really messy problem that often emerges from the conflict between the different alternative worlds projected by conflicting congeries of desire and/or conflicting value systems which exist and operate within the psyche of the same individual. The agent comes to a clear judgment or attitude (intention) as to what is the best course of action, all things considered, and yet either fails to enact it or intentionally chooses to enact a less preferable or even a contradictory alternative. He calls this a case of "weakness of will," and admits that it often involves "self-deception."

This messy problem was clearly perceived by Kierkegaard, and he also interprets it as a matter of weak or "corrupted" will and of self-deception. In fact, he finds this failure of "will" (as the self's choice/decision) to be *the key* to the reality of freedom, of that freedom which is definitive of selfhood. And in one way of looking at it, he makes this phenomenon the centrepiece of his major and normative work (*Sickness*). He says, "In the life of the spirit there is no standing still; ... everything is actuation." Or as he puts it earlier, "every moment that a self exists, it is in a-process-of-becoming [*i Vorden*]."[22] So the agent continuously faces an either/or. Ideally, one enacts one's ethical-religious perception of the good immediately. As Davidson says, it is reasonable to expect that one will perform one's unconditional judgment as to what is indicated by all the evidence (internal and external). But the fact is that a person often chooses intentionally not to do so. The self does not succeed in "excluding the thought of any other possibility" than the one indicated by its "inner necessity," its "absolute telos," the "command of love." And this ambivalence of "willing," either succeeding or failing in the transition, is profoundly revealing of the indeterminancy that resides precisely at this critical point in the transition from knowing the good to doing it, from unconditional intention to action.

So we face the key question: what determines the outcome of this conflict? Is it simply a matter of the psychic-physical strength of the desires or motives that drive the competing possibilities, interests, or concerns? Where is the turning point located, and what happens there? Again, we turn to our passages in *Sickness* to see how Kierkegaard analyses this failure. But our focus will be limited to only a part of his analysis because here again we listen to Kierkegaard as he straddles the borderline between humanist and theologian. His major treatment of the failure or corruption of willing lies within part two of *Sickness*, entitled "Despair is Sin." And for Kierkegaard "sin" is a strictly and exclusively *Christian* idea and understanding (just as is "faith" in the "eminent sense"). "Christianity very consistently assumes that neither paganism nor the natural human being knows what sin is; in fact, it assumes that there has to be a revelation from God to show what sin is."[23]

---

22 *Sickness*, pp. 224f, 163; (KW 19:94, 30); SV 15:146, 88; (11:205, 143).
23 Ibid., p. 220; (KW 19:89); SV 15:142; (11:201).

So this interpretation of Kierkegaard's concept of the self will consider "despair" only later in an interpretation of Kierkegaard as theologian, and so under the topic of "My Self: A Failure" (sinner) because Kierkegaard defines despair as a state of "disrelationship" in the self traceable to a disrelationship between the self and God. And this breach between the self and God is characterized by Kierkegaard strictly as "sin," that is, as the human failure to live with God in the relationship of faith. And the peculiarity of this faith-relationship is based by Kierkegaard strictly on the Christian understanding that human existence is "a gift" from God because God is our creator, that is, we are a "creation out of nothing"—a peculiarly Christian notion that Kierkegaard exposits very carefully. Of course Kierkegaard sees analogies to the Christian understandings of creation, sin, and faith in traditions other than the Christian. And when this study comes to the topics of self as "Gift," as "Failure," and as "In need of the Eternal" (fulfilled in "faith/love"), it will want to make as much of those analogies as possible, because, after all, Christian faith and life does not claim to be anything more than a realization of what is already present as a potentiality in the human as such.

At this point, therefore, we will restrict comment to those materials that describe the struggle of "willing" within the possibilities of the universal human capacity for ethical-religious consciousness, and therefore "willing" as a struggle whose description is recognizable as general human experience. The material on "willing" is primarily in the context of Kierkegaard's discussion of sin, but is clearly rooted in a significant passage at the very beginning of his analysis of "despair seen under the determinant: consciousness," that is, "despair that ... is conscious of having a self in which there is something eternal," an analysis that is mainly couched in the language of religiousness A. And this description of "willing" will lead us to Kierkegaard's materials on "self-deception" which are in discourses written (at least partially) from the point of view of universal human nature.

Kierkegaard is making the point that when a person does something contrary to what he really thinks is best, one's consciousness of one's condition (state) is not an either/or, that is, totally aware or totally ignorant. "Actual life is too complex," so one most often dwells in a "many-nuanced half-darkness," not quite clear whether the source of one's confusion lies within oneself or derives from something outside that could be altered. Usually one diverts one's attention away from this dilemma by becoming very busy in work and/or amusements and thus "tries to keep oneself in the dark" about what one is doing. On the other hand, "one may fully realize that one is working this way in order to sink one's soul in darkness," and one does so with "shrewd calculation" and "psychological insight." But this situation or condition of one's self-consciousness raises a basic question: is one "free" enough in this confused state of consciousness to be held responsible? For this consideration, Kierkegaard lays down a fundamental principle: "In all darkness and ignorance there is a dialectical interplay between knowing and willing," and in trying to understand our own or another's actions, we must not "err by accentuating knowing exclusively or willing exclusively."[24]

However, he does not apply this principle to the question of responsibility until much later in part two on sin. At this point he is assuming that one has arrived at "ethical and ethical-religious perception [*Erkjenden*]" of "the right" (*det Rette*), and that one is just at the point of entering into the appropriate "decisions and conclusions" which one will now "stamp" on one's action. How can one fail in this movement? Does one not automatically/rationally do what one knows is best? Is not decision the product of insight, without any intervening mysterious episode of vacillating "willing"? Socrates argued that if someone understands what is right, then that understanding quickly induces one to do it. "When someone does not do what is right, then neither has one understood what is right."[25]

Kierkegaard agrees that "the good must be done immediately, as soon as it is perceived" (a point he stresses throughout the authorship). But he also insists that the "doing" is not part of the perceiving. Between the element of "excluding" (all other possibilities) and the element of "stamping" (on one's actions), one must come to a "completely decisive resolve" to do it. But this personal individual decision of the whole self does not emerge from a mathematical-like or logical-like or scientific-like calculation which has only one inevitable, right answer. Neither does the "resolve" refer to what takes place in the slow and agonizing process, partly unconscious, by which one has already arrived at the perception of the good demanded by one's "inner necessity," etc. (or as Davidson would put it, the formation of an "unconditional evaluative attitude" or intention). Rather, at this critical juncture a dialectic comes into play. There is either a yielding or a resisting in respect to the perception of the good.

24 Ibid., p. 181; (KW 19:48); SV 15:104; (11:160).
25 Ibid., p. 223f.; (KW 19:92f.); SV 15:145; (11:203f.).

The "yielding" consists in what we have previously described a number of times as the turning or concentration of one's "evaluative attention" totally and exclusively on the one-thing-needful as perceived ethically and ethical-religiously. But here we are interested in Kierkegaard's analysis of the failure of resolve through what he calls a "darkening of [one's] ethical and ethical-religious knowing" of the good, or a "corruption of willing," because the *failure* shows that doing what one knows to be the good is not inevitable or necessitated.

The resisting, he says, does not usually take the form of a wild and rebellious "doing the opposite of what perceiving understands" to be the good. Rather, it happens in the subtle, sometimes hardly conscious, seemingly innocent asking whether I should not make sure that this is what I really *want* to do? Are there not better alternatives? In the transition from knowing to doing one turns one's attention to another voice that asks the question, "what does willing think [*synes*, feel] about the perception?" Or, as one would normally say, "how do *I* feel about it?" And the result is that "the perception simmers down" or cools off. This questioning of the absolute demand for instantaneous enactment of the perceived one-thing-needful arises, as we have heard, from the voices of one's "lower nature," that is, from the cool, objective, disinterested perspectives of the metaphysical or scientific perception of truth, or from the imperious, sensuous immediacy of the aesthetic claim that truth is a matter of *my* taste and its satisfaction. The self's consciousness listens to these voices and makes the seemingly innocuous response of "letting some time to elapse, an interim" in order to reconsider. But Kierkegaard insists that what is actually happening is a gradual "darkening" (*dunkel*) or obscuring of the self's perception of the good. "Willing ... almost appears to be in collusion" with these voices. "Gradually, willing's objection to this development lessens. ... And when knowing has been duly darkened, knowing and willing can better understand each other; eventually they agree completely, for now knowing has come over to the side of willing and admits that what it wants is entirely right."[26] So the process ends in one's being truly ignorant of the right, convinced that there is a better alternative.

The key question returns. How does the event of resisting the perception of the good demonstrate the freedom of the event of yielding to the perception of the good? Is not the question of indeterminacy and causation simply shifted to a different point? To answer this question

26 Ibid., p. 225; (KW 19:94); SV 15:146f.; (11:205).

Kierkegaard asks: is one's ignorance of the good "original" or a "resultant"? He agrees that if one is really and originally totally ignorant of the good, then one cannot be held responsible for doing what is wrong. But if ignorance of the good is the result "of one's [own] efforts to darken one's knowing," and "if it is assumed that one was clearly aware [*bevidst*] of what one was doing when one began to darken one's knowing," then the failure "is not in the knowing but in the willing."

Then he makes an important point about his analysis of how "willing," that is, how the fully conscious self deliberately delays doing what it knows is right (or at least what is the best thing to do, all things considered) by taking time to consider other conflicting alternatives. He contends that this analysis demonstrates that at the beginning there is a point of indeterminacy in the turning of one's attention away from the perceived right (good) thing and toward the "aesthetic" concerns of the sensuous and/or the "metaphysical" concerns of the abstract intellect, and that this turning is "voluntary" in the sense that it is the *self* that is doing it at the most intensely conscious centre of subjectivity. It is *I* who comes to a resolve, or it is *I* who avoids or rejects ("darkens") perception of the good and thus "cools off" the resolve; the only "cause" lies within and at the conscious centre of *my self*, not outside. And this freedom and responsibility are perfectly clear to anyone who "has the courage to declare that a person knowingly does wrong, knows what is right and does the wrong," who acknowledges the distinction between "not *being able* to understand and not *willing* to understand."[27]

This analysis of the deliberate "wilful" darkening of one's understanding of what is the good and right one-thing-needful occurs, as noted, in the context of Kierkegaard's Christian definition of "sin" before God. But before he came to this topic in *Sickness* he had analysed the same phenomenon several times as a case of what he calls "self-deception." And in some ways these depictions of how self-deception occurs are more subtle and more fully and sharply defined than those of "the corruption of willing" in *Sickness*. Furthermore, they occur in the context of discussions that are clearly based on the assumptions of the ethical-religious experience of universal humanity. We find these depictions in *Postscript* (1845), *Upbuilding Discourses in Various Spirits* (1846), and *Works of Love* (1847). The contents of these materials will be presented topically rather than sequentially.

---

27 Ibid., pp. 219, 225f.; (KW 19:88, 95); SV 15:141, 147; (11:199f., 205f.).

First of all, it is important to note that Kierkegaard carefully limits those types of human behaviour where it is proper to speak of self-deception. He recognizes that not every case of living in deception or under an illusion is self-instigated. Often there are persons who are validly ignorant of the truth and the good, because they have been "deprived either of the opportunity or the capacity to learn," but whose ignorance is subject to change into knowledge when they are confronted by the truth and "more and more is learned."[28] We have also heard him argue that one must distinguish between relative ends (goods) and absolute infinite or "eternal" ends and goods. And he is not focusing, he says, on the "choices" in the former realm of human behaviour. Indeed, "in relation to finitude (for example, physical well-being)" one makes only "finite decisions," which "are in a certain sense too small for one to approach from the infinite." Therefore, "to be compelled is the only help in finite matters," but "freedom's choice is the only deliverance in the infinite." For example, he admits some confusion when he is accused of "pride and arrogance" because "I am not making my life more comfortable and am not looking for financial security." On one's motivations in such "finite" matters, he blandly admits, "Well, who knows oneself in this way." But as to "infinite" matters in his own life, "It seems to me that something higher is constantly moving within me; I believe that I cannot justify anything else but continuing to serve it as long as possible."[29]

So for Kierkegaard self-deception occurs only when one is about to make the authentic leap of freedom, that is to say, when one is coming to a conclusion and decision in regard to the infinite/eternal dimension of the human self in its finite/temporal existence. "In the infinite sense, only one deception is possible, self-deception."[30] Furthermore, it must be remembered, that any decision about infinite/eternal matters presupposes self-consciousness, that is, "subjectivity" which confronts the occasion with "infinite, personal, passionate interestedness." But what is it in such an occasion that gives rise to the possibility of an inclination toward self-deception? Kierkegaard's answer: the entire multiple complexity of the given structure of the human self as a synthesis of the infinite and the finite, of the temporal and the eternal, of possibility and

---

28 *Upbuilding Discourses in Various Spirits*, "Part One: An Occasional Discourse" (*Purity of Heart*), p. 52; (KW 15:23); SV 11:29; (8:133).

29 *Journals*, 1253; VIII^1 A 178; 6805; X^4 A 559.

30 *Works of Love*, p. 223; SV 12:228; (9:226).

necessity. The resolution of the interplay of these multiple dimensions (when the individual faces the need to act in the face of a consciously perceived absolute good) reveals an irreducible condition of indeterminacy, because in every such occasion the individual may either succeed or fail in the resolution. And when the resolution requires a decision about an infinite or absolute good, the failure, Kierkegaard argues, always involves an element of self-deception. So it is precisely the self's openness to *either* self-deception *or* self-fulfilment that is the ground of Kierkegaard's assertion: "The self is freedom." In other words, the fact that I may deliberately and responsibly deceive myself about what I know I ought to do in a certain situation means, conversely, that if I choose to do what I know I ought to do, then I do that also deliberately and responsibly, that is, voluntarily and freely. This point on freedom comes out in several ways in Kierkegaard's analysis and description of self-deception.

As introduction, however, it is important to note again and more fully where Kierkegaard locates the occurrence of self-deception in the general structure of the self, namely, at the same point where "willing" occurs in the dialectic between one's "higher" and "lower" natures. In our own contemporary discussion of and debate about self-deception, the conception of the general structure of the self determines whether self-deception is even a viable concept, and if so, what elements of the self are involved and how they interact in order for genuine self-deception to occur.[31] In this debate two sharply opposing conceptions of the self's structure have emerged. On the one hand the self is viewed as "rationally integrated, automatically scanning and correcting its beliefs." In such a picture self-deception is paradoxical, incoherent, irrational. A rational person simply does not deliberately lie to oneself. Hence so-called self-deception is explained by "weakened conditions of unity, transparency, truthfulness, reflexivity" in one's central rationality, and is therefore reduced to cases of ignorance, conflict, or error.[32]

On the other hand the self is viewed as "a loosely organized system composed of relatively autonomous subsystems," for which "rational integration is a task and an ideal rather than a starting point." In its radical version as the homuncular theory, this view sees the subsytems as "themselves composed of increasingly simple, independent subsystems,

---

31 This fact becomes vividly clear in reading the twenty-four essays in *Perspectives on Self-Deception*, ed. Brian P. McLaughlin and Amélie Oksenberg Rorty.

32 A.O. Rorty, "The Deceptive Self: Liars, Layers, and Lairs," in ibid., pp. 12, 14, 16.

eventually reaching a level of relatively mechanical, subpersonic, specialized proto-intentional functions." Each subsystem may have "its own beliefs, goals, plans and strategies," and hence some degree of intentionality. This view does not deny that integration of the subsystems is desirable up to a point and under some circumstances, because "for some purposes a central panoptical monitor is adaptive." But it is also true that "we are also well served by autonomous and automatically triggered subsystems," and by the fact that they sometimes fail to communicate. "Compartmentalization, self-manipulated focusing, selective insensitivity, blind persistence, canny unresponsiveness—capacities and habits that undermine integration—have enormous benefits."[33]

In this second picture of the self, self-deception is easily understood as failure to integrate the subsystems, and the central system of coordination is not really to blame. "Even the capacities for critical, rational reflection are subdivided into subsystems." Hence self-deception "is a natural by-product of functional structures and strategies," and usually nothing more than "an unintended, tangential consequence." On this assumption, "there is no difficulty in explaining how a person can believe contradictions, can be aware and not aware of herself as holding contradictory views, and can adopt conflicting policies and strategies." This picture of the self "has demystified self-deception so thoroughly that it has evaporated. ... [I]t has abandoned the identity of the deceiver and the deceived." Self-deception "turn[s] out to be nothing more than ignorance, conflict, nonintegration, or compartmentalization."[34] So subscribers to this picture of the self analyse such phenomena as cases of wishful thinking, rationalization, motivational strength, bad faith, repression, denial, etc., rather than intentional and responsible self-deception.

The majority of philosophers and psychologists, however, view the self neither *simply* as a panoptical scanner and corrector for the purpose of rational integration of all one's systems, nor *simply* as "a problematically yoked-together bundle of partly autonomous systems."[35] Rather, they see the self as some kind of a combination of the two pictures. A strong

---

33 Ibid., pp. 12, 17ff. On the homuncular theory, see also, in the same book, Stephen L. White, "Self-Deception and Responsibility for the Self," as a whole, but particularly pp. 452ff. A "homunculus" is a "little man," and hence the theory that a human being has hidden away beneath the surface one or more little persons (subsystems) which are relatively independent of each other.

34 Ibid., pp. 17, 21f.

35 Ibid., p. 17; quotation is from Daniel Dennett.

statement of this latter view has been formulated by Amélie Oksenberg Rorty. She argues that "self-deception resists evaporation and reduction." We naturally recognize it as occuring in others as well as in ourselves, especially as we reflect about our past actions. This recognition is directly tied to the fact that we also recognize ourselves in both of the above pictures: both as rational integrator and as semiconscious and semi-independent systems of physical, psychological, and intellectual drives and interests. And it is precisely the disjunction and interplay of these two levels or dimensions or perspectives of ourselves that we find to be "essential to thinking of ourselves as responsible agents and responsible believers." Our innate and highly valued sense of being responsible for our selves as well as for our individual actions requires that we be "committed to and actively capable of rational integration" in order "to avoid false beliefs, correct them where possible, and suspend judgment when necessary," even while we often depend, for our survival and well-being, on the instinctive or automatic and not-rationally-controlled operation of physical, psychological, emotional and intellectual subsystems that are integral parts of our selves.

In other words, we assume that each of the "we" is identified with some central or main system whose "critical rationality" has the power and authority to judge (evaluate), legislate (decide), and execute (enact) in order to integrate suggestions and demands from subsystems, and to correct distortions when they occur. It is just this relationship between the two pictures of the self that opens up the possibility of full authentic self-deception. "When the first picture is projected onto the second, the self is deceived by itself when its subsystems uncharacteristically, persistently, and systematically resist the correction and integration that is readily available to them."[36]

How, then does Kierkegaard's picture of the structure of the self and its self-deception fit into these pictures of the self? Or rather, do they shed some light on his analysis and depiction of the self as self-deceiver? In most general terms he pictures the total self as passing through a series of "stages" (aesthetic, ethical, religious), and he views them as cumulative, that is, each stage catching up and carrying forward each

---

36 Ibid., pp. 12f., 16, 22–5. The given character and importance of the sense of "choice" and "responsibility" in human nature, and the inability of the homuncular view of the self to give it its due and to make sense of it, is developed in different ways in essays by several authors in *Perspectives on Self-Deception*. See especially those by Ronald B. de Sousa, Stephen L. Darwell, and Stephen L. White.

previous stage. He also argues that it is possible to get stuck at one stage or to resist inclusion or consideration of one or both of the other stages. But in *Postscript* (as we have seen) Kierkegaard largely deserts the language of "stages" and refers repeatedly (some eighty times) to the diverse "spheres" of human existence and their interrelationships. And although his "spheres" include aesthetic, ethical, and religious, he diversifies the concept and perceives more complex relationships among the various spheres than he had attributed to the relationships between the "stages."

For example, toward the end of *Postscript* he lists seven distinct "spheres" as: "immediacy; finite common sense; irony; ethics, with irony as incognito; humour; religiousness [A], with humour as incognito; and finally the Christian [religiousness B]."[37] Kierkegaard no doubt arranges these in what he considers to be an ascending order, and the notion of "stages" is still present in his insistence that "If one gains the religious, then it is assumed that one has passed through the ethical," and that "Religiousness A must first be present before there can be any question of becoming aware of the dialectical [religiousness] B."[38] Actually, his designation of spheres of human existence is even more diverse. And when he describes the interactions that take place among these spheres, he perceives very complex and often confusing phenomena. In other words, in the language of our contemporary philosophy of action and self-deception, Kierkegaard is recognizing that the self is composed of a variety of subsystems that are often in conflict. And, as we have seen, he does not see any of them as evil as such, and hence to be eliminated from the total system. Rather, each has a part to play and is to be caught up and carried forward into the total integration of the self, either as "stages" or as "spheres." But this integration is not a sure thing. It is a complicated, difficult, and indeterminate process, involving agonized decisions and choices, also failures and need for corrections.

For example, nowhere in the above list is there any recognition of that sphere of human existence of which the whole of *Postscript* is organized as a critique, namely, what Kierkegaard variously calls objective reflection, the intellectual, the philosophical, abstract speculative thought, and the latter's refinement as self-referential abstract truth in mathematics and logic. The terms "immediacy" (*Umiddelbarhed*) and

---

37 *Postscript*, p. 473n; (KW 12.1:531n); SV 10:204n; (7:464n).
38 Ibid., pp. 347, 494; (KW 12.1:388, 556); SV 10:83, 226; (7:336, 486).

"finite common sense" (*endelig Forstandighed*) hardly capture what is distinctive of this sphere and how it relates to the ethical and the religious. Granted, both the aesthetist (*det Æsthetiske*) and the intellectual or thinker (*det Intellectuelle* or *Tænker*) restrict their concept of "truth" to that which can be "immediately" known either through sense apprehension or rational conceptualization. But Kierkegaard so clearly and consistently differentiates the methodology of abstract conceptual thinking from that of the aesthetic experience and representation that, in one key passage, he does separate out "the sphere of intellectuality" (*Intellectualitetens Sphære*).

In his chapter on the "subjective thinker" (*Postscript*) he argues at length that "If the particular spheres are not decisively kept apart from each other, everything is confused."[39] That is to say, each sphere must respect the integrity of every other sphere and not try to annul other spheres by assimilation. And the ultimate problem for the self is to discover and to implement that order of the stages or spheres that brings true harmony for the totality of human existence, that is, for the totality of the particular, unique, individual, human self (spirit). What is the final "stage" that completes the process of "becoming" one's self? What sphere is the final concentric circle that includes, preserves, and fulfils all the other spheres within it? Obviously, for Kierkegaard it is the religious stage or sphere. Our interest here is not how that happens but how the struggle toward this end sets the stage for self-deception.

In this key passage Kierkegaard (i.e. Climacus) is arguing (again) that human "actuality" cannot be subsumed or understood in *purely* aesthetic or intellectual (conceptual) or even ethical terms but *also* integrally includes the sphere of religious faith. But, he says, "In our day everything is blended together; one answers aesthetic [questions] ethically, [questions of] faith intellectually, and so forth. One gets to the end of all such matters, and yet one has paid no attention [to the question:] in which sphere does each question find its [appropriate] answer. In the world of the spirit this produces great confusion." He also draws another key distinction in that he sees the ethical and the religious standing together against the attempts of the aesthetic and the intellectual perspectives to claim exclusive and ultimate truth about reality. "Faith's analogy to the ethical consists of infinite interestedness." And even though their focus of interest differs, they agree in that both "condemn every *posse* which is not an *esse*," while both aesthetics and abstract thought seek to resolve

---

39 Ibid., p. 290; (KW 12.1:325); SV 10:30; (7:280).

every *esse* into a *posse*.⁴⁰ Or as Kierkegaard likes to put it, from the aesthetic and intellectual point of view, possibility is "higher" than actuality, whereas the ethical-religious perspective contends that actuality is the end goal and therefore "higher" than possibility for the state of individual human existence.

This latter distinction between a "higher" level of truth and an implied "lower" level of truth is an important one for Kierkegaard in depicting the structure of the self that makes self-deception possible. This terminology first appears in *Either/Or*, but just to make a brief undeveloped distinction between romantic (aesthetic) "first love" and that same love "transfigured ... into a higher sphere" by "coming into relation with the ethical and the religious."⁴¹ But this language and its application to love are picked up again and developed more fully in *Works of Love*. In a key passage Kierkegaard contrasts a "lower sphere-of-ideas [representations] [*Forestillingskreds*]" with "the highest good and the greatest blessedness." To call this sphere of ideas "lower" does not imply "evil" or "wrong" as such and therefore to be eliminated. Rather, they have the quality of being "earthly" or "worldly" and hence temporal and relative. They are to be set in relationship with the "higher" or "highest" truth for an existing human individual and thus become "transfigured."⁴² In *Postscript* Climacus makes this point by saying that one must maintain only a relative relationship with relative ends, and that "the most general expression for madness [is] that the individual has an absolute relationship to what is relative."⁴³

What are the implications of this distinction between "higher" and "lower" for Kierkegaard's view of the structure of the self? As noted above, his designation of a variety of spheres that can influence human decisions and actions relatively independently of each other suggests our contemporary concept of autonomous subsystems each of which plays a legitimate and helpful role in the total functioning of the self. But his persistent insistence on the need and the ideal of control and coordination of the various stages and spheres points to his assumption of a central system comprised of conscious surveillance, evaluation, decision, and (if indicated) correction. In contemporary language, he assumes that the self is a panoptical scanner with legislative, judicial, and

---

40 Ibid., p. 288; (KW 12.1:324); SV 10:29; (7:279).
41 *Either/Or*, 2:57f.; (KW 4:56f.); SV 3:57f.; (2:52).
42 *Works of Love*, pp. 223–6; SV 12:228–32; (9:226–30).
43 *Postscript*, pp. 377 f.; SV 10:11f.; (7:366).

executive powers, and that it is this "system" which makes the self to be a "free" and responsible agent. And he agrees with A.O. Rorty that this system "cannot just be one among the system of subsystems" but is *superimposed* onto the subsystems, and that its *power* "must be a direct function of its rational authority, rather than of the vicissitudes of its psychological and physical history" (although, as will be seen below, Kierkegaard would substitute "ethical" for "rational").[44]

However, the way in which Kierkegaard (in his depiction of the structure of the self) defines the content and operation of the "higher" and "lower" spheres differentiates his picture from that in our contemporary philosophy of action and hence changes the nature of self-deception. For example, A.O. Rorty notes that the psychological salience of suggestions from one's subsystem(s) does not always reflect one's beliefs and priorities, and that one's "magnetized attention" does not always accord with one's "general all-things-considered attitudes." So "relevance and importance ... can vary independently," and it is precisely "this feature of psychological structures [that] ... makes both self-deception and *akrasia* possible."[45] In other words, the "autonomy" and "responsibility" that come with one's "rational integrative authority" lie *in between* the "salience" asserted by one's subsytems and the "importance" claimed by one's beliefs and priorities. And it is precisely in this dialectic that Kierkegaard also locates the possibilities of freedom and (i.e., *or*) self-deception. But for Kierkegaard the dialectic is not a moment simply of rational decision but of the more complex event of "willing."

This complexity of the moment is supported in different ways by other contributors to *Perspectives on Self-Deception*. Stephen L. Darwell points out that the interest of moral philosophers in self-deception has varied widely, and he contends that this variety reflects "fundamentally different approaches to the question of what it is right to do." He distinguishes four theories: (1) the right is a matter of an intrinsic sense of ought or duty; (2) the right is what produces good consequences; (3) the right is a matter of moral *character* (virtue); (4) the right is a matter of the individual's *constitution* which makes the person responsible for one's own moral integrity (making judgments). Clearly, it is the "constitutionalists" who are especially interested in the question of self-deception. For such a view self-deception is something a person does, a choice for which one is responsible. "[A] person represents his thought, be-

---

44 A.O. Rorty in *Perspectives on Self-Deception*, pp. 24f.
45 Ibid., p. 18.

liefs, aims, and intentions to himself as though they were well grounded, ... when in fact they ... are the result of quite different factors, and the person is in a position to know this." So self-deception involves *judgment* in which one "disregard[s] or explain[s] away conflicting evidence, to focus on supporting evidence."[46] This analysis provides another description of what Kierkegaard calls "darkening of the will" in that it requires the element of evaluation and decision. But it does not clearly assign a "higher" significance to the ethical.

Ronald B. de Sousa comes to similar conclusions but in a very different way. He agrees that the question of self-deception "cannot be pried apart from the question of *human nature*. ... [W]e make some things valuable by caring about them, but at least some of these things we should not care about if we thought there was nothing 'out there' objectively *worth* caring about. What is authentic and what is phony has much to do with individual autonomy; but the cult of individual autonomy can itself be phony, if it takes no account of the constraints and possibilities of human nature."[47] He also makes the very helpful point that "rationality" in human action is of three different kinds or levels: (1) strategic, which assesses the probable value of an action's consequences; (2) cognitive, which assesses the correlation of an intended action with some "true" objective state of the world; (3) axiological, which assesses "the appropriateness of an emotion to its object," in that the emotion is a "quasi-cognition" of the value of that object.[48] Again, what Kierkegaard means by "willing" involves deciding what is "worth caring about," and this decision calls into play one's "axiological rationality" by which one recognizes what actions are worth caring about with all one's "inward, passionate, infinite interestedness."

So de Sousa concentrates on how we can distinguish between "authentic emotions" and "hypocritical ... self-deceived emotions." Emotions are hard to access, but one way to attack them is by "consciousness raising," that is, by "the bringing into consciousness of facts about myself which then come up for endorsement as avowed parts of my identity." Although propositional description is a limited way of getting at the content of emotions, yet "a change of belief can radically alter an emotion," and "we can regestalt ... early paradigms" of belief from which we

---

46 Stephen L. Darwell, "Self-Deception, Autonomy, and Moral Constitution," in *Perspectives on Self-Deception*, pp. 409, 413, 415f.

47 Ronald B. de Sousa, "Emotion and Self-Deception," in *Perspectives on Self-Deception*, p. 337.

48 Ibid., pp. 326f.

learned our emotions. Indeed, "it is in searching out assumptions about emotions ... that we are most likely to transform and reform experienced content and emerge from self-deception." At this point "philosophical analysis merges with psychoanalysis" to strengthen therapy.[49] Again, this view of inward reflection about beliefs in what is of ultimate "value" or "worth," reflection that is passionately involved with its subject matter, is certainly what Kierkegaard means by that "subjective reflection" where freedom and self-deception lie waiting as dialectical possibilities.

Nevertheless, even though these various views of the self and its self-deception provide helpful interpretive tools for understanding Kierkegaard's distinction between "higher" and "lower" dimensions of the self, none of them bring into play that level or sphere of human nature where the individual is open to what Kierkegaard calls the "ethical-religious." Not even de Sousa's "axiological rationality" and its search for "authentic emotions" make room for a factor in human consciousness that *transcends* rationality of any kind, viz., the religious. The closest approximation to even a suggestion of such a factor in the texts of contemporary philosophy of action (as far as the present author is aware) is found in a closing, almost incidental remark by Donald Davidson in his essay "Paradoxes of Irrationality."

As we have seen (at the beginning of chapter 6), Davidson argues that a human being is a "person" in so far as there is "a coherent and plausible pattern in his [her] attitudes and actions." Such actions are "free" in so far as they are "intentional," that is, are the expression of that pattern of beliefs, desires, values, etc. that define who that person is. Such intentionality indicates that one is acting in accord with "the constitutive ideal of rationality." But one can also act intentionally contrary to this principle. Either out of "weakness of will" or by "self-deception" the agent acts in contradiction to one's "best standards of rationality." In both cases one follows the prompting of a ("lower") subsystem even though it is contrary to one's general ("higher") evaluative judgments and cognitive evidence. Hence such actions can only be judged to be "irrational."

But at the end of "Paradoxes of Irrationality" he notes another kind of mental process and action that is "irrational" in quite a different sense. This "more interesting and more important" case "is a form of self-criticism and reform that we tend to hold in high esteem, and that has even

---

49 Ibid., pp. 336–8.

been thought to be the very essence of rationality and the source of freedom. Yet it is clearly a case of mental causality that *transcends* reason (in the somewhat technical sense in which I have been using the concept)" (emphasis added). The "reasons" for change and transformation come not from within that "coherent and plausible pattern" of the agent's present attitudes (values, beliefs, desires, etc.) that define one's "rationality." Rather, they come from "an independent source, ... from a domain of values necessarily extrinsic to the contents of the views or values to undergo change." So from the point of view of the agent's present pattern of views and values, this source is "irrational" (POI 305).

It is precisely such a transcendent, independent, extrinsic domain of critique and reform (of what one essentially is in the "self's possibility" and the "self's necessity") that Kierkegaard calls "the religious"—even when this "transcendent" domain "speaks" to one's self "immanently" in the "inwardness" of one's own self-consciousness. And Kierkegaard agrees wholeheartedly that listening to and obeying this transcendent source and domain of critique and reform is truly "irrational," indeed appears "insane," to the normal human being who is trying to conduct his/her life according to "objective reflection" or according to some social-personal ethical standard of what is right and good. And the direct implication of Davidson's distinguishing between these two kinds of irrationality is that the true and normative location of the "rational" person or self is not in the intentionality of subsystems but is in the central coordinating system which seeks to resolve conflicts (in the total "network" of systems) as to what is the best thing to do in any particular situation. And, it should be noted, his "somewhat technical sense" of "reason" includes the consideration of both evaluative beliefs and cognitive evidence (DAD 143). So it is precisely this event of directing one's attention to the claims of evaluation and cognition (in order to adjudicate conflicts as to the "right") that Kierkegaard calls the dialectic of "willing."

But nowhere does Davidson explore the status of this transcendent "domain of values," or how it functions in the process by which the central "rational" system achieves "self-criticism and reform." As we have shown extensively, Kierkegaard provides elaborate and diverse analyses of this domain under the category of "the religious," characterizing it variously as: dealing with the infinite and the eternal; entering into silence and experiencing "death"; willing one thing through confession and repentance; the teleological suspension of the ethical; a passionate relationship to one's eternal blessedness; the transformation of one's existence by relating absolutely to the absolute; suffering that comes with dying away from the life of immediacy; freedom through the totality of guilt-consciousness; believing in "all-things-are-possible"; and finally and ultimately, the experience of affirmation and empowerment that comes with the recognition that *love* is the ultimate dynamic of reality ("God"). Now we must show how this specification of both the content (the "what") and the form (the "how") of the religious (as the transcendent "domain of values" in human self-consciousness) also affects Kierkegaard's analysis of the phenomenon of self-deception. But we are also to remember that we are interested in self-deception (at this point) only as evidence of the indeterminacy (the either/or) that obtains at the heart of the complex dialectic of "willing," that is, the turning of one's "evaluative attention" *either* toward the promptings of one's "lower" unintegrated subsystems (one's "aesthetic and metaphysical comprehension") *or* toward the calling of one's "higher" consciousness of that transcendent "domain of values" that offers self-criticism and reform (one's "ethical-religious comprehension").

Kierkegaard gradually developed his idea of self-deception over a three-year period, first in *Postscript* (1845), then in the discourse "On the Occasion of a Confessional" (in *Upbuilding Discourses in Various Spirits*, 1846), and finally in *Works of Love* (1847). In *Postscript* he (Climacus) is analysing the difficulties that human beings have in coming to the infinite decision to become absolutely committed to absolute ends, rather than absolutely committed to relative ends. He remarks on "how ingenious and inventive human beings are in order to evade an ultimate decision." Why? As he repeatedly argues throughout *Postscript*: because a decision about something ultimate, infinite, or absolute cannot be arrived at by a gradual accumulation of objective evidence that demonstrates conclusively what is the right or good thing. Rather, in decisions which involve ultimate ethical issues of value there always remains an element of uncertainty, a matter of judgment and commitment. So the transition to a conclusion requires a risky "leap" of decision, grounded on a belief in something absolute.

Humans generally like to be certain, or at least to have the assurance of probability. Cautiousness and prudence are praised as being wise. So they "make a feigned [pretended, false] movement or lunge in the direction of the absolute, while remaining totally within the relative, a feigned transition like the transition from eudaemonism to the ethical [while remaining] within eudaemonism." Thus they avoid the "infinite venture" which places them before "a yawning chasm, ... a gulf which reason [*Forstand*] cannot cross either forward or backward," but which can be crossed only by a risky decision made with "the passion of infinitude." Such persons are "deceived" (*narre*) into thinking they have gained everything when they have gained nothing. "For the perishable is nothing when it is past, and it is of its essence to pass away, quickly as the moment of sensuous enjoyment, the farthest possible remove from the eternal, a moment in time filled with emptiness." So they end in "avarice, vanity, envy, etc., ... essentially forms of madness."[50]

On the other hand, from this "finite" point of view, "to risk everything for the expectation of an eternal blessedness is the height of madness. On the contrary, to ask for certainty and definiteness is sagacity, because that is a subterfuge in order to avoid the strenuousness of risk-taking and action." So if I "am resolved to strive for the highest good," then with the passion of infinite I must embrace "uncertainty of knowledge with respect to an eternal blessedness." Nevertheless "there is a tranquillity and a restfulness in all this strenuousness, because it is no contradiction to relate absolutely to the absolute τελος, that is, with all one's might and in renunciation of everything else, but it is the absolute reciprocity of like-for-like."[51]

In this passage Climacus does not use the term self-deception, but seems to imply it as he describes the ingenuity and prevarication humans resort to in order to evade the agony of making a decision in the face of ethical uncertainty that cannot be assuaged by the methods of "aesthetic and metaphysical comprehension." But he does not raise the question that Anti-Climacus later faced up to, namely, does a human being *know*, is one *aware* when one begins to pretend (feign) to move toward the absolute but stops within the relative; that is, is one conscious of deliberately "darkening" one's "ethical-religious comprehension" of the absolute good, of the one-thing-needful?

This question is directly confronted by Kierkegaard in his discourse on confession. As we have seen, by "confession" he means the event in which a human being withdraws her attention from all the distractions of busy engagement with the world around, and concentrates one's mind in such a way as to "come to an understanding with oneself," that is, to be so totally and honestly open to oneself that one "gets to know something about oneself," even "what [one] tries to keep hidden in darkness." In the profound "silence" of this moment one becomes

---

50 *Postscript*, pp. 379, 378; (KW 12.1:423-4, 422); SV 10:113, 112; (7:367, 366).
51 Ibid., pp. 381f., 377; (KW 12.1:426, 422) SV 12:115, 112; (7:370, 366).

strangely aware that he is not alone. This uncovering or revealing of oneself to oneself occurs as if in the presence of "an all-knowing-one [*en Alvidende*]." Here is Kierkegaard's description of the experience of Davidson's transcendent "domain of values" which the person can use to accomplish "self-criticism and reform." But in this discourse as a whole Kierkegaard provides a methodology and a mood and orientation (religious) that occur nowhere in our philosophy of action and which philosophers in general seem reluctant to explore.

Indeed, says Kierkegaard, humans generally avoid this "silence" and its revealing because they do not like to look at what they have kept hidden in darkness, namely, "hate, anger, revenge, depression, despair, fear of the future, trust in the world, … pride, … envy." So when forms of this darkness assert themselves in their lives, they yield to the "seductive temptation" of claiming the "ostensible excuse" of being in "deceptive ignorance about oneself," that they had "forgotten the eternal." But Kierkegaard flatly rejects this excuse: "There is an ignorance about oneself which is equally tragic [*sørgelig*] for the learned and the simple, for both are bound by the same responsibility: this ignorance is called self-deception [*Selvbedrag*]. … To be ignorant of the fact that there is one thing, only one thing, that only one thing is needful, is yet to be in self-deception."[52]

One's responsibility for this deception of oneself, what makes it to be *self*-deception, is revealed to oneself precisely in the event of confession. In other words, if one has the courage to concentrate one's attention honestly on the totality of one's accumulated self that is open to conscious recollection, and if one takes this reflection with ultimate seriousness as "the one thing needful," then one is "taught to recognize many errors, disappointments, deceptions, and self-deceptions," and one "has striven to track down double-mindedness into its hidden ways, and to ferret out its secret." So Kierkegaard abjures his reader, "take account of your own life," and "the earnestness [*Alvor*] of this holy place will strengthen the will in holy resolve, while the presence of the-all-knowing-one makes self-deception impossible! … It will be as if [the occasion] spoke precisely to you."

Then Kierkegaard designates exactly when the moment of failure and hence responsibility occurs, that is, when and how the "darkening of the comprehension" of the good begins. He says: "it will be by your own ac-

---

52 *Upbuilding Discourses in Various Spirits*, "Part One: An Occasional Discourse" (*Purity of Heart*), pp. 47, 51–2; (KW 15:20, 22–3); SV 11:26, 28–9; (8:130, 132–3).

tivity [*Selvvirksomhed*] that you will be the one to whom the intimate 'thou' is spoken." So "above all let us not *withdraw any attention* from the decision ... of which every human being is capable, and which ... is the highest thing of all" (emphasis added). Rather, "to be serious [*Alvor*] is just this: to willingly *pay attention* in order to willingly act accordingly. This is the highest thing of all, and ... every human being is capable of it, *if he wills*" (emphasis added).[53] In other words, "willing" consists in concentrating one's "attention" (*Opmærksomhed*) or "paying attention" (*høre efter*), and the object of attention (that is determinative of one's selfhood in an ultimate or "eternal" sense) takes a couple of dialectical forms.

First, one *either* pays attention to the substance of one's self as revealed in "confession," *or* one obscures and ignores or avoids this revelation by deliberately dulling one's self-consciousness by burying oneself in the busyness of daily life with its demands to be sensible and prudent. Then, secondly, if one "willingly" faces the reality of oneself in "confession," then one *either* concentrates one's total attention on the demands and guidance (the "self-criticism and reform") that comes from one's "higher" transcendent "domain of values" with its "ethical and ethical-religious comprehension" (and then "self-deception is impossible"), *or* one "withdraws a measure of attention from [this] decision" and thus delays any decision while one listens to the voices coming from various other "lower" domains (subsystems) such as "the aesthetic and metaphysical" or "common sense" and social conformity.

Kierkegaard insists that the latter course consists precisely in deliberate, responsible deception of oneself by oneself, because there is enough consciousness of what one's self is doing (at that critical point of concentrating *or* withdrawing one's attention from what one's own "higher nature" says is the right and the good) to make this "decision" *free* ("voluntary") and therefore responsible. This either/or comprises the essential irreducible point of that particular kind of psychic/spiritual indeterminacy which defines what is meant by ascribing freedom and responsibility to the human being as agent. But before we spell this notion out more fully, we must see how Kierkegaard enriches his concepts of responsible choice and self-deception in *Works of Love*.

As we have seen at some length, in *Works of Love* Kierkegaard gives particular content to what is meant by the "ethical-religious" by asserting that spiritual or unconditional love is the ultimate dynamic of reality for

---

53 Ibid., pp. 178–9; (KW 15:122–3); SV 11:113–14; (8:216).

human existence. So instead of speaking of one's relationship with "the absolute" or "the eternal" or "an eternal blessedness" or "an all-knowing-one" or "all-things-are-possible," here he explores the reality of "love in-and-for-itself" as the "middle determinant" or "third party" in every human relationship (including one's relationship with oneself). "The highest good and the greatest blessedness" is precisely "to love in truth," and next, "to be loved." But this requires that one "believes" in "love itself," that one gives heed to the voice at the depth of one's conscience which commands the great law of life, "you shall love!" And, as we have seen, "love is deeply grounded in the nature [*Væsen*] of the human being, belongs essentially to the human being." So the question constantly presses (on us as well as on Kierkegaard in *Works of Love*): how can any human being *not* love? And Kierkegaard's answer from the first to the last page of *Works of Love* is: self-deception. And he gives a characterization of the "lower sphere-of-comprehension [*Forestillingskreds*] which has no intimation of true love, of love in and for itself," a characterization that is coordinate with his definition of true love. In this way the lower sphere gains more concrete content than being just "aesthetic and metaphysical," and the dialectical contrast and conflict between the higher and lower understandings of love set the locale and context that explain the possibility and character of self-deception.[54]

To say that authentic love is "in and for itself" means that the lover is concerned only for the well-being of the other human being, that is, concerned that the other be affirmed in her/his own unique identity and encouraged to be and become all that that identity holds in potentiality. Such love "seeks not its own." In contrast, the "lower view of love ... regards loving as a demand (reciprocated love is the demand), and [regards] this being loved (reciprocated love) as a temporal and earthly good—and yet, alas, as the highest bliss." But "as previously shown," this exclusive preferential loving and being loved is just another form of "self-loving" (*Selvkjerlig*).

To live at the level and in the perspective of this lower view seems to be natural to human beings and to be the generally accepted standard of human behaviour, even if it is an "illusion" and "deception" from the perspective of higher or "eternal" love. But Kierkegaard assumes here what he formulates so clearly in *Sickness*, that the self is a given and inescapable "synthesis of the temporal and the eternal," and therefore love in-and-for-itself, which is "the bond of the eternal," is by nature present

---

54 *Works of Love*, pp. 225, 155, 223; SV 12: 231, 152, 228; (9:229, 150, 226).

and operative in every human being. Hence, whenever human beings live in this state of illusion and deception, they have abandoned or "given up" love, and thus have arrived in this state by *self-deception*. "[T]o be deceived signifies simply and solely to quit loving, to the point of abandoning love in and for itself, and in this way to lose its intrinsic blessedness. Because in the infinite sense only one deception is possible, self-deception."[55]

But again the question presses, why? Indeed, *how* can and does self-deception happen? The background and situation of this event, Kierkegaard says, consist of "the ultimate and most terrible encounter/ conflict [collision, clash: *Sammenstød*]: that in the relationship of love there is an infinite difference in the perception of what love is." We have explored at length how Kierkegaard distinguishes between these ideas of love, the one being finite and temporal, the other infinite and eternal. But at this point he calls the one "worldly or merely human," and it finds expression in passionate love of the one-and-only, marriage, friendship, and other forms of commonality and affinity. The other love is determined by one's relationship to "God," that is, to "love-itself" which asserts itself as a dynamic that transcends the purely human-to-human relationship, but enters into that relationship as a third-determinant and so creates a love relationship that is threefold or triangular.

However, the ultimate conflict between them does not occur because they are mutually exclusive and antagonistic toward each other, but rather because humans attempt to engage in the former and to exclude the latter. Whereas, Kierkegaard argues, the very purpose and goal of love-itself is to "penetrate all relationships ... thereby transforming passionate-love and friendship" so that they too are delivered from simply being forms of self-love and become relationships in which each party honours and encourages the unique identity of the other(s), rather than trying to absorb the other(s) into one's own identity or to dominate and mould the other(s) into one's own image.[56] It is precisely at this point, when this demand of love-itself appears on the horizon of one's self-consciousness, that the possibility and "temptation" of self-deception occurs. There must be at least a dim awareness of this demand and of its *validity*, otherwise the notion of a deliberate and responsible deception of oneself by oneself has no substance and force (as we have

---

55 Ibid., p. 223; SV 12:228; (9:226).
56 Ibid., pp. 117f.; SV 12:112f.; (9:109f.).

heard Kierkegaard acknowledge in *Sickness*). So the moment of indeterminacy and freedom consists in the focusing and holding of one's attention on, *or* the weakening and withdrawing of one's attention from, the appearance and the reality of this demand by love-itself within the scope of one's self-consciousness. In *Works of Love* Kierkegaard repeatedly notes that "human beings very often invent evasions in order to escape" what is "grounded in [their] very nature"; "they discover deception—in order to deceive themselves." They stop short and remain within the "lower" conception of love, and hence "quit ... and abandon love in-and-for-itself."[57]

But *why* would anyone abandon that which promises "eternal blessedness"? Throughout *Works of Love* Kierkegaard has one clear answer: because the human being instinctively knows and intuitively hears a second demand implicit within the demand to love every other human being as one loves oneself, because "simultaneously the demand for self-denial and sacrifice is made infinite" (i.e., absolute). "Truly to love another human being is, with every sacrifice (even to become hated), to help the other person to love God," that is, to help the other person to know that transcendent love grants and affirms the ultimate dignity and worth of that person's unique identity.[58] In other words, every human being fears and resents and seeks to avoid every situation that requires one to forget, deny, and sacrifice one's own self-interest out of concern for the well-being of the other. Such action does not appear to be "reasonable" or "prudent," indeed appears to be "madness" to the "normal" human individual in the pursuits of everyday life. Perhaps in exceptionally dire circumstances, one might feel moved to be self-sacrificial for one's beloved or one's children (because, Kierkegaard says, one really thinks of them as extensions of oneself), but it is ridiculous to expect and demand that such an "attitude" should penetrate and transform every human relationship.

So the goal and function of so-called self-deception (in regard to the validity of love's demand) are to secure the fundamental and very "reasonable" value of self-preservation as the primary principle of human existence. But, Kierkegaard argues, this view simply raises the question as to what is "rational" and what is "irrational," what is "sanity" and what is "madness." Here again we must recall Kierkegaard's repeated insistence that the methodologies of aesthetics and of the "objective

---

57 Ibid., pp. 155, 223; SV 12:152, 228; (9:150, 226).
58 Ibid., pp. 118f.; SV 12:113f.; (9:110f.).

reflection" of logic and abstract speculative thought cannot capture and comprehend the essential characteristics of individual human existence in time/space. These methods simply ignore or deny the ultimate importance of ethical decision and "religious" belief in the fulfilment of human potentiality. They cannot recognize that there is a valid indispensable role for the leap of decision on the basis of belief and in the face of uncertainty when the individual faces a choice among alternative actions and when the choice cannot be made *simply* on the basis of facts or logical coherence but also involves one's ultimate values, one's sense of right, one's vision of the ultimate dynamic of reality (love).

Kierkegaard's point is that the denial of the reality of the ethical-religious dimension or sphere of human nature is the basic essential self-deception which closes off the possibility of attaining authentic "eternal blessedness" for the human being. By means of this self-deception I may gain the "whole world," that is, a stable marriage and family, economic success, social distinction, political power, etc., but thereby, at the same time, I lose and destroy my only opportunity to become *my self* in my unique integrity, in freedom and responsibility. Therefore, in terms of the total scope of human nature and its fulfilment, this denial is what is "irrational" and "insane." So he speaks of "how foolish and irrational [*uforstandig*] is that busyness which thinks that knowing [in the aesthetic or conceptual sense] is superior to believing, because it is precisely believing all things which secures the lover ... against being deceived."[59] The depths and the subtlety of this human "madness" are explored by Kierkegaard only when he brings to bear on it the Christian understanding of the human state in "sin" and "despair." But at this point we must push the question one more time: *how* does this self-deception occur?

Every human being instinctively wants to *be* loved, that is, to be understood, accepted, and affirmed in one's absolutely distinctive identity, in and for oneself. Furthermore, everyone wants to be helped to remain and to become ever more fully what one's self is in potentiality. So everyone "knows," in a fundamental even though inchoate way, what "love-itself" (in-and-for-itself) is. But when the need and the demand to be loved comes not *from* me but *to* me from an other, then the implicit need and demand that I forget, deny, and sacrifice my own self-concern (out of pure and unalloyed concern for the other) disturbs me, my self feels

---

[59] Ibid., p. 225; SV 12:231; (9:229).

threatened. Am I to believe in a "love-itself" which has the right and the power to make such a demand on me?

At this point, Kierkegaard says, one either believes and risks all in the "leap" of decision, or one looks for a way out. And every way out is an illusion and a deception. The illusions are readily at hand: a voice from the body urging "the life of the senses is the only 'real' life," or a voice from the social milieu proclaiming "take care of number one," or "if you don't take care of yourself, no one else will." But *how* do you deceive yourself into believing the illusions? Kierkegaard's answer: you employ and appeal to a kind of shrewd, commonsense wisdom or prudence (*Kløgt* or *Klogskab*). We have heard him say (in *Sickness*) that one may "sink one's soul in darkness ... with a certain keen discernment and shrewd [*klog*] calculation, with psychological insight," and yet not be fully aware of the consequences.[60] In the opening pages of *Works of Love* he provides a fuller analysis of this shrewdness.[61]

This prudence takes the form of raising the question of what one can really believe, and accepts the usual wisdom that one should believe only what one can "see by means of one's physical eyes." Obviously, one cannot see "love-itself," so should one believe in it? Prudence says that I should avoid "being deceived by believing what is untrue," that is, what cannot be proved by sense or by reason. But this "superficiality of shrewdness, ... the flattering conceit [that I] cannot be deceived," leads me into the deeper and more dangerous deception of "not believing what is true," namely, that there is indeed such a thing as a "love" which I truly know affirms my self in-and-for-itself. In this deception I "shrewdly" deny such a claim, or at least ignore it, because I cannot "see" it (aesthetically and rationally). And I cannot see it (thus) because I do not want to hear its demand upon *me*, so I simply *refuse* to listen (ethically-religiously) to the voice of love-itself which is built into the very structure and dynamic of my human existence as such. But, "To cheat oneself out of love is the most terrible deception; it is an eternal loss for which there is no reparation, either in time or eternity."

Where, then, does this deception have its origin? Precisely at the point when I become disturbed by hearing the demand of love that I love others in the same way as I desire to be loved (in-and-for-myself), and I withdraw my awareness from this demand and "shrewdly" turn my attention to the wisdom of the world (my "lower" nature), namely:

60 *Sickness*, p. 181; (19:48); SV 15:104; (11:160).
61 The following is from *Works of Love*, pp. 23ff.; SV 12:11ff.; (9:9ff.).

believe only what you can "see." "To the worldly prudence [*Kløgt*] of temporality love may seem to be a burden, and therefore in the temporal world it may seem to the sensualist a great relief to cast this bond of eternity away." And, indeed, "In the temporal world one may succeed in getting along without love, ... without discovering the self-deception." But since love is what "really binds the temporal and the eternal," the person "who ingeniously deceived himself by cleverly falling into the snare of cleverness [*Klogskab*], alas, even if throughout his entire life he has in his own conceit considered himself happy, what has he not lost when in eternity it appears that he deceived himself! ... [H]e cannot escape discovering that he has lost everything."

So not only is the "lower perception" of love as "self-love" arrived at through self-deception, but this self-love is also in itself a state of deception or illusion because one ends in losing oneself (in the antagonisms and isolation of envy, fear, hate, deceit, insatiable appetites, etc.) rather than in securing ("saving," "finding," "becoming") oneself. And even the "true lover" can be "drawn down out of love into the lower world of mean-mindedness and wrangling" by allowing one's vanity to resent and to resist the attempt of others to deceive him/her. So the true lover must "believe all things," that is, believe in the absolute power of love-itself to protect and maintain itself, and so be content that one does not deceive oneself, even though in a purely temporal sense one may be deceived by others.[62]

Thus we come to the end of our lengthy analysis of self-deception as the key to the ambivalence of "willing" and therefore as revelatory of the indeterminacy that resides precisely at the critical point in the transition from knowing the good to doing it in actuality. A summary statement of the import of this analysis is in order because it will also serve as a final clarification of "freedom" as the "leap," and therefore will bring to a close the entire treatment of freedom as event.

We have isolated the decisive "leap" (that is the essence of "freedom") as comprised of that resolve or decision which carries one's knowledge of and firm intention to do the "good" across the "breach" into enactment of that intention in actuality. We have argued that the possibility of *failure* to make this leap is the key to the reality of that freedom (which is definitive of selfhood) if and when that failure is caused by intentional self-deception, because such self-deception indicates a basic dialectic and ambivalence in "willing" which in turn assumes an

62 Ibid., pp. 224f.; SV 12:230f.; (9:228f.).

irreducible indeterminacy at the point when transition from knowing the good to doing it is demanded. The blunt fact of indecision entails the reality of decision. Finally, we have noted again and again that the decisive factor at this point of indeterminacy is the turning and concentration of one's attention this way or that.

A rigid determinist who views the human psyche as operating in strict accord with the laws of physical causality, however, would simply push the question one step further backward and ask: what causes me to turn my attention this way or that? Is it not simply that the motivational strength of one object of attention is greater than that of the other? If I skip an important committee meeting in order to play tennis, is this not just a case of my desire to play tennis being stronger than my sense of duty to fulfil my social obligations? Kierkegaard, and several of the philosophers of action we have quoted, would argue that the sense of guilt and responsibility that self-conscious persons have after the fact of an ethical failure (to follow one's "higher" values or one's "unconditional judgment" of what is best in the light of "all things considered") is clear evidence of the "free choice" a person had in the act of self-deception which lead to the failure.

For example, in July of 1990 a senator and a congressman in the United States congress were found guilty of violating the ethical rules of their respective houses. On television before the nation both confessed their guilt and responsibility. The congressman said that his actions were "dumb, dumb, dumb. ... I should have known better and I now do." The senator admitted his failures and commented that this day marked a new beginning in his life: he would now pay secondary attention to the demands of his office and give primary attention to his task of being a man, a human person. A fellow senator spoke to the issue by saying that he knew the accused senator as a man of noble ideals, honour and trust, who worked hard for the welfare of others. Hence the unethical actions did not follow the logic that informed the character and life of the man he knew the senator to be. And yet he also knew that the senator was fully aware of what he was doing and had followed his actions through to the end, and therefore he deserved to be censured. It is precisely the ambivalence and contradiction between (1) one's character and ideals and (2) one's conscious and intentional actions that posit the reality of indeterminacy at the point where one turns one's attention this way or that.

Is then this turning of attention purely arbitrary and capricious? Is this event of willing absolutely "free" in the sense of being uncaused? By using several different themes developed by Kierkegaard at different points in his authorship, we have demonstrated that he clearly and consistently gives a negative answer to these questions, that for him a bare and blank "free will" (*liberum arbitrium*) is a "chimera" and "illusion." And we have interpreted these Kierkegaardian materials by using our contemporary philosophy of action, especially as formulated by Donald Davidson, to show how an action can be said to be "caused" and yet also free and responsible.

Probably the best key to Kierkegaard's understanding of the "causation" that occurs in a free responsible action lies in his concept of "the unconditional" (see "The Leap as a Passionate Transition" and note 66 in chapter 6). He flatly states, "that which determines [*bestemmer*] me is simply and solely the unconditioned, I cannot do otherwise." And the unconditioned is "being-in-and-for-itself" or "sheer transparent subjectivity," which is achieved when "one … has totally interpenetrated oneself" so that "one becomes conscious of oneself so thoroughly so that no accidental element escapes him/her." Even though such transparency is never perfectly attained, yet "one becomes so luminous that one cannot hide from oneself, … as if one were transparent." And at the height/depth of this luminous self-transparency there appears the eternal, love in-and-for-itself which makes all-things-possible, encouraging and enabling the self to be faithful to itself in self-forgetting love. Then one is able to ignore and not to be determined (caused) by the voices of the "world-around" with their demand for consideration of "reasons" and "grounds" and "probability" and future goals or "purposes." Rather, one's actions ("works") are "caused" by one's "having the courage to be oneself before God [the eternal, love-itself]," and this is freedom.

Obviously, the opposite of this "being-in-and-for-itself" is what Kierkegaard calls "doublemindedness," in which one has a certain grasp and acceptance of the absolute and unconditional but at the same time commits oneself to it only "up to a point" or "to a certain degree," because of other more practical considerations which press into one's consciousness from the world around and which demand so much of one's time and energy. Hence one cannot "will one thing" with "purity [singleness] of heart," because one does not concentrate one's mind (attention) on one's "hidden" and "inner" world and being and thus gain the "time and tranquillity for gaining transparency, which is needed for understanding oneself in willing one thing." Rather, one buries oneself in the "busyness" of this world with its "mass of connections, stimuli and hindrances" and its interest in "the many" with its "externality and comparison and indulgence and excuse and evasion."

How does this analysis of "the unconditional" answer the question: what causes the turning of my attention *either* to my inward world of absolute being-in-and-for-itself *or* to the outward world of relative, reasonable, finite probabilities? How is the turning free and yet not capricious and arbitrary? Before trying to answer that question in general terms, let me (the author) step out from behind the editorial "we," and give two illustrations from my own life, one of an unconditional action, one of an act of self-deception. After all, this book is entitled *My Self*, and claims that Kierkegaard's method is phenomenological, that is, an interpretation of the phenomena of the events of one's own inward self-consciousness.

After completing a doctorate in theology, I had spent the last twenty years of my adult life in teaching. I was forty-eight years old, happily married, with two sons, engaged in a number of social and political causes, often invited to be a lecturer and conference speaker. But the central focus of my mind and heart was in teaching and writing. Having written numerous articles and essays of both a popular and scholarly nature, and having published five books in six years, I was happily convinced that my calling in life was in scholarly research and its interpretation at both a popular and a technical level. To that end I had recently begun to learn Danish in order to support my growing fascination with the writings of Søren Kierkegaard.

Suddenly this contented world was shattered. I was asked by the Board of Trustees of the seminary, where I had been teaching for the last thirteen years, to become its acting president. It was a crisis situation and I felt obliged to acquiesce. But when the former president resigned, I publicly announced that I would not be a candidate for the position because my clear calling for which I had spent my life preparing was in the field of teaching and writing. Nobody argued with me. But after almost a year went by and several persons had refused the position, I began to feel gentle pressures to change my mind. I was in a profound dilemma. Here was no conflict between a clearly higher calling and some crude, vulgar impulses of my lower nature, although some lower motives made themselves felt: my distaste for the minutiae of administration, money raising, public relations, etc., and on the other hand the attraction of the position's prestige, honour, power, and salary. But these I succeeded in ignoring, turning my "attention" away from them. My conflict was between two legitimate calls upon my talents and abilities. I asked a friend what I should do. His answer, "Do what you want to do." I wanted, with all my heart, to continue in the pleasant and yet important work of teaching and writing. Yet, I also wanted, with all my heart, to do my "duty" in solving the crisis which the seminary confronted, because while I believed in the importance of my teaching and writing, I also profoundly believed in the important role the seminary was playing in the life of the church and in its mission in the world. When the search committee of the board heard of my indecision, it called me to a meeting and urged me to accept the position of president. I did. What "determined" my decision? In what sense was it "free"?

Kierkegaard faced a similar question when he considered abandoning his writing to become a pastor, but stayed with his writing. And as we have heard, his answer was, "Well now, who knows oneself in this way?" When faced with a decision about matters in the realm of the "infinite," the decision cannot be made with certainty, neither the certainty of rational conclusion from objective evidence, nor the certainty of visible demonstration of the good, nor the certainty of socially approved standards. Rather, such a decision requires a "leap" into an uncertain future based on what one fundamentally believes, against reason and common sense and social demand. So Kierkegaard went on to say, "It seems to me that something higher is constantly moving within me, [which prompts] me to believe that I cannot justify anything else but continuing to serve it as long as possible." He knew his decision was a "venture [risk]," especially since the writing that remained for him was his public polemic against "official Christianity." Was his decision free? As he was about to start that polemic, he wrote, "Freedom, the voluntary, self-determination, etc. are implied by the words—enter by the narrow gate—for here it is left to the individual alone [*En selv*] whether one will or will not."[63]

What then determined or caused my decision? Was it free? The conflict for me was between two profoundly inward and "infinite" demands of my ultimate beliefs, and both were "unconditional" in their respective domains. On the one hand, my "inner necessity" demanded that I honour and remain faithful to my own integrity as a person, to do what the gestalt of my "self's possibility" demanded, namely, to use my gifts and capacities to the utmost in service of my calling to teach and to write. On the other hand, hovering "above" everything else in my self-consciousness was also my ultimate and unconditional belief (my "inner ne-

[63] *Journals*, 6805, X⁴ A 559; 1275, XI¹ A 24.

cessity") that my honouring of my own self's integrity should not be self-serving but should be used, expended, and if need be "sacrificed" in the service of others—at least, that was what I thought and hoped I believed, was what I at least taught was the ultimate truth for every human person.

In the particular situation which I faced, where the seminary faced and participated in the dynamics of the social confusions and revolutions of the late 1960s, I was confronted with the demand that "the service of others" which most needed to be met was not in my teaching and writing but in helping to see this institution (these people) through the storms of faith and ideology and social relationships that threatened its structural stability, communal cohesion, spiritual integrity, and the fulfilment of its own calling. Against all of my own inclinations and common sense and good rational arguments, I fastened my attention on this "higher" sense of duty and accepted the job. More than fifteen years later, at retirement, my retrospective judgment was that I had done the "right thing." But it was with a great feeling of relief and joy that I then turned to "will one thing" with all my heart and all my strength, namely, to write this interpretation of Kierkegaard.

Was my decision free? The sense of duty, "because" of which I did it, was *mine*. The decision was *mine*. That is to say, my double sense of duty operated purely within the domain of my own recognition of what defined *me, my self*, what was "essential" to my being me, stripped of all that was incidental and accidental and extraneous to my being the self I am. And the decision that emerged from the moment of indecision was not dictated by the intrusion of any force or compulsion from outside that essential self, not even a voice telling me clearly what was "God's will." In the silence "before God," I knew that "God's will" was that *I* choose to do what the ultimate dynamic of love demanded. So later, when there came the trials, agonies, nastiness, mistakes, disappointments that are inevitable in such a job, I could not blame my decision on the influence of fellow faculty members or of friends on the board, or on "fate," or even on "God," because it was *I* (my "self") who turned with fear and trembling in the silence to listen to the voice of love-itself.

Of course, others looking at this decision from the outside, or reading this account of that decision, could easily contend that my "sense of duty" to others was inculcated into my core being over the years in such a way that it automatically took charge of the direction of my life. Still others would sneer at the whole account and see the decision as a self-serving one, my self seeking to satisfy my (undoubted) fantasies of prestige and power and financial reward. How, then, does this account of my decision, as being "determined by the unconditional," clarify what caused the turning of my attention toward the demand that I accept the administrative job in order to "serve others," rather than toward the many voices which counselled me that my teaching and writing were the "higher" calling? This account isolates that moment or instant in which it became clear to me that the urgency and uniqueness of the need for me to accept that job outweighed the importance of the contributions I could make as teacher and writer in the total scheme of things (seminary/church/world) to which I had committed my life. Whether this "unconditional judgment" was correct would only be revealed in the future (as Kierkegaard pointed out to his journal as he struggled with the decision to stay with his writing). What then held my attention to *this* judgment as my "unconditional," so that I did not listen to (although I heard) the voices muttering in various of my "subsystems" and asking: will you really be "happy" in this job, and will you really find that "self-fulfilment" which after all is the be-all and end-all of every human life? The only possible answer to this question (in the light of the psychic evidence which, in recollection, is open only to me) is this: what held my attention to and what kept my attention from wandering from this particular judgment as my "unconditional" was *me*, my self, the total "I" which I was at that particular juncture of time/space in the ongoing process of my becoming. And the "weighing" of the alternatives by my self could not possibly be described as a careful rational balancing of evidence which yielded a convincing probability as to the best possible outcome in all my "possible worlds." Rather, that weighing could only be described as a passionate, personal, deeply concerned "leap," made in profound uncertainty, but enabled and empowered by the certainty of my "faith" as to what is ultimately "infinite" and "eternal" for me as an existing human individual. So this decision was "free" and "indeterminate" in the sense that it occurred solely within, and hence was determined by, my "self" and its own vision of the "unconditional."

These uncertainties about motivation are precisely what makes the alternative of self-deception so important for the clarification of the reality of a free indeterminate choice and decision. For Kierkegaard, the indeterminacy of freedom is given to us in order that we might be free *for* (something), not in order that we might be free *from* (something): free *for* choosing the absolute and the good, free *for* loving unconditionally, not free *from* everything and everybody, not freedom as an end in itself and for itself. And yet this negative possibility of the misuse of freedom is precisely the clearest sign of the reality of the positive possibility of freedom in the act of self-denying love.

As Kierkegaard repeatedly asserts in *Postscript*, "The positive is constantly [present] in the negative, and the negative is [its] signification [*Kjendet*]." Indeed, he sees this condition as integral to the existence of "the human." "The negativity that is in existence, or rather the negativity of the existing subject ... is grounded in the subject's synthesis, in its being an existing infinite spirit. Infinitude and the eternal are the only certainty, but since it is in the subject, it is in existence, and the primary expression for this [condition] is its duplicity [*Svig*] and that tremendous contradiction: that the eternal becomes, that it comes into existence [*bliver til*]."[64] In other words, the possibilty of failure is inherent in (necessary for) the possibility of human self-fulfilment in freedom.[65] But, as we have heard Kierkegaard say, the misuse of freedom (as act) does not lead to and secure freedom (as state), but just the opposite: the imprisonment of the self in the self-destructive forces of hate, envy, greed, lust, etc. So let us turn to my other example which shows the other side of the coin of freedom: failure.

While I was president of the seminary, my wife and I had become good friends of an elderly (and very rich) couple who supported the seminary generously and had it in their wills. We visited them several times a year. Even after I retired they continued to want us to visit them. Our reasons for doing so were mixed. On the one hand, we knew that they loved us, trusted us, and in a sense needed our friendship. On the other hand, I was sensitive to the fact that we were their continuing tie to the seminary, and that without our visits they might lose interest in the seminary and drop it from their wills. So both the demands of love and the demands of duty to the seminary "required" our continuing visits.

Five years after my retirement we returned from a five-month stay in England, and I knew with absolute clarity that we should visit them as soon as possible. She had indicated in a letter to us that they both were in ill health and desired to see us very much. But we let over four

---

64 *Postscript*, pp. 467, 75f.; (KW 12.1:524, 82); SV 10:198, 9:70; (7:457, 63).

65 This view of things will be spelled out under the topic of "My Self: A Failure," and hence has tremendous implications for Kierkegaard's interpretation of the Christian understanding of "sin." In this connection, it is interesting to note that biologists have pointed out that if the first amoeba (living organism) that appeared on this planet had been "perfect" and therefore had not had the possibility of making a "mistake" in its reproduction (a mutation), then there would still be nothing but amoebas on earth.

months slip by without going. Then the phone call came: she had died very suddenly. My "visit" was to speak at her memorial service. Her husband was ill and in the hospital. When I went to see him, almost his first words were, "What took you so long?" What was the answer? I knew with absolute clarity that I had utterly failed to do what I *knew* to be "the one-thing-needful," and that it was *my* failure, my responsibility. In the words of Kierkegaard, it was a case of my "darkening [my] understanding" of what was the one thing needful. In the language of philosophy of action, it was a case of "weakness of will" aggravated by "self-deception." How did it work?

We arrived home shortly before Christmas, and we had to get ready for family who were visiting us during the holidays. Certainly, our friends would not expect us at that time. But then the first "weakness of will" manifested itself in my decision not to call them to wish them merry Christmas because I knew I would have to commit us to a date for the visit, and I was reluctant. Why? Because of a mixture of things: flying would be difficult because of weather conditions in January, living with them was physically comfortable but personally awkward; entertaining them was a strain because of lack of common interests, etc. Yet, when confronted by clear recognition of the demands of love and duty, this reluctance was usually overcome. In this case it was not, because the "darkening" and self-deception gradually took place.

The first failure was in putting off the decision until later, with every good intention to resolve it later, in January, then in February, etc. As Kierkegaard says, there is only one "time" in which to make decisions about "infinite" matters, namely, not the worldly sequential time of human beings with its "tomorrow," but the time of "the eternal" which is: "straightway!" "now!" But how could I not know that? By turning my attention ever so slightly to listen for just an instant to the voices of my "aesthetic" and "rational" self, my "knowing" was obscured. We were tired from the long flight home from London and from entertaining during the holidays. We too were getting older and needed to recuperate. Moreover, I had an article to write with a March deadline, and my work was important. We had reservations for a week in Yosemite made a year before, and we could not disappoint our friends who were accompanying us. And in February and then in March it was even easier to find "reasons." So in the end these urgings of my "lower nature" persuaded my clear knowledge-of-the-good that the demands of love and duty were not absolute and unconditional. Did our friends really need us, since they had lots of family and friends where they lived? Was it not the job of the new seminary president to keep in touch? Surely, they would not change their will just because of the "delay" of our visit. The process of my own self-deception was complete.

But when the telephone call came, in that instant the lie and its guilt were revealed, undeniably. My failure affirmed that originally I was truly free to go visit them, now, straightway. I deliberately deceived myself, and therefore I *chose* not to go. Ah, the fear and trembling as one faces the "breach," the "yawning chasm" that lies between the good intention and its enactment in actuality, because one may *fail* to make the "leap." "The self is freedom." I am what I do in the instant of decision in the face of infinite possibility. If there was doubt and unclarity about the motivation of my positive decision to intend and to do the "good" dictated by my vision of the "unconditional," there can be no doubt about the vivid and undeniable conviction of my personal responsibility for my failure to heed that unconditional.

Now let us restate the implications of these examples in general terms and interpret them in the conceptuality and terminology of philosophy of action.

Kierkegaard would argue that the turning of my attention to the demands and desires of the "lower" dimensions (subsystems) of my self is "voluntary" in that the turning is what I will (want/choose) to do even in the face of "knowing better" (the demands of total evidence), that is, even though the "higher" dimensions (rational/ethical evaluation of alternatives) prompt or urge me otherwise. Therefore I recognize as "intentional" and assume responsibility for such actions. And when called to task for my "irresponsibility" (either overtly by circumstances or inwardly by conscience), I see and acknowledge that I cannot blame it on external circumstances or on my lower desires operating within my total self. Rather, I admit that I intentionally deceived myself into thinking that I had good reasons for doing what I did.

Conversely, when I follow the demands of the "higher" dimensions of my self and accept the self-denial and sufferings involved, this turning of my attention away from all other voices external to this judgment of what is the best thing to do (all-things-considered and unconditionally), in order to concentrate purely and wholly on the transcendent voice of love-itself, is also "voluntary." The "necessity" of doing so ("I cannot do otherwise") is *unconditional* as to *what* I do, but is *conditional* as to *how* (or *whether*) I do it: *if* I will (want/choose) to be faithful to the integrity of my selfhood as affirmed by love-itself, *then* I cannot do otherwise than to love others as I am loved, and to do so concretely, here and now in the specific conditions I confront with the specific personal resources I bring to them. This conditional "necessity" (if ... , then ...) lies at the heart of my inner self-consciousness and awaits my free resolve to stamp it upon my action.

In this mode or state of my being, the turning of my attention is not arbitrary and capricious, does not happen de novo or in a vacuum. Nor is it caused irrationally by subconscious physical/psychic conditions or subsystems beyond my control. Rather, it is done by *me*, consciously and intentionally, *because* of who *I am* at that particular moment in the continuous process of my becoming. Hence my later coming to a sense of failure in the light of my higher and better self (as I listen to the voice of transcendent love-itself), and to a sense of my responsibility for my "deception," is also who *I am*. And I come to my most vivid sense of freedom and of becoming my self when I willingly and gladly submit unconditionally to the demands of that love, concretely, here and now. Freedom and the voluntary comprise a possibility just in that moment of dialectical ambiguity and indeterminacy as to which way my total self will move at any single juncture where the relative conditions of my finitude come under the the demands of infinite, absolute, unconditional love (truth, goodness) at the centre of my conscious, passionate, interested subjectivity.

What, then, of the contention that all these complexities of human decision-making can be adequately explained by applying to psychological events the same principles of causal determination that are used in the purely physical, chemical, and biological realms, and the contention that even these principles can finally be reduced to mathematical and formally logical formulas, and that therefore any sense of freedom and responsibility is an illusion?

The first important point to remember (from all the foregoing) is that, while Kierkegaard insists on an irreducible polarity in the makeup of the individual human being (finite/infinite), he does not subscribe to a dualism that differentiates between body and mind (soul) as two separable entities which function independently of each other. As has been repeatedly demonstrated, he insists (with Hegel) that the human "spirit" or "self" is an indivisible synthesis and unity of finitude and infinitude, of temporal and eternal. So while the infinite/eternal self always functions as finite/temporal, the finite/temporal sphere of being may be devoid of an operative infinite/eternal. The infinite/eternal dimensions require consciousness and then self-consciousness and eventually the emergence of ethical/religious sensitivity. In our contemporary language, all chemical events are physical, but not all physical events are chemical; all biological events are physical and chemical, but not all physical and chemical events are biological; all mental events are physical, chemical, and biological events, but not all physical, chemical, and biological events are mental events. Each level or scheme of things has, in Davidson's terminology, its "disparate commitments" and its own "proper source of evidence."

On the other hand, it is even more important to remember that, while Kierkegaard consistently insists that the religious act is always ethical, and that the ethical act is always concrete and specific, fulfilled in "the infinitely little things of the deed [of love, of course] which can be accomplished this very day, this very hour, this very minute,"[66] yet it is always his central and supreme interest to show that this act is free, voluntary. That is to say, the act issues from and is determined by one's "subjectivity," which, while being ethical and religious, is definitively inward, personal, passionate, infinite, earnest, interested decision for and commitment to the unconditional.

Therefore, this act cannot be accounted for *simply* by reference to one's physical/biological makeup, instincts, capacities, learned abilities, social conditioning, and personal history—no matter how unique; nor can it be accounted for *merely* in the terms of universal scientific, philosophical, or psychic-sociological principles, even though abstracted from a million examples of similar behaviour by a million human beings. The qualitative dimensions of an ethical/religious decision and action by a unique subject/self/spirit in the unique conditions of its time/space can never be caught or explained *merely* within the abstract quantitative categories of the "lower" levels or spheres or schemata of complex but unified human nature. This sphere of decision/action has its own unique and "disparate commitments" which have no parallel in the spheres of abstract scientific and metaphysical thought, and therefore it is its own "proper source of evidence" which can be gleaned only by its own methodology of analysis, depiction, and communication. And Kierkegaard presents his entire authorship, in its extreme diversity of content and form, as an example of this methodology (although he admits to a few cases of "more direct" expression and communication).

What Kierkegaard is thus expressing in the terminology and categories peculiar to his own intellectual and literary milieu, we have often attempted (above) to interpret in the conceptuality of our own current

---

66 *Sickness*, p. 165; (KW 19:32); SV 15:89; (11:145).

philosophy of action. One final effort will be made here in order to show that Kierkegaard's depiction of the unique vicinage and character of freedom is not so strange and isolated after all, that his own formulation of "existentialism" is still au courant in some philosophical venues, but also in order to clarify our insistence that Kierkegaard's characterization of freedom comprises a position properly called "indeterminism." For this purpose we will draw upon the position of Donald Davidson (as summarized at the beginning of chapter 6).

Davidson admits that the most that a psychological philosophy can achieve is to provide an "ontological reduction" rather than a "definitional reduction" of the complicated process by which an intentional action is produced by a human individual. But such an analysis is adequate to explain "the possibility of autonomous action in a world of causality" by referring the action to "a desire, value, purpose, goal, or aim the person had, and a belief connecting the desire with the action to be explained." And this reference is the sphere or realm that Kierkegaard also appeals to as the source of "voluntary" (autonomous) actions. Davidson recognizes that many want and seek a more exact "definition" of just how intentional actions occur "by substitut[ing] for desires and beliefs more directly observable events," or by constructing "a theory that deals directly with the relations between actions, and treats wants and thoughts as theoretical constructs." But, he says, "a theory of action inspired by this idea has no chance of explaining complex behaviour unless it succeeds in inferring or constructing the patterns of thoughts and emotions of the agent" (which are not theoretical but particular and unique for each agent) and then "assume[s] that beliefs and values do not change over time," whereas it is obvious that "merely making choices (with no reward or feedback) alters future choices" (EAE 233ff.).

In other words, the enterprise of explaining intentional actions in terms of purely "physical phenomena" that "can be brought under deterministic laws" is nothing more than a theoretical possibility that can never be demonstrated because of the very nature of psychological phenomena. "Psychological concepts have an autonomy relative to the physical," because "psychological events and states often have causes that have no natural psychological descriptions," namely, "an irreducible normative element in all attributions of attitudes." Therefore, we cannot "expect ever to be able to explain and predict human behaviour with the kind of precision that is possible in principle for physical phenomena" (EAE 240f., 230f.). It also follows that "mental concepts connected with propositional attitudes cannot be incorporated into a system of exceptionless laws," because "strict laws do not deploy disposition terms nor do they use causal concepts" such as desires, values, and beliefs (EOD 245f.). Here in these words is a more technical exposition of precisely what Kierkegaard observed in the phenomena of his own self-analysis, namely, that the temporal processive character of becoming "self" cannot be caught in abstract concepts, and that inward passionate decisions (unconditional judgments) that express normative ethical/religious sensitivities cannot be reduced to the exceptionless laws of nature and history.

As we have seen, Davidson concludes that "thought, desire and voluntary action can[not] be brought under deterministic laws, as physical phenomena can." So we are left with "the indeterminacy that results from the absence of a clear line between the analytic and the synthetic" (EOD 245). Or again, "[s]ince psychological phenomena do not constitute a closed system, ... they are not, even in theory, amenable to precise prediction or subsumption under deterministic laws. The limit thus set on the social sciences is not set by nature, but by us when we decide to view [human beings] as rational agents with goals and purposes, and as subject to moral evaluation" (EAE 239). Such a conclusion is intensified to an absolute degree by Kierkegaard when he insists that this limit is indeed set by that "nature" which has produced human nature with its inherent capacity and ultimate task of becoming self (spirit), and when he insists that human beings are not simply rational and moral agents but are also inherently open to and in need of a "religious" relationship with "the eternal" as "love-itself."

As we have argued several times, Kierkegaard makes a unique contribution to this analysis of human decision-making in several ways. We have noted that his depiction (in the terms of religiousness A) of the nature of the openness of human consciousness to what Davidson calls "criticism and reform" from a "transcendent ... domain of values" is much more complicated and more psychologically profound than anything found in contemporary philosophy of action. It would be an interesting and worthwhile project to translate the basic elements of Kierkegaard's religiousness A into the language and conceptuality of philosophy of action in order to see how far this philosophy could be pressed into recognizing and exploring what Kierkegaard calls "religiousness" as an element in human consciousness which can be isolated as clearly as the element of "intention" (including such elements as: the "breach" between the ethical and the religious, the nature of the transcendent as "infinite" and "eternal," the need for and character of "silence" in the presence of the eternal, the nature of "faith" in the relationship with the eternal, the power of the eternal as the "all-knowing one" to enable "confession" and "repentance," and the power of the eternal to impart "encouragement" so that one has "courage" to be and become oneself).

But more relevant to our concluding topic (of the indeterminacy at the heart of human subjectivity in action) is the uniqueness of Kierkegaard's characterization of "willing" as central to voluntary action and self-deception. Davidson has a less centralized and unified picture of the self's struggle to come to a valid "all-out unconditional judgment" that forms an intentional action. On the one side he sees operating in the self's subsystems semi-independent intentional motivations which are subrational ("irrational") if compared with the rational all-things-considered judgment of the "coherent pattern" of values and beliefs that define the individual as responsible person. But this comparison may not take place, and the person will commit an irrational act. On the other side he pictures the rational self as occasionally being open to "criticism and reform" from a superrational ("irrational") domain of values that is transcendent to the rational self.

Kierkegaard, on the other hand, sees the fully intentional and therefore truly free and voluntary act as emerging from a strenuous exertion and struggle at the unifying heart of inward, passionate, infinite, interested subjectivity, and this struggle involves the interplay of all three levels or spheres of the self: the "lower" self concerned with the aesthetic and metaphysical; the self conscious of itself as an "infinite" gestalt of the "self's possibilities"; the higher ethical-religious self. He contends that the leap of freedom in the decision to act involves simultaneously all three elements that are separated by Davidson: (1) resistance of the irrational demands of "lower" subsystems of the self, (2) the "rational" deduction of what one's gestalt (coherent pattern) of definitive ("infinite") values demands, and (3) the opening of the self to critique and reform from a transcendent domain of values (the eternal). And for Kierkegaard it is precisely in the complexity of the interplay of these three elements (in the conscious struggle of self to come to a decision and to the courage to act) that there is located the unanalysability and unpredictability and hence the indeterminacy and freedom of the human act. It is *I*, my self, who came to this decision, here and now, in this particular event in this particular situation. This interplay is the source and the validity of the undeniable, inescapable sense that "I am responsible," both in the act of weakness of will and self-deception and in the act of obedience to the unconditional.

In the face of our comprehensive analysis of Kierkegaard's understanding of "my self," it is totally untenable to characterize Kierkegaard as a determinist whose god is "fate" and "necessity." Yet a number of interpreters have clearly labelled Kierkegaard as a determinist, one of whom is Kresten Nordentoft, whose study of *Kierkegaard's Psychology* we have referred to a number of times. Nordentoft is certainly correct in saying that Kierkegaard does not propose "free will in the indeterministic sense" of *liberum arbitrium* by which one can define good and evil for oneself, and which "gives man the possibility of autonomous, assumption-free self-determination."[67] He also acknowledges that while true "freedom" consists in yielding to and living in human dependence on God, yet the human being is also free to disobey God and to declare one's independence of God (pp. 111ff.). But he insists that Kierkegaard does not picture this human failure as the act of the individual but as a corporate state of the human race which each individual has to "discover" as true for him/herself.

Obviously, he has trouble with some materials in *The Concept of Anxiety* which do not seem to support this thesis. So he accuses the book of being "inconsistent" and "unclear" when its "formulations may be read as the expression of a radical indeterminism, which is supposed to make it possible to speak psychologically about the individual as the cause of, and therefore guilty in, his own actions." This view, he argues, "is not Kierkegaard's intention," and "his real meaning cannot be that a leap takes place within the psychological development." Rather, "What he speaks of is a spring from a psychological to a non-psychological way of viewing this development."[68] Clearly, these interpretations are mistaken from the point of view of our exposition of the same materials. If the individual is not "the cause of his own actions," what is? And if the leap of decision (as described in both *Anxiety* and *Postscript*) does not occur in one's "psychological development," where does it take place? And we have shown that when Haufniensis says that sin "presupposes itself" (as does freedom), and that "sin cannot be explained by anything antecedent to it, anymore than can freedom," what he means is that both freedom and its failure in sin are "caused" by decisions ("actions") of the

---

67 K. Nordentoft, *Kierkegaard's Psychology*, pp. 89, 113.
68 Ibid., p. 169.

individual self in its most interior and definitive being and not by anything antecedent or exterior to that self.

Nordentoft seeks to buttress his interpretation by arguing that in *The Sickness unto Death* "Sin ... is not an action, but a state." Therefore, "the fall into sin does not consist of the individual's becoming guilty by means of one or another individual action, ... but in becoming aware of himself as guilty." He insists that in *The Concept of Anxiety* Haufniensis tried to have it both ways: "in part he wants to explain the action as a product of the condition; in part he will not let go of the idea of freedom all the same, and therefore ... the development is in actuality discontinuous, and the chain of causality is broken." But this "inconsistent" and "self-contradictory" position is corrected, Nordentoft argues, in both *Postscript* and *Sickness*.

Climacus, he claims, shows that guilt arises from "an incorrect starting position" in that humans do not know what they are supposed to be and become. So, "Guilt is not due to the fact that the individual wills what is wrong, but ... *is discovered*. ... For the guilt which is discovered ... is naturally also present where it has not been discovered. But this fundamental (ontological) guilt is thus not due in the literal (psychological) sense to the individual himself." And, he argues, Anti-Climacus insists that "despair is a state, that despair is sin," and therefore he has abandoned Haufniensis' "legalistic concept of sin" and his "moralistic, particularistic conception of guilt as an individual action." How, then, according to Nordentoft, does Kierkegaard explain how the human race got into this "fallen" and "guilty" state? He says, "If [Kierkegaard] is able to speak of guilt as an ethical reality, he is not building upon the indeterminist notion of a free choice. ... The assertion of ethics is that man is guilty even in the actions of which he himself cannot be proven to be the cause (and it is precisely this which makes it possible for Kierkegaard to employ determinism as a working psychological hypothesis). Only if one becomes 'guilty by means of fate,' is there any meaning in speaking of guilt. This is why Judge William speaks of repenting oneself back into the race. ... If guilt is to be substantiated by referring to actions of which the individual himself can be proven to be the source, it can never be substantiated."[69]

---

[69] For the last two paragraphs, see ibid., pp. 174, 169, 170f., 174, 170. The phrase "guilty by means of [*ved*] fate" is from *The Concept of Anxiety*, p. 87; (KW 8:97); SV 6:185; (4:367). The reference to Judge William is from *Either/Or*, 2:220f.; (KW 4:216f.); SV 3:201; (2:194).

It is quite unsupportable (astounding!) that Nordentoft ascribes to Kierkegaard the idea that "one became guilty by fate." He clearly ignores (or misunderstands) the two paragraphs that immediately follow this statement (in *The Concept of Anxiety*). Kierkegaard labels the ordinary notion of "fate" as a misunderstanding because it identifies fate with necessity, whereas "fate is precisely the unity of necessity and the accidental." As soon as the human individual is known as "spirit" (self), then "fate" is replaced by "providence," because (as we have seen above) providence makes use of the accidental (*Tilfældige*) to appeal to and to guide the human being in his/her freedom. Hence, "the contradiction that one became guilty by fate" perishes when a deeper sense of sin and guilt emerges, because "The concepts of sin and guilt posit precisely the single-individual [*Enkelte*] as the single-individual. There is no question of any relation to the whole world or to all the past."

In other words, human failure and the guilt involved have as their presupposition nothing but the action of the single-individual as such, not that individual's (undeniable) involvement in its "whole world" and all its "past." And Kierkegaard rightly anticipates Nordentoft's position: "A misunderstanding of this contradiction [that one became guilty by fate] will result in a misunderstanding of the concept of hereditary sin; rightly understood, it gives the true concept, in the sense that every individual is both oneself and the race, and the subsequent individual is not essentially different from the first." Here Haufniensis is recalling his earlier position that "what holds true of the innocence of the subsequent individual also holds true of Adam. All of this obtains [*er*] only for freedom, and obtains only as the single-individual himself posits sin by the qualitative leap." So now in the later passage, he can make his point and insist that it is *freedom* that fails and "collapses" in the face of "fate" (necessity plus the accidental), because it is "[freedom's] actuality" that now "rises up, but with the explanation that it became guilty. ... So sin comes neither as a necessity nor as an accident [i.e., not as *fate*], and therefore what corresponds to the concept of sin is: providence."[70]

Nordentoft's contention that in *The Concept of Anxiety* Kierkegaard's explication of sin, guilt, and freedom is "unclear," "inconsistent," and "self-contradictory" simply cannot be demonstrated, nor can his proposal that Anti-Climacus "corrects" Haufniensis in *Sickness*. In his reading of *Anxiety* Nordentoft sets up a false either/or between sin as individual acts and as a state of being. What Kierkegaard describes is sin

---

70 *The Concept of Anxiety*, pp. 88, 55; (KW 8:61, 98); SV 6:153, 185; (4:332, 367f.).

as a *qualitative* act in which one's relation with God is broken, and he then shows how this qualitative act manifests itself *quantitatively* in both individual and corporate human existence. Humans vary in the weight of quantitative sinfulness under which they live, but this objective condition does not affect the fact that each individual becomes involved subjectively in sin (as a state) by the same qualitative, free, responsible *act* of sin. And this position is never deserted or corrected by Kierkegaard in the entire authorship or in the journals. So Nordentoft is mistaken in his insistence that in *Sickness* despair and sin are seen simply as a state or universal condition which has befallen human beings without their knowledge or responsible involvement. As we have shown at length, in his concept of self-deception and in his analysis of how "willing" is involved in the "darkening of understanding" of the good, Kierkegaard contends that humans are responsible and guilty because their failure is voluntary. Hence, in *Sickness* one of Kierkegaard's main theses is that sin is not a negation, not simply a "state" of ignorance or a lack of something, but rather is a "position" that the individual freely takes up against the truth that "all-things-are-possible," out of weakness or defiance. And he derides "the determinist, the fatalist" whose "God is necessity," and who therefore "has lost God and thus his self."[71]

Nordentoft has too rigid a conception or definition of "determinism" and "indeterminism." He is certainly correct that Kierkegaard is not an "indeterminist" in the sense of attributing to the human being the capacity of defining arbitrarily for oneself what is "good" and what is "evil" and the capacity to choose either one freely and with impunity. But he is totally mistaken in his contention that Kierkegaard views human beings' "dependence upon God" as meaning that they are "fated" in their fall into sin and in their delivery from sin and hence have no freedom and responsibility for either. Kierkegaard is indeed a "determinist" in believing that my actions are subject to limits set on my "infinitude" and "possibility," and that my actions are "caused" by my own "intentions" and by my submission of those intentions to the criticism and reform of "the eternal." But he is an indeterminist in his stubborn insistence that at the heart of the event of the transition from intention to action there is an unpredictable either/or: I may or may *not* submit to my vision of what love-itself demands that I should do, here and now, in this particular set of circumstances. At this juncture eternal love-itself may en-courage me

---

[71] *Sickness*, pp. 227–31, 173; (KW 19:96–100, 40); SV 15:148–52, 97; (11:207–11, 152).

with all its sovereign power and may help me see that apart from love there is absolutely no "life" at all in the eternal sense. And yet, in this moment, even "God" leaves me alone, so that it is "my self" who makes the decision. Why? Because love is a relationship only in equality, and "it is the god's concern to bring about equality"; "because this is the inscrutableness of love, that in earnestness and truth and not in jest it wills to be the equal of the beloved, and it is the omnipotence of resolving love to be capable of that." So, omnipotent love waits with bated breath as it asks the lowliest, most fallible beloved, "Do you really love me?", out of concern that the beloved may "make a mistake, ... become weary and lose his/her bold confidence," and thus be "offended." And yet sovereign love "knows that ... any easier way would be a deception [*Bedrag*]."[72]

Kierkegaard's characterization of human determinacy/indeterminacy in these terms, and his location of it at the heart of individual subjectivity, comprise precisely the grounds for our claim that his "method" for exploring and depicting the "truth" of human existence is phenomenological. This truth is not discovered and described by "quantitative calculation" which is ultimately proved by objectively observable data. Rather, this truth emerges from observations of the phenomena of one's own subjectivity (the "mental/spiritual") as composed of a gestalt ("coherent pattern") of one's definitive and essential beliefs, values, desires, ideals, commitments, attitudes, etc., but more particularly from observations of how one's subjectivity operates when confronted by the demand to come to an ethical decision and action. These observations can be compared with those reported by others, but, Kierkegaard says, "the only actuality about which an existing individual is more than cognitive [*vivende om*] is one's own actuality," that is, "one's own ethical [actuality]." All cognition of others' actuality produces only speculative possibilities. "The ethical as the inward [*Indvortes*] cannot be viewed by anyone who stands outside; it can be carried out only by the particular subject, who can then know about what dwells within him/her, the only actuality which does not become possibility by being known, and [which] can be known not by simply being thought, since it is one's own actuality."[73]

That brand of determinism, which declares that the human sense of free decision and responsibility is nothing but an illusion, runs counter to the reports by countless numbers of the most sensitive human beings

---

72 *Fragments*, p. 34, 39ff.; (KW 7:28, 32f.); SV 6:30, 33f.; (4:196, 200).
73 *Postscript*, pp. 280, 284; (KW 12.1:316, 320); SV 10:22, 26; (7:271, 275).

about the phenomena of their own subjectivity. The proponents of this determinism are simply ignoring what Davidson calls "the appropriate evidence" for valid description of those mental events which lead to ethical intentional actions. Take for example the testimony of two Russian dissidents recently released and allowed to talk freely because of the policy of glasnost.

Nathan Sheransky, being interviewed on television, was shown a film of prisoners being set free from the gulag where he had spent a number of years. There was a scene of three prisoners sitting and talking in a bare cell, with no chairs or mattresses, no toilet, or reading matter, or window onto the outside world. He was asked how he felt, seeing that place. "Nostalgia," he replied, "for my alma mater, where I had good times because I had good friends. We had the best conversations I have ever had, because we were reduced to the fundamentals. Then you come to know yourself. You come to know what is essential when everything extraneous has been stripped away: love, basic moral values."

At a very different point in the intellectual spectrum we have the witness of the words and actions of Andrei Sakharov, the nuclear physicist who helped produce the first Soviet thermonuclear bomb. A noted Russian has said, "For us he was a figure of the inner spirit. Just the bare facts of his life, the way he suffered for all of us, gave him an authority that no one else had." A reviewer of his recently published books says he had "a firsthand appreciation of both the laws of the universe and man's tragic ability to turn progress into catastrophe. He held in mind, it seems, a picture, even a music, of eternity. ... Almost accidentally, Sakharov reveals [in his *Memoirs*] how his understanding of even the most speculative notions of the universe helped form a moral understanding, a sense of accountability." Then he quotes Sakharov: "We should not minimize our sacred endeavors in the world, where, like faint glimmers in the dark, we have emerged for a moment from the nothingness of unconsciousness into material existence. We must make good the demands of reason and create a life worthy of ourselves and of the goals we dimly perceive." Though standing apart from official religion, "yet I am unable to imagine the universe and human life without some guiding principle, without a source of spiritual 'warmth' that is nonmaterial and not bound by physical laws."[74]

A very different but eloquent testimony comes from the anthropologist and paleontologist Loren Eiseley, in a posthumous collection of a

---

74 David Remnick, "The Struggle for Light," in *the New York Review of Books*, 16 August 1990, p. 3.

few of his many writings, *The Star Thrower*. It is impossible to communicate second-hand the mystical power of his accounts of his encounters with nature. For example, he tells of coming upon a small fox pup in its den under the worn timbers of an abandoned boat. The little fox snatches a bone in its mouth and invites the man to play with it. Eiseley accepts, and with a bone in his mouth rolls around in the sand with the pup. Suddenly he realizes that he is staring into "the front of the universe," face-to-face. In the face of "the wide-eyed innocent fox inviting me to play, with the innate courtesy of its two paws placed appealingly together, along with a mock shake of the head," it happened: "The universe was swinging in some fantastic fashion around to present its face, and the face was so small that the universe itself was laughing."

He can also make his point very directly. In commenting on the very definitions of the essence of "the human," he notes, "There are also those who have categorized [the human] as the sole religious animal or, finally, as *Homo duplex*, the creature composed of flesh and spirit. The appeal of this last definition gives me pause, even though I am a professional anthropologist who must employ the diction of his trade. For is it not true ... that man, in becoming aware of nature, has entered upon a confused and endless exploration, a transcendental search for order? Both the theologian and the scientist, each in his way, pursue that quest." He concludes, "Tomorrow lurks in us, the latency to be all that was not achieved before. That is what lead proto-man, five million years ago, to start upon a journey, at a time when night and day were strange and miraculous, as was the trumpeting of mammoths or the march of reindeer. It was for this that man adorned his caves in the morning of time. It was for this that he worshipped the bear. For man had fallen out of the secure world of instinct into a place of wonder."

This collection concludes with an exploration of "The Inner Galaxy," in which the main theme is love. He refers to "the brooding mystery that the poet Dante impelled into his great line: 'the love that moves the sun and other stars.'" He ends on a wild and lonely seashore, contemplating his own approaching death. His thoughts are of a love that "now ... was breaking free, at last, of my worn body, still containing but passing beyond those other loves. ... We would win, I thought steadily, if not in human guise then in another, for love was something that life in its infinite prodigality could afford."[75]

It is such reports of the phenomena of the inward subjective visions and decisions of unique human spirits that are the only "appropriate

---

75 Loren Eiseley, *The Star Thrower*, pp. 63f., 217, 301, 310f.

evidence" for characterizing the freedom, the unpredictability, the ultimate responsibility of each individual, and thereby establishing each one's infinite and eternal worth and dignity. It must have been such incontrovertible "evidence" that led Carl Sagan to make a comment when the pictures sent back by Voyagers I and II showed not the slightest sign of life on Jupiter and Saturn. "These pictures," he said, "underscore the rarity and preciousness of human life, and our responsibility to care for this little blue dot in the universe."

I (the present author) know of no more profound or complex or revealing or convincing depiction of what makes human life so precious as does that depiction found in the writings of Søren Kierkegaard. The power of the truth of his picture came home to me some years ago when a good friend came to me for help. He said, "I have to do something this afternoon which leaves me in an impossible quandary, because I just don't know what to do. A dear friend of mine, sixty-six years old and at the peak of her abilities and full of the joy of life, has suddenly discovered that her body is riddled with cancer, and she has but a short time to live. She is depressed and bitter, it all seems so unfair because she has so many things she still wants to do. And I just don't know what to say to her."

I mumbled something like, "I'm sure the right thing will come to you when you are actually there with her"—after all, he was one, outstanding Christian minister seeking to console another Christian minister in a dilemma which they both had faced innumerable times in counselling people of their parish in that inevitable crisis that comes to every human being, while I was just an abstract theoretical professor of theology. "No! No!" he cried out with some anguish. "I am asking for help! You're always talking about how wonderful and profound that Kierkegaard guy is. Now, just what does he have to offer when a person is in the final desperate need?"

I was shocked and taken aback. I, too, felt in "desperate need" as I hurriedly cast my mind across Kierkegaard's vast corpus, seeking for something directly relevant to my friend's dilemma. What I came up with went something like this.

Kierkegaard's concept of "eternal life" is not about a future life after the death of the body, "up there" some place in "heaven." I have never found it helpful to those facing death or grieving the death of another to try to give "proofs" of life-after-death. The only ground for hope in a future continuing life is the experience of "eternal life" here and now. So how does one have that experience? What does it consist in?

The key statement of Kierkegaard is in *The Concept of Anxiety*. He has been characterizing the ordinary human sense of "time" as having a negative relationship to the past and future. The past is something dead and gone, about which one can do nothing. The future is uncertain and not yet here, filling one with fear and anxiety. So, temporally, one's present "moment" is a void that instantly vanishes as it flicks into the past. The only way people try to hang onto the "present" is to spatialize it. You locate yourself in reference to things. The only solution to this dilemma, Kierkegaard says, is "the concept ... which makes all things new," namely, "the fulness of time." And "the fulness of time is the moment as the eternal, and yet this eternal is at once the future and the past."[76]

Then, for my friend, I interpreted all these abstruse notions in my favourite figurative language for Kierkegaard's key idea. It is like this: you reach with one arm and hand backward into all your life of the past, all that you have been and done, and bring it forward into the present moment. You don't leave anything out, you accept as "yours" both all the good and all the bad. You accept your self for who you have been. Then, at the very same time, you reach forward with your other hand to accept all that hangs as possibility in your (*your*) future but you grasp with all your vigour and determination one thing most needful and bring it backward into the present moment (as Kierkegaard puts it in *Sickness*: "to accomplish the infinitely little things of the deed which can be accomplished this very day, this very hour, this very minute"). And thus you experience "the fulness of time," because your "moment" that was so empty except for despair now becomes "the moment as the eternal." Hence it is a "religious" moment, because your have "repented" all your past and know that it is accepted (forgiven), and because you have "believed" in risking to do your future *now*, and you know that "all-things-are-possible." This is the experience of "eternal life" here and now.

Well, my friend looked at me quizzically, and I was afraid I hadn't really helped him. But later at the memorial service for his friend, he brought his eulogy for her to a close by telling how he had recounted my words to her that very afternoon. And what was her reaction? He told it in these words:

---

76 *The Concept of Anxiety*, pp. 76f., 81; (KW 8:85, 90); SV 6:174, 178; (4:355, 360).

As we talked about this, her face grew alive and reflective as it did when she was excited with a fresh thought. A few days later she told me she had had a beautiful dream which gave her tremendous comfort. Whatever the outcome of this illness, more years or early death, everything was all right. She felt support beneath her over the abyss. Then she swept the room with her eyes and her arm, encompassing the scores of cards arranged for her to see. "I have reached out," she said, "and drawn all the past to me and it is forgiven. All the days I was difficult or contentious, all the fears and all the failures. It is all forgiven. Really. For the first time in my life I really believe all this love—of my family and friends—all these cards. And the future? The next possibility? I'm ready for that."

She had experienced eternity, eternal life, her "eternal blessedness"—here and now.

I know this account verges into Kierkegaard's "theology," but I believe that what is recounted here is a possibility of any and every human spirit under the impact of that love-itself which comes selflessly from an other. The story serves as a good transition from "Kierkegaard the Humanist" to "Kierkegaard the Theologian." And I for one am eager to explore how much of the peculiarly Christian notions of the self, as "given" (created), as "failure" (sinner), and as "in need of the eternal" (the graces of faith and love), are open to appropriation by any seeker after the truth of human existence. But before we can make this transition, we are compelled to "pause," as was predicted at the beginning of this study of what we called "the basic anthropology" of Kierkegaard as humanist (pp. 11ff. in chapter 1 above). We must pause to ask, in retrospect, whether we have really found in Kierkegaard's writings and journals an "anthropological ontology" which has been derived (by him) by means of a generally available phenomenological method, and which has been formulated in this study without dependence on those Kierkegaardian materials that are clearly theological (in a Christian sense).

Obviously, the author of this present study believes that he has found such an ontology and by such a method. And we will not try to summarize the materials adduced throughout the study in support of this thesis. But the question that must be commented on in the transition between Kierkegaard's anthropology and his theology is this: what does it mean to grant his anthropology the status of being an "ontology" as distinct from being a "theology"?

Interlude:
Ontology and Theology

"Ontology" is not a widely used word or concept in contemporary philosophy. The dominance of the perspectives of formal logic and linguistic analysis in the schools of philosophy in the academic scene has largely relegated traditional metaphysics and its interest in ontology to a purely historical account of the past. But some scientists and philosophers of science have not been satisfied with the reduction of truth to matters of formal methodology and abstractions expressed in mathematical formulae. The two authors of *Principia Mathematica* separated and took quite opposite paths. Bertrand Russell followed the route of logical science and ended in a kind of scepticism about most questions of general human interest. A.N. Whitehead pursued the questions of cosmology and produced *Process and Reality*, in which many ultimate metaphysical and religious questions are openly explored. So some of the traditional interests of a philosophical exploration of "being" get expressed by him when he says that "cosmology is the effort to frame a scheme of the general character of the present stage of the universe," or that "speculative reason ... seeks to build a cosmology expressing the general nature of the world as disclosed in human interests," or that "metaphysics seeks to discover the general ideas which are indispensably relevant to the analysis of everything that happens."[1] Similar interests and concepts are to be found in the writings of the scientist Michael Polanyi, in such books as *Personal Knowledge*, *The Tacit Dimension*, and *Knowing and Being*. And of course the existentialist philosophy of Martin Heidegger and Jean-Paul Sartre and the philosophical theology of Paul Ricoeur make the nature of being a central issue.

---

1 A. N. Whitehead, *The Function of Reason*, pp. 76, 85; *Religion in the Making*, p. 7.

An even more interesting suggestion has been made more recently by Stephen Hawking and a few of his colleagues.[2] Hawking has said, "The odds against a universe like ours emerging out of something like the Big Bang are enormous. I think there are clearly religious implications whenever you start to discuss the origins of the universe. There must be religious overtones." Hawking assumes that "all the features of our everyday world, the subatomic world and the cosmos itself, are determined by a few basic physical laws and constants." Hawking, Brandon Carter, and a few others have discerned and described the "extremely delicate balance" among the basic forces that operate among the masses of elementary particles that make up "nature" or the universe. There are four forces that are especially important in determining (or in making possible) the kind of life that has emerged on our planet. They are: the strong force that holds the constituents of the nucleus together (quarks, protons, neutrons), the much weaker electromagnetic force that keeps electrons in orbit around the nucleus, the still weaker force that causes radioactive decay, and gravity which is the weakest force of all. It is the precise balance of relative strengths of these forces in interaction with each other that, Hawking points out, explains the fact that "the growth of the universe ... has been at just the proper rate to allow galaxies and stars to form," and to provide the proper time "for complex biological phenomena, such as mankind, to develop. If gravity were less powerful," and at the same time were not "so much weaker than the other three forces," then "matter would not have congealed into stars and galaxies and the universe would be cold and empty."

How to explain all this and the even more puzzling fact of the emergence of order out of the chaos of entropy (perpetual decay)? How did the universe "get wound up in the first place"? Hawking's answer is that it is precisely our presence in the universe that explains it. "This principle can be paraphrased as, 'Things are as they are because we are.'" In other words, the particular "conditions and parameters" of our particular universe are what make it "possible for intelligent life to develop and ask the question, 'Why is the universe as we observe it?' The only answer will be that if it were otherwise, there would be nobody to ask the question." Brandon Carter has labelled this basic concept of Hawking's the "anthropic principle." And John Wheeler ("the physicist's physicist") has embraced and developed this principle with enthusiasm, and

2 All the following material is derived from John Boslough, *Stephen Hawking's Universe* (New York: Avon Books, 1985), pp. 109–13; see also p. 76.

"agrees with Hawking and Carter that our universe is uniquely finetuned to produce life, even if in just one small, lost corner." He "even suggests that a universe in which life has failed to evolve is a failed universe."

Kierkegaard never deserted his single "category" of the individual human self in order to use his considerable talent of "speculative reason" to construct a general scheme of all the abstract "categories" (as he called them) which are relevant to the analysis of the universe as a whole. He gives us only an occasional brief formulation of one or another of them that is relevant to the aspect of human nature that is under his analysis. We have heard him say (while writing *Postscript*) that what is needed for a clarification of "the relationship between logic and ontology is an examination of the concepts: possibility, actuality, and necessity."[3] So all of his material summarized in the extended treatment of possibility and necessity (in chapter 5 above) comprises his treatment of logic's modal categories and has implications for his "ontology."

His concept of ontology would certainly fit into Whitehead's definition of metaphysics as the "discovery of the general ideas which are indispensably relevant to the analysis of everything that happens," but only in a restricted sense. And Hawking's "anthropic principle" certainly would support Kierkegaard's insistence that the power which has given being to the individual human being is the same power that has given being "to all things." But Kierkegaard's focus is not on "everything that happens" or on "the general character of the universe" or even on "the general nature of the world as disclosed to [*all*] human interests." Rather, he would agree with Davidson's thesis that the "basic physical laws and constants" of the universe have made possible the emergence of a limited "region" or sphere within nature, namely, the psychical, that operates according to its own "laws," which presume but are not restricted to the physical, chemical, and biological "laws" of the rest of nature. And, Kierkegaard argues, the peculiar structure or dynamic in the universe called "love" has actually created that "order" in the universe that supports the unique being of the individual human self. And he would also agree with Davidson that the "appropriate evidence" for understanding the operation of the human psyche is not at all like the cool, objective, abstract data used to test scientific theory. Rather, for this sphere it consists of inward subjective reports of the ethical-religious

---

3 *Journals*, 199, VI B 54:21.

struggles that take place in the formation and accomplishment of intentional actions.

So one would have to say that Kierkegaard limits himself to a "regional" ontology. In *Postscript* he makes explicit what is implicit in all his other writings, namely, that the "being" on which his "human interest" is focused is not that which is disclosed to "abstract thinking" or "objective reflection" as practised in mathematics, formal logic, or the natural sciences. Rather, Kierkegaard seeks to comprehend ultimate being as disclosed in "subjective reflection" when human thinking (including especially the imagination) focuses on one "region" of the universe, namely, the "sphere" of the human self as essentially involved in ethical-religious action.

However, it is not in *Postscript* that he draws the implications of his modal concepts (possibility, necessity) for the nature of being, even though that is precisely the book in which we might have expected it. Typically he waits until two years later, when he is writing some upbuilding discourses on love, to provide some "reflections" on his understanding of the ultimate "being" that conditions "everything that happens" in and to that peculiar and unique reflection of being, namely, the human individual self. So in summarizing his analysis and depiction of the disclosure of "love-itself" in the love-relationship between human beings (in chapter 7), we spoke of his "anthropological ontology" and "ontology of love." This terminology is fitting in the light of his declaration that love-itself (God) "gives me being, indeed gives all things, gives all things being." Indeed, we said, love gains "ontological status" when he insists that "the ground and foundation of the life of the spirit ... is precisely love; love is the origin of all ... and the deepest ground of the life of the spirit." And Kierkegaard "deepens his ontology of love," we said, when he says that the "reduplication," that becomes manifest in the love-relationship of the triad of lover-beloved-loveitself, is based on and reflective of the reduplication that exists in "the eternal" in that "the eternal *is* not merely in its qualities, but is *in itself* in its qualities, ... *is* in itself as simultaneously it has qualities." (See text above at notes 41–55 and 66–8 of chapter 7.)

In summary, then, Kierkegaard is engaged throughout his authorship in a kind of "ontological quest," in a search for those "general ideas which are indispensably relevant to the analysis of everything that happens" within the "sphere" of human selfhood, in search for "the general nature of the world as disclosed to human interest" in becoming self. And the key ideas that he finds most relevant are: the basic assumption that the human being is "constructed" precisely for the task of "becoming self"; the basic inescapable experience of "angst" with its dialectic of sympathy/antipathy toward this task; "freedom" as the necessary correlate to angst; the disturbance of primitive human immediacy by consciousness of the dimension of the infinite in tension with one's finitude, by consciousness of openness to the eternal within oneself in opposition to one's temporality; the resulting discovery that "truth" is subjectivity; the emergence of freedom in the dialectic of the self's possibility and the self's necessity; coming to the sense of the requirement of self-annihilation and of totality of guilt-consciousness when the eternal takes on the more specific guise of being "all-things-are-possible"; coming to the awareness that my own eternal blessedness as a being of infinite dignity and worth (my own proper self-love) can only be established and maintained by an "other," namely, love-itself as the ultimate universal dynamic of reality; and finally, the discovery (or revelation) of love-itself, which occurs only in my love-relationship with other human beings.

We have seen and heard Kierkegaard the humanist argue that all of the dynamics and structures of human existence (stated in the foregoing paragraph) are present and operative in every human individual, and also are (to a certain degree) open to the conscious experience and realization of every human individual. So now we are ready to ask and to explore what Kierkegaard the theologian has to add to this analysis of human selfhood. What additional insights are peculiar to specifically Christian faith and tradition? Do these insights assume and build on Kierkegaard's humanistic ontology of the self? Or do they wipe the slate clean and produce a totally new ontology, with a totally different understanding of "the general nature of the world," and hence with its own unique set of "general ideas" that explain "everything that happens"? And whatever these insights turn out to be, can they be understood and grasped and used only by those who stand within the concrete historical experience of Christian "faith"? The height and depth and complexity of Kierkegaard's humanistic ontology, as analysed and summarized in this study thus far, will make the answering of these questions no simple or facile task, as we explore the topics suggested by Kierkegaard himself, namely, My Self: A Gift; My Self: A Failure; My Self: In Need of the Eternal-in-Time.

Finally, the uniqueness of this ontology lies in the fact that every one of the expressions of it (as stated in the previous paragraph) is a piece of a whole. Each one interpenetrates and depends upon all the others. The whole adds up to more than its parts, and there is no expression or description or analogy that is adequate for capturing the whole. This character of Kierkegaard's vision of the self is of crucial importance, and it brings our characterization of Kierkegaard's ontology into conflict with one of the serious previous attempts to depict that whole. I (the present author) have in mind John W. Elrod's study, *Being and Existence in Kierkegaard's Pseudonymous Works*. There is much in this work with which I agree, and there are a number of his theses with which I would want to argue, but here I will concentrate on his delimitation of Kierkegaard's ontology.

Elrod argues that Kierkegaard's ontology is integrally ethical but not religious and therefore is purely "philosophical." He of course acknowledges that Kierkegaard's central focus is the religious. "By maintaining that Kierkegaard's ontology is philosophical, I do not wish to deny that he is fundamentally concerned with religion." Nevertheless, "I shall argue that [his] exploration of [human] existence gives rise to an ontology, because Kierkegaard is attempting to establish the priority of the self apart from any religious beliefs with respect to what the self is *qua* self." So although Kierkegaard seeks to "rediscover the meaning of being religious" and "is vitally interested in Christianity," yet "his understanding of Christianity and his ontology are formally distinct." So, "the concept of human being developed by Kierkegaard in his doctrine of the self omits the reality of God. For Kierkegaard, the God question is an existential question, not an ontological one. Discussions of God appear in his descriptions of the ethical-religious stage of existence, not in his ontology."[4] From what totally non-religious materials, then, does Elrod derive this ontology of the self?

The clue is given when he says, "The concept of existence in Kierkegaard's ontology does not primarily refer to the dialectically opposing poles of the self; i.e., to the existence-essence distinction, but to the decisive act by which the existing individual actualizes possibility in the contingent and becoming realm of being."[5] But certainly the "opposing poles" are present in the given structure of the self prior to that "decisive act" and are operative in that act. Indeed, one cannot even *try* to "actualize possibility" without being caught in the dialectic of each of these poles: infinite/finite, possible/necessary, temporal/eternal. In the entire foregoing analysis of "My Self: A Task," I have shown again and again that the "infinite" inevitably projects itself as the "possible,"

---

4 John W. Elrod, *Being and Existence in Kierkegaard's Pseudonymous Works*, pp. 19f., 70n.
5 Ibid., pp. 20f.

and the "possible" always appears as the "future," and the "future" is the incognito of the "eternal." These opposing poles are precisely the structural elements, the inescapable dynamics of the "being" of the self, that make every human being "naturally fitted" (*anlagt*) to become a self, to become *its* self.

In considering the relation of ontology and religion, the key pole in the synthesis of the self κατα δυναμιν (given in potentiality) is the "eternal." It has been shown above, in a number of different languages of Kierkegaard, that the "eternal" is a synonym for the transcendent "other," for "all-things-are-possible," for "love-itself," and that this "other" is present immanently in the forms of religiousness A. Elrod avoids this dilemma by conveniently taking literally Haufniensis' statement that "spirit is the eternal" to mean that "spirit *itself* is the eternal" (emphasis added). So later he says, "Religiousness A assumes that the individual is eternal. This assumption hinges on the notion that the self is divine."[6] Elrod sees no "breach" (*Brud*) in the God-relationship of religiousness A, no entering into a "silence" that means "death" of the self's adequacy, no "totality of guilt" that leads to the "annihilation" of the self in order to "make room for God," no repentance that allows the God-relationship to guide the self into any measure of true freedom. Elrod deals with these aspects of religiousness A, but depicts them simply as movement of the self within the self.

This view of the eternal and of the individual's relationship to it (in religiousness A) is hardly supported in the context in which Haufniensis says, "spirit is the eternal." That very sentence goes on to say that the self as spirit realizes the synthesis of its bipolarity "only when spirit posits the first synthesis [of finite/ infinite] along with the second synthesis of the temporal and the eternal." And the relation of these two syntheses had been explicated just a few pages before: "As for the latter synthesis, it is immediately striking that it is formed differently from the former. In the former, the two factors [*Momenter*] of the synthesis were soul [psyche] and body, and spirit is the third, and yet in such a way that one can speak of a synthesis only when spirit is posited. The latter synthesis has only two factors, the temporal and the eternal. Where is the third [factor]? And if there is no third, there really is no synthesis," but only the contradiction between the two. The direct implication is that the third factor that unites (overcomes the contradiction between) the temporal

6 Ibid., pp. 66, 204.

and the eternal is not the same as the third factor that unites soul (infinite) and body (finite), namely, the human spirit or self. What then is it?

Haufniensis' answer is "the moment," in which "time and eternity touch each other," which therefore is "an atom of eternity, ... the first reflection of eternity in time." But Kierkegaard (Climacus) provided a clearer answer in *Fragments* (published four days before *The Concept of Anxiety*) where he says, "the reason and the paradox meet happily in the moment. ... And the third [factor] in which this happens (because it does not occur in the reason which is disengaged, or in the paradox which bestows itself, therefore [occurs] in something) is that happy passion to which we will now give a name. ... We will call it *faith*."[7] And although in *Fragments* Climacus is speaking of Christian faith, in *Postscript* he also uses "faith" for the sphere of religiousness A when he says that the definition of truth as "objective uncertainty held fast in appropriation by the most passionate inwardness" is "a paraphrase for faith. Without risk there is no faith." So we have gone to great pains to show that Kierkegaard assumes that there is a kind of "breach" within the immanence of religiousness A, namely, between the self-conscious human being and the "eternal" or "god" who "speaks" in the "silence" when the human person negates him/herself as impotent in order to "make room for God." As abundantly illustrated above, Kierkegaard ascribes to religiousness A a much more profound and positive level of ethical-religious sensitivity and accomplishment than does Elrod. The strangest thing about Elrod's depiction of both religiousness A and B is the total absence of any mention of Kierkegaard's concept of love (*Works of Love* is not even mentioned in the bibliography). It was precisely in his exposition of love-itself that we found some of Kierkegaard's profoundest formulations of his ontology.

The point to this discussion of Elrod's characterization of Kierkegaard's ontology is to emphasize that Kierkegaard's understanding of *human* "being" is essentially and integrally "religious." That is to say, God, the eternal, all-things-are-possible, love-itself is at the heart of the structure/dynamic of what "is," insofar as what "is" is reflected in and experienced by human being. Kierkegaard the humanist knows that every human being is essentially and integrally and inescapably open to the eternal because of the very structure given to every human being. So finally we are equipped to answer the question raised early in this study

---

7 For this and the previous paragraph, *The Concept of Anxiety*, pp. 81, 76; (KW 8:90, 85); SV 6:178, 173; (4:360f., 355); *Fragments*, pp. 72f.; (KW 7:59); SV 6:56; (4:224).

(p. 25 of chapter 2), "whether Kierkegaard's anthropology contains an ontology which is independent of and separable from his theology." The answer is that his anthropological ontology is independent of his (Christian) theology, but this ontology includes the human's openness to and relationship with the eternal (religiousness A). In the context of the above question, we note that in *Sickness* Kierkegaard first proceeds to his analysis of the self by abstracting what he calls the factors or constituent-elements (*Momenter*) of the synthesis without regard to whether the self is conscious or not. And in this section he eliminates any consideration of the factors temporal/eternal, which can only mean that he does not consider the eternal to be a constituent element of the human being as such. "I" am not eternal in my own right, on my own. This point would seem to support Elrod's thesis that Kierkegaard's ontology does not include a religious dimension. But the matter is not that simple.

In the opening paragraph of *Sickness* Kierkegaard flatly declares that the self *is* a synthesis of the temporal and the eternal just as truly as it is a synthesis of the infinite and the finite and of possibility (freedom) and necessity. Does he then contradict himself when he eliminates the dyad of temporal/eternal in the section where he begins his analysis of the forms of despair? He answers this question in the first paragraph of that section. He says that the self as a synthesis is basically composed of infinitude and finitude. But he does not conceive of these two fundamental factors as inert and immutable substances or as static and causal conditions. Rather, they are in a relationship of opposition and tension, out of which emerges the dialectic of possibility and necessity, in which dialectic arises consciousness of the self and the will to become the self. In other words, "the relation relates to itself, which is freedom." But, as we have seen, the "possible" is "future," and this awareness raises the issue of one's relationship also to one's past, and thus one is caught in the dilemma of temporality, and then of decision and choice, and hence of risk and belief. The future is "the first incognito of the eternal." So "the relation which relates to itself" faces, in fear and trembling, its need also to relate simultaneously to "the power that established it."

All these "syntheses" and "relationships" that define what the self *is* are a seamless unity. No one of them is "ontologically" independent of any of the others. So the dialectic of temporal/eternal is integral to the "being" of the self, even though the self is not eternal as such, because the self is not and cannot become itself except in relationship with the eternal, the power that not only established the self but which is always present in and to the self, whether or not the self is aware of it or desires it. So the ontology of the self is not an exploration of static substances or conditions but of dynamic active relationships among given factors. The human self is ontologically involved in the dynamic interactive relationship of its temporality with the eternal.[8]

This leaves us with the question (which we have asked before): what does Christian faith/love and its "theology" (reflection about itself) add to Kierkegaard's humanist understanding of the self and its task of becoming itself? How are "Christian reflections" (theology) different from philosophical and psychological analyses of the human condition? With these questions we will begin (and probably end) our consideration of Kierkegaard as Theologian and of the latter's depiction not of the *discovery* of My Self but of the *recovery* of My Self.

---

[8] This concept of "being" is certainly in accord with contemporary philosophy and science for which the whole notion of immutable "substances" or even "laws" is now meaningless as they explore the unending and changing processes of the universe. As Kierkegaard says, the self is always *i Vorden*, in the process of becoming, or it is not the self.

Bibliography

PRIMARY SOURCES

Danish

Søren Kierkegaards Papirer. First edition, ed. P.A. Heiberg and V. Kuhr. Copenhagen: Glydendalske Boghandel, 1912.
– Second enlarged edition, 25 volumes or part-volumes, ed. Niels Thulstrup. Copenhagen: Gyldendal, 1968.
Søren Kierkegaards Samlede Værker. First edition, 15 volumes, ed. A.B. Drachmann, J.L. Heiberg, and H.O. Lange. Copenhagen: Glydendalske Boghandel, 1901–6.
– Third edition, 20 volumes, ed. Peter P. Rohde. Copenhagen: Glydendal, 1962.

English Translations in the Series "Kierkegaard's Writings"

Edited by Howard V. Hong and Edna H. Hong. Published in Princeton by Princeton Univerity Press. Translations are by Howard and Edna Hong unless otherwise noted. Translations incomplete as of date of publication of this book.

KW 1: *Early Polemical Writings.* Trans. Julia Watkin. 1990.
KW 2: *The Concept of Irony.* 1989.
KW 3: *Either/Or,* Part I. 1987.
KW 4: *Either/Or,* Part II. 1987.
KW 5: *Eighteen Upbuilding Discourses.* 1990.
KW 6: *Fear and Trembling; Repetition.* 1983.
KW 7: *Philosophical Fragments; Johannes Climacus.* 1985.
KW 8: *The Concept of Anxiety.* Trans. Reidar Thomte in collaboration with Albert B. Anderson. 1980.

KW 10: *Three Discourses on Imagined Occasions.* 1993.
KW 11: *Stages on Life's Way.* 1988.
KW 12: *Concluding Unscientific Postscript to Philosophical Fragments.* 1992.
KW 13: *The Corsair Affair.* 1982.
KW 14: *Two Ages: A Literary Review.* 1978.
KW 15: *Upbuilding Discourses in Various Spirits.* 1993.
KW 19: *The Sickness unto Death.* 1980.
KW 20: *Practice in Christianity.* 1991.
KW 21: *For Self-Examination; Judge for Yourself!* 1990.
KW 25: *Letters and Documents.* Trans. Henrik Rosenmeier. 1978.

Other English Translations

These translations were used in the writing of this book and are listed in chronological order, as is roughly done in KW, but here the chronology followed is that of the actual composition of the works as worked out by Niels Jørgen Cappelørn and Alastair McKinnon in *Kierkegaardiana* 9 (1974), 133-46.

The Concept of Irony. Trans. Lee M. Capel. Bloomington: Indiana University Press, 1968.
Either/Or, vol. 1. Trans. David F. Swenson and Lillian Marvin Swenson with revisions by Howard A. Johnson. Garden City, New York: Doubleday Anchor Books, 1959.
Either/Or, vol. 2. Trans. Walter Lowrie with revisions by Howard A. Johnson. Garden City, New York: Doubleday Anchor Books, 1959.
Johannes Climacus. Trans. T.H. Croxall. Stanford: Stanford University Press, 1958, 1967. (Not in *SV* but in *Papirer* IV B 1, pp. 103-50.)
Fear and Trembling. Trans. Walter Lowrie. Garden City, New York: Doubleday Anchor Books, 1954.
Repetition. Trans. Walter Lowrie. New York: Harper Torchbooks, 1941.
Edifying Discourses, vols. 1-4. Trans. of *Eighteen Upbuilding Discourses* by David F. Swenson and Lillian Marvin Swenson. Minneapolis: Augsburg Publishing House, 1943-4.
Philosophical Fragments. Trans. David F. Swenson. Princeton: Princeton University Press, 1942.
– Trans. David F. Swenson, rev. Howard V. Hong. Princeton: Princeton University Press, 1962. (Referenced in notes.)
The Concept of Dread. Trans. Walter Lowrie. Princeton: Princeton University Press, 1957.
Thoughts on Crucial Situations in Human Life: Three Discourses on Imagined Occasions. Trans. David F. Swenson. Minneapolis: Augsburg Publishing House, 1941.

Stages on Life's Way. Trans. Walter Lowrie. New York: Schocken Books, 1967.
Concluding Unscientific Postscript. Trans. David F. Swenson and Walter Lowrie. Princeton: Princeton University Press, 1941, 1974.
The Present Age. Trans. Alexander Dru. New York: Harper Torchbooks, 1962. This is a translation of less than half of Kierkegaard's work entitled *Two Ages: A Literary Review* (KW 14).
The following three books are translations of Parts 1, 2, and 3 respectively of *Upbuilding Discourses in Various Spirits* (KW 15):
– *Purity of Heart.* Trans. Douglas V. Steere. New York: Harper Torchbooks, 1938, 1948.
– *Consider the Lilies.* Trans. A.S. Aldworth and W.S. Ferrie. London: C.W. Daniel Co., 1940.
– *Gospel of Sufferings.* Trans. A.S. Aldworth and W.S. Ferrie. Cambridge, England: James Clarke and Co., 1955, 1982.
On Authority and Revelation: The Book on Adler. Trans. Walter Lowrie. Princeton: Princeton University Press, 1955. (Not in sv but in *Papirer* VII^2, pp. 3–230.)
Works of Love. Trans. Howard and Edna Hong. New York: Harper Torchbooks, 1962.
Of the Difference between a Genius and an Apostle (with *The Present Age* as listed above). Trans. Alexander Dru. New York: Harper Torchbooks, 1962. This item is one of *Two Minor Ethical-Religious Essays* written in 1847. The other essay, *Has a Man the Right to Let Himself Be Put to Death for the Truth?*, may be found in the British edition of Dru's *The Present Age* (Oxford: Oxford University Press, 1940).
Christian Discourses. Trans. Walter Lowrie. New York: Oxford University Press, 1961.
The Sickness unto Death (with *Fear and Trembling* as listed above). Trans. Walter Lowrie. Garden City, New York: Doubleday Anchor Books, 1954. (Referenced in notes.)
– Trans. Alastair Hannay. London: Penguin Books, 1989.
Training in Christianity. Trans. Walter Lowrie. Princeton: Princeton University Press, 1944.
The Lilies of the Field and the Birds of the Air (with *Christian Discourses* as listed above). Trans. Walter Lowrie. New York: Oxford University Press, 1961.
Three Discourses at the Communion on Fridays: The High Priest—The Publican—The Sinner (with *Christian Discourses* as listed above). Trans. Walter Lowrie. New York: Oxford University Press, 1961.
The Point of View for My Work as an Author and *My Work as an Author.* Trans. Walter Lowrie. New York: Harper Torchbooks, 1962.
For Self-Examination. Trans. Edna and Howard Hong. Minneapolis: Augsburg Publishing House, 1959.

Armed Neutrality and *An Open Letter.* Trans. Howard and Edna Hong. New York: Simon and Schuster, 1968.
Attack upon Christendom. Trans. Walter Lowrie. Boston: Beacon Press, 1959.

SELECTED SECONDARY SOURCES

Cole, J. Preston. *The Problematic Self in Kierkegaard and Freud.* New Haven: Yale University Press, 1971.
Come, Arnold B. *Trendelenburg's Influence on Kierkegaard's Modal Categories.* Montreal: Inter Editions, 1991.
Elrod, John W. *Being and Existence in Kierkegaard's Pseudonymous Works.* Princeton: Princeton University Press, 1975.
Evans, C. Stephen. *Passionate Reason.* Bloomington: Indiana University Press, 1992.
Fenger, Henning. *Kierkegaard, The Myths and Their Origins.* New Haven: Yale University Press, 1980. Trans. by George C. Schoolfield of *Kierkegaard-Myter og Kierkegaard-Kilder.* Odense: Odense Universitetsforlag, 1976.
Ferreira, M. Jaimie. *Transforming Vision.* Oxford: Clarendon Press, 1991.
Gouwens, David J. *Kierkegaard's Dialectic of the Imagination.* New York: P. Lang, 1989.
Hannay, Alastair. *Kierkegaard.* London: Routledge and Kegan Paul, 1982.
Holl, Jann. *Kierkegaards Konzeption des Selbst.* Meisenheim am Glan: Anton Hain, 1972.
Johnson, Howard A. and Niels Thulstrup, eds. *A Kierkegaard Critique.* New York: Harper and Brothers, 1962.
Kirmmse, Bruce H. *Kierkegaard in Golden Age Denmark.* Bloomington: Indiana University Press, 1990.
Lowrie, Walter. *Kierkegaard.* London: Oxford University Press, 1938.
Lübcke, Poul. "Modalität und Zeit bei Kierkegaard und Heidegger." In *Text und Context,* Sonderreihe, Band 15. Copenhagen-München: Wilhelm Fink Verlag, 1983.
Malantschuk, Gregor. *Fra Individ til den Enkelte.* Copenhagen: C.A. Reitzels Boghandel, 1978.
– *Frihedens Problem i Kierkegaards Begrebet Angest.* Copenhagen: Rosenkilde og Bagger, 1971.
– *Kierkegaard's Truth.* Princeton: Princeton University Press, 1971. Trans. by Howard and Edna Hong of *Dialekik og Eksistens hos Søren Kierkegaard.* Copenhagen: Hans Reitzels Forlag, 1968.
– *Kierkegaard's Way to the Truth: An Introduction to the Authorship of Søren Kierkegaard.* Montreal: Inter Editions, 1987. Trans. by Mary Michelsen of *Indførelse i Søren Kierkegaards Forfatterskab.* Copenhagen: Munksgaard.

McCarthy, Vincent A. *The Phenomenology of Moods in Kierkegaard*. The Hague: Martin Nijhoff, 1978.
McKinnon, Alastair. *Kierkegaard Indices*. Leiden: E.J. Brill, 1970–73.
Nordentoft, Kresten. *Kierkegaard's Psychology*. Pittsburgh: Duquesne University Press, 1978.
Ostenfeld, Ib. *Søren Kierkegaard's Psychology*. Waterloo, Ontario: Wilfrid Laurier University Press, 1978. Trans. and ed. by Alastair McKinnon from *Søren Kierkegaards Psykologi*. Copenhagen: Rhodos, 1972.
Rohde, H.P., ed. *Auktionsprotokol over Søren Kierkegaards Bogsamling* and *The Auctioneer's Sales Record of the Library of Søren Kierkegaard*. Trans. Helen Fogh. København: Det Kongelige Bibliotek, 1967.
Schrader, George A. *Existential Philosophers: Kierkegaard to Merleau-Ponty*. New York: McGraw-Hill, 1967.
Sløk, Johannes. *Die Anthropologie Kierkegaards*. Copenhagen: Rosenkilde und Bagger, 1954.
Smith, Joseph H., ed. *Kierkegaard's Truth: The Disclosure of the Self*. New Haven: Yale University Press, 1981.
Shmuëli, Adi. *Kierkegaard and Consciousness*. Trans. Naomi Handelman. Princeton: Princeton University Press, 1971.
Swenson, David F. *Something about Kierkegaard*. Minneapolis: Augsburg, 1941
Taylor, Mark C. *Journeys to Selfhood: Hegel and Kierkegaard*. Berkeley: University of California Press, 1980.
Thompson, Josiah. *Kierkegaard*. London: Victor Gollancz, 1974.
Theunissen, Michael. *Der Begriff Ernst bei Søren Kierkegaard*. Freiburg: Alber, 1958.
Thulstrup, Niels. *Kierkegaard's Relation to Hegel*. Princeton: Princeton University Press, 1980. Trans. by George. L. Stengren of *Kierkegaards Forhold til Hegel*. Copenhagen: Glydendal, 1967.
Walsh, Sylvia I. "Forming the Heart: The Role of Love in Kierkegaard's Thought." In *The Grammar of the Heart*. Ed. Richard H. Bell. San Francisco: Harper and Row, 1988.
Westphal, Merold. *Kierkegaard's Critique of Reason and Society*. Macon: Mercer University Press, 1987.

RELATED SOURCES

Aristotle. *Organon: Analytica Posteriora*; trans. in *The Basic Works of Aristotle*, ed. Richard McKeon. New York: Random House, 1941.
Davidson, Donald. *Essays on Actions and Events*. New York: Clarendon Press, 1980.
– "Paradoxes of Irrationality." In *Philosophical Essays on Freud*. Ed. R. Wolheim and J. Hopkins. New York: Cambridge University Press, 1982.

– "Deception and Division." In *Action and Events: Perspectives on the Philosophy of Donald Davidson*. Ed. E. LePore and B.P. McLaughlin. New York: B. Blackwell, 1985.
Eiseley, Loren. *The Star Thrower*. New York: Harcourt Brace Jovanovitch, 1978.
Hampshire, Stuart. *Innocence and Experience*. Cambridge, Mass.: Harvard University Press, 1989.
Kalkar, Chr. H., ed. *Bibelen eller den hellige Skrift*. Copenhagen, 1847.
Kneale, William and Martha. *The Development of Logic*. Oxford: Clarendon Press, 1964.
Lessing, G.E. *Schriften II*. Frankfurt am Main: Insel Verlag, 1967.
McCawley, James D. *Everything That Linguists Have Always Wanted to Know about Logic—But Were Ashamed to Ask*. Chicago: University of Chicago Press, 1981.
McLaughlin, Brian P., and Amélie Oksenberg Rorty, eds. *Perspectives on Self-Deception*. Berkeley: University of California Press, 1988.
Newton-Smith, W.H. *Logic: An Introductory Course*. London: Routledge and Kegan Paul, 1985.
Niebuhr, Reinhold. *An Interpretation of Christian Ethics*. New York: World Publishing Company, 1963; copyright 1935 by Harper and Brothers.
N. T. ved Kong Frederik den Siettes. Copenhagen: Kongelige Baisenhuses Forlag, 1841.
Parker, Robert B. *The Judas Goat*. New York: Dell Publishing Co., 1978.
Rosenstock, Gershon G. *F.A. Trendelenburg: Forerunner of John Dewey*. Carbondale: Southern Illinois University Press, 1964.
Tillich, Paul. *Systematic Theology, Volume I*. Chicago: University of Chicago Press, 1951.
Trendelenburg, Adolph. *Logische Untersuchungen*. 1st ed. Berlin: 1840; 3rd ed. Leipzig: Verlag von S. Hirzel, 1870.
– *Die logische Frage in Hegel's System*. Leipzig: F.A. Brockhaus, 1843.
– *Elementa logices Aristotelicae*. Berlin: W. Weber, 1842
– *Erläuterungen zu den Elementen der aristotelischen Logik*. Berlin: Rowalt, 1842.
– *Geschichte der Kategorienlehre*. Berlin, 1846.
– *Historische Beiträge zur Philosophie*. Berlin: Verlag von G. Bethge, 1867.
Vermazen, Bruce, and Merrill B. Hintikka, eds. *Essays on Davidson: Actions and Events*. Oxford: Clarendon Press, 1985.
Whitehead, Alfred North. *The Function of Reason*. Princeton: Princeton University Press, 1929; or Beacon Paperback edition, 1958.
– *Religion in the Making*. New York: Macmillan, 1926; or Meridian edition, 1960.

Index

accidental: *see* "fortuitous"
Aristotle, 82, 142, 144, 146–8, 148, 183–4, 243–4, 317, 319–21, 328, 339

contingent: *see* "fortuitous"

Davidson, Donald, 234–41, 257, 271–3, 324–5, 410n18, 413–14, 417, 429–30, 433, 442, 451–4, 460, 467

Elrod, John, 470–4

Fenger, Henning, 80n73
Ferreira, M. Jaime, 154n34
faith, 15–16, 26, 113, 116, 135, 261; and action, 401–7; and the "leap," 242, 244–9, 258, 281–2; and love, 331–2, 367, 393; and reason, 81–3; in religiousness A versus B, 304–10, 321–2; as "third" factor, 127–30, 288
fortuitous/accidental/contingent: as concrete self, 32; related to the "essential" and "eternal" in human-being, 259–260, 264–5, 275–6, 316; and fate, 457–8; as integral to human-being, 20–3, 146–8, 153, 159–60; related to "necessity," 190, 212; as outward occasion, 91–3; related to "possibility," 163–70, 174, 177, 179; related to thinking, 185
freedom, 16, 20, 24, 27–8, 36, 42–3, 46, 49–50, 53, 56–9, 63, 70, 79, 83, 104, 108, chapter 4 passim, chapter 5 passim, chapter 6 passim, 324, 327, 346, 353–4,

357–8, 366, 373, 377, 392, 397, chapter 8 passim

governance, 191–5, 197–8, 201–2, 214–16
guilt/ethical impotence, 52, 58–9, 254, 279, 291–8, 304, 309, 316

Hannay, Alastair, 335n16, 338–9, 345
Hegel, G.W.F., 4, 7, 18, 21, 27–30, 42, 49, 51–2, 74, 81–2, 85–8, 90, 109, 140–3, 146, 173, 178–9, 182–5, 190, 217, 220, 243–5, 251, 255, 265, 282, 309–10, 326, 450
Heidegger, Martin, 11, 50, 54, 282
Hong, Howard V. and Edna H., 8, 10, 25, 180n72, 181n75, 186n84, 187n85, 191, 243n13, 267, 274n66, 284n82, 295n97, 320n134, 322, 324n1, 335n16, 336n18, 353n44, 364n69, 377n85

imagination: basic function of, 161–3; and consciousness, 36–40, 47, 66; and the "infinite self," 76–7; and inwardness, 20–1; limitations of, 176–7, 204, 209–13, 218–19, 226–7; and "self's possibility," 43, 133, 138, 151–6, 166–8; and "subjective reflection," 98–100, 151–63
innocence, 15, 30–1, chapter 3 section A, 254, 457

Jacobi, Friedrich H., 242

Kant, Immanuel, 18, 140–1, 152, 178

leap, 31, 145, 212, 221, 229, chapter 6 passim, chapter 8 passim; and freedom, decision, 49, 70, 93, 109, 139, 143, 153, 163, 168, 175, 186, 189, 204; in the "transition," 107–8, 116–17, 148, 150, 220, 224, 392, 397
Lessing, Gotthold, 242–3 and note 11, 250
logic, 27, 30, 42, 49, 82–5, 93, 124, 134–5, 140–50, 168–9, 178–90, 202–3, 221–2, 242, 244–5, 251, 265, 314
Lowrie, Walter, 8, 10
Lübcke, Poul, 140

Malantschuk, Gregor, 18, 22
Martensen, Hans L., 19, 140–1, 145, 178, 182
McCawley, James D., 222n148, 223n149, 224n150, 226n151
McKinnon, Alastair, 243 and n10, 245n16, 281n79, 403n5

necessity, chapter 5 passim; "actuality is the unity of possibility and necessity," 27–8, 296–7; and fate, 457–9; and God, 133–4; and the historical past, 112–13, 120, 122–6; and immediacy, 29–30; "inner necessity" and "self's necessity," 241, 256–7, 262–3, 332–3, 338, 341, 362, 369, 392, 410, 444–5, 449–50; and possibility (general definition), 40–5, 110–11, 115, 135
Nordentoft, Kresten, 34, 39, 455–8

philosophy of action, 67, 212, 223, 228, 411, 424, 433, 442; summary of, 234–41; "caused" action, 256–7; and passion, 271–3; and self-deception, 426–31, 448–54; and "weakness of will," 414, 415
possibility, chapter 5 passim (especially 137–77, 220–2); in the breach, gap, 398–9; and communication, 105–6; and freedom, 24, 112–13, 122; and the future/eternal, 125–35; and God, 133–4, 247, 294–6, 349, 351, 353, 385, 398, 401–2, 405, 408–9, 431, 434–5, 458–9, 463; and the inner self, 96–7; and the leap of freedom, 244–5, 252, 254–5, 414, 446; and love, 331–2; and necessity (general definition), 40–4; and objective reflection, 87–8; and reflection, 72–3, 76–7; as the "self," 256–63

reduplication, 210, 359, 363–70, 373, 390, 393, 458
religiousness: and Kierkegaard's anthropology, 11–13, 15–16, 48, 59–60, 470–72; and the ethical, 268–9, 281–323, 372; and the eternal, 128–35, 248, 277; religiousness A (general), 101–2, 158, 261–2, 279, 281–323, 374; religiousness B (general), 284–5; religiousness A and B, relation of, 281–5, 333–5, 338–40, 393–4, 408, 424
repentance, 121, 277–81, 400–1, 454, 456, 463

Sartre, Jean-Paul, 50, 282
Schelling, Friedrich W.J., 141–2
self, definitions of, 4–6, 12–15, 102–3, 109–11, 113–14, 118–25, 129–30, 131, 155–8, 161–2, 203–21
self-deception, 238, 281, 415–40, 447–9, 454–7
sexuality, 74–6, 349, 373–4
Sløk, Johannes, 140n7
social/society: "crowd," "mass," 326–9, 373, 438; as "finitude," 32–6, 47, 102–3, 320–1, 326–7; and the individual, 62–3, 66–78, 103–4, 115–16, 172–5, 204, 224; limitations of Kierkegaard's view, 374–6, 385–7; and preferential love, 347–8; as realm of "necessity," 179–80, 201; distinct from "self's necessity" and "freedom," 224, 226–9, 240, 269, 281, 292, 314, 412–13, 451–3
stages/spheres: in general, 17, 128–9, 315, 317, 326, 334, 346, 351, 424–6, 438, 454; of the aesthetic/immediacy, 6; of the ethical, 218, 224, 249, 263, 279; of faith (religiousness B), 16, 279; freedom versus thinking, 179–80, 399; imagination and feeling versus thinking, 86, 98, 151–2; infinite versus faith, 246; pure thinking, 88; religiousness A, 60, 128–9, 263, 277, 281, 283–5, 290–4, 296, 451; religiousness A versus B, 308–9; transi-

tion from ethical to religiousness, 297–302, 305, 399–400

Taylor, Mark C., 15, 27–9, 72n55, 81–3, 86, 90, 103–4, 220, 310

Tennemann, Wilhelm G., 142–3, 145, 183, 242–4

Thompson, Josiah, 13–14, 79

Trendelenburg, Friedrich Adolph, 142–5, 148, 183–6, 339

Westphal, Merold, 102n118, 327n7, 376n84